COBOL Application Debugging under MVS

COBOL and COBOL II

Ranade IBM Series

H. MURPHY • *Assembler for Cobol Programmers: MVS, VM,* 0-07-044129-4

H. BOOKMAN • *Cobol II,* 0-07-006533-0

J. RANADE • *DB2: Concepts, Programming, and Design,* 0-07-051265-5

J. SANCHEZ • *IBM Microcomputers Handbook,* 0-07-054594-4

M. CARATHANASSIS • *Expert MVS/XA JCL: A Complete Guide to Advanced Techniques,* 0-07-009816-6

P. DONOFRIO • *CICS: Debugging, Dump Reading and Problem Determination,* 0-07-017606-X

T. EDDOLLS • VM Performance Management, 0-07-018966-8

P. KAVANAGH • *VS Cobol II for Cobol Programmers,* 0-07-033571-0

T. MARTYN • *DB2/SQL: A Professional Programmer's Guide,* 0-07-040666-9

S. PIGGOTT • *CICS: A Practical Guide to System Fine Tuning,* 0-07-050054-1

N. PRASAD • *IBM Mainframes: Architecture and Design,* 0-07-050686-8

J. RANADE • *Introduction to SNA Networking: A Guide to VTAM/NCP,* 0-07-051144-6

J. RANADE • *Advanced SNA Networking: A Professional's Guide for Using VTAM/NCP,* 0-07-051143-8

S. SAMSON • *MVS: Performance Management,* 0-07-054528-6

B. JOHNSON • *MVS Concepts and Facilities,* 0-07-032673-8

A. WIPFLER • *Distributed Processing in the CICS Environment,* 0-07-071136-4

A. WIPFLER • *CICS Application Development Programming,* 0-07-071139-9

J. RANADE • *VSAM: Concepts, Programming, and Design,* Second Edition, 0-07-051244-2

J. RANADE • *VSAM: Performance, Design, and Fine Tuning,* Second Edition, 0-07-051245-0

J. SANCHEZ • *Programming Solutions Handbook for IBM Microcomputers,* 0-07-054597-9

P. DONOFRIO • *CICS Programmer's Reference,* 0-07-017607-8

M. CARATHANASSIS • *Expert MVS/ESA JCL: A Guide to Advanced Techniques,* 0-07-009820-4

J. RANADE • *DOS to OS/2: Conversion, Migration, and Application Design,* 0-07-051264-7

K. BRATHWAITE • *Relational Databases: Concepts, Design and Administration,* 0-07-007252-3

R.H. JOHNSON, R.D. JOHNSON • *DASD: IBM's Direct Access Storage Devices,* 0-07-032674-6

M. MARX, P. DAVIS • *MVS Power Programming,* 0-07-040763-0

G. HOUTEKAMER, P. ARTIS • *MVS I/O Subsystems: Configuration Management and Performance Analysis,* 0-07-002553-3

A. KAPOOR • *SNA: Architecture, Protocols, and Implementation,* 0-07-033727-6

D. SILVERBERG • *DB2: Performance, Design, and Implementation,* 0-07-057553-3

R. CROWNHART • *IBM's Workstation CICS,* 0-07-014770-1

C. DANEY • *Programming in REXX,* 0-07-015305-1

G. GOLDBERG, P. SMITH • *The REXX Handbook,* 0-07-028682-8

A. WERMAN • *DB2 Handbook for DBAS,* 0-07-069460-5

R. LEFKON, J. KNEILING, P. SOMERS • *Understanding CICS Internals,* 0-07-037040-0

A. FRIEND • *COBOL Application Debugging under MVS: COBOL and COBOL II,* 0-07-022453-6

L. BRUMBAUGH • *VSAM: Architecture, Theory, and Applications,* 0-07-008606-6

COBOL Application Debugging under MVS

COBOL and COBOL II

Alan Friend

McGraw-Hill, Inc.

New York St. Louis San Francisco Auckland Bogotá
Caracas Lisbon London Madrid Mexico Milan
Montreal New Delhi Paris San Juan São Paulo
Singapore Sydney Tokyo Toronto

Library of Congress Cataloging-in-Publication Data

Friend, Alan.
COBOL application debugging under MVS : COBOL and COBOL II / by Alan Friend.
p. cm.—(J. Ranade IBM series)
Includes index.
ISBN 0-07-022453-6
1. COBOL (Computer program language) 2. IBM MVS. 3. Debugging in computer science. I. Title. II. Series.
QA76.73.C25F75 1992
005.13'3—dc20 92-6470
CIP

1 2 3 4 5 6 7 8 9 0 DOH/DOH 9 8 7 6 5 4 3 2

ISBN 0-07-022453-6

The sponsoring editor for this book was Jerry Papke, the editing supervisor was David E. Fogarty, and the production supervisor was Pamela A. Pelton. This book was set in Century Schoolbook by North Market Street Graphics.

Printed and bound by R. R. Donnelley & Sons Company.

To the memory of my late father, Jules, a man of many interests and talents who was always ahead of his time

Contents

Part 2 Dump Reading 141

Preface

It is said that COBOL is an easy language to understand because it "reads like English," and that COBOL programs are easy to maintain and debug because COBOL is "self-documenting." Why then do so many experienced COBOL programmers tremble at the thought of getting a COBOL ABEND, particularly when it requires interpreting and solving an MVS dump?

Many COBOL detractors, particularly those familiar with Assembler, claim that many COBOL programmers are ignorant of the nuts and bolts of the operating system, the significance of the PSW, and even the concept of base-displacement addressing. Typically, schools offering courses in business programming skills and computer technology do not give COBOL students in-depth training in this material. In fact, COBOL students often receive only a minimum of information about COBOL compiler options and debugging tools. Much of their debugging knowledge comes from on-the-job experience.

Many supporters of the newer fourth-generation languages say that details about the operating system and other "techie stuff" should be transparent to the programmer, and that debugging tools are now so sophisticated that it takes little effort to solve an ABEND. They assert that the age of the technician is over. They even suggest that COBOL has outlived its usefulness. To paraphrase Mark Twain, however, "the reports of COBOL's death are greatly exaggerated." Considering the enormous investment by big business in COBOL systems, and the continuing upgrading of COBOL's features in each new version and release, it appears that the language will be with us for quite a while.

It may not be imperative that every COBOL programmer be a supertechnician or a systems programmer, but it is certainly important that the programmer be well-versed in the principles of sound program design, testing, and debugging; have a basic feel for the purpose and function of the operating system; and be knowledgeable about the arsenal of available debugging tools.

This book, then, is for OS/VS COBOL or VS COBOL II programmers, from the beginning level to the experienced level. It fills the gaps in the typical COBOL programmer's training by presenting materials that enable him or her to function more effectively.

THE PURPOSE OF THIS BOOK

There are many excellent COBOL books which are very explicit about the syntax and use of COBOL language elements. Few, however, give adequate information about compiler options, testing procedures, or debugging facilities. Books devoted exclusively to COBOL debugging are almost nonexistent. This book fills the void. It includes a discussion of compiler options useful in debugging; analysis of completion codes and MVS operating system concepts; detailed examples of symbolic COBOL dumps; MVS hexadecimal storage dumps and Abend-AID reports; descriptions and instructions for the use of the interactive debuggers TESTCOB, COBTEST, and XPEDITER; and guidelines for writing, testing, and debugging COBOL programs.

The book is an outgrowth of a series of COBOL debugging courses which I developed for New York Life Insurance Company. The first was a hands-on workshop for OS/VS COBOL programmers on utilizing compiler output and reading MVS storage dumps. It evolved to hands-on workshops for COBOL II programmers on compiler options, dump reading, and interactive debugging facilities. During the last revision of my student handouts, I decided to expand my course-ware into a single, full-blown debugging book for OS/VS COBOL and COBOL II programmers.

The book cannot, and is not meant to, replace the official documentation from the companies and vendors cited. Readers should refer to the manuals from those companies and vendors for additional information.

OPERATING SYSTEM ENVIRONMENT

The book was written primarily for COBOL programmers in the MVS/XA or MVS/ESA operating system environments using either batch processing, TSO, or TSO/ISPF. Most of the concepts also apply to MVS/370. Users of CMS running under VM will also benefit from the book.

The book is intended for programmers using IBM's OS/VS COBOL Releases 2.3 and 2.4 and VS COBOL II Releases 2, 3.0, 3.1, and 3.2. The differences between COBOL II Releases 3.0, 3.1, and 3.2 are insignificant for our purposes; Release 3.1 is intended basically for VM compatibility and Release 3.2 for DOS/VSE compatibility. Unless otherwise noted, references to Release 3 apply equally to Releases 3.0, 3.1, and 3.2.

FOR WHOM THIS BOOK WAS WRITTEN

The reader should be familiar with the COBOL language, either OS/VS COBOL or VS COBOL II. A basic understanding of JCL and hexadecimal notation is assumed. It will be helpful for the reader to have access to a hexadecimal calculator. The book was written for:

- Programmers with a basic understanding of either version of COBOL who need an overview of debugging techniques and program design.

- Programmers experienced in either version of COBOL who need to know specific techniques and tools for debugging COBOL programs.
- Programmers familiar with OS/VS COBOL who need information about COBOL II debugging differences.
- Students in a second-level COBOL course, either at colleges or in corporate training programs.

All of those mentioned should become more valuable members of the COBOL community by reading and applying the materials presented in this book.

ORGANIZATION

This book is divided into three parts. Part 1, Basic COBOL Debugging, deals with condition codes, system and user completion codes, COBOL compiler options and compiler output, program design and testing considerations, and specific COBOL language debugging features. Part 1 concludes with a recommended debugging procedure. This first part of the book presents enough material to enable the programmer or programming student to design, test, and debug programs without getting heavily into operating system concepts.

Part 2, Dump Reading, explains and gives specific examples of symbolic COBOL dumps, Abend-AID reports, MVS operating system concepts, MVS symptom and hexadecimal storage dumps, and multimodule ABENDs. It discusses the benefits and drawbacks of different types of dumps and reports. The four chapters on MVS concepts and dumps describe how an ABEND occurs, significant system control blocks for debugging purposes, and how to use this information to solve a variety of ABENDs. Part 2 is for the programmer or student who needs a framework for understanding and interpreting dumps when either the debugging aids discussed in Part 1 are not available or are insufficient to solve especially difficult ABENDs.

Part 3, Interactive Debugging, describes and gives usage examples of TESTCOB, COBTEST, and XPEDITER/TSO. This part brings the reader up-to-date on the benefits of interactive testing and debugging.

Each chapter ends with a summary and review questions. This makes the book ideal for the programmer who wants to learn on his or her own, or for use in a COBOL debugging course. Learning is more effective when knowledge is utilized and applied; therefore, many of the questions are designed to enable the reader to interpret and apply the material presented.

The book includes over 15 complete programs written in OS/VS COBOL and COBOL II. They are used in specific debugging and dump-solving examples.

Alan Friend

Acknowledgments

I would like to acknowledge a number of people for their help and support. Special thanks go to Harvey Bookman, President of Bookman Consulting, Inc., who encouraged me to write articles for *Mainframe Journal* (now *Enterprise Systems Journal*) and provided a thorough technical review of the manuscript for this book. Our many discussions have been both enlightening and stimulating.

Sincere thanks also to longtime friend and experienced COBOL programmer Maddy Deleon. Her comments and suggestions helped me make this book clearer and more concise.

My colleague Nelson Richardson, who always keeps abreast of new developments in operating systems, gave me valuable insights into MVS concepts.

Kim Loehrke, Product Manager, and Claudia Mazur, Support Analyst, both at Compuware Corporation, provided examples and lent their technical expertise towards the material in Chap. 7.

I wish to thank Norman Minov, now at Loral Electronic Systems, for the encouragement he gave me when I first contemplated entering the data processing field.

Many people at McGraw-Hill helped see this book through to completion. Jay Ranade, Series Editor, was the moving force behind this project. David Fogarty did an excellent job in editing and in coordinating the preparation of the book. Thanks also to the many others at McGraw-Hill who worked behind-the-scenes to make this book a reality.

Thank you to my wife Rosalie Friend and daughter Julia Friend for their support. Rosalie's patience and encouragement made this long project easier and more pleasant. Julia eagerly typed some of the manuscript and lifted my spirits when I got bogged down with the many details.

COBOL Application Debugging under MVS

COBOL and COBOL II

Part

1

Basic COBOL Debugging

Chapter

1

First Steps: Condition Codes, Completion Codes, and System Messages

Many programmers, both experienced and inexperienced, shudder at the thought of attempting to solve a system dump. While dump reading is certainly a valuable skill, there is a lot more to successful debugging than that. Often, information from other sources and debugging tools will be quite helpful and may even enable a programmer to debug a program more quickly and more easily. One thing that separates the excellent programmer from the average programmer is the ability to make maximum use of all debugging information and tools. This includes knowing which information or tools to use at what time. There is no reason for any programmer to shy away from utilizing these aids, even system dumps. This book presents information about the techniques and tools which will help the COBOL programmer to become more proficient at debugging.

With that said, let's get started.

1.1 GETTING STARTED

Some say that debugging is an art; others that it is a science. The implication is that art is a flexible, creative activity while science requires a methodical and logical mind set. Not wishing to get into that old, artificial "art versus science" controversy, I believe that both of these approaches are important and that neither one has to exist to the exclusion of the other.

Effective debugging is largely developed through experience working with logical problem-solving procedures. Creativity comes in later when you learn to amend and adapt basic debugging procedures to the specific problem at hand. Debugging expertise increases with experience.

Consider the example of an abnormal termination of a COBOL application system accompanied by an S806 completion code from the MVS operating system. Inexperienced programmers will most likely need to look up the meaning of this code and then methodically go through a step-by-step procedure to find the name of the module which terminated and to locate the failing instruction in that module. More experienced programmers will take shortcuts. They will know that this completion code means that a requested module could not be found. Perhaps a CALL statement in the COBOL program was at fault or a supervisor routine required by the system was missing. They will probably bypass their normal stepwise debugging procedure and go directly to the linkage-editor output, the contents of certain general-purpose registers, and the job control language (JCL) to gather necessary information which will lead to the incriminating COBOL CALL statement or the service request in the faulty COBOL module.

Of course, not all debugging centers on uncovering the cause of an abnormal ending for a program. One of the most difficult aspects of debugging involves correcting programs which terminate normally but produce bad output. There may be no system messages indicating that anything is wrong. Consider the example of an Internal Revenue Service program which incorrectly reported a taxpayer's dividend income (an actual case). The error was noticed after the irate taxpayer (me) complained that the IRS was falsely accusing him of not paying income taxes on his entire dividend income. A situation like this may be discovered only when the programmer or user notices bad output. It must be stressed that errors like this should not occur, but unfortunately they sometimes do occur. Conscientious desk-checking, computer runs using carefully formulated test data, and structured walk-throughs should eliminate logic errors in the program, but even so it is possible that improper input to the program may make things go awry.

Faced with invalid output from a seemingly correct program, inexperienced programmers may not know where to turn. Sometimes they may make guesses and attempt code changes by trial-and-error to see what happens. Often this makes matters worse. Without a careful plan or procedure to follow, this "creative" guesswork may waste time and resources.

The expert knows that it is necessary to follow a logical plan for gathering pertinent data relating to the problem at hand. He or she may examine the input data set, judiciously place DISPLAY statements at key points in the COBOL program, or initiate a TRACE. Clearly, the expert programmer has an advantage over the novice because the expert can modify the debugging process based on sound debugging principles combined with a wealth of past experience.

Is the expert programmer's ability to zero-in on the essentials an art? Intuition? Science? Luck? Let's call it knowledge built from a broad background of experience. There is nothing magical about being good at debugging. Once you have learned the general steps to take when a problem occurs, almost all problems can be solved. If you have encountered certain types of abnormal terminations or processing errors before, you will know what to look for and will be able to shorten the problem-solving process when the problem recurs. Those few problems which are particularly elusive may require more sophisticated techniques and more extensive knowledge in order to solve them, but they too should yield.

I must stress that effective debugging starts with a carefully conceived, logical plan. Guesswork and haphazard "fixes" usually don't work.

The approach in this book will be to start with a knowledge base of useful debugging information provided by the system. This will include discussions of completion codes, system messages, and compiler output. We will then explore the tools and resources available to the COBOL programmer for problem solving. You will learn to utilize various compiler options and to interpret compiler output, read different types of dumps, and make use of interactive debugging facilities. Along the way we will develop a debugging procedure and demonstrate how it can be used. Examples will be given throughout the book wherever necessary for clarification.

1.2 FIRST STEPS TO SUCCESSFUL DEBUGGING

Programmers often submit a just-completed program for execution the first time and sit on the edge of their seats waiting for the operating system to return a condition code or completion code. These codes indicate whether the operating system or COBOL has detected problems. Inexperienced programmers may breathe a sigh of relief to see a condition code of 0, assuming that this indicates that the job completed perfectly; this is not always the case. Likewise, inexperienced programmers may not realize that there is a difference between condition codes and completion codes. The next section explains the significance of condition codes, completion codes, and various system messages.

1.3 CONDITION CODES

A *condition code* is returned to the operating system at the conclusion of a job step by the program which is executing. The value of the condition code, sometimes called return code, depends on the program logic, and may be a function of specific conditions which are tested within the program's processing. Thus the COBOL compiler, which is a program whose primary function is to translate the COBOL source code into machine instructions and produce an object module, may return condition codes of 0000, 0004, 0008, 0012, or 0016. The value 0000 represents the highest success level for the compiler, while 0016 represents the lowest. The full significance of COBOL compiler condition codes will be discussed in detail in Sec. 1.6.

You can also specify a condition code to be returned to the operating system or other calling program from an application program. In COBOL this is done by coding

```
MOVE nnnn TO RETURN-CODE
```

where *nnnn* is any numeric value less than 4095 which you choose to use. RETURN-CODE is a special COBOL register with an implicit definition of PIC S9999 COMP. Typically, you will test a condition and move a value based on the results of the condition test to RETURN-CODE just prior to issuing a GOBACK, STOP RUN, or EXIT PROGRAM. The value in this register is passed as the condition code to the calling program when control returns to that calling program. When STOP RUN or GOBACK is coded, the calling program may be the operating system. EXIT PROGRAM never returns control to the operating system. Examination of the value of the condition code may provide information about the condition which was tested just before the application program terminated.

As we have seen, condition codes can be used to give you an indication of the success of a job step. This can be vital in debugging. Obviously, the meanings of the codes must be documented. Condition code meanings for operating system programs are given in the IBM manuals for those programs. See the *IBM OS/VS COBOL Compiler and Library Programmer's Guide, VS COBOL II Application Programming Guide,* and *Linkage Editor and Loader User's Guide* for the appropriate COBOL compiler and for the linkage-editor. Condition codes for application programs must be well documented in order to be of use. Unfortunately, debugging is sometimes hindered by careless or missing documentation for application systems.

The condition code can be utilized to control execution of subsequent job steps. Letters "A" and "B" in Fig. 1.1 show how the JCL COND parameter is coded in the IBM cataloged procedure COB2UCLG. This is the compile, link, and go procedure for COBOL II. Letter "A" points to the EXEC statement for the LKED step. This step executes the linkage-editor, an operating system service program. The purpose of the linkage-editor is to create an executable load

```
//COB2     EXEC  PGM=IGYCRCTL,PARM='OBJECT',REGION=1024K
//STEPLIB   DD   DSNAME=SYS1.COB2COMP,DISP=SHR
//SYSPRINT  DD   SYSOUT=A
//SYSLIN    DD   DSNAME=&&LOADSET,UNIT=SYSDA,DISP=(MOD,PASS),
//               SPACE=(TRK,(3,3)),DCB=(BLKSIZE=80,LRECL=80,RECFM=FB)
//SYSUT1    DD   UNIT=SYSDA,SPACE=(CYL,(1,1))
//SYSUT2    DD   UNIT=SYSDA,SPACE=(CYL,(1,1))
//SYSUT3    DD   UNIT=SYSDA,SPACE=(CYL,(1,1))
//SYSUT4    DD   UNIT=SYSDA,SPACE=(CYL,(1,1))
//SYSUT5    DD   UNIT=SYSDA,SPACE=(CYL,(1,1))
//LKED     EXEC  PGM=IEWL,PARM='LIST,XREF,LET,MAP',COND=(5,LT,COB2),<---- (A)
//               REGION=512K
//SYSLIN    DD   DSNAME=&&LOADSET,DISP=(OLD,DELETE)
//          DD   DDNAME=SYSIN
//SYSLMOD   DD   DSNAME=&&GOSET(GO),DISP=(,PASS),UNIT=SYSDA,
//               SPACE=(CYL,(1,1,1))
//SYSLIB    DD   DSNAME=SYS1.COB2LIB,DISP=SHR
//SYSUT1    DD   UNIT=SYSDA,SPACE=(CYL,(1,1))
//SYSPRINT  DD   SYSOUT=A
//GO       EXEC  PGM=*.LKED.SYSLMOD,COND=((5,LT,COB2),(5,LT,LKED))<---- (B)
//STEPLIB   DD   DSNAME=SYS1.COB2LIB,DISP=SHR
//SYSABOUT  DD   SYSOUT=A
//SYSDBOUT  DD   SYSOUT=A
//SYSUDUMP  DD   SYSOUT=A
```

Figure 1.1 The COBOL II Compile, Link, and Go procedure showing the use of the COND parameter.

module from the object module previously created by the compiler. Notice that the COND parameter is coded

```
COND=(5,LT,COB2)
```

This specifies that if 5 is less than the condition code returned by the prior COB2 step, don't execute the current step. The COB2 step is the COBOL II compile step. In other words, the current link-edit step is to be executed only if the condition code returned by the compile step is 5 or less. A condition code of 0004 indicates a warning from the compiler, while anything higher means that the compiler found more serious errors in the COBOL program source code. It would not be wise to request the linkage-editor to produce a load module from an object module which will most likely cause incorrect processing or an abnormal ending if it is executed. Thus this COND parameter saves time and system resources by preventing you from invoking the linkage-editor when the compiler has found problems with the program source code.

Similarly, note the COND parameter on the EXEC card for the GO step ("B" in Fig. 1.1). The GO step executes the load module produced by the prior LKED step. This time the COND parameter is written as

```
COND=((5,LT,COB2),(5,LT,LKED))
```

This controls execution of the GO step based on the condition codes returned previously by either the compiler or the linkage-editor. Figure 1.2 shows a job in which the LKED and GO steps were not executed because the condition code from the COB2 step was 0008 (see letter "A"). Notice the messages at "B" and "C" which indicate that these steps were not run because of condition codes.

You can code the COND parameter in your application JCL to control job step flow in the same manner as is done in the COB2UCLG procedure.

In addition, the condition code from a COBOL subprogram can be examined by the calling program to determine what processing occurred or what conditions were found in the subprogram. Consider the following statements in a subprogram:

```
000100        IF ERROR-CONDITION
000200            MOVE 1234 TO RETURN-CODE.
000300        GOBACK.
```

If the test is true, the value 1234 is moved to the subprogram's RETURN-CODE register just before the subprogram transfers control back to the calling program. The contents of the subprogram's RETURN-CODE register are automatically stored in the RETURN-CODE register of the calling COBOL program when control returns to the calling program. The calling program can test the contents of its RETURN-CODE register just as it can for any data name. Thus a statement such as

```
IEF236I ALLOC. FOR DMPCB24 COB2 S1
IEF237I D96   ALLOCATED TO STEPLIB   - SYS1.COB2COMP
                                   .
                                   .
                                   .
IEF142I DMPCB24 COB2 S1 - STEP WAS EXECUTED - COND CODE 0008 <------------- (A)
IEF285I    SYS1.COB2COMP                                   KEPT
IEF285I    VOL SER NOS= 77RESA.
IEF285I    COB2.S1.SYSPRINT                                SYSOUT
IEF285I    SYS90136.T100953.RA000.DMPCB24.LOADSET          PASSED
IEF285I    VOL SER NOS= WKSH72.
IEF285I    SYS90136.T100953.RA000.DMPCB24.R0000002         DELETED
IEF285I    VOL SER NOS= WK7701.
IEF285I    SYS90136.T100953.RA000.DMPCB24.R0000003         DELETED
IEF285I    VOL SER NOS= WKSH02.
IEF285I    SYS90136.T100953.RA000.DMPCB24.R0000004         DELETED
IEF285I    VOL SER NOS= WKSH04.
IEF285I    SYS90136.T100953.RA000.DMPCB24.R0000005         DELETED
IEF285I    VOL SER NOS= WKSH03.
IEF285I    SYS90136.T100953.RA000.DMPCB24.R0000006         DELETED
IEF285I    VOL SER NOS= WKSH02.
IEF285I    MY.COBOL.LIB                                    KEPT
IEF285I    VOL SER NOS= TSOY10.
IEF373I STEP /COB2     / START 90136.1009
IEF374I STEP /COB2     / STOP  90136.1009 CPU    0MIN 00.27SEC SRB    0MIN 00.03SEC VIRT    144K SYS    196K EXT    32768K SYS    8960K
TAPE EXCPS          0        TAPE EXCPS PER CPU SECOND          0
DISK EXCPS        189        DISK EXCPS PER CPU SECOND        700
AVERAGE WORKING SET SIZE          484K

IEF202I DMPCB24 LKED S1 - STEP WAS NOT RUN BECAUSE OF CONDITION CODES <------------- (B)
IEF272I DMPCB24 LKED S1 - STEP WAS NOT EXECUTED.
IEF373I STEP /LKED     / START 90136.1009
IEF374I STEP /LKED     / STOP  90136.1009 CPU    0MIN 00.00SEC SRB    0MIN 00.00SEC VIRT    0K SYS    0K EXT    0K SYS    0K
THERE IS NO CPU TIME FOR THIS STEP

IEF202I DMPCB24 GO S1 - STEP WAS NOT RUN BECAUSE OF CONDITION CODES <------------- (C)
IEF272I DMPCB24 GO S1 - STEP WAS NOT EXECUTED.
IEF373I STEP /GO       / START 90136.1009
IEF374I STEP /GO       / STOP  90136.1009 CPU    0MIN 00.00SEC SRB    0MIN 00.00SEC VIRT    0K SYS    0K EXT    0K SYS    0K
THERE IS NO CPU TIME FOR THIS STEP

IEF237I 7F0   ALLOCATED TO SYS00001 - SYS90136.T100957.RA000.DMPCB24.R0000001
IEF285I    SYS90136.T100957.RA000.DMPCB24.R0000001         KEPT
IEF285I    VOL SER NOS= WKSH72.
IEF285I    SYS90136.T100953.RA000.DMPCB24.LOADSET          DELETED
IEF285I    VOL SER NOS= WKSH72.
IEF375I  JOB /DMPCB24 / START 90136.1009
IEF376I  JOB /DMPCB24 / STOP  90136.1009 CPU    0MIN 00.27SEC SRB    0MIN 00.03SEC
```

Figure 1.2 Job log showing a condition code and system message.

```
000100        IF RETURN-CODE EQUAL 1234
000200           PERFORM 0900-SUB-PROG-ERROR.
```

permits the calling program to determine what processing it will do based on information returned to it by the subprogram. If either the calling or called program terminates abnormally and issues a request for a system storage dump, the contents of the appropriate RETURN-CODE special registers can be examined in the dump. This will be discussed further in Sec. 2.2.1.6.

1.4 COMPLETION CODES

1.4.1 Types of Premature Program Termination

A major portion of debugging involves identifying and fixing the errors that prevented a program from running to a normal end-of-job. Basically, there are two reasons for premature program termination. First, the hardware or central processing unit (CPU) detected a critical error condition, or second, the software, which may be a system program or application program, found an error condition. In the first case, known as a *program interrupt* or *program exception,* an exit routine receives control when a specified event occurs and normally issues the ABEND macro instruction, which terminates the task, requests a system dump, and returns a completion code. One of the most common exceptional conditions encountered is a data exception. This means that an instruction was attempting an operation with invalid internal (packed) decimal data. Perhaps a field defined as COMP-3 was not initialized or had unpacked data placed in it before the instruction was attempted. Other program interrupts include the operation exception, resulting from an attempt to execute an instruction having an invalid operation code, and the protection exception, caused by accessing storage not allocated to the program.

Some program interruptions, such as decimal overflow, fixed-point overflow, exponent underflow, and significance exception can be disabled if specific bits in the Program Status Word (PSW) are set to zero. Note, however, that this cannot be done by COBOL programs. The PSW will be discussed further in Sec. 8.1.

The second reason for premature program termination, caused when software issues the ABEND macro, is often referred to as an *ab*normal *end*ing, or ABEND. Note that while a program interrupt may occur unexpectedly whenever the hardware detects an error condition, an ABEND occurs when the software deliberately invokes the ABEND macro instruction as a result of the software's logic finding some error condition true.

1.4.2 Types of Completion Codes

Completion codes, also known as ABEND codes, are issued when the job step ABENDs or a program interrupt occurs. Either the system or the application program issues the ABEND macro and returns the code when a task or address space is terminated due to some error condition. Normally, a hexadecimal storage dump and a very concise symptom dump, about 10 lines long, are requested through the DUMP parameter in the ABEND macro instruction. The symptom dump summarizes key information from the storage dump. Although the symptom dump will always appear within the job log (unless your installation has changed certain defaults), a DD statement must be provided in the JCL for the storage dump. Usually the //SYSUDUMP DD statement is coded. These dumps are valuable debugging aids and will be discussed fully in Part 2 of this book.

You may also see a reason code associated with the completion code. The reason code points to a more detailed explanation of the error which was encountered.

Completion codes appear in the job log in one of the two formats shown below.

```
IEF450I job-name step-name - ABEND=Sxxx Uyyyy REASON=zzzzzzzz
```

or

```
IEF472I job-name step-name - COMPLETION CODE - SYSTEM=xxx
                                USER=yyyy REASON=zzzzzzzz
```

Notice that there are two types of completion codes: system completion codes and user completion codes. The system completion codes may begin with the letter "S," as shown in the first example above, followed by a three-digit hexadecimal number (represented by *xxx* in the example). The user completion codes may start with the letter "U" followed by a four-digit decimal number (represented by *yyyy* in the example). The second example has a slightly different format; instead of the S or U prefix, the codes are clearly identified as being either system or user completion codes.

If an ABEND occurs, either the system code or the user code, with its accompanying reason code, will contain a value which you can look up in the appropriate documentation to find diagnostic information about the reason for the ABEND. The other completion code will have a value of 0. If a program interrupt occurs, a system code will always be produced.

The characters IEF*nnn*I at the extreme left in each of the previous examples indicate that these messages came from the operating system program known as the job scheduler. More about the different types of system messages will be given at the end of this chapter. System and user completion codes are discussed more fully in the next two sections. See Fig. 1.3 for an actual example of a completion code in the job log.

1.4.2.1 System completion codes

System completion codes are issued when MVS determines that the task or address space cannot continue processing correctly. As stated at the beginning of Sec. 1.4.2, the system issues the ABEND macro instruction, terminating the job step and requesting a dump. The numeric code specified in the macro instruction becomes the system completion code. The reason code contains a value other than zero only if the REASON keyword is coded on the ABEND macro instruction. Note that for 0C*x* type program interrupts, the last digit in the completion code is a hexadecimal number indicating the cause of the interruption, and that the reason code always matches this digit. Thus the completion code for a data exception would appear as

```
ABEND=S0C7 U0000 REASON=00000007
```

or

```
COMPLETION CODE - SYSTEM=0C7 USER=0000 REASON=00000007
```

All system completion codes, together with reason codes, are documented in the *IBM MVS Message Library: System Codes* manual (use the manual appropriate for your installation's version of MVS, i.e., MVS, MVS/XA, or MVS/

```
IEF472I DMPCB21 GO S1 - COMPLETION CODE - SYSTEM=0C7 USER=0000 REASON=00000007
```

Figure 1.3 A system completion code as it appears in the job log.

ESA). You can find a description of the condition which caused the ABEND, often with suggestions for fixing the problem, by looking up the code in that manual. For example, an S013 is a system completion code described in the system codes manual as an OPEN problem. One possible reason for this problem is that conflicting Data Control Block (DCB) information was passed to the OPEN macro and it ABENDed when trying to open a file in the COBOL program.

Some of the more common system completion codes which may occur in COBOL programs are also discussed briefly in the *IBM OS/VS COBOL Compiler and Library Programmer's Guide.* The more common system completion codes are summarized in Appendix B of this book.

1.4.2.2 User completion codes

User completion codes occur when the problem program determines that it cannot continue processing because an error condition exists. In COBOL, a subroutine in the OS/VS COBOL or COBOL II subroutine libraries, invoked when the COBOL program branches to it to request a COBOL service, may detect an error. The subroutine then supplies a numeric code which becomes part of the ABEND macro instruction. The ABEND macro terminates the job step, returns the number as a user completion code, and requests a dump. The meanings of these user completion codes can be found in the *IBM OS/VS COBOL Compiler and Library Programmer's Guide* and the *IBM VS COBOL II Application Programming: Debugging* manual. Thus, U0519 in OS/VS COBOL means that execution has reached the bottom of the PROCEDURE DIVISION without finding a GOBACK, STOP RUN, or EXIT PROGRAM. There is an error in the control flow logic of the program, perhaps because of a GO TO to the last paragraph instead of a PERFORM, or a fall through to the last paragraph without a program-terminating statement at the end. This is equivalent to a user completion code of U1037 in COBOL II.

Application programs can also supply user completion codes. How this is done in COBOL is explained in the next section. It must be noted that user completion codes are of little use unless their specific meanings are understood. Certainly a programmer encountering an unexpected ABEND should be given as much information as possible to aid the debugging process. The codes and their significance should be carefully documented during application design. The programmer can then get information relating to the error condition which generated that particular user code by consulting the documentation for that application. Note that user completion codes for non-IBM systems are not given in the *IBM MVS Message Library: System Codes* manual, nor in the two IBM COBOL manuals referred to above.

1.4.3 Forcing an ABEND

It might seem that you would never wish to have your programs ABEND. Certainly an abnormal termination implies that something went seriously wrong during program execution. It may sometimes be desirable, however, to terminate processing and get a storage dump if some error condition is found by the program's logic. Consider the code below, where TABLE-ERROR is one of the 88-level names for an error status field.

```
000100 01   ERROR-STATUS        PIC X VALUE ZERO.
000200      88 NO-ERROR               VALUE ZERO.
000300      88 IN-REC-ERROR           VALUE '1'.
000400      88 TABLE-ERROR            VALUE '2'.
                 .
                 .
                 .
```

In case the program logic detects a serious error in processing a table, there may be no point in continuing processing. The value 2 might be moved to ERROR-STATUS and a call to ILBOABN0 requested. ILBOABN0 is a routine in the COBOL subroutine libraries for both OS/VS COBOL and COBOL II. It invokes the ABEND macro, which terminates the program and issues a user completion code and a dump. A parameter is passed to ILBOABN0 in the CALL instruction, and the parameter is then passed back to the operating system to become the user completion code. In the following example, the COBOL program moves the value 3333 to a field in its WORKING-STORAGE SECTION immediately before issuing the call (the field should be coded as shown). The value 3333 becomes the user completion code.

```
000080 01   USER-COMP-CODE              PIC S9(4) COMP.
                 .
                 .
                 .
000100      IF TABLE-ERROR
000110          MOVE 3333 TO USER-COMP-CODE
000120          CALL 'ILBOABNØ' USING USER-COMP-CODE.
```

Certain completion codes are already used by various subroutines in the COBOL subroutine libraries and should be avoided when choosing a parameter to be passed to ILBOABN0. For OS/VS COBOL, do not use 0187, 0203, 0295, 0303, 0304, 0519, 1301, 3361, 3440, or 3505. For COBOL II, avoid values from 1000 to 1999. Also note that a value above 4095 should not be chosen since an internal algorithm will convert the value to a completion code which will not match the passed parameter.

Remember that all user completion codes used in application programs should be documented so that they can provide useful information to those who must analyze the problem.

```
13:57:51  + IGZ020I -01 A USER LOGIC ERROR HAS OCCURRED.  NEITHER FILE STATUS NOR  <---- (A)
13:57:51  + IGZ020I -02 A DECLARATIVE WAS SPECIFIED IN PROGRAM 'ZT803C05', FOR
13:57:51  + IGZ020I -03 FILE 'CARDFLE' AT RELATIVE LOCATION X'05D0'.
13:57:51  IEA995I SYMPTOM DUMP OUTPUT
13:57:51   ABEND CODE  USER= 1020 TIME=13.57.06 SEQ=01528 CPU=0000 ASID=003A
13:57:51   PSW AT TIME OF ERROR  078D1000   0000FF4A  ILC 2  INTC 0D
13:57:51     ACTIVE LOAD MODULE=GO          ADDRESS=00006C98  OFFSET=000092B2
13:57:51     DATA AT PSW  0000FF44 - 00181610  0A0D47F0  C0F84820
13:57:51     GPR  0-3  80000000  800003FC  000003FC  00016598
13:57:51     GPR  4-7  0000D6A0  0000DD88  00006CEC  000162EC
13:57:51     GPR  8-11 0000FC44  0000004C  0000DD88  00007044
13:57:51     GPR 12-15 5000FE62  000150B0  50009778  0000FE30
13:57:52   END OF SYMPTOM DUMP
13:57:53  + IGZ038I AN ABEND WAS INTERCEPTED BY THE COBOL EXECUTION TIME ABEND
13:57:53  +          HANDLER.
13:57:53  +   THE COMPLETION CODE WAS = 'U1020'   THE PSW AT ABEND WAS =
13:57:53  +          '078D10000000FF4A'
13:57:53  +   THE GP REGISTERS AT ENTRY TO ABEND WERE
13:57:53  +      REGS 0-3    - '80000000  800003FC  000003FC  00016598'
13:57:53  +      REGS 4-7    - '0000D6A0  0000DD88  00006CEC  000162EC'
13:57:53  +      REGS 8-11   - '0000FC44  0000004C  0000DD88  00007044'
13:57:53  +      REGS 12-15  - '5000FE62  000150B0  50009778  0000FE30'

                               .
                               .
                               .

13:57:54  JOB 8355 IEF450I DMPCB25 GO S1 - ABEND=S000 U1020 REASON=00000000
13:57:54           TIME=13.57.08
13:57:54 IAT5110 JOB 8355 (DMPCB25 ) USES     D WKSH04 SYS88316.T135709.RA000.DMPCB25.R0000001
13:57:54  JOB 8355 IEF404I DMPCB25 - ENDED - TIME=13.57.09
13:57:54 IAT5400 JOB 8355 (DMPCB25 ) IN BREAKDOWN
```

Figure 1.4 A portion of the job log showing IGZ messages from the COBOL II subroutine library, an IEA symptom dump, and a completion code.

1.5 SYSTEM MESSAGES

Our discussion so far has focused on the types of messages known as condition codes and completion codes. There are additional messages, however, which may be returned by various components of the operating system. These are prefixed by specific letters which identify their sources. The messages are printed in the job log in a format similar to that shown below (see Figs. 1.2 and 1.4 for actual examples).

```
XXXnnnI text of message.
```

In the example above, *XXX* represents the letters identifying the origin of the message, while *nnn* represents the message number. Often these messages are simply for informational purposes. In the event of an error condition, however, the message text may supply enough information to help you fix the problem. Note the IGZ message from the COBOL II subroutine library shown at "A" in Fig. 1.4. It clearly shows a problem with the DDNAME CARDFLE in a statement at a hexadecimal offset of 05D0 in program ZT803C05. The *IBM VS COBOL II Application Programming: Debugging* manual gives additional information. It states that there is an I/O logic error, and that the error in question is usually the result of an operation which is not valid for the file, such as a WRITE into a file opened for INPUT or a START to a VSAM ESDS.

Also recall from our earlier discussion of completion codes that the IEF450I and IEF472I messages from the job scheduler supply completion codes and reason codes in the message text.

It is sometimes helpful to know what system component produced the message. Some message prefixes, with their origins follow:

Prefix	Source
IDA	VSAM
IDC	Access Method Services (IDCAMS)
IEA	Supervisor
IEC	Data management
IEF	Job scheduler
IEW	Linkage-editor
IGY	VS COBOL II compiler
IGZ	Run-time routines in the VS COBOL II subroutine library
IKF	OS/VS COBOL compiler and run-time routines in the OS/VS COBOL subroutine library

The following IBM manuals give additional information about these messages:

MVS Message Library: System Messages

OS / VS COBOL Compiler and Library Programmer's Guide

VS COBOL II Application Programming: Debugging

For information about messages from other software, both IBM and non-IBM, see the appropriate documentation for that software.

1.6 MESSAGES FROM THE COBOL COMPILERS

We have already seen that the COBOL compiler may give condition codes of 0000, 0004, 0008, 0012, or 0016, depending on the kind of error it found in the COBOL source code. While a code of 0000 specifies that no problems were found, anything higher may indicate that something is wrong with the program; these problems should be carefully examined. COBOL programmers are usually conscientious about correcting the errors associated with codes of 0008, 0012, and 0016, but many programmers ignore the warning messages that accompany condition codes of 0004. While it is true that some warning messages may have no impact on proper program functioning, some may identify problems which should be fixed.

For example, the warning level diagnostic message "IKF4096I-W STATEMENT WILL NEVER BE EXECUTED," coming from the OS/VS COBOL compiler, indicates that a control flow logic error may be encountered if the program is executed.

Diagnostics are formatted as shown below:

```
nn III999999-Y Message text
```

where *nn* represents the source code line number of the statement in error, *III* is either IKF or IGY depending on which COBOL compiler was used, and *999999-Y* represents the message number and message level. Thus "W" in the IKF4096I-W message above means that this was a warning message coming from the OS/VS COBOL compiler.

The severity level of the diagnostic messages and their associated condition codes differ according to whether the OS/VS COBOL or VS COBOL II compiler is invoked. This will be discussed in detail in the two sections that follow.

1.6.1 OS/VS COBOL Compiler Diagnostics

Message levels and condition codes for the OS/VS COBOL compiler are as follows:

W, or Warning, means that the problem is not serious enough to hinder execution of the program. Unexpected results may occasionally occur, however, if the program is run. A condition code of 0004 is generated if this is the highest message level in the program.

C, or Conditional, means that the compiler found a problem and made an assumption. In some cases this assumption may correct the error. The statement containing the problem is retained. A conditional-level diagnostic returns a condition code of 0008 if it is the highest message level in the program.

E, or Error, indicates that the compiler detected a serious error and probably did not attempt a corrective assumption. The statement in error is discarded. A condition code of 0012 is generated if E is the highest message level in the program.

D, or Disaster, means that the error is so serious that the compiler did not continue processing. This severity level produces a 0016 condition code.

The type of diagnostic obtained depends on which compiler options are in effect. FLAGW specifies that all diagnostics from the warning-level and higher are to be listed. FLAGE indicates that all error-level and higher diagnostics are to be listed.

If compiler diagnostics have been produced, they will appear at the end of the compiler output (see Fig. 1.5). A complete listing of diagnostic error messages, together with descriptive text, can be generated by adding a job statement to the JCL and running a job as shown in Fig. 1.6.

```
CARD   ERROR MESSAGE

78     IKF5011I-W    AN INTERMEDIATE RESULT OR A SENDING FIELD MIGHT HAVE ITS HIGH ORDER DIGIT POSITION
                     TRUNCATED.
99     IKF3001I-E    TOTAL-LINEE NOT DEFINED. DISCARDED.
```

Figure 1.5 Diagnostics from the OS/VS COBOL compiler.

```
//S1      EXEC COBUC
//*********************************************************************
//*  SOURCE CODE IS OS/VS COBOL                                        *
//*********************************************************************
//COB.SYSIN   DD *
       ID DIVISION.
       PROGRAM-ID.     ERRMSG.
       REMARKS.  THIS PROGRAM WILL RESULT IN A LISTING OF ALL
                 COMPILER DIAGNOSTICS AND THEIR EXPLANATIONS.
       ENVIRONMENT DIVISION.
       DATA DIVISION.
       PROCEDURE DIVISION.
      **************************************************************
      *  THE SAME RESULTS CAN BE ACHIEVED BY CHANGING THE          *
      *  PROGRAM-NAME OF ANY PROGRAM TO 'ERRMSG', HOWEVER          *
      *  THE FOLLOWING COMPILER OPTIONS MUST BE IN EFFECT:         *
      *      NOCSYNTAX, NODECK, NODMAP, NOSTATE, NOSYNTAX,         *
      *      NOSXREF, NOTERM, NOTEST, NOXREF, NOFLOW, NOLOAD,      *
      *      NOOPTIMIZE, NOPMAP.                                   *
      ************************************************************ *
              GOBACK.
/*
//
```

Figure 1.6 Job which will generate a complete listing of OS/VS COBOL compiler diagnostics.

1.6.2 COBOL II Compiler Diagnostics

The COBOL II compiler message levels and their corresponding condition codes are

I, or Informational, indicates either a message for your information or a coding inefficiency that you can choose to change. It will not cause the program to run incorrectly. This message level gives a 0000 condition code if this is the highest message level in the program.

W, or Warning, means that the statement syntax is correct, but there is potential for error if it is executed. This message is accompanied by a condition code of 0004 if this is the highest-level diagnostic in the program.

E, or Error, means that there is a definite error, but the compiler tried to correct it. There is a possibility that the program will run correctly. A condition code of 0008 is generated if it is the highest message level in the program.

S, or Severe, represents a serious error. The compiler may have tried to correct it, but it is likely that program execution will be incorrect. If this is the most serious diagnostic in the program, a 0012 condition code is produced.

U, or Unrecoverable, means that the error is so serious that the compiler could not continue processing. A condition code of 0016 is generated.

In addition to producing diagnostic messages at the end of the compiler output, COBOL II permits generation of embedded diagnostics at the location in the source code where the error appears. The FLAG compiler option is used. The format is

```
FLAG(x[,y])
```

where *x* means that messages with a severity level of *X* or more are to be printed at the end of the source listing, and where *y* means that messages having a severity level of *Y* and above are to be embedded in the source code. Note that it is only necessary to code *y* if you desire embedded messages; messages at the end of the source listing will always be produced if FLAG is in effect.

Examples of the embedded diagnostics for a program can be seen in Fig. 1.7. Notice that sometimes a message may appear a few lines below the actual line in error. The line number is always identified, however. The diagnostics at the end of the listing, along with statistics generated by the compiler, are shown in Fig. 1.8.

A complete listing of the compiler diagnostic messages with their explanations can be generated by adding a job statement to the JCL and running a job as shown in Fig. 1.9.

```
  000101  011400 0100-READ.
  000102  011500       READ TEST-FILE INTO WS-TEST-RECORD
  000103  011600         AT END MOVE 1 TO SW-EOF
  000104  011610                 EXHIBIT  WS-EMP-NO

==000104==> IGYPS0084-S   < EXHIBIT > WAS RESTRICTED FROM USAGE BY THE INSTALLATION CONTROL FACILITY.

  000105  011620       END-READ.

==000104==> IGYPS2121-S   < EXHIBIT > WAS NOT DEFINED AS A DATA-NAME. THE STATEMENT WAS DISCARDED.


  000107  011700 0100-EXIT.
  000108  011800        EXIT.

  000110  012000 0200-PROCESS.
  000111  012100       MOVE WS-EMP-NO TO PRT-EMP-NUM
  000112  013000       MOVE WS-FIRST-NAME TO PRT-FIRST

==000111==> IGYPS2121-S   < PRT-EMP-NUM > WAS NOT DEFINED AS A DATA-NAME. THE STATEMENT WAS DISCARDED.

  000113  013100       MOVE WS-LAST-NAME TO PRT-LAST
  000114  013200       WRITE PRINT-FILE-REC FROM PRINT-LINE AFTER ADVANCING 2 LINES
  000115  013300       MOVE SPACES TO PRINT-LINE
  000116  013400       MOVE WS-STREET TO PRT-STREET
  000117  013500       WRITE PRINT-FILE-REC FROM PRINT-LINE AFTER ADVANCING 1 LINES
  000118  013600       MOVE SPACES TO PRINT-LINE
  000119  013700       MOVE WS-CITY-STATE TO PRT-CITY-STATE
  000120  013800       MOVE WS-ZIP-CODE TO PRT-ZIP-CODE
  000121  013900       WRITE PRINT-FILE-REC FROM PRINT-LINE AFTER ADVANCING 1 LINES
  000122  014000       MOVE SPACES TO PRINT-LINE
  000123  014100       ADD 1 TO EMP-CNT
  000124  014200       PERFORM 0100-READ THROUGH 0100-EXIT.
  000125  014300 0200-EXIT.
  000126  014400        EXIT.

  000128  014600 0300-TOTAL.
  000129  014700       MOVE EMP-CNT TO PRT-TOTAL
  000130  014800       MOVE 'TOTAL NO. OF EMPLOYEES' TO PRT-DATA
  000131  014900       WRITE PRINT-FILE-REC FROM PRINT-LINE AFTER ADVANCING 2 LINES.

  000133  015800 0300-EXIT.
  000134  015900        EXIT.
```

Figure 1.7 Embedded diagnostics, generated by the VS COBOL II compiler.

```
LINEID  MESSAGE CODE  MESSAGE TEXT ( IMBEDDED MESSAGES MAY BE IDENTIFIED BY THE <*> PRECEDING THE MESSAGE CODE )

        IGYDS0015-I   DIAGNOSTIC MESSAGES WERE ISSUED DURING PROCESSING OF COMPILER OPTIONS. THESE MESSAGES ARE LOCATED AT THE
                      BEGINNING OF THE LISTING.

   104 *IGYPS0084-S   < EXHIBIT > WAS RESTRICTED FROM USAGE BY THE INSTALLATION CONTROL FACILITY.

   104 *IGYPS2121-S   < EXHIBIT > WAS NOT DEFINED AS A DATA-NAME. THE STATEMENT WAS DISCARDED.

   111 *IGYPS2121-S   < PRT-EMP-NUM > WAS NOT DEFINED AS A DATA-NAME. THE STATEMENT WAS DISCARDED.

TOTAL MESSAGES     INFORMATIONAL     WARNING     ERROR     SEVERE     TERMINATING

      5                 2                                    3
* STATISTICS FOR COBOL PROGRAM SAMPLE1 :

*    SOURCE RECORDS =  434
*    DATA DIVISION STATEMENTS = 127
*    PROCEDURE DIVISION STATEMENTS = 229
```

Figure 1.8 Diagnostics at the end of the listing, generated by the VS COBOL II compiler. One informational message, not shown, is at the beginning of the listing.

1.7 SUMMARY

Successful debugging requires following a planned, logical procedure which may be modified to suit the specific problem at hand.

Understanding the information provided by the system is important in debugging. This information includes condition codes, completion codes, system messages, and compiler diagnostics.

Condition codes indicate how successful the execution of a job step has been. The JCL COND parameter can be utilized to control execution of job steps based on condition codes returned from prior steps. You can also specify a condition code within your COBOL program which will be passed back to the calling program or the operating system. COBOL's special RETURN-CODE register can be examined to determine the value of a COBOL program condition code.

Completion codes occur when a job step either ABENDs or a job step fails due to a program exception. The ABEND macro is invoked, with generation of a completion code, a message, and a dump. System completion codes are returned by operating system programs. They are documented in the *IBM MVS Message Library: System Codes* manual. (Also see Appendix B of this book.) User completion codes, which may be returned by routines in the COBOL subroutine libraries or by the application program, are described in the IBM COBOL manuals or in the documentation supplied with the specific application. You can request a system dump with a user completion code by placing a call to ILBOABN0 at any point within the COBOL application program.

The COBOL compiler generates diagnostic messages with accompanying condition codes. All diagnostic messages should be examined, and corrections made to the source code where necessary. The messages and their corresponding condition codes differ according to which COBOL compiler is used. You can generate complete compiler diagnostic listings with explanations by running the jobs shown in Fig. 1.6 or Fig. 1.9.

```
//S1      EXEC COB2UC
//***************************************************
//*  SOURCE CODE IS COBOL II                        *
//***************************************************
//COB2.SYSIN   DD *
       ID DIVISION.
       PROGRAM-ID.    ERRMSG.
      ************************************************
      *  THIS PROGRAM WILL RESULT IN A LISTING OF ALL *
      *  COMPILER DIAGNOSTICS AND THEIR EXPLANATIONS. *
      ************************************************
       ENVIRONMENT DIVISION.
       DATA DIVISION.
       PROCEDURE DIVISION.
      ************************************************
      *  THE SAME RESULTS CAN BE ACHIEVED BY CHANGING *
      *  THE PROGRAM-NAME OF ANY PROGRAM TO 'ERRMSG.' *
      ************************************************
               GOBACK.
/*
//
```

Figure 1.9 Job which will produce a complete listing of VS COBOL II compiler diagnostics.

REVIEW QUESTIONS

1. Is debugging an art? Give the reasons for your position.

2. What are the differences between a condition code and a completion code?

3. Describe how a condition code can be utilized to control execution of a job containing many job steps. Give an example.

4. Consider the following situation: A programmer wishes to display an error message and then terminate a main COBOL program if the subprogram it called finds the value "INACTIVE" in FIELD-A. Code the appropriate COBOL statements in both programs.

5. Explain the difference between a system completion code and a user completion code.

6. Write the necessary COBOL code to terminate a COBOL program with a user completion code of 4444 if no record is found when a READ statement is executed.

7. How can the origin of messages in the job log be identified? Where do the following messages come from?

- **a.** IEA995I
- **b.** IGZ038I
- **c.** IKF717I-D
- **d.** IEF686I

8. List the condition codes and their corresponding message levels generated by:

- **a.** the OS/VS COBOL compiler
- **b.** the VS COBOL II compiler

Chapter

2

Compiler Options and Compiler Output

As indicated in the previous chapter, the primary function of the COBOL compiler is to translate the COBOL source code into object code which can be processed by the computer. It is surprising, however, how few COBOL programmers take advantage of all the compiler has to offer. In addition to allowing such things as generation of optimized code, use of either static or dynamic calls to subroutines, and control over how binary fields are truncated during arithmetic operations, the compiler provides a wealth of useful debugging aids. These include maps, cross-reference listings, interactive debugging capability, and even options which identify the statement which was executing at the time the program crashed. Some options may already be in effect, either because they are IBM defaults or they have been set by the installation. You can see which are in effect for a compilation by consulting the "options in effect" listing in the compiler output. You may then activate additional options or override existing ones. Options are usually inactivated by using the prefix NO in front of an option name when passing a parameter to the compiler.

This chapter will concentrate on those compiler options and compiler output which are most useful for debugging.

2.1 COMPILER OPTIONS USEFUL IN DEBUGGING

Depending on the version of COBOL being used, different compiler options must be selected. Occasionally, a particular option will give virtually the same output regardless of which IBM compiler is used. In some cases, however, the name of the option may be the same for the different compilers but the output is different; the differences may range from minimal to significant. In other cases, the option may be available in one version of the COBOL compiler and not in another version.

To make it easier for the reader to find the options appropriate for the version of COBOL being used, OS/VS COBOL compiler options will be reviewed separately from COBOL II options. Also, in the discussion of COBOL II options, differences between Release 2 and Release 3 will be noted. If there is an abbreviation for an option, it will be given in parentheses.

2.1.1 OS/VS COBOL Compiler Options

To verify which compiler options are in effect, refer to the "options in effect" listing after compiling your program. Depending on which options were requested, this listing is either at the end of the compiler output or embedded somewhere in the middle of the compiler output, generally after the PMAP or CLIST listing (see Fig. 2.1). The options can be changed by passing parameters to the compiler through the JCL, as shown in the following example for the COBUCLG procedure:

```
//S1     EXEC COBUCLG,PARM.COB='PMAP,FLOW'
```

In this example the options PMAP and FLOW are passed as parameters to the COB step in the procedure. COB is the compile step.

Following are OS/VS COBOL compiler options which can provide assistance in debugging a program. They are listed alphabetically.

CLIST (CLI). This option gives a condensed listing of the PROCEDURE DIVISION. It includes the source line number for each COBOL verb, the hexadecimal offset into the program for the first Assembler instruction generated by the verb, and, if the VERB compiler option is in effect, the name of the verb. If VERB is not in effect, the word "verb" is substituted for each actual verb name. CLIST and the PMAP compiler option are mutually exclusive. More will be said about CLIST in Sec. 3.3.1.

COUNT (COU). When this is in effect, code is generated which will produce a verb execution summary at the end of program execution. This option implies that the VERB option is also in effect. If the VERB option was not explicitly requested, it will automatically be put into effect as a result of requesting COUNT. For each verb, the COUNT output includes the statement number, procedure name, last block of verbs executed (denoted with an asterisk), verb name, number of times the verb was executed, and the percentage of executions relative to the execution of all verbs in the program. A sorted summary of

```
*OPTIONS IN EFFECT*     SIZE =  196608  BUF =   28672  LINECNT = 57  SPACE1, FLAGW, NOSEQ,   SOURCE
*OPTIONS IN EFFECT*       DMAP, NOPMAP,   CLIST, NOSUPMAP, NOXREF,   SXREF,   LOAD, NODECK, APOST, NOTRUNC, NOFLOW
*OPTIONS IN EFFECT*     NOTERM,   NUM, NOBATCH, NONAME, COMPILE=01, NOSTATE, NORESIDENT, NODYNAM, NOLIB, NOSYNTAX
*OPTIONS IN EFFECT*     NOOPTIMIZE, NOSYMDMP, NOTEST,   VERB,   ZWB, SYST, NOENDJOB, NOLVL
*OPTIONS IN EFFECT*     NOLST , NOFDECK,NOCDECK, LCOL2,  L120,   DUMP ,   ADV , NOPRINT,
*OPTIONS IN EFFECT*     NOCOUNT, NOVBSUM, NOVBREF, LANGLVL(2)
```

Figure 2.1 Options in effect for an OS/VS COBOL compile.

all verbs by type (e.g., all ADD verbs, all MOVE verbs, etc.) is also given. This includes a static count (how many times this verb type exists in the program), dynamic count (how many of this verb type is actually executed, e.g., 11 of the 13 occurrences of ADD), total number of executions for this type of verb, and the percent this verb type was executed with respect to the execution of all verbs in the program (see Fig. 2.2). COUNT requires both SYSDBOUT and SYSCOUNT DD statements in the JCL.

The COUNT option is helpful in debugging because it clearly shows which code has and which code has not been executed. If statements were never executed, this may indicate a problem with control flow logic.

DMAP (DMA). The DMAP compiler option generates a DATA DIVISION map. The output includes the source name and internal name for each DATA DIVISION identifier, the level (01, 02, 03, etc.), the base locator cell number (these cells contain the base address in storage from which this identifier can be accessed), the displacement from the base address in storage for this identifier, the item's definition in Assembler-like terms, its USAGE, and additional miscellaneous information about the identifier (e.g., is it the subject of REDEFINES?). DMAP output will be discussed fully in Sec. 3.1.1.

FLOW (FLO). This compiler option initiates a trace of procedures executed before an abnormal termination of the program. You can specify the number of procedures to be traced from 1 to 99. If FLOW is requested at compile time, the number of procedures traced can be set at execution time. The option can also be turned off at run time. The FLOW output contains the program name, the statement number being executed at the time of the ABEND, the PSW and completion code, and the line numbers of the procedures executed before the ABEND occurred. The line numbers appear in first-in first-out order, with the most recently executed procedure last (see Fig. 2.3). The SYSDBOUT DD statement is required in the JCL if FLOW is used.

Because FLOW shows the logical flow of control of the program before an ABEND, it may aid you in determining how execution got to the ABENDing instruction. Perhaps the ABEND is caused by an endless loop, a branch to the wrong procedure, or some other incorrect flow of control.

LISTER feature. A number of compiler options are used to control the lister feature. The lister produces a reformatted source listing which includes cross-references and indenting conventions imposed by the lister. Optionally, the lister can be requested to produce a new source deck which reflects the reformatted source listing. Note that if compilation (generation of an object module) is requested, the results may be different than if a normal compilation were done. For example, the SKIP and EJECT statements will be ignored, the SUPPRESS option of the COPY statement will have no effect, and too many consecutive comment statements (approximately 80 or more) may terminate the lister. Complete information about the lister feature is given in the *IBM OS/VS COBOL Compiler and Library Programmer's Guide.*

Options used with the lister feature are

```
                     COBOL EXECUTION STATISTICS    PROG1

STATEMENT PROCEDURE-NAME                  L
NUMBER                                    B VERB ID          VERB COUNT           PERCENT
--------- ------------------------------ - ---------------- ------------------- -------
 15800    0000-MAINLINE
 16000                                      OPEN                                1   0.125
 16200                                      MOVE                                1   0.125
 16300                                      READ                                1   0.125
 16400                                      MOVE                                0   0.000
 16500                                      MOVE                                1   0.125
 16600                                      PERFORM                             1   0.125
 16700                                      IF                                  1   0.125
 16800                                      DISPLAY                             0   0.000
 16900                                      PERFORM                             1   0.125
 17100                                      PERFORM                             1   0.125
 17200                                      CLOSE                               1   0.125
 17320                                    * DISPLAY                             1   0.125
 17400                                    * MOVE                                1   0.125
 17500                                    * STOP                                1   0.125
 18000    0100-COMPARE-SEQ-NO
 18100                                      ADD                                32   4.030
 18200                                      MOVE                               32   4.030
 18300                                      IF                                 32   4.030
 18400                                      PERFORM                             1   0.125
 18500                                      ELSE
 18600                                      IF                                 31   3.904
 18700                                      PERFORM                             0   0.000
 18900                                      ELSE
 19000                                      IF                                 31   3.904
                                                 .
                                                 .
                                                 .
                     COBOL EXECUTION STATISTICS    TOTALS

VERBS EXECUTED TOTALS                                              794
VERB              STATIC COUNT DYNAMIC COUNT VERB EXECUTIONS PERCENT
----------------  ------------ ------------- --------------- -------
ADD                         13            11             166  20.906
CLOSE                        1             1               1   0.125
DISPLAY                      2             1               1   0.125
EXIT                         6             5              68   8.564
IF                          10             9             160  20.151
MOVE                        27            22             241  30.352
OPEN                         1             1               1   0.125
PERFORM                     12             6              37   4.659
READ                         2             2              33   4.156
STOP                         1             1               1   0.125
WRITE                       14            13              85  10.705
TOTALS                      89            72             794
                     END OF COBOL EXECUTION STATISTICS
```

Figure 2.2 Output from the COUNT compiler option in OS/VS COBOL showing static and dynamic verb counts and verb execution statistics.

LSTONLY (LSTO) or LSTCOMP (LSTC). LSTONLY requests a reformatted listing with no compilation. LSTCOMP requests both a reformatted listing and a compilation.

FDECK. This option specifies that a copy of the reformatted source listing is to be written to the SYSPUNCH data set as well as to the normal data set for compiler output.

```
PROGRAM          PROG1
LAST PSW BEFORE ABEND = FF850007C000B764      SYSTEM COMPLETION CODE = 0C7
                                                         FLOW TRACE
PROG1      019600 018000 021700 023700 019600 018000 021700 023700 019600 018000 021700 023700 019600 018000 021700
PROG1      023700 019600 018000 021700 023700 019600 018000 021700 025900 027900 023700 019600 018000 021700 023700
PROG1      019600 018000 021700 023700 019600 018000 021700 023700 019600 018000 021700 023700 019600 018000 021700
PROG1      023700 019600 018000 021700 023700 019600 018000 021700 023700 019600 018000 021700 023700 019600 018000
PROG1      021700 023700 019600 018000 021700 023700 019600 018000 021700 023700 019600 018000 021700 025900 027900
PROG1      023700 019600 018000 021700 023700 019600 018000 021700 023700 019600 018000 021700 023700 019600 018000
PROG1      021700 023700 019600 018000 021700 023700 019600 018000 021700
                                                  END OF COBOL DIAGNOSTIC AIDS
```

Figure 2.3 Output from the FLOW compiler option for an ABENDing program in OS/VS COBOL.

CDECK. This option requests expansion of copy members and commenting out of COPY statements.

LCOL1 or LCOL2. The first option causes the PROCEDURE DIVISION part of the listing to be in single-column format while the second option causes the PROCEDURE DIVISION listing to be in double-column format.

L120 or L132. These options indicate whether the length of each line in the reformatted listing is to be 120 or 132 characters long.

Figure 2.4 shows output obtained when the LCOL2 and L132 options were in effect.

NUM. Normally the compiler-generated source line numbers are used in error messages. NUM specifies that line numbers appearing in columns 1 through 6 of the input source module are to be used instead. This is helpful when you wish to have line numbers in the compiler output match the line numbers that may have been inserted in those columns in the edit session of the source code; it makes it easier to find the correct line in the source dataset so that errors can be fixed.

PMAP (PMA). This option generates a map of the PROCEDURE DIVISION. If the VERB compiler option is in effect, the COBOL name of each verb is shown. Also given is the source line number for the verb, a full Assembler-language expansion, hexadecimal object code, and information about the operands and the hexadecimal offset into the program for each Assembler instruction. If VERB is in effect, the listing also includes the name of the procedure which contains the COBOL verb. When VERB is not in effect, blanks will appear in place of verb and procedure names. The PMAP and CLIST compiler options are mutually exclusive. Use of the PMAP option will be discussed fully in Sec. 3.3.2.1.

SOURCE (SOU). The SOURCE option causes the COBOL source module to be listed. If NUM is not in effect, both the compiler-generated line numbers and the numbers appearing in columns 1 through 6 of the input source code are shown; the compiler-generated numbers are at the far left of the listing with the numbers from source columns 1 through 6 to their right. If NUM is in effect, only the numbers appearing in columns 1 through 6 of the input source module are listed.

```
PP 5740-CB1 RELEASE 2.4                    IBM OS/VS COBOL  JULY  1, 1982          9.39.43  DATE JUN 25,1991

   1        TABOSVS1          9.39.43        JUN 25,1991
```

YOUR PROGRAM HAS BEEN LISTED, SUMMARIZED, PUNCHED AND/OR COMPILED, DEPENDING ON THE OPTIONS YOU SELECTED. THIS PAGE DESCRIBES THE OUTPUTS OF THE LISTER FEATURE -

DETAIL LISTING

THIS BASIC LISTING SHOWS YOUR RE-FORMATTED PROGRAM WITH ADDED INFORMATION (NUMBERS, LETTERS, ETC.). NUMBERS ARE USED IN THREE WAYS -

1. STATEMENTS ARE NUMBERED ON THE LEFT. EACH SECTION, DIVISION, PARAGRAPH, LEVEL-INDICATOR, INDEX-DEFINITION, VERB OR 'ELSE' IS GIVEN A NEW NUMBER (AND A NEW LINE.
2. TO THE RIGHT OF A STATEMENT DEFINING A NAME IS A LIST OF THE NUMBERS THAT REFER TO THAT NAME.
3. TO THE RIGHT OF A STATEMENT THAT REFERS TO NAMES IS A LIST OF THE DEFINING STATEMENT NUMBERS. THESE POINTERS MAY BE FOLLOWED BY A SLASH AND CROSS-REFERENCES. UNDEFINED NAMES HAVE POINTERS OF ZERO.

LETTERS CLASSIFY REFERENCES, SHOW ERRORS, OR MARK FOOTNOTES. CROSS-REFERENCE SUFFIXES SHOW TYPE -

A - ALTER
B - (ALTER) TO PROCEED TO
C - DATUM CHANGED (BUT NOT READ OR WRITTEN)
D - REDEFINES OR RENAMES (OR 'DEBUG')
E - OPEN, CLOSE, ETC. (OR ENV-DIVISION REFERENCE)
G - GO TO
P - PERFORM
Q - DATUM QUERIED BY IF, UNTIL OR WHEN
R - READ, ACCEPT, ETC.
T - (PERFORM) THRU
U - DATUM UNCHANGED (SOURCE FOR MOVE, ADD, ETC.)
W - WRITE, DISPLAY, GENERATE, ETC.
X - SUBSCRIPT, INDEX OR 'DEPENDING ON' VARIABLE

AN 'E' IN COLUMN-7 SHOWS AN ERRONEOUS STATEMENT. A LETTER AFTER A CROSS-REFERENCE LIST IN THE DATA DIVISION SHOWS THAT THE LIST CONTINUES IN A FOOTNOTE. A LETTER AS POINTER IN THE PROCEDURE DIVISION SHOWS THAT THE FULL DATA DEFINITION (WITH REFERENCES) IS REPRINTED AS A FOOTNOTE (ON THE SAME OR A RECENT PRIOR PAGE).

THE LISTING IS INDENTED TWO SPACES PER LEVEL (UP TO EIGHT LEVELS). STATEMENT CONTINUATIONS ARE INDENTED SIX MORE SPACES. PROCEDURE DIVISION INDENTATION SHOWS THE RANGE OF (NESTED) 'IF', 'SEARCH' AND OTHER TESTING VERBS. (NOTE - 'ELSE' AND 'WHEN' ARE ALIGNED WITH THE MATCHING 'IF' AND 'SEARCH'.)

'VALUE', 'PIC', 'COMP', ETC., ARE ALIGNED, WHERE POSSIBLE, INTO COLUMNS TOWARD THE RIGHT SIDE OF EACH LINE. THIS ALIGNMENT HIGHLIGHTS PATTERNS ON THE RIGHT AND THE RARER 'REDEFINES' OR 'OCCURS' TOWARD THE LEFT.

STATEMENT AND CARD NUMBERS

STATEMENT NUMBERS IN THIS LISTING CORRESPOND TO THE FIRST FIVE DIGITS OF THE SIX-DIGIT NUMBER USED FOR COMPILER DIAGNOSTICS, REFORMATTED SOURCE CARDS, ETC. THUS, STATEMENT '317' WILL BE PUNCHED INTO CARD NUMBER '003170' AND STATEMENT '9307' WILL BE DIAGNOSED AS CARD NUMBER '093070'.

LISTING LINES WITHOUT STATEMENT NUMBERS (E.G., CONTINUATIONS OR *-COMMENTS) CORRESPOND TO CARDS WITH CARD NUMBERS INCREMENTED BY ONE FROM THE LAST CARD NUMBER THAT DID CORRESPOND TO A NUMBERED LINE. FOR EXAMPLE, STATEMENT '1304' AND TWO FOLLOWING LINES WITHOUT NUMBERS ARE 'PUNCHED' INTO CARDS '013040', '013041' AND '013042'.

SUMMARY PAGES

THIS CONDENSED LISTING SHOWS HOW MAJOR PARTS OF THE PROGRAM REFER TO EACH OTHER. THE SUMMARY LISTING FACILITATES INITIAL STUDY OF A LARGE UNFAMILIAR PROGRAM BY SHOWING GENERAL STRUCTURE, HIGHLIGHTING EXCEPTIONS, AND AIDING THE PLANNING FOR THE BEST DETAILED STUDY.

THE MAJOR PARTS OF A PROGRAM ARE SECTIONS, FD'S, SD'S, RD'S, ETC. FOR EACH MAJOR PART THERE IS A TITLE LINE, A SET OF SUMMARY ENTRIES AND (IF NEEDED) TOTALS FOR ERRONEOUS STATEMENTS, FOR REFERENCES TO UNDEFINED NAMES AND/OR (RARELY) FOR 'LOST DATA'.

SUMMARY ENTRIES CONTAIN BASIC TOTALS FORMED WITH A LETTER (SHOWING TYPE OF REFERENCE), A DASH AND A COUNT OF THE NUMBER OF REFERENCES OF THAT TYPE BETWEEN A SPECIFIC PAIR OF MAJOR PARTS. BASIC TOTALS FOR OTHER REFERENCE TYPES ARE PRINTED ON THE SAME LINE, AND THE LIST OF BASIC TOTALS IS PRECEDED BY A TOTAL COUNT FOR ALL TYPES OF REFERENCES BETWEEN THE TWO MAJOR PARTS.

SPECIFIC WORDS ARE USED TO SHOW THE DIRECTION OF REFERENCES. 'INTRA' SHOWS REFERENCES WITHIN THE MAJOR PART. 'TO' OR 'FROM' FOLLOWED BY A STATEMENT-NUMBER SHOW REFERENCES TO OR FROM THAT OTHER MAJOR PART.

```
 2        TABOSVS1          9.39.43        JUN 25,1991

  1 IDENTIFICATION DIVISION.
  2   PROGRAM-ID. TABOSVS1.
  3   AUTHOR. ALAN FRIEND.
  4   DATE-WRITTEN. 4 / 1 / 91.
  5   DATE-COMPILED. JUN 25,1991.
  6 ENVIRONMENT DIVISION.
  8 INPUT-OUTPUT SECTION.
  9   FILE-CONTROL.
 10     SELECT EMPFILE                                          16
              ASSIGN TO EMFILE.
 11     SELECT OUTFILE                                          23
              ASSIGN TO OUTFILE.
 12     SELECT DEPTFILE                                         30
              ASSIGN TO DEFILE.
```

Figure 2.4 Part of the output from the OS/VS COBOL Lister Feature. (*Continued*)

```
3         TABOSVS1          9.39.43         JUN 25,1991


13 DATA DIVISION.
15 FILE SECTION.
16 FD  EMPFILE                                                      10E,128E,141R,150E,207R
         RECORDING MODE IS F
         RECORD CONTAINS 80 CHARACTERS
         LABEL RECORDS ARE OMITTED
         BLOCK CONTAINS 0 RECORDS
         DATA RECORD IS EMPREC.
22   01  EMPREC                              PIC X(80).
23 FD  OUTFILE                                                      11E,128E,150E
         RECORDING MODE IS F
         RECORD CONTAINS 100 CHARACTERS
         LABEL RECORDS ARE OMITTED
         BLOCK CONTAINS 0 RECORDS
         DATA RECORD IS OUTREC.
29   01  OUTREC                              PIC X(100).            175W,202W,225W,241W,246W,254W
30 FD  DEPTFILE                                                     12E,128E,131R,150E,159R
         RECORDING MODE IS F
         RECORD CONTAINS 32 CHARACTERS
         LABEL RECORDS ARE OMITTED
         BLOCK CONTAINS 0 RECORDS
         DATA RECORD IS DEPTREC.
36   01  DEPTREC                             PIC X(32).
```

Figure 2.4 *(Continued)*

Obviously, it is usually necessary to have the source code available if the program must be reviewed or debugged. Also, having the source listing helps to tell which program statements are referred to in compiler diagnostic messages.

STATE (STA). This option specifies the number of the COBOL statement being executed at the time of an ABEND. In addition, the PSW at the time of the ABEND and the completion code are given (see Fig. 2.5). This is a very useful compiler option since it pinpoints the ABENDing COBOL instruction. The SYSDBOUT DD statement must be included in the execution JCL when STATE is to be put into effect.

SXREF (SXR). The SXREF option provides a sorted cross-reference of data names and procedure names, each in a separate list. Included is the line number in the source code where the item is defined as well as all line numbers where the item is referenced in PROCEDURE DIVISION statements (see Fig. 2.6). It is similar to the listing from the XREF option except that the SXREF output is in alphabetical order.

This option is particularly helpful because it allows you to find all occurrences of an item easily. SXREF and the XREF option are mutually exclusive.

SYMDMP (SYM). If SYMDMP is in effect, a COBOL-formatted dump of the DATA DIVISION and selected portions of COBOL's internal data area are generated if the program ABENDs. Dynamic dumps of specific data names can also be requested at strategic points during program execution. A compile-time SYSUT5 DD statement must be provided; this gives additional work

```
4        TABOSVS1         9.39.43        JUN 25,1991


37 WORKING-STORAGE SECTION.
  ***************************************************************
  *         ACCUMULATORS AND SWITCHES                           *
  ***************************************************************
42 01  MISC.
43    05  ACCUMULATORS                                COMP-3.
44      10  LN-CTR                  PIC 99            VALUE 60.      177C,204C,220Q,227C,238Q,243C,248C
45      10  PG-CTR                  PIC 9(3)          VALUE ZERO.    173C,174U
46      10  NO-DEPT-EMP             PIC S99           VALUE ZERO.    189C,215C,236U
47      10  EMP-SALARY              PIC S9(6)V99      VALUE ZERO.    217C,218U
48      10  DEPT-SALARY             PIC S9(9)V99      VALUE ZERO.    189C,218C,236U
49      10  AVE-DEPT-SALARY         PIC S9(6)V99      VALUE ZERO.    189C,236C,240U,245U
50      10  TOT-NO-EMP              PIC S9(6)V99      VALUE ZERO.    215C,250U
51      10  TOT-SALARY              PIC S9(9)V99      VALUE ZERO.    218C,250U
52      10  AVE-TOT-SALARY          PIC S9(6)V99      VALUE ZERO.    250C,253U
53    05  DEPT-HOLD                 PIC 99            VALUE ZERO.    145C,186Q,228C
54    05  SW-EOF                    PIC 9             VALUE ZERO.    135C,143C,161C,209C
55      88  NO-MORE-DEPT-RECORDS       VALUE 1.                      136Q,140Q
56      88  NO-MORE-EMP-RECORDS        VALUE 2.                      147Q,249Q
57    05  SEARCH-ERROR-SW           PIC 9             VALUE ZERO.    146C,188C,198C
58      88  NO-MATCH                   VALUE 1.
59      88  MATCH                      VALUE 2.                      205Q
  ***************************************************************
  *                  TABLE DEFINITION                           *
  *   FIRST RECORD DETERMINES NUMBER OF TABLE ENTRIES           *
  ***************************************************************
64 01  FIRST-REC.                                                    131R
65    05  NO-OF-ENTRIES             PIC 99.                          68X,137Q
66    05  FILLER                    PIC X(30).
67 01  DEPT-TABLE.
68    05  DEPT-REC    OCCURS 5 TO 15 TIMES DEPENDING ON NO-OF-ENTRIES 65/159R,193U
                                                        INDEXED BY
71            DEPT-IND.                                              137C,137Q,159X,192C,199X,200X,201X
72      10  DEPT-CODE               PIC XX.                          199Q,200U
73      10  DEPT-NAME               PIC X(30).                       201U
  ***************************************************************
  *             INPUT RECORD AREA                               *
  ***************************************************************
76 01  EMPREC-WS.                                                    141R,207R
77    05  EMPNO-WS.                                                  195W,222U
78      10  EMP-DEPT-WS             PIC XX.                          145U,186Q,196W,199Q,228U
79      10  EMP-LEVEL-WS            PIC X(3).
80    05  EMP-NAME-WS               PIC X(25).                       223U
81    05  EMP-SALARY-WS             PIC 9(6)V99.                     217U,224U
82    05  FILLER                    PIC X(42).
  ***************************************************************
  *                    PRINT LINES                              *
  ***************************************************************
86 01  HEADER-1.                                                     175W
87    05  FILLER                    PIC X(32)         VALUE SPACES.
88    05  FILLER                    PIC X(36)         VALUE
                          'D E P A R T M E N T   L I S T I N G'.
90    05  FILLER                    PIC X(25)         VALUE SPACES.
91    05  FILLER                    PIC X(4)          VALUE 'PAGE'.
                                          .
                                          .
                                          .
```

Figure 2.4 *(Continued)*

```
   6        TABOSVS1        9.39.43        JUN 25,1991

121 PROCEDURE DIVISION.
    *****************************************************************
    *   PROGRAM INITIALIZATION, LOAD DEPARTMENT TABLE, BEGIN TO *
    *   PROCESS EMPLOYEE RECORDS IF TABLE SUCCESSFULLY LOADED.  *
    *****************************************************************

127    1000-INIT.
128      OPEN INPUT EMPFILE DEPTFILE OUTPUT OUTFILE       16,30,23
131      READ DEPTFILE INTO FIRST-REC AT END                 30,64
133        DISPLAY 'TABLE FILL ERROR - DEPARTMENT FILE EMPTY'
134        DISPLAY '*** PROGRAM TERMINATED ***'
135        MOVE 1 TO SW-EOF.                                    54
136      IF NOT NO-MORE-DEPT-RECORDS                            55
137        PERFORM 1000-LOAD-TABLE THRU                        158
                 1000-LOAD-TABLE-EXIT VARYING DEPT-IND      166,71
                 FROM 1 BY 1 UNTIL DEPT-IND GREATER THAN        71
                 NO-OF-ENTRIES.                                 65
140      IF NOT NO-MORE-DEPT-RECORDS                            55
141        READ EMPFILE INTO EMPREC-WS AT END                16,76
143          MOVE 2 TO SW-EOF                                   54
144          DISPLAY 'EMPLOYEE FILE EMPTY'.
145      MOVE EMP-DEPT-WS TO DEPT-HOLD                       78,53
146      MOVE 2 TO SEARCH-ERROR-SW                              57
147      PERFORM 3000-COMPARE-PROCESS THRU 3000-EXIT       185,210
             UNTIL NO-MORE-EMP-RECORDS                          56
149      PERFORM 6000-DEPT-SUMMARY THRU                        235
             6000-DEPT-SUMMARY-EXIT                            256
150      CLOSE EMPFILE OUTFILE DEPTFILE                   16,23,30
153      GOBACK.
    *****************************************************************
    *  LOAD DEPARTMENT TABLE                                        *
    *****************************************************************

158    1000-LOAD-TABLE. 137P
159      READ DEPTFILE INTO DEPT-REC (DEPT-IND) AT END  30,68,71
161        MOVE 1 TO SW-EOF                                     54
162        DISPLAY 'TABLE FILL ERROR - NO. OF TABLE '
               'ENTRIES LESS THAN VALUE IN '
               'NO-OF-ENTRIES FIELD'
165        DISPLAY '*** PROGRAM TERMINATED ***'.

166    1000-LOAD-TABLE-EXIT. 137T
168      EXIT.
    *****************************************************************
    *  HEADER ROUTINE                                               *
    *****************************************************************

172    2500-HEADER. 221P,239P,252P
173      ADD 1 TO PG-CTR                                        45
174      MOVE PG-CTR TO PG-OUT                               45,92
175      WRITE OUTREC FROM HEADER-1 AFTER ADVANCING PAGE     29,86
177      MOVE 1 TO LN-CTR.                                      44
178    2500-EXIT. 221T,239T,252T
179      EXIT.
    *****************************************************************
    *  COMPARE EMPLOYEE DEPARTMENT NUMBER WITH DEPARTMENT TABLE *
    *  ENTRIES; REFORMAT AND WRITE EMPLOYEE RECORD IF THERE IS A *
    *  MATCH AND DISPLAY ERROR MESSAGE IF NO MATCH                  *
    *****************************************************************

185    3000-COMPARE-PROCESS. 147P
186      IF EMP-DEPT-WS GREATER THAN DEPT-HOLD                  78,53
187        PERFORM 6000-DEPT-SUMMARY THRU                         235
                 6000-DEPT-SUMMARY-EXIT                           256
188        MOVE 2 TO SEARCH-ERROR-SW                               57
189        MOVE ZERO TO NO-DEPT-EMP DEPT-SALARY                 46,48
               AVE-DEPT-SALARY                                     49
192        SET DEPT-IND TO 1                                       71
193        SEARCH DEPT-REC                                         68
194          AT END
195            DISPLAY 'ERROR FOR EMPLOYEE NO. ' EMPNO-WS          77
196            DISPLAY 'EMPLOYEE DEPARTMENT NO. ' EMP-DEPT-WS      78
                 ' NOT IN DEPARTMENT TABLE'
198            MOVE 1 TO SEARCH-ERROR-SW                           57
199          WHEN DEPT-CODE (DEPT-IND) IS EQUAL TO              72,71
                 EMP-DEPT-WS                                       78
200            MOVE DEPT-CODE (DEPT-IND) TO                     72,71
                 DEPT-CODE-OUT                                     97
201            MOVE DEPT-NAME (DEPT-IND) TO                     73,71
                 DEPT-NAME-OUT                                     99
202            WRITE OUTREC FROM SUBHEADER-1 AFTER              29,93
                 ADVANCING 3
204            ADD 3 TO LN-CTR.                                    44
205      IF MATCH                                                  59
206        PERFORM 5000-DETAIL THRU 5000-EXIT.                214,229
207      READ EMPFILE INTO EMPREC-WS AT END                     16,76
209        MOVE 2 TO SW-EOF.                                       54

210    3000-EXIT. 147T
211      EXIT.
    *****************************************************************
    *              WRITE DETAIL LINE.                               *
    *****************************************************************

214    5000-DETAIL. 206P
215      ADD +1 TO NO-DEPT-EMP TOT-NO-EMP                       46,50
217      MOVE EMP-SALARY-WS TO EMP-SALARY                       81,47
218      ADD EMP-SALARY TO DEPT-SALARY TOT-SALARY            47,48,51
220      IF LN-CTR GREATER THAN 55                                 44
221        PERFORM 2500-HEADER THRU 2500-EXIT.                172,178
222      MOVE EMPNO-WS TO EMPNO-OUT                            77,103
223      MOVE EMP-NAME-WS TO EMP-NAME-OUT                      80,105
224      MOVE EMP-SALARY-WS TO EMP-SALARY-OUT                  81,107
225      WRITE OUTREC FROM DETAIL-1 AFTER ADVANCING 2          29,101
227      ADD 2 TO LN-CTR                                           44
228      MOVE EMP-DEPT-WS TO DEPT-HOLD.                         78,53
                                   .
                                   .
                                   .
```

Figure 2.4 *(Continued)*

space to the compiler. Also, the execution-time DD statements SYSDBOUT and SYSDBG are required. The SYSDBG dataset will contain programmer-specified control statements needed for proper operation of the SYMDMP option. Output from SYMDMP appears on the SYSDBOUT dataset.

SYMDMP is an invaluable debugging aid since it shows the contents of DATA DIVISION fields and file information in a format that is easier to read than in a hexadecimal storage dump. For an abnormal program termination, it also gives the completion code and the number of the statement being executed. SYMDMP will be discussed fully in Sec. 6.1.

```
PROGRAM          PROG1
LAST PSW BEFORE ABEND = FF850007C000BAAC       SYSTEM COMPLETION CODE = 0C7
LAST CARD NUMBER/VERB NUMBER EXECUTED -- CARD NUMBER 022900/VERB NUMBER 01.
                                               END OF COBOL DIAGNOSTIC AIDS
```

Figure 2.5 Output from the STATE compiler option for an ABENDing OS/VS COBOL program.

TEST (TES). If the OS/VS COBOL interactive debugger TESTCOB is to be used, then the TEST compiler option must be requested. A compile-time SYSUT5 DD statement must be provided as well. When TEST is in effect, FLOW, STATE, COUNT, SYMDMP, or BATCH options cannot be specified. TESTCOB will be discussed in Chap. 12.

VBSUM (VBS). This option gives a sorted summary of the verbs used in the program, specifying how many times each type of verb occurs (see Fig. 2.7). It is similar to the static verb count given in the summary portion of the COUNT compiler option output. VBSUM implies that VERB is also in effect; it will be turned on even if it wasn't explicitly requested.

VBSUM can be helpful because it quickly identifies the frequencies with which verbs were coded, and this may suggest areas for improving program efficiency and eliminating potential logic problems. For example, multiple OPEN and CLOSE statements for a file may be less efficient and more error-prone than a single OPEN and a single CLOSE for that file.

VBREF (VBR). The VBREF compiler option gives a sorted cross-reference listing of all verbs used in the program. Included is the number of times each type of verb occurs as well as all line numbers where the verb is referenced in PROCEDURE DIVISION statements (see Fig. 2.8). This is especially helpful because it allows you to find quickly all occurrences of statements containing verbs which may need to be examined. This option implies that VERB and VBSUM are also in effect; they will be put into effect even if they were not explicitly requested.

VERB (VER). The VERB option causes verb names to be listed with CLIST compiler output, and both verb names and procedure names to be listed with PMAP compiler output. If VERB is not in effect, the word "verb" will be listed in place of the actual verb name in the CLIST output, and blanks will appear instead of verb and procedure names in the PMAP listing. Without VERB in effect, the CLIST and PMAP output are almost useless. VERB will automatically be in effect if COUNT, SYMDMP, STATE, TEST, VBREF, or VBSUM are in effect.

XREF (XRE). This option generates a cross-reference listing of data names and procedure names, each in a separate list. Included is the line number in the source code where the item is defined as well as all line numbers where the item is referenced in PROCEDURE DIVISION statements. It is similar to the SXREF listing except that the items are not listed alphabetically, but in the order in which they appear in the source code. XREF is helpful because it allows you to find all occurrences of an item which must be examined. XREF and SXREF are mutually exclusive.

As you can see, many of the options described above can take a good deal of the work out of debugging an OS/VS COBOL program. Your choice of options will depend on many factors. First, your personal preference must be considered. Do you prefer to use the NUM option so that line numbers in columns 1 through 6 of the source code will be used when printing diagnostic messages, or is it sufficient to specify NONUM so that the compiler will use its own numbering scheme instead?

Next, efficiency must be considered. A sorted cross-reference (SXREF) causes more compilation overhead than a normal cross-reference (XREF). The TEST option will degrade program performance, and is not advisable for production jobs. Thus if compile time is an issue, options which require extra system resources should not be used. If program execution time is important, as it usually is, then many options which cause the program to use extra system resources at execution time should be used only during program development and testing, not for production runs.

Some options may be chosen based on the type of listing desired. Perhaps the PMAP option is needed because you wish to determine what operands are used

```
                                         CROSS-REFERENCE DICTIONARY

DATA NAMES                          DEFN      REFERENCE

AMOUNT-COL                          008900
COL-HDR-1                           008300    027000
COL-HDR-2                           009200    027200
COMMENT-TOT                         011400
COMMENTS                            010900    018200   024500
                               .
                               .
                               .
PROCEDURE NAMES                     DEFN      REFERENCE

0000-MAINLINE                       015800
0100-COMPARE-SEQ-NO                 018000    016900
0100-COMPARE-SEQ-NO-EXIT            019600    016900
0200-SEQ-NO-EQUAL                   020200    018400
0200-SEQ-NO-EQUAL-EXIT              021400    018400
0300-SEQ-NO-GREATER                 021700    019100
0300-SEQ-NO-GREATER-EXIT            023700    019100
0400-SEQ-NO-LESS                    024000    018700
0400-SEQ-NO-LESS-EXIT               025300    018700
0500-HEADER-ROUT                    025900    016600   020900   022000   023200   024800   028800   029400
                               .
                               .
                               .
```

Figure 2.6 Sorted cross-reference listing produced by the SXREF compiler option in OS/VS COBOL.

```
                                    CROSS-REFERENCE DICTIONARY

VERBS                          OCCURS

 ADD                           000013
 CLOSE                         000001
 DISPLAY                       000002
 EXIT                          000006
 IF                            000010
 MOVE                          000027
 OPEN                          000001
 PERFORM                       000012
```

Figure 2.7 Static verb count generated by the VBSUM compiler option for an OS/VS COBOL program.

in an ABENDing Assembler instruction generated by a COBOL verb. Maybe the CLIST option is sufficient because you only need to know which COBOL verb was executing at the time of an ABEND. Perhaps embedded cross-references make the use of the lister feature more desirable than XREF or SXREF.

2.1.2 VS COBOL II Compiler Options

This section explains COBOL II compiler options which can prove helpful in debugging a program. To verify which are in effect, refer to the "options in effect" listing after compiling the program. This listing appears at the beginning of the compiler output (see Fig. 2.9). You can request options or override existing ones by passing parameters to the compiler through the JCL or by coding the PROCESS statement right before the IDENTIFICATION DIVISION header. The following example shows how to pass parameters to the compiler for the COB2UCLG procedure:

```
//S1     EXEC COB2UCLG,PARM.COB2='LIST,FLAG(I,I)'
```

In this case, the options LIST and FLAG(I,I) are passed to the COB2 step, which is the compile step in the procedure.

The PROCESS statement is coded as shown in the following example. The compiler options OFFSET and XREF are requested.

```
000100 PROCESS OFFSET,XREF
000200 IDENTIFICATION DIVISION.
```

CBL can be used as a synonym for PROCESS.

Options passed to the compiler through the PROCESS statement take precedence over those passed through the JCL. For easy reference, the options discussed here are presented in alphabetical order.

FDUMP (FDU). The FDUMP compiler option produces a COBOL-formatted dump if the program ABENDs. The DATA DIVISION dump is easier to understand than a hexadecimal system dump and gives extensive information about files and fields. Also included is the completion code, the PSW, the source line number of the statement in the program which was executing at the time of the ABEND, and the contents of the general-purpose registers. FDUMP is a valuable debugging tool since it provides essential information in an easy-to-read format. Since FDUMP output appears on the SYSDBOUT dataset, a SYSDBOUT execution-time DD statement must be included in the JCL. Also, the STAE run-time option must be in effect and the TEST compiler option must not be in effect. More will be said about FDUMP in Sec. 6.2.

LIST. This compiler option generates a PROCEDURE DIVISION map showing the COBOL verbs with their source code line numbers together with an Assembler-language expansion for each of the COBOL verbs. Also included is hexadecimal object code, information about the operands, and the hexadecimal offset into the program for each Assembler instruction. The name of the procedure containing the COBOL verb is shown as well. The LIST and OFFSET compiler options are mutually exclusive. LIST will be discussed more fully in Sec. 3.3.2.2.

MAP. The MAP option produces a map of the DATA DIVISION. The output for each DATA DIVISION identifier includes the source line number, field name and level (01, 05, 10, etc.), the base locator cell number (these cells contain the base address in storage from which each identifier can be accessed), the displacement from the base address in storage for this identifier, the displacement from the beginning of the structure (group-level item) containing this identifier, its definition in Assembler-like terms, its USAGE, and additional miscellaneous information about the identifier (e.g., is it the subject of REDEFINES?).

```
                                   CROSS-REFERENCE DICTIONARY

VERBS                      OCCURS  REFERENCE

 ADD                       000013  018100  020300  020700  021200  021800  022400  022900  023500  024100  025100
                                   026600  027700  029200
 CLOSE                     000001  017200
 DISPLAY                   000002  016800  017320
 EXIT                      000006  019700  021500  023800  025400  028000  030600
 IF                        000010  016700  018300  018600  019000  020800  021900  023100  024700  028700  029300
 MOVE                      000027  016200  016400  016500  017400  018200  019400  020400  020500  020600  022100
                                   022500  022600  022700  022800  023000  024200  024300  024400  024500  026000
                                   026100  026700  027400  028900  029500  029600  029700
 OPEN                      000001  016000
 PERFORM                   000012  016600  016900  017100  018400  018700  019100  020900  022000  023200  024800
                                   028800  029400
```

Figure 2.8 Output from the VBREF compiler option in OS/VS COBOL showing a static count and cross-reference listing of verbs.

```
Options in effect:
    ADV
    APOST
  NOAWO
    BUFSIZE(4096)
  NOCMPR2
  NOCOMPILE(S)
    DATA(31)
  NODBCS
  NODECK
  NODUMP
  NODYNAM
  NOEXIT
  NOFASTSRT
  NOFDUMP
    FLAG(I)
  NOFLAGMIG
  NOFLAGSAA
  NOFLAGSTD
    LANGUAGE(EN)
  NOLIB
    LINECOUNT(60)
  NOLIST
    MAP
  NONAME
    NUMBER
    NUMPROC(NOPFD)
    OBJECT
    OFFSET
  NOOPTIMIZE
    OUTDD(SYSOUT)
  NORENT
  NORESIDENT
  NOSEQUENCE
    SIZE(MAX)
    SOURCE
    SPACE(1)
  NOSSRANGE
  NOTERM
  NOTEST
    TRUNC(OPT)
  NOVBREF
  NOWORD
  NOXREF
    ZWB
```

Figure 2.9 Compiler options in effect listing at the beginning of a COBOL II Release 3 program.

The DATA DIVISION listing for Release 3 is slightly different from that for Release 2. Also, the Release 3 MAP option generates a nested program map. Nested programs are a Release 3 feature which allows programs to be nested, or contained within one another, and CALLed with the efficiency of a PERFORM rather than a CALL.

The MAP option will be discussed more fully in Sec. 3.1.2 and the nested program map more fully in Sec. 3.2.

NUMBER (NUM). The NUMBER compiler option causes the compiler to use the line numbers in columns 1 through 6 of the input source module for error messages. When NUMBER is not in effect, compiler-generated source line numbers are used instead. Having NUMBER in effect is helpful because the line numbers in the compiler output match the line numbers that may have been inserted in columns 1 through 6 when the source code was edited, making it easier to find the correct line in the source dataset so that errors can be fixed.

OFFSET (OFF). This compiler option generates a condensed PROCEDURE DIVISION listing. Included is the name and source line number for every COBOL verb, and the hexadecimal offset into the program for the first Assembler instruction generated by the verb. OFFSET and LIST are mutually exclusive. More will be said about OFFSET in Sec. 3.3.1.

SOURCE (S). SOURCE causes the COBOL source module to be listed. When the NUM option is not in effect, the compiler-generated source line numbers appear at the far left of the listing, followed by the numbers which were in columns 1 through 6 of the input source code. When NUM is in effect, only the line numbers in columns 1 through 6 are shown.

SOURCE must be in effect in order to get embedded compiler diagnostic messages. The Release 3 compiler also prints a column grid at the top of each page, program level (PL) and statement level (SL) nesting numbers, and, if the XREF option is specified, an abbreviated cross-reference listing at the right of the source code (see Fig. 2.10). Note that since Release 3 permits lowercase characters in the source code, you may get source code listings in mixed (upper and lower) case. (The LANGUAGE compiler option controls the listing of upper- and lowercase.)

It is usually necessary to have the source listing in order to tell which program statements are referred to in compiler diagnostic messages. The Release 3 source listing is particularly useful because it also provides nesting-level information and optional embedded cross-references.

SSRANGE (SSR). The SSRANGE option generates code which checks table subscripts and indexes at run time to be sure that they do not refer to items which are out of range of their assigned storage. In addition, SSRANGE checks that variable-length items defined with the OCCURS DEPENDING ON clause do not exceed their maximum defined lengths. In Release 3, SSRANGE also checks that expressions using reference modification contain valid starting positions and lengths.

Be cautious in using this option; note that rather than checking a subscript or index for a valid table occurrence, it checks the resulting address of the table element. This means for example, that it is possible for an item referenced with the subscript (1, 1, 13) in a three-dimensional table defined as having a maximum subscript of (15, 10, 12) to be considered within the range of the table. In this case, although the address of the item may be well within the bounds of the table's storage, we see that the third-level subscript (13) is erroneous; it is too large.

```
LineID  PL SL  ----+-*A-1-B--+----2----+----3----+----4----+----5----+----6----+----7-|--+----8  Cross Reference
000146         014700  01 MISC                                      GLOBAL.
000147         014800     05 INPUT-DATE.
000148         014900        10 YY                 PIC 99.
000149         015000        10 MM                 PIC 99.
000150         015100        10 DD                 PIC 99.
000151         015200     05 WS-SAVE-CUST-NO       PIC S9(5)    VALUE ZERO.                        IMP
000152         015300     05 WS-SAVE-CUST-TOT      PIC S9(4)V99 VALUE ZERO USAGE COMP-3.           IMP
000153         015400     05 COUNTERS     USAGE    COMP-3.
000154         015500        10 REC-READ           PIC S999     VALUE ZERO.                        IMP
000155         015600        10 REC-PROCESSED      PIC S999     VALUE ZERO.                        IMP
000156         015700        10 CUST-NO-ERROR      PIC S999     VALUE ZERO.                        IMP
000157         015800        10 REC-OUT-OF-SEQ     PIC S999     VALUE ZERO.                        IMP
000158         015900        10 PAGE-CT            PIC S99      VALUE ZERO.                        IMP
000159         016000        10 LINE-CT            PIC S99      VALUE +60.
                                                .
                                                .
                                                .
LineID  PL SL  ----+-*A-1-B--+----2----+----3----+----4----+----5----+----6----+----7-|--+----8  Cross Reference
000254  1      025500 IDENTIFICATION DIVISION.
000255  1      025600  PROGRAM-ID.  SUMMARY-REPORT.
000256  1      025700  AUTHOR.      ALAN FRIEND.
000257  1      025800 ENVIRONMENT DIVISION.
000258  1      025900 DATA DIVISION.
000259  1      026000 PROCEDURE DIVISION.
000260  1      026100     IF LINE-CT GREATER THAN 50                                               159
000261  1  1   026200        CALL 'HEADER-ROUTINE'                                                 224
000262  1      026300     END-IF
000263  1      026400     MOVE WS-SAVE-CUST-TOT TO WS-CUST-TOT                                     152 114
000264  1      026500     MOVE SPACES TO WS-COLUMN-1                                               IMP 180
                                                .
                                                .
                                                .
```

Figure 2.10 Source code listing generated by the SOURCE compiler option for a COBOL II Release 3 program. Because XREF was also in effect, an embedded cross-reference listing was produced at the right.

If an out-of-range condition is found when SSRANGE is in effect, the program is terminated and the message "IGZ007 The reference to variable length group *?* by verb number *?* on line *?* addressed an area outside the maximum defined length of the group" will appear in the job log. (The preceding message is generated in Release 3; the wording for the Release 2 message is slightly different.) This can be advantageous in testing and debugging a program since it gives a specific and meaningful message instead of allowing the program to terminate with a S0C4 protection exception or even run to completion. The code generated by the SSRANGE compiler option can be disabled at execution time by specifying the NOSSRANGE run-time option.

TEST (TES). The TEST option must be specified if the COBOL II interactive debugger COBTEST is to be used. When TEST is in effect, the compiler options RES, NOFDUMP, NOOPTIMIZE and OBJECT are also put into effect. COBTEST will be discussed in Chap. 13.

VBREF. This option produces a sorted cross-reference listing of all verbs used in the program. It gives a count of how many times each type of verb occurs as well as all line numbers where the verb is referenced in the PROCEDURE DIVISION (see Fig. 2.11). This is very helpful because it allows you to quickly locate all occurrences of statements containing a verb which may need to be examined.

```
COUNT   CROSS-REFERENCE OF VERBS        REFERENCES

    5   ADD. . . . . . . . . . . . . .  205 206 211 234 252
    1   CLOSE. . . . . . . . . . . . .  185
    3   COMPUTE. . . . . . . . . . . .  200 203 208
    2   DISPLAY. . . . . . . . . . . .  171 178
    1   EXIT . . . . . . . . . . . . .  219
    1   GOBACK . . . . . . . . . . . .  187
    3   IF . . . . . . . . . . . . . .  165 174 233
    8   MOVE . . . . . . . . . . . . .  166 168 195 196 197 198 199 202
    3   MULTIPLY . . . . . . . . . . .  223 225 227
```

Figure 2.11 Output from the VBREF compiler option in COBOL II. It gives a static count and cross-reference listing of verbs.

XREF (X). XREF gives a sorted cross-reference of data names and procedure names in two separate lists. Included is the line number in the source code where the item is defined as well as all line numbers where the item is referenced in PROCEDURE DIVISION statements (see Fig. 2.12). In Release 3, specifying the SOURCE and XREF compiler options produces an abbreviated embedded cross-reference listing at the right side of the source code listing as well as the full cross-reference listing later in the compiler output. Items which are undefined (referring to a data item or procedure name which does not exist, causing a compiler error), duplicate defined (a procedure name defined more than once or a data name defined more than once and used without qualification, causing a compilation error—the item causing the error is the one that is flagged), implicitly defined (figurative constants or COBOL special registers), or externally defined (external program names referred to in a CALL statement, not to be confused with the EXTERNAL attribute for files and data items) are noted in the embedded listing (see Fig. 2.10). The embedded listing does not give all references to an item; it only indicates where it was defined.

Note that in Release 3.1, you can specify XREF, XREF(FULL), or XREF(SHORT). XREF and XREF(FULL) yield the same results; they are the same as XREF under Release 3.0. XREF(SHORT) prints only the explicitly referenced variables in the cross-reference listing.

XREF in Release 3 and 3.1 also produces a cross-reference of programs, including the main program, nested programs, and external (nonnested) programs (see Fig. 2.13).

XREF is quite helpful because it allows you to quickly find all occurrences of an item which must be examined. The Release 3 version is particularly useful because of the extra information provided.

Using the right compiler options can make your job a lot easier. Your choices depend on your personal preference, efficiency considerations, and the type of compiler listings desired.

For ease in finding references while reading a Release 3 source listing, for example, you might prefer to have an embedded cross-reference listing. Thus the SOURCE and XREF options should be specified.

```
An "M" preceding a data-name reference indicates that the data-name is modified by this reference.

 Defined    Cross-reference of data names     References

     134    COUNTERS
      84    DETAIL-LINE-1. . . . . . . . . .  240
      93    DETAIL-LINE-2. . . . . . . . . .  242
     102    DETAIL-LINE-3. . . . . . . . . .  244
     118    DETAIL-LINE-4. . . . . . . . . .  246
     121    DETAIL-LINE-5. . . . . . . . . .  248
     124    DETAIL-LINE-6. . . . . . . . . .  250
     141    DOMESTIC-COPIES-1. . . . . . . .  M198 201 206
     142    DOMESTIC-COPIES-2. . . . . . . .  M199 204 206
     143    DOMESTIC-COPIES-3. . . . . . . .  M207 210 231
      71    DOMESTIC-CP-1. . . . . . . . . .  198 229
      73    DOMESTIC-CP-2. . . . . . . . . .  199 230
      64    DOMESTIC-INFO
     146    DOMESTIC-MONEY-INT . . . . . . .  M200 202 M203 205 M208 211
                                                .
                                                .
                                                .
Context usage is indicated by the letter preceding a procedure-name reference.
These letters and their meanings are:
    A = ALTER (procedure-name)
    D = GO TO (procedure-name) DEPENDING ON
    E = End of range of (PERFORM) through (procedure-name)
    G = GO TO (procedure-name)
    P = PERFORM (procedure-name)
    T = (ALTER) TO PROCEED TO (procedure-name)
    U = USE FOR DEBUGGING (procedure-name)

 Defined    Cross-reference of procedures     References

     162    0000-MAINLINE
     193    0100-PROCESS-RECORD. . . . . . .  P180
     218    0100-PROCESS-RECORD-EXIT . . . .  E181
     221    0200-PRINT . . . . . . . . . . .  P213
     253    0200-PRINT-EXIT. . . . . . . . .  E213
                                                .
                                                .
                                                .
```

Figure 2.12 Sorted cross-reference listing of data names and procedures produced by the XREF compiler option in COBOL II.

In terms of compilation efficiency, NOXREF rather than XREF might be chosen. Certain options, such as TEST and SSRANGE, use extra system resources at run time and might be better utilized for program development and testing rather than for programs going into production.

2.2 INTERNAL COBOL TABLES

There are a number of internal data areas, or control blocks, which are used to maintain the COBOL environment for a program. These control blocks contain addresses and data needed for the COBOL program to function properly, such as the address of the program's WORKING-STORAGE SECTION and the

Defined	Cross-reference of programs	References
020600	CHECK-CUST-NO.	022000 018600
EXTERNAL	ERRORS	021400
022500	HEADER-ROUTINE	025000 019500 026200
002600	PROG1.	027800
025600	SUMMARY-REPORT	027700 017900

Figure 2.13 Cross-reference listing of programs generated by the XREF compiler option for a COBOL II Release 3 program.

characteristics of program input/output files. Understanding how to read these control blocks can provide you with valuable debugging information which is difficult, if not impossible, to find elsewhere. Following is a discussion of those control blocks relevant for COBOL program debugging.

2.2.1 Task Global Table

The Task Global Table (TGT) is used to keep track of information which is required by the system during execution of the COBOL program. It contains a great deal of information which is helpful for an understanding of how COBOL operates internally as well as information which is essential for effective COBOL program debugging. This information includes pointers to the base locator (BL) cells, the value of the RETURN-CODE special register, and pointers to temporary storage areas. A listing of the TGT is included in the compiler output whenever a PROCEDURE DIVISION map or condensed PROCEDURE DIVISION listing is requested, and in OS/VS COBOL, whenever a DATA DIVISION map is requested as well.

The TGT has a fixed-length portion followed by a variable-length portion. The fixed-length portion consists of fields which are fixed in length. The variable-length portion contains fields which may be fixed or variable in length, or not be present at all, depending on the specific requirements of each program.

Although the function of the TGT is essentially the same in both OS/VS COBOL and COBOL II, the format of the listing, the names of many of the fields, and the information provided in some of the fields differs. Also, some fields may appear in one version of the TGT and not in the other. Specific differences will be given in the sections that follow.

2.2.1.1 The TGT in OS/VS COBOL

Figure 2.14 shows a typical TGT listing for an OS/VS COBOL program. Notice that it identifies each field and gives its hexadecimal offset from the beginning of the COBOL program.

The variable portion of the TGT in an OS/VS COBOL program, starting with the field labeled BL CELLS, lists all fields, even if some of them are not used by the program. A field which is not used has a length of zero. This becomes readily apparent because the offset of the following field is listed as being the same as that of the field in question.

MEMORY MAP	
TGT	00888
SAVE AREA	00888
SWITCH	008D0
TALLY	008D4
SORT SAVE	008D8
ENTRY-SAVE	008DC
SORT CORE SIZE	008E0
RET CODE	008E4
SORT RET	008E6
WORKING CELLS	008E8
SORT FILE SIZE	00A18
SORT MODE SIZE	00A1C
PGT-VN TBL	00A20
TGT-VN TBL	00A24
RESERVED	00A28
LENGTH OF VN TBL	00A2C
LABEL RET	00A2E
RESERVED	00A2F
DBG R14SAVE	00A30
COBOL INDICATOR	00A34
A(INIT1)	00A38
DEBUG TABLE PTR	00A3C
SUBCOM PTR	00A40
SORT-MESSAGE	00A44
SYSOUT DDNAME	00A4C
RESERVED	00A4D
COBOL ID	00A4E
COMPILED POINTER	00A50
COUNT TABLE ADDRESS	00A54
RESERVED	00A58
DBG R11SAVE	00A60
COUNT CHAIN ADDRESS	00A64
PRBL1 CELL PTR	00A68
RESERVED	00A6C
TA LENGTH	00A71
RESERVED	00A74
PCS LIT PTR	00A7C
DEBUGGING	00A80
CD FOR INITIAL INPUT	00A84
OVERFLOW CELLS	00A88
BL CELLS	00A88
DECBADR CELLS	00A94
FIB CELLS	00A94
TEMP STORAGE	00A98
TEMP STORAGE-2	00AA8
TEMP STORAGE-3	00AB8
TEMP STORAGE-4	00AB8
BLL CELLS	00AB8
VLC CELLS	00AC0
SBL CELLS	00AC0
INDEX CELLS	00AC0
SUBADR CELLS	00AC0
ONCTL CELLS	00AC0
PFMCTL CELLS	00AC0
PFMSAV CELLS	00AC0
VN CELLS	00AF0
SAVE AREA =2	00B20
SAVE AREA =3	00B20
XSASW CELLS	00B2C
XSA CELLS	00B2C
PARAM CELLS	00B2C
RPTSAV AREA	00B3C
CHECKPT CTR	00B3C

Figure 2.14 The TGT in OS/VS COBOL.

In OS/VS COBOL, the TGT is printed whenever the DMAP, PMAP, or CLIST compiler options are in effect. It is normally pointed to by general-purpose register 13. It physically exists in the load module after the WORKING-STORAGE code or, if there are any Data Control Blocks (DCBs), after the DCBs (when DCBs exist, they are located after WORKING-STORAGE in the load module), and right before the Program Global Table (PGT) (the PGT is located just before PROCEDURE DIVISION code in the load module). The TGT can be found right after the DATA DIVISION MAP in the compiler output listings.

2.2.1.2 The TGT in VS COBOL II

The TGT for a nonreentrant (NORENT compiler option) COBOL II Release 3 program is shown in Fig. 2.15. The format of the TGT for Release 2 is the same. It specifies the hexadecimal offset of each field from the beginning of the program as well as from the start of the TGT itself, and gives a brief explanation of the field. The variable portion of the COBOL II TGT lists only the fields needed by each program.

The TGT in COBOL II appears in the compiler output whenever the LIST or OFFSET options are in effect. The listing is near the end of the compiler output, after the location of the internal tables used by FDUMP or TEST is given (if the programmer specified those compiler options), which in turn follows the PROCEDURE DIVISION map or OFFSET listing. Although the IBM *VS COBOL II Application Programming Guide* implies that the TGT is included when MAP is in effect, this is not the case; only the hexadecimal offset and length of the TGT are printed.

The physical location of the TGT depends on whether the RENT or NORENT compiler option is in effect. RENT causes the program to be reentrant so it can be shared by many users concurrently. As such, both the TGT and WORKING-STORAGE SECTION are then in storage outside the bounds of the rest of the COBOL II program. For this reason, the TGT listing does not and cannot show the offsets of its fields relative to the beginning of the program when RENT is in effect.

When NORENT is in effect, the program is nonreentrant. Thus the TGT is physically part of the program's storage area. It is located after the PROCEDURE DIVISION code and before the WORKING-STORAGE SECTION.

2.2.1.3 Base locator cells for files and WORKING-STORAGE

Probably the most frequently referenced TGT fields for debugging purposes are the base locator cells. As already mentioned in our discussion of compiler options, these cells contain the base addresses in storage from which COBOL data items, either files or WORKING-STORAGE areas, can be accessed. Each base locator cell is a fullword (4 bytes) in length.

In OS/VS COBOL, the TGT lists base locator cells for files first, with one cell assigned to each program input or output file. Following them are the cells for the WORKING-STORAGE SECTION. In both cases, the cells are referred to as BL cells.

```
            *** TGT MEMORY MAP ***
PGMLOC   TGTLOC

000B18   000000   72 BYTE SAVE AREA
000B60   000048   TGT IDENTIFIER
000B68   000050   TGT LEVEL INDICATOR
000B69   000051   RESERVED - 3 SINGLE BYTE FIELDS
000B6C   000054   32 BIT SWITCH
000B70   000058   POINTER TO RUNCOM
000B74   00005C   POINTER TO COBVEC
000B78   000060   POINTER TO PROGRAM DYNAMIC BLOCK TABLE
000B7C   000064   NUMBER OF FCB'S
000B80   000068   WORKING STORAGE LENGTH
000B84   00006C   POINTER TO PREVIOUS TGT IN TGT CHAIN
000B88   000070   ADDRESS OF IGZESMG WORK AREA
000B8C   000074   ADDRESS OF 1ST GETMAIN BLOCK (SPACE MGR)
000B90   000078   FULLWORD RETURN CODE
000B92   00007A   RETURN CODE SPECIAL REGISTER
000B94   00007C   SORT-RETURN SPECIAL REGISTER
000B96   00007E   MERGE FILE NUMBER
000B98   000080   RESERVED - 4 HALF WORD FIELDS
000BA0   000088   PROGRAM MASK OF CALLER OF THIS PROGRAM
000BA1   000089   PROGRAM MASK USED BY THIS PROGRAM
000BA2   00008A   RESERVED - 2 SINGLE BYTE FIELDS
000BA4   00008C   NUMBER OF SECONDARY FCB CELLS
000BA8   000090   LENGTH OF THE VN(VNI) VECTOR
000BAC   000094   ADDRESS OF IGZEBST TERMINATION ROUTINE
000BB0   000098   DDNAME FOR DISPLAY OUTPUT
000BB8   0000A0   SORT-CONTROL SPECIAL REGISTER
000BC0   0000A8   POINTER TO COM-REG SPECIAL REGISTER
000BC4   0000AC   CALC ROUTINE REGISTER SAVE AREA
000BF8   0000E0   ALTERNATE COLLATING SEQUENCE TABLE PTR.
000BFC   0000E4   ADDRESS OF SORT G.N. ADDRESS BLOCK
000C00   0000E8   ADDRESS OF IGZCLNK DYNAMIC WORK AREA
000C04   0000EC   CURRENT INTERNAL PROGRAM NUMBER
000C08   0000F0   POINTER TO 1ST IPCB
000C0C   0000F4   RESERVED
000C10   0000F8   POINTER TO ABEND INFORMATION TABLE
000C14   0000FC   POINTER TO FDMP/TEST FIELDS IN THE TGT
000C18   000100   ADDRESS OF START OF COBOL PROGRAM
000C1C   000104   POINTER TO VN'S IN CGT
000C20   000108   POINTER TO VN'S IN TGT
000C24   00010C   POINTER TO FIRST PBL IN THE PGT
000C28   000110   POINTER TO FIRST FCB CELL
000C2C   000114   WORKING STORAGE ADDRESS
000C30   000118   POINTER TO FIRST SECONDARY FCB CELL

            *** VARIABLE PORTION OF TGT ***

000C34   00011C   BACKSTORE CELL FOR SYMBOLIC REGISTERS
000C3C   000124   BASE LOCATORS FOR SPECIAL REGISTERS
000C44   00012C   BASE LOCATORS FOR WORKING-STORAGE
000C48   000130   BASE LOCATORS FOR LINKAGE-SECTION
000C50   000138   BASE LOCATORS FOR FILES
000C58   000140   VARIABLE NAME (VN) CELLS
000C64   00014C   PERFORM SAVE CELLS
000C70   000158   FCB CELLS
000C78   000160   INTERNAL PROGRAM CONTROL BLOCKS
000C88   000170   TEMPORARY STORAGE-1
000C98   000180   TEMPORARY STORAGE-2
```

Figure 2.15 The TGT memory map in COBOL II.

In COBOL II, a distinction is made between base locator cells for files and base locator cells for WORKING-STORAGE. They are known as BLF and BLW cells, respectively.

Each of the base locator cells for WORKING-STORAGE can reference up to 4K of WORKING-STORAGE; an additional cell is needed for every 4K of storage beyond the first 4K. In all cases, the TGT specifies the offset of the first cell only. To find the offsets of succeeding cells, add 4 bytes for each cell after the first.

In OS/VS COBOL, the first cell is referred to as BL cell 1. It is listed in the DATA DIVISION map as BL=1. In COBOL II, however, the cells are numbered from zero. Thus the DATA DIVISION map refers to the first base locator cell for files as BLF=0000 and the first cell for WORKING-STORAGE as BLW=0000.

We will give an example of how to find a field in a dump using base locator cells in our discussion of reading the DATA DIVISION map, Sec. 3.1.3.

2.2.1.4 Base locator cells for the LINKAGE SECTION

The TGT also lists base locator cells for the LINKAGE SECTION. They are referred to as BLL cells in both OS/VS COBOL and COBOL II, and they are similar in function to the base locator cells already discussed. Each is a fullword in length, and each contains the base address for an 01-level in the program's LINKAGE SECTION, with an additional cell for every 4K bytes of storage beyond the first 4K for that 01-level. In OS/VS COBOL sort files are also referenced by BLL cells; this is not readily apparent from the IBM documentation.

In OS/VS COBOL the first two BLL cells are reserved for COBOL's internal use. Since the cells are numbered starting with 1, the first cell used to access any LINKAGE SECTION item is referred to as BLL=3 in the DATA DIVISION map.

In COBOL II, only the first BLL cell is needed for COBOL's internal use. Since the cells are numbered from zero, the first cell listed in the DATA DIVISION map is referred to as BLL=0001.

2.2.1.5 Temporary storage

Sometimes a COBOL instruction will use a field in a temporary storage area rather than an identifier defined in the COBOL source code as one of its operands. The temporary storage areas are used by COBOL as intermediate work areas when it becomes necessary for the program to convert or store data items. For example, if an ADD instruction operates on fields having different usage clauses, such as DISPLAY numeric and COMP-3, it is necessary for COBOL to generate an extra instruction, the Assembler PACK instruction, to pack the DISPLAY field. The PACK converts the COBOL field into a packed decimal format, with temporary storage used to hold the receiving field in the PACK instruction. This intermediate field in temporary storage is used in place of the DISPLAY field in the ADD. If the ADD causes a Data Exception (S0C7), it may be helpful for you to examine the intermediate field in temporary storage.

In OS/VS COBOL, there are four temporary storage areas. TEMP STORAGE (the first area) is used for arithmetic computations, as shown in the previous example. TEMP STORAGE-2 is used for nonarithmetic operations, such as editing numeric data or executing a STRING instruction. TEMP STORAGE-3 is utilized for aligning numeric fields defined with the SYNC clause. TEMP STORAGE-4 is used when the SEARCH ALL statement is executed.

COBOL II also has temporary storage areas. TEMPORARY STORAGE-1 is used for execution of SEARCH ALL. TEMPORARY STORAGE-2 is used for processing both arithmetic and nonarithmetic instructions. It also holds the parameters which are passed in the COBOL II CALL BY CONTENT statement. TEMPORARY STORAGE-3 is used to hold a parameter list, a list of the addresses which are passed when a CALL BY REFERENCE is executed. TEMPORARY STORAGE-4 is used for the EVALUATE statement.

2.2.1.6 Return code

In Sec. 1.3 we explained the importance of the COBOL RETURN-CODE special register in COBOL program debugging. We mentioned that a program may specify a condition code to be passed back to a calling program via the RETURN-CODE register, and that the contents of the register can be examined if the program ABENDs. The TGT contains a field for the RETURN-CODE register.

In OS/VS COBOL the field is a halfword (2 bytes) in length and is called RET CODE. The value in RET CODE is the contents of the RETURN-CODE special register.

In COBOL II, the field in the TGT for the RETURN-CODE special register is, appropriately enough, called RETURN CODE SPECIAL REGISTER. It is also one-halfword long.

2.2.1.7 Sort Return code

Just as it may be valuable for you to know the value of the RETURN-CODE special register, it may also be valuable to know the condition code returned from a SORT/MERGE operation.

In OS/VS COBOL, the TGT field called SORT RET is a halfword which receives the condition code returned by a SORT/MERGE program.

In COBOL II, the TGT field called SORT-RETURN SPECIAL REGISTER receives the condition code from a SORT/MERGE operation. It is also a halfword in length.

2.2.1.8 Variable-length cells

It may be important in debugging to know how long variable-length data items, defined with the OCCURS . . . DEPENDING ON clause, are at the time of an ABEND.

The field VLC points to the first variable-length cell in an OS/VS COBOL TGT. There is one cell for each item coded with an OCCURS DEPENDING ON clause, in the order in which they appear in the program. Each cell contains the current length of its associated variable-length item. Each VLC is a half-word in length, since a table defined with the OCCURS . . . DEPENDING ON clause can be up to 32K in length.

The VARIABLE-LENGTH CELLS field points to the first variable-length cell in a COBOL II TGT. It is similar in function to the VLC in OS/VS COBOL, although it is a fullword in length because a table can be up to 16 MB in COBOL II.

2.2.1.9 Index cells

You may need to know which entry in a table is being processed if a program involving table-handling ABENDs. COBOL programmers sometimes avoid using indexes in table-handling, opting for subscripts instead, because finding the value of an index in a hexadecimal dump seems more difficult. If indexes are used, however, the TGT has a field which points to them.

Once the value of an index has been found, it must be converted into a table-entry number. It is important to understand that indexes are displacements from the beginning of the table rather than occurrence numbers. Also, they appear in a hexadecimal dump in binary, as though they were defined as PIC S9(9) COMP fields. To convert the value of an index to a table-entry occurrence number, divide its decimal value by the length of the table entry and add 1. For example, if the index is hexadecimal 10 (decimal 16) and the table entries are each 8 bytes in length, the index refers to the third entry in the table (16 divided by 8 equals 2, plus 1 gives 3).

In the OS/VS COBOL TGT, the field labeled INDEX CELLS contains the current value of the first implicitly defined table index. Each INDEX CELL is a fullword, with a cell for each implicitly defined index in the order in which they are coded in the program.

In COBOL II, the TGT field called INDEX CELLS is used to hold the values of implicitly defined indexes, as described for the INDEX CELL field in OS/VS COBOL.

2.2.1.10 FIB cells and FCB cells

Knowing the characteristics (e.g., record length) and current status (open or closed) of files can be invaluable when debugging programs having I/O problems. Several control blocks directly or indirectly provide this type of information. They are the FILE INFORMATION BLOCK (FIB) and FILE CONTROL BLOCK (FCB), both of which are internal COBOL control blocks, and the DATA CONTROL BLOCK (DCB), which is a system control block. The first two will be discussed in depth in Sec. 2.2.3 and the last one will be covered in Chap. 9.

The OS/VS COBOL compiler creates a FIB for every VSAM file used by the program. The TGT in OS/VS COBOL contains a field called FIB CELLS. As the program starts executing, this field contains the offset of the first FIB. There is a cell, each a fullword in length, for each FIB. When each VSAM file is opened by the program, an FCB is created, and the FIB cell in the TGT is adjusted to point to the corresponding FCB instead of the FIB. In order to tell whether a FIB cell is pointing to a FIB or an FCB, examine the first byte at the address pointed to by the FIB cell. A '1' in the first byte indicates a FIB, while an 'F' indicates an FCB.

In COBOL II, there are FIBs and FCBs for non-VSAM as well as VSAM files. The TGT field NUMBER OF FCBs indicates how many FCBs exist for the program. IBM gave the field called POINTER TO FIRST FCB CELL a rather misleading name; this field gives the offset to the beginning of the FCB pointer list, not to the first FCB cell. The pointer list is composed of 4-byte addresses; each is the actual address of an FCB. The first address in the pointer list is the address of the first FCB, the second is the address of the second FCB, and so on. Within each FCB is a pointer to its corresponding FIB.

2.2.1.11 The SAVE AREA

A SAVE AREA exists in every COBOL program. It is used to store addresses and general-purpose register contents when the current program is called by the operating system or another program. COBOL automatically handles the SAVE AREA internally. The SAVE AREA provides information which may be helpful when debugging ABENDs, particularly multimodule ABENDs. It occupies the first 72 bytes of the TGT, and is normally pointed to by the address in general-purpose register 13. We will discuss it more completely in Sec. 11.1.

2.2.2 The Program Global Table

The Program Global Table (PGT) contains information referenced by instructions in the COBOL program's PROCEDURE DIVISION at execution time. This information includes pointers to cells as well as maps of literals used during execution. The PGT is included in the compiler output when a DATA DIVISION map, PROCEDURE DIVISION map, or condensed PROCEDURE DIVISION map is produced.

Data in the PGT is never intentionally modified by instructions in the program. Also, the size of the PGT is variable in length, depending on the needs of the program.

The function of some of the fields in the PGT, the type of information provided, and the format of the PGT listing differ in the two versions of COBOL.

2.2.2.1 The PGT in OS/VS COBOL

Figure 2.16 shows a PGT listing for an OS/VS COBOL program. All of the fields in the PGT are variable in length, and may not exist at all if they are not needed by the program. Notice that the listing briefly identifies each field and gives its hexadecimal offset from the beginning of the program.

In OS/VS COBOL, the PGT listing is generated whenever the DMAP, PMAP, or CLIST compiler options are in effect. It is normally pointed to by general-purpose register 12. Physically, it exists in the load module after the TGT and just before the PROCEDURE DIVISION code. The PGT listing

```
                PGT                              00B48

          OVERFLOW CELLS                         00B48
          VIRTUAL CELLS                          00B48
          PROCEDURE NAME CELLS                   00B6C
          GENERATED NAME CELLS                   00B90
          DCB ADDRESS CELLS                      00C44
          VNI CELLS                              00C4C
          LITERALS                               00C80
          DISPLAY LITERALS                       00CDF
```

Figure 2.16 A PGT listing for an OS/VS COBOL program.

appears after the literal pool, which in turn follows the TGT listing in the compiler output.

The most important field in the OS/VS COBOL PGT for debugging purposes is the one labeled DCB ADDRESS CELLS. As previously mentioned, the DCBs are system control blocks which contain information about I/O files. A DCB is created as a storage location within the COBOL object module by the compiler for every non-VSAM file defined in the program. Some of the information for a DCB comes from the program's FD for the file. More information about the DCB will be given in Chap. 9.

The first 4 bytes of the DCB ADDRESS CELLS field points to the first DCB cell. The first cell contains the address of the first DCB. Each succeeding 4 bytes points to another DCB cell, with each cell containing the address of its corresponding DCB. The cells appear in the same order as the program's FDs.

2.2.2.2 The PGT in VS COBOL II

Figure 2.17 shows a PGT listing for a COBOL II Release 2 program. Notice that the listing specifies the offsets of the Constant Global Table (CGT), any system literals used, and the base locator for procedure code (PBL). This is followed by the literal pool map for system literals in hexadecimal and EBCDIC format. The length of the PGT in COBOL II is variable.

The PGT listing for COBOL II is generated whenever the MAP, LIST, or OFFSET compiler options are specified. It follows the DATA DIVISION map when MAP is in effect, the program source code listing when OFFSET and NOMAP are present, and the Assembler listing of COBOL II's program initialization code when LIST is in effect. Physically, the PGT exists near the beginning of the load module, after the COBOL II initialization code and before the CGT.

The PGT may be useful when, in the absence of a full or condensed PROCEDURE DIVISION map, the beginning of the program's object code needs to be located in a hexadecimal dump. Notice in Fig. 2.17 that the PGT gives the offset from the start of the program for the beginning of the code addressed by PBL cell number 1, and specifies that the statement is at line 149 in the source module. This is the first Assembler instruction generated by the first COBOL verb in the PROCEDURE DIVISION. Be aware that in Release 3, the PBL will

```
PROGRAM GLOBAL TABLE BEGINS AT LOCATION 000080 FOR 00001C BYTES
THE PGT CONTAINS 000001 CELL(S) FOR ADDRESSABILITY TO THE CGT
PBL1    AT LOCATION 0003B6 FOR LINE 149

LITERAL POOL MAP FOR SYSTEM LITERALS IN THE PGT:
000080  (LIT+0)        40404040 40404040 40404040 40404040 4040000C          |        ..        |
```

Figure 2.17 A PGT listing for a COBOL II program. It includes a map of system literals.

indicate the first line in the IDENTIFICATION DIVISION rather than in the PROCEDURE DIVISION. The Assembler instruction will be the first one generated internally by COBOL itself, typically to initialize fields coded with VALUE clauses by the programmer.

2.2.3 I/O Control Blocks

We have already described COBOL and system control blocks which contain information about I/O files. When debugging programs with I/O problems, it is important to have access to this information. We will now go into greater depth about the COBOL I/O control blocks.

2.2.3.1 The FCB in OS/VS COBOL

Section 2.2.1.10 explained how to use the TGT to find the FCBs for VSAM files used by the program. At hexadecimal offset 60 in the FCB is the file status code from the last VSAM I/O operation. At offset 63 you can find either the error code from the VSAM Access Control Block (ACB) if an OPEN or CLOSE was just done, or the feedback code from the VSAM Request Parameter List (RPL).

2.2.3.2 The FIB and FCB in COBOL II

In COBOL II, FCBs and FIBs are created for non-VSAM as well as VSAM files. The FCB is used by COBOL II to control an input or output data set and contains information such as the address of the current record and the address of the system control block for the file.

Once the first FCB has been located in a hexadecimal dump, additional FCBs will be found immediately after it. You can verify that this is, indeed, an FCB by looking at the EBCDIC portion of the dump; the characters "FCB" will appear in the first 3 bytes. The number of the FCB will appear in the following 2 bytes in the hexadecimal portion of the dump.

In order to determine to which file an FCB pertains, it is necessary to find its corresponding FIB. The FIB contains permanent characteristics of a file, including, at hexadecimal offset 6, its DDname. To locate an FCB's associated FIB, look at hexadecimal offset A4 in the FCB. There you will find the address of the pointer to the FIB. At the pointer you will find the actual address of the FIB. After going to that address in the dump, you can verify that this is really a FIB by looking at the first 3 bytes in the EBCDIC portion. The characters "FIB" will appear.

If the proper DDname has been found in the FIB, it is necessary to go back to its associated FCB to gather information about the file. At hexadecimal offset AC in the FCB is the address of the current record. At hexadecimal displacement 78 is the address of the system control block, either a DCB for non-VSAM files or a VSAM ACB for VSAM files. They contain additional information about the file. See Chap. 9 for a more detailed discussion of the DCB.

2.2.4 Literals

The COBOL compiler places literals used by the program into literal pools. There are literal pools for system literals as well as pools for literals coded in the PROCEDURE DIVISION. Although uncommon, it is possible that a literal may be overlaid by an improperly subscripted or indexed field during table processing. When the literal is later referenced by an instruction, a program exception or incorrect result may occur. Consider the numeric literal "+1" in the instruction:

```
ADD +1 TO PAGE-COUNT
```

If PAGE-COUNT is defined in the DATA DIVISION as a packed field, then the literal should also be packed and should appear as hexadecimal 1C in the literal pool. If the literal has been overlaid by unpacked data, then a data exception (S0C7) will occur when the ADD is executed. This is more likely in OS/VS COBOL since the literal pool comes after WORKING-STORAGE in the load module; in COBOL II the literal pool comes before WORKING-STORAGE.

2.2.4.1 OS/VS COBOL literal pool

In the OS/VS COBOL compiler output the literal pool is divided into two areas: LITERAL POOL (HEX) and DISPLAY LITERALS (BCD). The first area includes literals coded by the programmer in the PROCEDURE DIVISION. An example might be the "N" in the statement

```
MOVE 'N' TO EOF-SWITCH
```

The second area contains literals coded in DISPLAY statements. Values in the pool are given in hexadecimal, two hexadecimal characters per byte.

Figure 2.18 shows how the literal pool is formatted. Letter "A" points to the hexadecimal offset from the beginning of the program of the first byte in the pool (00C80). Letter "B" indicates that this is decimal offset 0 from the start of the pool (LIT + 0). The actual hexadecimal value of this literal is 00, shown by letter "C" in the figure.

The pool appears in the compiler output listings between the TGT and the PGT. In the load module, it exists as part of the PGT.

2.2.4.2 VS COBOL II Constant Global Table

The COBOL II CGT contains a map of program literals. The format is shown in Fig. 2.19. The hexadecimal offset from the beginning of the program for the

```
LITERAL POOL (HEX)

00C80 (LIT+0)     00001C40  205B2020  20214B20  20053C05  5C2C0000  000C4020
00C98 (LIT+24)    206B2020  208C057C  40202020  10000000  1C000000  48140000
00CB0 (LIT+48)    005C5C40  E2C5D8E4  C5D5C3C5  40C5D9D9  D6D97A40  D9C5C3D6
00CC8 (LIT+72)    D9C440D5  D6E340D7  D9D6C3C5  E2E2C5C4  405C5C00  000001

      DISPLAY LITERALS (BCD)

00CDF (LTL+95)    '**** EMPTY FILE **** ASSEMBLER PROGRAM CALLED - CONTROL '
00D17 (LTL+151)   'RETURNED **'
```

Figure 2.18 The literal pool map in an OS/VS COBOL program.

first byte in the pool (000A8) is pointed to by letter "A". The decimal offset from the beginning of the pool for this byte is shown by letter "B" (LIT + 0). The hexadecimal value of this byte is 00, pointed to by letter "C". Since the EBCDIC equivalent of 00 is an unprintable character, it is represented by ".", indicated by letter "D".

The CGT literal pool can be found after the PGT system literals listing in the compiler output. Physically, it exists after the PGT in the load module.

2.3 SUMMARY

There are many compiler options which can provide information and assistance in testing and debugging COBOL programs. The following chart summarizes the most useful ones in OS/VS COBOL.

Option	Description
CLIST	Produces a condensed listing of the PROCEDURE DIVISION.
COUNT	Gives a verb count and verb execution statistics.
DMAP	Generates a DATA DIVISION map.
FLOW	Gives a trace of program flow before an ABEND.
NUM	Uses line numbers in columns 1 through 6 for messages.
PMAP	Produces a full PROCEDURE DIVISION map.
SOURCE	Generates a source code listing.
STATE	Gives the line number of the ABENDing COBOL statement.
SXREF	Gives a sorted cross-reference of data and procedure names.
SYMDMP	Generates a symbolic COBOL dump in the event of an ABEND.
TEST	Permits interactive debugging with TESTCOB.
VBSUM	Gives a summary of verbs used in the program.
VBREF	Generates a cross-reference and use count of verbs.
VERB	Prints verb names in CLIST and PMAP output.
XREF	Produces a cross-reference of data and procedure names.

Some of the COBOL II compiler options which are useful for testing and debugging are similar to those in OS/VS COBOL, while others are quite different in what they do and how they format their output. The following chart summarizes the COBOL II options.

Option	Description
FDUMP	Generates a symbolic COBOL dump in the event of an ABEND.
LIST	Produces a full PROCEDURE DIVISION map.
MAP	Generates a DATA DIVISION map.
NUMBER	Uses line numbers in columns 1 through 6 for messages.
OFFSET	Produces a condensed listing of the PROCEDURE DIVISION.
SOURCE	Generates a source code listing.
SSRANGE	Checks for out-of-range subscripts and indexes.
TEST	Permits interactive debugging with COBTEST.
VBREF	Generates a cross-reference and use count of verbs.
XREF	Gives a sorted cross-reference of data and procedure names.

A number of internal COBOL control blocks may provide you with useful debugging information. The TGT has pointers to the different base locator cells, temporary storage, the RETURN-CODE register, the Sort RETURN-CODE register, variable-length cells, index cells, FIB cells, and FCB cells. The TGT also contains the SAVE AREA, used in subprogram linkage.

The OS/VS PGT points to the DCBs. DCBs are system control blocks containing important information about files.

In COBOL II, the PGT gives offsets to the CGT and PBL. The PBL points to the program's object code. The COBOL II PGT also has a map of system literals.

The FIB and FCB are two COBOL I/O control blocks. When debugging OS/VS COBOL programs they can supply information about VSAM files. In COBOL II, they contain information pertaining to both VSAM and non-VSAM files used by the program. In addition, the COBOL II FCB points to the DCB for a non-VSAM file or the ACB for a VSAM file.

The compiler creates pools for system literals and literals coded in the PROCEDURE DIVISION. In rare instances you may need to examine a program literal to verify its value. In OS/VS COBOL, literals used in data manipulation instructions are in the pool labeled LITERAL POOL (HEX); those used in DISPLAY statements can be found in the pool labeled DISPLAY LITERALS (BCD). In COBOL II program literals are in the CGT.

```
   (A)       (B)            (C)                                                                             (D)
LITERAL POOL MAP FOR LITERALS IN THE CGT:

0000A8  (LIT+0)     00000002 00000001 00000000 83969789 85A24081 A2A2A494 85844086 969940A3   |...........copies assumed for t|
0000C8  (LIT+32)    8885A285 4085A781 94979385 A25DC5D5 C440D6C6 40C6C9D3 C540D6D5 40C6C9D9   |hese examples)END OF FILE ON FIR|
0000E8  (LIT+64)    E2E340D9 C5C1C496 95408193 93408396 978985A2 408186A3 8599C4D6 D4C5E2E3   |ST READon all copies afterDOMEST|
000108  (LIT+96)    C9C340E2 C1D3C5E2 4060D5D6 40D7C1D9 D440D7C1 E2E2C5C4 969540A3 88854086   |IC SALES -NO PARM PASSEDon the f|
000128  (LIT+128)   8999A2A3 D5C5E340 D9C5C3C5 C9D7E3E2 969540A3 88854095 85A7A340 40839697   |irstNET RECEIPTSon the next  cop|
000148  (LIT+160)   8985A240 407E4D94 81A78994 A4944040 D3C9E2E3 40D7D9C9 C3C5D9D6 E8C1D3E3   |ies  =(maximum  LIST PRICEROYALT|
000168  (LIT+192)   E840E2E8 E2D6E4E3 40404040 407E4040 40D78187 85401000 0C001C10 0C060C05   |Y SYSOUT     =   Page ..........|
000188  (LIT+224)   6C8C0000 01380000 00020000 012C0000 00010000 01300000 00020000 00000000   |%...............................|
0001A8  (LIT+256)   00008000 00004020 5B202020 6B212020 4B202040 20206B21 20204B20 20402020   |...... .$...,..... ..,...... ..|
0001C8  (LIT+288)   6B212020 40404020 5B21204B 20204021 2120204B 20080000 00402021 20040000   |,...   .$..... .......... ......|
0001E8  (LIT+320)   00400000 40800000 000025C0 00014000 08080000 1400C640 00010002 80000140   |. .. ......... .......F ....... |
000208  (LIT+352)   00001908 00001400 3AFF0140 00000E08 00001400 76FF8000 01000280 00800000   |.......... .....................|
000228  (LIT+384)   000040C0 00014000 07080000 1400C602 40000808 00001400 C6090001 3C000009   |.. ... .......F. .......F.......|
000248  (LIT+416)   00013800 00                                                               |..;..                           |
```

Figure 2.19 A literal pool map for literals in the CGT for a COBOL II program.

REVIEW QUESTIONS

1. A programmer said to her colleague, "Only system programmers need to understand COBOL compiler options." Does the author agree or disagree with this statement? How does the author support his position? Do you agree or disagree? How would you support your position?

2. Name the compiler option which directs the compiler to use the source line numbers in columns 1 through 6 for error messages in

a. OS/VS COBOL
b. COBOL II

3. Which compiler options identify the statement number of an ABENDing instruction in

a. OS/VS COBOL
b. COBOL II

4. Describe what the FLOW compiler option does in an OS/VS COBOL program.

5. What is the purpose of the COBOL II compiler option SSRANGE? What limitation should you be aware of when using this option?

6. What compiler options produce cross-reference listings of data names, procedure names, and verbs in

a. OS/VS COBOL
b. COBOL II

7. How does a full PROCEDURE DIVISION listing differ from a condensed PROCEDURE DIVISION listing?

8. Specify the compiler option that produces each of the following listings.

a. DATA DIVISION map in OS/VS COBOL
b. PROCEDURE DIVISION map in OS/VS COBOL
c. Condensed PROCEDURE DIVISION listing in OS/VS COBOL
d. DATA DIVISION map in COBOL II
e. PROCEDURE DIVISION map in COBOL II
f. Condensed PROCEDURE DIVISION listing in COBOL II

9. What useful debugging information can be found in

a. The TGT?
b. The PGT?
c. Literal pools?

10. Name the COBOL I/O control blocks and the useful debugging information they contain in

a. OS/VS COBOL
b. COBOL II

Chapter

3

Reading and Using COBOL Maps

The last chapter described COBOL compiler options, compiler output, and COBOL control blocks which aid you in debugging. Although some compiler options allow you to debug programs at the source level, such as those which generate COBOL-formatted dumps or which permit use of the IBM interactive debuggers, it is rare to find these options in effect for programs running in production. Also, many debugging tools from non-IBM vendors are not set up to assist the programmer in debugging at the COBOL source level. It thus becomes important for you to be able to read and utilize the DATA DIVISION and PROCEDURE DIVISION maps which can be requested at compile time. They provide a way to locate COBOL identifiers and verbs. In COBOL II Release 3, the nested program map can be helpful as well. This chapter will show how COBOL maps can be used.

3.1 THE DATA DIVISION MAP

Very often in debugging an ABEND it is necessary to identify the operands used by the instruction which was executing at the time the ABEND occurred and to know the contents of those operands. The DATA DIVISION map provides information which is essential for locating DATA DIVISION items in a hexadecimal storage dump. As mentioned, some compiler options are especially useful for debugging at the COBOL source level. They may be able to identify the fields used by an ABENDing instruction and even display the contents of the fields, but all too often these options are not in effect at the time a program terminates abnormally during a production run. Debuggers from non-IBM vendors are usually not COBOL-specific; they may merely identify the fields by indicating their offsets into the object module without supplying the COBOL source names. In addition, other data names which you may wish to examine may not have been made available by the tool.

Therefore, it is important for you to be able to utilize the information provided in the DATA DIVISION map. The map contains an entry for every file name and data name coded in the program's FILE SECTION, WORKING-STORAGE SECTION, and LINKAGE SECTION. It identifies the base locator cell containing the base address for each item as well as the displacement of that item from its base address. Adding the displacement to the base address gives the item's address in storage.

The DATA DIVISION map contains other information as well. The information provided and the format of the listing varies with the version of COBOL used.

3.1.1 OS/VS COBOL DATA DIVISION Map

The DMAP compiler option in OS/VS COBOL generates a map of the program's DATA DIVISION. Following is a description of fields in the DMAP listing shown in Fig. 3.1.

INTRNL NAME. This field is at the left and is repeated in the middle of the map. It is the internal name generated by the COBOL compiler to represent the COBOL name coded in the source module. This internal name is used in the object code listing produced by the PMAP compiler option.

LVL. This is what IBM calls the "normalized" level number. It may not reflect the actual level number which you coded, but rather shows the hierarchy of a structure beginning with a level of 01 and incremented by 1 until level-49 is reached. Usually programmers leave gaps in the level numbers to allow for easy insertion of additional levels if the need should arise. If you have coded level numbers of 01, 05, and 10 for a group item, it will appear in the map with

INTRNL NAME	LVL	SOURCE NAME	BASE	DISPL	INTRNL NAME	DEFINITION	USAGE	R	O	Q	M
DNM=1-440	FD	OGK-STUDENT-FILE	DCB=01		DNM=1-440		QSAM				F
DNM=1-470	01	OGK-STUDENT-RECORD	BL=1	000	DNM=1-470	DS 80C	DISP				
DNM=2-000	SD	OGK-SORT-FILE			DNM=2-000						F
DNM=2-025	01	OGK-SORT-REC	BLL=3	000	DNM=2-025	DS 0CL80	GROUP				
DNM=2-050	02	OGK-SORT-LAST-NAME	BLL=3	000	DNM=2-050	DS 15C	DISP				
DNM=2-078	02	OGK-SORT-ST-MAJOR	BLL=3	00F	DNM=2-078	DS 4C	DISP-NM				
DNM=2-108	02	FILLER	BLL=3	013	DNM=2-108	DS 61C	DISP				
DNM=2-119	FD	OGK-REPORT-FILE	DCB=02		DNM=2-119		QSAM				F
DNM=2-148	01	OGK-LIST-OUT	BL=2	000	DNM=2-148	DS 133C	DISP				
DNM=2-170	77	FILLER	BL=3	000	DNM=2-170	DS 24C	DISP				
DNM=2-184	77	WS-SUB	BL=3	018	DNM=2-184	DS 2C	COMP				
DNM=2-200	77	WS-OGK-END-OF-FILE	BL=3	01A	DNM=2-200	DS 3C	DISP				
DNM=2-228	77	WS-EOF-SORT	BL=3	01D	DNM=2-228	DS 3C	DISP				
DNM=2-249	01	WS-OGK-STUDENT-RECORD	BL=3	020	DNM=2-249	DS 0CL80	GROUP				
DNM=2-283	02	OGK-ST-NAME	BL=3	020	DNM=2-283	DS 15C	DISP				
DNM=2-304	02	OGK-ST-MAJOR	BL=3	02F	DNM=2-304	DS 4C	DISP-NM				
DNM=2-326	02	OGK-ST-NUM-OF-COURSES	BL=3	033	DNM=2-326	DS 2C	DISP-NM				
DNM=2-357	02	OGK-COURSE-TABLE	BL=3	035	DNM=2-357	DS 0CL5	GROUP		O		
DNM=2-386	03	OGK-ST-COURSE-NUM	BL=3	035	DNM=2-386	DS 3C	DISP				
DNM=2-416	03	OGK-ST-COURSE-GRD	BL=3	038	DNM=2-416	DS 1C	DISP				
DNM=2-446	03	OGK-ST-COURSE-CRD	BL=3	039	DNM=2-446	DS 1C	DISP-NM				
DNM=2-476	02	OGK-ST-MAJOR-NME	BL=3	05D	DNM=2-476	DS 10C	DISP				
DNM=3-000	02	FILLER	BL=3	067	DNM=3-000	DS 9C	DISP				
DNM=3-014	02	WS-OGK-ST-CRD-PTS	BL=3	070	DNM=3-014	DS 3P	COMP-3				

Figure 3.1 OS/VS COBOL DATA DIVISION map generated when DMAP is in effect.

the normalized level numbers 01, 02, and 03. Levels 66, 77, and 88 as well as FD, SD, RD, and CD appear as coded in the program.

SOURCE NAME. This is the actual data name for the item as it appears in the source module.

BASE. This specifies the name and number of the base locator cell for data items, or the number of the DCB for files. We briefly mentioned DCBs in Sec. 2.2.2.1; their full significance will be covered in Chap. 9. As mentioned in Chap. 2, a base locator cell is a fullword which contains the base address for the data item. BL means base locator cell, while BLL indicates a base locator cell for LINKAGE SECTION items. Note that sort files are also referenced by the BLL cells. This is not evident from IBM's OS/VS COBOL manuals. Except for BLL cells, the cells appearing in the map are numbered beginning at 1. Since BLL cells 1 and 2 are used internally by COBOL, the map lists BLL cells starting with number 3 (also see Fig. 3.11).

DISPL. This gives the hexadecimal displacement from the base address for this item in storage.

DEFINITION. This gives the definition for each data item in an Assembler-like format. See Fig. 3.2 for an explanation of the symbols used in this column.

USAGE. This indicates the USAGE for data names, or the file access method for files. See Fig. 3.2 for a list of possible usages.

The columns on the far right in Fig. 3.1 give additional information about the items. A letter under the corresponding column means:

R This data name redefines another data name.

O An OCCURS clause has been coded for this item.

Q This data name is the object of an OCCURS DEPENDING ON clause or contains the object of an OCCURS DEPENDING ON clause.

M A letter in this column specifies the format of the records in this file. F means fixed, V means variable, U means undefined, and S means spanned.

3.1.2 VS COBOL II DATA DIVISION Map

In COBOL II, the MAP compiler option generates a DATA DIVISION map. Figure 3.3 shows the MAP listing for a COBOL II, program; (a) is for Release 3 and (b) is for Release 2. The format for a Release 2 compile is somewhat different from that for Release 3, mainly sparser column headings and the absence of a Data Definition Attribute key. However, the program information provided is the same. In the following discussion the column headings refer to Release 3, with the corresponding headings for Release 2 in parentheses.

SOURCE LINEID (LINE). This gives the source line number of the statement which defines the data item.

HIERARCHY AND DATA NAME (LEVEL NUMBER AND SOURCE NAME). This gives the normalized level number and the data name coded in the source module.

DESCRIPTION	DEFINITION	USAGE
Group (fixed length)	DS 0CLn	GROUP
Group (variable length)	DS VCl=n	GROUP
Alphabetic	DS nC	DISP
Alphanumeric	DS nC	DISP
Alphanumeric Edited	DS nC	AN-EDIT
Numeric Edited	DS nC	NM-EDIT
External Decimal	DS nC	DISP-NM
Internal Decimal	DS nP	COMP-3
Binary (halfword)	DS 2C	COMP
Binary (halfword, sync)	DS 1H	COMP
Binary (fullword)	DS 4C	COMP
Binary (fullword, sync)	DS 1F	COMP
Binary (doubleword)	DS 8C	COMP
Binary (doubleword, sync)	DS 2F	COMP
Internal Floating Point	DS 4C	COMP-1
Internal Floating Point, sync	DS 1F	COMP-1
Internal Floating Point	DS 8C	COMP-2
Internal Floating Point, sync	DS 1D	COMP-2
External Floating Point	DS nC	DISP-FP
Index-name	blank	INDEX-NAME
File (FD)	blank	File Access Method
Sort definition (SD)	blank	blank
Level 88	blank	blank

Notes: "n" is the number of bytes being defined, except in variable-length groups, where it represents a variable-length cell number.

"P" means packed.

"C" means character.

Figure 3.2 Definition and usage terms used in OS/VS COBOL DMAP output.

```
Data Division Map
Data Definition Attribute codes (rightmost column) have the following meanings:
    D = Object of OCCURS DEPENDING     G = GLOBAL                              S = Spanned file
    E = EXTERNAL                       O = Has OCCURS clause                   U = Undefined format file
    F = Fixed length file              OG= Group has own length definition     V = Variable length file
    FB= Fixed length blocked file      R = REDEFINES                           VB= Variable length blocked file
Source   Hierarchy and                                      Base       Hex-Displacement  Asmblr Data                 Data Def
LineID   Data Name                                          Locator    Blk   Structure   Definition   Data Type      Attributes
  2200  PROGRAM-ID ERRORS ------------------------------------------------------------------------------------------------*
  4700  FD ERRORS-FILE . . . . . . . . . . . . . . . . . .             001                            QSAM           FB
  5300  01 ERRORS-FILE-REC . . . . . . . . . . . . . . . .  BLF=0000   000               DS 133C      Display
  5533  77 LAST-DAY. . . . . . . . . . . . . . . . . . . .  BLW=0000   000               DS 2C        Disp-Num
  6200     02 RPT-TYPE. . . . . . . . . . . . . . . . . . . BLW=0000   04F   0 000 04F   DS 62C       Display
  6240  01 DETAIL-LINE . . . . . . . . . . . . . . . . . .  BLW=0000   090               DS 0CL133    Group
  6241     02 FILLER. . . . . . . . . . . . . . . . . . . . BLW=0000   090   0 000 000   DS 48C       Display
  6250     02 FILLER. . . . . . . . . . . . . . . . . . . . BLW=0000   0C0   0 000 030   DS 21C       Display
  6260     02 FILLER. . . . . . . . . . . . . . . . . . . . BLW=0000   0D5   0 000 045   DS 15C       Display
  6270     02 NUM-OUT-SEQ . . . . . . . . . . . . . . . . . BLW=0000   0E4   0 000 054   DS 3C        Num-Edit
  6280     02 FILLER. . . . . . . . . . . . . . . . . . . . BLW=0000   0E7   0 000 057   DS 46C       Display
  6700  01 RPT-HDR-1 . . . . . . . . . . . . . . . . . . .  BLL=0001   000               DS 0CL133    Group
  6710     02 FILLER. . . . . . . . . . . . . . . . . . . . BLL=0001   000   0 000 000   DS 53C       Display
  6720     02 COMPANY-NM-1. . . . . . . . . . . . . . . . . BLL=0001   035   0 000 035   DS 16C       Display
  6730     02 COMPANY-NM-2. . . . . . . . . . . . . . . . . BLL=0001   045   0 000 045   DS 64C       Display
  6800  01 RPT-HDR-2 . . . . . . . . . . . . . . . . . . .  BLL=0002   000               DS 0CL133    Group
  6900     02 FILLER. . . . . . . . . . . . . . . . . . . . BLL=0002   000   0 000 000   DS 11C       Display
  7000     02 DAY-OF-MONTH. . . . . . . . . . . . . . . . . BLL=0002   00B   0 000 00B   DS 2C        Disp-Num
  7100     02 FILLER. . . . . . . . . . . . . . . . . . . . BLL=0002   00D   0 000 00D   DS 111C      Display
  7200     02 PAGE-NO . . . . . . . . . . . . . . . . . . . BLL=0002   07C   0 000 07C   DS 5C        Num-Edit
  7300     02 FILLER. . . . . . . . . . . . . . . . . . . . BLL=0002   081   0 000 081   DS 4C        Display
  7400  01 NUM-BAD-REC . . . . . . . . . . . . . . . . . .  BLL=0003   000               DS 2P        Packed-Dec
```

(a)

```
DATA DIVISION MAP
LINE    LEVEL NUMBER AND SOURCE NAME                       BASE      DISPL   STRCT DISP   DEFINITION   USAGE        R O D F
  4700  FD ERRORS-FILE . . . . . . . . . . . . . . . . . .           001                               QSAM              FB
  5300  01 ERRORS-FILE-REC . . . . . . . . . . . . . . . . BLF=0000  000                  DS 133C      DISPLAY
  5533  77 LAST-DAY. . . . . . . . . . . . . . . . . . . . BLW=0000  000                  DS 2C        DISP-NUM
  6200     02 RPT-TYPE. . . . . . . . . . . . . . . . . . . BLW=0000  04F     0 000 04F    DS 62C       DISPLAY
  6240  01 DETAIL-LINE . . . . . . . . . . . . . . . . . . BLW=0000  090                  DS 0CL133    GROUP
  6241     02 FILLER. . . . . . . . . . . . . . . . . . . . BLW=0000  090     0 000 000    DS 48C       DISPLAY
  6250     02 FILLER. . . . . . . . . . . . . . . . . . . . BLW=0000  0C0     0 000 030    DS 21C       DISPLAY
  6260     02 FILLER. . . . . . . . . . . . . . . . . . . . BLW=0000  0D5     0 000 045    DS 15C       DISPLAY
  6270     02 NUM-OUT-SEQ . . . . . . . . . . . . . . . . . BLW=0000  0E4     0 000 054    DS 3C        NUM-EDIT
  6280     02 FILLER. . . . . . . . . . . . . . . . . . . . BLW=0000  0E7     0 000 057    DS 46C       DISPLAY
  6700  01 RPT-HDR-1 . . . . . . . . . . . . . . . . . . . BLL=0001  000                  DS 0CL133    GROUP
  6710     02 FILLER. . . . . . . . . . . . . . . . . . . . BLL=0001  000     0 000 000    DS 53C       DISPLAY
  6720     02 COMPANY-NM-1. . . . . . . . . . . . . . . . . BLL=0001  035     0 000 035    DS 16C       DISPLAY
  6730     02 COMPANY-NM-2. . . . . . . . . . . . . . . . . BLL=0001  045     0 000 045    DS 64C       DISPLAY
  6800  01 RPT-HDR-2 . . . . . . . . . . . . . . . . . . . BLL=0002  000                  DS 0CL133    GROUP
  6900     02 FILLER. . . . . . . . . . . . . . . . . . . . BLL=0002  000     0 000 000    DS 11C       DISPLAY
  7000     02 DAY-OF-MONTH. . . . . . . . . . . . . . . . . BLL=0002  00B     0 000 00B    DS 2C        DISP-NUM
  7100     02 FILLER. . . . . . . . . . . . . . . . . . . . BLL=0002  00D     0 000 00D    DS 111C      DISPLAY
  7200     02 PAGE-NO . . . . . . . . . . . . . . . . . . . BLL=0002  07C     0 000 07C    DS 5C        NUM-EDIT
  7300     02 FILLER. . . . . . . . . . . . . . . . . . . . BLL=0002  081     0 000 081    DS 4C        DISPLAY
  7400  01 NUM-BAD-REC . . . . . . . . . . . . . . . . . . BLL=0003  000                  DS 2P        COMP-3
```

(b)

Figure 3.3 DATA DIVISION maps for *(a)* COBOL II Release 3 and *(b)* COBOL II Release 2. The MAP option generates them.

What IBM calls the normalized level number may not reflect the actual level number as coded by the programmer, but rather shows the hierarchy of a structure starting with a level of 01 and incremented by 1 until level-49 is reached. Many programmers leave gaps in the level numbers for a group item, such as level-01, level-05, and level-10. This makes it easy to insert additional levels in the structure. The group item and its subordinate fields will appear in the map with the normalized level numbers 01, 02, and 03. Levels 66, 77, and 88 as well as the indicators FD and SD appear as coded in the program.

BASE LOCATOR (BASE). This specifies the base locator cell containing the base address for the item. A base locator cell, as discussed in Chap. 2, is a fullword which contains the base address for the item. BLF is a base locator cell for files, BLW a base locator cell for WORKING-STORAGE, BLL a base locator cell for LINKAGE SECTION items, BLV a base locator cell for variably located data, and BL is a base locator for special COBOL registers. In Release 3, BLS is a base locator cell for sort items and BLX is a base locator cell for external data items. Some base locator cells may not appear in this column; BL cells, for example, will be found in the PROCEDURE DIVISION map instead. Except for BLL cells, cells appearing in the DATA DIVISION map are numbered starting with 0; since BLL cell 0000 is used internally by COBOL, the map begins with BLL cell 0001. (Also see Fig. 3.13.)

HEX DISPLACEMENT BLK (DISPL). This is the hexadecimal displacement from the base address for this item in storage.

HEX DISPLACEMENT STRUCTURE (STRCT DISP). This is the hexadecimal displacement from the beginning of the structure (group item) containing this item.

ASMBLR DATA DEFINITION (DEFINITION). This gives the definition for each data item in an Assembler language format. See Fig. 3.4 for an explanation of the symbols used in this column.

DATA TYPE (USAGE). This indicates the COBOL USAGE for data names or the file access method for files. See Fig. 3.4 for an explanation of the terms in this column.

DATA DEF ATTRIBUTES (R O D F). These appear at the far right in both parts of Fig. 3.3 and specify data definition attribute codes. For Release 3, the meanings of the codes are given at the top of the DATA DIVISION map. For Release 2, a code may appear under the appropriate column R, O, D, or F; only the codes R, O, D, F, FB, V, VB, S, and U are valid and they have the same meanings as in Release 3.

3.1.3 Using a DATA DIVISION Map to Find a Field in a Dump

3.1.3.1 Overview of hexadecimal storage dumps

Before we find a DATA DIVISION field in a dump, we need to take a brief look at how a storage dump is formatted. Figures 3.5 and 3.6 illustrate portions of the compiler output for the program we will use in Sec. 3.1.3.2. Figure 3.7 shows part of the storage dump for the same program. The dump was produced when the program ABENDed while running under the MVS/ESA operating system.

The leftmost column contains hexadecimal storage addresses. Notice that they all end in 0. This column is followed by eight columns giving the contents of storage in hexadecimal form; two hexadecimal characters represent 1 byte. Each column has eight hexadecimal characters, representing 4 bytes of storage. The eight columns show a total of 32 bytes of storage on each line.

DESCRIPTION	DEFINITION	USAGE RELEASE 2	DATA TYPE RELEASE 3
Group (fixed length)	DS 0CLn	GROUP	GROUP
Group (variable length)	DS VCl=n	GRP-VARLEN	GRP-VARLEN
Alphabetic	DS nC	DISPLAY	ALPHABETIC
Alphanumeric	DS nC	DISPLAY	DISPLAY
Alphanumeric Edited	DS nC	AN-EDIT	AN-EDIT
Numeric Edited	DS nC	NUM-EDIT	NUM-EDIT
External Decimal	DS nC	DISP-NUM	DISP-NUM
Internal Decimal	DS nP	COMP-3	PACKED-DEC
Binary (halfword)	DS 2C	COMP	BINARY
Binary (halfword, sync)	DS 1H	COMP	BINARY
Binary (fullword)	DS 4C	COMP	BINARY
Binary (fullword, sync)	DS 1F	COMP	BINARY
Binary (doubleword)	DS 8C	COMP	BINARY
Binary (doubleword, sync)	DS 2F	COMP	BINARY
Internal Floating Point	DS 4C	COMP-1	COMP-1
Internal Floating Point	DS 8C	COMP-2	COMP-2
Index	DS 4C	INDEX	INDEX
Index-name	blank	INDEX-NAME	INDEX-NAME
Pointer	DS 4C	POINTER	POINTER
File (FD)	blank	QSAM or VSAM	QSAM or VSAM
Sort Definition (SD)	blank	SORT	SORT
Level 88	blank	blank	blank

Notes: "n" is the number of bytes being defined, except in variable-length groups, where it represents a variable-length cell number.

"P" means packed.

"C" means character.

Figure 3.4 Definition and usage terms used in COBOL II MAP output.

```
                                     .
                                     .
                                     .
000072         007200  01 SWITCHES.
000073         007300     05 SW-EOF                            PIC X       VALUE 'N'.
000074         007400        88 END-OF-FILE                                VALUE 'Y'.
000075         007500     05 SW-NM-LEN-ERR                     PIC X       VALUE 'N'.
000076         007600        88 NAME-LENGTH-ERROR                          VALUE 'Y'.
                                     .
                                     .
                                     .
```

(a)

```
                                           .
                                           .
                                           .
72    01 SWITCHES. . . . . . . . . . . . . . . . . . . . BLW=0000   010              DS OCL2      Group
73       02 SW-EOF. . . . . . . . . . . . . . . . . . . . BLW=0000   010    0 000 000  DS 1C        Display
74       88 END-OF-FILE . . . . . . . . . . . . . . . .
75       02 SW-NM-LEN-ERR . . . . . . . . . . . . . . . . BLW=0000   011    0 000 001  DS 1C        Display
76       88 NAME-LENGTH-ERROR . . . . . . . . . . . . .
                                           .
                                           .
                                           .
```

(b)

Figure 3.5 (*a*) Partial listing of a COBOL II Release 3 program's WORKING-STORAGE section, and (*b*) the corresponding portion of its DATA DIVISION map.

Letter "A" in the figure points to address 0000B240. The first two hexadecimal characters in the first storage column represent the contents of the byte at address 0000B240. It is hexadecimal D1, pointed to by letter "B" in the figure. The contents of the next byte, at address 0000B241, are shown in the next two character positions on that line. In the figure, this byte contains hexadecimal 4C.

The dump is formatted with storage for addresses ending with 0 at the beginning of the first storage column. Storage for addresses ending with 4 (B244 in the example) are at the beginning of the second storage column, storage for addresses ending with 8 are at the beginning of the third storage column, and storage for addresses ending with C are at the beginning of the fourth storage column. A larger space follows the fourth storage column. The beginning of the fifth column represents the byte in storage at an address hexadecimal 10 (decimal 16) bytes beyond that at the beginning of the line, so that once again storage for addresses ending in 0 appear at the beginning of the fifth storage column (B250 in the example), storage for those ending in 4 are at the beginning of the sixth column, storage for addresses ending with 8 are at the beginning of the seventh column, and storage for addresses ending with C are at the beginning of the eighth column. The address at the start of the next line is hexadecimal 20 (32 decimal) bytes greater than the address at the beginning of the line right above it.

On the far right is an EBCDIC translation of each of the preceding 32 bytes of storage on that line. If a byte is not a printable character, as might be the

```
                 *** TGT MEMORY MAP ***
         PGMLOC  TGTLOC

         0008A0  000000  72 BYTE SAVE AREA
         0008E8  000048  TGT IDENTIFIER
                                   .
                                   .
                                   .

                 *** VARIABLE PORTION OF TGT ***
 (A)
         0009BC  00011C  BACKSTORE CELL FOR SYMBOLIC REGISTERS
         0009D4  000134  BASE LOCATORS FOR SPECIAL REGISTERS
      -->0009DC  00013C  BASE LOCATORS FOR WORKING-STORAGE
         0009E0  000140  BASE LOCATORS FOR LINKAGE-SECTION
         0009E8  000148  BASE LOCATORS FOR FILES
         0009F0  000150  BASE LOCATORS FOR VARIABLY LOCATED DATA
         0009F4  000154  VARIABLE NAME (VN) CELLS
                                   .
                                   .
                                   .
```

Figure 3.6 A portion of the TGT for the program illustrated in Fig. 3.5.

case with a packed number, a period is printed. The translation of the byte shown at letter "B" in the figure, hexadecimal D1, is "J" (pointed to by letter "C"). The next storage position in the dump contains hexadecimal value 4C. This may have been a packed +4 but it is equivalent to "<" in EBCDIC. A period was printed instead, based on a limited set of characters which was available for output devices years ago (see letter "D" in Fig. 3.7).

3.1.3.2 Finding a COBOL field in a dump

As an example of how to use the information available in a map of the DATA DIVISION, let us now consider a program written in COBOL II Release 3. Although the maps look different in the other versions of COBOL, the technique we will demonstrate is the same. Assume that it is necessary to learn the contents of a field at the time the program ABENDs, and that we must find it in a hexadecimal storage dump. See Fig. 3.5*a* for a partial listing of the program's WORKING-STORAGE SECTION. The field we are interested in is SW-EOF. A portion of the DATA DIVISION map is shown in Fig. 3.5*b*. We see from the map that SW-EOF is displaced hexadecimal 10 from the base address in BLW cell 0000. It is also defined as a 1-byte character display, which is how it was coded in the program's WORKING-STORAGE SECTION.

We must find the location of BLW cell 0000 in the dump. To do so we look in the TGT for the offset into the program of the first BLW cell, which is cell number 0000. The relevant portion of the TGT is shown in Fig. 3.6 (note that either the OFFSET or LIST compiler options must have been specified in order to get a listing of the TGT in COBOL II). The hexadecimal offset, shown at "A" in the figure, is 0009DC. If we had wanted the next cell, which is BLW cell 0001, we would have added 4 to this offset because each cell is a fullword (4 bytes) in length.

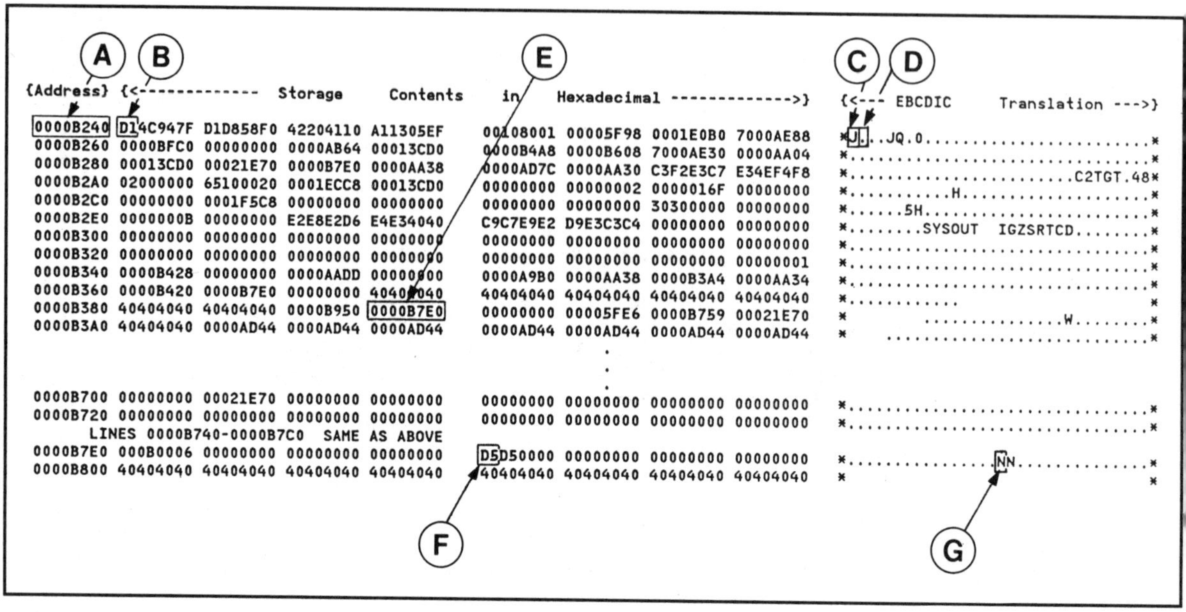

Figure 3.7 Part of the hexadecimal storage dump produced when a program ABENDed.

To find the actual address of BLW cell 0000 we must add its offset into the program to the beginning address of the program in the load module. We will go over how to find the program's beginning address in Sec. 8.7.4. For now, assume that we have found it to be hexadecimal 0000A9B0. Adding 0009DC to 0000A9B0 gives 0000B38C.

We can now look in the dump for address 0000B38C, which is the location of BLW cell 0000. It is shown at "E" in Fig. 3.7. The cell contains the value 0000B7E0, which is the base address for SW-EOF. Adding SW-EOF's displacement of 10 to 0000B7E0 gives us its actual address, 0000B7F0. We look at this address, shown at "F" in the figure. Because SW-EOF is a 1-byte character display field, its contents is D5. This hexadecimal value is equivalent to "N" in EBCDIC. The "N" is also seen at letter "G" in the EBCDIC portion of the dump at the right. Notice that this value is the same as that coded in the program's value clause.

3.2 THE NESTED PROGRAM MAP IN COBOL II RELEASE 3

As mentioned in Sec. 2.1.2, the MAP compiler option in COBOL II Release 3 also supplies you with a nested program map if there are nested programs. This map indicates where each nested program is defined in the source code, the nesting level of each program, program attribute information, and whether its PROCEDURE DIVISION header contains a USING clause. A key for program attribute codes is given at the top of the map. Figure 3.8 shows a nested program map; an explanation of the map follows.

SOURCE LINEID. This gives the line number of the source statement that defines the program.

NESTING LEVEL. This specifies how deeply the program is nested. No level number is given for the first program, since this is the main program, which is not nested.

PROGRAM NAME FROM PROGRAM-ID PARAGRAPH. This identifies the program. The names are indented to show the depth of the nesting.

PROGRAM ATTRIBUTES. This indicates whether the program has the COMMON or INITIAL attribute, and whether the USING clause is coded in the PROCEDURE DIVISION header.

Because a COBOL II Release 3 program can contain nested programs, the logical flow and physical structure can become quite complex. This map makes it easy to identify the nested programs and get a clearer representation of the overall structure.

3.3 PROCEDURE DIVISION INFORMATION

One of the first questions you may ask when a program terminates abnormally is what instruction was executing. Output from certain compiler options may identify the COBOL statement, but the output may not be available at the time the program ABENDs because the options were not in effect at compile time. Products from non-IBM vendors may do a good job of pinpointing the ABENDing instruction, but they don't always do it at the COBOL source code level. Often they merely give the offset into the program of the instruction.

It is therefore important for you to know how to obtain PROCEDURE DIVISION information from the output available from the COBOL compiler. This information includes a condensed PROCEDURE DIVISION listing or a full PROCEDURE DIVISION listing, and a verb cross-reference listing. The format of these listings and the information provided depend on which version of COBOL is used.

```
Nested Program Map
Program Attribute codes (rightmost column) have the following meanings:
    C = COMMON
    I = INITIAL
    U = PROCEDURE DIVISION USING...
Source Nesting                                                        Program
LineID Level    Program Name from PROGRAM-ID paragraph                Attributes
  2600          PROG1 . . . . . . . . . . . . . . . . . . . . . . . .
 20600     1      CHECK-CUST-NO . . . . . . . . . . . . . . . . . . .
 21400     2        ERROR-ROUTINE . . . . . . . . . . . . . . . . . .
 22500     1      HEADER-ROUTINE. . . . . . . . . . . . . . . . . . . C
 25600     1      SUMMARY-REPORT. . . . . . . . . . . . . . . . . . .
```

Figure 3.8 A nested program map in COBOL II Release 3.

3.3.1 The Condensed PROCEDURE DIVISION Listing

When the offset of the ABENDing instruction is known, the condensed PROCEDURE DIVISION listing can be used to find out what COBOL verb was executing. First, you must understand that each COBOL verb generates one or more Assembler instructions. The offset points to one of these Assembler instructions and your job is to find the COBOL verb which generated it. The condensed PROCEDURE DIVISION listing shows the source line number of each COBOL verb and the hexadecimal offset into the program of the first Assembler instruction generated by that verb.

The CLIST compiler option produces the condensed listing of the PROCEDURE DIVISION in OS/VS COBOL. If the VERB option is also in effect, the name of each COBOL verb is given; otherwise the word "verb" is substituted for the actual verb name.

In COBOL II, the OFFSET compiler option generates the condensed PROCEDURE DIVISION listing. The actual name of each verb is always given.

The format of the condensed listing is almost identical in OS/VS COBOL, COBOL II Release 2, and COBOL II Release 3. Figure 3.9 shows the listing for a COBOL II Release 3 program. The column labeled LINE # indicates the source line number for the COBOL verb, the column labeled HEXLOC shows the offset of its first Assembler instruction, and the column labeled VERB identifies the verb. The column headings are the same in COBOL II Release 2; the condensed listing has no headings in OS/VS COBOL.

As an example of how to use the condensed listing, let us assume that a non-IBM debugger has stated that the hexadecimal offset of the ABENDing instruction is 594. [Note that the offset of the next sequential instruction (NSI), which is the next instruction which would have executed, is often given instead.] Looking at Fig. 3.9 we see that there is no offset of 594; the closest offsets listed are 58E and 59E, indicated by "A" and "B" in the figure. The offset we are interested in falls between them. Recalling that a COBOL verb may generate many Assembler instructions, and that the offset in the condensed listing represents the first of those instructions, we realize that offset 594 must

```
(B)                                                                             (A)
LINE #  HEXLOC  VERB         LINE #  HEXLOC  VERB         LINE #  HEXLOC  VERB
000099 00050E DISPLAY        000100 00051C OPEN           000103 000548 READ
000105 000586 SET            000107 00058A PERFORM        000118 00058E IF
000119 00059E MOVE           000120 00059E MOVE           000122 0005AE ADD
000123 0005C0 ADD            000124 0005CC IF             000125 0005D6 PERFORM
000147 0005D6 ADD            000148 0005E2 MOVE           000149 0005F2 MOVE
000150 0005F2 MOVE           000151 000614 WRITE          000127 000648 READ
000129 000686 SET            000109 000692 PERFORM        000133 000692 DIVIDE
000135 0006AA MOVE           000136 0006BC WRITE          000138 0006F4 MOVE
000139 000712 MOVE           000140 00071E WRITE          000142 000750 MOVE
000143 000762 WRITE          000110 000794 CLOSE          000113 0007C0 DISPLAY
000114 0007CA GOBACK
```

Figure 3.9 A condensed PROCEDURE DIVISION listing in COBOL II Release 3 generated by the OFFSET option.

represent one of the Assembler instructions generated by the verb whose offset is shown as 58E. We therefore conclude that the COBOL verb being executed is the IF at line number 118 in the source module.

The rule for locating the proper COBOL verb is to find the verb whose offset matches that of the ABENDing Assembler instruction, or whose offset is the closest one which is smaller than that of the ABENDing Assembler instruction.

3.3.2 The PROCEDURE DIVISION Map

Usually the condensed listing of the PROCEDURE DIVISION is sufficient for finding the COBOL verb in the source code. Occasionally, however, it may be necessary to examine the actual Assembler instruction which was executing at the time of the ABEND. In this case, having the full map of the PROCEDURE DIVISION is desirable. The full map gives the source line number for each COBOL verb along with a full Assembler-language expansion for each verb. The hexadecimal offset into the program for each Assembler instruction, the hexadecimal object code, and information about the operands is also provided. Because so much information is given, the full PROCEDURE DIVISION map listing is many times the size of a condensed listing. It also requires more system resources to generate.

Besides showing a full Assembler expansion of your program statements, the PROCEDURE DIVISION map shows similar information for the initialization code used by the COBOL compiler to set up the proper run-time environment. This code is always present in a COBOL program. Although the function of the initialization routine is similar, the actual code differs in OS/VS COBOL and COBOL II.

There are some differences in the PROCEDURE DIVISION maps in OS/VS COBOL and COBOL II; the maps for each version of COBOL will be discussed in the following sections.

3.3.2.1 OS/VS COBOL PROCEDURE DIVISION map

The PMAP compiler option produces the PROCEDURE DIVISION map in OS/VS COBOL. If the VERB option is also in effect, the name of each COBOL verb and the name of the procedure containing the verb are given as well. If VERB is not in effect, blanks will appear in place of verb and procedure names.

Figure 3.10 shows part of an OS/VS COBOL PROCEDURE DIVISION map. The line number, shown at letter "A" in Fig. 3.10, is the number of the source line containing the verb or procedure shown in the next column. The source line number is shown only with the first Assembler instruction generated for each verb.

Letter "B" points to the column containing the verb or procedure name associated with the line number to the left. Names preceded by an asterisk (*) are procedure names.

The next column, indicated by letter "C" in Fig. 3.10, contains the hexadecimal displacement from the beginning of the program module for the instruction shown on this line.

```
  (A)          (B)            (C)  (D)          (E)              (F)                          (G)

15500    *0100-COMPARE-SEQ-NO
                   000F00                            PN=01   EQU   *
15600    ADD       000F00  FA 10 6 511 C 138                 AP    511(2,6),138(1,12)    DNM=4-328       LIT+0
15700    MOVE      000F06  92 40 6 2BE                       MVI   2BE(6),X'40'          DNM=3-233
                   000F0A  D2 2D 6 2BF 6 2BE                 MVC   2BF(46,6),2BE(6)      DNM=3-233+1     DNM=3-233
15800    IF        000F10  F2 74 D 210 6 000                 PACK  210(8,13),000(5,6)    TS=01           DNM=2-0
                   000F16  F2 74 D 218 6 508                 PACK  218(8,13),508(5,6)    TS=09           DNM=4-256
                   000F1C  F9 22 D 215 D 21D                 CP    215(3,13),21D(3,13)   TS=06           TS=014
                   000F22  58 F0 C 064                       L     15,064(0,12)          GN=08
                   000F26  07 7F                             BCR   7,15
15900    PERFORM   000F28  58 00 D 280                       L     0,280(0,13)           VN=04
                   000F2C  50 00 D 244                       ST    0,244(0,13)           PSV=4
                   000F30  58 00 C 068                       L     0,068(0,12)           GN=09
                   000F34  50 00 D 280                       ST    0,280(0,13)           VN=04
                   000F38  58 10 C 02C                       L     1,02C(0,12)           PN=03
                   000F3C  07 F1                             BCR   15,1
                   000F3E                            GN=09   EQU   *
```

Figure 3.10 A portion of an OS/VS COBOL PROCEDURE DIVISION map generated by the PMAP option.

Letter "D" points to the hexadecimal object code for the instruction.

In the column to the right of the object code, at letter "E" in the figure, is either a procedure-name (PN) number or compiler-generated-name (GN) number. There is a number listed only for procedures which are referenced in other PROCEDURE DIVISION statements.

An Assembler-like translation of the object code instruction is given next, pointed to by letter "F." Note that these are not true Assembler instructions; the displacements are shown in hexadecimal notation rather than in the decimal notation that an Assembler programmer would actually code.

At letter "G" in the figure is compiler-generated information about the operands in the instruction on this line. Figure 3.11 gives information about the symbols used in this column.

3.3.2.2 VS COBOL II PROCEDURE DIVISION map

In COBOL II, the LIST compiler option produces the PROCEDURE DIVISION map. Figure 3.12 shows a portion of a PROCEDURE DIVISION map for a COBOL II Release 3 program. The formats of the maps in Release 2 and in Release 3 are identical. An explanation of the format for the map illustrated in Fig. 3.12 follows.

At letter "A" in the figure is the source line number and the COBOL verb, paragraph name, or section name. Paragraph or section names have an asterisk (*) in front of them.

On the line below the COBOL verb is the hexadecimal displacement from the beginning of the program for the generated instruction given on this line. It is indicated by letter "B" in Fig. 3.12.

SYMBOL	DEFINITION
BL	Base locator cell
BLL	Base locator cell for LINKAGE SECTION
CKP	Checkpoint counter
DBGC	Debug statement number
DBGI	Debug information pointer
DCB	DCB address cell
DEC	DECB address cell
DNM	COBOL internal data name
FIB	FIB address cell
GN	Generated procedure name
INX	Index cell number
LIT	Literal in literal pool
ON	ON statement counter
OVF	Overflow cell
PBL	Procedure block for Optimizer
PFM	PERFORM counter
PN	Procedure name
POV	PGT overflow cell
PRM	Parameter
PSV	PERFORM save area

Figure 3.11 Symbols used in OS/VS COBOL PMAP and DMAP output. *(Continued)*

Letter "C" points to the hexadecimal object code for the instruction.

In the column following the object code, at letter "D" in the figure, is the compiler-generated name (GN) number for code sequences.

Letter "E" points to an Assembler translation of the object code instruction.

At letter "F" in the figure is compiler-generated information about the instruction's operands. Information about the symbols used can be found in Fig. 3.13.

3.3.2.3 Analyzing a COBOL verb in the PROCEDURE DIVISION map

Now that we have seen what a PROCEDURE DIVISION map shows, here is an example of how it might be used. A COBOL II Release 3 program was com-

SYMBOL	DEFINITION
SAV	Save area cell
SA2	I/O error save cell
SA3	OPEN parameter cell
SBL	Secondary base locator
SBS	Subscript address
SSVE	Sort save area
SWT	Cell for COBOL internal switches
TLY	Tally cell
TOV	TGT overflow cell
TS	Temporary storage area
TS2	Temporary storage-2 area
TS3	Temporary storage-3 area
TS4	Temporary storage-4 area
V (routine name)	VCON (address constant for external routine)
VLC	Variable length cell
VN	Variable name procedure cell
VNI	Variable name initialization
WC	Working cell
XSA	Exhibit save area
XSW	Exhibit switch

Figure 3.11 *(Continued)*

piled, linked, and executed with no apparent errors. Sometime later it was recompiled. When the program was executed again with the same input data set it ABENDed with an S0C7 completion code (data exception).

A portion of the PROCEDURE DIVISION map for the recompiled program is shown in Fig. 3.14*a*. The instruction causing the ABEND was determined to be the CP Assembler instruction generated by the IF statement at line 118 in the source code (see letter "A" in Fig. 3.14*a*). This is a "Compare Packed" instruction. The preceding Assembler instruction, PACK, packed the field STUDENT-GRADE. Apparently one of the operands in the CP instruction contained invalid packed data, causing the ABEND.

Why did the program ABEND the second time and not the first? Look at the

```
                                    (D)                      (E)                                                      (F)
(A)-> 000099  *0000-MAINLINE
      000100   OPEN                (C)
(B)->   00051C  5830 D158 <-              L    3,344(0,13)         FCB=1
        000520  D202 3034 A0A3            MVC  52(3,3),163(10)     (FCB=1)+52                       PGMLIT AT +147
        000526  5840 D15C                 L    4,348(0,13)         FCB=2
        00052A  D202 4034 A14D            MVC  52(3,4),333(10)     (FCB=2)+52                       PGMLIT AT +317
        000530  5850 D160                 L    5,352(0,13)         FCB=3
        000534  D202 5034 A14D            MVC  52(3,5),333(10)     (FCB=3)+52                       PGMLIT AT +317
        00053A  58F0 21E4                 L    15,484(0,2)         V(IGZEQOC )
        00053E  4110 A168                 LA   1,360(0,10)         PGMLIT AT +344
        000542  05EF                      BALR 14,15
        000544  5880 D12C                 L    8,300(0,13)         BLF=0
      000103   READ
        000548  5840 D158                 L    4,344(0,13)         STUDENT-FILE
        00054C  9200 40C9                 MVI  201(4),X'00'        FCB=1
        000550  9200 40B3                 MVI  179(4),X'00'        FCB=1
        000554  D203 4074 A146            MVC  116(4,4),326(10)    FCB=1                            PGMLIT AT +310
        00055A  58F0 403C                 L    15,60(0,4)          FCB=1
        00055E  055F                      BALR 5,15
        000560  9500 40C9                 CLI  201(4),X'00'        FCB=1
        000564  4770 B11E                 BC   7,286(0,11)         GN=17(000572)
        000568  5010 D12C                 ST   1,300(0,13)         BLF=0
        00056C  1881                      LR   8,1
        00056E  47F0 B136                 BC   15,310(0,11)        GN=4(00058A)
        000572                   GN=17    EQU  *
        000572  9510 40C9                 CLI  201(4),X'10'        FCB=1
                                                .
                                                .
                                                .
```

Figure 3.12 Part of a PROCEDURE DIVISION map for a COBOL II program. It is produced by the LIST option.

PROCEDURE DIVISION map for the program when it was compiled the first time (see Fig. 3.14*b*). The same COBOL instruction that caused the problem, the IF at line 118, generated different Assembler instructions (see letter "B" in Fig. 3.14*b*). There is an OI instruction. This is the "Or Immediate," and it changed the rightmost portion of last byte of the field, which was packed in the previous PACK instruction to "F." This byte contains the sign of the field. The OI instruction changed the sign portion of this byte to a hexadecimal F. This means that even if the field in question originally had an invalid sign, it will have been altered to a valid sign, avoiding a potential S0C7 ABEND! It turns out that the input file contained one record with spaces in STUDENT-GRADE. When this field was packed, the hexadecimal 40, equivalent to a space in EBCDIC, was changed to 04 in the last byte of the field. The OI instruction converted the 4, which is an invalid sign, to an F, which is a valid sign. In the packing process, the rest of STUDENT-GRADE became zeros because the 4's were stripped off. Although the program appeared to have run successfully the first time, it had actually produced bad output because of the faulty field in that record.

What was different in the two compiles? The first time, when the program did not ABEND, the compiler option NUMPROC(NOPFD) was used (equivalent to NOPFDSGN in Release 2). This option assumes that there is "no preferred sign," and it generates the OI instruction to convert whatever is in the sign position to an F (NUMPROC is also affected by the NUMCLS installation option; see Sec. 7.1.2).

SYMBOL	DEFINITION	RELEASE
BL=n	Base locator cell for special registers	2, 3
BLF=n	Base locator cell for files	2, 3
BLL=n	Base locator cell for LINKAGE SECTION	2, 3
BLV=n	Base locator cell for variably located data	2, 3
BLW=n	Base locator cell for WORKING-STORAGE	2, 3
BLX=n	Base locator cell for EXTERNAL data	3
CBL=n	Base locator cell for CGT	2, 3
CLLE@=	Load list entry address in TGT	2, 3
EVALUATE=n	EVALUATE boolean cell number in TGT	2, 3
FCB=n	FCB address	2, 3
GN=n(hhhh)	Generated procedure name with its offset from beginning of the program	2, 3
IDX=n	Index cell number	2, 3
ODOSAVE=n	OCCURS DEPENDING ON save cell number	2, 3
OPT=dddd	Optimizer temporary storage cell	2, 3
PBL=n	Base locator cell for procedure code	2, 3
PFM=n	PERFORM x TIMES cell	2, 3
PGMLIT AT + dddd	Displacement for program literal from beginning of literal pool	2, 3
PSV=n	PERFORM save cell number	2, 3

Figure 3.13 Symbols used in COBOL II LIST and MAP output.

The second time, when the program did ABEND, the NUMPROC(PFD) option was in effect (equivalent to the PFDSGN compiler option in Release 2). This option assumes that one of the "preferred signs," C, D, or F, is present. The compiler does not generate the OI instruction since there is no need to convert the value in the sign position to an F. Although this option produces more efficient code, it does not "protect" the program from ABENDing when the sign is not C, D, or F. Actually, unless the programmer is certain that all numeric data used by the program are valid, it would be wise to use this option to permit an S0C7 ABEND to occur. This may avoid the danger of producing bad output data, as happened in the situation just described. In our example, unbeknownst to the programmer, the installation had changed the default compiler options for the compile procedure! The problem might never have been found without an analysis of the instructions shown in the PROCEDURE DIVISION map.

SYMBOL	DEFINITION	RELEASE
RBKST=n	Backstore cell for symbolic registers	2, 3
SYSLIT AT + dddd	Displacement for system literal from beginning of system literal pool	2, 3
TGT FDMP TEST INFO AREA + dddd	Information area used when FDUMP and TEST are in effect	2, 3
TGTFIXD=dddd	Offset from beginning of the fixed portion of the TGT	2, 3
TOV=n	TGT overflow cell number	2, 3
TS1=dddd	Temporary storage-1 area in subpool 1	2, 3
TS2=dddd	Temporary storage-2 area in subpool 2	2, 3
TS3=dddd	Temporary storage-3 area in subpool 3	2, 3
TS4=dddd	Temporary storage-4 area in subpool 4	2, 3
V (routine name)	VCON (address constant for external routine)	2, 3
VLC=n	Variable length cell used for length of ODO field	2, 3
VN=n	Variable name procedure cell used for ALTER	2, 3
VNI=n	Variable name initialization	2, 3
WHEN=n	EVALUATE WHEN cell number in TGT	2, 3

Notes: "n" represents the number of the entry

"dddd" represents the decimal offset from the beginning of the entry

"hhhh" represents the hexadecimal offset from the beginning of the program

Figure 3.13 *(Continued)*

3.3.3 COBOL Initialization Code

The initialization code generated by the COBOL compiler is listed whenever a PROCEDURE DIVISION map is requested. Among other things, this code provides for standard program linkage by storing the contents of the calling program's general-purpose registers; we will come back to this further into the book.

Some useful debugging information from the initialization code includes the version of the compiler used, the date and time of the compilation, and the program name. If during the course of program testing several compilations were done, it can be important to verify which of the several versions you are looking at. Although this information appears in the header at the top of each page of compiler output, you can find the initialization code information in a hexadecimal storage dump if the compiler output is not readily available.

```
                                              (A)
000116  *0100-PROCESS-RECORD
000118  IF
   00058E  F212 D18E 8014          PACK 398(2,13),20(3,8)       OPT=6                     STUDENT-GRADE
   000594  F911 9044 D18E          CP   68(2,9),398(2,13)       SAVE-STUDENT-GRADE        OPT=6
   00059A  47D0 B15A               BC   13,346(0,11)            GN=5(0005AE)

                                                (a)
(B)
000116  *0100-PROCESS-RECORD
000118  IF
   000592  F212 D18E 8014          PACK 398(2,13),20(3,8)       OPT=6                     STUDENT-GRADE
   000598  960F D18F               OI   399(13),X'0F'           OPT=7
   00059C  F911 9044 D18E          CP   68(2,9),398(2,13)       SAVE-STUDENT-GRADE        OPT=6
   0005A2  47D0 B160               BC   13,352(0,11)            GN=5(0005B8)

                                                (b)
```

Figure 3.14 Part of a PROCEDURE DIVISION map for a COBOL II Release 3 program (*a*) compiled with the NUMPROC(PFD) option, and (*b*) again with the NUMPROC(NOPFD) option. The OI instruction is generated when NUMPROC(NOPFD) is in effect.

3.3.3.1 OS/VS COBOL initialization code

Three initialization routines are generated by the OS/VS COBOL compiler. The first, known as INIT1, is always at the beginning of the program in the load module. However, it is located near the end of the PROCEDURE DIVISION map listing; it can be found by looking for INIT1 at hexadecimal offset 000000 (see Fig. 3.15). The significant information in this code is the program name and the time-date stamp. It is necessary for you to translate the hexadecimal notation to understand it.

As an example, refer to Fig. 3.15. At hexadecimal offset 00000C are the characters "D7D9D6C7F1404040." This translates to "PROG1", which is the name of the present program. The program name is always found at this offset.

At offset 000088 is the beginning of the time-date stamp. Figure 3.15 shows the characters "F1F64BF0F54BF2F9" at offset 000088. This is the time of compilation, "16.05.29." At offsets 000090 and 000098 are the characters "D5D6E540F1F66B40" and "F1F9F9F0", respectively. This is the compilation date "NOV 16, 1990." The time and date are always found at these positions in INIT1.

3.3.3.2 VS COBOL II initialization code

The initialization code generated by the COBOL II compiler is well-commented compared to that generated by the OS/VS COBOL compiler (see Fig. 3.16). It is almost identical in Release 2 and Release 3. Although it is located physically at the beginning of the program in the load module, the code appears as a separate section in the PROCEDURE DIVISION map listing, after the DATA DIVISION map and before the PGT.

You can verify which compiler options were in effect by looking at the bit settings in the 4 bytes starting at hexadecimal offset 2C in the COBOL II initialization code; the settings are documented in the IBM *VS COBOL II Application Programming: Debugging* manual. You must first translate the hexadecimal val-

```
000000  90 EC D 00C          INIT1   STM    14,12,00C(13)
000004  18 5D                        LR     5,13
000006  05 F0                        BALR   15,0
000008  45 80 F 010                  BAL    8,010(0,15)
00000C  D7D9D6C7F1404040             DC     X'D7D9D6C7F1404040'
000014  E5E2D9F1                     DC     X'E5E2D9F1'
000018  07 00                        BCR    0,0
00001A  98 9F F 024                  LM     9,15,024(15)
00001E  07 FF                        BCR    15,15
000020  96 02 1 034                  OI     034(1),X'02'
000024  07 FE                        BCR    15,14
000026  41 F0 0 001                  LA     15,001(0,0)
00002A  07 FE                        BCR    15,14
00002C  0000161A                     ADCON  L4(INIT3)
000030  00000000                     ADCON  L4(INIT1)
000034  00000000                     ADCON  L4(INIT1)
000038  00000B48                     ADCON  L4(PGT)
00003C  00000888                     ADCON  L4(TGT)
000040  00000CF2                     ADCON  L4(START)
000044  000015DA                     ADCON  L4(INIT2)
000048                               DS     15F
000084  00000000                     DC     X'00000000'
000088  F1F64BF0F54BF2F9             DC     X'F1F64BF0F54BF2F9'
000090  D5D6E540F1F66B40             DC     X'D5D6E540F1F66B40'
000098  F1F9F9F0                     DC     X'F1F9F9F0'
```

Figure 3.15 Initialization code in an OS/VS COBOL program.

ues in these bytes into binary digits. For example, the byte at hexadecimal 2C in the initialization code illustrated in Fig. 3.16 contains hexadecimal E0, or binary 11100000. These bit settings mean that ADV, APOST, DATA(31), NODECK, NODUMP, NODYNAM, NOFASTSRT, and NOFDUMP were in effect.

The initialization code can also be used to determine the program name, the compiler used, and the date and time of compilation. In the code shown in Fig. 3.16, the program name "DMPCB23" appears at hexadecimal offset 5, the compiler used is listed as "C2" (representing COBOL II) at offset D, and the version, release, and modification of the compiler is designated as "1.3.0" at offset 11. Also, the date of the compilation is shown as "11/01/90" at hexadecimal offset 17 and the time of the compile is "08.21.08" at offset 20. This all appears in easy-to-read EBCDIC character format. The information is always found at these positions in the initialization code.

3.4 SUMMARY

Understanding how to read COBOL maps is essential in debugging. These maps provide information about the DATA DIVISION, the PROCEDURE DIVISION, and, in COBOL II Release 3, nested program structure.

Knowledge of the DATA DIVISION map enables you to locate DATA DIVISION items in a hexadecimal storage dump. This map specifies base locator cells, displacements, and data definitions for all items in a program's DATA DIVISION. By using the base address found in the appropriate base locator cell

```
000000                    DMPCB23  DS    0H
                                   USING *,15
000000  47F0 F070                  B     112(,15)                    BYPASS CONSTANTS. BRANCH TO @STM
000004  23                         DC    AL1(35)                     SIGNATURE: LEN. PGM. I.D. CHARS.
000005  C4D4D7C3C2F2F340           DC    C'DMPCB23 '       @EPNAM:              PROGRAM NAME
00000D  40C3F240                   DC    C' C2 '                                COMPILER = COBOL II
000011  F14BF34BF040               DC    C'1.3.0 '                              VERSION/RELEASE/MOD.
000017  F1F161F0F161F9F0           DC    C'11/01/90 '                           DATE COMPILED
000020  F0F84BF2F14BF0F8           DC    C'08.21.08'                            TIME COMPILED
000028  00000054                   DC    A(*+44)           @APARM:              A(@PARMS)
00002C  E06A8C0C0080               DC    X'E06A8C0C0080'                        INFO. BYTES 1-6
000032  0000420C010B               DC    X'0000420C010B'                        INFO. BYTES 7-12
000038  810040000800               DC    X'810040000800'                        INFO. BYTES 13-18
00003E  0000000004                 DC    X'0000000004'                          INFO. BYTES 19-23
000043  00                         DC    X'00'                                  RESERVED
000044  0000001C                   DC    X'0000001C'                            # DATA DIV. STMTS.
000048  0000001F                   DC    X'0000001F'                            # PROC. DIV. STMTS.
00004C  0000                       DC    X'0000'                                INFO. BYTES 24-25
00004E  0000                       DC    2X'00'                                 RESERVED
000050  40404040                   DC    C'    '                                USER LEVEL INFO (LVLINFO)
000054  00000000                   DC    A(DMPCB23)        @PARMS: 1) MAIN ENTRY POINT ADDRESS
000058  00000080                   DC    A(PGT)                    2) PGT ADDRESS
00005C  000007D8                   DC    A(TGT)                    3) TGT ADDRESS
000060  00000005                   DC    A(*-91)                   4) A(@EPNAM)= E. P. NAME ADDRESS
000064  00000000                   DC    A(DMPCB23)                5) CURRENT ENTRY POINT ADDRESS
000068  00000428                   DC    A(START)          @BRVAL: PROCEDURE CODE ADDRESS
00006C  00000000                   DC    V(IGZENRI)                INITIALIZATION ROUTINE
000070  90EC D00C                  STM   14,12,12(13)      @STM:   SAVE CALLER'S REGISTERS
000074  5810 F028                  L     1,40(,15)                 GET ADDR. OF PARMLIST FROM @APARM
000078  98EF F068                  LM    14,15,104(15)             LOAD ADDRESSES FROM @BRVAL
00007C  07FF                       BR    15                        DO ANY NECESSARY INITIALIZATION
```

Figure 3.16 Initialization code for a COBOL II Release 3 program.

and adding it to the item's displacement, you can locate the item in the dump.

Hexadecimal storage dumps are formatted with addresses in the leftmost column, the contents of storage given in hexadecimal notation in the next eight columns, and the EBCDIC translation of the storage contents on the extreme right.

A nested program map is available in COBOL II Release 3. It gives each program name, where it is defined, its nesting level, and its attributes. Because a nested program structure can be very complex, this map makes it easier to decipher the overall structure of the source module.

Information about a program's PROCEDURE DIVISION can be found in either the condensed listing or the full PROCEDURE DIVISION map. The condensed listing gives the hexadecimal offset of the first Assembler instruction and the source line number for each COBOL verb in the program. If the offset of the Assembler instruction causing the ABEND has been determined, then the COBOL verb which generated that instruction can be found.

The full map of the PROCEDURE DIVISION provides the source line number for each COBOL verb together with a full Assembler-language expansion for the verb, the hexadecimal offset for each Assembler instruction generated by the verb, the hexadecimal object code for each Assembler instruction, and information about the operands. The condensed PROCEDURE DIVISION listing is usually sufficient for locating the COBOL verb that was executing when the program ABENDed; however, if you are faced by a seemingly obscure problem, the full PROCEDURE DIVISION map may be vital for examining the actual Assembler instruction involved.

Besides giving information about the verbs coded by the programmer, the PROCEDURE DIVISION map shows information about the initialization code generated by the COBOL compiler to set up the proper run-time environment. Some important things found in the initialization code include the program name, the compiler version used, and the date and time of compilation.

REVIEW QUESTIONS

1. Why is it important for a COBOL programmer to know how to use the DATA DIVISION map?

2. Which compiler option generates a DATA DIVISION map in:
a. OS/VS COBOL?
b. COBOL II?

3. **a.** What are base locator cells?
b. Name the different base locator cells and describe their purposes in OS/VS COBOL.
c. Name the different base locator cells and describe their purposes in COBOL II.
d. Describe what steps must be taken to find the address of a base locator cell in a hexadecimal storage dump.

4. Answer the following questions about a hexadecimal storage dump.
a. Which column contains addresses?
b. How many bytes of storage are mapped out per line?
c. Where is the EBCDIC translation of the hexadecimal contents of each byte of storage?
d. How are the contents of a byte represented in the EBCDIC portion of the dump if the byte contains an unprintable character?

5. Refer to Fig. 3.17 for this question.
a. Which OS/VS COBOL compiler option produced this listing? What is the comparable option in COBOL II?
b. If the offset of an ABENDing instruction is 0008EE, what COBOL verb was executing? What is the source line number of the statement containing the verb?
c. What OS/VS COBOL compiler option would you request in order to be able to examine the Assembler instruction at offset 000AFC?
d. Which COBOL II compiler option would be needed to examine the Assembler instruction at offset 000AFC?

142	ENTRY	0008C0	144	DISPLAY	0008D8	146	CALL	0008EC
149	IF	000926	151	DISPLAY	000936	152	GOBACK	00094A
153	OPEN	000974	154	MOVE	0009B2	155	PERFORM	0009C6
157	CLOSE	0009F2	158	DISPLAY	000A74	159	GOBACK	000A88
161	WRITE	000AB2	162	ADD	000AFC			

Figure 3.17 A portion of the compiler output for an OS/VS COBOL program.

6. Use the information in Fig. 3.18 to find the contents of the field PROCESS-SWITCH in an OS/VS COBOL program which ABENDed. The starting address of the program is A1A0.

7. Refer to Fig. 3.19 in order to find the contents of the field REC-READ IN COUNTERS at the time a COBOL II program ABENDed. The beginning of the COBOL program is at the hexadecimal address A608.

8. Explain why it is important for you to know how to use the PROCEDURE DIVISION information provided by the compiler. What two types of PROCEDURE DIVISION listings can the programmer request from the compiler?

9. What does the COBOL II Release 3 nested program map show? Explain how this map can be of use to the programmer.

10. What helpful information can be found in COBOL's initialization code?

```
INTRNL NAME   LVL SOURCE NAME                   BASE    DISPL  INTRNL NAME   DEFINITION   USAGE     R  O  Q  M
DNM=1-088     FD  IN-FILE                       DCB=01         DNM=1-088                  QSAM               F
DNM=1-111     01  IN-RECORD                     BL=1    000    DNM=1-111     DS 1000C     DISP
DNM=1-132     01  DATA-AREA                     BL=2    000    DNM=1-132     DS 0CL1069   GROUP
DNM=1-155     02  FILLER                        BL=2    000    DNM=1-155     DS 32C       DISP
DNM=1-166     02  PACKED-INPUT-DATA             BL=2    020    DNM=1-166     DS 0CL3      GROUP
DNM=1-201     03  RECORDS-READ                  BL=2    020    DNM=1-201     DS 3P        COMP-3
DNM=1-226     02  CONTR-REC                     BL=2    023    DNM=1-226     DS 0CL1000   GROUP
DNM=1-253     03  RECORD-NUMBER                 BL=2    023    DNM=1-253     DS 4C        COMP
DNM=1-276     03  FILLER                        BL=2    027    DNM=1-276     DS 996C      DISP
DNM=1-290     02  PROCESS-SWITCH                BL=2    40B    DNM=1-290     DS 1C        DISP
DNM=1-317     88  CONTINUE-PROCESSING                          DNM=1-317
DNM=1-345     88  END-PROCESSING                               DNM=1-345
DNM=1-376     02  RECORD-CODE                   BL=2    40C    DNM=1-376     DS 1C        DISP
```

(a)

```
                 MEMORY MAP

          TGT                              005F0

       SAVE AREA                           005F0
       SWITCH                              00638
                           .
                           .
                           .
       DEBUGGING                           007E8
       CD FOR INITIAL INPUT                007EC
       OVERFLOW CELLS                      007F0
       BL CELLS                            007F0
       DECBADR CELLS                       007F8
```

(b)

```
0000A240 5C5C5CE6 D6D9D2C9 D5C740E2 E3D6D9C1   C7C540E2 E3C1D9E3 E240C8C5 D9C55C5C   *...WORKING STORAGE STARTS HERE..*
0000A260 00049C00 00000440 40404040 40404040   40404040 40404040 40404040 40404040   *.......                         *
0000A280 40404040 40404040 40404040 40404040   40404040 40404040 40404040 40404040   *                                *
    LINES 0000A2A0-0000A620  SAME AS ABOVE
0000A640 40404040 40404040 404040E8 D5000000   5C5C4040 40404040 1C400000 40404040   *           YN.....       . ..   *
                                                   .
                                                   .
                                                   .
0000A960 00000000 00000000 00000000 00000000   0000AA54 00000000 00000000 00000000   *................................*
0000A980 00000000 00000000 00000000 00000000   0000FB90 0000A240 00000000 00000000   *....................    ........*
0000A9A0 00000000 00000018 00000000 00000000   00000000 00000000 00000000 0000AC7E   *................................*
```

(c)

Figure 3.18 Information for an OS/VS COBOL program which ABENDed.

```
Data Division Map
Data Definition Attribute codes (rightmost column) have the following meanings:
    D = Object of OCCURS DEPENDING    G = GLOBAL                           S = Spanned file
    E = EXTERNAL                      O = Has OCCURS clause                U = Undefined format file
    F = Fixed length file             OG= Group has own length definition  V = Variable length file
    FB= Fixed length blocked file     R = REDEFINES                        VB= Variable length blocked file
Source   Hierarchy and                                    Base       Hex-Displacement  Asmblr Data                     Data Def
LineID   Data Name                                        Locator    Blk   Structure   Definition    Data Type         Attributes
     2   PROGRAM-ID DMPCB24 ---------------------------------------------------------------------------------------------------*
    10    FD PRINT-FILE. . . . . . . . . . . . . . . . .              001                             QSAM              FB
    16    01 PRINT-FILE-REC. . . . . . . . . . . . . . . BLF=0000     000               DS 133C       Display
    17    FD IN-FILE . . . . . . . . . . . . . . . . . .              001                             QSAM              FB
    23    01 IN-FILE-REC . . . . . . . . . . . . . . . . BLF=0001     000               DS 80C        Display
    26    01 PRINT-OUT . . . . . . . . . . . . . . . . . BLW=0000     000               DS 0CL133     Group
    27      02 CTRL-CODE . . . . . . . . . . . . . . . . BLW=0000     000   0 000 000   DS 1C         Display
    28      02 CARD-INFO . . . . . . . . . . . . . . . . BLW=0000     001   0 000 001   DS 132C       Display
    29    01 PRINT-SUMMARY . . . . . . . . . . . . . . . BLW=0000     088               DS 0CL48      Group
    30      02 FILLER. . . . . . . . . . . . . . . . . . BLW=0000     088   0 000 000   DS 19C        AN-Edit
    32      02 REC-READ. . . . . . . . . . . . . . . . . BLW=0000     09B   0 000 013   DS 3C         Num-Edit
    33     '02 FILLER. . . . . . . . . . . . . . . . . . BLW=0000     09E   0 000 016   DS 23C        AN-Edit
    35      02 REC-WRITTEN . . . . . . . . . . . . . . . BLW=0000     0B5   0 000 02D   DS 3C         Num-Edit
    36    01 WS-IN-FILE. . . . . . . . . . . . . . . . . BLW=0000     0B8               DS 0CL80      Group
    37      02 FILLER. . . . . . . . . . . . . . . . . . BLW=0000     0B8   0 000 000   DS 80C        Display
    38    01 SAVE-AREA . . . . . . . . . . . . . . . . . BLW=0000     108               DS 0CL135     Group
    39      02 REC-NO. . . . . . . . . . . . . . . . . . BLW=0000     108   0 000 000   DS 2P         Packed-Dec
    40      02 CTRL-CODE . . . . . . . . . . . . . . . . BLW=0000     10A   0 000 002   DS 1C         Display
    41      02 CARD-INFO . . . . . . . . . . . . . . . . BLW=0000     10B   0 000 003   DS 132C       Display
    42    01 COUNTERS. . . . . . . . . . . . . . . . . . BLW=0000     190               DS 0CL4       Group
    43      02 REC-READ. . . . . . . . . . . . . . . . . BLW=0000     190   0 000 000   DS 2P         Packed-Dec
    44      02 REC-WRITTEN . . . . . . . . . . . . . . . BLW=0000     192   0 000 002   DS 2P         Packed-Dec
```

(a)

```
           *** TGT MEMORY MAP ***
    PGMLOC  TGTLOC

    000548  000000  72 BYTE SAVE AREA
    000590  000048  TGT IDENTIFIER
                          .
                          .
                          .

           *** VARIABLE PORTION OF TGT ***

    000664  00011C  BASE LOCATORS FOR SPECIAL REGISTERS
    00066C  000124  BASE LOCATORS FOR WORKING-STORAGE
    000670  000128  BASE LOCATORS FOR LINKAGE-SECTION
    000674  00012C  BASE LOCATORS FOR FILES
    00067C  000134  VARIABLE NAME (VN) CELLS
                          .
                          .
                          .
```

(b)

```
0000AC60 0000A618 0000A6A0 0000AC94 0000A69C   0000ACAC 0000AFE0 00000000 40404040   *............................    *
0000AC80 0000B180 0000AFE0 00000000 00000000   00000000 0000A8D0 0000A8D0 0000A8D0   *................................*
                                                   .
                                                   .
                                                   .
0000B060 00000000 00000000 E3D6E3C1 D340D9C5   C3D6D9C4 E240D9C5 C1C44000 0000E3D6   *........TOTAL RECORDS READ ...TO*
0000B080 E3C1D340 D9C5C3D6 D9C4E240 E6D9C9E3   E3C5D540 40000000 00000000 00000000   *TAL RECORDS WRITTEN  ...........*
0000B0A0 00000000 00000000 00000000 00000000   00000000 00000000 00000000 00000000   *................................*
     LINES 0000B0C0-0000B140  SAME AS ABOVE
0000B160 00000000 00000000 00000000 00000000   00000000 00000000 F0000000 00000000   *........................0.......*
0000B180 00000000 00000000 00000000 00000000   00000000 00000000 E2E8E2D6 E4E34040   *.......................SYSOUT  *
```

(c)

Figure 3.19 Information for a COBOL II program which ABENDed.

Chapter

4

Additional COBOL Debugging Tips and Techniques

There are a number of COBOL language features which are a great help in testing and debugging COBOL programs. These include the ability to display the contents of fields at any point during program execution, control how many times a portion of code is to be executed, trace program flow, execute alternate code, test file status conditions, and automatically invoke COBOL file I/O error routines and programmer-coded error routines.

Some of these features are considered indispensable by almost all COBOL programmers, while others are hardly ever used. In this chapter we will take a look at both the commonly used and the rarely used features, pointing out how they may be utilized to their best advantage.

4.1 COBOL VERBS USEFUL FOR DEBUGGING

COBOL verbs helpful in testing and debugging include DISPLAY, TRACE, EXHIBIT, and ON. Note that all of these verbs are allowed in OS/VS COBOL, but that only DISPLAY is available in COBOL II.

4.1.1 The DISPLAY Verb

DISPLAY is probably the most widely used of the debugging verbs. It permits you to display the contents of DATA DIVISION fields, some special COBOL registers, literals, and figurative constants on a variety of output devices. Numeric binary and packed data are automatically converted to EBCDIC characters as though they were defined as USAGE DISPLAY so they can be easily read. Note that assumed decimal points, coded as "V" in the picture clause, do not get translated into actual decimal points and will not appear in the output. Also, positive signed numbers are printed without the sign and negative signed numbers appear with a low-order sign overpunch. For example, if three packed items having values of –67, +67, and 67 are displayed, they will appear as 6P, 67, and 67, respectively. The P appears in the first item because the rightmost byte in the packed field contains 7D. The D represents a negative sign. When it is unpacked before being displayed, the 7D is changed to D7, which is equivalent to P in EBCDIC. The third item is an implicit positive number and is displayed, as is the explicitly defined positive-signed number, without a sign.

DISPLAY is intended for transferring low-volume data to an output device. No SELECT . . . ASSIGN clause, FD, OPEN statement, or CLOSE statement is coded in the program for the output.

The contents of the operands in the DISPLAY statement are transferred in a left to right order, with no formatting, to the output device. Thus, you must insert blanks as part of a literal if spaces are desired preceding or following the contents of a field or register. For example, if FLD-A is defined as PIC S9(3) COMP-3 and contains the value +7, then the statement

```
000100          DISPLAY 'THE CONTENTS OF FLD-A = '
000200                  FLD-A
000300                  ' BEFORE PROCESSING.'
```

will yield output which looks like this:

```
THE CONTENTS OF FLD-A = 007 BEFORE PROCESSING.
```

DISPLAY will cause the printer to advance before printing. In COBOL II Release 3, however, DISPLAY permits an optional WITH NO ADVANCING clause. This provides some flexibility in formatting the output since it means that data from a subsequent DISPLAY statement can be made to appear on the same line as the output from the current DISPLAY statement.

Since by default output from DISPLAY is sent to the file or device assigned to the SYSOUT DD statement in the JCL, it may be hard to read the output from DISPLAY statements if another program is also using SYSOUT. As an example, messages from the internal sort program normally use SYSOUT. This means that output from DISPLAY will be intermixed with output from the sort program. COBOL II permits you to specify a different output device or file by coding the compiler option OUTDD. Thus, specifying OUTDD(DISPOUT) causes output from DISPLAY statements to be sent to the file or device associated with the DISPOUT DD statement. In OS/VS COBOL you can specify a different DD statement to which messages from the sort program are to be routed. The COBOL statement

```
MOVE 'SORTOUT' TO SORT-MESSAGE
```

sends sort messages to a device or file associated with the SORTOUT DD statement.

A DISPLAY statement is typically used when you need to know the contents of a field at predefined points in the program's processing. DISPLAY should not be used as a substitute for WRITE; it is considered poor programming practice to DISPLAY all output records instead of WRITEing them. This is because of DISPLAY's limited formatting and editing capabilities, and because other DISPLAYed output will be mixed in with the output records.

Another use for DISPLAY is to give messages relating to program flow during program testing. If you haven't written all the code for a procedure, simply coding the paragraph or section header followed by a DISPLAY statement is sufficient to determine if the procedure has indeed been reached. The following example illustrates this:

```
000100      PERFORM 9000-ERROR-ROUTINE.
                    .
                    .
                    .

000800 9000-ERROR-ROUTINE.
000900      DISPLAY 'PROGRAM HAS REACHED 9000-ERROR-ROUTINE'.
```

4.1.2 Additional Debugging Verbs Available in OS/VS COBOL

EXHIBIT. This verb is similar in its function and use to DISPLAY. It gives a formatted display of the operands coded in the statement, with the output going to whatever device is associated with the SYSOUT DD statement. It also allows you to automatically monitor the values in a field. Because of the formatting, EXHIBIT involves more system overhead than DISPLAY.

EXHIBIT can be coded with either the NAMED, CHANGED, or CHANGED NAMED options. CHANGED or CHANGED NAMED causes the value of an identifier to be displayed the first time the EXHIBIT statement is encountered. For each subsequent execution of that EXHIBIT statement, the value is displayed only if the value of the identifier has changed since the previous execution. If more than one identifier is coded in an EXHIBIT using the CHANGED or CHANGED options, only the value of the identifier that changed is displayed.

When NAMED or CHANGED NAMED is coded for an identifier, the output is formatted with the source name of the identifier followed by a space, an equal sign, another space, and then the current value. If FLD-A, defined as PIC S9(3) COMP-3, has a value of +7, then the statement

```
000200          EXHIBIT NAMED FLD-A
```

produces the following:

```
FLD-A = 007
```

If CHANGED without the NAMED option is coded, the values of the operands are placed in fixed columnar positions in the order in which they were coded in the statement. If FLD-B, defined as PIC X(10), contains a changed value of 'NEW RECORD' and FLD-C, defined as PIC 9(3), has a changed value of 68, then the statement

```
           EXHIBIT CHANGED FLD-B FLD-C
```

results in

```
NEW RECORD 068
```

TRACE. For testing and debugging, the TRACE verb is probably second only to DISPLAY in popularity among OS/VS COBOL programmers. It is invoked by coding READY TRACE at any point in the PROCEDURE DIVISION. TRACE enables you to see the flow of control of the program. RESET TRACE turns off a previously invoked TRACE.

After a READY TRACE has been executed, a list of either paragraph and section names (if the VERB compiler option is in effect), or statement numbers of the paragraph and section headers (if VERB is not in effect) is displayed each time the paragraph or section begins execution. The names or numbers appear left to right in the order in which the paragraphs or sections are executed. They appear on the system's logical output device, usually the printer.

TRACE helps you learn if the correct procedure paths are taken for specified program logic. A disadvantage, however, is that it does not report which path is taken for IF . . . ELSE statements within a paragraph or section. A combination of DISPLAY or EXHIBIT and TRACE will do this. Because the output from TRACE can be voluminous, you may want to conditionally set and reset TRACE.

ON. ON allows you to specify statements to be executed at predetermined points or intervals. The compiler sets up a counter for the ON statement and initializes it to zero. Each time the ON statement is reached, the counter is automatically incremented by one. Thus instead of executing a statement each time it is encountered, you may wish to execute it the tenth time only, or perhaps the tenth time and every twenty times thereafter, or possibly the tenth time and every twenty times after that until a condition is met. This may save unnecessary program processing time, particularly when a program is being tested and it is not necessary to obtain complete program output.

In the examples that follow, the programmer is sampling the results of program processing at specific intervals instead of monitoring the data continuously.

```
           ON 10
               DISPLAY 'TENTH RECORD CONTAINS 'EMP-RECORD
           ON 10 AND EVERY 20
               EXHIBIT NAMED FLD-A
           ON 10 AND EVERY 20 UNTIL 130
               PERFORM 0500-TAKE-SAMPLE
```

4.1.3 VS COBOL II Debugging Verbs

DISPLAY is the only one of the four debugging verbs we mentioned that is available in COBOL II. ON and EXHIBIT are not valid in the COBOL II language, but the functions they perform in OS/VS COBOL are readily available in the COBOL II interactive debugger COBTEST. Although READY TRACE and RESET TRACE are accepted by the COBOL II compiler, they are checked for syntax only; READY TRACE does not actually cause any tracing action to occur in a COBOL II program. I think it would have been better to have simply removed TRACE from the language the way ON and EXHIBIT were removed. The tracing function is, however, available in COBTEST.

As can be seen, it becomes rather important to learn how to use COBTEST, since the COBOL II language is quite deficient in debugging verbs. COBTEST will be covered fully in Chap. 13.

4.2 DEFINING WORKING-STORAGE BOUNDARIES

If it becomes necessary to look at a hexadecimal dump, a very simple technique often makes it easier to locate the program's WORKING-STORAGE SECTION. You can code an alphanumeric FILLER item with a distinctive VALUE clause as the first entry in the WORKING-STORAGE SECTION and another one as the last entry in WORKING-STORAGE. It is a good idea to include the program name in the VALUE clause so that there will be no doubt as to which program's storage is being viewed. By scanning down the EBCDIC portion on the right-hand side of the dump for the literals coded in the VALUE clauses, you can readily find the boundaries of the program's WORKING-STORAGE. The following example illustrates this.

```
000100 WORKING-STORAGE SECTION.
000110 01    FILLER         PIC X(32)
000120           VALUE 'PROGRAM1 WORKING-STORAGE STARTS'.
                             .
                             .
                             .
000900 01    FILLER         PIC X(32)
000910           VALUE 'PROGRAM1 WORKING-STORAGE ENDS   '.
```

Some COBOL programmers frown upon this practice, saying that it is a crutch for novices; it may not be very useful in a huge dump with multiple programs (do you really want to scan the EBCDIC portion of a 2000-page dump?). Also, it is possible that the literals in the literal pool may mistakenly be thought to be the actual location of WORKING-STORAGE. Experienced programmers point out that the location of WORKING-STORAGE and its length are given as part of the compiler output listing whenever a DATA DIVISION or PROCEDURE DIVISION map is requested. I find that defining the boundaries of WORKING-STORAGE is most useful in small dumps.

4.3 FILE STATUS

The file status clause allows you to determine the success of an I/O operation. To obtain this information, code a FILE STATUS clause in the SELECT . . . ASSIGN statement for the file. The FILE STATUS clause identifies a WORKING-STORAGE field which will receive the status code. The field name is up to you, but the field must be defined as 2 bytes, either PIC X(2) or PIC 9(2) USAGE DISPLAY. The first byte represents status key 1. It gives general information about the results of the just-completed I/O request. The second byte represents file status key 2. It will contain more detailed information about the general I/O status reported in file status key 1. COBOL automatically places a value in the 2-byte file status field after the execution of every I/O request for the file.

It is typical to interrogate file status fields after all I/O verbs, including OPEN, CLOSE, READ, and WRITE, and base subsequent program processing on the values found. This allows you to trap possible I/O error conditions, and perhaps branch to an error routine. File status can be used in conjunction with the EXCEPTION/ERROR DECLARATIVE. Declaratives will be discussed in Sec. 4.6.

File status can be used for both QSAM and VSAM files. It is not critical to request status information for QSAM files since many I/O error conditions will cause an ABEND, halting program execution. It is essential, however, that every VSAM file have a file status field which is checked after every I/O request. Otherwise VSAM file I/O errors may go undetected by the program, yet the program may continue processing. The program will not ABEND, and any erroneous results may be difficult to uncover.

An additional file status field is offered in COBOL II. It returns more detailed information from VSAM. This COBOL II VSAM status field will be discussed in Sec. 4.3.2.

4.3.1 File Status in OS/VS COBOL

OS/VS COBOL file status values with their associated meanings are shown for VSAM and non-VSAM files in Fig. 4.1.

Figure 4.2 illustrates the use of file status in an OS/VS COBOL program. The program changes, adds, and deletes records in a VSAM file. For the sake of simplicity, the keys for the records to be processed have been coded in the program rather than being read from an input file. The file status field is examined after every VSAM I/O request with messages displayed whenever it is not 00. A file status of 22 occurred on the WRITE VSAM-FILE-REC statement at line 10700 because PROJECT-NAME COBDEBUG was a duplicate key.

Since duplicates were not allowed, the record could not be added. File status 23 occurred on the DELETE at line 12200 because the record with PROJECT-NAME ISAMBOOK was not found. Notice that the program did not ABEND, and that if the file status were not checked, you might never have known that these records were not processed.

KEY 1	MEANING	KEY 2	MEANING	FILE TYPE
0	Successful completion	0	No further information	VSAM, Non-VSAM
		2	Duplicate key and duplicates allowed	VSAM
1	End of file	0	No further information	VSAM, Non-VSAM
2	Invalid Key	0	No further information	VSAM
		1	Sequence error	VSAM
		2	Duplicate key and duplicates not allowed	VSAM
		3	No record found	VSAM
		4	Boundary violation on WRITE to indexed or relative file (no space to add record)	VSAM
3	Permanent I/O error (data check, parity check, transmission error)	0	No further information	VSAM
		4	Boundary violation on WRITE to sequential file (no space to add record)	VSAM, Non-VSAM
9	Other errors	0	No further information	VSAM
		0	OPEN or CLOSE failed (possible missing DD statement on OPEN)	Non-VSAM
		1	Password failure	VSAM
		2	Logic error (such as attempt to OPEN a file already open, OPEN a file closed with a lock, CLOSE a file already closed or never opened, READ after end-of-file, READ, WRITE, or REWRITE unopened file or file opened in wrong mode)	VSAM, Non-VSAM
		3	Resource not available	VSAM
		4	Sequential record not available	VSAM
		5	File information invalid or incomplete	VSAM
		6	No DD statement	VSAM
		7	File was not properly closed previously; a verify was therefore implicitly issued, and the file was then opened successfully.	VSAM

Figure 4.1 OS/VS COBOL file status codes.

```
000100 IDENTIFICATION DIVISION.
000200  PROGRAM-ID. VSAMSTAT.
000300  AUTHOR. ALAN FRIEND.
000400 DATE-COMPILED. OCT 16,1990.

000600 ENVIRONMENT DIVISION.
000700  INPUT-OUTPUT SECTION.
000800  FILE-CONTROL.
000900      SELECT VSAM-FILE ASSIGN TO VSAMDD
001000                       FILE STATUS IS FILE-STATUS
001100                       ORGANIZATION IS INDEXED
001200                       ACCESS MODE IS DYNAMIC
001300                       RECORD KEY IS PROJECT-NAME.

001500 DATA DIVISION.
001600 FILE SECTION.
001700 FD   VSAM-FILE
001800      LABEL RECORDS ARE OMITTED
001900      RECORD CONTAINS 123 CHARACTERS
002000      BLOCK CONTAINS 0 RECORDS.
002100 01   VSAM-FILE-REC.
002200      05 FILLER                   PIC X(1).
002300      05 PROJECT-NAME.
002400         10 PRIM-KEY              PIC X.
002500         10 FILLER                PIC X(7).
002600      05 FILLER                   PIC X(21).
002700      05 CREATE-DATE              PIC X(8).
002800      05 FILLER                   PIC X(60).
002900      05 AUTHOR-ID                PIC X(8).
003000      05 FILLER                   PIC X(17).

003200 WORKING-STORAGE SECTION.
003300*****************************************************************
003400*  FILE STATUS FIELD AND OPERATION-ATTEMPTED FIELD
003500*****************************************************************
003600 01   STATUS-OPERATION-FIELDS.
003700      05  FILE-STATUS             PIC X(2).
003800      05  OPERATION-FLD           PIC X(9)  VALUE SPACES.

004000 PROCEDURE DIVISION.

004200*****************************************************************
004300*  PROCESS VSAM FILE USING THE PRIME KEY "PROJECT-NAME"
004400*****************************************************************

004600 0000-MAINLINE.
004700      OPEN I-O VSAM-FILE
004800      IF FILE-STATUS =  '00'
004900         PERFORM 0100-PROCESS THRU 0100-PROCESS-EXIT
005000         CLOSE VSAM-FILE
005100         IF FILE-STATUS NOT EQUAL '00'
005200            DISPLAY 'FILE STATUS = ' FILE-STATUS
005300                    ' CLOSE ERROR'
005400         ELSE
005500            NEXT SENTENCE
005600      ELSE
005700         DISPLAY 'FILE STATUS = ' FILE-STATUS
005800                 ' OPEN ERROR: PROGRAM TERMINATED'.
005900      GOBACK.

006100*****************************************************************
006200*        THIS PARAGRAPH BRANCHES TO CHANGE, ADD,
006300*        AND DELETE ROUTINES.
006400*****************************************************************

006600 0100-PROCESS.
006700      PERFORM 0110-CHANGE      THRU 0110-CHANGE-EXIT
006800      PERFORM 0120-ADD         THRU 0120-ADD-EXIT
006900      PERFORM 0130-DELETE      THRU 0130-DELETE-EXIT.

007100 0100-PROCESS-EXIT.
007200      EXIT.
```

Figure 4.2 An OS/VS COBOL program illustrating (*a*) the use of file status for VSAM processing; (*b*) with the output from the DISPLAY statement at lines 13600 through 13900. (*Continued*)

```
*****************************************************************
*        CHANGE FIELDS IN AN EXISTING RECORD
*****************************************************************

 0110-CHANGE.
     MOVE 'DICTPROJ' TO PROJECT-NAME
     READ VSAM-FILE
     IF FILE-STATUS = '00'
        MOVE 'WILS0019' TO AUTHOR-ID
        REWRITE VSAM-FILE-REC
        IF FILE-STATUS NOT EQUAL '00'
           MOVE 'REWRITE' TO OPERATION-FLD
           PERFORM 0200-DISPLAY-ERR-MSG THRU
                   0200-DISPLAY-ERR-MSG-EXIT
        ELSE
           NEXT SENTENCE
     ELSE
        MOVE 'READ' TO OPERATION-FLD
        PERFORM 0200-DISPLAY-ERR-MSG THRU
                0200-DISPLAY-ERR-MSG-EXIT.

 0110-CHANGE-EXIT.
     EXIT.

*****************************************************************
*        ADD A RECORD TO THE VSAM FILE
*****************************************************************

 0120-ADD.
     MOVE SPACES TO VSAM-FILE-REC
     MOVE 'COBDEBUG' TO PROJECT-NAME
     MOVE 'FRIE4033' TO AUTHOR-ID
     MOVE '09/28/90' TO CREATE-DATE
     WRITE VSAM-FILE-REC
     IF FILE-STATUS NOT EQUAL '00'
        MOVE 'WRITE' TO OPERATION-FLD
        PERFORM 0200-DISPLAY-ERR-MSG THRU
                0200-DISPLAY-ERR-MSG-EXIT.

 0120-ADD-EXIT.
     EXIT.

*****************************************************************
*       DELETE A RECORD FROM THE VSAM FILE
*****************************************************************

 0130-DELETE.
     MOVE 'ISAMBOOK' TO PROJECT-NAME
     DELETE VSAM-FILE RECORD
     IF FILE-STATUS NOT EQUAL '00'
        MOVE 'NONE' TO AUTHOR-ID
        MOVE 'DELETE' TO OPERATION-FLD
        PERFORM 0200-DISPLAY-ERR-MSG THRU
                0200-DISPLAY-ERR-MSG-EXIT.

 0130-DELETE-EXIT.

*****************************************************************
*       DISPLAY ERROR MESSAGES WITH THE FILE STATUS.
*****************************************************************

 0200-DISPLAY-ERR-MSG.
     DISPLAY 'FILE-STATUS = ' FILE-STATUS '    '
             OPERATION-FLD ' ERROR ON RECORD: '
             'PROJECT NAME = ' PROJECT-NAME '    '
             'AUTHOR-ID = ' AUTHOR-ID.

 0200-DISPLAY-ERR-MSG-EXIT.
     EXIT.
```

(a)

```
FILE-STATUS = 22   WRITE    ERROR ON RECORD: PROJECT NAME = COBDEBUG  AUTHOR-ID = FRIE4033
FILE-STATUS = 23   DELETE   ERROR ON RECORD: PROJECT NAME = ISAMBOOK  AUTHOR-ID = NONE
```

(b)

Figure 4.2 *(Continued)*

4.3.2 File Status in VS COBOL II

In COBOL II there is a second file status clause which may be used to get more detailed information from VSAM. When used, it must be defined after the standard file status in the SELECT . . . ASSIGN clause for the file. It must then be coded in WORKING-STORAGE as three binary fields defined as PIC 9(2) COMP. The following example shows both the standard and VSAM file status fields coded in a program's WORKING-STORAGE SECTION:

```
01   STATUS AREA.
     05 STANDARD-FILE-STATUS      PIC X(2).
     05 VSAM-FILE-STATUS.
        10 VSAM-R15-RETURN-CODE   PIC 9(2) COMP.
        10 VSAM-FUNCTION-CODE     PIC 9(2) COMP.
        10 VSAM-FEEDBACK-CODE     PIC 9(2) COMP.
```

The name VSAM-FILE-STATUS and the names assigned to the three fields constituting VSAM-FILE-STATUS are up to your discretion; the names used in the preceding example indicate the source of the VSAM information. See Fig. 4.3 for the meanings of the VSAM register-15 return codes, function codes, and feedback codes. For additional information about these codes, refer to the IBM manuals *VSAM Administration: Macro Instruction Reference* and *VSAM Administration Guide.*

Values in the VSAM file status field are set only when the standard status field is not 00. In addition, the function code and feedback code are filled in with valid information only when the register-15 return code is not zero; there is no guarantee that they will contain accurate information when the return code is zero.

Figure 4.4 gives the standard file status values and their meanings for COBOL II Release 2 and Release 3 for VSAM and non-VSAM files. New status codes have been added in Release 3; they provide more detailed and meaningful information than was previously given in either OS/VS COBOL or COBOL II Release 2.

An example of the use of both of the standard and VSAM file status fields in a COBOL II program is given in Fig. 4.5. The program is similar to the OS/VS COBOL program shown in Fig. 4.2. It changes, adds, and deletes VSAM records. To simplify the example, the keys for the records to be processed are coded in the program rather than being read from an input file. The standard file status is examined after every VSAM I/O request. If the value is not 00, a message, the standard file status, and the three VSAM codes are displayed.

Notice that a standard file status of 22 occurred on the WRITE VSAM-FILE-REC statement at line 12100. This value indicates that the record could not be added because PROJECT-NAME COBDEBUG was a duplicate key and duplicates were not allowed. The VSAM register-15 return code of 08 means that there was a logic error, and the feedback code 08 means the same thing as the standard file status of 22: an attempt was made to add a record with a dupli-

RETURN CODE IN REGISTER 15	MEANING
0	VSAM request completed successfully.
4	For an OPEN request, the OPEN completed successfully; however, a warning message was issued. For a CLOSE request, the CLOSE failed.
8	There was a logical error; refer to the logical error feedback codes.
12	There was a physical error; refer to the physical error feedback codes.

(a)

FUNCTION CODE	MEANING
0	There was an attempt to access the base cluster and the upgrade set status is correct.
1	There was an attempt to access the base cluster and the upgrade set status may be incorrect.
2	There was an attempt to access the alternate index over a base cluster and the upgrade set status is correct.
3	There was an attempt to access the alternate index over a base cluster and the upgrade set status may be incorrect.
4	Upgrade processing was attempted and the upgrade set status is correct.
5	Upgrade processing was attempted and the upgrade set status may be incorrect.

(b)

FEEDBACK CODE	MEANING
0	For an OPEN request, either the file is already open or the DDNAME is invalid.
4	For a CLOSE request, the data set is already closed. For other I/O requests, there is either a logical error because an end-of-file condition was reached during sequential or skip sequential processing, or the key in use is greater than the highest key in the data set, or there is a physical error during a READ for a data set.
8	There is either a logical error because an attempt was made to store a record with a duplicate key, or there is a duplicate record for an alternate index that has the UNIQUE key option, or there is a physical error during a READ for an index set.
12	There is either a logical error due to a key sequence error during KSDS or RRDS processing, or there is a physical error during a READ for a sequence set.
16	There is either a logical error because a record was not found, or there is a physical error during a WRITE for a data set.
20	There is either a logical error because a control interval needed by the program was already in use by another program, or there was a physical error during a WRITE for an index set.

Figure 4.3 VSAM register 15 return codes, function codes, and selected feedback codes. *(Continued)*

FEEDBACK CODE	MEANING
24	There was physical error during a WRITE for a sequence set.
28	There was a logical error because of an out-of-space condition. Either an attempt was made to increase the size of a data set processed with SHROPT=4 and DISP=SHR, or space does not exist for a secondary allocation.
36	There was a logical error because the key specified is not valid for the data set. This only occurs if specific key ranges are defined for the data set.
40	There was a logical error because there was insufficient virtual storage in the address space to complete the request.
68	There was a logical error during attempted processing of a data set that was not allowed when the data set was opened (e.g., a WRITE to a data set opened for INPUT).
72	There was a logical error due to a keyed access request on an ESDS.
80	There was a logical error on an attempt to DELETE a record from an ESDS.
92	There was a logical error because of a REWRITE or DELETE request on a record without a prior READ.
96	There was a logical error on an attempt to update the prime key of a KSDS.
100	A warning is issued because an empty alternate index which is part of an upgrade set was encountered during OPEN.
104	A warning is issued during OPEN because the time stamp in the data set and its time stamp in the catalog do not match.
108	Either a discrepancy in the time stamp in a data component and in an index component was found during OPEN, or there was a logical error due to an attempt to process with an invalid record length.
112	There is a logical error because the specified key length is either too large or is equal to zero.
116	Either the data set had not been properly closed and an implicit VERIFY was unsuccessful during OPEN, or there was a logical error because a request other than WRITE was issued for a data set opened for OUTPUT.

Figure 4.3 *(Continued)*

cate key. The standard file status 23 occurred when the DELETE at line 13900 was attempted. This value means that the record with PROJECT-NAME ISAMBOOK could not be found. VSAM's register-15 return code of 08 indicates that there was a logic error, and the feedback code 16 again specifies that the record was not found.

Although some of the extended VSAM codes merely duplicate the information given by the standard file status codes, there are many cases, especially in Release 3, when the extended VSAM codes give you much more specific debugging information than can be gotten from the standard file status codes alone.

FEEDBACK CODE	MEANING
118	The data set had not been properly closed and an implicit VERIFY was successful during OPEN.
128	The DD statement is missing for the file during an OPEN.
136	There was insufficient virtual storage in the address space for work areas, control blocks or buffers during OPEN or CLOSE.
144	Either there was an uncorrectable I/O error when VSAM was reading or writing a catalog record during OPEN or CLOSE, or there was a logical error because an invalid pointer exists in an alternate index and there is no associated base record.
148	Either an error occurred during CLOSE when VSAM was searching the catalog, or there was a logical error because the maximum number of pointers was exceeded in the alternate index.
152	There was a logical error because not enough buffers were available to process the request when shared resources were used.
156	There was a logical error due to an invalid control interval during keyed processing.
168	An OPEN error occurred because another program had the data set open or the data set could not be opened for the type of processing requested.
180	There was an OPEN error because a VSAM catalog specified in the JCL does not exist or is not open.
184	There was an uncorrectable error when VSAM was completing an I/O request during OPEN or CLOSE.
192	There was a logical error because an invalid record number was used.
196	An attempt was made to access data via an empty path during OPEN.
232	Reset was specified for a non-reusable data set that was not empty during OPEN.

(c)

Figure 4.3 *(Continued)*

Also note that the program in Fig. 4.5 did not ABEND. If the file status were not checked after every VSAM I/O request, you might never have known that some records were never processed.

4.4 DEBUGGING PACKETS IN OS/VS COBOL

Debugging packets are a little-used feature in OS/VS COBOL. They allow you to group together alternate statements for a given PROCEDURE DIVISION

KEY 1	MEANING	KEY 2	MEANING	FILE TYPE	RELEASE
0	Successful completion	0	No further information	VSAM, Non-VSAM	2, 3
		2	Duplicate key and duplicates allowed	VSAM	2, 3
			For a READ, the next record has the same key. For a WRITE or REWRITE, there is at least one other record with the same key in the alternate index.		3
		4	A READ was successful, but the length of the record did not conform to the fixed file attributes for the file. Thus the record may have been truncated.	VSAM, Non-VSAM	3
		5	An OPEN was successful for an OPTIONAL file which does not exist. If OPEN mode is I-O or EXTEND, the file has been created.	Non-VSAM	3
		7	Either an OPEN with the NO REWIND clause or a CLOSE with the NO REWIND, REEL/UNIT, or FOR REMOVAL clause was issued, but the file was on a non-reel device.	Non-VSAM	3
1	End of file	0	AT END was reached on a sequential READ when all records have been processed, or when the first READ was issued on a non-existent OPTIONAL file.	VSAM, Non-VSAM	2, 3
		4	A sequential READ was issued for a relative file and the number of significant digits in the record number was greater than the size of the relative key data item.	VSAM	3
2	Invalid key	0	No further information	VSAM	2
		1	A sequence error was found for sequentially accessed indexed file. Either the prime key was changed after the last successful READ and before the next REWRITE, or the ascending requirements for successive record keys was violated.	VSAM	2, 3
		2	A duplicate key error occurred because an attempt was made to create a duplicate key in a relative file, or an attempt was made to create a duplicate key in an indexed file in which duplicates are not allowed.	VSAM	2, 3
		3	No record was found in an attempt to randomly READ a file, or an optional input file was not present on a START or random READ statement.	VSAM	2, 3

Figure 4.4 Standard file status codes for COBOL II. *(Continued)*

KEY 1	MEANING	KEY 2	MEANING	FILE TYPE	RELEASE
		4	There was a boundary violation on a WRITE to an indexed or a relative file, or a sequential WRITE was issued for a relative file and the number of significant digits in the record number was greater than the size of the relative key data item.	VSAM	2, 3 3
3	Permanent error condition	0	No further information	VSAM, Non-VSAM	2, 3
		4	Boundary violation on WRITE to sequential file: no space to add record	VSAM, Non-VSAM	2, 3
		5	An OPEN with the I-O, INPUT, or EXTEND clause was attempted on a non-optional file that was not present.	VSAM, Non-VSAM	3
		7	An OPEN was attempted with options which were incompatible with the file. Possible reasons are: - EXTEND or OUTPUT clauses were specified but the file does not allow WRITE, - the I-O clause was specified but either READ or WRITE is not permitted, - the INPUT clause was specified but READ is not allowed.	VSAM, Non-VSAM	3
		8	An OPEN was issued for a file previously CLOSEd with LOCK.	VSAM, Non-VSAM	3
		9	OPEN was unsuccessful because of conflicts between the FD in the program and the actual file attributes. The attributes include: - file organization, - prime key position, - alternate key position, - maximum record size, - record type, - block size, - code set.	VSAM, Non-VSAM	3
4	Logic error conditions	1	OPEN was attempted for a file already open	VSAM, Non-VSAM	3
		2	CLOSE was attempted for a file that was not open	VSAM, Non-VSAM	3

Figure 4.4 *(Continued)*

KEY 1	MEANING	KEY 2	MEANING	FILE TYPE	RELEASE
		3	READ wasn't successful before a REWRITE on a mass storage file	Non-VSAM	3
			READ wasn't successful before a REWRITE or DELETE for an indexed or relative file in sequential access mode	VSAM	3
		4	An attempt was made to REWRITE a record which was not the same size as the record being replaced, or an attempt was made to WRITE or REWRITE a record that was larger than the largest or smaller than the smallest record allowed by the RECORD IS VARYING clause in the FD for the file.	VSAM, Non-VSAM	3
		6	A sequential READ was issued on a file open for input or I-O, but there was no valid next record because the preceding READ either caused an AT END condition or was unsuccessful without causing an AT END condition.	VSAM, Non-VSAM	3
		7	A READ was attempted on a file not open for input or I-O.	VSAM, Non-VSAM	3
		8	A WRITE was attempted on a file not open in output, I-O, or extend mode.	VSAM, Non-VSAM	3
		9	A DELETE or REWRITE was issued for a file not open in I-O mode.		3
9	Other implementation dependent errors	0	No further information	VSAM, Non-VSAM	2, 3
		1	Password failure	VSAM	2, 3
		2	Program logic error	VSAM, Non-VSAM	2, 3
		3	Resource not available	VSAM	2, 3
		4	Sequential record not available	VSAM	2
		5	File information invalid or incomplete	VSAM	2, 3
		6	No DD statement specified	VSAM	2, 3
		7	OPEN was successful and file integrity was verified	VSAM	2, 3

Figure 4.4 *(Continued)*

```
000100 IDENTIFICATION DIVISION.
000200  PROGRAM-ID. VSAMCOB2.
000300  AUTHOR. ALAN FRIEND.
000400 DATE-COMPILED. 12/28/90.

000600 ENVIRONMENT DIVISION.
000700  INPUT-OUTPUT SECTION.
000800  FILE-CONTROL.
000900     SELECT VSAM-FILE ASSIGN TO VSAMDD
001000                      FILE STATUS IS FILE-STATUS  VSAM-STATUS
001100                      ORGANIZATION IS INDEXED
001200                      ACCESS MODE IS DYNAMIC
001300                      RECORD KEY IS PROJECT-NAME.

001500 DATA DIVISION.
001600 FILE SECTION.
001700 FD  VSAM-FILE
001800     RECORD CONTAINS 123 CHARACTERS.
001900 01  VSAM-FILE-REC.
002000     05 FILLER                          PIC X(1).
002100     05 PROJECT-NAME.
002200        10 PRIM-KEY                     PIC X.
002300        10 FILLER                       PIC X(7).
002400     05 FILLER                          PIC X(21).
002500     05 CREATE-DATE                     PIC X(8).
002600     05 FILLER                          PIC X(60).
002700     05 AUTHOR-ID                       PIC X(8).
002800     05 FILLER                          PIC X(17).

003000 WORKING-STORAGE SECTION.
003100*****************************************************************
003200*  FILE STATUS FIELDS AND OPERATION-ATTEMPTED FIELD             *
003300*****************************************************************
003400 01  STATUS-OPERATION-FIELDS.
003500     05  FILE-STATUS                    PIC X(2).
003600     05  VSAM-STATUS.
003700         10  VSAM-R15-RETURN-CODE       PIC 9(2) COMP.
003800         10  VSAM-FUNCTION-CODE         PIC 9(2) COMP.
003900         10  VSAM-FEEDBACK-CODE         PIC 9(2) COMP.
004000     05  OPERATION-FLD                  PIC X(9)  VALUE SPACES.

004200 PROCEDURE DIVISION.

004400*****************************************************************
004500*  PROCESS VSAM FILE USING THE PRIME KEY "PROJECT-NAME"         *
004600*****************************************************************

004800 0000-MAINLINE.
004900     OPEN I-O VSAM-FILE.
005000     EVALUATE FILE-STATUS
005100        WHEN    '00'
005200           PERFORM 0100-PROCESS THRU 0100-PROCESS-EXIT
005300           CLOSE VSAM-FILE
005400           IF FILE-STATUS NOT EQUAL '00'
005500              MOVE 'CLOSE' TO OPERATION-FLD
005600              DISPLAY 'FILE STATUS =  ' FILE-STATUS '    '
005700                      OPERATION-FLD
005800              PERFORM  0300-VSAM-ERROR THRU
005900                       0300-VSAM-ERROR-EXIT
006000           END-IF
006100        WHEN  OTHER
006200           MOVE 'OPEN' TO OPERATION-FLD
006300           DISPLAY 'FILE STATUS =  ' FILE-STATUS '    '
006400                   OPERATION-FLD
006500           PERFORM  0300-VSAM-ERROR THRU
006600                    0300-VSAM-ERROR-EXIT
006700     END-EVALUATE
006800     GOBACK.
```

Figure 4.5 A COBOL II program (*a*) which uses both standard and VSAM file status codes; (*b*) with the output from the DISPLAY statements at lines 15600 through 15900 and 16900 through 17100. (*Continued*)

```
007000******************************************************************
007100*        THIS PARAGRAPH BRANCHES TO CHANGE, ADD, DELETE, AND     *
007200*        DISPLAY-RECORD ROUTINES.                                *
007300******************************************************************

007500 0100-PROCESS.
007600     PERFORM 0110-CHANGE     THRU 0110-CHANGE-EXIT
007700     PERFORM 0120-ADD        THRU 0120-ADD-EXIT
007800     PERFORM 0130-DELETE     THRU 0130-DELETE-EXIT.

008000 0100-PROCESS-EXIT.
008100     EXIT.

008300******************************************************************
008400*        CHANGE FIELDS IN AN EXISTING RECORD                     *
008500******************************************************************

008700 0110-CHANGE.
008800     MOVE 'DICTPROG' TO PROJECT-NAME.
008900     READ VSAM-FILE.
009000     EVALUATE FILE-STATUS
009100        WHEN    '00'
009200           MOVE 'WILS0019' TO AUTHOR-ID
009300           REWRITE VSAM-FILE-REC
009400              IF FILE-STATUS NOT EQUAL '00'
009500                 MOVE 'REWRITE' TO OPERATION-FLD
009600                 PERFORM 0200-DISPLAY-ERR-MSG THRU
009700                         0200-DISPLAY-ERR-MSG-EXIT
009800                 PERFORM  0300-VSAM-ERROR THRU
009900                          0300-VSAM-ERROR-EXIT
010000              END-IF
010100        WHEN  OTHER
010200           MOVE 'READ' TO OPERATION-FLD
010300           PERFORM 0200-DISPLAY-ERR-MSG THRU
010400                   0200-DISPLAY-ERR-MSG-EXIT
010500           PERFORM  0300-VSAM-ERROR THRU
010600                    0300-VSAM-ERROR-EXIT
010700     END-EVALUATE.

010900 0110-CHANGE-EXIT.
011000     EXIT.

011200******************************************************************
011300*        ADD A RECORD TO THE VSAM FILE                           *
011400******************************************************************

011600 0120-ADD.
011700     MOVE SPACES TO VSAM-FILE-REC
011800     MOVE 'COBDEBUG' TO PROJECT-NAME
011900     MOVE 'FRIE4033' TO AUTHOR-ID
012000     MOVE '09/28/90' TO CREATE-DATE
012100     WRITE VSAM-FILE-REC
012200     IF FILE-STATUS NOT EQUAL '00'
012300        MOVE 'WRITE' TO OPERATION-FLD
012400        PERFORM 0200-DISPLAY-ERR-MSG THRU
012500                0200-DISPLAY-ERR-MSG-EXIT
012600        PERFORM  0300-VSAM-ERROR THRU
012700                 0300-VSAM-ERROR-EXIT
012800        END-IF.

013000 0120-ADD-EXIT.
013100     EXIT.
```

Figure 4.5 *(Continued)*

```
*****************************************************************
*      DELETE A RECORD FROM THE VSAM FILE                        *
*****************************************************************

 0130-DELETE.
     MOVE 'ISAMBOOK' TO PROJECT-NAME
     DELETE VSAM-FILE RECORD
     IF FILE-STATUS NOT EQUAL '00'
        MOVE 'NONE' TO AUTHOR-ID
        MOVE 'DELETE' TO OPERATION-FLD
        PERFORM 0200-DISPLAY-ERR-MSG THRU
                0200-DISPLAY-ERR-MSG-EXIT
        PERFORM  0300-VSAM-ERROR THRU
                 0300-VSAM-ERROR-EXIT
        END-IF.

 0130-DELETE-EXIT.
     EXIT.

*****************************************************************
*      DISPLAY ERROR MESSAGES WITH THE FILE STATUS.              *
*****************************************************************

 0200-DISPLAY-ERR-MSG.
     DISPLAY 'FILE-STATUS = ' FILE-STATUS '    '
             OPERATION-FLD ' ERROR ON RECORD: '
             'PROJECT NAME = ' PROJECT-NAME '    '
             'AUTHOR-ID = ' AUTHOR-ID.

 0200-DISPLAY-ERR-MSG-EXIT.
     EXIT.

*****************************************************************
*  DISPLAY REGISTER-15 RETURN CODE, FUNCTION CODE AND FEEDBACK   *
*  CODE                                                          *
*****************************************************************

 0300-VSAM-ERROR.
     DISPLAY 'VSAM-R15-RETURN-CODE = ' VSAM-R15-RETURN-CODE
     DISPLAY 'VSAM-FUNCTION-CODE   = ' VSAM-FUNCTION-CODE
     DISPLAY 'VSAM-FEEDBACK-CODE   = ' VSAM-FEEDBACK-CODE.

 0300-VSAM-ERROR-EXIT.
     EXIT.
```

(a)

```
FILE-STATUS = 22    WRITE      ERROR ON RECORD: PROJECT NAME = COBDEBUG    AUTHOR-ID = FRIE4033
VSAM-R15-RETURN-CODE = 08
VSAM-FUNCTION-CODE   = 00
VSAM-FEEDBACK-CODE   = 08
FILE-STATUS = 23    DELETE     ERROR ON RECORD: PROJECT NAME = ISAMBOOK    AUTHOR-ID = NONE
VSAM-R15-RETURN-CODE = 08
VSAM-FUNCTION-CODE   = 00
VSAM-FEEDBACK-CODE   = 16
```

(b)

Figure 4.5 *(Continued)*

paragraph or section without deleting or commenting out the original statements. The packets are clustered together immediately following the original program source code. Each begins with a DEBUG statement which refers to a paragraph or section name in the program. When the program is run, the statements following the DEBUG statement are executed as soon as the named paragraph or section is reached in the normal flow of control for the program. After the code in the debugging packet is executed, the program continues with the original statements in the paragraph or section. Logically, it is as though the statements in the debugging packet were inserted between the paragraph or section header and the original code.

Figure 4.6 illustrates the use of a debugging packet. The programmer needed to change paragraph 0300-TOTAL in order to call the subprogram OVERMAX in the event that the total number of company employees equals or exceeds the maximum allowed. Note in the figure that in order to bypass the original statements in paragraph 0300-TOTAL, a GO TO statement was placed as the last statement in the packet in order to transfer control to 0300-EXIT. Notice that syntactically, the DEBUG statement is not followed by a period.

Debugging packets may be used when it is desirable to test changes to a program by replacing entire paragraphs or sections. Because the packets are coded in one place at the end of the source module, it is easier to find and remove them after the program has been tested.

4.5 DEBUGGING LINES

Both OS/VS COBOL and COBOL II allow you to specify lines which are to be recognized only when the appropriate switch is set. These are known as debugging lines, and they must be coded with the letter D in column 7 of the source code. They may appear in the ENVIRONMENT DIVISION (after the OBJECT-COMPUTER paragraph), DATA DIVISION, or PROCEDURE DIVISION.

The debugging lines are activated by a compile-time switch. The switch is placed in effect by coding WITH DEBUGGING MODE in the SOURCE-COMPUTER paragraph of the ENVIRONMENT DIVISION's CONFIGURATION SECTION. The format is

```
SOURCE-COMPUTER. computer-name WITH DEBUGGING MODE.
```

Computer-name is treated as a comment for documentation purposes only.

When the compile-time switch is in effect, all debugging lines are compiled and become part of the object module. They will execute when the program is run. If the compile-time switch is not in effect, all debugging lines are treated as comments.

Debugging lines are helpful when it is necessary to test numerous lines in the COBOL source module. Rather than inserting test lines and then commenting them out with asterisks in column 7 when they are no longer needed, all of the lines to be tested can be marked as debugging lines. They can be activated or deactivated by either coding or removing the WITH DEBUGGING MODE clause in the SOURCE COMPUTER paragraph. This is much easier than searching for all the lines and then either removing or inserting asterisks.

```
IDENTIFICATION DIVISION.
 PROGRAM-ID.    DEBGPACK.
 AUTHOR.        ALAN FRIEND.
 DATE-WRITTEN. JANUARY 1986.
DATE-COMPILED. OCT 12,1990.

ENVIRONMENT DIVISION.
 CONFIGURATION SECTION.
  SOURCE-COMPUTER. IBM-370.
  OBJECT-COMPUTER. IBM-370.
 INPUT-OUTPUT SECTION.
  FILE-CONTROL.
    SELECT TEST-FILE  ASSIGN TO INFILE.
    SELECT PRINT-FILE ASSIGN TO PRTFILE.

DATA DIVISION.
 FILE SECTION.
 FD TEST-FILE
    RECORDING MODE IS F
    RECORD CONTAINS 80 CHARACTERS
    BLOCK CONTAINS 0 RECORDS
    LABEL RECORDS ARE OMITTED.
 01 TEST-FILE-REC                       PIC X(80).

 FD PRINT-FILE
    RECORDING MODE IS F
    RECORD CONTAINS 133 CHARACTERS
    BLOCK CONTAINS 0 RECORDS
    LABEL RECORDS ARE OMITTED.
 01 PRINT-FILE-REC                      PIC X(133).

WORKING-STORAGE SECTION.

*****************************************************************
*    MAXIMUM CONSTANT VALUES.
*****************************************************************

 01 CONSTANT-VALUES.
    05 EMP-NUMBER-MAX                   PIC 9(5)  VALUE 3600 COMP-3.
    05 LINE-CNT-MAX                     PIC 9(3)  VALUE 55   COMP-3.

*****************************************************************
*    END-OF-FILE SWITCH AND COUNTERS
*****************************************************************

 01 SWITCH-AND-COUNTERS.
    05 LINE-CNT                         PIC 9(3)  VALUE 60   COMP-3.
    05 EMP-CNT                          PIC 9(5)  VALUE ZERO COMP-3.
    05 SW-EOF                           PIC X     VALUE 'N'.
       88 NO-MORE-RECORDS                         VALUE 'Y'.
```

Figure 4.6 An OS/VS COBOL program which makes use of a debugging packet. (*Continued*)

4.6 DECLARATIVE PROCEDURES

DECLARATIVES can be used in OS/VS COBOL as well as in COBOL II Release 2 and Release 3. The EXCEPTION/ERROR DECLARATIVE enables you to trap I/O errors and attempt to recover from them. Specific procedures are coded within the program and are executed if an I/O error is encountered.

```
005200*****************************************************************
005300*    OUTPUT PRINT LINE
005400*****************************************************************

005600  01 PRINT-LINE                         PIC X(133) VALUE SPACES.
005700  01 PRT-LINE1 REDEFINES PRINT-LINE.
005800     05 FILLER                          PIC X.
005900     05 PRT-EMP-NO                      PIC 9(5).
006000     05 FILLER                          PIC X(5).
006100     05 PRT-FIRST                       PIC X(30).
006200     05 PRT-LAST                        PIC X(20).
006300     05 FILLER                          PIC X(72).
006400  01 PRT-LINE2 REDEFINES PRINT-LINE.
006500     05 FILLER                          PIC X(11).
006600     05 PRT-STREET                      PIC X(20).
006700     05 FILLER                          PIC X(102).
006800  01 PRT-LINE3 REDEFINES PRINT-LINE.
006900     05 FILLER                          PIC X(11).
007000     05 PRT-CITY-STATE                  PIC X(25).
007100     05 PRT-ZIP-CODE                    PIC 9(5).
007200     05 FILLER                          PIC X(92).
007300  01 PRT-LINE4 REDEFINES PRINT-LINE.
007400     05 FILLER                          PIC X(60).
007500     05 PRT-DATA                        PIC X(27).
007600     05 PRT-TOTAL                       PIC 9(5).
007700     05 FILLER                          PIC X(41).

007900  01 WS-TEST-RECORD.
008000     05 WS-EMP-NO                       PIC 9(5).
008100     05 WS-NAME.
008200        10 WS-LAST-NAME                 PIC X(15).
008300        10 WS-FIRST-NAME                PIC X(15).
008400     05 WS-ADDRESS.
008500        10 WS-STREET                    PIC X(15).
008600        10 WS-CITY-STATE                PIC X(15).
008700        10 WS-ZIP-CODE                  PIC 9(5).

008900 PROCEDURE DIVISION.

009100*****************************************************************
009200* THIS PROGRAM READS AN INPUT EMPLOYEE FILE AND PRINTS OUT A
009300* FORMATTED REPORT OF EMPLOYEE NUMBERS, NAMES, ADDRESSES AND
009400* TOTAL NUMBER OF EMPLOYEES.
009500*****************************************************************

009700 0000-MAINLINE.

009900     OPEN INPUT  TEST-FILE
010000          OUTPUT PRINT-FILE.
010100     PERFORM 0100-READ THROUGH 0100-EXIT.
010200     PERFORM 0200-PROCESS THROUGH 0200-EXIT
010300       UNTIL NO-MORE-RECORDS.
010400     PERFORM 0300-TOTAL THROUGH 0300-EXIT.
010500     CLOSE TEST-FILE
010600           PRINT-FILE.
010700     GOBACK.
```

Figure 4.6 *(Continued)*

```
 0100-READ.
         READ TEST-FILE INTO WS-TEST-RECORD
             AT END MOVE 'Y' TO SW-EOF.
 0100-EXIT.
           EXIT.

 0200-PROCESS.
         IF LINE-CNT GREATER THAN LINE-CNT-MAX
               MOVE 'COMPANY EMPLOYEE LISTING' TO PRINT-LINE
               WRITE PRINT-FILE-REC FROM PRINT-LINE AFTER ADVANCING PAGE
               MOVE 1 TO LINE-CNT.
         MOVE SPACES TO PRINT-LINE.
         MOVE WS-EMP-NO TO PRT-EMP-NO.
         MOVE WS-FIRST-NAME TO PRT-FIRST.
         MOVE WS-LAST-NAME TO PRT-LAST.
         WRITE PRINT-FILE-REC FROM PRINT-LINE AFTER ADVANCING 2 LINES.
         MOVE SPACES TO PRINT-LINE.
         MOVE WS-STREET TO PRT-STREET.
         WRITE PRINT-FILE-REC FROM PRINT-LINE AFTER ADVANCING 1 LINES.
         MOVE SPACES TO PRINT-LINE.
         MOVE WS-CITY-STATE TO PRT-CITY-STATE.
         MOVE WS-ZIP-CODE TO PRT-ZIP-CODE.
         WRITE PRINT-FILE-REC FROM PRINT-LINE AFTER ADVANCING 1 LINES.
         ADD 4 TO LINE-CNT.
         ADD 1 TO EMP-CNT.
         PERFORM 0100-READ THROUGH 0100-EXIT.
 0200-EXIT.
           EXIT.

 0300-TOTAL.
         MOVE 'COMPANY EMPLOYEE LISTING' TO PRINT-LINE
         WRITE PRINT-FILE-REC FROM PRINT-LINE AFTER ADVANCING PAGE.
         MOVE SPACES TO PRINT-LINE.
         MOVE EMP-CNT TO PRT-TOTAL.
         MOVE 'TOTAL NO. OF EMPLOYEES' TO PRT-DATA.
         WRITE PRINT-FILE-REC FROM PRINT-LINE AFTER ADVANCING 2 LINES.

 0300-EXIT.
           EXIT.

 DEBUG 0300-TOTAL

*****************************************************************
* THIS DEBUGGING PACKET REPLACES 0300-TOTAL.
* IT CHECKS THE TOTAL NUMBER OF EMPLOYEES, PRINTS THE TOTAL AND
* CALLS 'OVERMAX' IF TOTAL EQUALS OR EXCEEDS EMP-NUMBER-MAX.
*****************************************************************

         IF EMP-CNT LESS THAN EMP-NUMBER-MAX
               MOVE 'COMPANY EMPLOYEE LISTING' TO PRINT-LINE
               WRITE PRINT-FILE-REC FROM PRINT-LINE AFTER ADVANCING PAGE
               MOVE SPACES TO PRINT-LINE
               MOVE EMP-CNT TO PRT-TOTAL
               MOVE 'TOTAL NO. OF EMPLOYEES' TO PRT-DATA
               WRITE PRINT-FILE-REC FROM PRINT-LINE AFTER
                    ADVANCING 2 LINES
         ELSE
               DISPLAY 'NUMBER OF EMPLOYEES TOO LARGE: LAYOFFS NEEDED'
               CALL 'OVERMAX'  USING EMP-CNT EMP-NUMBER-MAX PRINT-LINE
               DISPLAY 'OVER MAXIMUM EMPLOYEE NUMBER REPORT GENERATED'.
         GO TO 0300-EXIT.
```

Figure 4.6 *(Continued)*

The debugging DECLARATIVE gives you the ability to monitor various program elements during execution. COBOL gives control to procedures coded within debugging sections when the specified program elements are referenced during program execution. You also have access to the DEBUG-ITEM special register. COBOL places status information about the item being monitored in this register. More will be said about DEBUG-ITEM in Sec. 4.6.2. Note that IBM's documentation for COBOL II Release 3 states that the debugging section is an obsolete language element and may be deleted in future releases.

In order to use these features a DECLARATIVE section must be written. This is done by coding the key word DECLARATIVES on the line after the PROCEDURE DIVISION header, a programmer-defined section header on the next line, a USE sentence, and then whatever code is to be executed if the appropriate condition should arise. As many EXCEPTION/ERROR and debugging sections, each consisting of its own section header, its own USE statement, and its own executable COBOL statements can be coded as is necessary. The entire DECLARATIVE section is terminated with the key words END DECLARATIVES. An example of the format follows:

```
000100 PROCEDURE DIVISION.
000200 DECLARATIVES.
000300 section-name-1 SECTION.
000400      USE sentence-1.
000500 Paragraph headers optional
000600      COBOL statements
000700
000600 section-name-2 SECTION.
000700      USE sentence-2.
000800 Paragraph headers optional
000900      COBOL statements
001000 END DECLARATIVES.
```

4.6.1 USE Statement

The USE statement identifies the function of the section in which it appears and defines the conditions which will cause the COBOL statements immediately following it within that section to be executed. After the section is executed, control returns to the routine which activated it.

There are several formats for USE; those pertinent to debugging COBOL programs are USE AFTER EXCEPTION/ERROR and USE FOR DEBUGGING.

4.6.1.1 The USE AFTER EXCEPTION/ERROR statement

The USE AFTER EXCEPTION/ERROR statement specifies a procedure to be executed in the event of I/O errors on both QSAM and VSAM files. This is in addition to the standard system procedures. More specifically, the EXCEPTION/ERROR procedure will be executed either after a standard system I/O error routine has completed, when an INVALID KEY or AT END condition occurs if those options were coded in the I/O statement, or if an error condition occurs which has a FILE STATUS of 90 or above. Typical errors may include those occurring during execution of a READ, WRITE, REWRITE, START, or DELETE statement, an attempt to OPEN a file already opened, or an unsuccessful CLOSE of an open file. A word of caution: when a file is initially opened, the current DECLARATIVE has not yet been established. Thus no DECLARATIVE can receive control if a CLOSE is issued for a file that has never been opened. However, if a file has been previously opened, the last previously established DECLARATIVE procedure will receive control. To clarify this, the statement OPEN INPUT IN-FILE establishes a DECLARATIVE procedure for IN-FILE. Assume the file is opened without error. If an error occurs during later processing of IN-FILE, the DECLARATIVE procedure established when the file was opened for input will gain control.

You can specify files by name in the USE statement or specify all files opened for INPUT, all files opened for OUTPUT, all direct-access files opened in I-O mode, or all files opened in EXTEND mode. The general format for the statement is

```
USE AFTER STANDARD {EXCEPTION} PROCEDURE ON xxx
                   {  ERROR  }
```

The words STANDARD and ON are optional. EXCEPTION and ERROR are synonymous, and one or the other must be coded. The *xxx* must be replaced by one or more file names, INPUT, OUTPUT, I-O, or EXTEND.

Figure 4.7 shows how the EXCEPTION/ERROR DECLARATIVE might be used to trap I/O errors and continue processing in an OS/VS COBOL program which processes a VSAM file. This is the same program shown in Fig. 4.2 except that it has been modified to use both the EXCEPTION/ERROR DECLARATIVE and FILE STATUS. The error processing is now located in one place, in the DECLARATIVE section.

If an I/O error occurs in a program and neither a DECLARATIVE nor FILE STATUS was coded, a message similar to the one that follows may be printed in the job log if COBOL itself intercepts the error.

IGZ020I A user logic error occurred. Neither FILE STATUS nor a declarative was specified for file 'CARDFLE' in program 'IOERROR' at relative location X'076C'. The I-O status code was '47'.

This message came from a routine in the COBOL II Release 3 subroutine library. When the same program was run under COBOL II Release 2, a similar message appeared but without the file status code. When run under OS/VS COBOL, the system ABENDed the program with no message from COBOL.

In OS/VS COBOL, an optional GIVING clause can be coded in the USE statement. This allows you to receive a 136-byte descriptive message after an I/O error on a READ, WRITE, REWRITE, or START statement. For example,

```
USE AFTER STANDARD ERROR PROCEDURE ON FILE-1
  GIVING DATA-NAME-1  DATA-NAME-2
```

```
IDENTIFICATION DIVISION.
 PROGRAM-ID. VSAMDECL.
 AUTHOR. ALAN FRIEND.
DATE-COMPILED. OCT 16,1990.

ENVIRONMENT DIVISION.
 INPUT-OUTPUT SECTION.
 FILE-CONTROL.
     SELECT VSAM-FILE ASSIGN TO VSAMDD
                      FILE STATUS IS FILE-STATUS
                      ORGANIZATION IS INDEXED
                      ACCESS MODE IS DYNAMIC
                      RECORD KEY IS PROJECT-NAME.

DATA DIVISION.
FILE SECTION.
FD  VSAM-FILE
    LABEL RECORDS ARE OMITTED
    RECORD CONTAINS 123 CHARACTERS
    BLOCK CONTAINS 0 RECORDS.
01  VSAM-FILE-REC.
    05 FILLER                     PIC X(1).
    05 PROJECT-NAME.
       10 PRIM-KEY                PIC X.
       10 FILLER                  PIC X(7).
    05 FILLER                     PIC X(21).
    05 CREATE-DATE                PIC X(8).
    05 FILLER                     PIC X(60).
    05 AUTHOR-ID                  PIC X(8).
    05 FILLER                     PIC X(17).

WORKING-STORAGE SECTION.
*****************************************************************
*  FILE STATUS FIELD AND OPERATION-ATTEMPTED FIELD
*****************************************************************
01  STATUS-OPERATION-FIELDS.
    05  FILE-STATUS               PIC X(2).
    05  OPERATION-FLD             PIC X(9)  VALUE SPACES.

PROCEDURE DIVISION.

DECLARATIVES.

*****************************************************************
*      DISPLAY ERROR MESSAGES WITH THE FILE STATUS.
*****************************************************************

D0100-VSAM-FILE-ERROR SECTION.
    USE AFTER STANDARD ERROR PROCEDURE ON VSAM-FILE.
        IF OPERATION-FLD = 'OPEN'
           DISPLAY 'FILE STATUS = ' FILE-STATUS
                   ' OPEN ERROR: PROGRAM TERMINATED'
        ELSE
           IF OPERATION-FLD = 'CLOSE'
              DISPLAY 'FILE STATUS = ' FILE-STATUS
                      ' CLOSE ERROR'
           ELSE

              DISPLAY 'FILE-STATUS = ' FILE-STATUS '    '
                      OPERATION-FLD ' ERROR ON RECORD: '
                      'PROJECT NAME = ' PROJECT-NAME '    '
                      'AUTHOR-ID = ' AUTHOR-ID.
END DECLARATIVES.
```

Figure 4.7 The EXCEPTION/ERROR DECLARATIVE used in an OS/VS COBOL program.

```
***************************************************************
*  PROCESS VSAM FILE USING THE PRIME KEY "PROJECT-NAME"
***************************************************************

 0000-MAINLINE.
     MOVE 'OPEN' TO OPERATION-FLD
     OPEN I-O VSAM-FILE
     IF FILE-STATUS =  '00'
        PERFORM 0100-PROCESS THRU 0100-PROCESS-EXIT
        MOVE 'CLOSE' TO OPERATION-FLD
        CLOSE VSAM-FILE.
     GOBACK.

***************************************************************
*       THIS PARAGRAPH BRANCHES TO CHANGE, ADD,
*       AND DELETE ROUTINES.
***************************************************************

 0100-PROCESS.
     PERFORM 0110-CHANGE     THRU 0110-CHANGE-EXIT
     PERFORM 0120-ADD        THRU 0120-ADD-EXIT
     PERFORM 0130-DELETE     THRU 0130-DELETE-EXIT.

 0100-PROCESS-EXIT.
     EXIT.

***************************************************************
*       CHANGE FIELDS IN AN EXISTING RECORD
***************************************************************

 0110-CHANGE.
     MOVE 'DICTPROJ' TO PROJECT-NAME
     MOVE 'READ' TO OPERATION-FLD
     READ VSAM-FILE
     IF FILE-STATUS = '00'
        MOVE 'WILS0019' TO AUTHOR-ID
        MOVE 'REWRITE' TO OPERATION-FLD
        REWRITE VSAM-FILE-REC.

 0110-CHANGE-EXIT.
     EXIT.

***************************************************************
*       ADD A RECORD TO THE VSAM FILE
***************************************************************

 0120-ADD.
     MOVE SPACES TO VSAM-FILE-REC
     MOVE 'COBDEBUG' TO PROJECT-NAME
     MOVE 'FRIE4033' TO AUTHOR-ID
     MOVE '09/28/90' TO CREATE-DATE
     MOVE 'WRITE' TO OPERATION-FLD
     WRITE VSAM-FILE-REC.

 0120-ADD-EXIT.
     EXIT.

***************************************************************
*      DELETE A RECORD FROM THE VSAM FILE
***************************************************************

 0130-DELETE.
     MOVE 'ISAMBOOK' TO PROJECT-NAME
     MOVE 'NONE'  TO AUTHOR-ID
     MOVE 'DELETE' TO OPERATION-FLD
     DELETE VSAM-FILE RECORD.

 0130-DELETE-EXIT.
     EXIT.
```

Figure 4.7 *(Continued)*

The field DATA-NAME-1 is coded in the WORKING-STORAGE SECTION and DATA-NAME-2 in either the WORKING-STORAGE or LINKAGE SECTION. For complete details on the GIVING option see the IBM *OS / VS COBOL Compiler and Library Programmer's Guide.* The GIVING option is not available in COBOL II.

COBOL II Release 3 allows the GLOBAL clause in the USE statement. For example,

```
USE GLOBAL AFTER STANDARD ERROR PROCEDURE ON FILE-2
```

There are rules of precedence for execution of the first qualifying DECLARATIVE when nested programs are coded in COBOL II Release 3. See the IBM *VS COBOL II Application Programming: Language Reference, Release 3* manual for details.

4.6.1.2 The USE FOR DEBUGGING statement

The USE FOR DEBUGGING statement enables you to monitor elements in the COBOL program during execution. In OS/VS COBOL, these may include files, identifiers, and procedures. In COBOL II, only procedures may be monitored, and in COBOL II Release 3 debugging sections are only valid in the outermost program when nested programs are coded. Also recall that IBM's documentation for Release 3 indicates that the debugging section is an obsolete language element and may be deleted in future releases. Because of the limitations of USE FOR DEBUGGING in COBOL II, it may be wise to avoid it in COBOL II programs.

COBOL passes control to procedures within debugging sections whenever specified program elements are referenced during program execution. You also have access to status information about the item being monitored in the DEBUG-ITEM special register.

The general format for the USE FOR DEBUGGING statement is

```
USE FOR DEBUGGING ON xxx
```

The words FOR and ON are optional. In OS/VS COBOL the *xxx* must be replaced by one or more identifiers, file names, or procedure names, or one or more occurrences of ALL REFERENCES OF identifier name (the words REFERENCES and OF are optional), or one or more occurrences of ALL PROCEDURES. In COBOL II *xxx* can be one or more procedure names or ALL PROCEDURES.

The rules for the points during program execution at which the USE FOR DEBUGGING procedures gain control are complex. They are summarized in Fig. 4.8. The figure specifies the operand in the USE FOR DEBUGGING statement and indicates whether the COBOL statement containing that operand or the USE FOR DEBUGGING procedures execute first.

OPERAND IN USE FOR DEBUGGING STATEMENT	WHEN THE USE FOR DEBUGGING STATEMENT EXECUTES
file-name-a	after READ file-name-a and the AT END or INVALID KEY phrase is not executed after CLOSE, DELETE, OPEN or START file-name-a.
identifier-a	before REWRITE or WRITE identifier-a, and after the FROM option move if it was coded before RELEASE identifier-a, and after the FROM option move if it was coded after every initialization, modification or evaluation of identifier-a when it is named in the VARYING clause of a PERFORM, or in any of the AFTER or UNTIL clauses of a PERFORM after any other COBOL statement that explicitly refers to identifier-a which causes its value to change. If the statement or phrase containing identifier-a is not executed, the debugging section is not executed.
ALL REFERENCES OF identifier-a	before any GO TO DEPENDING ON identifier-a control occurs, and before any associated debugging section for procedure-name is executed before REWRITE or WRITE identifier-a, and after the FROM option move if it was coded before RELEASE identifier-a, and after the FROM option move if it was coded after every initialization, modification or evaluation of identifier-a when it is named in the VARYING clause of a PERFORM, or in any of the AFTER or UNTIL clauses of a PERFORM after any other COBOL statement that explicitly refers to identifier-a. If the statement or phrase containing identifier-a is not executed, the debugging section is not executed.
procedure-name-a	before every execution of procedure-name-a after execution of an ALTER statement referring to procedure-name-a.
ALL PROCEDURES	before each execution of every non-debugging procedure after execution of every ALTER statement except those in DECLARATIVE procedures.

Figure 4.8 Rules showing the points at which the USE FOR DEBUGGING procedures gain control in a program.

Figure 4.9 demonstrates use of the DEBUGGING DECLARATIVE. The OS/VS COBOL program processes employee records based on the value of a parameter passed from the JCL. A value of "A" represents active employees, while a value of "I" represents inactive employees who may have an employment status of either "TERMINATE" or "LEAVE."

Lines 8300 through 9200 ensure that the passed parameter is valid before any record is processed. This code gains control after the OPEN statement at

```
000100 IDENTIFICATION DIVISION.
000200  PROGRAM-ID.   USEDEBG.
000300  AUTHOR.       ALAN FRIEND.
000400  DATE-WRITTEN. OCT., 1990.
000500 DATE-COMPILED. OCT 18,1990.

000700 ENVIRONMENT DIVISION.
000800  CONFIGURATION SECTION.
000900  SOURCE-COMPUTER. IBM-370 WITH DEBUGGING MODE.
001000  INPUT-OUTPUT SECTION.
001100   FILE-CONTROL.
001200     SELECT INFILE    ASSIGN TO  INFILE.
001300     SELECT OUTFILE   ASSIGN TO  OUTFILE.

001500 DATA DIVISION.
001600  FILE SECTION.
001700  FD INFILE
001800     RECORDING MODE IS F
001900     RECORD CONTAINS 80 CHARACTERS
002000     BLOCK CONTAINS 0 RECORDS
002100     LABEL RECORDS ARE OMITTED
002200     DATA RECORD IS INFILE-REC.
002300  01 INFILE-REC.
002400     05 INFILE-REC-NO         PIC S9(5).
002500     05 INFILE-REC-TYPE       PIC X.
002600     05 EMPLOYEE-DATA.
002700        10 LAST-NAME-IN       PIC X(15).
002800        10 FIRST-NAME-IN      PIC X(10).
002900        10 DEPT-ID-IN         PIC X(5).
003000        10 EMP-STATUS-IN      PIC X(10).
003100        10 DATE-RETURN-IN     PIC X(8).
003200        10 SALARY-IN          PIC 9(6)V99.
003300     05 FILLER                PIC X(18).
003400  FD OUTFILE
003500     RECORDING MODE IS F
003600     RECORD CONTAINS 100 CHARACTERS
003700     BLOCK CONTAINS 0 RECORDS
003800     LABEL RECORDS ARE OMITTED
003900     DATA RECORD IS OUTFILE-REC.
004000  01 OUTFILE-REC.
004100     05 OUTFILE-REC-NO        PIC 9(5).
004200     05 EMPLOYMENT-STATUS.
004300        10 LAST-NAME-OUT      PIC X(15).
004400        10 FIRST-NAME-OUT     PIC X(10).
004500        10 EMP-STATUS-OUT     PIC X(10).
004600     05 FILLER                PIC X.
004700     05 SCHED-RET             PIC X(16).
004800     05 FILLER                PIC X.
004900     05 DATE-RETURN-OUT       PIC X(10).
005000     05 FILLER                PIC X(32).

005200  WORKING-STORAGE SECTION.

005310*****************************************************************
005320*    END-OF-FILE SWITCH AND COUNTERS
005330*****************************************************************

005350  01 SWITCH-AND-COUNTERS.
005500     05 SW-EOF                PIC X         VALUE 'N'.
005600        88 NO-MORE-RECORDS                  VALUE 'Y'.
005700     05 COUNTERS          COMP-3.
005800        10 DETAIL-LINE-CNT    PIC S99       VALUE +60.
005900        10 PAGE-CNT           PIC S99       VALUE ZERO.
006000        10 RECORDS-WRITTEN    PIC S9(5)     VALUE ZERO.

006010*****************************************************************
006020*    REPORT HEADER LINES
006030*****************************************************************

006100  01 HEADER-LINE-1.
006200     05 FILLER                PIC X(10)     VALUE SPACES.
006300     05 REPT-DATE             PIC X(8).
006400     05 FILLER                PIC X(15)     VALUE SPACES.
006500     05 FILLER                PIC X(34)
006600                VALUE 'EMPLOYEE STATUS REPORT - QUARTERLY'.
006700     05 FILLER                PIC X(15)     VALUE SPACES.
006800     05 FILLER                PIC X(5)      VALUE 'PAGE '.
006900     05 HEADER-PAGE-NO        PIC Z9.
007000     05 FILLER                PIC X(11)     VALUE SPACES.
007100  01 HEADER-LINE-2            PIC X(100)    VALUE ALL '*'.
```

Figure 4.9 (*a*) An OS/VS COBOL program which utilizes the debugging DECLARATIVE. (*b*) Output from the DISPLAY statements at lines 8600 and 8900, and (*c*) from lines 9700 through 10400.

```
007300  LINKAGE SECTION.

007500  01 PASSED-PARM.
007600      05 FILLER                 PIC S9(4)    COMP SYNC.
007700      05 INPARM                 PIC X.

007900 PROCEDURE DIVISION USING PASSED-PARM.

008100 DECLARATIVES.

008210*****************************************************************
008220* VALIDATE PASSED PARM AND TERMINATE PROGRAM IF NOT "A" OR "I"
008230*****************************************************************
008300 CHECK-PASSED-PARM SECTION.
008400      USE FOR DEBUGGING ON INFILE
008500      IF INPARM NOT EQUAL 'A' AND 'I'
008600         DISPLAY 'INVALID PASSED PARM '
008700                 INPARM
008800                 '. IT MUST BE "A" OR "I".'
008900         DISPLAY '** PROGRAM TERMINATED **'
009000         CLOSE INFILE
009100               OUTFILE
009200         GOBACK.

009400 MONITOR-EMPLOYEE-STATUS SECTION.

009420*****************************************************************
009430* MONITOR PARAGRAPH WHICH PROCESSES RECORDS OF INACTIVE EMPLOYEES
009431* TO DISPLAY MESSAGES AFTER EVERY RECORD READ IF EMP-STATUS-IN
009432* IS NOT EQUAL TO "TERMINATE" OR "LEAVE".
009440*****************************************************************
009500      USE FOR DEBUGGING ON 0300-PARA-INACTIVE
009600      IF EMP-STATUS-IN NOT EQUAL 'TERMINATE' AND 'LEAVE'
009700         DISPLAY 'PARAGRAPH BEING MONITORED IS '  DEBUG-NAME
009800         DISPLAY 'IT IS UNDER CONTROL OF A '      DEBUG-CONTENTS
009900         DISPLAY 'IT RECEIVES CONTROL FROM LINE ' DEBUG-LINE
010000         DISPLAY 'EMP-STATUS-IN '
010100                 EMP-STATUS-IN
010200                 ' IN RECORD NUMBER '
010300                 INFILE-REC-NO
010400                 ' IS INVALID. IT MUST BE "TERMINATE" OR "LEAVE" '.
010500 END DECLARATIVES.

010600*****************************************************************
010700*     MAINLINE CONTROL PARAGRAPH - HOUSE-KEEPING, READ EACH
010800*     RECORD AND PROCESS BASED ON VALUE IN INPARM PASSED AS A
010900*     PARAMETER FROM THE JCL.
011000*****************************************************************

011200 0100-MAINLINE.
011400      OPEN INPUT  INFILE
011500           OUTPUT OUTFILE
011600      MOVE CURRENT-DATE TO REPT-DATE
011700      READ INFILE
011800           AT END MOVE 'Y' TO SW-EOF.
011900      IF INPARM EQUAL 'A'
012000         PERFORM 0200-PARA-ACTIVE
012100            UNTIL NO-MORE-RECORDS
012200      ELSE
012300         IF INPARM EQUAL 'I'
012400            PERFORM 0300-PARA-INACTIVE
012500               UNTIL NO-MORE-RECORDS.
012600      CLOSE INFILE
012700            OUTFILE
012800      GOBACK.

013600*****************************************************************
013700*  PRINT REPORT OF ACTIVE EMPLOYEES, WHO HAVE INPUT RECORDS WITH
013710*  A VALUE OF "A" IN INFILE-REC-TYPE.
013800*****************************************************************

014000 0200-PARA-ACTIVE.
014200      IF DETAIL-LINE-CNT GREATER THAN +55
014300         PERFORM 0400-HEADER-RTN.
014400      IF INFILE-REC-TYPE EQUAL 'A'
014500         MOVE SPACES          TO OUTFILE-REC
014600         MOVE INFILE-REC-NO   TO OUTFILE-REC-NO
014700         MOVE LAST-NAME-IN    TO LAST-NAME-OUT
014800         MOVE FIRST-NAME-IN   TO FIRST-NAME-OUT
014900         MOVE 'ACTIVE'        TO EMP-STATUS-OUT
015000         WRITE OUTFILE-REC
015100         ADD +1 TO DETAIL-LINE-CNT  RECORDS-WRITTEN.
015200      READ INFILE
015300           AT END MOVE 'Y' TO SW-EOF.
```

Figure 4.9 *(Continued)*

```
015410*****************************************************************
015420*  PRINT REPORT OF INACTIVE EMPLOYEES, HAVING INPUT RECORDS WITH
015430*  A VALUE OF "I" IN INFILE-REC-TYPE AND A VALUE OF EITHER "LEAVE"
015431*  OR "TERMINATED" IN EMP-STATUS-IN
015440*****************************************************************

015500 0300-PARA-INACTIVE.
015700     IF DETAIL-LINE-CNT GREATER THAN +55
015800        PERFORM 0400-HEADER-RTN.
015900     IF INFILE-REC-TYPE EQUAL 'I'
016000        MOVE SPACES          TO OUTFILE-REC
016100        MOVE INFILE-REC-NO   TO OUTFILE-REC-NO
016200        MOVE LAST-NAME-IN    TO LAST-NAME-OUT
016300        MOVE FIRST-NAME-IN   TO FIRST-NAME-OUT
016400        MOVE EMP-STATUS-IN   TO EMP-STATUS-OUT
016500        MOVE 'SCHEDULED RETURN' TO SCHED-RET
016600        IF EMP-STATUS-IN EQUAL 'TERMINATE'
016700           MOVE 'TERMINATED'      TO DATE-RETURN-OUT
016800           WRITE OUTFILE-REC
016900           ADD +1 TO DETAIL-LINE-CNT  RECORDS-WRITTEN
017000        ELSE
017100           IF EMP-STATUS-IN EQUAL 'LEAVE'
017200              MOVE DATE-RETURN-IN TO DATE-RETURN-OUT
017300              WRITE OUTFILE-REC
017400              ADD +1 TO DETAIL-LINE-CNT  RECORDS-WRITTEN.
017500     READ INFILE
017600          AT END MOVE 'Y' TO SW-EOF.

017800*****************************************************************
017900* HEADER ROUTINE PERFORMED WHEN DETAIL-LINE-CNT GREATER THAN 55.
018000*****************************************************************

018200 0400-HEADER-RTN.
018400     ADD +1 TO PAGE-CNT
018500     MOVE PAGE-CNT TO HEADER-PAGE-NO
018600     WRITE OUTFILE-REC FROM HEADER-LINE-1
018700        AFTER ADVANCING PAGE
018800     WRITE OUTFILE-REC FROM HEADER-LINE-2
018900        AFTER ADVANCING 1 LINE
019000     MOVE +2 TO DETAIL-LINE-CNT.
```

(a)

```
INVALID PASSED PARM B. IT MUST BE "A" OR "I".
** PROGRAM TERMINATED **
```

(b)

```
PARAGRAPH BEING MONITORED IS 0300-PARA-INACTIVE
IT IS UNDER CONTROL OF A PERFORM LOOP
IT RECEIVES CONTROL FROM LINE 012400
EMP-STATUS-IN ACTIVE   IN RECORD NUMBER 10001 IS INVALID. IT MUST BE "TERMINATE" OR "LEAVE"
```

(c)

Figure 4.9 *(Continued)*

lines 11400 and 11500 has executed. Figure 4.9*b* shows the output from the DISPLAY statements when the value was "B." Note that "INFILE" was coded on line 8400 rather than the identifier "INPARM" because the DISPLAY statements at lines 8600 through 8900 would have been activated only if the identifier "INPARM" had changed when line 8500 was executed. Alternatively, line 8400 could have been written

```
USE FOR DEBUGGING ON ALL REFERENCES OF INPARM
```

in order to have gotten the desired results; the USE statement would have been activated by line 11900.

Lines 9400 through 10400 check the value of the employment status in the field EMP-STATUS-IN for inactive employees. The check is done after each record is read and before the paragraph which processes inactive employee records (0300-PARA-INACTIVE) is executed. Figure 4.9*c* shows the output from the DISPLAY statements when a record for an inactive employee had an incorrect value of "ACTIVE" for the employment status. Notice that several fields in the DEBUG-ITEM special register (see Sec. 4.6.2) are DISPLAYed.

Debugging sections are activated by compile-time and object-time switches. First, the compile-time switch must be placed in effect by coding WITH DEBUGGING MODE in the SOURCE-COMPUTER paragraph as is done when activating debugging lines (see Sec. 4.5). When the compile-time switch is in effect, all debugging sections are compiled and become part of the object module. If the compile-time switch is not in effect, all debugging sections are treated as comments.

In order for debugging sections which have been compiled to be executed, an object-time switch must be in effect. This is done by specifying DEBUG on the EXEC statement in the JCL. DEBUG is the IBM default. Note that the object-time switch will have no effect on execution unless the compile-time switch has been placed in effect. Coding NODEBUG on the EXEC statement inhibits execution of the debugging sections. (Note that the object-time switch has no effect on debugging lines; they are always active if they have been compiled with the compile-time switch.)

4.6.2 DEBUG-ITEM Special Register

As previously mentioned, access is given to the DEBUG-ITEM Special Register when the USE FOR DEBUGGING statement is coded. This register contains status information about the item being monitored by the USE statement. The implicit description of DEBUG-ITEM is as follows:

```
01  DEBUG-ITEM.
    02  DEBUG-LINE      PICTURE IS X(6).
    02  FILLER          PICTURE IS X    VALUE SPACE.
    02  DEBUG-NAME      PICTURE IS X(30).
    02  FILLER          PICTURE IS X    VALUE SPACE.
    02  DEBUG-SUB-1     PICTURE IS S9999
                        SIGN IS LEADING SEPARATE CHARACTER.
    02  FILLER          PICTURE IS X    VALUE SPACE.
    02  DEBUG-SUB-2     PICTURE IS S9999
                        SIGN IS LEADING SEPARATE CHARACTER.
    02  FILLER          PICTURE IS X    VALUE SPACE.
    02  DEBUG-SUB-3     PICTURE IS S9999
                        SIGN IS LEADING SEPARATE CHARACTER.
    02  FILLER          PICTURE IS X    VALUE SPACE.
    02  DEBUG-CONTENTS  PICTURE IS X(n).
```

DEBUG-ITEM is variable in length and is dependent on the length of the character string placed in DEBUG-CONTENTS.

DEBUG-ITEM must not be coded anywhere in the source module. The contents of its fields may, however, be used for whatever debugging logic the programmer wishes. Note that only one DEBUG-ITEM register is established by COBOL regardless of how many debugging sections are coded, and that DEBUG-ITEM and its subordinate fields may be referred to only in debugging sections.

COBOL assigns values to the fields in DEBUG-ITEM as shown in Fig. 4.10.

4.6.3 A Few Final Observations on Using DECLARATIVE

As can be seen, the DECLARATIVE is a powerful tool for testing and debugging. It allows you to keep the debugging code together in one place at the beginning of the PROCEDURE DIVISION where it can be readily found. The debugging DECLARATIVE can be activated at will by using the compile-time and object-time switches. However, it takes careful planning and some experience to use DECLARATIVE properly. Perhaps that is why this feature is not widely used by COBOL programmers. Additional information about DECLARATIVE can be found in these IBM manuals:

IBM VS COBOL for OS / VS

OS / VS COBOL Compiler and Library Programmer's Guide

VS COBOL II Application Programming: Language Reference

VS COBOL II Application Programming Guide

4.7 ADDITIONAL THOUGHTS ON USING COBOL LANGUAGE DEBUGGING AIDS

Of all the debugging aids discussed, DISPLAY is probably the easiest to use and the most helpful in a variety of situations. It can be used alone or in combination with other techniques. It is available in both OS/VS COBOL and COBOL II.

EXHIBIT NAMED (not available in COBOL II) can perform the same functions as DISPLAY, giving neatly formatted output. It is more costly, however, in terms of utilization of system resources. The extra formatting it provides when giving the contents of identifiers or registers can easily be achieved by including descriptive literals in DISPLAY statements.

EXHIBIT CHANGED or CHANGED NAMED (OS/VS COBOL only) is quite helpful when it is desirable to monitor how fields are changing during program execution. Again, however, system overhead may need to be considered. With some planning, DISPLAY may be used in conjunction with the ON verb (not available in COBOL II) to obtain results reasonably close to that from EXHIBIT CHANGED or EXHIBIT CHANGED NAMED.

The TRACE verb may be helpful when it is necessary to follow the flow of control in an OS/VS COBOL program. Its use is limited because it does not show which path is taken when there is a choice of paths through a paragraph.

ITEM WHICH CAUSES EXECUTION OF THE DEBUG SECTION	VALUE IN DEBUG-LINE IS NUMBER OF COBOL STATEMENT REFERRING TO:	DEBUG-NAME CONTAINS: (see note)	DEBUG-CONTENTS CONTAINS:
file-name-a	file-name-a	file-name-a	For READ, contents of record. For other references, spaces.
identifier-a	identifier-a	identifier-a	Contents of identifier-a when control transfers to debug section.
procedure-name-a in an ALTER reference	ALTER statement	procedure-name-a	procedure-name-n in TO PROCEED TO phrase
GO TO procedure-name-a	GO TO statement	procedure-name-a	Spaces
procedure-name-a in a SORT/MERGE INPUT or OUTPUT procedure	SORT/MERGE statement	procedure-name-a	The literal "SORT INPUT", "SORT OUTPUT" or "MERGE OUTPUT" depending on what was coded.
procedure-name-a in a USE procedure	statement which causes execution of the USE procedure	procedure-name-a	The literal "USE PROCEDURE".
PERFORM statement transfer of control	this PERFORM statement	procedure-name-a	The literal "PERFORM LOOP".
implicit transfer of control from the previous sequential procedure	the previous statement executed in the previous sequential procedure. If a section header precedes this procedure and control passes through the section header, the statement number is that of the section header.	procedure-name-a	The literal "FALL THROUGH".
the first execution of the first nondeclarative procedure	the line number of the first nondeclarative procedure name	first nondeclarative procedure name	The literal "START PROGRAM".
Note: DEBUG-SUB-1, DEBUG-SUB-2 and DEBUG-SUB-3 contain the occurrence number of each level of DEBUG-NAME if it is indexed or subscripted. If DEBUG-NAME is not indexed or subscripted, these fields contain spaces.			

Figure 4.10 Assignment of fields in the DEBUG-ITEM register.

File status is essential when dealing with VSAM files. It is recommended that it always be used with VSAM processing since failure to use it can result in erroneous program output which may be difficult to detect.

The USE FOR DEBUGGING statement is quite powerful and is also the most complicated tool presented here. Using it incorrectly can be worse than not using it at all. Thus it is important that you understand its rules and be able to interpret its output. As previously mentioned, IBM suggests in its COBOL II Release 3 manuals that debugging sections will most likely not be supported in future releases. Because of its complexity and questionable future, it is recommended that COBOL programmers refrain from using it. Alternate coding within the PROCEDURE DIVISION can get the same results and is probably easier to understand (as witnessed by the needlessly complex examples given in Sec. 4.6.1.2).

How should you select which of the tips and techniques presented in this chapter to use for testing and debugging a program? Choose the techniques which are easiest to understand and use, which most readily give the desired results for the specific programming situation, and which are least costly in terms of system overhead. Part of the choice, of course, depends on your personal style and how comfortable you are with a particular technique.

4.8 SUMMARY

Several techniques and COBOL language features can be utilized to make COBOL program debugging a bit easier.

The DISPLAY verb can be used in both OS/VS COBOL and COBOL II to view the contents of DATA DIVISION fields and special registers at strategic points in the program's processing. It can also permit you to display literal messages to show the logical flow of control of the program.

Additional debugging verbs available in OS/VS COBOL but not in COBOL II are EXHIBIT, TRACE, and ON. Most of their functions can be achieved through the use of the interactive debugger COBTEST when working with COBOL II programs.

EXHIBIT is similar to display except that it generates formatted output when giving the contents of fields or literals. It can also be set up to monitor an identifier and show the contents when they change.

TRACE can be turned on or off at any point in the program's processing by coding READY TRACE and RESET TRACE, respectively. It allows you to see the program's logical flow of control.

The ON verb permits you to control the frequency with which a COBOL statement will be executed.

In order to simplify locating the range of WORKING-STORAGE data in a hexadecimal dump, VALUE clauses containing alphanumeric literals can be coded at the beginning and end of WORKING-STORAGE to make its beginning and end more conspicuous in the EBCDIC portion of the dump.

File status supplies you with information regarding how successfully an I/O operation has completed. It can be used for both QSAM and VSAM files, but it is much more critical to request status information for VSAM files since many potential I/O error conditions may go undetected otherwise. There is a standard file status in both OS/VS COBOL and COBOL II, with additional VSAM file status information in COBOL II.

DEBUGGING PACKETS, which are only available in OS/VS COBOL, let you test new versions of paragraphs without deleting or commenting out the original code. The packets are placed together at the end of the source module.

DEBUGGING LINES provide an alternative to inserting lines of test code which will be commented out with asterisks or removed when the testing is concluded. DEBUGGING LINES are activated or deactivated with a compile-time switch.

DECLARATIVEs enable you to group I/O error routines as well as other debugging routines at the beginning of the PROCEDURE DIVISION. The USE AFTER EXCEPTION/ERROR statement is coded when I/O error procedures are desired. The USE FOR DEBUGGING statement is required when other error procedures are to be coded. The USE FOR DEBUGGING procedures are activated by both compile-time and object-time switches.

You should select which of the debugging techniques presented here to use based on system efficiency considerations, ease of use, the results desired, and your knowledge and personal preferences. DISPLAY is quite versatile and simple to use for testing and debugging both OS/VS COBOL and COBOL II programs. The USE FOR DEBUGGING statement is rather complex and it is recommended that it be avoided if possible, particularly in COBOL II where IBM has indicated that it may not be supported in future releases. The other tools and techniques may be used as the need arises.

REVIEW QUESTIONS

1. Name the COBOL debugging verbs which are available in:
a. OS/VS COBOL
b. COBOL II

2. Write code which will:
a. Display the contents of FIELD-A preceded by the literal "The contents of FIELD-A is" and followed by the literal "after processing.".
b. Execute paragraph 5000-PRINT-RECORD the fifth through the tenth time source line 200 is reached in an OS/VS COBOL program.
c. Print the name and contents of FIELD-B in an OS/VS COBOL program only if the value of FIELD-B changes.
d. Execute the alternate code MOVE FIELD-A TO FIELD-B in paragraph 5000-PRINT-RECORD, bypassing the original code, in an OS/VS COBOL program.

3. How are debugging lines designated in a COBOL program? Write the COBOL code necessary to activate them.

4. How can a record of the flow of control of an OS/VS COBOL program be initiated and then turned off from within the program? Are there any limitations to this technique? Explain.

5. Write the ENVIRONMENT DIVISION and DATA DIVISION code required to:
a. Obtain file status information for a file called FILE-1 which is associated with the DD statement FILE1DD in an OS/VS COBOL program.
b. Obtain standard and VSAM file status information for a file called FILE-2 which is associated with the DD statement FILE2DD in a COBOL II program.

6. Explain the purpose of checking the file status for files in a COBOL program. Why is it especially important to do this for VSAM files?

7. Answer the following questions about DECLARATIVEs.

a. What is the purpose of the EXCEPTION/ERROR DECLARATIVE in a COBOL program?

b. What is the purpose of the debugging DECLARATIVE in a COBOL program?

c. Where are DECLARATIVEs located in a COBOL program?

d. What marks the beginning of the DECLARATIVE section?

e. What marks the end of the DECLARATIVE section?

f. What code is required within a DECLARATIVE section?

g. How is a debugging DECLARATIVE activated?

8. How should a programmer decide which COBOL language techniques to use for testing and debugging a program?

Chapter

5

Putting It All Together: Developing, Testing, and Debugging a COBOL Program

Many COBOL language books are quite explicit about the use and syntax of COBOL language elements and about the desirability of writing structured programs. Few, however, give sufficient guidance in designing and testing a program. The old adage "an ounce of prevention is worth a pound of cure" is certainly true when it comes to programming; it makes more sense to carefully design and thoroughly test a program before it is moved into production than to have to deal with a nasty production ABEND at 3 A.M.

In this chapter we will cover general program design concepts, COBOL program testing, and COBOL program debugging. For the testing and debugging sections we will refer to many of the COBOL techniques discussed in previous chapters.

5.1 DESIGNING THE PROGRAM

Good program design does not occur by accident. It requires a thorough understanding of the program requirements and a method for achieving them through efficient, error-free, and easily maintainable program code. There are tools and methodologies whose purposes are to help the project team to attain these objectives.

5.1.1 Design Tools

Design of an application system should start at the highest level, where the main application functions are established, and flow downward into more specific subtasks. The subtasks may be individual programs within the system, or sections, paragraphs, and even individual statements within a program. There are many design tools which can assist the application development team.

They should enable the team to see the whole picture clearly, from the overall functions down to the specifics of each subtask.

One design approach used to build an overall structured specification for a system is known as structured analysis. It encompasses the high- and low-level aspects of the system, using data flow diagrams, a data dictionary, structured English, decision tables, and decision trees. It is a quite sophisticated technique which has gained popularity among analysts. Its use is beyond the scope of this book, but I mention it here to make you aware of its importance.

We will now look briefly at some of the other widely used tools which are commonly utilized at the lower levels for application program design.

Hierarchy chart. This is similar to an organization chart. The top level is broken down into manageable pieces which are shown at lower levels. The hierarchy chart illustrated in Fig. 5.1 is for a program that calculates employee compensation.

HIPO diagram. This combines the *h*ierarchy chart with an *i*nput-*p*rocess-*o*utput diagram (HIPO). It gives a graphic representation of the program from the major high-level functions down to detailed lower-level functions. Figure 5.2*a* shows the hierarchy chart, which is often referred to as a "visual table of contents" in the HIPO methodology. Figure 5.2*b* illustrates overview diagrams for box 3.0 in the visual table of contents. The detail diagrams for box 3.1 are shown in Fig. 5.2*c*.

Flowchart. The flowchart uses standard symbols to represent the logic flow of a program. It clearly indicates the decision-making steps and sequence of processing within the program. In the flowchart illustrated in Fig. 5.3 you can see the logic for a program that reads, edits, and writes records until the end of the input file is reached.

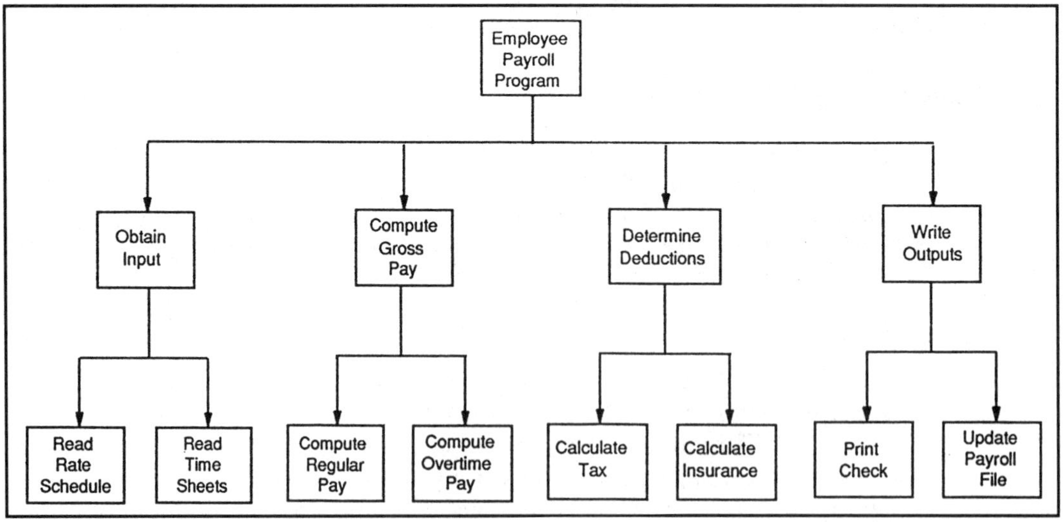

Figure 5.1 A hierarchy chart for a program that calculates employee compensation.

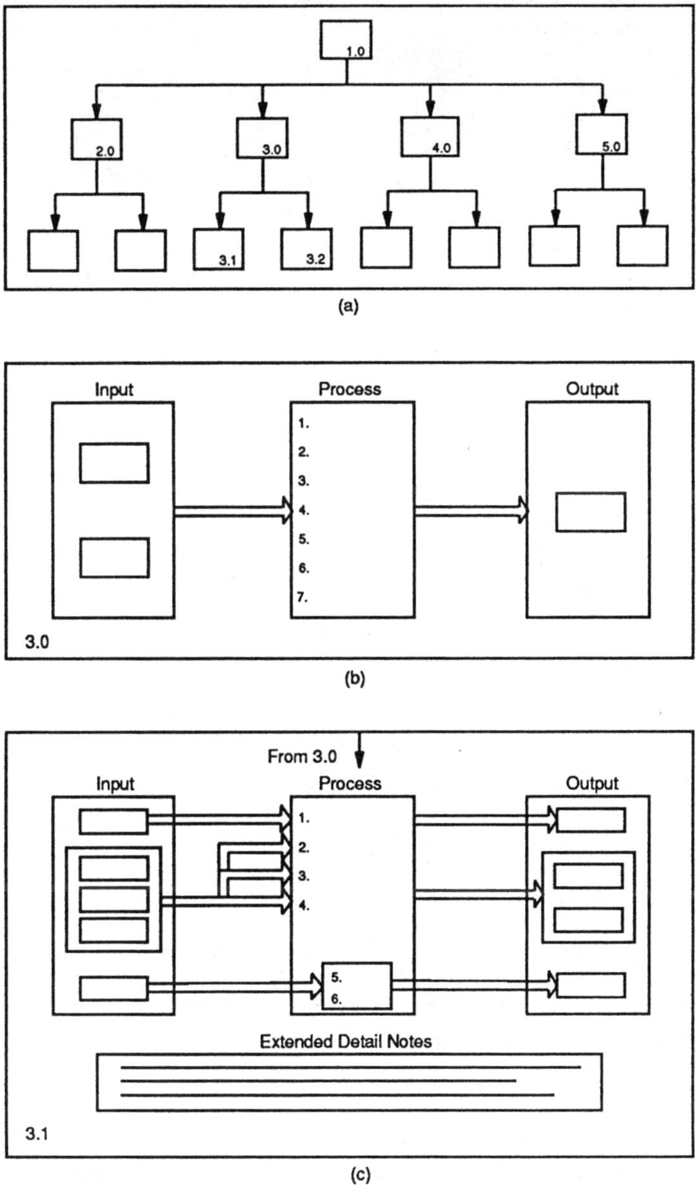

Figure 5.2 A HIPO diagram consisting of (*a*) a visual table of contents; (*b*) overview diagrams; and (*c*) detail diagrams.

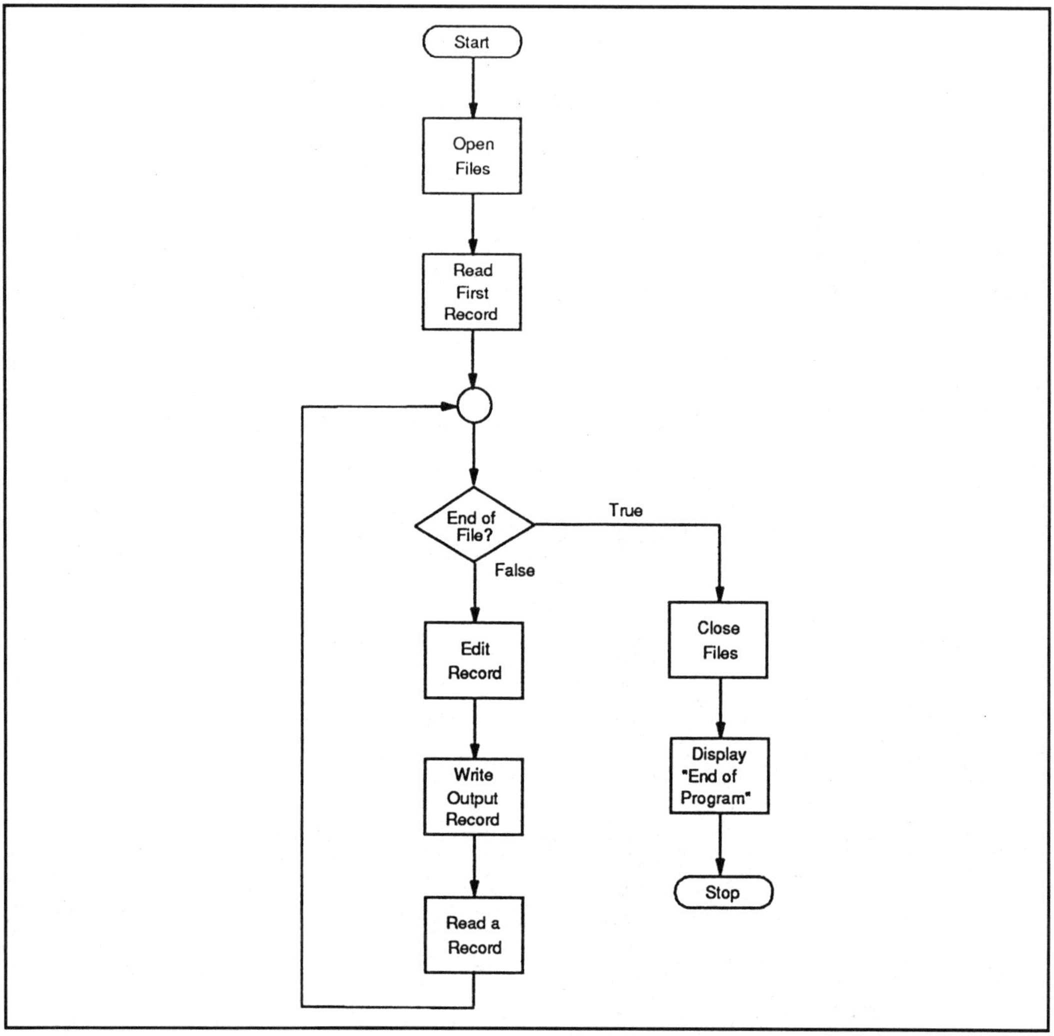

Figure 5.3 A flowchart for a program that reads, edits, and writes records.

Nassi-Schneiderman chart. This also uses a set of standard graphic representations to show the program logic. The symbols are different from those in a flowchart. The Nassi-Schneiderman chart in Fig. 5.4 shows a program which reads, edits, checks for errors, and writes records until the end of the input file is encountered. A summary is written at the end of the job.

Pseudocode. Pseudocode is written in English with a number of specific indentation rules and key words (such as END) to show the procedural steps in a program. It can show program logic in whatever detail is deemed necessary. The pseudocode in Fig. 5.5 is for a program which reads sales records, computes the salesperson's commission and total salary, and prints a check

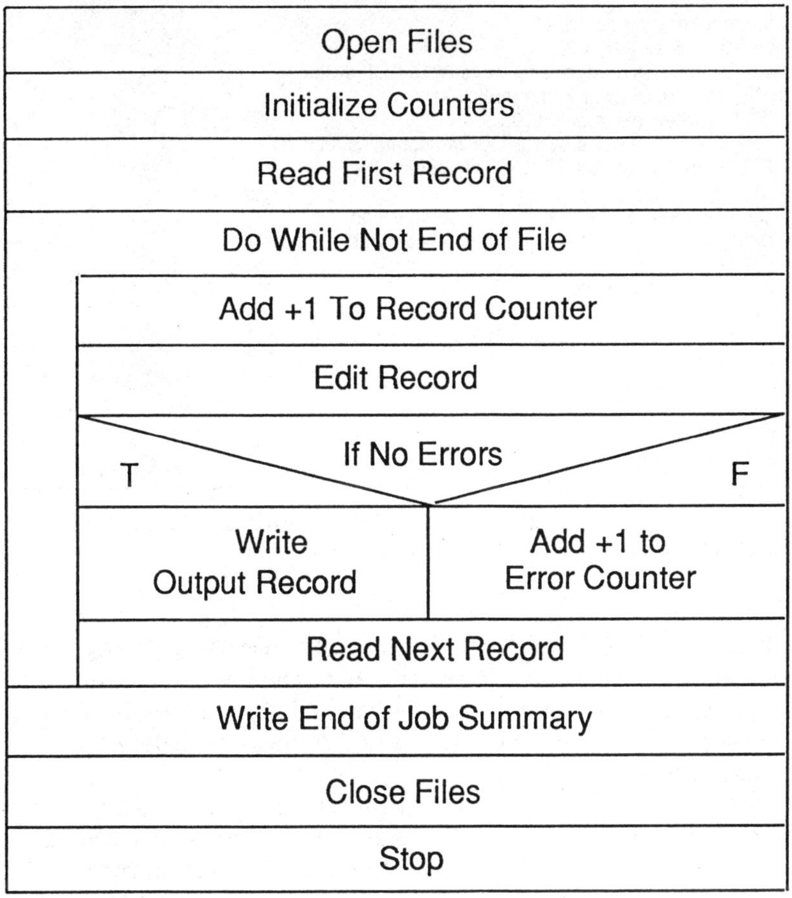

Figure 5.4 A Nassi-Schneiderman chart depicting a program that reads, edits, and writes records. It also checks for error conditions and writes a summary report.

until end-of-file is reached. It writes a payroll summary report at the end of the job.

5.1.2 Top-down Development

Top-down development is an approach to system and program design that considers the major function of the application first, then its subordinate functions, and so on until the lowest-level functions are addressed. The top level gives the general, overall picture, and each successively lower level gives increasingly more specific functions. This approach implies that modularization will be used to define and implement each subfunction. Typically, after the hierarchy of the entire system or program has been laid out (perhaps using a hierarchy chart as explained in Sec. 5.1.1), each level is completed and tested

```
Open input and output files
Initialize EOF switch to 'N'
Read first sales-record; at end move 'Y' to EOF switch
PERFORM until EOF switch equal 'Y'
   IF      sales less than $1000
   THEN  multiply sales by 5.5% giving commission
   ELSE  multiply sales by 10% giving commission
   ENDIF
   Calculate total pay equal salary + commission
   Move salesperson name and total pay to check
   Print check
   Add 1 to checks written
   Move total pay to total payroll amount
   Read next sales-record; at end move 'Y' to EOF switch
ENDPERFORM
Write summary payroll report
Close files
Terminate program
```

Figure 5.5 Pseudocode showing the logic for a program which reads records, calculates salesperson compensation, writes checks, and produces a payroll summary report.

before proceeding to the next lower level. The advantage to using this approach is that the top levels can be coded and tested before the lower levels are completed. As the lower levels are completed, they can be inserted into the existing structure and tested immediately. This allows design flaws to be detected early in the development cycle.

When using top-down development for creating a COBOL program, the main control paragraph may be written first, then each PERFORMed procedure may be coded and tested in turn. It is not necessary to complete all the code for a paragraph which executes a subfunction. A "stub" can be written to serve as a placeholder. The stub may simply be a DISPLAY statement which indicates that this part of the program has been reached (also see Sec. 4.1.1). The following example illustrates this.

```
PROCEDURE DIVISION.
0000-MAINLINE.
    OPEN INPUT IN-FILE
         OUTPUT PRINT-FILE
    READ IN-FILE INTO WS-IN-FILE
      AT END MOVE 'Y' TO EOF-SWITCH.
    PERFORM 0100-PROCESS
      UNTIL END-OF-FILE.
    CLOSE IN-FILE
          OUT-FILE.
    GOBACK.
```

```
000220 0100-PROCESS.
000230     PERFORM 0200-CHECK-ITEM-NUMBER.
000240     PERFORM 0300-CHECK-CUSTOMER-STATUS.
000250     READ IN-FILE INTO WS-IN-FILE
000260       AT END MOVE 'Y' TO EOF-SWITCH.
000270
000280 0200-CHECK-ITEM-NUMBER.
000290     DISPLAY 'PROGRAM REACHED 0200-CHECK-ITEM-NUMBER'.
000300
000310 0300-CHECK-CUSTOMER-STATUS.
000320     DISPLAY 'PROGRAM REACHED
000330              0300-CHECK-CUSTOMER-STATUS'.
```

The DISPLAY statements at lines 000290 and 000320 indicate that program control has reached these paragraphs. The actual code will be written later after the logic for 0000-MAINLINE and 0100-PROCESS has been written and tested.

5.1.3 Structured Programming

In 1966 C. Bohm and G. Jacopini published a paper ("Flow Diagrams, Turing Machines and Languages with Only Two Formation Rules," *Communications of the ACM,* Vol. 9, May, 1966) which formed the basis for the structured programming concept. They stated that a truly structured program is built of only three logic structures which can be combined in an endless variety of ways. They also stated that there is only one entry and one exit for each structure and for the program as a whole. There is an absence of out-of-line branches in a structured program. Because the GO TO statement represents a nonreturning branch, the term "GO-TO-less programming" has become synonymous with structured programming.

Implicit in the structured approach is ease of maintenance. A structured program should be easy to read, with logic structures flowing sequentially from top to bottom. Years of experience using the structured programming technique have demonstrated that it leads to programs which are easier to maintain and more error-free than other programming methods.

5.1.3.1 The structured program constructs

The three logic structures defined by Bohm and Jacopini are sequence, selection, and iteration. They are shown symbolically in Fig. 5.6.

Sequence means that individual statements or blocks of code are executed one after another in the order in which they appear in the program. In Fig. 5.6*a* the process boxes "A" and "B" might represent two COBOL statements, respectively, such as

```
MOVE FLD-A TO FLD-B
COMPUTE FLD-D = 1.5 * FLD-B / FLD-C
```

which are executed sequentially.

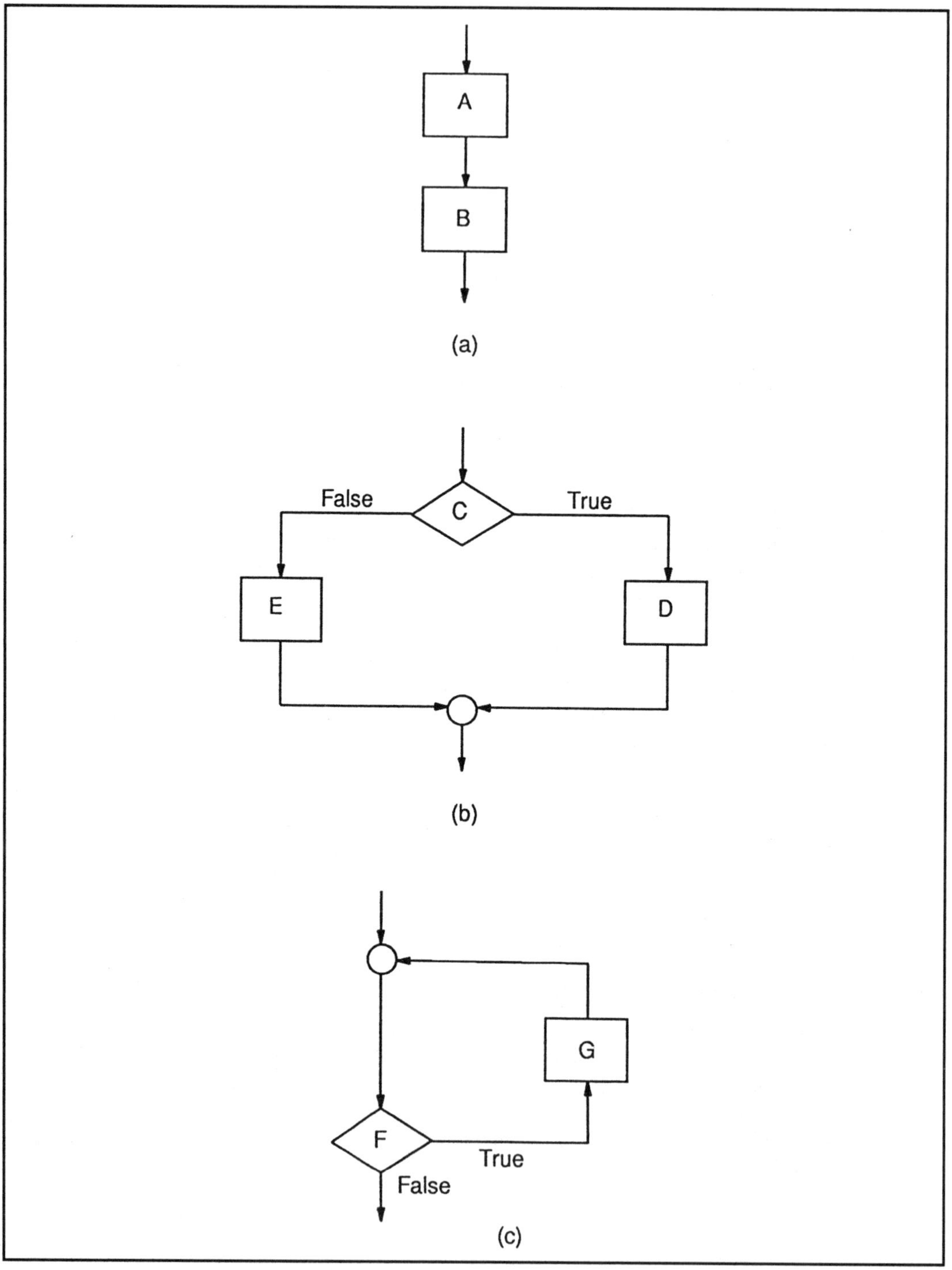

Figure 5.6 The three valid logic structures in a structured program are (*a*) sequence; (*b*) selection; and (*c*) iteration.

Selection is a decision-making construct. A condition is tested with the direction of the flow of control depending on whether the result of the test is true or false. In Fig. 5.6*b*, the condition represented at "C" might be a COBOL IF . . . ELSE statement or a COBOL II EVALUATE statement with the process box "D" being executed for a true condition and process box "E" being executed for a false condition. The following two coding examples illustrate selection.

```
IF ERROR-SWITCH = 'Y'
   MOVE ERROR-MESSAGE TO PRINT-LINE
ELSE
   MOVE OUTPUT-RECORD TO PRINT-LINE.

EVALUATE ERROR-SWITCH
   WHEN 'Y'        MOVE ERROR-MESSAGE TO PRINT-LINE
   WHEN  OTHER     MOVE OUTPUT-RECORD TO PRINT-LINE
END-EVALUATE
```

Iteration is the looping mechanism. Figure 5.6*c* shows process box "G" being executed as long as condition "F" continues to be true. When the condition becomes false, flow of control passes to the next sequential statement or block of code. Note that this is referred to as "Do While". This might be coded in COBOL as

```
PERFORM 0300-PROCESS-PARAGRAPH
   UNTIL END-OF-FILE.
MOVE NUMBER-RECORDS-PROCESSED TO PRINT-LINE.
```

In the preceding COBOL example, the condition is tested before paragraph 0300-PROCESS-PARAGRAPH is entered, and the paragraph continues to be repeatedly executed while we are not at END-OF-FILE (while not END-OF-FILE is true). When we reach END-OF-FILE (not END-OF-FILE is false), control passes to the MOVE statement.

5.1.3.2 GO TO and PERFORM statements

As already mentioned, an ideally structured program should flow downward using combinations of the three logic constructs. As such, branches should be restricted. The COBOL GO TO statement, which is a nonreturning branch to another procedure, is considered by many to be the epitome of poorly structured programming. Excessive branching makes a program difficult to read, forcing you to flip back and forth from procedure to procedure, often pages apart in the source listing, in order to follow the logic flow. Also, excessive branching degrades execution performance; sequential execution is more efficient (we will discuss instruction fetching and execution in Sec. 8.3).

An additional problem with unrestricted use of GO TOs is that it is possible for a poorly written program to inadvertently cause execution to fall into an area of code which was not intended at that point in program flow. Debugging such a program can become a nightmare because control flow may continue to drop through procedures until another GO TO transfers control to a totally different portion of code way out in left field. Needless time may be wasted trying to discover how execution got to that point.

I have found that many installations, conscious of the desirability of the structured approach, permit COBOL programmers to code GO TO only as a means of transferring control to an exit paragraph. This removes some of the danger inherent in wild branches into never-never land caused by unwisely coded GO TOs, and may be quite useful when done properly. In the following example, an error condition found in FLD-A causes processing of lines 000630 through 000690 to be bypassed. The exit at line 000710 will cause a return to the PERFORM at line 000400. Because the PERFORM 0300-PROCESS-PARAGRAPH is performed THRU 0300-PROCESS-PARAGRAPH-EXIT, and the only GO TO is to the exit, control returns to the PERFORM statement which invoked the procedure. Assuming that there is no other statement which invokes 0300-PROCESS-PARAGRAPH, such as PERFORM 0300-PROCESS-PARAGRAPH or GO TO 0300-PROCESS-PARAGRAPH, the danger of accidentally falling into the paragraphs following line 000710 is eliminated.

```
000400      PERFORM 0300-PROCESS-PARAGRAPH
000410          THRU 0300-PROCESS-PARAGRAPH-EXIT
000420              UNTIL END-OF-FILE OR PROCESS-ERROR.
                        .
                        .
                        .
000500 0300-PROCESS-PARAGRAPH.
                        .
                        .
                        .
000600      IF FLD-A NOT NUMERIC
000610          MOVE 'Y' TO PROCESS-ERROR-SWITCH
000620          GO TO 0300-PROCESS-PARAGRAPH-EXIT.
000630      MOVE FLD-A TO . . .
                        .
                        .
                        .
000680      READ IN-FILE
000690           AT END MOVE 'Y' TO EOF-SWITCH.
000700 0300-PROCESS-PARAGRAPH-EXIT.
000710      EXIT.
```

Note that while many installations restrict GO TOs, there is seldom any constraint on PERFORM statements. In fact, PERFORM is often commended as being integral and desirable in modular programming. Although the PERFORM . . . UNTIL has a legitimate place in creating the iterative structure, excessive and indiscriminate PERFORMs of other procedures in the program have the same drawbacks as any other branching; they make the program hard to read and they adversely affect program efficiency. I find it absurd that many COBOL programmers will PERFORM a paragraph which contains a single statement, such as a WRITE, at one or two places in the PROCEDURE DIVISION, claiming that this increases modularity and makes it a more structured program. Let reason and common sense prevail when coding a COBOL program. Remember the goals of structured programming: ease of maintenance and fewer errors as well as improved execution efficiency.

COBOL II has a feature which makes it easier to write structured programs. The in-line PERFORM is ideal since it permits a loop to be coded in-line with no need to branch to an out-of-line procedure.

5.1.3.3 The NEXT SENTENCE solution

For a shop that totally forbids GO TO statements, including GO TO EXIT paragraphs, the NEXT SENTENCE clause can enable you to bypass code in a paragraph and get to an exit point. This is particularly easy to do in COBOL II.

A sentence in COBOL is defined as a statement or series of statements terminated by a period. When NEXT SENTENCE is executed, control is transferred to whatever follows the first period encountered. Since the only period which is required in a COBOL II paragraph is at the very end of the paragraph, NEXT SENTENCE can effectively cause a branch to the following paragraph, which can be the exit point of the procedure. Consider the following example, which is a modification of the example given in Sec. 5.1.3.2:

```
000400      PERFORM 0300-PROCESS-PARAGRAPH
000410          THRU 0300-PROCESS-PARAGRAPH-EXIT
000420              UNTIL END-OF-FILE OR PROCESS-ERROR
                                .
                                .
                                .
000500 0300-PROCESS-PARAGRAPH.
                                .
                                .
                                .
000600      IF FLD-A NOT NUMERIC
000610          MOVE 'Y' TO PROCESS-ERROR-SWITCH
000620      END-IF
000630      IF PROCESS-ERROR
000640          NEXT SENTENCE
000650      END-IF
000660      MOVE FLD-A TO . . .
                                .
                                .
                                .
```

```
000720       READ IN-FILE
000730           AT END MOVE 'Y' TO EOF-SWITCH
000740       END-READ.
000750 0300-PROCESS-PARAGRAPH-EXIT.
000760       EXIT.
```

Notice that the only period in paragraph 0300-PROCESS-PARAGRAPH is at the very end (at line 000740). The END-IF at line 000650 in combination with the NEXT SENTENCE at line 000640 transfers control to the EXIT statement at line 000760, and control then returns to the PERFORM at line 000400.

Be cautious if you use this technique. Remember to code a period only at the end of a paragraph; use explicit scope terminators (e.g., END-IF) rather than periods to terminate conditional statements or you may change the processing logic.

5.2 TESTING THE COBOL PROGRAM

When I first learned COBOL in school, instructors placed importance on flowcharting program logic. After figuring out the processing logic I would carefully fill in COBOL coding sheets, review my code, and only then key in the program at the terminal. As I became more experienced, I followed the example of my colleagues and switched to the "quick-and-dirty" approach; for a relatively simple program or a one-shot job, the program was thought out in my head and keyed in directly at the terminal. Perhaps an existing COBOL program was copied and modified for the present purposes. Sometimes the time savings in not going through the formal flowcharting and pencil-and-paper coding process was lost in debugging the program and correcting mistakes which may have been easily caught if everything had been carefully worked out before touching the keyboard. I am older and wiser now, and although I may not need to write every bit of code on paper first, I certainly heed the wisdom of planning ahead.

5.2.1 Think Before Coding

As discussed at the beginning of this chapter, it is important to go through a design process. When program stubs are utilized, the higher levels of the program can be coded and tested before completing the code associated with the stubs. This helps to uncover errors in the early stages of program development.

You should be aware of what conditions need to be checked during program processing. Do fields on input records need to be examined for numeric values? Must file status be checked? Is it necessary to DISPLAY any messages? Many of the techniques discussed in Chap. 4 can be utilized for this testing.

Desk-checking and walk-throughs should be a part of the overall test process. Desk-checking refers to the process of stepping through the program on paper. Do this before keying it in and attempting to compile and execute it. Think through the logic flow and examine every possible path to be sure that it is correct. Look for spelling errors.

Walk-throughs are verbal reviews of the program. In a walk-through, you may explain the program logic to other members of the project team. This sharing may raise questions and uncover flaws in the program design or program code which you overlooked. Again, it is better to fix errors before submitting the program for compilation and execution. A program which does not pass the desk-checking or walk-through processes will certainly not make it through the computer with the correct results.

5.2.2 Inspecting the Source Code with Software Tools

Once problems discovered in desk-checking and walk-throughs have been corrected, the program may be keyed in, compiled, and optionally run through various software tools designed to inspect source code for quality. An example of one such tool is INSPECTOR from Language Technology, Inc. This tool examines OS/VS or COBOL II source code for such things as complexity, structure, potential problems such as recursion, the number of specific verbs such as GO TOs and PERFORMS, the number of comment lines, and the size of the program. It generates reports which you can use to improve the program.

A companion to INSPECTOR is PINPOINT, also from Language Technology, Inc. This product actually zeros in on potential problems, generating in-line comments and numerous cross-reference tables.

INSPECTOR and PINPOINT should not be used unless the program has been compiled successfully. This is because these products look for compiler errors and may terminate processing if any are found.

5.2.3 Compiling the Program

The first time compilation is attempted, there may be errors which must be corrected before the compiler can create an object module. Some of these may simply be the result of misspellings, while others may represent logic errors. The COBOL compiler gives many diagnostic messages identifying these errors, varying from warnings to extremely serious errors. As discussed in Sec. 1.6, you should review all compiler diagnostic messages and make the appropriate changes to the source code.

In order to reduce overhead when submitting a program to the compiler the first time, the compiler can be requested to perform a syntax check on the source module without attempting to generate an object module. In OS/VS COBOL this is done by using either the SYNTAX or CSYNTAX compiler option. SYNTAX causes the compiler to check the code for syntax errors without any attempt to generate object code. CSYNTAX requests syntax checking with conditional generation of object code. If no errors exceed the C level, an object module is created. If one or more errors are at E level or higher, no object code is generated.

In COBOL II, the NOCOMPILE option with or without parameters can be chosen. NOCOMPILE with no parameters causes the compiler to syntax check the source code only, with no generation of object code. NOCOMPILE(W), NOCOMPILE(E), or NOCOMPILE(S) requests syntax checking with conditional generation of object code. If the compiler finds an error of the level specified in parentheses or higher, it does not generate object code.

5.2.4 Executing with Test Data

Once the program has passed scrutiny in the previously mentioned steps and has been successfully compiled, it is time to execute the program using a test input file. The test data may have been prepared along with development of the application specifications; if not, it must be prepared now. The test file should include all types of input which may conceivably be found in "live" production data. It is important to include valid data as well as data which are invalid but plausible and even wildly improbable. The entire range of input which the program is designed to handle should be part of the test file. For example, if a numeric field having values between 10 and 1000 is to be processed, be sure to include those values as well as values in between in the test data.

You should be aware of what results to expect when the test data are processed. Executing the program with this test file and comparing the output with the expected results will help ensure that the program is producing correct output and is handling error conditions properly.

5.3 DEBUGGING THE COBOL PROGRAM

It is unfortunate but true that, as Robert Burns wrote, "the best laid schemes o' mice and men gang aft a-gley." Thus unexpected program logic errors or failures caused by insufficient validation of input data may be found during testing. The problems must be diagnosed and removed before the program is ready for production.

Program errors generally fall into three categories: successful program termination with incorrect output, abnormal termination with correct output up to the point where the program terminated, and abnormal program termination with incorrect program output.

5.3.1 Incorrect Output

The first category is sometimes the most difficult to debug because there may be no messages from COBOL or the system to indicate that anything is wrong. I mentioned earlier an example where bad program output went unnoticed until it was too late (Sec. 1.1). Hopefully these types of errors will be caught during testing before the program is moved to production. If, as discussed in Sec. 5.2.4, the program is executed with carefully formulated test data and the expected results are compared with the actual output, these errors will be discovered and eliminated. To debug when errors are found, many of the techniques presented in Chap. 4 may be used. DISPLAY statements, tracing facilities, file status checks, alternate debugging code, or debugging procedures may be added to the program, which can then be recompiled and retested. Also, as discussed in Chap. 2, the program may be recompiled and then executed using various compiler options such as COUNT (OS/VS COBOL) or SSRANGE (COBOL II).

5.3.2 Basic ABEND Debugging Steps

The errors resulting in abnormal program termination may yield to techniques presented in the last section. Here is a suggested sequence of steps for solving ABENDs:

1. Determine the nature and location of the ABEND.
   - Scan the job log for a completion code. Check appropriate documentation to learn the meaning of this code.
   - Determine which step ABENDed.
   - See if you had a clean compile and link. Be sure to examine all messages from the compiler and linkage-editor.
   - Look for system or COBOL messages in the job log.
2. Review your actions.
   - Were you modifying program statements or logic? Did you execute the wrong code (debugging statements, for example)?
   - Did you use the wrong input data set?
3. Examine your program output.
   - Is it complete?
   - Does it match expected results?
   - Does it seem plausible (for example, is it correct for an employee to earn a negative salary)?
4. Review the output from any COBOL debugging aids which were in effect.
   - File status codes.
   - DISPLAY, EXHIBIT, or READY TRACE statements in OS/VS COBOL.
   - DISPLAY statements in COBOL II.
   - Output from interactive debuggers (TESTCOB in OS/VS COBOL or COBTEST in COBOL II).
   - Compiler options which were in effect (COUNT, FLOW, STATE, or SYMDMP in OS/VS COBOL, and FDUMP or SSRANGE in COBOL II).
5. Check to see if the JCL is correct.
   - Did you compile using the correct version of COBOL?
   - Are you executing the intended program?
   - Are you using the correct input data sets?
   - Were expected data sets passed from previous steps?
   - Is the JOBLIB/STEPLIB correct?

6. If the problem has not yet been resolved, analyze the dump.
   - Look at the SYMDMP output in OS/VS COBOL or the FDUMP output in COBOL II (see Chap. 6 for a discussion of COBOL formatted dumps).
   - Look at the SYMPTOM dump in the job log (see Chap. 10).
   - If necessary, examine the system dump (see Chap. 10).

5.3.3 Solving a COBOL ABEND

Let us now put our knowledge to work. We will follow the procedure outlined in the last section to solve a COBOL ABEND.

A COBOL program reads input data consisting of student names and grades. It produces a report giving the grade average for a group of students, the number of students failing (having a grade below 65), and the name and grade of the student with the lowest grade. It also prints a notice to each student who has gotten a failing grade.

The output from the job is shown in Fig. 5.7. It includes JCL, relevant portions of the job log and compiler output, any program output which was generated, and any execution-time dump output. Where necessary, the numbers of the debugging steps we will follow are printed and circled in the appropriate places in the figure for easy reference.

1. Determine the nature and location of the ABEND.
   a. The completion code USER =1037 occurred on the GO step of the procedure executed in step S1 of the JCL.
   b. The previous compile step returned an 0004 condition code.
   c. Looking for messages from the compiler reveals a Warning level diagnostic message at the beginning of the compiler output indicating that there was a compiler option conflict: the OFFSET option was discarded in favor of the LIST option requested in the JCL; the COBOL II Release 2 compiler was run in this job. Otherwise, the compile was satisfactory.
   d. The link-edit step returned a 0000 condition code.
   e. The COBOL II run-time message IGZ037I FLOW OF CONTROL IN PROGRAM 'DMPCB22' IS PROCEEDING BEYOND THE LAST LINE OF THE PROGRAM. THE PROGRAM IS TERMINATED is found, together with a symptom dump.
2. Review your actions.
   a. This was the first time the program was put through the compile, link, and go procedure.
   b. The correct input data set was used.
3. Examine your program output.
   a. The program contains a DISPLAY statement 'PROGRAM BEGINNING' at line 000099 and another DISPLAY statement 'PROGRAM ENDING' at line 00113.
   b. There is a series of WRITE statements at lines 000136, 000140, 000143, and 000151.

```
//S1       EXEC COB2UCLG,PARM.COB2='XREF,LIST,OPTIMIZE,FDUMP',              00010000
//              REGION=512K                                                 00010100
//***********************************************************              00011000
//*  SOURCE CODE IS COBOL II                                *              00020000
//***********************************************************              00021000
//COB2.SYSIN    DD DSN=MY.PROGLIB.COBOL(DMPCB22),DISP=SHR                  00030004
//LKED.SYSLIB DD DSN=SYS1.COB2LIB,DISP=SHR                                 00033000
//GO.REPTFLE  DD SYSOUT=A                                                  00050001
//GO.NOTFLE   DD SYSOUT=A                                                  00050103
//GO.STUDFLE  DD *                                                         00051001
/*                                                                         00054000
//GO.SYSDBOUT DD SYSOUT=A                                                  00055000
//SYSUDUMP    DD SYSOUT=A                                                  00070000
//SYSOUT      DD SYSOUT=A                                                  00070200
                                        .
                                        .
                                        .
IEF142I DMPCB22 COB2 S1 - STEP WAS EXECUTED - COND CODE 0004  <------------ 1b
                                        .
                                        .
                                        .
IEF142I DMPCB22 LKED S1 - STEP WAS EXECUTED - COND CODE 0000  <------------ 1d
                                        .
                                        .
                                        .
 IGZ037I FLOW OF CONTROL IN PROGRAM 'DMPCB22' IS PROCEEDING BEYOND THE
         LAST LINE OF THE PROGRAM.  THE PROGRAM IS TERMINATED.
IEA995I SYMPTOM DUMP OUTPUT
  USER COMPLETION CODE=1037
 TIME=13.52.18  SEQ=00382  CPU=0000  ASID=0069
 PSW AT TIME OF ERROR  078D1000   00020FD2  ILC 2  INTC 0D                 <-- 1e
   ACTIVE LOAD MODULE=GO          ADDRESS=0000A1D8  OFFSET=00016DFA
   DATA AT PSW  00020FCC - 00181610  0A0D47F0  C0F84820
   GPR  0-3  80000000  8000040D  0000040D  00025590
   GPR  4-7  00013F10  0001BB74  4000A528  0000A2FC
   GPR  8-11 0001EBF4  00000090  0001BB74  0000A4D8
   GPR 12-15 50020EEA  000240B0  50010000  00020EB8
 END OF SYMPTOM DUMP
                                        .
                                        .
                                        .
IEF472I DMPCB22 GO S1 - COMPLETION CODE - SYSTEM=000 USER=1037 REASON=00000000 <-- 1a
                                        .
                                        .
                                        .
```

Figure 5.7 A COBOL program which ABENDed. Shown are portions of the JCL, job log, compiler listings, program output, and dump output. (*Continued*)

   c. The only output produced was from the DISPLAY statement at line 000099. Thus program output is incomplete.

4. Review the output from any COBOL debugging aids which were in effect.
   a. As mentioned in step 3*a,* the DISPLAY statement at the beginning of the program was executed, but the one at the logical end of the program was not.
   b. The FDUMP compiler option was requested.
   c. Although we will look more closely at the FDUMP option in Chap. 6, we can certainly see that there is a significant message at the beginning of the FDUMP output: ABEND ADDRESS IS OUTSIDE OF MAINLINE COBOL CODE. This agrees with the IGZ message we saw in step 1*e.* Also, the offset of the 'START OF THE INSTRUCTION SEQUENCE FOR THE CURRENT CALL' is 000005DC.
   d. The LIST compiler option was in effect. We find that the Assembler instruction at offset 000005DC was generated by the WRITE verb at line 000151 in the source code.

```
PP 5668-958 REL. 2.0, 09/08/86, IBM VS COBOL II.                         DATE 05/14/90  TIME 13.51.56   PAGE     1

        IGYOS4013-I    AN OPTIONS PARAMETER LIST WAS FOUND AS INPUT TO THE COMPILER AND WAS PROCESSED.

(1c) -> IGYOS4020-W    OFFSET   OPTION DISCARDED DUE TO OPTION CONFLICT RESOLUTION. LIST     OPTION FROM COMPILER INPUT PARMLIST
                       TAKES PRECEDENCE.


PP 5668-958 REL. 2.0, 09/08/86, IBM VS COBOL II.                         DATE 05/14/90  TIME 13.51.56   PAGE     2
*OPTIONS IN EFFECT*
    ADV
    APOST
    BUFSIZE(4096)
  NOCOMPILE(S)
    DATA(31)
  NODECK
  NODUMP
  NODYNAM
  NOFASTSRT
    FDUMP <---------------------- (4b)
    FLAG(I)
  NOLIB
    LINECOUNT(60)
    LIST <----------------------- (4d)
    MAP
  NONUMBER
    OBJECT
  NOOFFSET
    OPTIMIZE
    OUTDD(SYSOUT  )
  NOPFDSGN
  NORENT
  NORESIDENT
  NOSEQUENCE
    SIZE(MAX)
    SOURCE
    SPACE(1)
  NOSSRANGE
  NOTERM
  NOTEST
  NOTRUNC
  NOVBREF
  NOWORD
    XREF <----------------------- (4f)
    ZWB
```

Figure 5.7 *(Continued)*

e. Going to line 000151 in the source code shows that this is the last statement in the last paragraph, 0300-MESSAGE, in the PROCEDURE DIVISION. So far we know that we ABENDed because the flow of control dropped through the bottom of the program. The question now is, how did execution reach this last statement in the program?

f. The XREF compiler option was in effect. Looking at the cross-reference of procedure names shows that the last program paragraph, 0300-MESSAGE, is referenced by a GO TO at line 125.

g. Line 125 is indeed GO TO 0300-MESSAGE. It is executed when the condition tested by the IF statement at line 000124 is true. A STUDENT-GRADE of less than +65 is supposed to cause a branch to 0300-MESSAGE, which prints a message to the student. We have found a logic error in the program. Probably a PERFORM was intended instead of a GO TO; after

```
PP 5668-958 REL. 2.0, 09/08/86, IBM VS COBOL II.                    DATE 05/14/90  TIME 13.51.56   PAGE     3

  000001         IDENTIFICATION DIVISION.
  000002         PROGRAM-ID.    DMPCB22.
  000003         AUTHOR.        ALAN FRIEND.
  000004         DATE-WRITTEN. 01/05/90
  000005         DATE-COMPILED. 05/14/90.

  000007         ENVIRONMENT DIVISION.
  000008         CONFIGURATION SECTION.
  000009         INPUT-OUTPUT SECTION.
  000010         FILE-CONTROL.
  000011             SELECT  STUDENT-FILE    ASSIGN  TO  STUDFLE.
  000012             SELECT  REPORT-FILE     ASSIGN  TO  REPTFLE.
  000013             SELECT  NOTICE-FILE     ASSIGN  TO  NOTFLE.
  000014         DATA DIVISION.
  000015         FILE SECTION.
  000016         FD  STUDENT-FILE
  000017             BLOCK CONTAINS  0  RECORDS
  000018             LABEL RECORDS ARE OMITTED
  000019             RECORDING MODE IS F
  000020             RECORD CONTAINS  80 CHARACTERS
  000021             DATA RECORD IS STUDENT-RECORD.
  000022         01  STUDENT-RECORD.
  000023             05  STUDENT-NAME                  PIC X(20).
  000024             05  STUDENT-GRADE                 PIC 999.
  000025             05  FILLER                        PIC X(57).
  000026         FD  REPORT-FILE
  000027             BLOCK CONTAINS  0  RECORDS
  000028             LABEL RECORDS ARE OMITTED
  000029             RECORDING MODE IS F
  000030             RECORD CONTAINS 133 CHARACTERS
  000031             DATA RECORD IS PRINT-RECORD.
  000032         01  PRINT-RECORD                      PIC  X(133).
  000033         FD  NOTICE-FILE
  000034             BLOCK CONTAINS  0  RECORDS
  000035             LABEL RECORDS ARE OMITTED
  000036             RECORDING MODE IS F
  000037             RECORD CONTAINS 133 CHARACTERS
  000038             DATA RECORD IS PRINT-RECORD.
  000039         01  NOTICE-RECORD                     PIC  X(133).
```

Figure 5.7 *(Continued)*

paragraph 0300-MESSAGE executed control would return to the statement at line 000127 so processing could continue with a READ of the next record. The problem is solved!

5.4 SUMMARY

Carefully designing and testing a whole application system as well as individual programs pays great dividends in terms of fewer maintenance problems and less risk of future ABENDs.

A number of design techniques and tools make it easier for members of the project team to see the overall project requirements as well as its specific subtasks clearly. One design procedure currently in vogue is known as structured analysis. It is used to build an overall structured specification for a system, encompassing both its high- and low-level aspects.

Some other widely used tools commonly utilized at the lower levels for application program design include hierarchy charts, HIPO diagrams, flowcharts, Nassi-Schneiderman charts, and pseudocode.

Top-down development of the system or the individual program helps break its construction and testing into manageable pieces. First the overall, top-level portion can be written and tested, followed by each of the lower levels. Thus it is not necessary to wait for the entire application to be finished before

```
PP 5668-958 REL. 2.0, 09/08/86, IBM VS COBOL II.              DMPCB22   DATE 05/14/90  TIME 13.51.56   PAGE    4

          WORKING-STORAGE SECTION.
          01  FILLER                              PIC X(32)
                                  VALUE 'DMPCB22 WORKING-STORAGE BEGINS'.
          01  ACCUMULATORS                        COMP-3.
              10  TOT-GRADE                       PIC S9(7)  VALUE +0.
              10  AVERAGE-GRADE                   PIC S9(03)V99.
              10  NUMBER-STUDENTS                 PIC S9(03) VALUE +0.
              10  NUMBER-FAILING                  PIC S9(03) VALUE +0.
          01  WORK-AREAS.
              05  SAVE-STUDENT-NAME               PIC X(20).
              05  SAVE-STUDENT-GRADE              PIC S9(03)  COMP-3
                                                          VALUE +101.
          01  SWITCHES.
              05  SW-EOF                          PIC X      VALUE 'N'.

                  88  NO-MORE-RECORDS                        VALUE 'Y'.
          01  PRINT-LINES.
              05  DETAIL-LINE.
                  10  FILLER                       PIC X(11)
                                                         VALUE SPACES.
                  10  PRINT-NAME                   PIC X(20).
                  10  FILLER                       PIC X(11)
                                                         VALUE SPACES.
                  10  PRINT-GRADE                  PIC Z99B(4).
                  10  PRINT-MESSAGE                PIC X(64)
                                                         VALUE SPACES.
              05  AVERAGE-GRADE-LINE.
                  10  FILLER                       PIC X(11)
                                                         VALUE SPACES.
                  10  FILLER                       PIC X(24)
                                        VALUE 'FINAL STUDENT AVERAGE = '.
                  10  PRINT-AVERAGE-GRADE          PIC Z99.99.
                  10  FILLER                       PIC X(44)
                                                         VALUE SPACES.
              05  LOWEST-GRADE-LINE.
                  10  FILLER                       PIC X(11)
                                                         VALUE SPACES.
                  10  FILLER                       PIC X(23)
                                        VALUE 'LOWEST STUDENT GRADE = '.
                  10  PRINT-LOWEST-GRADE           PIC Z99.99.
                  10  FILLER                       PIC X(02)
                                                         VALUE SPACES.
                  10  FILLER                       PIC X(16)
                                        VALUE 'STUDENT NAME IS '.
                  10  PRINT-LOWEST-NAME            PIC X(27).
              05  NUMBER-FAILING-LINE.
                  10  FILLER                       PIC X(11)
                                                         VALUE SPACES.
                  10  FILLER                       PIC X(29)
                                VALUE 'NUMBER OF FAILING STUDENTS = '.
                  10  PRINT-NUMBER-FAILING         PIC ZZ9.
                  10  FILLER                       PIC X(39)
                                                         VALUE SPACES.
          01  FILLER                              PIC X(32)
                                  VALUE 'DMPCB22 WORKING-STORAGE ENDS  '.
```

Figure 5.7 *(Continued)*

verifying the correctness of the higher levels. When using this approach to writing a COBOL program, the lower levels may simply be "stubs" consisting of DISPLAY statements; these DISPLAYs can be placeholders for future code, giving messages indicating that specific points in the program have been reached.

Many years of experience using the technique of structured programming have demonstrated that it leads to programs which are easier to maintain and more error-free than those produced by other programming methods.

A truly structured program is built of only three types of logic structures: sequence, selection, and iteration. They can be combined in an endless variety of ways.

A structured program should be easy to read, and as such it avoids branching as much as possible. This becomes a dilemma in COBOL programming

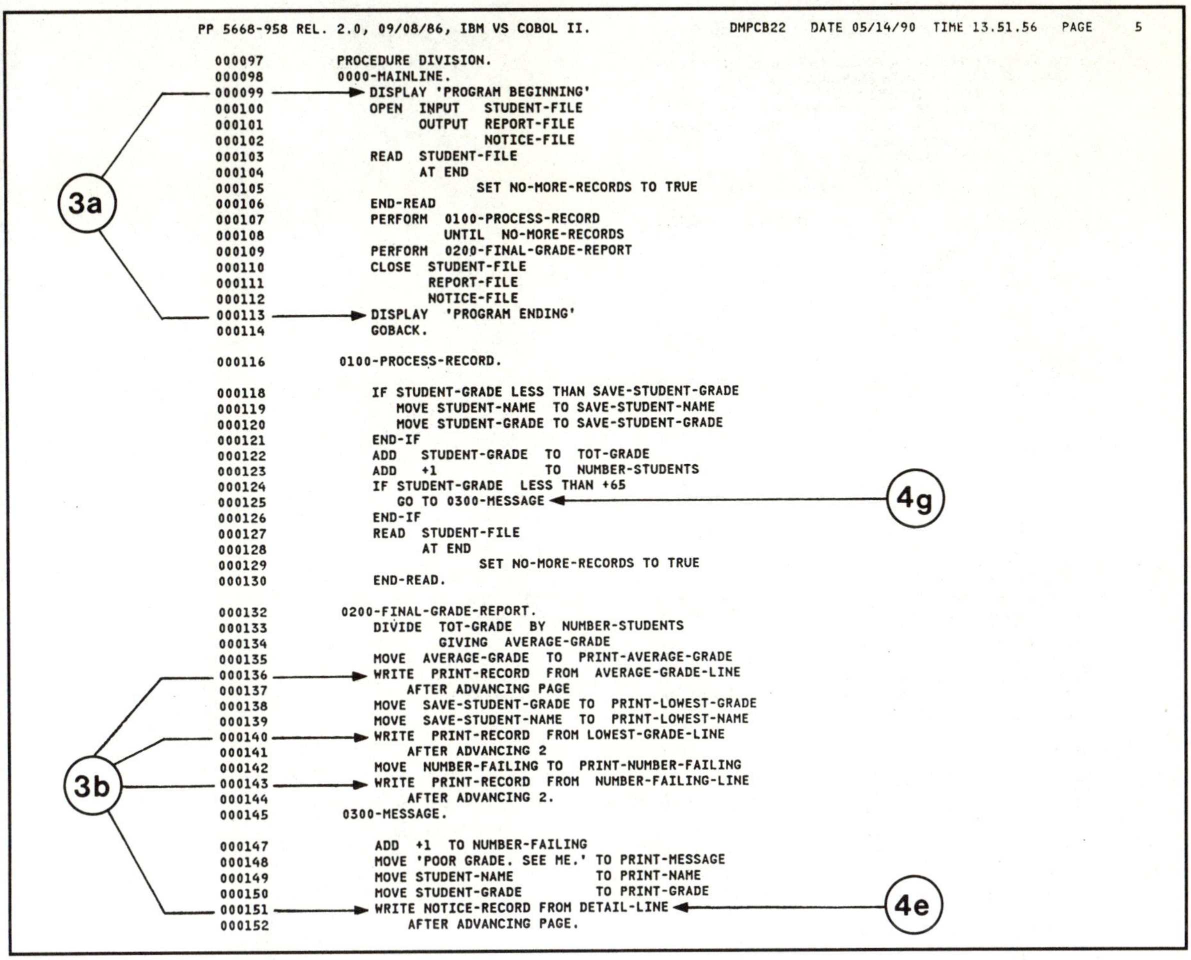

```
PP 5668-958 REL. 2.0, 09/08/86, IBM VS COBOL II.          DMPCB22   DATE 05/14/90   TIME 13.51.56   PAGE   5

       PROCEDURE DIVISION.
       0000-MAINLINE.
           DISPLAY 'PROGRAM BEGINNING'
           OPEN  INPUT   STUDENT-FILE
                 OUTPUT  REPORT-FILE
                         NOTICE-FILE
           READ  STUDENT-FILE
                 AT END
                        SET NO-MORE-RECORDS TO TRUE
           END-READ
           PERFORM  0100-PROCESS-RECORD
                    UNTIL  NO-MORE-RECORDS
           PERFORM  0200-FINAL-GRADE-REPORT
           CLOSE  STUDENT-FILE
                  REPORT-FILE
                  NOTICE-FILE
           DISPLAY  'PROGRAM ENDING'
           GOBACK.

       0100-PROCESS-RECORD.

           IF STUDENT-GRADE LESS THAN SAVE-STUDENT-GRADE
              MOVE STUDENT-NAME  TO SAVE-STUDENT-NAME
              MOVE STUDENT-GRADE TO SAVE-STUDENT-GRADE
           END-IF
           ADD   STUDENT-GRADE  TO  TOT-GRADE
           ADD   +1             TO  NUMBER-STUDENTS
           IF STUDENT-GRADE  LESS THAN +65
              GO TO 0300-MESSAGE
           END-IF
           READ  STUDENT-FILE
                 AT END
                        SET NO-MORE-RECORDS TO TRUE
           END-READ.

       0200-FINAL-GRADE-REPORT.
           DIVIDE  TOT-GRADE  BY  NUMBER-STUDENTS
                   GIVING  AVERAGE-GRADE
           MOVE  AVERAGE-GRADE  TO  PRINT-AVERAGE-GRADE
           WRITE  PRINT-RECORD  FROM  AVERAGE-GRADE-LINE
               AFTER ADVANCING PAGE
           MOVE  SAVE-STUDENT-GRADE TO  PRINT-LOWEST-GRADE
           MOVE  SAVE-STUDENT-NAME  TO  PRINT-LOWEST-NAME
           WRITE  PRINT-RECORD  FROM LOWEST-GRADE-LINE
               AFTER ADVANCING 2
           MOVE  NUMBER-FAILING TO  PRINT-NUMBER-FAILING
           WRITE  PRINT-RECORD  FROM  NUMBER-FAILING-LINE
               AFTER ADVANCING 2.
       0300-MESSAGE.

           ADD  +1  TO NUMBER-FAILING
           MOVE 'POOR GRADE. SEE ME.' TO PRINT-MESSAGE
           MOVE STUDENT-NAME          TO PRINT-NAME
           MOVE STUDENT-GRADE         TO PRINT-GRADE
           WRITE NOTICE-RECORD FROM DETAIL-LINE
               AFTER ADVANCING PAGE.
```


Figure 5.7 *(Continued)*

because many COBOL programmers equate branching with the use of the GO TO statement and instead make overliberal use of PERFORMs. Although the PERFORM may be less likely to cause control to fall through the bottom of the program than indiscriminate use of GO TOs, excessive PERFORM statements make a program difficult to read and may degrade execution efficiency. Some shops permit coding GO TOs to exit paragraphs but put no restrictions at all on PERFORM statements. Sequential instruction execution is easier to do in COBOL II because of the in-line PERFORM statement.

A program cannot be considered ready for production until it has gone through extensive testing. This requires that the programmer be familiar with the program design and the execution-time conditions that may be encountered. All factors which may compromise successful completion of program execution should be tested for when coding the program.

```
PP 5668-958 REL. 2.0, 09/08/86, IBM VS COBOL II.                DMPCB22   DATE 05/14/90  TIME 13.51.56   PAGE     7

THE LETTER PRECEDING A PROCEDURE-NAME REFERENCE INDICATES THE CONTEXT IN WHICH THE PROCEDURE-NAME IS USED.
THESE LETTERS AND THEIR MEANINGS ARE:
    A = ALTER (PROCEDURE-NAME)
    D = GO TO (PROCEDURE-NAME) DEPENDING ON
    E = END OF RANGE OF (PERFORM) THRU (PROCEDURE-NAME)
    G = GO TO (PROCEDURE-NAME)
    P = PERFORM (PROCEDURE-NAME)
    T = (ALTER) TO PROCEED TO (PROCEDURE-NAME)
    U = USE FOR DEBUGGING (PROCEDURE-NAME)

 DEFINED   CROSS-REFERENCE OF PROCEDURES   REFERENCES

     98     DUMMY-SECTION
     98    0000-MAINLINE
    116    0100-PROCESS-RECORD. . . . . .  P107
    132    0200-FINAL-GRADE-REPORT. . . .  P109
    145    0300-MESSAGE . . . . . . . . .  G125  <---- (4f)
                                                  .
                                                  .
                                                  .

000145  *0300-MESSAGE
                                                  .
                                                  .
                                                  .
(4d)
000151  WRITE
    0005AA  5820 D138            L    2,312(0,13)             BLF=2
    0005AE  D270 2000 9050       MVC  0(113,2),80(9)                              DETAIL-LINERD
    0005B4  D213 2071 C000       MVC  113(20,2),0(12)                             SYSLIT AT +0D+113
    0005BA  5840 D184            L    4,388(0,13)             NOTICE-FILE
    0005BE  9200 40B3            MVI  179(4),X'00'            FCB=3
    0005C2  9212 40F9            MVI  249(4),X'12'            FCB=3
    0005C6  92A8 40F8            MVI  248(4),X'A8'            FCB=3
    0005CA  0530                 BALR 3,0
    0005CC  5030 D13C            ST   3,316(0,13)             TGT FDMP/TEST-INFO. AREA +0
    0005D0  5830 D05C            L    3,92(0,13)              TGTFIXD+92
    0005D4  58F0 308C            L    15,140(0,3)             V(IGZCSPA )
    0005D8  05EF                 BALR 14,15
    0005DA  0540                 BALR 4,0
    0005DC  5040 D13C            ST   4,316(0,13)             TGT FDMP/TEST-INFO. AREA +0
    0005E0  58F0 31CC            L    15,460(0,3)             V(IGZEMSG )
                                                  .
                                                  .
                                                  .
(1c)
PP 5668-958 REL. 2.0, 09/08/86, IBM VS COBOL II.                DMPCB22   DATE 05/14/90  TIME 13.51.56   PAGE    18

LINEID  MESSAGE CODE   MESSAGE TEXT ( IMBEDDED MESSAGES MAY BE IDENTIFIED BY THE <*> PRECEDING THE MESSAGE CODE )

        IGYDS0015-I    DIAGNOSTIC MESSAGES WERE ISSUED DURING PROCESSING OF COMPILER OPTIONS. THESE MESSAGES ARE LOCATED AT THE
                       BEGINNING OF THE LISTING.

TOTAL MESSAGES     INFORMATIONAL     WARNING     ERROR     SEVERE     TERMINATING

        3                2              1
                                                  .
                                                  .
                                                  .

PROGRAM BEGINNING  <---- (3c), (4a)
                                                  .
                                                  .
                                                  .

               --- VS COBOL II FORMATTED DUMP AT ABEND ---

                          PROGRAM      DMPCB22

COMPLETION CODE = U1037       PSW AT ABEND = 078D100000020FD2

ABEND ADDRESS IS OUTSIDE OF MAINLINE COBOL CODE  <----
OPTIMIZATION IN EFFECT FOR THIS PROGRAM                      (4c)
RELATIVE ADDR. OF START OF INSTRUCTION SEQUENCE FOR CURRENT CALL: 000005DC  <----
                                                  .
                                                  .
                                                  .
```

Figure 5.7 *(Continued)*

The testing process includes desk-checking and walk-throughs. Software tools, such as INSPECTOR and PINPOINT, may help evaluate the quality of the code, pointing out areas where the potential for problems exists. It is also important to check all compiler diagnostic messages, even warning-level messages, to be sure that the program is free of errors. To reduce system overhead, the program can be run through the COBOL compiler using the option that checks syntax only, without generating object code.

Once the program appears to be error-free, it should be executed using carefully formulated input files. The data should mimic production data in order to test all conditions which may be encountered when the program goes "live."

If the program results are not correct, the program must be debugged. One of the hardest types of problems to fix is the case where the program terminates successfully but produces erroneous output. This is where extensive testing with carefully designed input data is crucial. If the actual program output does not match the expected output, it may be necessary to recompile and reexecute after adding COBOL debugging features (as described in Chap. 4) or requesting various compiler options (see Chap. 2) in order to locate the trouble spots.

If an ABEND occurs, the problem may be found by following a step-by-step debugging plan. A suggested sequence of steps is: determine the type and location of the ABEND, review your actions, examine your program output, review the output from any COBOL debugging aids which were in effect, check to be sure the JCL is correct, and if the problem has not yet been resolved, analyze any dumps that were produced.

REVIEW QUESTIONS

1. Name tools which help a programmer to design a program.

2. What is top-down development? Describe the advantages in using this approach.

3. Name the logic constructs which are valid in a structured program. Describe the purpose of each one.

4. Structured programming is sometimes referred to as "GO-TO-less programming."
- **a.** Why is GO TO often considered to be a characteristic of poorly structured programs?
- **b.** What is the role of the COBOL PERFORM statement in structured programming?
- **c.** What are the author's opinions about the use of GO TO and PERFORM in a COBOL program? Evaluate his reasons.

5. Write code to:
- **a.** Execute an in-line loop in a COBOL II program while ERROR-SWITCH = N.
- **b.** Branch to paragraph 0800-PROCESS-TABLE-EXIT, bypassing the rest of the code in the present paragraph. The present paragraph is to be invoked by a PERFORM of the present paragraph THRU 0800-PROCESS-TABLE-EXIT.

6. What are the goals of structured programming? How does branching influence these goals?

7. Describe:

a. Desk-checking

b. Walk-throughs

8. A programmer is reported to have said, "My program is perfect! I desk-checked it, no problems were uncovered in the walk-through, and all compiler errors were removed. Let's save time; we can forget about executing it with test data, and move it right into production." Do you approve? Why?

9. List the steps which the author suggests for debugging a COBOL program.

Part

2

Dump Reading

Chapter

6

COBOL Formatted Dumps

Of all the different types of dumps available to the COBOL programmer, the COBOL formatted dump is one of the least used. Knowing the distaste that so many COBOL programmers have for reading hexadecimal system dumps, it would seem that such a "user-friendly" COBOL dump should be a welcome tool. If it is necessary for you to find the contents of a field defined in a program's storage area, it is easier and quicker to locate it in the COBOL formatted dump than in a system dump because the fields are identified by their COBOL source names, and their contents are given in character and hexadecimal notation. Using the compiler option which provides a COBOL formatted dump will increase the size of the object module, but the effect on execution efficiency is minor. When the OPTIMIZE compiler option is used, the reduction in execution efficiency is insignificant (I recommend using OPTIMIZE for production jobs). Unless there are severe storage constraints, using this debugging aid can be justified when a program is under development and even when it goes into production.

This chapter will discuss in detail OS/VS COBOL and COBOL II formatted dumps, showing how they can be used to solve ABENDs.

6.1 THE OS/VS COBOL FORMATTED DUMP

The SYMDMP compiler option requests a symbolic formatted dump of the DATA DIVISION and selected portions of COBOL's internal data areas if an OS/VS COBOL program ABENDs. In addition, dynamic dumps of specified data names can be requested at any point during execution of the program.

Besides the formatted dump of the DATA DIVISION, the ABEND dump includes a message giving the completion code and number of the statement being executed at the time of the ABEND, and selected portions of the TGT.

A number of DD statements must be included in the JCL in order for SYMDMP to work. Figure 6.1 shows the JCL to invoke SYMDMP when execut-

```
//S1       EXEC COBUCLG,PARM.COB='SYMDMP,SXREF,CLIST'
//**************************************************
//*  SOURCE CODE IS OS/VS COBOL                     *
//**************************************************
//COB.SYSIN    DD DSN=MY.PROGLIB.COBOL(PROG1),DISP=SHR
//COB.SYSUT5   DD UNIT=TSWK,SPACE=(CYL,(1,1),RLSE),
//            DISP=(NEW,PASS)
//GO.CUSTFILE DD DSN=INPUT.PROG1.DATA,DISP=SHR
//GO.PRTFILE   DD SYSOUT=A
//GO.SYMDEBUG     DD DSN=*.COB.SYSUT5,DISP=OLD
//GO.SYSDBOUT DD SYSOUT=A
//GO.SYSDBG    DD *
     PROG1,SYMDEBUG,HEX
     139,WS-CUST-NO-INPUT
     166,ON 1,10,101(HEX),WS-CUST-REC,REC-READ
/*
//SYSOUT        DD SYSOUT=A
//
```

Figure 6.1 JCL for requesting an OS/VS COBOL formatted dump when executing COBUCLG.

ing the COBUCLG procedure. SYSUT5 is required at compile time in order to hold the file that stores the SYMDMP information produced during compilation. The file is passed to GO.SYMDEBUG at execution time. SYMDEBUG is a programmer-assigned name. GO.SYSDBG contains SYMDMP execution-time control statements which you code. They may be coded in-line as shown, or placed in a dataset assigned to SYSDBG. The output from SYMDMP appears on the dataset allocated to GO.SYSDBOUT. You can also specify a SYSDTERM DD statement, which is allocated to the terminal. This will cause dynamic dump output, which is interruptible, to be written to the terminal, while the ABEND output will go to the dataset assigned to SYSDBOUT; the ABEND dump output can then be listed at the terminal after the ABEND has completed.

6.1.1 SYMDMP Control Statements

Two types of control statements are used to determine the type of processing which SYMDMP will do. One is the program-control statement. This is required if an ABEND dump, a dynamic dump, or both are requested. The other is the line-control statement. This is needed only if dynamic dumps are requested. Control statements can begin in any column, but cannot extend beyond column 71. If a control statement needs to be continued to the next line, a nonblank character must be placed in column 72 of the statement being continued.

6.1.1.1 The program-control statement

The format for the program-control statement follows:

```
program-id,ddname [,ENTRY  ] [,HEX  ] [,PDS]
                  [,NOENTRY] [,NOHEX]
```

When selected, the parameters shown in uppercase must be spelled as shown. Parameters in lowercase are names defined by you. Items in brackets are optional. Underlined options are the defaults.

Program-id is always required, and must be the name coded in the IDENTIFICATION DIVISION of the OS/VS COBOL program compiled with the SYMDMP option. It must be the first parameter on the control statement.

DDname is required and must appear after the program-id. The DDname is the execution-time DDname of the file which was passed from the compile-time SYSUT5 DD statement.

The rest of the program-control statement parameters are optional. Commas are not needed to account for them if they are not coded.

The ENTRY option provides a trace of a program name, specified in the program-id parameter, each time the program is entered. The name of the program is displayed when it is entered. This is helpful when several programs are in the same load module. NOENTRY is the IBM default.

HEX specifies the format of DATA DIVISION items for an ABEND dump. HEX will cause level-01 items to be given in hexadecimal notation, with identifiers subordinate to the 01-level to be given in EBCDIC whenever printable. Level-77 items are given in both hexadecimal and EBCDIC notation. If HEX is not specified, 01-level item names are given and the elementary identifiers as well as level-77 items are given in EBCDIC notation wherever printable; if they are unprintable, they are provided in hexadecimal notation. The IBM default is NOHEX.

PDS permits you to indicate that the file associated with the execution-time DDname of the file which was passed from the compile-time SYSUT5 DD statement is a partitioned dataset. SYMDMP then assumes that program-id is a member of the partitioned dataset. This permits a COBOL run unit containing many programs compiled with SYMDMP to specify PDS on their program-control statements so they can all use the same partitioned dataset, with each program-id a unique member in that dataset. Note that the partitioned dataset should not be compressed, and its members should not be altered in any way. This is because the file created at compile time on SYSUT5 contains device-dependent relative block addresses, which makes it unmovable. Attempts to alter the partitioned dataset will cause error messages. If it is necessary to modify a member in the existing partitioned dataset, the program must be recompiled.

You can see in Fig. 6.1, letter "A," how the program-control statement was actually coded on the SYSDBG DD statement for a program which ABENDed. The resulting dump will be examined in Sec. 6.1.2.

6.1.1.2 The line-control statement

The line-control statement allows you to customize the processing which SYMDMP will do for a dynamic dump. The format is

```
                                          ⎧ [,(HEX)  ]                                ⎫
                                          ⎪ [,(NOHEX)] [,ALL]                         ⎪
line-num[,(verb-num)][,ON a[,b[,c]]]      ⎨                                           ⎬
                                          ⎪ ⎧[,(HEX)  ]                          ⎫    ⎪
                                          ⎩ ⎩[,(NOHEX)], name1 [THRU name2]...   ⎭    ⎭
```

When specified, the parameters shown in uppercase must be spelled as shown. Parameters in lowercase are names defined by you. Items in brackets are optional, while stacked items enclosed in braces mean that one of those items must be chosen. Underlined items are the defaults.

Line-num must always be coded. It indicates the line number in the PROCEDURE DIVISION source code where the dynamic dump is to be taken. The number must be that of a section or paragraph header, a conditional verb (e.g., IF), or an imperative verb (e.g., MOVE). The dump is taken prior to the execution of that line.

Verb-num is used to specify at which verb on the line indicated by the line-num parameter the dump is to be taken. It is not required, and if not coded is assumed to be 1.

The parameter ON a[,b[,c]] is similar to the COBOL ON statement described in Sec. 4.1.2. It allows you to limit the taking of the dump to specific instances of execution of the code. For example, if "a" is 10, "b" is 20, and "c" is 100, then the first dynamic dump will be taken the tenth time line-num is executed, and additional dumps will be taken every twentieth time thereafter until after the hundredth execution of line-num has occurred.

HEX specifies the format of DATA DIVISION items for a dynamic dump. HEX will cause level-01 items to be given in hexadecimal notation, with identifiers subordinate to the 01-level to be given in EBCDIC whenever printable. Level-77 items are given in both hexadecimal and EBCDIC notation. If HEX is not specified, 01-level names are given, whereas identifiers subordinate to the 01-level and level-77 items are given in EBCDIC notation if printable and in hexadecimal if they are unprintable. If HEX is not specified and if "name-1," representing a group item, has been coded, neither the group nor its subordinate items will be given in hexadecimal. The IBM default is NOHEX.

You can designate specific data names to be dumped by coding them where name-1[THRU name-2]. . . is shown in the format example. For a table, specifying the name of the item coded on the OCCURS clause without any subscript dumps every occurrence.

Specifying ALL gives the same output as that provided when an ABEND dump is produced for the program specified in the "program-id" parameter on the program-control statement.

Figure 6.1 shows several line-control statements coded after the program-control statement. The first statement, at letter "B," specifies that the field named WS-CUST-NO-INPUT is to be dumped just before source line number 139 is executed. The second statement, indicated by letter "C," means that WS-CUST-REC and REC-READ are to be dumped in hexadecimal format the first time line 166 is reached, and every tenth time thereafter until after the 101st time line 166 is reached.

6.1.2 Solving an ABEND Dump Generated by SYMDMP

The program which was executed by the JCL shown in Fig. 6.1 ABENDed with a system completion code of 0C7, a data exception. The complete program is shown in Fig. 6.2, and portions of the SYMDMP output data appearing on SYSDBOUT is shown in Fig. 6.3.

The first page of the output indicates that no errors were found in the SYMDMP control statements (see Fig. 6.3*a*).

Following that is a key showing the codes used in the dump with their meanings.

Next we see the dynamic dumps requested by the first and second line-control statements. SYMDMP indicates which line-control statements produced the output, but when ON is coded it does not specify which occurrence of the ON parameter was executing. That is why, for the second statement, the programmer requested the contents of REC-READ, which is a counter for records read, as well as the contents of group item WS-CUST-REC, which includes the record number in field WS-CUST-NO-INPUT. As you see in the figure, the information provided for each item includes the hexadecimal storage address (LOC), source line number (CARD), normalized level number (LV), source name (NAME), data type (TYPE), and contents in the format requested on the line-control statement (VALUE) (see Fig. 6.3*b*).

The next page shows the name of the program, the PSW, the completion code, and the statement which was executing at the time of the ABEND (see Fig. 6.3*c*). Notice that verb number 1 on source line number 202 was being executed when the S0C7 ABEND occurred.

The next part of the SYMDMP output shows the hexadecimal addresses and contents of the fields in the TGT, followed by the COBOL-formatted ABEND dump showing the files, data names, and indexes in the program's DATA DIVISION (Fig. 6.3*d*). File information includes the OPEN/CLOSE status, file organization, last I/O operation, file status, and, for non-VSAM files, contents of the DCB. The information for the rest of the items in the DATA DIVISION is formatted the same way as for the items in the dynamic dump.

Looking at line 202 in the source code, flagged by SYMDMP as the place where the program ABENDed, we see the statement

```
ADD WS-AMT-INPUT TO WS-SAVE-CUST-TOT.
```

Since an S0C7 completion code means that invalid packed data were being used, we need to examine the fields in the ADD statement.

WS-AMT-INPUT is listed in the dump as ND-OT, which the key defines as "numeric display overpunch sign trailing." It is an elementary field in group item WS-CUST-REC. Because HEX was specified on the program-control statement, the contents of the group item are given in hexadecimal notation and its subordinate fields are specified in EBCDIC wherever printable. Notice that the contents of WS-AMT-INPUT appears to be **.**. This certainly cannot be valid data since we know that the field is numeric. SYMDMP uses the asterisk in the EBCDIC representation of the field's value to indicate a conflict between the type and the actual contents of the field. We can look at the hexadecimal contents of the entire 01-level item to determine the actual value of WS-AMT-INPUT.

```
000100 IDENTIFICATION DIVISION.
000200  PROGRAM-ID.  PROG1.
000300  AUTHOR       ALAN FRIEND.
000400  DATE-WRITTEN AUGUST 1985.
000500 DATE-COMPILED. DEC 17,1990.

000700 ENVIRONMENT DIVISION.
000800  INPUT-OUTPUT SECTION.
000900   FILE-CONTROL.
001000     SELECT CUSTOMER-FILE ASSIGN TO UT-S-CUSTFILE.
001100     SELECT PRINT-FILE    ASSIGN TO UR-S-PRTFILE.

001300 DATA DIVISION.
001400  FILE SECTION.
001500  FD CUSTOMER-FILE
001600     RECORDING MODE IS F
001700     RECORD CONTAINS 80 CHARACTERS
001800     BLOCK CONTAINS 0 RECORDS
001900     LABEL RECORDS ARE OMITTED
002000     DATA RECORD IS CUST-FILE-REC.
002100  01 CUST-FILE-REC          PIC X(80).
002200  FD PRINT-FILE
002300     RECORDING MODE IS F
002400     RECORD CONTAINS 133 CHARACTERS
002500     BLOCK CONTAINS 0 RECORDS
002600     LABEL RECORDS ARE OMITTED
002700     DATA RECORD IS PRINT-FILE-REC.
002800  01 PRINT-FILE-REC         PIC X(133).

003000  WORKING-STORAGE SECTION.
003100*****************************************************************
003200*    INPUT CUSTOMER RECORD LAYOUT                                *
003300*****************************************************************
003400  01 WS-CUST-REC.
003500      05 WS-CUST-NO-INPUT     PIC 9(5).
003600      05 WS-ITEM-NO-INPUT     PIC X(5).
003700      05 WS-AMT-INPUT         PIC S99V99.
003800      05 FILLER               PIC X(66).
003900*****************************************************************
004000*     HEADER LINES                                               *
004100*****************************************************************
004200  01 WS-HEADERS.
004300      05 RPT-HDR-1.
004400         10 FILLER            PIC X(53)   VALUE SPACES.
004500         10 FILLER            PIC X(16)   VALUE 'FRIEND SOFTWARE '.
004600         10 FILLER            PIC X(64)   VALUE 'COMPANY, INC.'.
004700      05 RPT-HDR-2.
004800         10 FILLER            PIC X(8)    VALUE SPACES.
004900         10 DT                PIC X(8).
005000         10 FILLER            PIC X(39)   VALUE SPACES.
005100         10 FILLER            PIC X(14)   VALUE 'CUSTOMER ACTIV'.
005200         10 FILLER            PIC X(10)   VALUE 'ITY REPORT'.
005300         10 FILLER            PIC X(40)   VALUE SPACES.
005400         10 FILLER            PIC X(4)    VALUE 'PAGE'.
005500         10 PAGE-NO           PIC Z,ZZZ   VALUE ZERO.
005600         10 FILLER            PIC X(4)    VALUE SPACES.
005700      05 COL-HDR-1.
005800         10 FILLER            PIC X(10)   VALUE SPACES.
005900         10 FILLER            PIC X(8)    VALUE 'CUSTOMER'.
006000         10 FILLER            PIC X(23)   VALUE SPACES.
006100         10 FILLER            PIC X(4)    VALUE 'ITEM'.
006200         10 FILLER            PIC X(25)   VALUE SPACES.
006300         10 FILLER            PIC X(6)    VALUE 'AMOUNT'.
006400         10 FILLER            PIC X(24)   VALUE SPACES.
006500         10 FILLER            PIC X(33)   VALUE 'COMMENTS'.
```

Figure 6.2 Source code for the COBOL program compiled, linked, and executed by the JCL in Fig. 6.1.

```
006600     05 COL-HDR-2.
006700        10 FILLER            PIC X(11)   VALUE SPACES.
006800        10 FILLER            PIC X(6)    VALUE 'NUMBER'.
006900        10 FILLER            PIC X(23)   VALUE SPACES.
007000        10 FILLER            PIC X(93)   VALUE 'NUMBER'.
007100******************************************************************
007200*    REPORT OUTPUT LAYOUT                                        *
007300******************************************************************
007400  01 WS-REPORT-LINES.
007500     05 TRX-DETAIL-LINE.
007600        10 FILLER            PIC X(12)   VALUE SPACES.
007700        10 WS-CUST-NO-RPT    PIC  9(5)    VALUE ZERO.
007800        10 FILLER            PIC X(23)   VALUE SPACES.
007900        10 WS-ITEM-NO-RPT    PIC X(5).
008000        10 FILLER            PIC X(24)   VALUE SPACES.
008100        10 WS-AMT-RPT        PIC $ZZZZ.99.
008200        10 FILLER            PIC X(9)    VALUE SPACES.
008300        10 COMMENTS          PIC X(47).
008400     05 CUST-TOTAL-LINE.
008500        10 FILLER            PIC X(69)   VALUE SPACES.
008600        10 WS-CUST-TOT       PIC $ZZZZ.99.

008700        10 FILLER            PIC X(13)   VALUE SPACES.
008800        10 FILLER            PIC X(43)   VALUE 'CUSTOMER TOTAL'.
008900******************************************************************
009000*    REPORT FOOTINGS                                             *
009100******************************************************************
009200  01 WS-FOOTINGS.
009300     05  FOOTING-1.
009400        10 FILLER            PIC X(52)   VALUE SPACES.
009500        10 FILLER            PIC X(14)   VALUE 'TOTAL RECORDS '.
009600        10 FILLER            PIC X(16)   VALUE 'READ'.
009700        10 FILLER            PIC XX      VALUE '= '.
009800        10 NO-READ           PIC ZZZ.
009900        10 FILLER            PIC X(46)   VALUE SPACES.
010000     05 FOOTING-2.
010100        10 FILLER            PIC X(52)   VALUE SPACES.
010200        10 FILLER            PIC X(14)   VALUE 'TOTAL RECORDS '.
010300        10 FILLER            PIC X(16)   VALUE 'PROCESSED'.
010400        10 FILLER            PIC XX      VALUE '= '.
010500        10 NO-PROCESSED      PIC ZZZ.
010600        10 FILLER            PIC X(46)   VALUE SPACES.
010700     05 FOOTING-3.
010800        10 FILLER            PIC X(52)   VALUE SPACES.
010900        10 FILLER            PIC X(17) VALUE 'TOTAL RECORDS OUT'.
011000        10 FILLER            PIC X(13)   VALUE ' OF SEQUENCE'.
011100        10 FILLER            PIC XX      VALUE '= '.
011200        10 NO-OUT-OF-SEQ     PIC ZZZ.
011300        10 FILLER            PIC X(46)   VALUE SPACES.
011400******************************************************************
011500*    SAVE AREAS, TOTALS, COUNTERS, EOF-SWITCH                    *
011600******************************************************************
011700  01 MISC.
011800     05 WS-SAVE-CUST-NO      PIC  9(5)    VALUE ZERO.
011900     05 WS-SAVE-CUST-TOT     PIC S9(4)V99 VALUE ZERO USAGE COMP-3.
012000     05 COUNTERS    USAGE    COMP-3.
012100        10 REC-READ          PIC S999     VALUE ZERO.
012200        10 REC-PROCESSED     PIC S999     VALUE ZERO.
012300        10 REC-OUT-OF-SEQ    PIC S999     VALUE ZERO.
012400        10 PAGE-CT           PIC S99      VALUE ZERO.
012500        10 LINE-CT           PIC S99      VALUE ZERO.
012600     05 SWEOF                PIC X       VALUE SPACES.
```

Figure 6.2 *(Continued)*

```
012800 PROCEDURE DIVISION.
012900******************************************************************
013000*    MAINLINE CONTROL PARAGRAPH                                  *
013100******************************************************************
013200 0000-MAINLINE.

013400     OPEN INPUT  CUSTOMER-FILE
013500          OUTPUT PRINT-FILE.
013600     MOVE CURRENT-DATE TO DT.
013700     READ CUSTOMER-FILE INTO WS-CUST-REC
013800        AT END MOVE '1' TO SWEOF.
013900     MOVE WS-CUST-NO-INPUT TO WS-SAVE-CUST-NO.
014000     PERFORM 0500-HEADER-ROUT THRU 0500-HEADER-ROUT-EXIT.
014100     IF SWEOF EQUAL TO '1'
014200        DISPLAY '**** EMPTY FILE ****'.
014300     PERFORM 0100-COMPARE-SEQ-NO THRU 0100-COMPARE-SEQ-NO-EXIT
014400        UNTIL SWEOF EQUAL TO '1'.
014500     PERFORM 0900-END-OF-JOB THRU 0900-END-OF-JOB-EXIT.
014600     CLOSE CUSTOMER-FILE
014700           PRINT-FILE.
014800     STOP RUN.

015000******************************************************************
015100*    COMPARE SEQUENCE NO. OF RECORD WITH PRECEDING SEQUENCE NO.  *
015200******************************************************************
015300 0100-COMPARE-SEQ-NO.
015400     ADD 1 TO REC-READ.
015500     MOVE SPACES TO COMMENTS.
015600     IF WS-CUST-NO-INPUT EQUAL TO WS-SAVE-CUST-NO
015700         PERFORM 0200-SEQ-NO-EQUAL THRU 0200-SEQ-NO-EQUAL-EXIT
015800       ELSE
015900          IF WS-CUST-NO-INPUT LESS THAN WS-SAVE-CUST-NO
016000              PERFORM 0400-SEQ-NO-LESS
016100                THRU 0400-SEQ-NO-LESS-EXIT
016200          ELSE
016300             IF WS-CUST-NO-INPUT GREATER THAN WS-SAVE-CUST-NO
016400               PERFORM 0300-SEQ-NO-GREATER
016500                 THRU 0300-SEQ-NO-GREATER-EXIT.
016600     READ CUSTOMER-FILE INTO WS-CUST-REC
016700        AT END MOVE '1' TO SWEOF.

016900 0100-COMPARE-SEQ-NO-EXIT.
017000     EXIT.

017200******************************************************************
017300*    PROCESS RECORDS BASED ON COMPARISON OF SEQUENCE NUMBER.     *
017400******************************************************************
017500 0200-SEQ-NO-EQUAL.
017600     ADD 1 TO REC-PROCESSED.
017700     MOVE WS-CUST-NO-INPUT TO WS-CUST-NO-RPT.
017800     MOVE WS-ITEM-NO-INPUT TO WS-ITEM-NO-RPT.
017900     MOVE WS-AMT-INPUT     TO WS-AMT-RPT.
018000     ADD WS-AMT-INPUT TO WS-SAVE-CUST-TOT.
018100     IF LINE-CT GREATER THAN 53
018200        PERFORM 0500-HEADER-ROUT THRU 0500-HEADER-ROUT-EXIT.
018300     WRITE PRINT-FILE-REC FROM TRX-DETAIL-LINE
018400        AFTER ADVANCING 1 LINE.
018500     ADD 1 TO LINE-CT.

018700 0200-SEQ-NO-EQUAL-EXIT.
018800     EXIT.
```

Figure 6.2 *(Continued)*

```
019000 0300-SEQ-NO-GREATER.
019100     ADD 1 TO REC-PROCESSED.
019200     IF LINE-CT GREATER THAN 55
019300        PERFORM 0500-HEADER-ROUT THRU 0500-HEADER-ROUT-EXIT.
019400     MOVE WS-SAVE-CUST-TOT TO WS-CUST-TOT.
019500     WRITE PRINT-FILE-REC FROM CUST-TOTAL-LINE
019600        AFTER ADVANCING 2 LINES.
019700     ADD 2 TO LINE-CT.
019800     MOVE ZERO TO WS-SAVE-CUST-TOT.
019900     MOVE WS-CUST-NO-INPUT TO WS-CUST-NO-RPT.
020000     MOVE WS-ITEM-NO-INPUT TO WS-ITEM-NO-RPT.
020100     MOVE WS-AMT-INPUT     TO WS-AMT-RPT.
020200     ADD WS-AMT-INPUT TO WS-SAVE-CUST-TOT.
020300     MOVE WS-CUST-NO-INPUT TO WS-SAVE-CUST-NO.
020400     IF LINE-CT GREATER THAN 53
020500        PERFORM 0500-HEADER-ROUT THRU 0500-HEADER-ROUT-EXIT.
020600     WRITE PRINT-FILE-REC FROM TRX-DETAIL-LINE

020700        AFTER ADVANCING 2 LINES.
020800     ADD 2 TO LINE-CT.

021000 0300-SEQ-NO-GREATER-EXIT.
021100     EXIT.

021300 0400-SEQ-NO-LESS.
021400     ADD 1 TO REC-OUT-OF-SEQ.
021500     MOVE WS-CUST-NO-INPUT TO WS-CUST-NO-RPT.
021600     MOVE WS-ITEM-NO-INPUT TO WS-ITEM-NO-RPT.
021700     MOVE WS-AMT-INPUT     TO WS-AMT-RPT.
021800     MOVE '** SEQUENCE ERROR: RECORD NOT PROCESSED **'
021900        TO COMMENTS.
022000     IF LINE-CT GREATER THAN 53
022100        PERFORM 0500-HEADER-ROUT THRU 0500-HEADER-ROUT-EXIT.
022200     WRITE PRINT-FILE-REC FROM TRX-DETAIL-LINE
022300        AFTER ADVANCING 2 LINES.
022400     ADD 2 TO LINE-CT.

022600 0400-SEQ-NO-LESS-EXIT.
022700     EXIT.

022900*****************************************************************
023000*    ROUTINE TO PRINT REPORT AND COLUMN HEADINGS.                 *
023100*****************************************************************
023200 0500-HEADER-ROUT.
023300     MOVE ZERO TO LINE-CT.
023400     MOVE SPACES TO PRINT-FILE-REC.
023500     WRITE PRINT-FILE-REC
023600        AFTER ADVANCING PAGE.
023700     WRITE PRINT-FILE-REC FROM RPT-HDR-1
023800        AFTER ADVANCING 1 LINE.
023900     ADD 1 TO PAGE-CT.
024000     MOVE PAGE-CT TO PAGE-NO.
024100     WRITE PRINT-FILE-REC FROM RPT-HDR-2
024200        AFTER ADVANCING 2 LINES.
024300     WRITE PRINT-FILE-REC FROM COL-HDR-1
024400        AFTER ADVANCING 2 LINES.
024500     WRITE PRINT-FILE-REC FROM COL-HDR-2
024600        AFTER ADVANCING 1 LINE.
024700     MOVE SPACES TO PRINT-FILE-REC.
024800     WRITE PRINT-FILE-REC
024900        AFTER ADVANCING 2 LINES.
025000     ADD 8 TO LINE-CT.

025200 0500-HEADER-ROUT-EXIT.
025300     EXIT.
```

Figure 6.2 *(Continued)*

```
025500*****************************************************************
025600*    END OF JOB ROUTINE PRINTS FINAL CUSTOMER TOTAL               *
025700*    AND STATISTICS ON RECORDS READ.                              *
025800*****************************************************************
025900 0900-END-OF-JOB.
026000     IF LINE-CT GREATER THAN 55
026100        PERFORM 0500-HEADER-ROUT THRU 0500-HEADER-ROUT-EXIT.
026200     MOVE WS-SAVE-CUST-TOT TO WS-CUST-TOT.
026300     WRITE PRINT-FILE-REC FROM CUST-TOTAL-LINE

026400        AFTER ADVANCING 2 LINES.
026500     ADD 2 TO LINE-CT.
026600     IF LINE-CT GREATER THAN 57
026700        PERFORM 0500-HEADER-ROUT THRU 0500-HEADER-ROUT-EXIT.
026800     MOVE REC-READ        TO NO-READ.
026900     MOVE REC-PROCESSED  TO NO-PROCESSED.
027000     MOVE REC-OUT-OF-SEQ TO NO-OUT-OF-SEQ.
027100     WRITE PRINT-FILE-REC FROM FOOTING-1
027200        AFTER ADVANCING 2 LINES.
027300     WRITE PRINT-FILE-REC FROM FOOTING-2
027400        AFTER ADVANCING 1 LINE.
027500     WRITE PRINT-FILE-REC FROM FOOTING-3
027600        AFTER ADVANCING 1 LINE.

027800 0900-END-OF-JOB-EXIT.
027900     EXIT.
```

Figure 6.2 *(Continued)*

There are several ways to find where WS-AMT-INPUT is located. We can consult the hexadecimal offsets listed in the LOC column of the dump, we can look at the DATA DIVISION map (if it is available), or we can go directly to the source code. Looking at the source code in Fig. 6.2 we learn that WS-AMT-INPUT starts 11 bytes from the beginning of WS-CUST-REC and is defined as PIC S99V99. Counting 11 bytes into the hexadecimal representation of the value of WS-CUST-REC, shown at letter "A" in Fig. 6.3*d*, we see that WS-AMT-INPUT contains spaces (40404040).

The same procedure can be used to examine the other operand in the ADD instruction, WS-SAVE-CUST-TOT. SYMDMP indicates that this field is NP-S, or "numeric packed decimal signed." It has valid packed data, +0000.00, shown at letter "B" in Fig. 6.3*d*.

We already know (see Sec. 2.2.1.5) that if one of the COBOL fields in the ADD instruction is packed and the other isn't, COBOL will generate instructions to convert the unpacked operand into a packed intermediate field. It will then use that intermediate field in an Assembler AP instruction (Add Packed). Since WS-AMT-INPUT contained spaces, the PACK instruction created an intermediate field with invalid packed data. This intermediate field caused the ABEND when the AP was executed.

SYMDMP also reports the contents of WS-CUST-NO-INPUT as 26283 and the value of REC-READ as +13. These fields contain the record number and total number of records read at this point in the program. Record 26283 in the input data set (see Fig. 6.4) has spaces starting in column position 11, which is the beginning of the field moved into WS-AMT-INPUT as a result of the READ . . . INTO statement.

```
                              SYMDMP CONTROL CARDS


PROG1,SYMDEBUG,HEX

139,WS-CUST-NO-INPUT

166,ON 1,10,101(HEX),WS-CUST-REC,REC-READ


                         NO ERRORS FOUND IN CONTROL CARDS

                                        (a)

                                   TYPE CODES USED IN SYMDMP OUTPUT

                         CODE      MEANING

                         A       = ALPHABETIC
                         AN      = ALPHANUMERIC
                         ANE     = ALPHANUMERIC EDITED
                         D       = DISPLAY (STERLING NONREPORT)
                         DE      = DISPLAY EDITED (STERLING REPORT)
                         F       = FLOATING POINT (COMP-1/COMP-2)
                         FD      = FLOATING POINT DISPLAY (EXTERNAL FLOATING POINT)
                         NB      = NUMERIC BINARY UNSIGNED (COMP)
                         NB-S    = NUMERIC BINARY SIGNED
                         ND      = NUMERIC DISPLAY UNSIGNED (EXTERNAL DECIMAL)
                         ND-OL   = NUMERIC DISPLAY OVERPUNCH SIGN LEADING
                         ND-OT   = NUMERIC DISPLAY OVERPUNCH SIGN TRAILING
                         ND-SL   = NUMERIC DISPLAY SEPARATE SIGN LEADING
                         ND-ST   = NUMERIC DISPLAY SEPARATE SIGN TRAILING
                         NE      = NUMERIC EDITED
                         NP      = NUMERIC PACKED DECIMAL UNSIGNED (COMP-3)
                         NP-S    = NUMERIC PACKED DECIMAL SIGNED
                         *       = SUBSCRIPTED
PROG1    AT CARD 000139
 LOC     CARD   LV NAME                             TYPE    VALUE

00A288  000035  02 WS-CUST-NO-INPUT                 ND      10549

PROG1    AT CARD 000166
 LOC     CARD   LV NAME                             TYPE    VALUE

        000034  01 WS-CUST-REC
00A288                                     (HEX)            F1F0F5F4 F9F0F3F0 F4F1F1F2    F2F2F240 40404040 40404040
00A2A0                                                      40404040 40404040 40404040    40404040 40404040 40404040
00A2B8                                                      --SAME--
00A2D0                                                      40404040 40404040
00A288  000035  02 WS-CUST-NO-INPUT                 ND      10549
00A28D  000036  02 WS-ITEM-NO-INPUT                 AN      03041
00A292  000037  02 WS-AMT-INPUT                     ND-OT   +12.22
00A296  000038  02 FILLER                           AN      2

00A799  000121  03 REC-READ                         NP-S    +001

PROG1    AT CARD 000166
 LOC     CARD   LV NAME                             TYPE    VALUE

        000034  01 WS-CUST-REC
00A288                                     (HEX)            F2F5F2F2 F7F0F3F4 F2F1F1F8    F2F4F040 40404040 40404040
00A2A0                                                      40404040 40404040 40404040    40404040 40404040 40404040
00A2B8                                                      --SAME--
00A2D0                                                      40404040 40404040
00A288  000035  02 WS-CUST-NO-INPUT                 ND      25227
00A28D  000036  02 WS-ITEM-NO-INPUT                 AN      03421
00A292  000037  02 WS-AMT-INPUT                     ND-OT   +18.24
00A296  000038  02 FILLER                           AN      0

00A799  000121  03 REC-READ                         NP-S    +011

                                                            (b)
```

Figure 6.3 SYMDMP output produced as a result of running the JCL in Fig. 6.1. The OS/VS COBOL program ABENDed. (*a*) SYMDMP control statements; (*b*) output codes key and dynamic dump output; (*c*) completion code and PSW; (*d*) DATA DIVISION dump. (*Continued*)

```
                                COBOL ABEND DIAGNOSTIC AIDS


PROGRAM        PROG1


LAST PSW BEFORE ABEND = FF850007C000B2AC     SYSTEM COMPLETION CODE = 0C7

LAST CARD NUMBER/VERB NUMBER EXECUTED -- CARD NUMBER 000202/VERB NUMBER 01.
                                                                    (c)


                                 DATA DIVISION DUMP OF PROG1


 TASK GLOBAL TABLE       LOC      VALUE

 SAVE AREA               00AA70   0030C4C2 00005FB0 00005BF8 4000D364   92DC5968 0000B0F4 00011EF0 8000A900
                         00AA90   00000086 1400A9E7 5000B7EE 1400A9E7   00000086 00000002 00000002 0000A1E8
                         00AAB0   0000AD14 6000D168
 SWITCH                  00AAB8   3902804B
                                              .
                                              .
                                              .
                                 DATA DIVISION DUMP OF PROG1


LOC      CARD    LV NAME                      TYPE    VALUE

         000010  FD CUSTOMER-FILE             QSAM    FILE: OPEN     ORGANIZATION: PHYSICAL SEQUENTIAL
                                                      LAST SUCCESSFUL I/O STMT: READ       FILE STATUS: 00
00A7E4                               DCB  00000000 00000000 05D20009 0FF6EDE6   002FE5A2 05013628 00004000 00012E30
00A804                                    4600CAF6 9000A7AC 00404800 008E19BC   12C1D088 00C27A40 09000001 00095B90
00A824                                    30013030 00012EE0 00019BC0 00019580   00000050 00000000 00000000 00D77490

019580   000021  01 CUST-FILE-REC             AN      26283

019580                                    (HEX)       F2F6F2F8 F3404040 40404040   40404040 40404040 40404040
019598                                                40404040 40404040 40404040   40404040 40404040 40404040
0195B0                                                --SAME--
0195C8                                                40404040 40404040

         000011  FD PRINT-FILE                QSAM    FILE: OPEN     ORGANIZATION: PHYSICAL SEQUENTIAL
                                                      LAST SUCCESSFUL I/O STMT: WRITE      FILE STATUS: 00
00A900                               DCB  00000000 00000000 00000000 00000000   00000000 01011EE8 00864000 00012188
00A920                                    4600CAF6 9400A8C8 00540048 008E1658   92DC5968 00000000 00000001 08090086
00A940                                    00000000 00012038 00011F76 00011F76   00000086 00000000 00000000 00000000

00A9E8   000028  01 PRINT-FILE-REC            AN
                                                               $  20.35            CUSTOMER TOTAL

00A9E8                                    (HEX)       40404040 40404040 40404040   40404040 40404040 40404040
00AA00                                                --SAME--
00AA18                                                40404040 40404040 40404040   40404040 40404040 405B4040
00AA30                                                F2F04BF3 F5404040 40404040   40404040 4040C3E4 E2E3D6D4
00AA48                                                C5D940E3 D6E3C1D3 40404040   40404040 40404040 40404040
00AA60                                                40404040 40404040 40404040   40
```

Figure 6.3 *(Continued)*

Thus, with the aid of the formatted OS/VS COBOL dump, we have quickly solved the ABEND.

6.2 THE COBOL II FORMATTED DUMP

In COBOL II, the FDUMP compiler option may be used to request a symbolic formatted dump if the program ABENDs. The dump includes extensive information about the DATA DIVISION as well as the contents of the general-pur-

```
                                                                                                  (A)
        000034  01 WS-CUST-REC
00A288                                      (HEX)         F2F6F2F8 F3404040 40404040   40404040 40404040 40404040
00A2A0                                                    40404040 40404040 40404040   40404040 40404040 40404040
00A2B8                                                    --SAME--
00A2D0                                                    40404040 40404040
00A288  000035  02 WS-CUST-NO-INPUT               ND      26283
00A28D  000036  02 WS-ITEM-NO-INPUT               AN
00A292  000037  02 WS-AMT-INPUT                   ND-OT   **.**
00A296  000038  02 FILLER                         AN

                                                  .
                                                  .
                                                  .

        000117  01 MISC
00A790                                      (HEX)         F2F5F5F0 F7000000 0C013C01   3C000C00 1C055C40
00A790  000118  02 WS-SAVE-CUST-NO                ND      25507
00A795  000119  02 WS-SAVE-CUST-TOT               NP-S    +0000.00 <---------------------------------------(B)
        000120  02 COUNTERS
00A799  000121  03 REC-READ                       NP-S    +013
00A79B  000122  03 REC-PROCESSED                  NP-S    +013
00A79D  000123  03 REC-OUT-OF-SEQ                 NP-S    +000
00A79F  000124  03 PAGE-CT                        NP-S    +01
00A7A1  000125  03 LINE-CT                        NP-S    +55
00A7A3  000126  02 SWEOF                          AN


                                           END OF COBOL DIAGNOSTIC AIDS

                                                       (d)
```

Figure 6.3 *(Continued)*

pose registers, the completion code, and the statement and verb number being executed when the ABEND occurred. Although the information provided in the Release 2 and Release 3 dumps is essentially the same, the formats differ slightly.

The TEST compiler option should not be specified when FDUMP is requested; otherwise, no formatted dump will be produced if the program ABENDs. Also, the STAE run-time option must be in effect. This is the IBM default but if the installation has changed it to NOSTAE, a formatted dump will not be generated (see Sec. 6.2.1).

Since the output from FDUMP is written to the file allocated to the SYSDBOUT DD statement, you must include SYSDBOUT in the JCL. Figure 6.5 shows JCL used to request a COBOL II formatted dump when executing the COB2UCLG procedure in the event that the COBOL II program ABENDs during the GO step.

6.2.1 The STAE and NOSTAE Run-Time Options

Before continuing our discussion of COBOL II formatted dumps, it is necessary to understand the STAE and NOSTAE run-time options. STAE instructs the COBOL II ABEND handler to take control if an ABEND occurs. This causes production of the COBOL II formatted dump on the SYSDBOUT DD dataset if the FDUMP compiler option was in effect.

```
105490304112222
107040714120363
125080410120374
144390402122292
161070709121360
178030431119216
187530260118296
207700466119265
237230345122296
245990362120443
252270342118240
255070486120350
2628300000
360270527117241
364930373118399
       .
       .
       .
```

Figure 6.4 Input data set for the COBOL program executed by the JCL in Fig. 6.1.

Even if FDUMP is not specified, STAE will provide additional debugging information. An IGZ message from the COBOL II subroutine library may be printed in the job log to indicate that the ABEND was intercepted by the COBOL II ABEND handler, and the completion code, PSW, and contents of the general-purpose registers at entry to the ABEND may be given (see Fig. 6.6).

If an appropriate dump DD statement is included in the JCL (SYSUDUMP is used at most installations), a system hexadecimal storage dump is produced.

If the SYSABOUT DD statement is present, additional ABEND information from COBOL II will be given. This information includes the program name, date and time of compilation, address of the TGT, contents of all base locator cells used by the program, and the contents of each index used (no index names

```
//S1      EXEC COB2UCLG,
//             PARM.COB2='XREF,FDUMP',
//             REGION=512K
//*****************************************************
//*  SOURCE CODE IS COBOL II                           *
//*****************************************************
//COB2.SYSIN  DD DSN=MY.PROGLIB.COBOL(PROG2),DISP=SHR
//GO.REPTFLE  DD SYSOUT=A
//GO.NOTFLE   DD SYSOUT=A
//GO.STUDFLE  DD DSN=INPUT.PROG2.DATA,DISP=SHR
//SYSOUT      DD SYSOUT=A
//SYSABOUT    DD SYSOUT=A
//SYSDBOUT    DD SYSOUT=A
//
```

Figure 6.5 JCL for requesting a COBOL II formatted dump when executing COB2UCLG.

```
IGZ038I AN ABEND WAS INTERCEPTED BY THE COBOL EXECUTION TIME ABEND
      HANDLER.
  THE COMPLETION CODE WAS = 'U1035'  THE PSW AT ABEND WAS =
      '478D100000021FA2'
  THE GP REGISTERS AT ENTRY TO ABEND WERE
     REGS 0-3    - '80000000  8000040B  0000040B  00026480'
     REGS 4-7    - '00014EC0  0001CB34  0000D4F8  00026480'
     REGS 8-11   - '00021C9C  00000088  0001CB34  00023F94'
     REGS 12-15  - '50021EBA  000250B0  50010BE0  00021E88'
```

Figure 6.6 IGZ message appearing in the job log when STAE is in effect for a COBOL II program which ABENDed.

are given) in hexadecimal notation (see Fig. 6.7). Thus even if FDUMP was not requested, you should always be sure that the SYSABOUT DD statement is included in the JCL if you use STAE.

STAE also cleans up and terminates the run-time environment, which can be thought of as an interface between the MVS operating system and the application program, before control is passed back to the operating system. The run-time environment consists of control blocks, library routines, and buffers. The four levels of this environment, from highest to lowest, are partition, thread, run-unit, and program. The program level is closest to the COBOL application program. The major control block at the program level is one we are already familiar with, the TGT (see Sec. 2.2.1).

If NOSTAE is in effect, no diagnostic information and no COBOL II dump are given. Also, the run-time environment is not cleaned up. NOSTAE might be

```
--- VS COBOL II ABEND Information ---

Program = 'PROG2' compiled on '12/17/90' at '10:36:43'
    TGT = '0000CE78'

Contents of base locators for files are:
    0-0002DDE8        1-0000D4A9        2-0000D531

Contents of base locators for working storage are:
    0-0000D5B8

Contents of base locators for the linkage section are:
    0-00000000

No variably located areas were used in this program.

No EXTERNAL data was used in this program.

No indexes were used in this program.

--- End of VS COBOL II ABEND Information ---
```

Figure 6.7 COBOL II ABEND information appearing on the SYSABOUT DD statement.

necessary if you want error recovery routines from another product to gain control without interference from COBOL II (refer to the product documentation).

6.2.2 Solving an ABEND Using FDUMP Output

We will now examine a COBOL II formatted dump. Figure 6.5 shows the JCL to compile, link, and execute a COBOL II Release 3 program using the FDUMP compiler option. When the program executed, it ABENDed with a system completion code of 0C7, a data exception. The program source code is shown in Fig. 6.8, and part of the output from FDUMP, appearing on the SYSDBOUT DD data set, can be seen in Fig. 6.9.

At the beginning of the formatted dump is the name of the program, the completion code, the PSW, and the number of the statement and verb which was executing at the time of the ABEND (see Fig. 6.9). The ABEND occurred when verb number 1 on source line number 122 was executing. If the OPTIMIZE compiler option is used, the hexadecimal offset from the beginning of the program for the next sequential instruction is given instead of the line and verb

```
LineID  PL SL  ----+-*A-1-B--+----2----+----3----+----4----+----5----+----6----+----7-|--+----8 Cross Reference
000001               IDENTIFICATION DIVISION.
000002               PROGRAM-ID.    PROG2.
000003               AUTHOR.        ALAN FRIEND.
000004               DATE-WRITTEN. 01/05/90
000005               DATE-COMPILED. 12/17/90.

000007               ENVIRONMENT DIVISION.
000008               CONFIGURATION SECTION.
000009               INPUT-OUTPUT SECTION.
000010               FILE-CONTROL.
000011                   SELECT  STUDENT-FILE    ASSIGN  TO  STUDFLE.                           16
000012                   SELECT  REPORT-FILE     ASSIGN  TO  REPTFLE.                           26
000013                   SELECT  NOTICE-FILE     ASSIGN  TO  NOTFLE.                            33
000014               DATA DIVISION.
000015               FILE SECTION.
000016               FD  STUDENT-FILE
000017                   BLOCK CONTAINS  0  RECORDS
000018                   LABEL RECORDS ARE OMITTED
000019                   RECORDING MODE IS F
000020                   RECORD CONTAINS  80 CHARACTERS
000021                   DATA RECORD IS STUDENT-RECORD.
000022               01  STUDENT-RECORD.
000023                   05  STUDENT-NAME                  PIC X(20).
000024                   05  STUDENT-GRADE                 PIC 999.
000025                   05  FILLER                        PIC X(57).
000026               FD  REPORT-FILE
000027                   BLOCK CONTAINS  0  RECORDS
000028                   LABEL RECORDS ARE OMITTED
000029                   RECORDING MODE IS F
000030                   RECORD CONTAINS 133 CHARACTERS
000031                   DATA RECORD IS PRINT-RECORD.
000032               01  PRINT-RECORD                      PIC X(133).
000033               FD  NOTICE-FILE
000034                   BLOCK CONTAINS  0  RECORDS
000035                   LABEL RECORDS ARE OMITTED
000036                   RECORDING MODE IS F
000037                   RECORD CONTAINS 133 CHARACTERS
000038                   DATA RECORD IS PRINT-RECORD.
000039               01  NOTICE-RECORD                     PIC X(133).
```

Figure 6.8 The COBOL II program compiled, linked, and executed by the JCL in Fig. 6.5.

```
LineID  PL SL  ----+-*A-1-B--+----2----+----3----+----4----+----5----+----6----+----7-|--+----8 Cross Reference
                    WORKING-STORAGE SECTION.
                    01  FILLER                                   PIC X(32)
                                             VALUE 'PROG2   WORKING-STORAGE BEGINS'.
                    01  ACCUMULATORS                             COMP-3.
                        10  TOT-GRADE                            PIC S9(7).
                        10  AVERAGE-GRADE                        PIC S9(03)V99.
                        10  NUMBER-STUDENTS                      PIC S9(03).
                        10  NUMBER-FAILING                       PIC S9(03).
                    01  WORK-AREAS.
                        05  SAVE-STUDENT-NAME                    PIC X(20).
                        05  SAVE-STUDENT-GRADE                   PIC S9(03)  COMP-3
                                                                         VALUE +101.
                    01  SWITCHES.
                        05  SW-EOF                               PIC X     VALUE 'N'.

                            88  NO-MORE-RECORDS                            VALUE 'Y'.
                    01  PRINT-LINES.
                        05  DETAIL-LINE.
                            10  FILLER                            PIC X(11)
                                                                        VALUE SPACES.        IMP
                            10  PRINT-NAME                        PIC X(20).
                            10  FILLER                            PIC X(11)
                                                                        VALUE SPACES.        IMP
                            10  PRINT-GRADE                       PIC Z99B(4).
                            10  PRINT-MESSAGE                     PIC X(64)
                                                                        VALUE SPACES.        IMP
                        05  AVERAGE-GRADE-LINE.
                            10  FILLER                            PIC X(11)
                                                                        VALUE SPACES.        IMP
                            10  FILLER                            PIC X(24)
                                                   VALUE 'FINAL STUDENT AVERAGE = '.
                            10  PRINT-AVERAGE-GRADE               PIC Z99.99.
                            10  FILLER                            PIC X(44)
                                                                        VALUE SPACES.        IMP
                        05  LOWEST-GRADE-LINE.
                            10  FILLER                            PIC X(11)
                                                                        VALUE SPACES.        IMP
                            10  FILLER                            PIC X(23)
                                                   VALUE 'LOWEST STUDENT GRADE = '.
                            10  PRINT-LOWEST-GRADE                PIC Z99.99.
                            10  FILLER                            PIC X(02)
                                                                        VALUE SPACES.        IMP
                            10  FILLER                            PIC X(16)
                                                   VALUE 'STUDENT NAME IS '.
                            10  PRINT-LOWEST-NAME                 PIC X(27).
                        05  NUMBER-FAILING-LINE.
                            10  FILLER                            PIC X(11)
                                                                        VALUE SPACES.        IMP
                            10  FILLER                            PIC X(29)
                                           VALUE 'NUMBER OF FAILING STUDENTS = '.
                            10  PRINT-NUMBER-FAILING              PIC ZZ9.
                            10  FILLER                            PIC X(39)
                                                                        VALUE SPACES.        IMP
                    01  FILLER                                   PIC X(32)
                                             VALUE 'PROG2   WORKING-STORAGE   ENDS'.
```

Figure 6.8 *(Continued)*

```
LineID  PL SL  ----+-*A-1-B--+----2----+----3----+----4----+----5----+----6----+----7-|--+----8 Cross Reference
000097               PROCEDURE DIVISION.
000098               0000-MAINLINE.
000099                   DISPLAY 'PROGRAM BEGINNING'
000100                   OPEN  INPUT   STUDENT-FILE                                          16
000101                         OUTPUT  REPORT-FILE                                           26
000102                                  NOTICE-FILE                                          33
000103                   READ  STUDENT-FILE                                                  16
000104                         AT END
000105      1                         SET NO-MORE-RECORDS TO TRUE                            56
000106                   END-READ
000107                   PERFORM  0100-PROCESS-RECORD                                        116
000108                            UNTIL  NO-MORE-RECORDS                                     56
000109                   PERFORM  0200-FINAL-GRADE-REPORT                                    132
000110                   CLOSE  STUDENT-FILE                                                 16
000111                          REPORT-FILE                                                  26
000112                          NOTICE-FILE                                                  33
000113                   DISPLAY  'PROGRAM ENDING'
000114                   GOBACK.

000116               0100-PROCESS-RECORD.

000118                   IF STUDENT-GRADE LESS THAN SAVE-STUDENT-GRADE                       24 51
000119      1                MOVE STUDENT-NAME  TO SAVE-STUDENT-NAME                         23 50
000120      1                MOVE STUDENT-GRADE TO SAVE-STUDENT-GRADE                        24 51
000121                   END-IF
000122                   ADD   STUDENT-GRADE  TO  TOT-GRADE                                  24 45
000123                   ADD   +1             TO  NUMBER-STUDENTS                            47
000124                   IF STUDENT-GRADE  LESS THAN +65                                     24
000125      1                PERFORM 0300-MESSAGE                                            145
000126                   END-IF
000127                   READ  STUDENT-FILE                                                  16
000128                         AT END
000129      1                         SET NO-MORE-RECORDS TO TRUE                            56
000130                   END-READ.

000132               0200-FINAL-GRADE-REPORT.
000133                   DIVIDE  TOT-GRADE  BY  NUMBER-STUDENTS                              45 47
000134                           GIVING  AVERAGE-GRADE                                       46
000135                   MOVE  AVERAGE-GRADE  TO  PRINT-AVERAGE-GRADE                        46 72
000136                   WRITE  PRINT-RECORD  FROM  AVERAGE-GRADE-LINE                       32 67
000137                       AFTER ADVANCING PAGE
000138                   MOVE  SAVE-STUDENT-GRADE TO  PRINT-LOWEST-GRADE                     51 80
000139                   MOVE  SAVE-STUDENT-NAME  TO  PRINT-LOWEST-NAME                      50 85
000140                   WRITE  PRINT-RECORD  FROM LOWEST-GRADE-LINE                         32 75
000141                       AFTER ADVANCING 2
000142                   MOVE  NUMBER-FAILING TO  PRINT-NUMBER-FAILING                       48 91
000143                   WRITE  PRINT-RECORD  FROM  NUMBER-FAILING-LINE                      32 86
000144                       AFTER ADVANCING 2.
000145               0300-MESSAGE.

000147                   ADD  +1  TO NUMBER-FAILING                                          48
000148                   MOVE 'POOR GRADE. SEE ME.' TO PRINT-MESSAGE                         65
000149                   MOVE STUDENT-NAME          TO PRINT-NAME                            23 61
000150                   MOVE STUDENT-GRADE         TO PRINT-GRADE                           24 64
000151                   WRITE NOTICE-RECORD FROM DETAIL-LINE                                39 58
000152                       AFTER ADVANCING PAGE.
```

Figure 6.8 *(Continued)*

```
--- VS COBOL II Formatted Dump at ABEND ---

Program = 'PROG2'

Completion code = 'S0C7'

PSW at ABEND = '478D10000000A6AA'

Line number or verb number being executed:  '0000122'/'1'

The GP registers at entry to ABEND were

     Regs  0 - 3  - '7000A590  0002DDE8  00015B38  0000D098'

     Regs  4 - 7  - '0000A5FC  7000A5C0  0000D531  0000D4A9'

     Regs  8 - 11 - '0002DDE8  0000D5B8  0000A0D8  0000A448'

     Regs 12 - 15 - '0000A0B8  0000CE78  70013234  80013244'

Data Division dump of 'PROG2'
000016 FD PROG2.STUDENT-FILE FD
FILE SPECIFIED AS:
  ORGANIZATION=SEQUENTIAL   ACCESS MODE=SEQUENTIAL
  RECFM=FIXED BLOCKED
CURRENT STATUS OF FILE IS:
  OPEN STATUS=INPUT
  QSAM STATUS CODE=00
000022 01 PROG2.STUDENT-RECORD AN-GR
000023 02 PROG2.STUDENT-NAME X(20)
      DISP    ===>MOPEY       MICHAEL
000024 02 PROG2.STUDENT-GRADE 999                                    INVALID DATA FOR THIS DATA TYPE
      DISP    HEX>444
                  000
000025 02 PROG2.FILLER X(57)
      DISP    ===>                                     00051100
000026 FD PROG2.REPORT-FILE FD
FILE SPECIFIED AS:
  ORGANIZATION=SEQUENTIAL   ACCESS MODE=SEQUENTIAL
  RECFM=FIXED BLOCKED
CURRENT STATUS OF FILE IS:
  OPEN STATUS=OUTPUT
  QSAM STATUS CODE=00
000032 01 PROG2.PRINT-RECORD X(133)
      DISP    ===>****************************************************************************************************
                                                                                  UNPRINTABLE CHARACTERS IN DATA
              HEX>0000000000000000000000000000000000000000000000000000000000000000000000000000000000000000000000000000
                  0000000000000000000000000000000000000000000000000000000000000000000000000000000000000000000000000000
              ===>*********************************
                                                                                  UNPRINTABLE CHARACTERS IN DATA
              HEX>000000000000000000000000000000000
                  000000000000000000000000000000000
```

Figure 6.9 FDUMP output generated as a result of running the JCL in Fig. 6.5. The COBOL II program ABENDed. (*Continued*)

number of the ABENDing statement. In the current example, this would be an Assembler instruction generated by the verb on line 122.

The contents of the general-purpose registers at entry to the ABEND appear next. In a Release 3 dump the contents of the floating-point registers would also be shown if they were used.

Next is the COBOL formatted dump of the program's DATA DIVISION, showing information about files, indexes (this program has none), and data names. For each data name, the following information is given:

1. Its source line number (at letter "A" in Fig. 6.9)
2. Its normalized level number (letter "B" in the figure)
3. The name of the item in the format program-name.item-name (letter "C")

```
000033 FD PROG2.NOTICE-FILE FD
FILE SPECIFIED AS:
  ORGANIZATION=SEQUENTIAL   ACCESS MODE=SEQUENTIAL
  RECFM=FIXED BLOCKED
CURRENT STATUS OF FILE IS:
  OPEN STATUS=OUTPUT
  QSAM STATUS CODE=00
000039 01 PROG2.NOTICE-RECORD X(133)
      DISP     ===>****************************************************************************************************
                                                                                  UNPRINTABLE CHARACTERS IN DATA
               HEX>0000000000000000000000000000000000000000000000000000000000000000000000000000000000000000000000000000
                   0000000000000000000000000000000000000000000000000000000000000000000000000000000000000000000000000000
               ===>*********************************
                                                                                  UNPRINTABLE CHARACTERS IN DATA
               HEX>000000000000000000000000000000000
                   000000000000000000000000000000000
000042 01 PROG2.FILLER X(32)
      DISP     ===>PROG2    WORKING-STORAGE BEGINS
000044 01 PROG2.ACCUMULATORS AN-GR
000045 02 PROG2.TOT-GRADE S9(7)<--------------(H)
                                                                                  INVALID SIGN - POSITIVE VALUE IS
      CMP3     ===>+0000000
               HEX>0000                                                                        \
                   0000                                                                         \------(I)
000046 02 PROG2.AVERAGE-GRADE S999V99
                                                                                  INVALID SIGN - POSITIVE VALUE IS
      CMP3     ===>+000.00
               HEX>000
                   000
000047 02 PROG2.NUMBER-STUDENTS S999
                                                                                  INVALID SIGN - POSITIVE VALUE IS
      CMP3     ===>+000
               HEX>00
                   00
000048 02 PROG2.NUMBER-FAILING S999
                                                                                  INVALID SIGN - POSITIVE VALUE IS
      CMP3     ===>+000
               HEX>00
                   00
000049 01 PROG2.WORK-AREAS AN-GR
000050 02 PROG2.SAVE-STUDENT-NAME X(20)
      DISP     ===>MOPEY        MICHAEL
000051 02 PROG2.SAVE-STUDENT-GRADE S999
      CMP3     ===>+000
000053 01 PROG2.SWITCHES AN-GR
000054 02 PROG2.SW-EOF X
      DISP     ===>N
000057 01 PROG2.PRINT-LINES AN-GR
000058 02 PROG2.DETAIL-LINE AN-GR
000059 03 PROG2.FILLER X(11)
      DISP     ===>
                                        .
                                        .
                                        .

--- End of VS COBOL II Formatted Dump at ABEND ---
```

Figure 6.9 *(Continued)*

4. Either a symbol indicating the data type (e.g., AN-GR which means alphanumeric group) or the PICTURE of the item (see letter "D" in the figure)
5. The data item's USAGE (letter "E")
6. The item's contents in EBCDIC or in hexadecimal if it is invalid or unprintable (shown at letter "F")
7. Possibly an informational message such as "INVALID DATA FOR THIS DATA TYPE" or "UNPRINTABLE CHARACTERS IN DATA" (letter "G")

Notice that FDUMP uses an asterisk in the EBCDIC representation of a field to signify a conflict between the data type and the actual contents of the field. Several fields in the current dump are flagged this way; however, they do not necessarily represent a problem. The two output records PRINT-RECORD and NOTICE-RECORD, for example, are PIC X items containing binary zeros. They were not initialized at the start of the program because they will have data moved into them before they are written.

Information about files includes OPEN/CLOSE status, file organization, and file status code.

Getting back to the problem at hand, we need to look at line 122 in the source code, flagged by FDUMP as the statement which was executing at the time of the ABEND. The statement is

```
ADD STUDENT-GRADE TO TOT-GRADE
```

We know that an S0C7 completion code means that an instruction was attempting an operation with invalid packed data. We therefore must examine the operands in the ADD statement.

STUDENT-GRADE is a field in the input record STUDENT-RECORD. FDUMP shows us that it is defined with a PICTURE clause of 999 and USAGE DISPLAY (DISP). The hexadecimal value of STUDENT-GRADE is given as 404040, which represents three spaces. Spaces are invalid in a numeric field, and the FDUMP message (at letter "G") gives us a message to that effect.

The contents of the STUDENT-NAME field for this record is listed in the dump as "MOPEY MICHAEL." In the input data set shown in Fig. 6.10 we see that the record for MOPEY MICHAEL does indeed have spaces in the STUDENT-GRADE field.

The other operand in the ADD instruction, TOT-GRADE, is listed in the dump as a COMP-3 field (CMP3) with a PICTURE of S9(7) (see letter "H"). It is an elementary field in the group item ACCUMULATORS. The EBCDIC value of TOT-GRADE is listed as +0000000 and the hexadecimal value is shown as 00000000. The FDUMP message (letter "I") alerts us that this is incorrect data for this field; the hexadecimal value indicates unsigned binary zeros rather than a properly packed number.

Looking at the source code in Fig. 6.8 we find that TOT-GRADE has not been initialized with a VALUE clause. We can look at the cross-reference listing to see if there was any attempt to initialize TOT-GRADE or the group item ACCUMULATORS in the PROCEDURE DIVISION; there was none (see Fig. 6.11).

```
                  .
                  .
                  .
MOPEY       MICHAEL
PETERS      ROBERT   085
REESE       THELMA   057
TAYLOR      GEORGE   100
WASHINGTON  ALFRED   099
WASHINGTON  MARTHA   087
```

Figure 6.10 Input data set for the COBOL II program executed by the JCL in Fig. 6.5.

```
An "M" preceding a data-name reference indicates that the data-name is modified by this reference.

 Defined    Cross-reference of data names    References

     44     ACCUMULATORS
     46     AVERAGE-GRADE. . . . . . . . .   M134 135
     67     AVERAGE-GRADE-LINE . . . . . .   136
                                               .
                                               .
                                               .
     53     SWITCHES
     45     TOT-GRADE. . . . . . . . . . .   M122 133
     49     WORK-AREAS
```

Figure 6.11 Cross-reference listing for the COBOL II program shown in Fig. 6.8.

We now see why the program ABENDed. Both fields used in the ADD statement contained invalid data, one because of an improper input record and the other because of failure to initialize a data item in the program. FDUMP made it easy to solve this ABEND.

6.3 SUMMARY

The COBOL formatted dump makes it easy for you to find information about a program's data areas since it identifies fields by their COBOL source names and is printed primarily in EBCDIC notation. It also provides ABEND information.

The OS/VS COBOL SYMDMP compiler option generates a dump of the DATA DIVISION and portions of COBOL's internal data areas if the program ABENDs. You can also request dynamic dumps of specific data names during program execution.

Several DD statements must be coded in the JCL when SYMDMP is to be used. SYSUT5 is required at compile time and its contents must be passed to an execution-time DD statement. SYSDBOUT is used to hold the SYMDMP output. SYSDBG must be coded to hold execution-time control statements.

```
//S1       EXEC COBUCLG
//**********************************************************
//*  SOURCE CODE IS OS/VS COBOL                            *
//**********************************************************
//COB.SYSIN    DD DSN=YOUR.PROGLIB.COBOL(TESTPROG),DISP=SHR
//GO.TRANSFLE  DD DSN=INPUT.TRANS.DATA,DISP=SHR
//MASTFILE     DD DSN=INPUT.MASTER.DATA,DISP=SHR
//REPTFLE      DD SYSOUT=A
//ERRORS       DD SYSOUT=A
//SYSOUT       DD SYSOUT=A
//SYSUDUMP     DD SYSOUT=A
//
```

Figure 6.12 JCL for executing COBUCLG.

There are two types of SYMDMP control statements: the program-control statement and the line-control statement. A program-control statement is always required, and line statements are required to request dynamic dumps.

When an ABEND dump is produced, SYMDMP also identifies the name of the program which was executing, the completion code, and the number of the COBOL statement which was executing when the program terminated.

The FDUMP compiler option is used to request a COBOL II formatted dump if a COBOL II program ABENDs. A SYSDBOUT DD statement is required in the JCL to hold the dump output. FDUMP output includes information about the DATA DIVISION, the contents of general-purpose registers, the completion code, and the source line number of the statement which was executing at the time of the ABEND.

When FDUMP is requested, the TEST compiler option should not be specified and the STAE execution-time option must be in effect. STAE invokes the COBOL II ABEND handler and cleans up the COBOL II run-time environment. The run-time environment serves as an interface between COBOL and the operating system. Even if the FDUMP compiler option was not in effect, it is helpful to have STAE in effect since it causes additional debugging information to be generated and sent to the SYSABOUT DD statement.

```
LOC      CARD    LV NAME                          TYPE    VALUE

         000007  FD PRINT-FILE                    QSAM    FILE: CLOSED   ORGANIZATION: PHYSICAL SEQUENTIAL
                                                          LAST SUCCESSFUL I/O STMT: UNKNOWN   FILE STATUS: 00
00A884                             DCB   00000000 00000000 00000000 00000000   00000000 00000001 00004000 00000001
00A8A4                                   42000001 0000A84C D7D9C9D5 E3C5D940   02000000 00000000 00000001 00000000
00A8C4                                   00000000 00000000 00000000 00000000   00000085 00000000 00000000 00000000

         000014  01 PRINT-RECORD                  AN

IKF182I  UNINITIALIZED OR INVALID BASE ADDRESS FOR DATA ITEM ABOVE.

         000017  01 WORK-AREAS
00A750                                    (HEX)           E3C5E2E3 D7D9D6C7 40E6D6D9   D2C9D5C7 60E2E3D6 D9C1C7C5
00A768                                                    40C2C5C7 C9D5E240 0350000C   010C0000 00000000 00000000
00A780                                                    00000000 00000000 0001985C   000C0000 02400C00 00000000
00A798                                                    00000000 00F14040 40404040   40404040 E3C8C540 C1D5E2E6
00A7B0                                                    C5D940C9 E2400000 00000000   00000000 00000040 40404040
00A7C8                                                    40404040 40404040 40404040   40404040 40404040 40404040
00A7E0                                                    --SAME--
00A810                                                    40404040 40404040 40404040   40404040 4040E85C 5C5CE6D6
00A828                                                    D9D2C9D5 C740E2E3 D6D9C1C7   C540C5D5 C4E240C8 C5D9C55C
00A840                                                    5C5C5C
00A750   000018  02 FILLER                        AN      TESTPROG WORKING-STORAGE BEGINS
         000020  02 INPUT-FIELDS
00A770   000021  03 BEGINNING-BALANCE             NP-S    +03500.00
00A774   000023  03 TIME-PERIOD                   NP-S    +010
00A776   000025  03 INTEREST-RATE                 NP-S    .00*
00A778   000026  03 ACCUMULATED-INTEREST          NP-S    00000.0*
00A77C   000027  03 HOLD-AREA                     NP-S    0000000.0*
00A781   000028  03 TOTAL-AMT                     NP-S    0000000.0*
                                                          .
                                                          .
                                                          .
```

Figure 6.13 A portion of the SYMDMP output for a program which ABENDed.

```
000174 03 SAMP2.FILLER X(44)
       DISP      ===>
000176 02 SAMP2.EMP-SALARY-LINE AN-GR
000177 03 SAMP2.FILLER X(11)
       DISP      ===>
000179 03 SAMP2.FILLER X(25)
       DISP      ===>LOWEST EMPLOYEE SALARY =
000181 03 SAMP2.PRINT-LOWEST-GRADE Z99,999.99
       DISP      ===>**********
                                                                        INVALID DATA FOR THIS DATA TYPE
                 HEX>0000000000
                     0000000000
000182 03 SAMP2.FILLER XX
       DISP      ===>
000184 03 SAMP2.FILLER X(17)
       DISP      ===>EMPLOYEE NAME IS
000186 03 SAMP2.PRINT-LOWEST-NAME X(27)
       DISP      ===>***************************
                                                                        UNPRINTABLE CHARACTERS IN DATA
                 HEX>000000000000000000000000000
                     000000000000000000000000000
000188 02 SAMP2.NUMBER-RECORDS-LINE AN-GR
000188 03 SAMP2.FILLER X(11)
       DISP      ===>
000190 03 SAMP2.FILLER X(29)
       DISP      ===>NUMBER OF EMPLOYEE RECORDS =
000192 03 SAMP2.PRINT-EMPLOYEE-RECORDS ZZ99
       DISP      ===>****
                                                                        INVALID DATA FOR THIS DATA TYPE
                 HEX>0000
                     0000
000193 03 SAMP2.FILLER X(39)
       DISP      ===>

                                        .
                                        .
                                        .
```

Figure 6.14 Part of the FDUMP output for a program which ABENDed.

REVIEW QUESTIONS

1. What are the advantages of debugging with symbolic COBOL formatted dumps? What are the disadvantages?

2. What is the function of the STAE option? Why must it be in effect if a COBOL II formatted dump is to be requested?

3. What do the following control statements instruct SYMDMP to do?

a. 150,ON 100,(HEX),ALL

b. SAMPPROG,PASSED,ENTRY,NOHEX

c. 200,ON 50,50,900,(NOHEX),FIELD-1 THRU FIELD-9

4. A programmer intends to compile, link, and execute a program named YOURPROG in the IDENTIFICATION DIVISION using the JCL shown in Fig. 6.12. Modify the JCL to do the following:

a. Request an OS/VS COBOL formatted dump in the event YOURPROG ABENDs.

b. Request the printing in hexadecimal format of the contents of the records in TRANSFLE the tenth time and then every twentieth time the READ statement at line 199 is reached. The file is referred to as TRANSACTION-FILE in the program's FD.

c. Request the values of the DATA DIVISION fields YOUR-FIELD-1 and YOUR-FIELD-2 to be given the tenth time through the twentieth time the statement at line 250 is reached.

5. Use Fig. 6.13 to answer the following questions about SYMDMP output:

a. What is the hexadecimal offset and source line number of the field BEGINNING-BALANCE?

b. What is the data type of TIME-PERIOD?

c. What does the asterisk mean in the field INTEREST-RATE? What are its contents in hexadecimal?

d. Was PRINT-FILE open or closed at the time of the ABEND?

6. Use Fig. 6.14 to answer the following questions about the FDUMP output shown.

a. At what line does EMP-SALARY-LINE appear in the source module? What is its data type?

b. What is the meaning of the asterisks and the message for the field PRINT-LOWEST-GRADE?

c. What does the message to the right of the field PRINT-LOWEST-NAME indicate?

Chapter

7

Debugging with Abend-AID

As an alternative to the hexadecimal system dumps generated by MVS, many shops install products from non-IBM vendors. One widely used tool is Abend-AID.* Before looking at MVS system dumps we will examine Abend-AID.

The Abend-AID product is designed to intercept MVS's dumping facilities and produce its own formatted dump and diagnostic reports when an ABEND occurs. Abend-AID may be customized to suit an installation's requirements. Some optional enhancements can also be added to the basic Abend-AID product. Although Abend-AID provides support for several languages and databases, we will look at the features common to all, and at those specific to COBOL. Examples in this chapter were run under Abend-AID Release 6.0.2.

7.1 BASIC Abend-AID FEATURES

Abend-AID receives control whenever a dump is requested because of an ABEND or a request by the programmer. Either the SYSUDUMP or SYSABEND DD statement must be present in the JCL, or both the SYSMDUMP and ABENDAID DD statements must be present. Compuware provides default options in Abend-AID's control structure; these determine the type of processing Abend-AID will do when it receives control.

7.1.1 The Abend-AID Control Structure

Abend-AID produces diagnostic information and dump formatting based on the options in effect in the control structure. This control structure consists of a five-level hierarchical system with options which can be modified by the installation or the programmer. The levels, in order of priority from lowest to highest, are selection tables, ABEND code table, user exits, JCL modification, and systemwide shutdown. Here is a brief description of each of the control structure levels.

*Abend-AID is a trademark of Compuware Corporation.

Selection tables. These tables are supplied by Compuware. They permit your installation to specify by particular program name or job name prefixes what type of processing Abend-AID is to do. Options include "dump," "no dump," and "ignore."

ABEND code table. This table is supplied by Compuware. It indicates what actions, such as the printing of an MVS system dump, Abend-AID is to take when it encounters specific ABENDs and the problem is either completely or partially diagnosed by Abend-AID. The table may be modified by your installation to tailor such things as program storage analysis and control block formatting.

User exits. The Abend-AID product allows the installation to specify three user exits. They permit the dynamic performance of special processing based on conditions for a particular job. The exits enable you to

- Override job and program tables or specify an alternate ABEND code table from that supplied by Compuware. This permits the installation to invoke its own specific error processing, such as produce a dump, Abend-AID report or neither, for specific ABENDs and job names.
- Change the name of the report data set, dynamically suppress output, or direct output to a particular output device. This is helpful because it allows you to customize output destinations by ABEND code, job name, or both.
- Print selected storage areas, such as control blocks or tables from user-written applications.

JCL modification. This allows a programmer to specify certain DD statements which will override default options specified in the global default table supplied by Compuware (this sets installation-wide defaults), the ABEND code table, the selection tables, or a user exit. Possible DD statements include:

DD statement	Description
`//ABENDAID DD SYSOUT=`	Alternate DD for Abend-AID output (many installations direct the Abend-AID output to the SYSUDUMP DD statement).* Also required for SNAP-AID (see Sec. 7.2.1).
`//ABNLALL DD DUMMY`	Forces formatting of all program storage and control blocks.
`//ABNLDUMP DD DUMMY`	Forces printing of the normal IBM dump in addition to the Abend-AID output.
`//ABNLENAB DD DUMMY`	Enables Abend-AID when it has been disabled in the CWGLOBAL table. This table is supplied by Compuware; it is used to establish installation-wide defaults, including formatting and printing options.
`//ABNLFMTD DD DUMMY`	Forces printing of only the formatted control blocks portion of the IBM dump (see Secs. 8.7 and 9.2).
`//ABNLHELP DD DUMMY`	Produces the Abend-AID help pages outlining how to use the Abend-AID output.
`//ABNLIGNR DD DUMMY`	Shuts off Abend-AID processing.

*NOTE: A SYSUDUMP/SYSABEND DD is still required to invoke Abend-AID. Users of SYSMDUMP must use the ABENDAID DD to get Abend-AID output. Abend-AID will not write to SYSMDUMP.

//ABNLINCL DD DUMMY	Causes all active load modules to be considered for CSECT inclusion via the CWINCLUD table. A CSECT is a relocatable program unit (see Secs. 10.3.1 and 11.4). The CWINCLUD table is supplied by Compuware; it allows you to specify that all CSECTS on the calling chain are to be shown, including those you would not normally see, such as those from IBM utility routines.
//ABNLNCBS DD DUMMY	Suppresses printing of the Abend-AID data management control blocks section.
//ABNLNODP DD DUMMY	Suppresses printing of the IBM dump after Abend-AID processing.
//ABNLNONE DD DUMMY	Opposite of //ABNLALL; suppresses printing of all program storage and control blocks.
//ABNLNWSP DD DUMMY	Suppresses printing of the Abend-AID program storage section.
//ABNLPCBS DD DUMMY	Forces printing of the Abend-AID data management control blocks section.
//ABNLSPRT DD DUMMY	Forces printing of the entire record if 'RECPRT=S' is in the CWGLOBAL table.
//ABNLSUPT DD DUMMY	Suppresses the inclusion of Abend-AID/COBOL information in the object deck.*
//ABNLSUPW DD DUMMY	Suppresses the placement of error/warning messages in the body of the Abend-AID/COBOL source listing.
//ABNLTERM DD SYSOUT=	Invokes the Abend-AID/ONLINE feature for 72-column output (we will discuss the ONLINE feature in Sec. 7.2.2).
//ABNLTERM DD DSN=	Specifies an Abend-AID report data set for Abend-AID output.
//ABNLWIDE DD DUMMY	Allows 121-column output when the default is 72 columns.
//ABNLWSPT DD DUMMY	Forces printing of the Abend-AID program storage section.

If two mutually exclusive DD statements are present in the JCL, the last one encountered will be the one that takes effect.

Systemwide shutdown. This level permits Abend-AID to be removed from the system to be sure that it is not causing a system problem.

7.1.2 Basic Abend-AID Reports

Abend-AID produces a report which provides information necessary to solve an ABEND. The report is composed of several parts: Next Sequential Instruction Section, Diagnostic Section, Program Area Section, Working Storage Section, and File Area. Generally, the most useful debugging information is found at the beginning of a section, followed by more detailed supporting data. The report sections will be described as we examine an actual Abend-AID report to solve an ABEND.

The system being tested consisted of two COBOL II programs compiled under Release 3.1. The main program, MAINPGM, processes employee time card records, writing an employee master record for each one. MAINPGM also writes records to a payroll report and calls SUBPGM1 to calculate employee savings plan amount. The called program, SUBPGM1, calculates the savings plan amount for each employee, based on gross pay and a savings factor passed from MAINPGM.

*NOTE: When this DD card is used, the enhanced Abend-AID/COBOL output will not be available at ABEND time (we will discuss the enhanced COBOL option in Sec. 7.2.3).

```
PP 5668-958 IBM VS COBOL II Release 3.1 09/19/89           MAINPGM   Date 05/17/91  Time 12:40:38   Page    2
 LineID  PL SL  ----+-*A-1-B--+----2----+----3----+----4----+----5----+----6----+----7-|--+----8 Map and Cross Reference

 000001               IDENTIFICATION DIVISION.                                         00010000
 000002               PROGRAM-ID.   MAINPGM.                                           00020000
 000003               AUTHOR.       A. PROGRAMMER.                                     00030000
 000004              *INSTALLATION. MYCOMPANY.                                         00040000
 000005              ***************************************************************** 00041000
 000006              *REMARKS.                                                         00050000
 000007              *   THIS PROGRAM PROCESSES PAYROLL TIME-CARD RECORDS AND          00060000
 000008              *   WRITES AN EMPLOYEE MASTER RECORD FOR EACH EMPLOYEE            00070000
 000009              *   TIME-CARD. IT ALSO CALCULATES THE SAVINGS PLAN BY             00080000
 000010              *   CALLING A COBOL SUBROUTINE.                                   00090000
 000011              ***************************************************************** 00100000
 000012               ENVIRONMENT DIVISION.                                            00110000
 000013               CONFIGURATION SECTION.                                           00120000
 000014               SOURCE-COMPUTER. IBM-370.                                        00130000
 000015               OBJECT-COMPUTER. IBM-370.                                        00140000
 000016               SPECIAL-NAMES.                                                   00150000
 000017                   C01 IS HOF.                                                  00160000
 000018               INPUT-OUTPUT SECTION.                                            00170000
 000019               FILE-CONTROL.                                                    00180000
 000020                   SELECT MASTER   ASSIGN TO UT-S-MASTER.                       00190002  25
 000021                   SELECT OUTLIST  ASSIGN TO UT-S-OUTLIST.                      00200002  32
 000022                   SELECT TIMECARD ASSIGN TO UT-AS-TIMECARD.                    00210002  39
 000023               DATA DIVISION.                                                   00220000
 000024               FILE SECTION.                                                    00230005
 000025               FD  MASTER                                                       00240000
 000026                       LABEL RECORDS ARE STANDARD                               00250000
 000027                       RECORDING MODE IS F                                      00260000
 000028                       RECORD CONTAINS 80 CHARACTERS                            00270000
 000029                       BLOCK CONTAINS 0 RECORDS                                 00280000
 000030                       DATA RECORD IS MSTR-RECORD.                              00290000
 000031               01  MSTR-RECORD          PIC X(80).                              00300000  BLF=0000+000          80C
 000032               FD  OUTLIST                                                      00310000
 000033                       LABEL RECORDS ARE STANDARD                               00320000
 000034                       RECORDING MODE IS F                                      00330000
 000035                       RECORD CONTAINS 133 CHARACTERS                           00340000
 000036                       BLOCK CONTAINS 10 RECORDS                                00350000
 000037                       DATA RECORD IS R-LINE.                                   00360000
 000038               01  R-LINE               PIC X(133).                             00370000  BLF=0001+000          133C
 000039               FD  TIMECARD                                                     00380000
 000040                       LABEL RECORDS ARE STANDARD                               00390000
 000041                       RECORD CONTAINS 80 CHARACTERS                            00410000
 000042                       DATA RECORD IS T-RECORD .                                00430000
 000043               01  T-RECORD             PIC X(80).                              00440000  BLF=0002+000          80C
 000044              ***************************************************************** 00441000
 000045              *  WORKING STORAGE:                                               00441100
 000046              ***************************************************************** 00441200
 000047               WORKING-STORAGE SECTION.                                         00442000
 000048               77  RECORD-CTR           PIC S999     COMP-3 VALUE +0.           00443000  BLW=0000+000          2P
 000049               77  OLD-EMPL-NUMB        PIC 9(8)            VALUE ZEROS.        00444000  BLW=0000+008          8C
                                                                                                 IMP
 000050               77  NET-PAY              PIC S9(5)V99 COMP-3.                    00445000  BLW=0000+010          4P
 000051               77  PAGE-CTR             PIC S999     COMP-3 VALUE ZEROS.        00446000  BLW=0000+018          2P
                                                                                                 IMP
 000052               77  TOTAL-CTR            PIC S9(7)V99 COMP-3.                    00447000  BLW=0000+020          5P
 000053               77  LINE-CTR             PIC S999     COMP-3 VALUE +56.          00448000  BLW=0000+028          2P
 000054               77  SAVINGS-AMT          PIC 9(5)V99.                            00449000  BLW=0000+030          7C
```

Figure 7.1 COBOL II compiler output for MAINPGM showing source code and portions of the XREF listing.

The source module for MAINPGM is shown in Fig. 7.1 and the source module for SUBPGM1 is shown in Fig. 7.2. The system ABENDed when it was run under MVS/XA with Abend-AID installed. The Abend-AID report is shown in Fig. 7.3.

At the beginning of the Abend-AID report we see that the completion code was S0C7 (letter "A" in Fig. 7.3). Following this, in the Next Sequential Instruction Section, we find that the next sequential instruction to be executed (NSI) is at hexadecimal displacement 0002D8 in SUBPGM1 (at letter "B" in the figure). Sometimes Abend-AID will also provide the displacement of the last I/O statement or CALL. This may be a helpful clue in determining what the program was doing prior to the ABEND.

```
PP 5668-958 IBM VS COBOL II Release 3.1 09/19/89              MAINPGM   Date 05/17/91  Time 12:40:38   Page     3
  LineID  PL SL  ----+-*A-1-B--+----2----+----3----+----4----+----5----+----6----+----7-|--+----8  Map and Cross Reference

 000055               ****************************************************************** 00449100
 000056               *  INPUT RECORD AND REDEFINE:                                        00449200
 000057               ****************************************************************** 00449300
 000058                01  TIME-RECORD.                                                  00450000  BLW=0000+038               0CL80
 000059                   03  EMPLOYEE-NO          PIC 9(8).                             00460000  BLW=0000+038,0000000 8C
 000060                   03  MONTH-CODE           PIC XX.                               00470000  BLW=0000+040,0000008 2C
 000061                   03  EMPLOYEE-NAME        PIC X(32).                            00480000  BLW=0000+042,000000A 32C
 000062                   03  GROSS-PAY            PIC 9(5)V99.                          00490000  BLW=0000+062,000002A 7C
 000063                   03  TOTAL-TAXES          PIC 9(4)V99.                          00500000  BLW=0000+069,0000031 6C
 000064                   03  SAVINGS-FACTOR       PIC V99.                              00510000  BLW=0000+06F,0000037 2C
 000065                   03  FILLER               PIC X(23).                            00520000  BLW=0000+071,0000039 23C
 000066     (B)        01  TIME-REC-NUM REDEFINES TIME-RECORD.                           00530000  BLW=0000+038               0CL80
                                                                                                   58
 000067                   03  FILLER               PIC X(8).                             00540000  BLW=0000+038,0000000 8C
 000068                   03  MONTH-NUM            PIC S99.                              00550000  BLW=0000+040,0000008 2C
 000069                   03  FILLER               PIC X(70).                            00560000  BLW=0000+042,000000A 70C
 000070               ****************************************************************** 00561000
 000071               *  HEADER LINES, DETAIL LINE AND TOTAL LINE:                         00562000
 000072               ****************************************************************** 00563000
 000073                01  HDR-LINE1.                                                    00570000  BLW=0000+088               0CL133
 000074                   03  FILLER               PIC X(58)  VALUE SPACES.              00580000  BLW=0000+088,0000000 58C
                                                                                                   IMP
 000075                   03  FILLER               PIC X(48)  VALUE 'PAYROLL REPORT'.    00590000  BLW=0000+0C2,000003A 48C
 000076                   03  FILLER               PIC X(19)  VALUE SPACES.              00600000  BLW=0000+0F2,000006A 19C
                                                                                                   IMP
 000077                   03  FILLER               PIC X(5)   VALUE 'PAGE '.             00610000  BLW=0000+105,000007D 5C
 000078                   03  PAGE-NO              PIC ZZZ.                              00620000  BLW=0000+10A,0000082 3C
 000079                01  HDR-LINE2.                                                    00630000  BLW=0000+110               0CL133
 000080                   03  FILLER               PIC X      VALUE SPACES.              00640000  BLW=0000+110,0000000 1C
                                                                                                   IMP
 000081                   03  FILLER               PIC X(35)  VALUE 'EMPLOYEE NAME'.     00650000  BLW=0000+111,0000001 35C
 000082                   03  FILLER               PIC X(18)  VALUE 'EMPLOYEE NUMBER'.   00660000  BLW=0000+134,0000024 18C
 000083                   03  FILLER               PIC X(17)  VALUE 'MONTH'.             00670000  BLW=0000+146,0000036 17C
 000084                   03  FILLER               PIC X(15)  VALUE 'GROSS PAY'.         00680000  BLW=0000+157,0000047 15C
 000085                   03  FILLER               PIC X(17)  VALUE 'TOTAL TAXES'.       00690000  BLW=0000+166,0000056 17C
 000086                   03  FILLER               PIC X(18)  VALUE 'SAVINGS PLAN'.      00700000  BLW=0000+177,0000067 18C
 000087                   03  FILLER               PIC X(10)  VALUE 'NET PAY'.           00710000  BLW=0000+189,0000079 10C
 000088                   03  FILLER               PIC X(2)   VALUE SPACES.              00720000  BLW=0000+193,0000083 2C
                                                                                                   IMP
 000089                01  OUTLIST-LINE.                                                 00730000  BLW=0000+198               0CL133
 000090                   03  FILLER               PIC X      VALUE SPACES.              00740000  BLW=0000+198,0000000 1C
                                                                                                   IMP
 000091                   03  R-EMPLOYEE-NAME      PIC X(32).                            00750000  BLW=0000+199,0000001 32C
 000092                   03  FILLER               PIC X(6)   VALUE SPACES.              00760000  BLW=0000+1B9,0000021 6C
                                                                                                   IMP
 000093                   03  R-EMPLOYEE-NO        PIC 9(8).                             00770000  BLW=0000+1BF,0000027 8C
 000094                   03  FILLER               PIC X(6)   VALUE SPACES.              00780000  BLW=0000+1C7,000002F 6C
                                                                                                   IMP
 000095                   03  MONTH                PIC X(9).                             00790000  BLW=0000+1CD,0000035 9C
 000096                   03  FILLER               PIC X(9)   VALUE SPACES.              00800000  BLW=0000+1D6,000003E 9C
                                                                                                   IMP
 000097                   03  R-GROSS-PAY          PIC $ZZ,ZZZ.99.                       00810000  BLW=0000+1DF,0000047 10C
 000098                   03  FILLER               PIC X(5)   VALUE SPACES.              00820000  BLW=0000+1E9,0000051 5C
                                                                                                   IMP
```

Figure 7.1 *(Continued)*

The Next Sequential Instruction Section also gives load module information, the program status word (PSW), the instruction length code (ILC), the entry point and load point addresses (EPA and LPA), and the contents of the general-purpose registers (none of this was included in Fig. 7.3 since we normally will not need to examine this information when we debug using Abend-AID output). Chapters 8 through 11 explain the significance of this information should it become necessary to use it.

We can now look at hexadecimal offset 2D8 in SUBPGM1 to find the NSI. In the OFFSET output, at letter "A" on page 5 in Fig. 7.2, we see that the NSI is one of the Assembler instructions generated by the MULTIPLY on line 41; the actual ABENDing instruction is the preceding Assembler instruction generated by the MULTIPLY statement. We see at letter "B" on page 2 in Fig. 7.2 that line 41 in the source module is

```
PP 5668-958 IBM VS COBOL II Release 3.1 09/19/89              MAINPGM   Date 05/17/91  Time 12:40:38   Page    4
  LineID  PL SL  ----+-*A-1-B--+----2----+----3----+----4----+----5----+----6----+----7-|--+----8 Map and Cross Reference

  000099                       03  R-TOTAL-TAXES        PIC $Z,ZZZ.99.                          00830000  BLW=0000+1EE,0000056 9C
  000100                       03  FILLER               PIC X(8)    VALUE SPACES.               00840000  BLW=0000+1F7,000005F 8C
                                                                                                          IMP
  000101                       03  R-SAVINGS-AMT        PIC $ZZ,ZZZ.99.                         00850000  BLW=0000+1FF,0000067 10C
  000102                       03  FILLER               PIC X(8)    VALUE SPACES.               00860000  BLW=0000+209,0000071 8C
                                                                                                          IMP
  000103                       03  R-NET-PAY            PIC $ZZ,ZZZ.99.                         00870000  BLW=0000+211,0000079 10C
  000104                       03  FILLER               PIC X(2)    VALUE SPACES.               00880000  BLW=0000+21B,0000083 2C
                                                                                                          IMP
  000105                    01  FINAL-LINE.                                                     00890000  BLW=0000+220         0CL133
  000106                       03  FILLER               PIC X(118) VALUE ' TOTAL NET PAY'.      00900000  BLW=0000+220,0000000 118C
  000107                       03  TOTAL-NET-PAY        PIC $Z,ZZZ,ZZZ.99.                      00910000  BLW=0000+296,0000076 13C
  000108                       03  FILLER               PIC X(2)    VALUE SPACES.               00920000  BLW=0000+2A3,0000083 2C
                                                                                                          IMP
  000109                   ***************************************************************** 00921000
  000110                   *  VARIABLES FOR MONTH NUMBER TO MONTH NAME CONVERSION:              00922000
  000111                   ***************************************************************** 00923000
  000112                    01  CONSTANTS.                                                      00930000  BLW=0000+2A8         0CL6
  000113                       03  BLANK-MONTH          PIC XX      VALUE '  '.                 00940000  BLW=0000+2A8,0000000 2C
  000114                       03  JAN                  PIC S99     VALUE +00.                  00950000  BLW=0000+2AA,0000002 2C
  000115                       03  DEC                  PIC S99     VALUE +13.                  00960000  BLW=0000+2AC,0000004 2C
  000116                    01  MONTH-TAB.                                                      00970000  BLW=0000+2B0         0CL108
  000117                       03  FILLER               PIC X(9)    VALUE 'JANUARY  '.          00980000  BLW=0000+2B0,0000000 9C
  000118                       03  FILLER               PIC X(9)    VALUE 'FEBRUARY '.          00990000  BLW=0000+2B9,0000009 9C
  000119                       03  FILLER               PIC X(9)    VALUE 'MARCH    '.          01000000  BLW=0000+2C2,0000012 9C
  000120                       03  FILLER               PIC X(9)    VALUE 'APRIL    '.          01010000  BLW=0000+2CB,000001B 9C
  000121                       03  FILLER               PIC X(9)    VALUE 'MAY      '.          01020000  BLW=0000+2D4,0000024 9C
  000122                       03  FILLER               PIC X(9)    VALUE 'JUNE     '.          01030000  BLW=0000+2DD,000002D 9C
  000123                       03  FILLER               PIC X(9)    VALUE 'JULY     '.          01040000  BLW=0000+2E6,0000036 9C
  000124                       03  FILLER               PIC X(9)    VALUE 'AUGUST   '.          01050000  BLW=0000+2EF,000003F 9C
  000125                       03  FILLER               PIC X(9)    VALUE 'SEPTEMBER'.          01060000  BLW=0000+2F8,0000048 9C
  000126                       03  FILLER               PIC X(9)    VALUE 'OCTOBER  '.          01070000  BLW=0000+301,0000051 9C
  000127                       03  FILLER               PIC X(9)    VALUE 'NOVEMBER '.          01080000  BLW=0000+30A,000005A 9C
  000128                       03  FILLER               PIC X(9)    VALUE 'DECEMBER '.          01090000  BLW=0000+313,0000063 9C
  000129                    01  MO-TAB REDEFINES MONTH-TAB.                                     01100000  BLW=0000+2B0         0CL108
                                                                                                          116
  000130                       03  MONTH-TABLE          PIC X(9)    OCCURS 12 TIMES.            01110000  BLW=0000+2B0,0000000 9C
  000131                   ***************************************************************** 01120000
  000132                   *  PROCEDURE DIVISION:                                               01121000
  000133                   ***************************************************************** 01123000
  000134                    PROCEDURE DIVISION.                                                 01130000
  000135                    START-HERE.                                                         01140000
  000136                        OPEN INPUT TIMECARD,                                            01150000  39
  000137                             OUTPUT MASTER, OUTPUT OUTLIST.                             01160000  25 32
  000138                        MOVE ZEROS TO TOTAL-CTR.                                        01170000  IMP 52
  000139                   ***************************************************************** 01171000
  000140                   *---- READ/PROCESS LOOP BEGINS HERE:                                 01173000
  000141                   ***************************************************************** 01180000
  000142                    GET-ANOTHER.                                                        01190000
  000143                        READ TIMECARD INTO TIME-RECORD AT END GO TO END-OF-JOB.         01200000  39 58 206  <---- (C)
  000144                        MOVE TIME-RECORD TO MSTR-RECORD.                                01210000  58 31
  000145                        ADD 1 TO RECORD-CTR.                                            01220001  48
```

Figure 7.1 *(Continued)*

```
MULTIPLY WS-SAVINGS-FACTOR BY WS-GROSS-PAY GIVING WS-SAVINGS-AMT.
```

Since an S0C7 is a data exception, i.e., an instruction attempted an operation on invalid packed data, we need to get information about the instruction's operands. The Diagnostic Section gives information about the causes of the ABEND and often suggests specific corrective actions. The message at letter "C" in the Diagnostic Section in Fig. 7.3 tells us that an S0C7 occurs when a COMP-3 field has an invalid digit (not 0 to 9), or its last byte contains an invalid sign (not F, C, or D).

The statement about the sign may be misleading; IBM system 370 hardware accepts A, B, C, D, E, and F as signs. In COBOL II Release 3 there is an installation option (NUMCLS(ALT)) which causes the compiler option NUMPROC(NOPFD) to accept A to F as signs for numeric class tests on fields

```
PP 5668-958 IBM VS COBOL II Release 3.1 09/19/89            MAINPGM   Date 05/17/91  Time 12:40:38   Page     5
 LineID  PL SL  ----+-*A-1-B--+----2----+----3----+----4----+----5----+----6----+----7-|--+----8 Map and Cross Reference

 000146               ****************************************************************** 01221000
 000147               *---- VALIDATE EMPLOYEE NUMBER:                                    01222000
 000148               ****************************************************************** 01223000
 000149                    IF EMPLOYEE-NO > OLD-EMPL-NUMB                                01230000  59 49
 000150       1                MOVE EMPLOYEE-NO TO OLD-EMPL-NUMB ELSE                    01240000  59 49
 000151       1                DISPLAY 'EMPLOYEE# SEQ ERROR  ', EMPLOYEE-NO, SPACE,      01250000  59 IMP
 000152       1                OLD-EMPL-NUMB UPON SYSOUT,  GO TO GET-ANOTHER.            01260000  49 142
 000153               ****************************************************************** 01261000
 000154               *---- MOVE STATIC VARIABLES TO OUTPUT LINE,                        01262000
 000155               *     CALL SUBPGM1 TO CALCULATE SAVINGS PLAN AMOUNT                01263000
 000156               *     PERFORM TOTAL PAY CALCUTION                                  01264000
 000157               ****************************************************************** 01265000
 000158                    MOVE EMPLOYEE-NO   TO R-EMPLOYEE-NO.                          01270000  59 93
 000159                    MOVE EMPLOYEE-NAME TO R-EMPLOYEE-NAME.                        01280000  61 91
 000160                    CALL 'SUBPGM1' USING GROSS-PAY, SAVINGS-FACTOR,               01290000  EXT 62 64 <---- (A)
 000161                                         SAVINGS-AMT, EMPLOYEE-NO.                01300000  54 59
 000162                    SUBTRACT TOTAL-TAXES SAVINGS-AMT                              01310000  63 54
 000163                                         FROM GROSS-PAY GIVING NET-PAY.           01320000  62 50
 000164                    MOVE GROSS-PAY   TO R-GROSS-PAY.                              01330000  62 97
 000165                    MOVE TOTAL-TAXES TO R-TOTAL-TAXES.                            01340000  63 99
 000166                    MOVE SAVINGS-AMT TO R-SAVINGS-AMT.                            01350000  54 101
 000167                    MOVE NET-PAY     TO R-NET-PAY.                                01360000  50 103
 000168                    ADD NET-PAY      TO TOTAL-CTR.                                01370000  50 52
 000169               ****************************************************************** 01371000
 000170               *---- DETERMINE NAME OF MONTH USING MONTH NUMBER                   01372000
 000171               ****************************************************************** 01375000
 000172                    IF MONTH-CODE = BLANK-MONTH                                   01380000  60 113
 000173       1              MOVE SPACES TO MONTH                                        01390000  IMP 95
 000174                    ELSE                                                          01400000
 000175       1                IF MONTH-NUM > JAN AND MONTH-NUM < DEC                    01410000  68 114 68 115
 000176       2                  MOVE MONTH-TABLE(MONTH-NUM) TO MONTH                    01420000  130 68 95
 000177       1                ELSE                                                      01430000
 000178       2                  MOVE SPACES TO MONTH.                                   01440000  IMP 95
 000179               ****************************************************************** 01441000
 000180               *---- IF AT END-OF-PAGE, PERFORM END-OF-PAGE PROCESSING,           01442000
 000181               *        ELSE WRITE DETAIL LINE                                    01443000
 000182               ****************************************************************** 01444000
 000183                    IF LINE-CTR > 55 THEN                                         01450000  53
 000184       1                ADD 1 TO PAGE-CTR                                         01460000  51
 000185       1                MOVE PAGE-CTR TO PAGE-NO                                  01470000  51 78
 000186       1                WRITE R-LINE FROM HDR-LINE1 AFTER ADVANCING HOF           01480000  38 73 17
 000187       1                WRITE R-LINE FROM HDR-LINE2 AFTER ADVANCING 3 LINES       01490000  38 79
 000188       1                MOVE SPACES TO R-LINE                                     01500000  IMP 38
 000189       1                WRITE R-LINE AFTER ADVANCING 3 LINES                      01510000  38
 000190       1                MOVE 1 TO LINE-CTR                                        01520000  53
 000191       1                ELSE NEXT SENTENCE.                                       01530000
 000192                    WRITE R-LINE FROM OUTLIST-LINE AFTER ADVANCING 1 LINE.        01540000  38 89
 000193                    ADD 1 TO LINE-CTR.                                            01550000  53
```

Figure 7.1 *(Continued)*

defined as USAGE COMP-3 or USAGE DISPLAY which also contain a sign in the picture clause. This option cannot be changed by the application programmer (contact your systems programmer to find out the status of NUMCLS at your installation). When NUMCLS(ALT) and NUMPROC(NOPFD) are in effect, an "invalid" sign will be converted to an F, thereby preventing a data exception (also see Sec. 3.3.2.3). [The COBOL II Release 2 compiler option NOPFDSGN is comparable to NUMPROC(NOPFD).] Referring to the "Execution / Debugging options in effect" messages in the Working Storage Section of Abend-AID's report (letters "D" on page 5 and "E" on page 8 in Fig. 7.3) informs us that the compiler option NUMPROC(NOPFD) was in effect for both programs, although it does not tell us the status of the NUMCLS installation option.

Going back to the Diagnostic Section (page 3 in Fig. 7.3) we are provided with information about the operand fields in error (at letters "F" and "G"). Notice that, at the time of this ABEND, both fields contained invalid numeric data: hexadecimal F0F06A7C7BF2F0 in the first one and hexadecimal

```
PP 5668-958 IBM VS COBOL II Release 3.1 09/19/89            MAINPGM   Date 05/17/91  Time 12:40:38   Page     6
 LineID  PL SL  ----+-*A-1-B--+----2----+----3----+----4----+----5----+----6----+----7-|--+----8 Map and Cross Reference

 000194                ****************************************************************** 01551000
 000195                *---- END OF READ AND PROCESS LOOP:                                 01551100
 000196                *       PERFORM AUDIT OF PROCESSED RECORD, AND GET ANOTHER          01552000
 000197                ****************************************************************** 01553000
 000198                 MSTR-RTN.                                                          01560000
 000199                     WRITE MSTR-RECORD.                                             01570000  31
 000200                     GO TO GET-ANOTHER.                                             01580000  142
 000201                 MSTR-EXIT.                                                         01590000
 000202                     EXIT.                                                          01600000
 000203                ****************************************************************** 01601000
 000204                *---- PERFORM END-OF-JOB PROCESSING                                 01602000
 000205                ****************************************************************** 01604000
 000206                 END-OF-JOB.                                                        01610000
 000207                     MOVE TOTAL-CTR TO TOTAL-NET-PAY.                               01620000  52 107
 000208                     WRITE R-LINE FROM FINAL-LINE AFTER ADVANCING 3 LINES.          01630000  38 105
 000209                     CLOSE  MASTER, OUTLIST, TIMECARD.                              01640000  25 32 39
 000210                     STOP RUN.                                                      01650000

PP 5668-958 IBM VS COBOL II Release 3.1 09/19/89            MAINPGM   Date 05/17/91  Time 12:40:38   Page     7

An "M" preceding a data-name reference indicates that the data-name is modified by this reference.

 Defined   Cross-reference of data names   References

                                                       .
                                                       .
                                                       .
      62   GROSS-PAY. . . . . . . . . . .  160 163 164
                                                       .
                                                       .
                                                       .
      64   SAVINGS-FACTOR . . . . . . . .  160
      43   T-RECORD
      66   TIME-REC-NUM
      58   TIME-RECORD. . . . . . . . . .  66 M143 144
      39   TIMECARD . . . . . . . . . . .  22 136 143 209
                                                       .
                                                       .
                                                       .
```

Figure 7.1 *(Continued)*

F07CFF in the second one. Abend-AID also states that the first field is located at displacement 20 from the start of BLW cell 00 and the second field is located at displacement 27 from the start of BLW cell 00. Knowing this, we can find the names of the COBOL fields in error. This is easy to do since the XREF and SOURCE compiler options in COBOL II Release 3.1 produce embedded cross-reference information. At letter "C" on page 2 in Fig. 7.2 we see that the fields used in the MULTIPLY statement are defined at lines 23 and 22 in the source listing. Examining those lines (see letter "D") verifies that the locations of the first and second fields indicated in Abend-AID's Diagnostic Section match those specified in the embedded cross-reference listing for WS-GROSS-PAY and WS-SAVINGS-FACTOR, respectively. Notice that both fields are defined as USAGE DISPLAY (the default). When COBOL performs arithmetic operations on such fields, it must generate extra instructions to pack the data and place it into intermediate work fields before actually doing the arithmetic operation. The Diagnostic Section does state that although the COBOL fields are in WORKING-STORAGE, contents of both COBOL fields were moved to temporary work fields. If we had a map of the Assembler instructions, we would see that the Assembler instruction peforming the multiplication expects valid packed data in the temporary work fields.

```
PP 5668-958 IBM VS COBOL II Release 3.1 09/19/89              SUBPGM1   Date 05/17/91  Time 12:40:17   Page     2
 LineID  PL SL  ----+-*A-1-B--+----2----+----3----+----4----+----5----+----6----+----7-|--+----8  Map and Cross Reference

 000001                IDENTIFICATION DIVISION.                                      00010000
 000002                PROGRAM-ID.  SUBPGM1.                                         00020000
 000003                INSTALLATION. MYCOMPANY.                                      00030000
 000004                AUTHOR.       A. PROGRAMMER.                                  00031001
 000005               ***************************************************************** 00032001
 000006               *REMARKS.                                                      00040000
 000007               *   THIS SUBROUTINE CALCULATES THE SAVINGS PLAN AMOUNT         00050001
 000008               *   BASED ON GROSS PAY AND SAVINGS FACTOR.                     00060001
 000009               ***************************************************************** 00061001
 000010                ENVIRONMENT DIVISION.                                         00070000
 000011                DATA DIVISION.                                                00080000
 000012               *                                                              00081001
 000013                WORKING-STORAGE SECTION.                                      00090004
 000014                01  CONSTANTS.                                                00100000  BLW=0000+000            0CL9
 000015                    03  MIN-FACTOR          PIC S9V99       VALUE +0.02.      00110000  BLW=0000+000,0000000 3C
 000016                    03  MAX-FACTOR          PIC S9V99       VALUE +0.15.      00120000  BLW=0000+003,0000003 3C
 000017                    03  ZERO-FACTOR         PIC S9V99       VALUE  0.00.      00130002  BLW=0000+006,0000006 3C
 000018                01  PRINT-VARIABLES.                                          00140000  BLW=0000+010            0CL11
 000019                    03  PRINT-FACTOR        PIC 9.99.                         00150000  BLW=0000+010,0000000 4C
 000020                    03  MIN-MAX-PRT         PIC X(7)        VALUE SPACES.     00160000  BLW=0000+014,0000004 7C
                                                                                               IMP
 000021                01  WORK-VARIABLES.                                           00170000  BLW=0000+020            0CL17
(D)---> 000022             03  WS-GROSS-PAY        PIC 9(5)V99     VALUE 0.          00180000  BLW=0000+020,0000000 7C
        000023             03  WS-SAVINGS-FACTOR   PIC 9V99        VALUE 0.          00190000  BLW=0000+027,0000007 3C
 000024                    03  WS-SAVINGS-AMT      PIC 9(5)V99     VALUE 0.          00200000  BLW=0000+02A,000000A 7C
 000025               *                                                              00201001
 000026                LINKAGE SECTION.                                              00210000
(G)---> 000027         77  GROSS-PAY               PIC 9(5)V99.                      00220000  BLL=0001+000            7C
        000028         77  SAVINGS-FACTOR          PIC V99.                          00230000  BLL=0002+000            2C
 000029                77  SAVINGS-AMT             PIC 9(5)V99.                      00240000  BLL=0003+000            7C
 000030                77  EMPLOYEE-NO             PIC 9(8).                         00250000  BLL=0004+000            8C
 000031               *                                                              00260000
 000032                PROCEDURE DIVISION USING GROSS-PAY, SAVINGS-FACTOR,           00270000  27 28
 000033                                         SAVINGS-AMT, EMPLOYEE-NO.            00280000  29 30
 000034               *                                                              00281001
 000035                CALC-SAVINGS.                                                 00282009
 000036               *                                                              00283001
(F)---> 000037             MOVE GROSS-PAY       TO WS-GROSS-PAY.                     00300000  27 22
        000038             MOVE SAVINGS-FACTOR  TO WS-SAVINGS-FACTOR.                00310000  28 23
 000039                    MOVE ZEROS           TO WS-SAVINGS-AMT.                   00320000  IMP 24
 000040                    MOVE SPACES          TO MIN-MAX-PRT.                      00330000  IMP 20
(B)---> 000041             MULTIPLY WS-SAVINGS-FACTOR BY WS-GROSS-PAY GIVING         00352010  23 22 <---(C)
 000042                       WS-SAVINGS-AMT.                                        00353010  24
 000043                    MOVE WS-SAVINGS-AMT TO SAVINGS-AMT.                       00360000  24 29
PP 5668-958 IBM VS COBOL II Release 3.1 09/19/89              SUBPGM1   Date 05/17/91  Time 12:40:17   Page     3
 LineID  PL SL  ----+-*A-1-B--+----2----+----3----+----4----+----5----+----6----+----7-|--+----8  Map and Cross Reference

 000044               ***************************************************************** 00361001
 000045               *--- VALIDATE SAVINGS FACTOR -- IF INVALID,                    00362001
 000046               *      SET SAVINGS AMOUNT TO ZERO AND PRINT A MESSAGE.         00363001
 000047               ***************************************************************** 00364001
 000048                    IF WS-SAVINGS-FACTOR > MAX-FACTOR THEN                    00370000  23 16
 000049        1              MOVE 'MAXIMUM' TO MIN-MAX-PRT                          00380000  20
 000050                    ELSE                                                      00390000
 000051        1           IF WS-SAVINGS-FACTOR < MIN-FACTOR AND                     00400000  23 15
 000052        1              WS-SAVINGS-FACTOR NOT EQUAL ZERO-FACTOR THEN           00410000  23 17
 000053        2                 MOVE 'MINIMUM' TO MIN-MAX-PRT                       00420005  20
 000054        2              ELSE NEXT SENTENCE.                                    00430000
 000055                    IF MIN-MAX-PRT NOT EQUAL SPACES THEN                      00440000  20 IMP
 000056        1                 MOVE ZEROS TO SAVINGS-AMT                           00450005  IMP 29
 000057        1                 MOVE WS-SAVINGS-FACTOR TO PRINT-FACTOR              00460005  23 19
 000058        1                 DISPLAY 'EMPLOYEE# ', EMPLOYEE-NO, ' OUT OF ',      00470005  30
 000059        1                 MIN-MAX-PRT ' RANGE, SAVINGS FACTOR SET FROM ',     00480005  20
 000060        1                 PRINT-FACTOR ' TO ZERO ' UPON SYSOUT                00490005  19
 000061        1              ELSE NEXT SENTENCE.                                    00500000
 000062                END-CALC-SAVINGS.                                             00501005
 000063                    GOBACK.                                                   00510000
```

Figure 7.2 COBOL II compiler output for SUBPGM1 showing source code and portions of the XREF and OFFSET listings. (*Continued*)

```
PP 5668-958 IBM VS COBOL II Release 3.1 09/19/89              SUBPGM1   Date 05/17/91  Time 12:40:17   Page    5

An "M" preceding a data-name reference indicates that the data-name is modified by this reference.

 Defined   Cross-reference of data names   References

      14   CONSTANTS
      30   EMPLOYEE-NO. . . . . . . . . . .  33 58
      27   GROSS-PAY. . . . . . . . . . . .  32 37
      16   MAX-FACTOR . . . . . . . . . . .  48
      15   MIN-FACTOR . . . . . . . . . . .  51
      20   MIN-MAX-PRT. . . . . . . . . . .  M40 M49 M53 55 59
      19   PRINT-FACTOR . . . . . . . . . .  M57 60
      18   PRINT-VARIABLES
      29   SAVINGS-AMT. . . . . . . . . . .  33 M43 M56
      28   SAVINGS-FACTOR . . . . . . . . .  32 38
      21   WORK-VARIABLES
 (E) ->22  WS-GROSS-PAY . . . . . . . . . .  M37 41
      24   WS-SAVINGS-AMT . . . . . . . . .  M39 M42 43
     ->23  WS-SAVINGS-FACTOR. . . . . . . .  M38 41 48 51 52 57
                                                   .
                                                   .
                                                   .
LINE #  HEXLOC  VERB               LINE #  HEXLOC  VERB                     LINE #  HEXLOC  VERB
000037 00029A MOVE                 000038 0002A4 MOVE                       000039 0002B2 MOVE
000040 0002B8 MOVE                 000041 0002BE MULTIPLY <---- (A)         000043 0002E2 MOVE
000048 0002EC IF                   000049 00030A MOVE                       000051 000314 IF
                                          .
                                          .
                                          .
```

Figure 7.2 *(Continued)*

At this point we need to ascertain how the invalid data got into WS-GROSS-PAY and WS-SAVINGS-FACTOR. Looking at the XREF listing for SUBPGM1 at letter "E" on page 5 in Fig. 7.2, we find that these fields were modified at lines 37 and 38. The statements at those lines (see letter "F" on page 2) are

```
000037          MOVE GROSS-PAY          TO WS-GROSS-PAY
000038          MOVE SAVINGS-FACTOR     TO WS-SAVINGS-FACTOR
```

GROSS-PAY and SAVINGS-FACTOR are defined in the LINKAGE SECTION (letter "G" in the same figure).

The Call Trace Summary in the Program Area Section of the Abend-AID report, shown at letter "H" on page 4 in Fig. 7.3, informs us that SUBPGM1 was called by MAINPGM. This section also gives attributes of the application programs in our system, and indicates that they both reside in the same load module. We next have to determine where the values came from that were passed to the fields GROSS-PAY and SAVINGS-FACTOR by MAINPGM.

The Working Storage Section of the Abend-AID report (excerpts from pages 5 to 11 of the report are shown in Fig. 7.3) provides information from the TGT, relevant base locator cell contents and related storage areas for both programs. We can find the definition and storage location of GROSS-PAY and SAVINGS-FACTOR at lines 27 and 28 in SUBPGM1's source listing (refer again to letter "G" on page 2 in Fig. 7.2) and then look up the contents in Abend-AID's storage listing.

GROSS-PAY is located at hexadecimal displacement 000 from the address in BLL cell 0001 and SAVINGS-FACTOR is located at hexadecimal displacement 000 from the address in BLL cell 0002. Both fields are numeric USAGE DISPLAY.

```
                              A B E N D - A I D                       PAGE 1

        FRIDAY     17 MAY 91                              910514-R 6.0.2

            ****************************************************************
            *          A b e n d - A I D   D i a g n o s t i c s           *
            *                                                              *
            *       Copyright (c) 1976, 1991 by Compuware Corporation      *
            *                    All Rights Reserved                       *
            *                                                              *
            *                    Licensed for use at:                      *
            *                      MY COMPANY NAME                         *
            *                  Company Number:  999999                     *
            ****************************************************************

            Model - 3090          OPSYS   - MVS/SP 3.1.3       Job   - AA0C2BA2
                                  CP FMID - JBB3313            Step  - GO
                                  System  - MVSA               Time  - 12.41.09

                             Completion Code - S0C7 <------------------------- (A)

        ------------------------------------------------------------------------------


                          *******************************************
                          *   Next Sequential Instruction Section   *
                          *******************************************

               The next sequential instruction to be executed in program
                         SUBPGM1 was at displacement 0002D8. <---------------- (B)

            The program was compiled on 17 MAY 91 and is 002036 bytes long.

                         It is part of load module MAIN2PGM.

               The module was loaded from STEPLIB library MY.COBOL.LOAD
               It was link edited on 17 MAY 91 and is 0064B8 bytes long.
                              A B E N D - A I D                       PAGE 3

                                ***********************
                                * Diagnostic Section *
                                ***********************


                               Both fields are in error

                               * First field in error * <--------------------- (F)

          Abend S0C7 was caused by data referenced at displacement 020 from the
          start of BLW cell 00 (X'0').  The field contains X'F0F06A7C7BF2F0'.
          Refer to the data division map in the program listing to locate the
          field name.

          The first field causing the abend is located in a temporary work field
          in the TGT.  The actual field in error is in Working-Storage of
          program SUBPGM1.

                               * Second field in error * <-------------------- (G)

          Abend S0C7 was caused by data referenced at displacement 027 from the
          start of BLW cell 00 (X'0').  The field contains X'F07CFF'.  Refer to
          the data division map in the program listing to locate the field name.

          The second field causing the abend is located in a temporary work
          field in the TGT.  The actual field in error is in Working-Storage of
          program SUBPGM1.

          Because the program is re-entrant, Working-Storage is located outside
          of the program.

          ----------------------------------------------------------------------


          S0C7, data exception, is caused when a computational-3 field has  \
          an invalid digit (not 0-9), or its last byte contains an invalid   } <---- (C)
          sign (not F, C, or D).                                             /
```

Figure 7.3 The basic Abend-AID report produced when the system composed of MAINPGM and SUBPGM1 ABENDed. (*Continued*)

```
                              A B E N D - A I D                    PAGE 4

                            *********************
                            * Call Trace Summary *
                            *********************

*****Calling*****           ***Return***          ******Called*******
Load-Mod    Program         Type   Value          Program    Load-Mod

*SYSTEM                                    Calls  MAINPGM    MAIN2PGM

MAIN2PGM    MAINPGM         DISP   000784  Calls  SUBPGM1    MAIN2PGM  *  <---- (H)

MAIN2PGM    SUBPGM1         DISP   0003D6  Calls  IGZETRM    IGZCPCO

                                                 Abending Program *

  ******************************************************************
  *                  Application Program Attributes                *
  ******************************************************************

  Load-Mod    Program    Compile Date   Length     Language

  MAIN2PGM    MAINPGM     17 MAY 91     00405E     VS COBOL II V1R3M1

  MAIN2PGM    SUBPGM1     17 MAY 91     002036     VS COBOL II V1R3M1
                                  A B E N D - A I D                    PAGE 5

          **********************************************************
          *          Data Division of Program MAINPGM              *
          *        Compiled on  17 MAY 91    at  12.40.38          *
          *                                                        *
          *                    VS COBOL II V1R3M1                  *
          *                                                        *
          *          Execution / Debugging options in effect       *
          *                                                        *
          *   NOADV           FDUMP                RESIDENT        *
          *   NOCMPR2        NOOPTIMIZE          NOSSRANGE         *
          *     DATA(31)      OUTDD(SYSOUT   )   NOTEST            *
          *   NODYNAM         NUMPROC(NOPFD)       TRUNC(OPT)      *  <---- (D)
          *   NOFASTSRT       RENT                 ZWB             *
          **********************************************************

                          Working-Storage Section

Working storage referenced by BLW cell    0 (X'0')

 DSPL Address    -------------- Data ---------------
00000 03407698   004C0000 00000000 F4F0F5F8 F8F2F9F9  .<......40588299
00010 034076A8   0707347C 00000000 001C0000 00000000  ...@............
00020 034076B8   00111320 5C000000 004C0000 00000000  ....*....<......
00030 034076C8   F0F1F8F0 F0F5F900 F4F0F5F8 F8F2F9F9  0180059.40588299
00040 034076D8   F1F2C4D6 C56B4040 E6C9D3D3 C9C1D440  12DOE,  WILLIAM
                                  .
                                  .
                                  .
```

Figure 7.3 *(Continued)*

```
                        A B E N D - A I D                       PAGE 8

          **********************************************************
          *            Data Division of Program SUBPGM1            *
          *          Compiled on  17 MAY 91    at  12.40.17        *
          *                                                        *
          *                     VS COBOL II V1R3M1                 *
          *                                                        *
          *         Execution / Debugging options in effect        *
          *                                                        *
          *   NOADV           FDUMP                 RESIDENT       *
          *   NOCMPR2       NOOPTIMIZE            NOSSRANGE        *
          *     DATA(31)      OUTDD(SYSOUT  )     NOTEST           *
          *   NODYNAM        [NUMPROC(NOPFD)]       TRUNC(OPT)     *   <-- E
          *   NOFASTSRT       RENT                  ZWB            *
          **********************************************************

                      Working-Storage Section

Working storage referenced by BLW cell   0 (X'0')

 DSPL Address   -------------- Data ---------------
00000 03407C00  F0F0C2F0 F1C5F0F0 C0000000 00000000  00B01E00{.......
00010 03407C10  00000000 40404040 40404000 00000000  ....      .....
00020 03407C20  F0F06A7C 7BF2F0F0 7CFFF0F0 F0F0F0F0  00 @#200@.000000
00030 03407C30  F0                                   0

                          Linkage Section

Linkage storage referenced by BLL cell   1 (X'1')
 (Length:  TO NEXT BLL CELL)

 DSPL Address   -------------- Data ---------------
00000 034076FA [F0F06A7C 7BF2F0]F0 F1F3F3F9 F0       00 @#20013390     <-- I

Linkage storage referenced by BLL cell   2 (X'2')
 (Length:  TO END OF CALLING PGM WS)

 DSPL Address   -------------- Data ---------------
00000 03407707 [7C6F]F2F3 F4F3F2F4 40404040 40404040  @?234324         <-- I
                                   .
                                   .
                                   .
```

Figure 7.3 *(Continued)*

The format of the storage area in the Abend-AID report is slightly different from the format of a hexadecimal MVS storage dump. Not only does it show storage addresses, hexadecimal storage contents and EBCDIC translations of the storage contents, but it also shows the hexadecimal displacements from the beginning of each pertinent base locator cell. This makes it easy to find contents of program fields. We find that GROSS-PAY contains hexadecimal F0F06A7C7BF2F0 and SAVINGS-FACTOR contains hexadecimal 7C6F (refer to letter "I" in the Abend-AID Working Storage Section for SUBPGM1 on page 8 in Fig. 7.3). In order to determine the source of the invalid numeric data, we need to find out how these fields were last updated in MAINPGM.

Examining the source code for MAINPGM in Fig. 7.1 shows us that the CALL statement at line 160 (letter "A" on page 5 in Fig. 7.1) passed the parameters in question, GROSS-PAY and SAVINGS-FACTOR, to SUBPGM1. GROSS-PAY and SAVINGS-FACTOR are elementary fields in TIME-RECORD (see letter "B" on page 3 in Fig. 7.1). The READ TIMECARD INTO TIME-RECORD. . . statement at line 143 in the source module, pointed to by letter "C" on page 4 in the figure, places values in these fields. We can also examine either the source code or the XREF listing to verify that these fields were not modified before they were passed to SUBPGM1 by the CALL at line 160.

```
                    A B E N D - A I D                                PAGE 16

     Data Management Control Blocks for DDNAME - TIMECARD

     DSNAME=CWV.CWS070.AA.TIMECARD

                                                            ACC METH=VSAM

File Excp Count=1


File Summary:

Access type........BASE CLUSTER
Dataset type.......ESDS
Processing type....ADR,AMODE31,NFX,DDN,NDF,SEQ,NCI,IN,NIS,NRM,NRS,NSR,
                   NUB

File errors........None

Current record:

00044F70   CHAR  4058829912DOE,  WILLIAM  T.                   00 @#200
           ZONE  FFFFFFFFFFCDC644ECDDCCD44E4444444444444444FF677FFF  <---- (J)
          DIGIT  4058829912465B006933914003B000000000000000000ACB200
                 1...5...10....*...20....*...30....*...40....*...50

00044FA2   CHAR  13390@?234324          01550023
           ZONE  FFFFF76FFFFFF444444444FFFFFFFF
          DIGIT  13390CF234324000000000001550023
                51...*...60....*...70....*...80                       (K)

Previous record:

0340E8A0   CHAR  4014003912JOHNSTONE, REGINALD B.             12003983
           ZONE  FFFFFFFFFFDDCDEEDDC64DCCCDCDC4C44444444444FFFFFFFF
          DIGIT  4014003912168523655B09579513402B00000000000012003983
                 1...5...10....*...20....*...30....*...40....*...50

0340E8D2   CHAR  1299215442344          01540023
           ZONE  FFFFFFFFFFFFF444444444FFFFFFFF
          DIGIT  1299215442344000000000001540023
                51...*...60....*...70....*...80

Last request:
ID.................GET
Request ECB........completed
Mode...............MOVE
Access.............SEQ
Misc...............Locate the record at the specified RBA
Current RBA........000000F0
```

Figure 7.3 *(Continued)*

The File Area portion of the Abend-AID report gives detailed information about each file used in the program. Looking at the information for TIME-CARD (Fig. 7.3, page 16 of the report), we find the contents of the current record. Using the decimal displacement grid allows us to find the locations of GROSS-PAY (at displacement 43) and SAVINGS-FACTOR (at displacement 56). We see at letters "J" and "K" that the contents of the fields are hexadecimal F0F06A7C7BF2F0 and 7C6F, respectively. These are not numeric data. Since we are viewing the entire input record, we can also identify the faulty record in the file.

Abend-AID has enabled us to solve this ABEND with relative ease. We found that the S0C7 was caused by bad input data read into the main program which was subsequently passed to and used in a MULTIPLY statement in the subprogram.

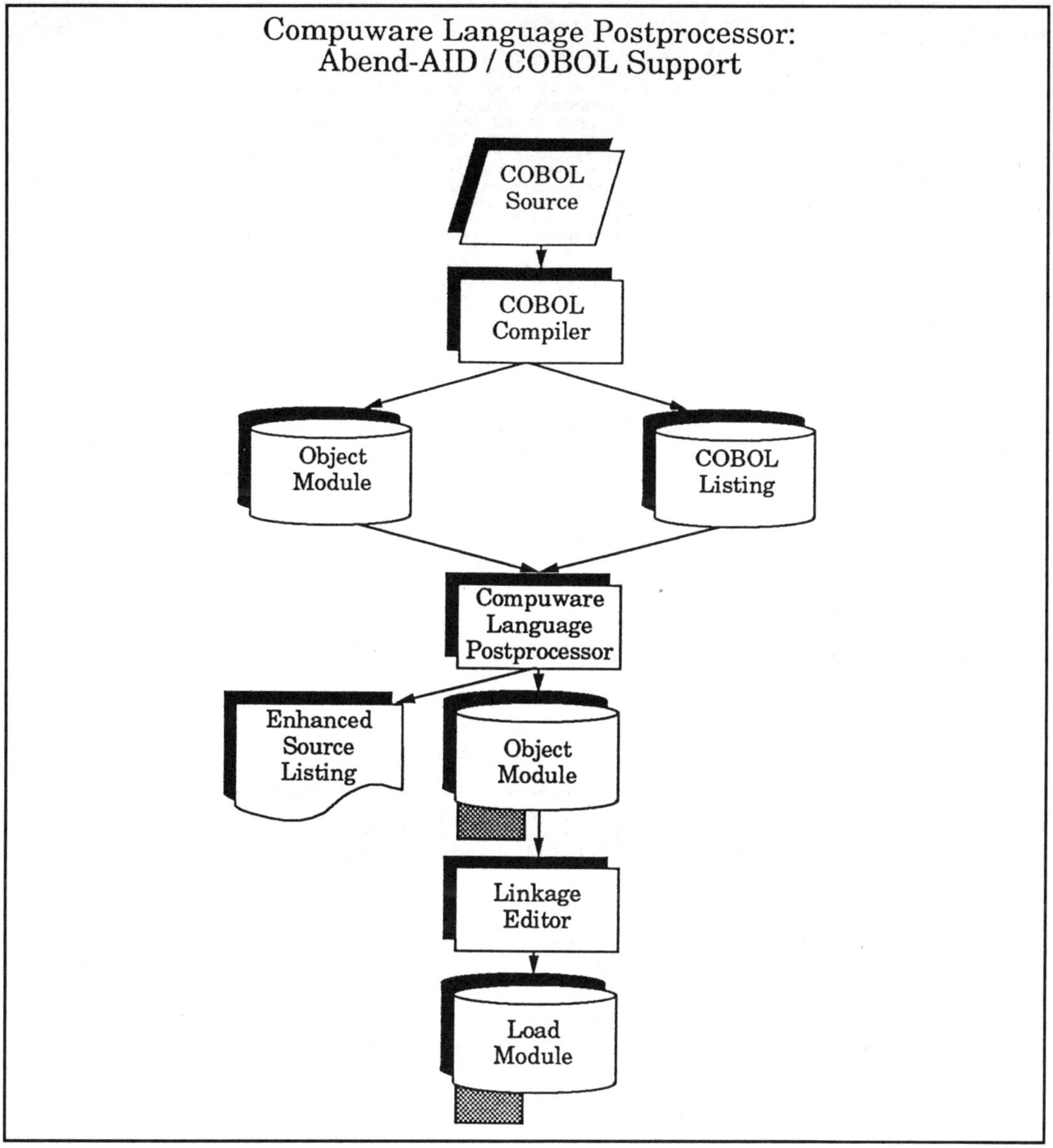

Figure 7.4 Processing which occurs to create the output required for generation of the Abend-AID/COBOL report.

```
                  COBOL PROCESSOR  MAINPGM    12:42:16 05/17/91   PAGE     1

                  COMPUWARE COBOL PROCESSOR*COMPUWARE COBOL PROCESSOR******************
                  COMPUWARE COBOL PROCESSOR*COMPUWARE COBOL PROCESSOR*   **************
                  COMPUWARE COBOL PROCESSOR*COMPUWARE COBOL PROCESSO*    **********  **
                  COMPUWARE COBOL PROCESSOR*COMPUWARE COBOL PROCESS*     **********  **
                  COMPUWARE COBOL PROCESSOR*COMPUWARE COBOL PROCES*   *  **  *******  **
                  COMPUWARE COBOL PROCESSOR*COMPUWARE COBOL PROCE*   **  **********  **
                  COMPUWARE COBOL PROCESSOR*COMPUWARE COBOL PROC*   ***  **  ****     **
                  COMPUWARE COBOL PROCESSOR*COMPUWARE COBOL PRO*         **  ***  **  **
                  COMPUWARE COBOL PROCESSOR*COMPUWARE COBOL PR*   *****  **  **  ***  **
                  COMPUWARE COBOL PROCESSOR*COMPUWARE COBOL P*   ******  **  ***  **  **
                  COMPUWARE COBOL PROCESSOR*COMPUWARE COBOL *   *******  **  ****     **
                  COMPUWARE COBOL PROCESSOR*COMPUWARE COBOL*****************************

                                    COMPUWARE COBOL PROCESSOR
                     COPYRIGHT (C) 1987 BY COMPUWARE CORPORATION, ALL RIGHTS RESERVED
                                    RELEASE 03.25.03 (10/10/90)
                                   LICENSED FOR USE AT: 999999
                                         MY COMPANY NAME


               * *   P O S T - P R O C E S S O R   O P T I O N S   I N   E F F E C T   * *

                              IBM VS COBOL II RELEASE 3.1 PP 5668-958
                                    OUTPUT(NODDIO,NOPRINT)

                                        P R O C E S S O R
                                      OUTPUT(NODDIO,PRINT)
                                     WARNINGS(FRONT,EMBED)
                        TEXT(FILE,WORKING-STORAGE,LINKAGE,REPORT,PROCEDURE)
                                      ERRORS(UPPER-CASE)

                          * *  C O B O L   O P T I O N S   I N   E F F E C T  * *

MAINPGM         * SOURCE STATISTICS     *DATA DIV SZ =     39  *PROC DIV SZ =      41  *SOURCE SIZE =    210
MAINPGM        NOADV                     APOST                NOAWO                  BUFSIZE(4096)
MAINPGM        NOCMPR2                 NOCOMPILE(E)             DATA(31)            NODBCS
MAINPGM        NODECK                  NODUMP                 NODYNAM               NOEXIT
MAINPGM        NOFASTSRT                 FDUMP                  FLAG(I)             NOFLAGMIG
MAINPGM        NOFLAGSAA               NOFLAGSTD                LANGUAGE(EN)          LIB
MAINPGM          LINECOUNT(60)         NOLIST                   MAP                 NONAME
MAINPGM        NONUMBER                  NUMPROC(NOPFD)         OBJECT                OFFSET
                                                    .
                                                    .
                                                    .
```

Figure 7.5 Output from the Compuware Language Postprocessor for MAINPGM showing Postprocessor options and portions of COBOL options in effect, and portions of the source listing.

7.2 ADDITIONAL Abend-AID FEATURES

There are a number of Abend-AID enhancements which may be helpful. Some are available with the basic Abend-AID package while others must be purchased and installed as add-on features.

Including the DD statement

```
//ABNLHELP DD DUMMY
```

in the JCL produces a one-page set of instructions on how to use the Abend-AID report in solving ABENDs. This is part of the basic Abend-AID product.

Several utility programs are provided to help in the installation and use of Abend-AID. The one of most value from a maintenance standpoint is the System Management Facility (SMF) Analysis Report program. This analyzes the number and type of ABENDs which occur on a system. Such information can provide a basis for making system improvements by identifying programs which may need to be reviewed and modified.

```
BASE DISPL STMT    SEQ.       COBOL PROCESSOR  MAINPGM     12:42:16 05/17/91    PAGE     3    IDENT.            FROM     THRU  LENGTH *
                  ----+-*A-1-B--+----2----+----3----+----4----+----5----+----6----+----7-|--+----8

          000001        IDENTIFICATION DIVISION.                                        00010000
          000002        PROGRAM-ID.   MAINPGM.                                          00020000
          000003        AUTHOR.       A.PROGRAMMER.                                     00030000
                                                        .
                                                        .
                                                        .
VSAM   FILE 000039        FD  TIMECARD                                                  00380000 ** FIXED LENGTH RECORDS **

*ERROR* IGYGR1213-I   The "LABEL" clause was processed as comments for this file definition.

          000040                LABEL RECORDS ARE STANDARD                              00390000
          000041                RECORD CONTAINS 80 CHARACTERS                           00410000
          000042                DATA RECORD IS T-RECORD .                               00430000
BLF=2   000 000043        01  T-RECORD              PIC X(80).                          00440000 T-RECORD                     80

          000047        WORKING-STORAGE SECTION.                                        00442000
                                                        .
                                                        .
                                                        .
BLW=0   038 000058        01  TIME-RECORD.                                              00450000 TIME-RECORD                  80
BLW=0   038 000059            03  EMPLOYEE-NO       PIC 9(8).                           00460000            1        8       8
BLW=0   040 000060            03  MONTH-CODE        PIC XX.                             00470000            9       10       2
BLW=0   042 000061            03  EMPLOYEE-NAME     PIC X(32).                          00480000           11       42      32
BLW=0   062 000062            03  GROSS-PAY         PIC 9(5)V99.                        00490000           43       49       7
BLW=0   069 000063            03  TOTAL-TAXES       PIC 9(4)V99.                        00500000           50       55       6
BLW=0   06F 000064            03  SAVINGS-FACTOR    PIC V99.                            00510000           56       57       2
BLW=0   071 000065            03  FILLER            PIC X(23).                          00520000           58       80      23
                                                        .
                                                        .
                                                        .
 000134              PROCEDURE DIVISION.                                             01130000
                                                        .
                                                        .
                                                        .
 000142              GET-ANOTHER.                                                    01190000
 000143                  READ TIMECARD INTO TIME-RECORD AT END GO TO END-OF-JOB.     01200000 READ      00069A GO           0006E2
                                                        .
                                                        .
                                                        .
 000160                  CALL 'SUBPGM1' USING GROSS-PAY, SAVINGS-FACTOR,             01290000 CALL      00074C
                                                        .
                                                        .
                                                        .
```

Figure 7.5 *(Continued)*

Four additional facilities, SNAP-AID, Compuware/SPF, Abend-AID/COBOL, and Abend-AID/XCS are valuable extras which can make debugging easier. They will be discussed in Secs. 7.2.1, 7.2.2, 7.2.3, and 7.2.4.

7.2.1 The SNAP-AID Facility

The SNAP-AID facility allows you to get an Abend-AID report at a prespecified point in the program execution even if the program does not ABEND. After the "Abend-AID Snapshot" is generated, the COBOL program continues execution.

There are some differences between the SNAP-AID report and a basic Abend-AID report. In the SNAP-AID report, the word "SNAP" appears in place of a completion code. Since there is no ABEND, there is no Diagnostic Section. The Next Sequential Instruction Section specifies the location of the instruction following the call to SNAP-AID.

To use SNAP-AID, code a CALL statement as follows:

```
CALL 'SNAPAID'
```

```
                                COBOL PROCESSOR  SUBPGM1    12:41:46 05/17/91   PAGE     1

                                COMPUWARE COBOL PROCESSOR*COMPUWARE COBOL PROCESSOR*******************
                                COMPUWARE COBOL PROCESSOR*COMPUWARE COBOL PROCESSOR*   ***************
                                COMPUWARE COBOL PROCESSOR*COMPUWARE COBOL PROCESSO*    ***********  **
                                COMPUWARE COBOL PROCESSOR*COMPUWARE COBOL PROCESS*     ***********  **
                                COMPUWARE COBOL PROCESSOR*COMPUWARE COBOL PROCES*   *  **  *******  **
                                COMPUWARE COBOL PROCESSOR*COMPUWARE COBOL PROCE*   **  ***********  **
                                COMPUWARE COBOL PROCESSOR*COMPUWARE COBOL PROC*   ***  **  ****     **
                                COMPUWARE COBOL PROCESSOR*COMPUWARE COBOL PRO*         **  ***  **  **
                                COMPUWARE COBOL PROCESSOR*COMPUWARE COBOL PR*   *****  **  **  ***  **
                                COMPUWARE COBOL PROCESSOR*COMPUWARE COBOL P*   ******  **  ***  **  **
                                COMPUWARE COBOL PROCESSOR*COMPUWARE COBOL *   *******  **  ****     **
                                COMPUWARE COBOL PROCESSOR*COMPUWARE COBOL*****************************

                                               COMPUWARE COBOL PROCESSOR
                                   COPYRIGHT (C) 1987 BY COMPUWARE CORPORATION, ALL RIGHTS RESERVED
                                               RELEASE 03.25.03 (10/10/90)
                                              LICENSED FOR USE AT: 999999
                                                    MY COMPANY NAME


                              * *   P O S T - P R O C E S S O R   O P T I O N S   I N   E F F E C T   * *

                                          IBM VS COBOL II RELEASE 3.1 PP 5668-958
                                                 OUTPUT(NODDIO,NOPRINT)

                                                   P R O C E S S O R
                                                  OUTPUT(NODDIO,PRINT)
                                                 WARNINGS(FRONT,EMBED)
                                    TEXT(FILE,WORKING-STORAGE,LINKAGE,REPORT,PROCEDURE)
                                                  ERRORS(UPPER-CASE)

                                     * *   C O B O L   O P T I O N S   I N   E F F E C T   * *

     SUBPGM1            * SOURCE STATISTICS      *DATA DIV SZ =      15   *PROC DIV SZ =      15   *SOURCE SIZE =       63
     SUBPGM1          NOADV                      APOST                  NOAWO                       BUFSIZE(4096)
     SUBPGM1          NOCMPR2                  NOCOMPILE(E)               DATA(31)                NODBCS
     SUBPGM1          NODECK                   NODUMP                   NODYNAM                   NOEXIT
     SUBPGM1          NOFASTSRT                  FDUMP                    FLAG(I)                 NOFLAGMIG
     SUBPGM1          NOFLAGSAA                NOFLAGSTD                  LANGUAGE(EN)              LIB
     SUBPGM1            LINECOUNT(60)          NOLIST                     MAP                     NONAME
     SUBPGM1          NONUMBER                   NUMPROC(NOPFD)           OBJECT                    OFFSET
                                                              .
                                                              .
                                                              .

  BASE DISPL STMT    SEQ.      COBOL PROCESSOR  SUBPGM1    12:41:46 05/17/91   PAGE     3    IDENT.          FROM    THRU  LENGTH *

                    ----+-*A-1-B--+----2----+----3----+----4----+----5----+----6----+----7-|--+----8

             000001          IDENTIFICATION DIVISION.                                        00010000
             000002          PROGRAM-ID.  SUBPGM1.                                           00020000
                                                               .
                                                               .
                                                               .
             000013          WORKING-STORAGE SECTION.                                        00090004
                                                               .
                                                               .
                                                               .
BLW=0    020 000021          01  WORK-VARIABLES.                                             00170000 WORK-VARIABLES            17
BLW=0    020 000022              03  WS-GROSS-PAY        PIC 9(5)V99   VALUE 0.              00180000              1      7      7
BLW=0    027 000023              03  WS-SAVINGS-FACTOR   PIC 9V99      VALUE 0.              00190000              8     10      3
BLW=0    02A 000024              03  WS-SAVINGS-AMT      PIC 9(5)V99   VALUE 0.              00200000             11     17      7
             000025         *                                                                00201001
             000026          LINKAGE SECTION.                                                00210000
BLL=1    000 000027          77  GROSS-PAY               PIC 9(5)V99.                        00220000 GROSS-PAY                  7
BLL=2    000 000028          77  SAVINGS-FACTOR          PIC V99.                            00230000 SAVINGS-FACTOR             2
BLL=3    000 000029          77  SAVINGS-AMT             PIC 9(5)V99.                        00240000 SAVINGS-AMT                7
BLL=4    000 000030          77  EMPLOYEE-NO             PIC 9(8).                           00250000 EMPLOYEE-NO                8
             000031         *                                                                00260000

 000032                  PROCEDURE DIVISION USING GROSS-PAY, SAVINGS-FACTOR,             00270000
                                                  SAVINGS-AMT, EMPLOYEE-NO.               00280000
 000034                 *                                                                 00281001
 000035                  CALC-SAVINGS.                                                    00282009
 000036                 *                                                                 00283001
 000037                      MOVE GROSS-PAY      TO WS-GROSS-PAY.                         00300000 MOVE        00029A
 000038                      MOVE SAVINGS-FACTOR TO WS-SAVINGS-FACTOR.                    00310000 MOVE        0002A4
 000039                      MOVE ZEROS          TO WS-SAVINGS-AMT.                       00320000 MOVE        0002B2
 000040                      MOVE SPACES         TO MIN-MAX-PRT.                          00330000 MOVE        0002B8
 000041                      MULTIPLY WS-SAVINGS-FACTOR BY WS-GROSS-PAY GIVING            00352010 MULTIPLY    0002BE
 000042                         WS-SAVINGS-AMT.                                           00353010
                                                               .
                                                               .
                                                               .
```

Figure 7.6 Output from the Compuware Language Postprocessor for SUBPGM1 showing Postprocessor options and portions of COBOL options in effect, and portions of the source listing.

```
                         A B E N D - A I D                         PAGE 1

FRIDAY      17 MAY 91                                      910514-R 6.0.2

       *****************************************************************
       *           A b e n d - A I D   D i a g n o s t i c s           *
       *                                                               *
       *       Copyright (c) 1976, 1991 by Compuware Corporation       *
       *                    All Rights Reserved                        *
       *                                                               *
       *                    Licensed for use at:                       *
       *                      MY COMPANY NAME                          *
       *                 Company Number:  999999                       *
       *****************************************************************

       Model - 3090        OPSYS   - MVS/SP 3.1.3       Job  - AA0C2CA2
                           CP FMID - JBB3313            Step - GO
                           System  - MVSB               Time - 12.42.55

                       Completion Code - S0C7

--------------------------------------------------------------------------------

                          ***************************
                          *   Instruction Section   *
                          ***************************

                 The statement being executed in program
                   SUBPGM1 was statement number 41.<------------------------ (A)

       The program was compiled on 17 MAY 91 and is 00216E bytes long.

                    It is part of load module MAIN2PGM.

          The module was loaded from STEPLIB library MY.COBOL.LOAD
          It was link edited on 17 MAY 91 and is 006828 bytes long.
```

Figure 7.7 The Abend-AID/COBOL report produced when the system composed of MAINPGM and SUBPGM1 ABENDed. (*Continued*)

If the COBOL program is compiled with the NODYNAM option, do one of the following in the link-edit step: include the Abend-AID load library (SYS1.ABENDAID, or the name your installation has chosen) in the SYSLIB DD statement, or code the INCLUDE statement to bring the SNAP-AID module into the load module. The appropriate DD statements for the link-edit step are as follows:

```
//SYSLIB  DD DSN=SYS1.ABENDAID,DISP=SHR
//        DD DSN=COBOL subroutine library,DISP=SHR
```

or

```
//SYSLIB  DD DSN=COBOL subroutine library,DISP=SHR
//OTHER   DD DSN=SYS1.ABENDAID,DISP=SHR
//SYSIN   DD *
 INCLUDE OTHER(SNAPAID)
/*
```

```
                         A B E N D - A I D                    PAGE 3

                        *********************
                        * Diagnostic Section *
                        *********************


                       Both fields are in error

                       * First field in error *

Abend S0C7 was caused by data referenced at position 1 thru 7 in field
'01  WORK-VARIABLES'.  The field contains X'F0F06A7C7BF2F0'.          <---- (B)

The first field causing the abend is located in a temporary work field
in the TGT.  The actual field in error is in Working-Storage of
program SUBPGM1.

                       * Second field in error *

Abend S0C7 was caused by data referenced at position 8 thru 10 in
field '01  WORK-VARIABLES'.  The field contains X'F07CFF'.            <---- (C)

The second field causing the abend is located in a temporary work
field in the TGT.  The actual field in error is in Working-Storage of
program SUBPGM1.

Because the program is re-entrant, Working-Storage is located outside
of the program.

----------------------------------------------------------------------

S0C7, data exception, is caused when a computational-3 field has
an invalid digit (not 0-9), or its last byte contains an invalid
sign (not F, C, or D).
```

Figure 7.7 *(Continued)*

The //ABENDAID DD statement must be coded in the execution step JCL. SNAP-AID output will be placed on the data set associated with this DD statement unless either another data set is designated on the //ABNLTERM DD statement, or an Abend-AID report data set is specified in the CWGLOBAL table and no overriding //ABNLTERM DD statement is coded.

7.2.2 Compuware/SPF

Abend-AID has an on-line report access feature called SPF. Compuware/SPF is menu-driven and requires that IBM's Interactive System Productivity Facility (ISPF) has been installed under the MVS, MVS/XA, or MVS/ESA operating system. For programmers familiar with ISPF, using Compuware/SPF is quite simple since the format and function of the panels are very similar to those of ISPF.

The Compuware/SPF Entry Panel is accessed through the ISPF Primary Option Menu. After specifying the location of the Abend-AID output on the Entry Panel, additional menus are then accessed to perform a variety of func-

```
                         A B E N D - A I D                     PAGE 5

          ***************************************************************
          *             Data division of program MAINPGM                *
          *           Compiled on  17 MAY 91    at  12.42.16            *
          *                                                             *
          *                   VS COBOL II V1R3M1                        *
          *                                                             *
          *          Execution / Debugging options in effect            *
          *                                                             *
          *    NOADV            FDUMP                 RESIDENT          *
          *    NOCMPR2        NOOPTIMIZE            NOSSRANGE           *
          *      DATA(31)       OUTDD(SYSOUT   )    NOTEST              *
          *    NODYNAM          NUMPROC(NOPFD)        TRUNC(OPT)        *
          *    NOFASTSRT        RENT                  ZWB               *
          ***************************************************************

                        Working-Storage Section

Working storage referenced by BLW cell 0 + 000

77 RECORD-CTR      (BLW 0 + 000)
           CHAR   <
           ZONE   04
          DIGIT   0C
                  1.

77 OLD-EMPL-NUMB      (BLW 0 + 008)
           CHAR   40588299
           ZONE   FFFFFFFF
          DIGIT   40588299
                  1...5...
                                 .
                                 .
                                 .
```

Figure 7.7 *(Continued)*

tions. These include displaying portions of the Abend-AID report at the terminal, printing the report, and accessing the help tutorial.

A useful feature is the ability to view the Abend-AID information at the terminal in narrow (72-column) format. This eliminates the need to scroll right and left to view an entire line of text. The print format can be chosen to be narrow or wide.

When using Compuware/SPF, the Abend-AID output must be saved in a special data set. This can be a default data set supplied by your installation or a data set assigned to the //ABNLTERM DD statement in the JCL. In either case, it must be a VSAM or BDAM data set which has been formatted before use.

7.2.3 Abend-AID COBOL Support

Abend-AID/COBOL (formerly called COBOL-AID) makes it easier for COBOL programmers coding in OS/VS COBOL or COBOL II to find the statement causing an ABEND and to identify the COBOL fields in the ABENDing state-

```
                        A B E N D - A I D                         PAGE 9

              ***********************************************************
              *          Data division of program SUBPGM1               *
              *        Compiled on  17 MAY 91     at  12.41.46          *
              *                                                         *
              *                  VS COBOL II V1R3M1                     *
              *                                                         *
              *       Execution / Debugging options in effect           *
              *                                                         *
              *   NOADV            FDUMP                RESIDENT        *
              *   NOCMPR2        NOOPTIMIZE           NOSSRANGE         *
              *     DATA(31)       OUTDD(SYSOUT  )    NOTEST            *
              *   NODYNAM          NUMPROC(NOPFD)       TRUNC(OPT)      *
              *   NOFASTSRT        RENT                 ZWB             *
              ***********************************************************

                         Working-Storage Section

      Working storage referenced by BLW cell 0 + 000

      01 CONSTANTS       (BLW 0 + 000)
                 CHAR   00B01E00{
                 ZONE   FFCFFCFFC
                DIGIT   002015000
                        1...5...1

      01 PRINT-VARIABLES      (BLW 0 + 010)
                 CHAR
                 ZONE   00004444444
                DIGIT   00000000000
                        1...5...10.

      01 WORK-VARIABLES      (BLW 0 + 020)
                 CHAR   00 @#200@ 0000000
                 ZONE   FF677FFF7FFFFFFFF
                DIGIT   00ACB200CF0000000
                        1...5...10....*..

                                    .
                                    .
                                    .
```

Figure 7.7 *(Continued)*

ment. This is because a Compuware Language Postprocessor is used to create an enhanced source code listing and provide several improvements in the basic Abend-AID report.

The Postprocessor uses both the COBOL compiler listing and the COBOL object module as input. Postprocessor output consists of the enhanced source listing and a new object module. The new object module contains a table which gives program displacements to COBOL statement numbers, base locator cell offsets to 77- and 01-level data, and relative positions of elementary fields within 01-level items. This additional information is carried through to the load module by the linkage-editor. Figure 7.4 shows the processing flow.

To demonstrate the differences between the basic Abend-AID output and output with COBOL support, the system described in Sec. 7.1.2 was run with

```
                         A B E N D - A I D                          PAGE 16

     Data Management Control Blocks for DDNAME - TIMECARD

     DSNAME=CWV.CWS070.AA.TIMECARD
                                                        ACC METH=VSAM

File Excp Count=1


File Summary:

Access type........BASE CLUSTER
Dataset type.......ESDS
Processing type....ADR,AMODE31,NFX,DDN,NDF,SEQ,NCI,IN,NIS,NRM,NRS,NSR,
                   NUB

File errors........None

Current record:

00044F70    CHAR  4058829912DOE, WILLIAM T.              00 @#200
            ZONE  FFFFFFFFFFCDC644ECDDCCD44E4444444444444444FF677FFF
            DIGIT 4058829912465B006933914003B000000000000000000ACB200
                  1...5...10....*...20....*...30....*...40....*...50

00044FA2    CHAR  13390@?234324          01550023
            ZONE  FFFFF76FFFFFF444444444FFFFFFFF
            DIGIT 13390CF2343240000000001550023
                 51...*...60....*...70....*...80
                                   .
                                   .
                                   .
```

Figure 7.7 *(Continued)*

Abend-AID/COBOL. Portions of the source listing output from the Compuware Language Postprocessor for MAINPGM are shown in Fig. 7.5 and portions of the output from the Postprocessor for SUBPGM1 are shown in Fig. 7.6. Notice the differences in the source listings from those shown in Figs. 7.1 and 7.2. The Postprocessor embeds compiler diagnostic messages, DATA DIVISION map information, and condensed PROCEDURE DIVISION map information in the source code. This eliminates the need for separate DATA DIVISION and PROCEDURE DIVISION maps. This enhanced source listing is similar to the type of source listing available under IBM's COBOL II Release 3 compiler.

The Abend-AID/COBOL report is illustrated in Fig. 7.7. There are a number of enhancements. The actual COBOL statement number of the instruction being executed at the time of the ABEND is given instead of the offset of the NSI (see letter "A" on page 1 in Fig. 7.7). The 77- or 01-level names and positions of the COBOL fields coded in the COBOL statement are provided instead of the locations of the temporary work fields (letters "B" and "C" on page 3). The report's Working-Storage Section identifies the relevant 77- and 01-level storage areas with the positions of the fields in error (see pages 9 and 10 in Fig. 7.7). All of this eliminates the need for translating hexadecimal displacements into decimal displacements and scanning COBOL compiler output looking for the instruction and fields involved in the ABEND.

7.2.4 Abend-AID/Extended COBOL Support

Abend-AID/Extended COBOL Support (Abend-AID/XCS, also referred to by Compuware as Abend-AID with Source Level Support) provides even more enhancements than Abend-AID/COBOL. The enhanced source listing produced by the Language Postprocessor is the same as that produced when Abend-AID/COBOL is used, but the Abend-AID report contains more detailed COBOL-specific information. In order to use Abend-AID/XCS, Abend-AID/COBOL and Compuware/SPF must be installed.

The Abend-AID/XCS report is produced by merging the source listing produced by the Postprocessor with the Abend-AID report through the SPF product. Note that if no source listing is available (as might be the case if a production load module ABENDs without its source listing being available) the program can simply be recompiled to get the Abend-AID source level support. It is not necessary to re-create the ABEND. The Abend-AID/XCS report can be viewed on-line through SPF or can be printed by choosing an option on an SPF screen.

To illustrate the enhancements provided by the XCS product, the same system used in Secs. 7.1.2 and 7.2.3 was run with Abend-AID/Extended COBOL Support. The source listings from the Compuware Language Postprocessor for both programs are the same as when Abend-AID/COBOL was in effect (see Figs. 7.5 and 7.6). The Abend-AID report, however, provides even more assistance than that produced under Abend-AID/COBOL. It is shown in Fig. 7.8. Notice that the complete COBOL statement being executed at the time of the ABEND, with its source line number, is given (see letter "A" on page 1 in Fig. 7.8). In the Diagnostic Section, the COBOL statement is repeated and the COBOL source names, level numbers, definitions, and contents of the fields used in the statement are provided (see letter "B" in the figure). The relevant program storage areas are laid out in even more detail than in the Abend-AID/COBOL report; the format is similar to the way it would appear in the actual COBOL program (see page 8 in Fig. 7.8). The Program Listing Section (page 10 in the figure) shows the COBOL source code for the entire paragraph in SUBPGM1 containing the statement which was executing when the program ABENDed. The extent of this listing can be selected through SPF. The information is so thorough that it takes virtually all the work out of finding the offending COBOL statement and fields. Of course, you still need to determine the root cause of the invalid data which caused the ABEND, as we did in Sec. 7.1.2.

7.3 MISCELLANEOUS NOTES ABOUT Abend-AID

It is unlikely that any debugging product can automatically and completely solve every ABEND. When Abend-AID cannot fully resolve a problem, it provides all the debugging information that it can and then automatically invokes MVS system dump services (unless this option is suppressed). With user completion codes (unfortunately, user completion codes are not always well documented), unless the installation has provided a macro for such a completion code, such as the Compuware supplied macro CWDIAGS which permits printing specific error messages, you may have to read and interpret the system dump. All the more reason for programmers to be able to handle system dumps when necessary; we will cover MVS concepts and dumps in the remainder of Part 2.

```
                          A B E N D - A I D                          PAGE 1

FRIDAY     17 MAY 91                                       910514-R 6.0.2

      ****************************************************************
      *          A b e n d - A I D   D i a g n o s t i c s          *
      *                                                              *
      *      Copyright (c) 1976, 1991 by Compuware Corporation       *
      *                    All Rights Reserved                       *
      *                                                              *
      *                    Licensed for use at:                      *
      *                      MY COMPANY NAME                         *
      *                 Company Number:  999999                      *
      ****************************************************************

      Model - 3090          OPSYS   - MVS/SP 3.1.3      Job  - AA0C2XB2
                            CP FMID - JBB3313           Step - GO
                            System  - MVSA              Time - 12.24.53

                        Completion Code - S0C7

-------------------------------------------------------------------------------


   LANGUAGE PROCESSOR INTERFACE RELEASE      = 03.25.03
   LANGUAGE PROCESSOR POST PROCESSOR RELEASE = 03.25.03


                          **************************
                          *   Instruction Section  *
                          **************************


                      The statement being executed was:

(A)------> 000041     MULTIPLY WS-SAVINGS-FACTOR BY WS-GROSS-PAY GIVING
           000042        WS-SAVINGS-AMT.

      This statement is contained in PARAGRAPH "CALC-SAVINGS" of
      program SUBPGM1.

      The program was compiled on 17 MAY 91 and is 002036 bytes long.


                   It is part of load module MAIN2PGM.

         The module was loaded from STEPLIB library MY.COBOL.LOAD
         It was link edited on 17 MAY 91 and is 0064B8 bytes long.
```

Figure 7.8 The Abend-AID/XCS report produced when the system composed of MAINPGM and SUBPGM1 ABENDed. *(Continued)*

```
                              A B E N D - A I D                          PAGE 3

                            *********************
                            * Diagnostic Section *
                            *********************

  Abend S0C7 occurred in program SUBPGM1 in the following statement

  000041            MULTIPLY WS-SAVINGS-FACTOR BY WS-GROSS-PAY GIVING
  000042               WS-SAVINGS-AMT.

               CURRENT VALUES OF FIELDS ON ABENDING STATEMENT
 LEVEL/FIELD NAME                       PICTURE/TYPE OFFS       VALUE
 ---------------------------------  ----------------- ----+----1----+----2
 02 WS-SAVINGS-AMT                       9(5)V99            0000000
(B) 02 WS-GROSS-PAY                    # 9(5)V99            00 @#20
    02 WS-SAVINGS-FACTOR               # 9V99              X'F07CFF'
 --------------------------------------------------------------------------
              ("#" - INDICATES FIELD CONTAINS INVALID DATA)

  The first field causing the abend is located in a temporary work field
  in the TGT.  The actual field in error is in Working-Storage of
  program SUBPGM1.

  The second field causing the abend is located in a temporary work
  field in the TGT.  The actual field in error is in Working-Storage of
  program SUBPGM1.

  Because the program is re-entrant, Working-Storage is located outside
  of the program.

  ----------------------------------------------------------------------

  S0C7, data exception, is caused when a computational-3 field has
  an invalid digit (not 0-9), or its last byte contains an invalid
  sign (not F, C, or D).
```

Figure 7.8 *(Continued)*

The preceding sections have discussed the basic and enhanced Abend-AID facilities. Many installations purchase only the basic version, assuming that its programmers have enough knowledge about debugging to carry the ball from there. The extra enhancements, while quite helpful, are not indispensable.

7.4 SUMMARY

Installations often purchase debugging products from non-IBM vendors in order to expand their testing and debugging capabilities. One commonly used product is Compuware's Abend-AID.

Abend-AID intercepts MVS's dumping facilities, generating its own formatted dump and diagnostic reports when an ABEND occurs. It can be tailored to an installation's requirements, with extra debugging enhancements added on to its basic facilities.

In order to use Abend-AID, either the SYSUDUMP or SYSABEND DD statement must be present in the JCL, or SYSMDUMP and ABENDAID DD state-

```
                           A B E N D - A I D                    PAGE 8

          **********************************************************
          *          Data Division of Program SUBPGM1              *
          *        Compiled on  17 MAY 91    at  12.23.36          *
          *                                                        *
          *                    VS COBOL II V1R3M1                  *
          *                                                        *
          *          Execution / Debugging options in effect       *
          *                                                        *
          *   NOADV            FDUMP                 RESIDENT      *
          *   NOCMPR2        NOOPTIMIZE            NOSSRANGE       *
          *     DATA(31)       OUTDD(SYSOUT  )     NOTEST          *
          *   NODYNAM          NUMPROC(NOPFD)        TRUNC(OPT)    *
          *   NOFASTSRT        RENT                  ZWB           *
          **********************************************************

                          Working-Storage Section

Working storage referenced by BLW cell   0 (X'0')
 LEVEL/FIELD NAME                     PICTURE/TYPE OFFS      VALUE
----------------------------------  ---------------- ----+----1----+----2
01 CONSTANTS
 02 MIN-FACTOR                      S9V99              +002
 02 MAX-FACTOR                      S9V99              +015
 02 ZERO-FACTOR                     S9V99              +000
01 PRINT-VARIABLES
 02 PRINT-FACTOR                    9.99               LOW-VALUES
 02 MIN-MAX-PRT                     X(7)               SPACES
01 WORK-VARIABLES
 02 WS-GROSS-PAY                    9(5)V99            00 @#20
 02 WS-SAVINGS-FACTOR               9V99             X'F07CFF'
 02 WS-SAVINGS-AMT                  9(5)V99            0000000

                              Linkage Section

Linkage storage referenced by BLL cell   1 (X'1')
 LEVEL/FIELD NAME                     PICTURE/TYPE OFFS      VALUE
----------------------------------  ---------------- ----+----1----+----2
77 GROSS-PAY                        9(5)V99            00 @#20

Linkage storage referenced by BLL cell   2 (X'2')
 LEVEL/FIELD NAME                     PICTURE/TYPE OFFS      VALUE
----------------------------------  ---------------- ----+----1----+----2
77 SAVINGS-FACTOR                   V99                @?

Linkage storage referenced by BLL cell   3 (X'3')
LEVEL/FIELD NAME                    PICTURE/TYPE OFFS      VALUE
----------------------------------  ---------------- ----+----1----+----2
77 SAVINGS-AMT                      9(5)V99            0180059

Linkage storage referenced by BLL cell   4 (X'4')
LEVEL/FIELD NAME                    PICTURE/TYPE OFFS      VALUE
----------------------------------  ---------------- ----+----1----+----2
77 EMPLOYEE-NO                      9(8)               40588299
                                          .
                                          .
                                          .
```

Figure 7.8 *(Continued)*

```
                         A B E N D - A I D                         PAGE 10

***********************************************************************
*                     Program Listing Section                         *
***********************************************************************

000035          CALC-SAVINGS.
000036         *
000037              MOVE GROSS-PAY       TO WS-GROSS-PAY.
000038              MOVE SAVINGS-FACTOR TO WS-SAVINGS-FACTOR.
000039              MOVE ZEROS           TO WS-SAVINGS-AMT.
000040              MOVE SPACES          TO MIN-MAX-PRT.
 ABND STMT ==>      MULTIPLY WS-SAVINGS-FACTOR BY WS-GROSS-PAY GIVING
000042                 WS-SAVINGS-AMT.
000043              MOVE WS-SAVINGS-AMT TO SAVINGS-AMT.
000044         *
000045         *--- VALIDATE SAVINGS FACTOR -- IF INVALID,
000046         *      SET SAVINGS AMOUNT TO ZERO AND PRINT A MESSAGE.
000047         *
000048              IF WS-SAVINGS-FACTOR > MAX-FACTOR THEN
000049                 MOVE 'MAXIMUM' TO MIN-MAX-PRT
000050              ELSE
000051              IF WS-SAVINGS-FACTOR < MIN-FACTOR AND
000052                 WS-SAVINGS-FACTOR NOT EQUAL ZERO-FACTOR THEN
000053                    MOVE 'MINIMUM' TO MIN-MAX-PRT
000054                 ELSE NEXT SENTENCE.
000055              IF MIN-MAX-PRT NOT EQUAL SPACES THEN
000056                    MOVE ZEROS TO SAVINGS-AMT
000057                    MOVE WS-SAVINGS-FACTOR TO PRINT-FACTOR
000058                    DISPLAY 'EMPLOYEE# ', EMPLOYEE-NO, ' OUT OF ',
000059                    MIN-MAX-PRT ' RANGE, SAVINGS FACTOR SET FROM ',
000060                    PRINT-FACTOR ' TO ZERO ' UPON SYSOUT
000061                 ELSE NEXT SENTENCE.
```

Figure 7.8 *(Continued)*

ments must be in the JCL. Default options for Abend-AID's control structure are provided by Compuware; they can be modified by the installation.

The Abend-AID control structure determines the type of processing and report formatting to be done. The control structure levels, in order from lowest priority to highest priority, are selection tables, ABEND code tables, user exits, JCL modification, and systemwide shutdown.

The programmer is most likely to use JCL modification to control such things as Abend-AID output destination, output formatting, or printing of Abend-AID help. The installation may use the other control structure elements to specify systemwide options or options for particular jobs and programs.

The basic Abend-AID report consists of several sections: the Next Sequential Instruction Section, the Diagnostic Section, the Program Area Section, the Working Storage Section, and the File Area. These provide enough information to enable you to solve most ABENDs.

There are a number of enhanced Abend-AID facilities which can make debugging an ABEND quicker and easier than by using just the basic product. They are SNAP-AID, Compuware/SPF, Abend-AID/COBOL (formerly called COBOL-AID), and Abend-AID/XCS.

SNAP-AID permits you to “snap” out an Abend-AID report and then continue processing. Compuware/SPF permits on-line viewing of the Abend-AID report. Both Abend-AID/COBOL and Abend-AID/XCS provide enhanced COBOL-specific information in the Abend-AID report; this enhanced information may speed up resolution of COBOL program ABENDs.

REVIEW QUESTIONS

1. What DD statement or statements must be coded in the JCL in order to use Abend-AID?

2. List the levels in the Abend-AID control structure in the order of their priority from highest to lowest. Which level are programmers most likely to use to specify options?

3. State the purpose of each of the following DD statements:
- **a.** //ABNLHELP DD DUMMY
- **b.** //ABENDAID DD SYSOUT= . . .
- **c.** //ABNLTERM DD SYSOUT= . . .
- **d.** //ABNLDUMP DD DUMMY
- **e.** //ABNLFMTD DD DUMMY
- **f.** //ABNLWIDE DD DUMMY
- **g.** //ABNLIGNR DD DUMMY
- **h.** //ABNLNODP DD DUMMY

4. What is the function of each of the following Abend-AID control structures?
- **a.** JCL modification
- **b.** ABEND code table
- **c.** Systemwide shutdown
- **d.** User exits
- **e.** Selection tables

5. Can an MVS system dump be obtained if Abend-AID is in effect? How?

6. Name the sections in a basic Abend-AID report. Briefly describe the type of information provided in each.

7. Assuming that the necessary JCL has been properly set up, describe the output which results from the following code in a COBOL program.

```
000100         DISPLAY 'ABOUT TO REQUEST ABEND-AID REPORT'
000200         CALL 'SNAPAID'
000300         DISPLAY 'RETURNED FROM ABEND-AID'
```

8. What is the function of the Abend-AID/SPF facility?

9. How does the Abend-AID report with the COBOL support option differ from the basic Abend-AID report?

10. How does the Abend-AID report with Extended COBOL support differ from the basic Abend-AID report?

Chapter

8

Overview of MVS Task Management Concepts

A detailed explanation of the MVS operating system, which for the current discussion includes MVS/XA and MVS/ESA, is too complex to be covered in depth in this book. Nevertheless, to read and interpret system dumps and to understand how the operating system handles ABENDs, we need to review some operating system concepts. This chapter will discuss the Program Status Word, object code, how MVS fetches and executes instructions, Interrupt Processing, and various Task Management control blocks.

8.1 THE PROGRAM STATUS WORD

The Program Status Word (PSW) is a special system register which contains information necessary for proper control of the central processing unit (CPU). The CPU executes machine instructions. There is only one active PSW per CPU in effect at any given time, although many system control blocks and storage areas have fields which store old PSWs or PSWs which may become active in the future.

The PSW is a doubleword in length. Some of its bits are shown in Fig. 8.1 and are described below.

Bit 1 is the Program Event Recording (PER) mask. When on, this feature monitors various events (e.g., successful execution of a branch instruction), registers, and main storage locations. The PER is generally used only by systems programmers and may be useful in diagnosing system problems.

Bit 5 controls the Dynamic Address Translation (DAT) feature. DAT is a combination of hardware and software which converts virtual addresses (see Sec. 8.5) into real central storage addresses as instructions are being executed. When this bit is set to 1, DAT is in effect.

Bit 6 controls the Input/Output mask and bit 7 the External mask. If bit 6 is on, the CPU will process I/O interruptions. If bit 7 is on, the CPU will process

BITS	DESCRIPTION	
01	(R) PER Mask	First Word
05	(T=1) DAT Mode	
06	(I) Input/Output Mask	
07	(E) External Mask	
08-12	PSW Key	
13	(M) Machine Check Mask	
14	(W=1) Wait State	
15	(P=1) Problem State	
16-17	(AS) Address Space Control	
18-19	(CC) Condition code	
20	Fixed-point Overflow Mask	Program Masks
21	Decimal Overflow Mask	Program Masks
22	Exponent Underflow Mask	Program Masks
23	Significance Mask	Program Masks
32	(A=1) 31 Bit Addressing Mode	Second Word
33-63	NSI Address: 33-63 if A=1 40-63 if A=0	

Figure 8.1 Important bits in the PSW under MVS/ESA.

external interruptions. If either bit is off, its associated interrupt cannot occur. A system control program may set these bits under certain conditions to disable these interrupts when other types of interrupts are being handled. Interrupt handling will be discussed in Sec. 8.4.

Bits 8 through 12 protect restricted system storage from alteration by application programs. This "protection key" can only be modified by a privileged instruction and usually only MVS supervisor routines can run in privileged mode.

Bit 13 works in a similar fashion to bits 6 and 7. It controls whether the CPU will recognize a machine check (the hardware has detected an error caused by a component failure) interruption.

When bit 14 is set to 1, the CPU is in a wait state. No instructions execute because all active programs are waiting for completion of some event. When an interrupt occurs, a new PSW will be loaded with this bit set to 0. The CPU will now be in running state and instructions can again execute.

Bit 15 is the problem/supervisor bit. When it is set to 1, the CPU is in the problem state; no privileged instructions can execute. This is the state in which application programs run. The instruction to load a new PSW is a privileged instruction, so an application program cannot get out of the problem state. When the bit is set to 0, the CPU is in privileged state. Bit 15 is 0 in the new PSW which is loaded when an interrupt occurs, and an operating system program will be given control and allowed to execute privileged instructions. When control is to return to an application program, a new PSW with bit 15 in the problem state becomes the active PSW.

Bits 16 and 17 designate what address space mode is in effect. In MVS/XA, only bit 16 is used; in MVS/ESA, both bits are used. Together with DAT, they control the handling of address translations within multiple address spaces. Our discussion assumes that primary mode, that is, the current instruction space, is in effect. COBOL programmers do not control address space mode selection.

The next two bits, 18 and 19, constitute the condition code which is set and interrogated by many machine instructions. It is set to 0, 1, 2, or 3 depending on the result obtained when the instructions are executed. For example, an AP (Add Packed) instruction sets the condition code to 0 when the result is zero, to 1 when the result is less than zero, to 2 when the result is greater than zero, and to 3 when the execution results in an overflow. Assembler programmers can use this code to control the instruction execution flow, and any programmer may find the code important in debugging. This is not the same condition code that we described in Chap. 1; unfortunately, IBM used the same term to represent two different things.

Bits 20 through 23 are program masks; bit 20 is the fixed-point overflow mask, bit 21 is the decimal overflow mask, bit 22 is the exponent underflow mask, and bit 23 is the significance mask. Each can be set off to disable its particular type of interrupt. Again, Assembler programmers can control these bits.

Bit 32 begins the second word of the PSW. It controls the addressing mode. When it is 0, 24-bit addressing is in effect; in this mode only 16 megabytes of real or virtual storage (see Sec. 8.5) may be addressed because only 24 bits of any address are used (also referred to as an address "below the line"). When this bit is 1, 31-bit addressing is in effect; in this mode 2 gigabytes of real or virtual storage may be addressed because 31 bits of any address are used (also referred to as an address "above the line"). OS/VS COBOL programs can use only 24-bit addresses; COBOL II programs can use either 24- or 31-bit addresses.

The remaining portion of the second word is the most important from a debugging standpoint; it contains the address of the next sequential instruction (NSI). This is the address of the Assembler instruction which is usually intended for execution at the conclusion of the current instruction. When 24-bit addressing is in effect, bits 40 through 63 contain the NSI address. If the 31-bit addressing mode is active, the address of the NSI is in bits 33 to 63. Of course, if the current instruction causes a branch, as when a COBOL PERFORM statement transfers control to a different paragraph, NSI will not be the next instruction executed; a different instruction address will have to be established. We will examine the steps which MVS takes when it is about to execute an instruction in Sec. 8.3.

8.2 UNDERSTANDING OBJECT CODE

Before discussing how instructions are fetched and executed, it will help to briefly examine how Assembler instructions are coded and how to interpret object code. The purpose here is not to teach you Assembler, but rather to provide a basis for understanding and appreciating what is to follow. Those who have been in the data processing field for some time will undoubtedly agree that many of the best COBOL programmers have some Assembler exposure. Knowledge of what happens at the Assembler level and below makes what COBOL is doing more meaningful. Enough said!

In Sec. 3.3.2, when illustrating the usefulness of PROCEDURE DIVISION maps, we indicated that a COBOL instruction generates Assembler instructions. The level below Assembler instructions contains machine instructions, represented by the hexadecimal object code shown in a PROCEDURE DIVISION map and a system storage dump.

A machine instruction consists of two main parts. The first is the operation code (Op Code). It specifies what operation is to be performed by the instruction. The second part defines the operands that are acted upon by the instruction. The Op Code always starts in the first byte; those most commonly found in COBOL modules are usually 1 byte long, although some MVS/XA and many new MVS/ESA instructions have 2-byte Op Codes.

We can look at the listing of machine instructions in IBM's *System/370 Extended Architecture Reference Summary, Enterprise Systems Architecture/370 Reference Summary* or *Principles of Operations* (use the publication for XA or ESA as appropriate) to see the Op Codes and operands. Figure 8.2 shows part of the listing, sorted alphabetically by mnemonic, from the *Enterprise Systems Architecture/370 Reference Summary* (see Appendix D for the full listing). An Assembler programmer would code the mnemonic followed by the operands represented by the symbols in the listing. The Op Code is given in hexadecimal notation; a machine instruction listing sorted by Op Code shows the Op Code and its associated mnemonic (see Appendix D).

To summarize the meanings of the symbols shown in the format column for the more common instructions, RR means a register to register operation, RRE is a register to register instruction which has an extended Op Code field, RX denotes a register and indexed storage instruction, RS is an operation involving a register and storage, SI is a storage with immediate operation (immediate means that the operand is contained within the instruction), S denotes an instruction which uses storage and an implied operand, SS is a storage to storage operation, and SSE denotes a storage to storage operation which has an extended Op Code field. In the operands column, R represents a

MACHINE INSTRUCTIONS

By Mnemonic

Mnemonic	Operands	Name	Format	Op Code	Class & Notes
A	$R_1, D_2(X_2, B_2)$	Add	RX	5A	c
AD	$R_1, D_2(X_2, B_2)$	Add Normalized (L)	RX	6A	c
ADR	R_1, R_2	Add Normalized (L)	RR	2A	c
AE	$R_1, D_2(X_2, B_2)$	Add Normalized (S)	RX	7A	c
AER	R_1, R_2	Add Normalized (S)	RR	3A	c
AH	$R_1, D_2(X_2, B_2)$	Add Halfword	RX	4A	c
AL	$R_1, D_2(X_2, B_2)$	Add Logical	RX	5E	c
ALR	R_1, R_2	Add Logical	RR	1E	c
AP	$D_1(L_1, B_1), D_2(L_2, B_2)$	Add Decimal	SS	FA	c
AR	R_1, R_2	Add	RR	1A	c
AU	$R_1, D_2(X_2, B_2)$	Add Unnormalized (S)	RX	7E	c
AUR	R_1, R_2	Add Unnormalized (S)	RR	3E	c
AW	$R_1, D_2(X_2, B_2)$	Add Unnormalized (L)	RX	6E	c
AWR	R_1, R_2	Add Unnormalized (L)	RR	2E	c
AXR	R_1, R_2	Add Unnormalized (L)	RR	36	c
BAKR	R_1, R_2	Branch and Stack	RRE	B240	q
BAL	$R_1, D_2(X_2, B_2)$	Branch and Link	RX	45	
BALR	R_1, R_2	Branch and Link	RR	05	
BAS	$R_1, D_2(X_2, B_2)$	Branch and Save	RX	4D	
BASR	R_1, R_2	Branch and Save	RR	0D	
BASSM	R_1, R_2	Branch and Save and Set Mode	RR	0C	
BC	$M_1, D_2(X_2, B_2)$	Branch on Condition	RX	47	
BCR	M_1, R_2	Branch on Condition	RR	07	
BCT	$R_1, D_2(X_2, B_2)$	Branch on Count	RX	46	
		⋮			
STH	$R_1, D_2(X_2, B_2)$	Store Halfword	RX	40	
STIDP	$D_2(B_2)$	Store CPU ID	S	B202	p
STM	$R_1, R_3, D_2(B_2)$	Store Multiple	RS	90	
STNSM	$D_1(B_1), I_2$	Store Then AND System Mask	SI	AC	p
STOSM	$D_1(B_1), I_2$	Store Then OR System Mask	SI	AD	p
STPT	$D_2(B_2)$	Store CPU Timer	S	B209	p
STPX	$D_2(B_2)$	Store Prefix	S	B211	p
STSCH	$D_2(B_2)$	Store Subchannel	S	B234	pc
STURA	R_1, R_2	Store Using Real Address	RRE	B246	p
SU	$R_1, D_2(X_2, B_2)$	Subtract Unnormalized (S)	RX	7F	c
SUR	R_1, R_2	Subtract Unnormalized (S)	RR	3F	c
SVC	I	Supervisor Call	RR	0A	
SW	$R_1, D_2(X_2, B_2)$	Subtract Unnormalized (L)	RX	6F	c
SWR	R_1, R_2	Subtract Unnormalized (L)	RR	2F	c
SXR	R_1, R_2	Subtract Normalized (E)	RR	37	c
TAR	R_1, R_2	Test Access	RRE	B24C	qc

Floating-point operand lengths:

- (E) Extended source and result.
- (E/L) Extended source, long result.
- (L/E) Long source, extended result.
- (L) Long source and result.
- (L/S) Long source, short result.
- (S/L) Short source, long result.
- (S) Short source and result.

Notes:

- c. Condition code set.
- i. Interruptible instruction.
- n. New condition code loaded.
- p. Privileged instruction.
- q. Semiprivileged instruction.
- x. Execution in problem state and supervisor state differs.
- y. Condition code may be set.
- z. Condition code is unpredictable.

Class (for instructions subject to vector-control bit. CR 0 bit 14)

- IC: Interruptible; (VCT – VIX) elements processed.
- IG: Interruptible; either (bit count in a general register) elements or (section-size – VIX) elements processed, whichever is fewer.
- IM: Interruptible; (VCT – VIX) elements processed, vector-mask mode.
- IP: Interruptible; (partial-sum-number – VIX) elements processed.
- IZ: Interruptible; (section-size) elements processed.
- NC: Not interruptible; (VCT) elements processed.
- NZ: Not interruptible; (section-size) elements processed.
- N0: Not interruptible; no elements processed (VSR/VAC housekeeping).
- N1: Not Interruptible; one element processed.

Figure 8.2 A portion of the listing of machine instructions under MVS/ESA.

register field, B a base register, X an index register, D a displacement, and L a length.

The actual formats of the instructions represented by the symbols in the format column together with the meanings of the symbols in the operands column are illustrated in Fig. 8.3. Unfortunately, the order in which the operands appear in the machine instructions is not the order shown in the operands column of Fig. 8.2, which is the way they are coded in Assembler. For example, an Add Decimal instruction (also referred to as Add Packed) is an SS instruction which is coded in Assembler as

```
AP D1(L1,B1),D2(L2,B2)
```

This is the way it appears in the PROCEDURE DIVISION map when generated by a COBOL ADD verb.

Op Code	L_1	L_2	B_1	D_1	B_2	D_2	
0	8	12	16	20	32	36	47

However, as can be seen in Fig. 8.3, the format is in the hexadecimal object code portion of the PROCEDURE DIVISION map or the system dump. An actual instruction coded in Assembler as

```
AP 531(5,13),88(4,6)
```

would appear in hexadecimal object code as

```
FA43D2136058
```

Note that each length in the hexadecimal object code will always be 1 byte less than the actual length coded in the Assembler instruction.

With this background, we can now see how a machine instruction appearing in hexadecimal notation corresponds to the Assembler instruction. Be aware that sometimes when a program ABENDs, particularly production jobs, a system dump may be all that is available for use in debugging. The ABENDing instruction will be given in hexadecimal notation. In order to find out what type of instruction it is, looking at the Op Code may be sufficient. Thus an S0C7 ABEND implies that something is wrong with an operand in an instruction involving packed fields. If the instruction executing at the time of the ABEND has an Op Code of FA, it is an Add Packed instruction probably generated by a COBOL ADD statement. If the Op Code is F9, it is a Compare Decimal instruction (also known as Compare Packed) which may have been generated by a COBOL IF verb.

However, if it is necessary to learn the location of the operands, further translation may be required. We will illustrate how this is done in the next two sections.

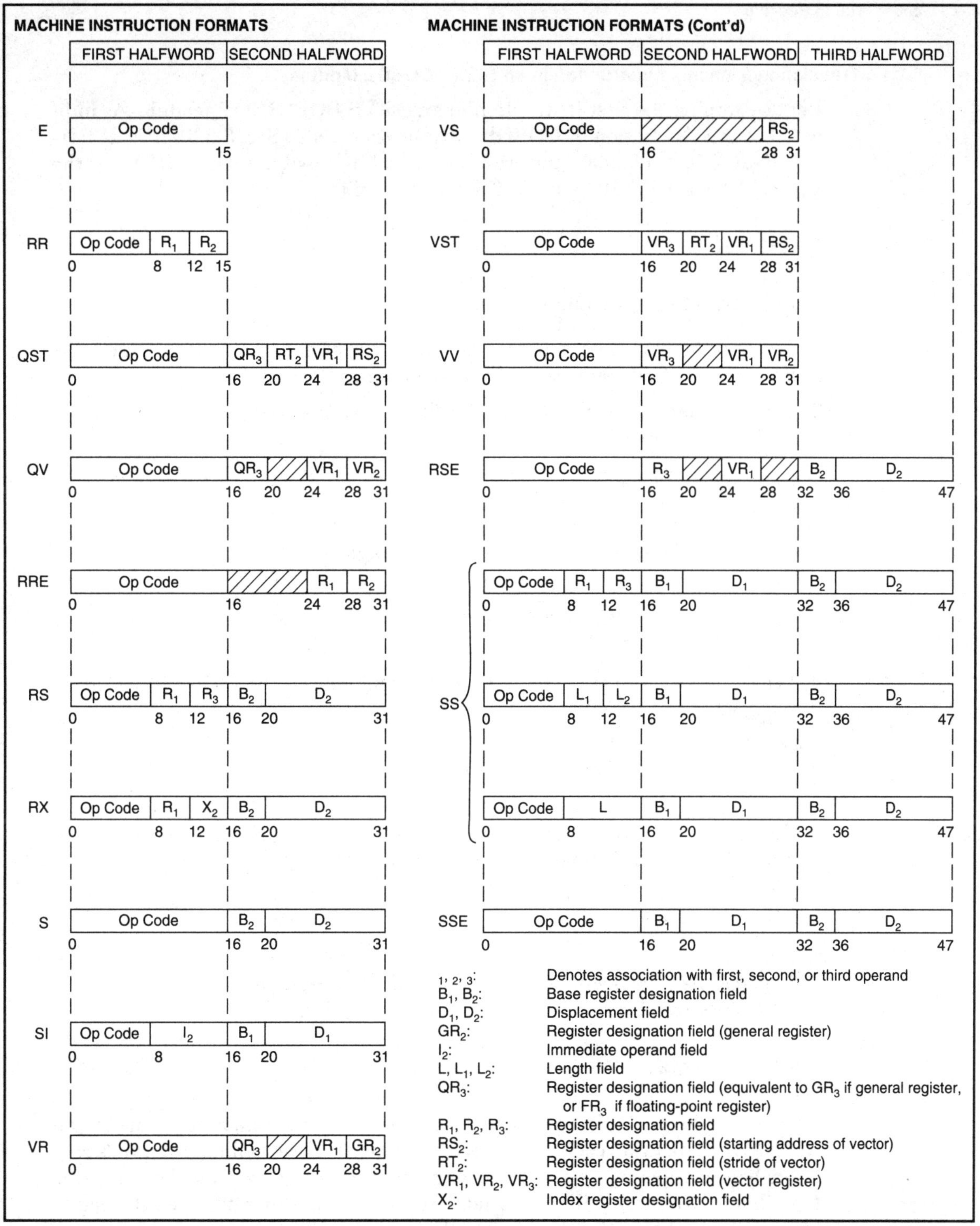

Figure 8.3 Format of the machine instructions under MVS/ESA.

8.2.1 Translating a Machine Instruction in an OS/VS COBOL Module

Let us examine the first instruction in an OS/VS COBOL load module. As indicated in our discussion of COBOL initialization code (Sec. 3.3.3), it is at hexadecimal offset 000000 and can be found by looking for INIT1 in the PROCEDURE DIVISION map. The instruction is

```
90ECD00C
```

To interpret this, we follow these steps:

1. Look up the Op Code to determine what type of instruction this is (see Fig. 8.2). The Op Code 90 is the STM instruction.
2. Write down the machine format for the instruction (see Fig. 8.3). STM is an RS instruction with the format

Op Code	R_1	R_3	B_2	D_2

0 8 12 16 20 31

3. Substitute the object code in the format diagram.

Op Code	R_1	R_3	B_2	D_2
90	E	C	D	00C

0 8 12 16 20 31

4. Look at the Operands column in Fig. 8.2 to see how this is coded in Assembler.

```
STM     R1,R3,D2(B2)
```

5. Substitute the hexadecimal object code from the machine format diagram in step 3 into the Assembler format shown in step 4.

```
STM     E,C,00C(D)
```

6. Replace the hexadecimal characters with their equivalent decimal characters, since this is the way it is coded in Assembler.

```
STM     14,12,12(13)
```

This is the Store Multiple instruction. Recall that a major function of the COBOL initialization code is to store the contents of the calling program's registers before allowing any other code in the program to execute. This ensures that this information will be available to the calling program when it regains control. This STM instruction stores the contents of general-purpose registers 14 through 12 (it wraps around, so that registers 14, 15, and 0 through 12 are included) in a storage area displaced 12 bytes from the base address in register 13. When the current program receives control, the address in register 13 points to the start of the calling program's Save Area. (If the calling program is written in COBOL, register 13 points to the beginning of COBOL's TGT; refer back to Fig. 2.14 and you will see that the Save Area is the first field in the TGT.) Thus the contents of the calling program's registers are stored beginning at word 4 (12-byte displacement) into the calling program's Save Area.

Refer to the initialization code in Fig. 3.15 to verify our results. Notice that the instruction at offset 000000 is indeed 90ECD00C, or STM 14,12,00C(13). The displacement is shown as hexadecimal 00C rather than 12 because the map has "Assembler-like" code rather than the true Assembler instructions.

8.2.2 Translating a Machine Instruction in a COBOL II Module

We can use the same technique presented in the previous section to translate any machine instruction. Let us now do it for the very first instruction in a COBOL II load module. As discussed in the section on COBOL initialization code (Sec. 3.3.3), we can find it in the PROCEDURE DIVISION map at hexadecimal offset 000000. The instruction is

```
47F0F070
```

These are the steps we need to follow:

1. Look up the Op Code to find out what instruction this is (see Fig. 8.2). The Op Code 47 is the BC instruction.
2. Write down the machine format for the instruction (see Fig. 8.3). We see that BC is an RX instruction having the following format:

Op Code	R_1	X_2	B_2	D_2
0	8	12	16	20 … 31

3. Substitute the object code in the format diagram.

Op Code	R_1	X_2	B_2	D_2
47	F	0	F	070
0	8	12	16	20 … 31

4. Looking at the Operands column in Fig. 8.2 shows us that the BC instruction is coded in Assembler as

```
BC     M1,D2(X2,B2)
```

Notice that register R1 is replaced by M1. This represents a mask rather than a register. A mask is a pattern of bits or characters which may be used to test or alter another field.

5. Now substitute the hexadecimal object code from the machine format diagram in step 3 into the Assembler format shown in step 4.

```
BC      F,070(0,F)
```

6. Replacing the hexadecimal characters with their equivalent decimal characters, the way an Assembler programmer would code it, gives

```
BC      15,112(0,15)
```

This is the Branch on Condition instruction. If the condition or conditions specified by the mask M1 are true, a branch to the location represented by D2(X2,B2) will take place. Each bit in the mask corresponds to one of the four possible condition codes (0, 1, 2, or 3) for the instruction (see Sec. 8.1). The mask 15 (equivalent to hexadecimal F or binary 1111) specifies an unconditional branch since it signifies that all possible conditions are specified, and therefore one of the conditions must always be met. The location to which control is transferred is 112 bytes past the address in register 15; since register 15 by convention contains the entry point address (EPA), the first instruction in a COBOL II module branches around a 112-byte area to another instruction.

What is this other instruction and why is there a branch around the 112-byte area? Look at the COBOL II initialization code in Fig. 3.16. First notice that the very first instruction is not coded as

```
BC      15,112(0,15)
```

but rather as

```
B       112(,15)
```

This is an extended mnemonic instruction which incorporates the BC 15, or "branch on condition 15" into the instruction; it is an alternate way of coding the BC 15 and achieves the same result.

Second, control is transferred to an instruction which is identical to the first instruction in an OS/VS COBOL load module. That instruction is Store Multiple; it stores the contents of the calling program's registers beginning in word 4 of the calling program's Save Area (see Sec. 8.2.1). The 112-byte area which is bypassed contains constants, not executable instructions. Thus the COBOL II initialization code starts out by doing essentially the same thing as the OS/VS COBOL initialization code; it ensures that the contents of the calling program's registers will be available to the calling program when it regains control.

8.3 FETCHING AND EXECUTING INSTRUCTIONS

We are now ready to look at how MVS fetches and executes instructions. Instruction fetching involves loading the object code from main storage located at the address indicated in the second word of the PSW. Execution involves carrying out the task specified by the instruction. A simplified, conceptual version of the sequence of events in the system is

1. The system gets the address of the NSI from the PSW. DAT is used to translate virtual addresses into real storage addresses (see Sec. 8.5 for a discussion of real and virtual storage).
2. The first half byte of the Op Code is examined to determine the instruction length so that the proper number of bytes can be fetched. All instructions are 2, 4, or 6 bytes in length. A hexadecimal value of 0 through 3 in the first half byte of the Op Code means 2 bytes, 4 through B means 4 bytes, and C through F means 6 bytes.
3. The instruction is fetched into the Arithmetic Logic Unit (ALU) of the CPU.
4. MVS then increments the instruction address in the PSW by the instruction length to give a new NSI address. Because the NSI has already been updated before the current instruction actually executes, the address in the second word of the PSW must be decreased by the instruction length to find the address of the current instruction if the instruction causes an ABEND.
5. The Op Code is now checked to see if this is a valid instruction. If it is not, an operation exception will occur (an S0C1 completion code).
6. If the instruction has been found to be valid, storage is now allocated in the ALU for the operands.
7. The addresses of the operands are determined based on the displacements and the addresses in the registers specified in the instruction.
8. The system fetches the operand data into ALU.
9. The operation specified by the instruction is now carried out.
10. The operand data are returned to storage and the appropriate condition code is set in bits 18 and 19 of the PSW if this is required by the instruction.
11. The cycle is repeated for the next instruction.

The procedure just outlined assumes that instructions are fetched one-by-one as needed and interpreted in the sequence described. Actually there is a prefetch process which allows instructions to be fetched and analyzed in advance. Thus, for the sake of efficiency, the NSI may be fetched while the ALU is executing the current instruction. If the current instruction involves a branch rather than normal sequential processing, the chain of events is altered; the system must then go back and fetch a different instruction. This is why branching is inefficient. Also, instructions are not necessarily fetched in the order in which they are conceptually executed, and may not be fetched as a single unit. For more detailed information, see *IBM System/370 Principles of Operation* or *Enterprise Systems Architecture/390 Principles of Operation.*

8.4 INTERRUPT PROCESSING

There is hardware as well as MVS system software designed to interrupt execution of whatever task has control of the CPU. You might think that you would never want your job interrupted, but interrupts are a normal part of the IBM mainframe computer operation. MVS supports multiprogramming (a technique which allows many jobs to appear to be executing at the same time) by interrupting whatever program is currently active if it does not need the CPU at a given instant (as when I/O is occurring) and giving control to another which may be ready to execute an instruction. Also, some interrupts may be necessary when the active program needs to switch control to a system routine to carry out a task for it (as when a COBOL program issues an OPEN instruction) or when, heaven forbid, an abnormal condition is detected by the hardware or software.

There are six types of interrupts; 4 are normal and 2 represent error conditions. All interrupts are asynchronous but one. Asynchronous interrupts occur at times which cannot be predicted by the program which is executing. The one interrupt which is synchronous occurs when the program knowingly transfers control to another routine. The interrupts are briefly described in the section which follows.

8.4.1 The Types of Interrupts

Input/output interrupt. The I/O interrupt occurs when the channel, which is an interface between an external I/O device and real storage, must inform the operating system that an I/O operation has completed. This interrupt is asynchronous.

Supervisor Call interrupt. This is the only type of interrupt which is synchronous. The program issuing a SuperVisor Call (SVC) does it deliberately at specific times in its processing, transferring control to the supervisor so that the supervisor can carry out some specific task (see Appendix C for a listing of SVCs). This, as explained in Sec. 1.4, includes the call to the ABEND macro (SVC 13) when the program which is currently running determines that an error condition exists. Assembler programmers can issue SVCs directly; a COBOL programmer does it indirectly, as when the COBOL OPEN statement is executed, thereby calling a COBOL library subroutine which issues the OPEN macro (SVC 19).

External interrupt. This interrupt is asynchronous and occurs for external reasons. Examples are when the interrupt key is pressed by the operator or when a malfunction alert occurs.

Restart interrupt. The restart interrupt is asynchronous and rarely occurs. It may be caused when the restart key on the hardware console is pressed by the operator.

Program interrupt. A program interrupt is asynchronous and represents an error condition. As discussed in Sec. 1.4, the hardware may detect an exceptional condition due to an invalid operation, such as a data exception, and call an exit routine to issue the ABEND macro; this in turn terminates the task, requests a system dump, and returns the appropriate system completion code. Program checks, which have 0Cx-type completion codes, are of this type. (See Appendix B for a listing of these and other common system completion codes.) The "x" is a hexadecimal number which comes from the program interrupt code. It is possible in Assembler to disable certain program interrupts by setting the appropriate bits in the PSW to 0. This cannot be done in COBOL.

Other program interrupts include those caused by Monitor Call interruptions from the Program Event Recording (PER) hardware, and page requests caused when DAT recognizes an invalid page reference and requests MVS to load the appropriate page into real storage.

Machine Check interrupt. This interrupt is asynchronous and occurs when the hardware detects an error condition caused by a component failure.

8.4.2 The PSW Switch

In all cases, after the interrupt processing is completed, the system must be able to resume from where it left off. To accomplish this, a PSW switch takes place, using the Old and New PSW fields which are in fixed storage in the Prefixed Save Area (PSA). The PSA may be in low core starting at address 00000000 or in some other location if there are multiple CPUs in the computer. There is an Old PSW and New PSW field for each type of interrupt. The Old PSW field serves as a save area for the PSW which was active before the interrupt occurred, while the New PSW field contains a preset PSW which will give control to the First Level Interrupt Handler (FLIH) for that type of interrupt. One of the first jobs of the interrupt routine is to save the interrupted program's registers.

Figure 8.4 illustrates the sequence of events for the PSW switch when an I/O interrupt occurs. At number "1," the hardware saves the currently active PSW by placing it in the I/O Old slot. At "2," the PSW from the I/O New field is loaded so that it is now active. It invokes the First Level Interrupt Handler (FLIH) for the Input/Output Supervisor (IOS). Part of the FLIH's processing, shown at "3," includes placing a copy of the interrupted program's PSW from the I/O Old field into the Old PSW field (OPSW) of its request block. (We will discuss request blocks in the section on control blocks later in this chapter.) It also saves the contents of the interrupted program's general-purpose registers. The IOS initiates the channel subsystem so that data transfer can occur. When the channel subsystem is done, it signals its completion by causing an I/O interrupt. IOS then continues. At the conclusion of its processing, IOS will transfer control to the system's dispatcher. The dispatcher will return control to the interrupted program's next sequential instruction address, taken from the saved PSW, when its turn is reached.

8.5 VIRTUAL STORAGE AND ADDRESS SPACES

MVS stands for multiple virtual storage. The term "virtual storage" implies that the storage does not really exist. The storage which is physically present in the processor is called real storage. Storage that exists on external media,

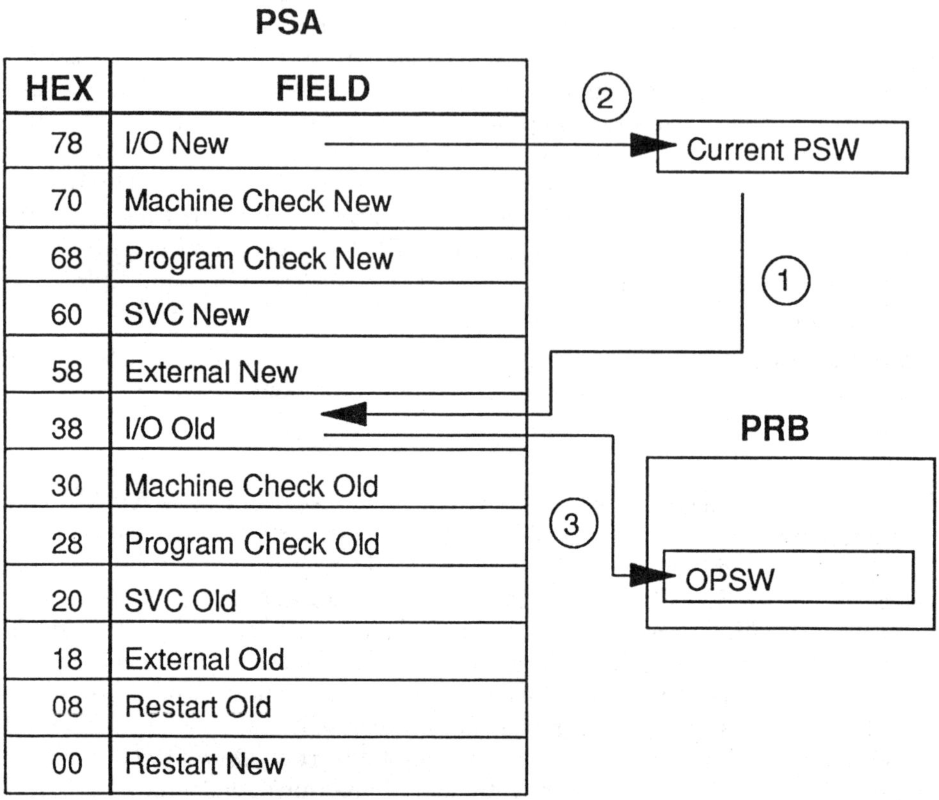

Figure 8.4 The PSW swap for an I/O interrupt.

such as tape drives or disk drives, is known as auxiliary storage. Conceptually, virtual storage combines both real and auxiliary storage, thereby giving the CPU more storage to work with than is apparently available. Each unique location is assigned a virtual address. MVS uses tables to keep track of where a program is in virtual storage.

In order for the processor to execute an instruction in a program, both the instruction and any data it references must be in real storage. Because it is not necessary to have an entire program in real storage in order to execute only one instruction, MVS transfers pieces of a program from the auxiliary storage devices into real storage when it is ready to execute those particular program instructions, and moves those pieces back out to auxiliary storage when the real storage is needed for another purpose. These program pieces are called *pages,* hence the term paging, which refers to the process of transferring pages into and out of real storage.

The complete range of virtual addresses which MVS assigns to a program is known as an address space. Every address space has a unique address space identification number (ASID) and a system control block known as the Address

Space Control Block (ASCB). The ASCB is created at the start of the job. Additional control blocks are associated with each ASCB.

8.6 TASKS

A task is the basic unit of work for MVS. It is a subdivision of a job and runs in the job's address space. MVS selects the address space with the highest priority and then selects the task with the highest priority within that address space for execution. The control block associated with a task is called a Task Control Block (TCB).

8.7 MVS CONTROL BLOCKS USED IN MANAGING TASKS

We have already alluded to two of the control blocks used by MVS: the ASCB and the TCB. Recall that a control block is a storage area containing data and pointers to other areas. Some control blocks are chained, with the first pointing to the second, the second pointing to the next, and so on. Often those further down the chain will point back up to previous control blocks. Only those most useful for debugging are discussed here.

Although control blocks can be found in the hexadecimal portion of a storage dump when an ABEND occurs, it is quite time consuming to do so. Fortunately, MVS provides most of the important control blocks at the beginning of a dump in a neatly formatted fashion. The control blocks are labeled, their storage dump addresses are given, control block field names along with the field contents are provided, and hexadecimal offsets from the start of the control blocks are shown. We will see what these formatted control blocks look like in Sec. 8.7.6.

The figures in the sections that follow show the names, lengths, and hexadecimal offsets from the beginning of the control block for important fields in dumps produced under MVS/XA or MVS/ESA. The field names given in IBM's *MVS/ESA Diagnosis: Data Areas* and *MVS/XA Debugging Handbook* have prefixes which identify which control blocks the fields are in; I have omitted these prefixes. Also note that the field names given in the manuals, and in the figures, do not always exactly match the names supplied in the formatted control blocks at the beginning of the dump. Although the names are similar, those used in the dump often indicate the purpose of the fields more clearly. Some fields in a control block are not labeled in the dump, so it is important to use the hexadecimal offsets to accurately find a desired field.

8.7.1 Address Space Control Block

The Address Space Control Block (ASCB) contains information needed by MVS to manage the address space. Each address space is identified by an address space identification number (ASID); MVS has a table of all its ASIDs with pointers to the corresponding ASCBs. The formatted ASCB for a job appears near the beginning of the formatted portion of the dump.

HEX OFFSET	LENGTH	DESCRIPTION
+1C	4	TNEW- Address of the TCB of the first ready task
+24	2	ASID- Address space identifier
+2B	1	DP- Dispatching priority range from 0 to 255
+D8	4	TCBS- Number of ready TCBs in address space

Figure 8.5 Some fields in the Address Space Control Block (ASCB).

Some of the ASCB fields which may be useful in order to get an overall perspective of the address space in a particular ABEND situation are shown in Fig. 8.5.

8.7.2 Task Control Block

The Task Control Block (TCB) contains the information that MVS needs to manage the task. The TCB is created by the ATTACH SVC when the task is begun. The TCB for the ABENDing task appears shortly after the ASCB in the formatted part of the dump. Useful fields are given in Fig. 8.6.

8.7.3 Request Blocks

A Request Block (RB) contains data and addresses needed by the system concerning a program or a supervisor routine. Information is stored there during interrupt processing. The stored information includes the contents of general-purpose registers, PSWs at interrupt time, instruction lengths, interrupt codes, and pointers to other control blocks.

Two types of request blocks found in a system dump are the Program Request Block (PRB) and the Supervisor Request Block (SVRB). The PRB contains information for a program which has been interrupted. The SVRB, created when a supervisor service is requested, contains information relating to that supervisor routine. It is longer than a PRB because it stores an extra set of registers.

A system dump will have at least three RBs in its request block chain. They appear in the formatted portion of the dump with the oldest first and the most recent last. The last two are the SVRBs for the routines that generated the dump and terminated the task. The third one up from the last may be a PRB or SVRB; it is the RB for the program (if it is a PRB) or supervisor routine (if it is a SVRB) that issued the ABEND macro (or SNAP macro).

Figure 8.7 shows request block fields which are important when solving an ABEND. A few fields have a negative offset; they begin before the "start" of the control block.

Two important fields are FLCDE and WLIC. In a PRB, FLCDE points to the Contents Directory Entry, a control block which provides load module information about the program (see next section). In both the PRB and SVRB, the last 2 bytes of the WLIC field indicates the interrupt code. In the PRB this code may be the hardware interrupt code (e.g., 04 for an S0C4 ABEND) or the hexadecimal SVC number of the routine that issued the ABEND. For example, a value of 37 (equivalent to decimal 55) in an S002 ABEND means that the End-of-Volume (EOV) SVC data management routine requested ABEND processing.

The last 2 bytes of the WLIC field in an SVRB represents the hexadecimal interrupt code of the SVC associated with this SVRB. A value of 33, for example, refers to SVC 51 (equivalent to hexadecimal 33); this is the SVC for the SNAP macro.

HEX OFFSET	LENGTH	DESCRIPTION
0	4	RBP- RP pointer: address of RB for executing program
+08	4	DEB- Address of the DEB queue
+0C	4	TIO- Address of the TIOT
+2C	4	JPQ- Address of last CDE in JPA control queue

Figure 8.6 Some of the important fields in the Task Control Block (TCB).

HEX OFFSET	LENGTH	DESCRIPTION
-18	8	RTPSW1- PSW at interrupt time in abending program's RB
-10	8	RTPSW2- ILC and interrupt code
-04	4	WLIC- 1 byte: Wait count 1 byte: Instruction length 2 bytes: Interrupt code
+0C	4	FLCDE- Address of CDE, if this is a PRB
+10	8	OPSW- User's old PSW
+1C	4	LINK- Address of previous RB or of TCB if this is first RB
+20	16	GPR0-3 - Save area for GP Registers 0-3
+30	16	GPR4-7 - Save area for GP Registers 4-7
+40	16	GPR8-11 - Save area for GP Registers 8-11
+50	16	GPR12-15 - Save area for GP Registers 12-15

Figure 8.7 Some of the important fields in a Request Block (RB).

8.7.4 Contents Directory Entry

A Contents Directory Entry (CDE) is created for every load module name and alias associated with the task. This control block contains important debugging information, including the name of the load module, its entry-point address (EPA), and a pointer to its associated entry in the Extent List (XTLST). We referred to the starting point of a program in Sec. 3.1.3.2 when we demonstrated how to find a COBOL field in a hexadecimal storage dump. The EPA is the logical "starting point" for the program execution; the CDE is one place where it can be found.

Some of the fields in the CDE are given in Fig. 8.8.

HEX OFFSET	LENGTH	DESCRIPTION
0	4	CHAIN- Address of next higher CDE in queue
+04	4	RRBP- Address of RB controlling module (if reusable), or RB at top of wait queue (if serially reusable)
+08	8	NAME- Name of this load module
+10	4	ENTPT- Module's Entry Point Address
+14	4	XLMJP- Address of Extent List for this module
+18	4	USE- 2 bytes: Total use count
+1C	1	ATTR- Module attributes (i.e., rent, in process of being loaded, etc.)
+1D	1	ATTR2- 2nd attribute field (i.e., module inactive, XTLST built, etc.)

Figure 8.8 A number of fields in the Contents Directory Entry (CDE).

HEX OFFSET	LENGTH	DESCRIPTION
+09	3	MSBLN- Load module's length
+0C	4	MSBAD- Load point address of the module

Figure 8.9 Two fields in the Extent List (XTLST).

8.7.5 Extent List

The Extent List (XTLST) gives information about the extent of a load module which has been loaded into virtual storage. There is one XTLST entry for each major CDE entry (a minor CDE is created if the IDENTIFY macro was used to name a module or when an alias is present), and the entry in the CDE has a pointer to its corresponding XTLST entry. For debugging purposes, the most useful information in the XTLST is the load module's length and load-point address (LPA), the physical beginning address of the program in storage. Figure 8.9 shows these two important XTLST fields.

8.7.6 Formatted Task Management Control Blocks in a Dump

Now that we have described a number of control blocks you are undoubtedly eager to see them in an actual system dump. Figure 8.10 shows parts of the formatted portion of a dump produced when a program ABENDed under the MVS/ESA operating system. Only the control blocks mentioned in the preceding sections are shown. The acronym for each control block appears at the upper left of that block, followed by its hexadecimal address. The arrows in the figure show how a control block points to the next one in the chain. For example, the field TNEW at offset +1C in the ASCB contains the address of the TCB of the first ready task (008F7100), and the arrow at letter "A" in the figure points to that TCB. You can look for the other fields described in Figs. 8.5 through Fig. 8.9 as well. We will see these control blocks in a complete system dump in Chap. 10, and will use them to help solve the ABEND.

8.8 SUMMARY

A basic knowledge of MVS operating system concepts can prove helpful in interpreting system dumps and understanding how ABENDs are handled.

The PSW contains information essential for proper control of the CPU. The settings most relevant for debugging purposes include those which determine the types of interrupts permitted, the condition code for certain Assembler

```
ASCB: 00F35980
       +0000  ASCB..... ASCB      FWDP..... 00F35700  BWDP..... 00F35C00  CMSF..... 00000000  SVRB..... 008FD610
       +0014  SYNC..... 00012074  IOSP..... 00000000  TNEW..... 008F7100  CPUS..... 00000001  ASID..... 004D
       +0026  R026..... 0000      LL5...... 00        HLHI..... 01        DPHI..... 00        DP....... 61
       +002C  TRQP..... 80FDC441  LDA...... 7FF15EB0  RSMF..... 00        R035..... 0000      TRQI..... 40
       +0038  CSCB..... 00F35B48  TSB...... 00000000  EJST..... 00000000  06C9BB00
       +0048  EWST..... A1E5DF9D  800A8445            JSTL..... 000000AC  ECB...... 808FDD60  UBET..... A1E5C125
       +005C  TLCH..... 00000000  DUMP..... 008FFD18  AFFN..... FFFF      RCTF..... 00        FLG1..... 00
       +0068  TMCH..... 00000000  ASXB..... 008FDF00  SWCT..... B118      DSP1..... 00        FLG2..... 00
       +0074  RSV...... 0000      SRBS..... 0000      R078..... 00000000  RCTP..... 008FE178  LOCK..... 00000000
       +0084  LSQH..... 00000000  QECB..... 00000000  MECB..... 40000000  OUCB..... 01C5E6D0  OUXB..... 01C5F888
       +0098  FMCT..... 0000      LEVL..... 02        FL2A..... 00        XMPQ..... 00000000  IQEA..... 00000000
       +00A4  RTMC..... 00000000  MCC...... 00000000  JBNI..... 00F56D50  JBNS..... 00F35B58  SRQ1..... 00
       +00B5  SRQ2..... 00        SRQ3..... 00        SRQ4..... 00        VGTT..... 00000000  PCTT..... 00000000
       +00C0  SSRB..... 0000      SMCT..... 00        SRBM..... 07        SWTL..... 00000478
       +00C8  SRBT..... 00000000  004E0000            LSMQ..... 00000000  LSPL..... 00000000  TCBS..... 00000001
       +00DC  TCBL..... 00000000  WPRB..... 008FEA58  NDP...... 61        TNDP..... FF        NTSG..... FF
       +00E7  IODP..... 60        LOCI..... 00000000  CMLH..... 00000000  CMLC..... 00000000  SS01..... 000000
       +00F7  SS04..... 00        ASTE..... 01AFB340  LTOV..... 7FFEC000  ATOV..... 7FFFE440  ETC...... 0000
       +0106  ETCN..... 0000      LXR...... 0000      AXR...... 0000      STKH..... 008FEA68  GQEL..... 00000000
       +0114  LQEL..... 03601420  GSYN..... 00000000  XTCB..... 008F7100  CS1...... 00        R121..... 000000
       +0124  GXL...... 035A6008  EATT..... 00000000  AD0923FF            INTS..... A1E5DF8D  CE575F43
       +0138  LL1...... 00        LL2...... 00        LL3...... 00        LL4...... 00        RCMS..... 00000000
       +0140  IOSC..... 00000009  PKML..... 0000      XCNT..... 01F4      NSQA..... 00000000  ASM...... 01C63050
       +0150  ASSB..... 01C5E800  TCME..... 00000000  GQIR..... 00000000  R15C..... 00000000  00000000  00000000
       +0168  CREQ..... 0000000A  RSME..... 01C5E988  AVM1..... 00        AVM2..... 00        AGEN..... 0000
       +0174  ARC...... 00000000  RSMA..... 01C5E880  DCTI..... 000001AE  TAXT..... 00000000  00000000
       +0188  SAXT..... 00000000  00000000            TCPT..... 00000000  00000000
       +0198  SCPT..... 00000000  00000000
                                                       .
          (A)                                          .
                                                       .
TCB: 008F7100
       +0000  RBP...... 008FD4C8  PIE...... 00000000  DEB...... 008E34C8  TIO...... 008D7000  CMP...... 940C7000
       +0014  TRN...... 00000000  MSS...... 7FFD4E68  PKF...... 80        FLGS..... 01000000  00
       +0022  LMP...... FF        DSP...... FF        LLS...... 008DF550  JLB...... 008FF1E0  JPQ...... 008DF570
 GENERAL PURPOSE REGISTER VALUES
    0-3  000000D8  7F73C5C8  00000078  00000000
    4-7  00000FE0  008D4774  008D43F9  008D4F7C
   8-11  00000000  008D4714  008D4774  008D4F7C
  12-15  821E6388  008CE030  821E64EA  00000000
       +0070  FSA...... 00005F98  TCB...... 00000000  TME...... 00000000  JSTCB.... 008F7100  NTC...... 00000000
       +0084  OTC...... 008F75E0  LTC...... 00000000  IQE...... 00000000  ECB...... 008FFBAC  TSFLG.... 20
       +0095  STPCT.... 00        TSLP..... 00        TSDP..... 00        RD....... 7FF15EE4  AE....... 7FFD4CE8
       +00A0  STAB..... 008FD180  TCT...... 808FF320  USER..... 008E2FD8  NDSP..... 00000000  MDIDS.... 00000000
       +00B4  JSCB..... 008F7344  SSAT..... 00FDB048  IOBRC.... 00000000  EXCPD.... 00000000  EXT1..... 00000000
       +00C8  BITS..... 00000000  DAR...... 00        RSV37.... 00        SYSCT.... 00        STMCT.... 00
       +00D0  EXT2..... 008F7258  AECB..... 00000000  XSB...... 008FD598  BACK..... 008F75E0  RTWA..... 7FFD6090
       +00E4  NSSP..... 00000000  XLAS..... 00000000  ABCUR.... 00        FJMCT.... 00        TID...... 00
       +00EF  RSV...... 00        XSCT..... 80000041  FOE...... 00000000  SWA...... 7FFD4748  STAWA.... 00000000
       +0100  TCBID.... TCB       RTM12.... 00000000  ESTAE.... 00000000  UKYSP.... 7FFD4490  SEQNO.... 0005
       +0112  AFFN..... FFFF      FBYT1.... 08        FBYT2.... 04        FBYT3.... 80        RSV...... 00
       +0118  RPT...... 00000000  VAT...... 00000000  SWASA.... 7FFECDD8  SVCA2.... 00000000  ERD...... 7FF15EF4
       +012C  EAE...... 7FFD41A8  ARC...... 00000007  GRES..... 00000000  STCB..... 7FFFE2D0
       +013C  TTIME.... 00000000  20B0EF00            R144..... 00000000  000000              LEVEL.... 03
       +014C  BDT...... 00000000  NDAXP.... 00000000  SENV..... 00000000
                                                       .
                                                       .
                                                       .
```

Figure 8.10 Portions of the formatted section of a system dump produced under MVS/ESA. Only control blocks discussed in this chapter are shown. (*Continued*)

```
PRB: 008F74E0
        -0020  XSB...... 008F7548  FLAGS2... 00000000  RTPSW1... 078D0000  0000ADAA           RTPSW2... 00060007
        -000C            03600070  FLAGS1... 02000000  WLIC..... 00060007
        +0000  RSV...... 00000000  00000000            SZSTAB... 00110082  FLCDE.... 008DF570
        +0010  OPSW..... 078D0000  0000ADAA            SQE...... 00000000  LINK..... 008F7100
        +0020  GPR0-3... FD00001A  00005FE0  00000040  008F87D4
        +0030  GPR4-7... 008F87B0  008F75E0  008D6FF8  FD000000
        +0040  GPR8-11.. 008FFB88  808FF320  00000000  008F75E0
        +0050  GPR12-15. 00E37CC2  00005F98  80E381E4  008FFBB8
        +0060  RSV...... 0000AA48  40404040

                                                   .
                                                   .
                                                   .
SVRB: 008FD358
        -0020  XSB...... 008FD428  FLAGS2... 00000000  RTPSW1... 00000000  00000000           RTPSW2... 00000000
        -000C            00000000  FLAGS1... 22000000  WLIC..... 00020033
        +0000  RSV...... 00000000  00000000            SZSTAB... 001ED022  FLCDE.... 00000000
        +0010  OPSW..... 070C1000  81F6C4A6            Q........ 00000000  LINK..... 008F74E0
        +0020  GPR0-3... 00000000  0000AB7B  00011B00  00000006
        +0030  GPR4-7... 0000B4C0  4000AD46  0000AA9C  00011B00
        +0040  GPR8-11.. 0001DE70  0000B698  0000AAD0  0000AD08
        +0050  GPR12-15. 0000AAC8  0000B120  4000AD96  0000BCF0
        +0060  EXSAVE... 00000000  0000AB7B  00000000  008F7100  008FD358  00F35980  00FEE180  01B91B28  7FFD6090
        +0084            FF000F70  40000101  940C7000  SCBB..... 00000000  00000000  00000000  838FD358  6400DB00
        +00A4  SXPTR.... 008FD418  FEPARM... 00000000  00000000  00000000  00000000  00000000  00000000
        +00C0  SCBX..... 00000000  00000000  00000000  008FD3B8

                                                   .
                                                   .
                                                   .
SVRB: 008FD4C8
        -0020  XSB...... 008FD598  FLAGS2... 00000000  RTPSW1... 00000000  00000000           RTPSW2... 00000000
        -000C            00000000  FLAGS1... 02000000  WLIC..... 00020078
        +0000  RSV...... 00000000  00000000            SZSTAB... 001ED022  FLCDE.... 00000000
        +0010  OPSW..... 070C1000  80E9FFB6            Q........ 00000000  LINK..... 008FD358
        +0020  GPR0-3... 008D5E68  7FFD6190  01F6D328  008E0ABC
        +0030  GPR4-7... 01F6C4BC  01F6C329  81F6B32A  7FFD6090
        +0040  GPR8-11.. 008D5E68  000C7000  008D5EC0  008D5EC0
        +0050  GPR12-15. 008E0760  7FFD6204  00F6EC24  00000000
        +0060  EXSAVE... AA540400  008D4270  00000000  00000000  00FEE180  00000000  00000000  00000000  830279C8
        +0084            00040000  00000000  00000000  SCBB..... 008FD180  00000000  16000000  838FD4C8  2400DB00
        +00A4  SXPTR.... 008FD588  FEPARM... E2D9E501  008F7100  00000000  00000000  00000000  00000000
        +00C0  SCBX..... 00000000  00000000  00000000  008D5E00

                                                   .
                                                   .
                                                   .
CDE
      008DF570  CHAIN.... 00000000  RRBP..... 008F74E0  NAME..... GO        ENTPT.... 0000AA48  XLMJP.... 008F73F0
         +0018  USE...... 0001      ATTRB.... 00        SP....... FB        ATTR..... 0B        ATTR2.... 20
         +001E  ATTR3.... 0000

                                                   .
                                                   .
                                                   .
XTLST
      008F73F0  LNTH..... 00000010  NRFAC.... 00000001  MSBLA.... 8000F5B8  MSBAD.... 0000AA48
                                                   .
                                                   .
                                                   .
```

Figure 8.10 *(Continued)*

instructions, and whether the CPU is running in problem state or privileged state. Of most importance to the COBOL programmer is the second word of the PSW, which contains the address of the NSI.

COBOL programmers who have background in Assembler are often better able to understand what COBOL is doing internally. Sometimes examining the Assembler instruction which caused an ABEND can help you debug the problem.

In order to convert hexadecimal object code into an Assembler instruction you must understand the format of both the object code and its corresponding Assembler instruction. The Op Code indicates the type of instruction. Looking at the Op Code may be all that is necessary to determine what the ABENDing instruction was doing. Further translation will usually be necessary to learn what operands were being used.

Instruction fetching involves loading the object code from main storage which is located at the address specified in the second word of the PSW. Execution involves carrying out the operation specified by the instruction. When debugging, it is important to remember that the address of the NSI is updated before the instruction is actually executed. Thus the address in the second word of the PSW must be decremented by the instruction length in order to find the address of the instruction executing at the time of the ABEND.

There are six types of interrupts; all are asynchronous except the Supervisor Call interrupt. Interrupts do not necessarily represent a problem. Some, such as the Input/Output interrupt, occur frequently during normal job flow. The Program interrupt and Machine Check interrupt result from error conditions detected by the hardware.

After an interrupt, the system must be able to resume processing at the point where it left off before the interrupt occurred. The hardware accomplishes this by saving the current PSW before control is given to the interrupt handler.

In order to carry out its functions, the system creates and maintains a series of control blocks. Those discussed in this chapter are the ASCB, TCB, PRB, SVRB, CDE, and XTLST. Many of them have fields which provide useful debugging information. These control blocks are formatted, with field names and offsets, in the first part of a system dump; you could also find them in the hexadecimal section of a storage dump. We will examine some of these control blocks again when we solve a system dump in Chap. 10.

REVIEW QUESTIONS

1. Explain the function of the PSW.

2. Why is it necessary for the operating system to save the current PSW during an interrupt? Explain how this is done.

3. Name two types of request blocks which can be found in the formatted portion of a system dump. Explain their functions.

4. What is an address space? What is the name of its system control block?

5. What is a task? What is the name of its system control block?

6. What information does the Op Code for a machine instruction provide?

7. Use Fig. 8.2, Fig. 8.3, and Appendix D in this book to help you convert each of the following machine instructions into Assembler.

- **a.** D2848000A010
- **b.** F911D1D6D1DE

8. Where can you find the address of the instruction which would have executed next if a program had not ABENDed?

9. At what point in the instruction fetch/execute cycle is the NSI updated? If an ABEND occurs, explain why you must subtract the length of the ABENDing instruction from the NSI to find the address of the ABENDing instruction.

10. List the six types of interrupts. Which of them represent error conditions?

11. Define:

- **a.** virtual storage
- **b.** real storage
- **c.** address space
- **d.** task
- **e.** control block

12. Give the purpose and acronym for each of the following system control blocks:

- **a.** Contents Directory Entry
- **b.** Extent List
- **c.** Request Block
- **d.** Supervisor Request Block
- **e.** Program Request Block

13. How can the request block for an ABENDing module be found in the formatted portion of a system dump?

14. Which control block can be used to find:

- **a.** The name of an ABENDing load module?
- **b.** The load-point address of the ABENDing module?
- **c.** The general-purpose register contents of the ABENDing program?
- **d.** The entry-point address of the ABENDing load module?

Chapter

9

Overview of MVS Data Management Concepts

In this chapter we will turn our attention to data management concepts of the MVS operating system. Again, because of the complexity of MVS, we will give only as much detail as is necessary to understand the management of data from a debugging perspective. We will not cover the new enhancements of MVS/ESA: data space and HIPERspace. A data space provides a greatly expanded storage area for data; access of data in a data space is very similar to access of data in the address space which uses the data space. The HIgh PERformance Space (HIPERspace) permits quicker access of large data sets through use of new system services.

MVS Data Management is responsible for storing and retrieving all data. It is important to know how MVS handles data when dealing with ABENDs involving input or output problems. Consequently, an overview of the creation and use of pertinent Data Management control blocks is in order.

9.1 JOB STARTUP

The Job Entry Subsystem (JES) is responsible for reading batch jobs, interpreting the JCL, scheduling execution, managing all printers, and routing the print output to the proper destination. At job startup time, the JES Interpreter creates a number of control blocks for managing the job, job steps, and information from the JCL. JES also assigns the job to an MVS initiator, which takes control of the job's address spaces before and after each job step executes. The initiator creates a table to identify DD statement information and file information for the job step.

9.2 CONTROL BLOCKS USED BY DATA MANAGEMENT

We have already mentioned that control blocks are system storage areas containing data as well as pointers to other areas. They are used by MVS to help manage its operation. Interrogating the contents of various control blocks can provide much useful information when it is necessary to solve an ABEND. Just as with the control blocks used by Task Management, the Data Management control blocks can be found in the hexadecimal portion of a storage dump produced when a program ABENDs. It is much easier and quicker, however, to refer to the control blocks in the formatted portion at the beginning of the dump. Here the control blocks are labeled and their storage addresses, field names, and field contents are provided. Hexadecimal displacements for the fields from the beginning of the control blocks are shown. Figure 9.5, described in Sec. 9.2.7, will illustrate these formatted control blocks in an actual dump.

For debugging purposes, it will often be helpful to look for the following information in the Data Management control blocks: the open/close status of a file, the logical record length (LRECL), the record format (RECFM), the physical block size (BLKSIZE) and physical extent information, the address of the current record in a file, the Residual Byte Count, the Channel Program Completion Code, and various error flags in the Channel Status Word (these terms will be defined in the sections which follow).

As I describe various Data Management control blocks in the sections that follow, I will indicate their more significant fields for debugging purposes. The figures will give each field's name, length, and hexadecimal offset from the beginning of the control blocks for dumps produced by MVS/ESA or MVS/XA. IBM's *MVS/ESA Diagnosis: Data Areas* and *MVS/XA Debugging Handbook* manuals show prefixes for field names which identify the control blocks in which they appear. I have not included these prefixes in the following figures. Also, the field name roots listed in the manuals and in the following figures do not always exactly match the names supplied in the formatted control blocks at the beginning of the dump. Often those used in the dump indicate the purpose of the fields more clearly. Because some fields in a formatted control block are unlabeled, it is important to use the hexadecimal offsets to accurately locate a desired field.

Some fields contain bit settings which represent important debugging information. I will give some of these bit settings, or their hexadecimal equivalents, in the following discussion; you can find additional information in the IBM manuals named in the preceding paragraph.

9.2.1 Data Control Block

There have been numerous references to the Data Control Block (DCB) in previous chapters. The DCB contains information about input and output files used by the program. There is one DCB for each non-VSAM file to be opened by a program (VSAM files use ACBs). It is established by the compiler in the COBOL program's storage area using information coded in the program's FD statement. Additional information is provided during the forward or backward merge (see Sec. 9.4.2 for a discussion of the merges).

The format of the DCB varies according to the file access method in use. The access method, and hence the DCB format, is shown to the right of the DCB label in the formatted portion of the dump.

The first five fullwords (up to hexadecimal offset 14 into the DCB) are dependent on the access method. They contain device-dependent information such as the disk address for a data set on DASD or the block count for a tape data set.

A good deal of helpful information about a file at the time of an ABEND is available in many of the fields following the first five fullwords; this section, up to hexadecimal offset +30, is common to all formats. The information in many fields is represented by bit settings. Values in the first byte of the DSORG field mean the following:

Bit setting	Hexadecimal value	Meaning
1000 0000	80	IS—Indexed sequential organization
0100 0000	40	PS—Physical sequential organization
0010 0000	20	DA—Direct organization
0001 0000	10	CX—BTAM or QTAM line group
0000 0010	02	PO—Partitioned organization
0000 0001	01	U—Unmovable; data contains location dependent information

Values in the RECFM field mean the following:

Bit setting	Hexadecimal value	Meaning
1110 0000	E0	Record-length indicator—ASCII
0010 0000	32	ASCII variable record length
1100 0000	C0	Record-length indicator
1000 0000	80	Fixed-length records
0100 0000	40	Variable-length records
1100 0000	C0	Undefined-length records
0010 0000	32	Track overflow
0001 0000	10	Blocked records
0000 1000	08	For fixed-length record format, standard blocks For variable-length record format, spanned records
0000 0110	06	Control character indicator
0000 0100	04	ASA control character
0000 0010	02	Machine control character
0000 0000	00	No control character
0000 0001	01	Key length was specified in DCB macro instruction

Starting at offset +30, the format again depends on the type of access method being used. The fields listed in Fig. 9.1 assume that the access method is QSAM (sequential).

If you are faced with an ABEND caused by a file problem, you should probably look first at the fields starting at hexadecimal offset +28. Notice that several of them have different names, lengths, and meanings depending on whether the file is not yet open or has already been opened. Before OPEN, the 8-byte field at offset +28 called DDNAM contains the file's DDname. The 1-byte field at offset +30 (for QSAM) called OFLGS should contain the hexadecimal value 02, indicating the file is closed. It is usually important to know whether the file in question is open or closed, and the DCB provides this information. Unfortunately, the DCB for a file does not appear in the formatted portion of a dump before it has been opened (we will come back to this in Sec. 9.2.3).

HEX OFFSET	LENGTH	DESCRIPTION
+14	1	BUFNO- Number of buffers for this data set
+18	2	BUFL- Length of buffer
+1A	2	DSORG- Data set organization
+24	1	RECFM- Record format
		FIELDS BEFORE OPEN
+28	8	DDNAM- Name on the DD card for this data set
+30	1	OFLGS- Open-routine flags: x'02' if file closed
+31	1	IFLG- Error condition flags used by IOS
+32	2	MACR- Macro instruction reference indicates type of access method
		FIELDS AFTER OPEN
+28	2	TIOT- Offset into TIOT to start of entry for DD card for this data set
+2A	2	MACRF- Same as MACR before open
+2C	1	IFLGS- Same as IFLG before open
+2D	3	DEBA- Address of the associated DEB
+30	1	OFLG- Same as 0FLGS before open: x'12' if file open-input x'92' if file open-output
+3E	2	BLKSI- Blocksize for this data set
+44	4	IOBA- Address of IOB prefix
+4D	3	RECA- Address of current or next logical record
+52	2	LRECL- Logical record length

Figure 9.1 Important fields in the Data Control Block (DCB).

After OPEN has been issued for a file, the information at hexadecimal offset +28 into the DCB becomes a 2-byte field called TIOT. It gives an offset into the Task Input Output Table (TIOT) to the start of the entry for the DD statement for the file (we will discuss the TIOT in Sec. 9.2.2). The TIOT contains the DDname, so this allows you to match the current DCB with the correct file. Again there is a 1-byte field at displacement +30 into the DCB (for QSAM) called OFLG, which gives the status of the current file; a hexadecimal value of 12 means the file is open for input and a value of 92 means it is open for output. There is also a pointer, the field DEBA, to this DCB's associated Data Extent Block (DEB); the DEB contains additional information about the opened file (see Sec. 9.2.4).

Other helpful fields in the DCB for QSAM files include BLKSI, RECA, and LRECL (see Fig 9.1).

9.2.2 Task Input Output Table

The TIOT is created by MVS device allocation routines. There is one TIOT for each job step. The TIOT provides I/O support routines with pointers to the Job File Control Blocks (JFCB) and their allocated devices. The JFCB contains logical file information from the JCL DD statement; it is used in the merges alluded to previously in the discussion of the DCB. Another field in the TIOT contains the address of the Unit Control Block (UCB) for the file (see Sec. 9.2.6).

Two important fields in the TIOT for debugging purposes are CSTEP and EDDNM (see Fig. 9.2). The first field gives the name of the job step, or the procedure step and job step. The second, EDDNM, provides the DDname of the file. We mentioned earlier that after OPEN for a file, the field called TIOT, at hexadecimal displacement +28 into the DCB, gives the offset into the TIOT for the start of the entry for the file's DD statement. Looking for the DDname in the EDDNM field of the TIOT and then matching the offset of the beginning of this TIOT entry with the offset specified in the TIOT field of the DCB ensures that you are examining the proper DCB for a file.

9.2.3 Finding the DCB for an Unopened File

We have referred to the fact that the DCB for an unopened file is not shown in the formatted portion of the dump (Sec. 9.2.1). Therefore, we have to look for the DCB in the hexadecimal portion of the dump. This requires a more roundabout journey.

Recall from our discussion of internal COBOL tables in Sec. 2.2 that the DCB is created at compile time and that there are fields in COBOL control blocks which point to the DCB; they are the DCB ADDRESS CELLS field in the PGT in OS/VS COBOL (see Sec. 2.2.2.1) and the FCB in COBOL II (see Sec. 2.2.3.2). To identify the correct DCB for a file in an OS/VS COBOL program, look for the name of the file and its corresponding DCB number in the DATA DIVISION map. The DCB is at the address pointed to by its corresponding DCB ADDRESS CELL.

HEX OFFSET	LENGTH	DESCRIPTION
0	8	CNJOB- Job name
+08	16	CSTEP- Job step name (8 bytes) OR Proc step name (8 bytes) and Job step name (8 bytes)
+19	1	ESTTA- Status byte A
+1C	8	EDDNM- DD Name
+24	3	EJFCB- Relative track address of the JFCB
+28	1	ESTB- Status byte B
+29	3	EFSRT- Address of the UCB
+2D	1	ESTTA- Status byte A
+30	8	EDDNM- DD Name

.

.

.

Figure 9.2 Important fields in the Task Input Output Table (TIOT). The fields from offsets +19 to +29 apply to the first DD statement; they are repeated for each additional DD.

Finding a data set's DCB in a COBOL II program is a more convoluted process. First find the field labeled POINTER TO FIRST FCB CELL in the fixed portion of the TGT. This leads you to the pointer list for FCBs. To be sure you have the correct FCB for the file you must find the FIB associated with this FCB and verify the DDname in the FIB. Then go back to the FCB to find the pointer to the DCB. Alternatively, for a program compiled with the NORENT option, look for the offsets of various DCBs following the variable portion of the TGT; offsets of FCBs are given here as well (the offsets of DCBs and FCBs are not available following the TGT listing for programs compiled with the RENT option). Sec. 2.2.1.10 and 2.2.3.2 give additional information.

In many dumps resulting from I/O errors, general-purpose register 2 contains the address of the DCB for the data set which was being processed at the time of the ABEND. We will discuss specific I/O ABENDs near the end of this chapter.

We will illustrate how to find the DCB when we solve an I/O ABEND in Chap. 10.

9.2.4 Data Extent Block

The Data Extent Block (DEB) is an extension of the information provided in the DCB. Its field DCBB at hexadecimal offset +19 has the address of its corresponding DCB (or ACB for a VSAM file). DCBB (for 24-bit address) is in the three low-order bytes of the field labeled DCBADR in the formatted DEB. A number of DEBs will be found in the formatted portion of the dump. DEBs are created by OPEN routines at file OPEN time and are taken off the DEB queue at CLOSE time. An opened non-VSAM data set has one DEB, and an opened VSAM data set has two or more DEBs according to its type and whether or not it has an alternate index. The structure for a DEB depends on the type of data set, access method, and device involved. The DEB for the most recently opened file appears first in the formatted part of the dump, and the one for the first file which was opened appears last. The DEBs are chained together.

The DEB contains information about the physical characteristics of the data set including DASD and tape device information, cylinder and track addresses for extents, and the type of file access method being used. The access method in effect is indicated by the field AMTYP in the prefix area at offset −03. Some of the access method codes you will often see are 01 for VSAM, 02 for Execute Channel Program (EXCP), 20 for Sequential Access Method (SAM), and 81 for Subsystem-JES.

The DEB also stores information from the Data Set Control Block (DSCB) in the DASD's Volume Table of Contents (VTOC), reducing how often the VTOC needs to be accessed.

The DEB is of most value when debugging OPEN, CLOSE, End-of-Volume (EOV), and DASD-related ABENDs. Figure 9.3 shows some fields in the DEB for a QSAM file on DASD.

HEX OFFSET	LENGTH	DESCRIPTION
-0F	7	DSCBA- Address of the DSCB
-04	1	LNGTH- Length of DEB in double words
-03	1	AMTYP- Access method type
00	4	TCBAD- Address of TCB
+04	4	DEBAD- Address of next DEB in the same task
+19	3	DCBB- Address of DCB associated with this DEB

DASD SECTION -- ONE FOR EACH EXTENT IN DATA SET
(Offsets are from the beginning of the section)

+00	4	UCBAD- Address of UCB associated with this extent
+06	2	STRCC- Cylinder address for start of an extent limit
+08	2	STRHH- READ/WRITE track address for start of an extent limit
+0A	2	ENDCC- Cylinder address for end of an extent limit
+0C	2	ENDHH- READ/WRITE track address for end of an extent limit
+0E	2	NNTRK- Number of tracks allocated to an extent for split cylinder file

Figure 9.3 Some of the important fields in the Data Extent Block (DEB) for a QSAM file on DASD. The DEB has different sections depending on the device, access method, and type of file.

9.2.5 Input/Output Block

There is one Input/Output Block (IOB) for each buffer for a data set. It is built at OPEN time for the file by the access method, and provides a work area for channel programs handling physical record transfers as well as for Data Management programs doing logical record transfers. The IOB is particularly useful when debugging I/O problems caused by hardware errors.

The DCB for the data set points (at hexadecimal offset +44) to the first IOB prefix, with all the IOBs for that data set chained together. The IOBs also have a field labeled DCBPB, which contains the address of the associated DCB.

The size and structure of the IOB depends on whether or not chained scheduling, which allows half of a program's buffers to be filled while the other half is being transferred, is in effect. The fields illustrated in Fig. 9.4 are for a QSAM file with normal scheduling.

The field FLAG1, at offset 00 into the IOB, has bit settings which may indicate problems; when bit 5 is on (hexadecimal 04), a permanent I/O error has occurred.

The channel program completion code appears in the IOB field ECBCC (offset +04 into the IOB). If it contains hexadecimal 00, 44, 48, or 7F, there was no error and you need to look at a different IOB. The field NIOBB, at hexadecimal offset –07 in the IOB, contains the address of the next IOB for the current DCB.

If a hardware problem is suspected, an important field in the IOB is the Channel Status Word (CSW). The low-order 7 bytes of the CSW, starting at hexadecimal offset +9 into the IOB, contains bit settings giving the status of the I/O device and the status of the last I/O operation. The channel is a separate computer which is an interface between external I/O devices and real storage. It is directed by a number of channel programs which contain Channel Control Words (CCW). A CCW consists of a command code, the address in virtual or real storage of the data being transferred, the length of the data, and a number of flags. The meanings of the bit settings for the CSW flags, CCW flags, and for the status of the I/O device and I/O operation can be found in the *System/370 Extended Architecture Reference Summary* and the *Enterprise Systems Architecture/370 Reference Summary.*

The last 2 bytes of the CSW, starting at offset +0E into the IOB, give the Residual Byte count. This is the number of bytes not transferred across the channel in the last I/O for this buffer. This may indicate whether or not the last records were completely written out when the program was terminated.

9.2.6 Other Data Management Control Blocks

Some additional Data Management control blocks may occasionally be useful in debugging. They include the Unit Control Block (UCB) and the Job File Control Block (JFCB).

The UCB describes the physical characteristics of an I/O device. There is one UCB per device. It is pointed to by the TIOT and the DEB for a data set.

The JFCB contains logical file information from the DD statement for a data set. This information is used in the merge when the DCB is completed (see Sec.

QSAM - NORMAL SCHEDULING

HEX OFFSET	LENGTH	DESCRIPTION
-08	1	NFLG1- Flag byte
-07	3	NIOBB- Address of next IOB for this DCB
-04	4	NECB- Event Control Block used by QSAM to indicate status of I/O event

STANDARD SECTION OF THE IOB

00	1	FLAG1- Status and error flag
+04	1	ECBCC- Channel Program Completion code. Also appears in 1st byte of ECB.
+05	3	ECBPB- Address of the ECB to be posted on completion of I/O
+09	7	CSW- Low-order 7 bytes of CSW reflecting status for this request
+0E	2	Last 2 bytes of CSW, giving the Residual byte count
+15	3	DCBPB- Address of the DCB associated with this IOB

Figure 9.4 Some important fields in the Input/Output Block (IOB) for a QSAM file with normal scheduling.

9.4.2). Rather than looking in the JFCB for DD statement parameters for a file, it is normally easier to go directly to the JCL. The TIOT points to the track address of the JFCB for a data set.

9.2.7 Formatted Data Management Control Blocks in a Dump

We are now ready to see how the formatted Data Management control blocks we have described appear in an actual system dump. Figure 9.5 shows parts of the formatted portion of a dump produced when a COBOL program using non-VSAM files ABENDed under the MVS/ESA operating system. The acronym for a control block appears at the upper left for that control block, with its hexadecimal storage location to the right. The arrows in the figure show how control blocks point to one another. For example, the field UCB in the entry beginning at offset +007C in the TIOT for DDname DISKFLE contains the address of the UCB (F9CF38). The arrow at letter "A" in the figure points to that UCB. You can look for the other fields described in Fig. 9.1 through Fig. 9.4 as well. We will see these control blocks again when we examine a complete system dump in the next chapter.

9.2.8 The OPEN/CLOSE/EOV Work Area

The OPEN, CLOSE, and EOV Data Management routines use a special work area acquired from storage in subpool 230 known as the OPEN/CLOSE/EOV (O/C/EOV) work area. The OPEN macro creates one for each DCB. Information from the DCB, JFCB, and the DSCB or tape labels used in the merge (described in Sec. 9.4.2) which completes the DCB will be found in this work area; information is copied to the work area from the various Data Management control blocks. If a Data Management ABEND occurs it may be more convenient to find certain data set information here rather than in the control blocks. The O/C/EOV work area for the file being processed at the time of a data management ABEND is pointed to by general-purpose register 4 in REGISTERS AT ENTRY TO ABEND right before the hexadecimal storage area for the active load modules in the dump, in the GPRS AT TIME OF ERROR listed under the RTM2WA SUMMARY, or in the GPR fields of the SVRB right below the request block which issued the ABEND.

Minimal documentation is available for the O/C/EOV work area, and IBM recommends not using this area for debugging. However, I have indicated offsets from the address in register 4 where some useful information in the O/C/EOV work area may be found (see descriptions of OPEN problems in Sec. 9.4.3).

9.3 VSAM CONSIDERATIONS

It is rare that an ABEND will occur when VSAM is in control. Recall (Sec. 4.3) that VSAM does not issue ABENDs; for I/O and other Data Management errors it returns a status code to the program instead. The COBOL program

```
TIOT: 008D8000
        JOB...... DEBUG22   STEP..... GO                S1

              LN-STA    DDNAME    TTR-STC   STB-UCB
        +0018 14010100  PGM=*.DD  8F070000  80F90C68
        +002C 14010100  STEPLIB   8EFC4000  80FBA278
        +0040 14010102  SYSABOUT  8EFAC000  80000000
        +0054 14010102  SYSDBOUT  8EF94000  80000000
        +0068 14010102  SYSUDUMP  8EF7C000  80000000
        +007C 14010100  DISKFLE   8EF64000  80F9CF38
        +0090 14010100  CARDFLE   8EF4C000  80F8D4C8
        +00A4 14010102  PRTFILE   8EF28000  80000000
        +00B8 14010102  SYSDBOUT  8EF10000  80000000
        +00CC 14010102  SYSUDUMP  8E5F4000  80000000
        +00E0 14010102  SYSOUT    8E5DC000  80000000
                                              .
                                              .
                                              .

-DEB-------------------------------------AT LOCATION  008E37C0
-----

-8      EXTNSION 008E3840 LENGTH   11       AMTYPE   81       TBLOF    0001
+0      TCBADR   008C24E8 NEXTDEB  008E3A48 IRBADR   088F9AF8 PATB     0F000900
+10     USRPG    00000000 RRQ      008D6E68 DCBADR   8F005558 APPADR   00E94000
+20     00FBA278 E2E2C9C2 00240000 D1C5E2F3
+30     00000000 00000000 00000000 00000000
+40     00000000 00000000 E2E2D6C2 001C0010
+50     008E37E4 00000000 008E3824 00000000
+60     00000000 001C0000 00000000 008E3DCC
+70     008E37C0 03832620 00000000 00000000


*** FOR THIS DEB THERE IS NO DCB, THE CONTROL BLOCK POINTED TO BY THE DEB IS AN ACB ***

-DEB-------------------------------------AT LOCATION  008E3A48
-----

-8      EXTNSION 008E3AC8 LENGTH   11       AMTYPE   81       TBLOF    0003
+0      TCBADR   008C24E8 NEXTDEB  008E35C4 IRBADR   088F9A40 PATB     0F000900
+10     USRPG    00000000 RRQ      0000B9B0 DCBADR   8F0056C0 APPADR   00E94000
+20     00FBA278 E2E2C9C2 00240000 D1C5E2F3
+30     00000000 00000000 00000000 00000000
+40     00000000 00000000 E2E2D6C2 001C0010
+50     008E3A6C 00000000 008E3AAC 00000000
+60     00000000 001C0000 00000000 008E3C0C
+70     008E3A48 038264C8 00000000 00000000


*** FOR THIS DEB THERE IS NO DCB, THE CONTROL BLOCK POINTED TO BY THE DEB IS AN ACB ***
```

Figure 9.5 Formatted Data Management control blocks in an MVS/ESA system dump. Only control blocks discussed in this chapter are shown.

can examine the status code to determine the nature of the problem (see Sec. 4.3.1 and Sec. 4.3.2 for a discussion of VSAM status codes, return codes, function codes, and feedback codes).

System messages returned by Data Management may be found in the job log. Common ones indicating VSAM problems include:

IEC070I An End-of-Volume (EOV) error occurred during processing for a VSAM data set.

IEC161I An error occurred during the OPEN macro processing for a VSAM data set.

IEC251I An error occurred during the CLOSE macro processing for a VSAM data set.

```
-DEB--------------------------------------AT LOCATION   008E35C4
-----

-24      DEBAVT    00FF854C 80D98B18 DEBPCIA  00FF854C DEBCEA   80D96000 DEBXCEA  00D96006
-10      PREFIX    00000001 2C000323 EXTNSION 008E36B0 LENGTH   11       AMTYPE   20        TBLOF     0002
+0       TCBADR    038C24E8 NEXTDEB  10000000 IRBADR   68000000 PATB     00001100
+10      USRPG     01000000 RRQ      FF000000 DCBADR   8F00B850 APPADR   048E35A0
+20      58F9CF38 00000000 00070000 00070001
+30      00010001 00000000 00000000 00000050
+40      F3C2C1D8 C1C10000 00000000 00000000
+50      00000000 00000000 00000000 00000000
+60      00F9CF38


-DCB-     (QSAM)                           AT LOCATION 0000B850
-----

+10      002EBB60 050247A8 00004000 00005808 4600F3DC 90019E84 007C4800 008E35C4
+30      12E3B2E8 20C6A508 0900F69C 00091810 30013030 00005870 00000000 00000000
+50      00000050 00000000 00000000 00D9AE48


-IOB-     (SAM,BPAM-NORMAL SCHEDULING)    AT LOCATION   00005878
-----

-8       010058B8 7F000000
+0       FLAG      0200     SENS     0000     ECBPT    00005874 CSW      00000000 00000000
+10      START     00000000 DCBPT    0000B850 RESTR    00000000 VARIABLE 00000000


-IOB-     (SAM,BPAM-NORMAL SCHEDULING)    AT LOCATION   000058C0
-----

-8       20005900 7F000000
+0       FLAG      0200     SENS     0000     ECBPT    000058BC CSW      000058F0 0C4014F0
+10      START     00000000 DCBPT    0000B850 RESTR    00000000 VARIABLE 00000000


-IOB-     (SAM,BPAM-NORMAL SCHEDULING)    AT LOCATION   00005908
-----

-8       20005948 42000000
+0       FLAG      0200     SENS     0000     ECBPT    00005904 CSW      00005938 01000000
+10      START     00000000 DCBPT    0000B850 RESTR    00000000 VARIABLE 00000000
```

Figure 9.5 *(Continued)*

IEC252I An error occurred during CLOSE macro processing (Temporary Close) for a VSAM data set.

If you are unable to get all the information needed to solve an ABEND from the various status codes and system messages, it is possible to gather a great deal of VSAM information from a number of system control blocks. VSAM uses many of the control blocks described in previous sections. In addition, there are a number of specialized VSAM control blocks which may be examined.

9.3.1 VSAM Access Method Control Block and VSAM DEBs

In order to identify the current record or obtain other VSAM file information from a dump, several VSAM control blocks must be considered. The first is the VSAM Access Method Control Block (ACB). This is the counterpart of the DCB for non-VSAM data sets. ACBs do not appear in the formatted portion at the

```
-IOB-     (SAM,BPAM-NORMAL SCHEDULING)    AT LOCATION  00005950
-----

-8        20005990 00000000
+0        FLAG     0200     SENS     0000     ECBPT    0000594C CSW      00000000 00000000
+10       START    00000000 DCBPT    0000B850 RESTR    00000000 VARIABLE 00000000


-IOB-     (SAM,BPAM-NORMAL SCHEDULING)    AT LOCATION  00005998
-----

-8        20005870 00000000
+0        FLAG     0200     SENS     0000     ECBPT    00005994 CSW      00000000 00000000
+10       START    00000000 DCBPT    0000B850 RESTR    00000000 VARIABLE 00000000



FOR DEB AT LOCATION 008E37C0
-------------------

*** FOR THIS DEB, THERE ARE NO UCBS ***


FOR DEB AT LOCATION 008E3A48
-------------------

*** FOR THIS DEB, THERE ARE NO UCBS ***


FOR DEB AT LOCATION 008E35C4
-------------------
                                                                  (A)

-UCB-     (DIRECT ACCESS TYPE)               AT LOCATION  00F9CF38
-----


 UCBPRFIX: 00F9CF08
          -0030  RSTEM.... 00        RSV...... 02        MIHTI.... 00        HOTIO.... 40        IOQF..... 00000000
          -0028  IOQL..... 00000000  SIDA..... 0001      SCHNO.... 03D8      PMCW1.... 289C      MBI...... 0317
          -001C  LPM...... C0        RSV...... 00        LPUM..... 80        PIM...... C0        CHPID.... 4A76FFFF
          -0014            00000000  LEVEL.... 01        IOSF1.... 08        MIHCT.... 0000      LVMSK.... 00000001
          -0008  LOCK..... 00000000  IOQ...... 00F6FF00

 UCBOB: 00F9CF38
          +0000  JBNR..... 41        FL5...... 8A        ID....... FF        STAT..... 8C        CHAN..... 0752
          +0006  FL1...... 00        FLB...... 00        NXUCB.... 00F9CFD8  WGT...... 00        NAME..... F7F5F2
          +0010  TBYT1.... 30        TBYT2.... 30        DVCLS.... 20        UNTYP.... 0E        FLC...... 00
          +0015  EXTP..... F9CEE8
```

Figure 9.5 *(Continued)*

beginning of a dump. It is therefore necessary to find the hexadecimal address of a file's ACB and look for it in the storage dump. The ACB is pointed to by the field DCBB at offset +19 into the "dummy" DEB. This field is the low-order 3 bytes of the field labeled DCBADR in the formatted DEB.

Recall that an opened VSAM data set has two or more DEBs according to its type and whether or not it has an alternate index (see Sec. 9.2.4 for a more complete discussion of the DEB). More specifically, a VSAM cluster (the term for an entire VSAM data set, including the data component and any indexes) has a "dummy" DEB which points to the cluster's ACB and a second DEB which describes the data component. For a VSAM KSDS there is a third DEB which gives the characteristics of the index component. If there are alternate indexes, there are two additional DEBs for each one. As can be seen, it is necessary to distinguish between the DEBs for non-VSAM data sets and the DEBs for VSAM data sets and then to find the dummy DEB for the VSAM cluster.

It is fairly easy to tell a non-VSAM DEB from a VSAM DEB in the formatted portion of a dump. The AMTYP field contains hexadecimal 01 if the DEB refers to a VSAM data set. The first DEB for the VSAM cluster, the "dummy" DEB, does not begin with the characters "DEBAVT." Also, DEBs pointing to ACBs have the words "FOR THIS DEB THERE IS NO DCB, THE CONTROL BLOCK POINTED TO BY THE DEB IS AN ACB" printed under them.

In order to be certain that you are working with the proper dummy DEB, go to the storage dump address specified in the field DCBB at offset +19 in the DEB. This is the location of the ACB associated with this DEB. At hexadecimal offset +28 into the ACB is the offset into the TIOT for this VSAM cluster. If the DDname given at that offset into the TIOT is that of the VSAM cluster of interest, then you have found the correct dummy DEB and ACB.

Figure 9.6 illustrates some useful fields in the ACB. Notice that the field DEB points back to the dummy DEB.

9.3.2 Access Method Block, Placeholder, and Request Parameter List

In order to find the current VSAM record, you must continue along the chain of VSAM control blocks for the current cluster. The DEB following the dummy DEB points to another VSAM control block, the Access Method Block (AMB) for the data component of the cluster. The DEB field DCBB, at hexadecimal offset +19, contains the address of the AMB.

Figure 9.7 shows some fields in the AMB. The field PH, at offset +C, points to the next VSAM control block in the chain called the Placeholder (PLH).

Figure 9.8 gives a number of fields in the PLH. The value at offset +3C into the PLH is the address of the current or next VSAM record. The field CRPL at hexadecimal offset +14 points to the next VSAM control block, the Request Parameter List (RPL).

The RPL contains a number of useful fields (see Fig. 9.9), including the object of our chaining. It is the field AREA at hexadecimal offset +20, which contains the address of the record work area for the current record or the address of the current record in the buffer.

Other information is available in these control blocks as well. Additional technical information about VSAM control blocks and diagnostic aids appears in the IBM *MVS VSAM Logic* manual. This manual is not readily available to applications programmers so you may have to borrow it from systems programmer colleagues.

9.4 I/O ABENDS

Now that we have seen where I/O information can be found in a system dump, we will turn our attention to some typical I/O problems that may occur. First we will discuss OPEN, then CLOSE, and finally some miscellaneous I/O items.

HEX OFFSET	LENGTH	DESCRIPTION
+10	2	BUFND- Number of data buffers
+12	2	BUFNI- Number of index buffers
+18	1	RECFM- Record format
+1A	2	DSORG- Data set organization
		FIELDS BEFORE OPEN
+28	8	DDNAM- Name on the DD card for this data set
		FIELDS AFTER OPEN
+28	2	TIOT- Offset into TIOT to start of entry for DD card for this data set
+2C	1	ERFL- Error flags
+2D	3	DEB- Address of the dummy DEB for this ACB
		NOT CHANGED BY OPEN
+30	1	OFLGS- OPEN/CLOSE flags
+31	1	ERFLG- Error flags. See OPEN and CLOSE Return Codes.
+32	2	INFLG- Indicator flags
+34	4	UJFCB- Address of the user JFCB
+3C	2	BLKSZ- Length of physical DASD record
+3E	2	LRECL- Length of user's record

Figure 9.6 Some of the important fields in the VSAM Access Method Control Block (ACB).

HEX OFFSET	LENGTH	DESCRIPTION
+0C	4	PH- Address of the PLACEHOLDER
+1C	4	IOBAD- Address of the IOB
+28	2	TIOT- Offset into TIOT to start of entry for DD card for this data set

Figure 9.7 Some fields in the VSAM Access Method Block (AMB).

9.4.1 OPEN Processing

Following is a summary of the events which occur when a file in a COBOL program is opened. If necessary refer to Sec. 8.4 to refresh your memory about interrupt processing and to Sec. 8.7 to review some of the Task Management control blocks.

1. The COBOL program issues an OPEN statement. This causes a branch to a routine in the COBOL subroutine library which then initiates an SVC 19 (OPEN) interrupt.
2. The PSW switch for an SVC occurs. An operating system instruction causes the system hardware to load a new PSW which puts the CPU into supervisor state. The supervisor state allows other called MVS operating system modules to execute privileged instructions.
3. The SVRB for the OPEN routine is created.
4. The RB pointer from the TCB is adjusted to point to the SVRB instead of the PRB. (Recall that this pointer has the address of the most recent RB.)
5. The old SVC PSW from the PSA is placed in the OPSW field of the PRB.
6. The contents of the general-purpose registers are stored in the GPR fields of the OPEN SVRB.
7. The SVC interrupt handler transfers control to the OPEN routine.
8. The OPEN routine:
   a. Performs the TIOT lookup
   b. Merges DCB information from various sources to create a complete DCB (see Sec. 9.4.2 for a discussion of the merge)
   c. Builds the DEB
   d. Obtains buffers for the file
   e. Builds the channel program
   f. Creates the pointers to the appropriate access method routine
   g. Primes the buffers if this file is being opened for input

HEX OFFSET	LENGTH	DESCRIPTION
+14	4	CRPL- Address of the current RPL
+34	4	BUFC- Address of current data Buffer Control Block
+3C	4	RECP- Address of current or next record

Figure 9.8 Some fields in the VSAM control block known as the Placeholder (PLH).

9. The OPEN routine then resets the values of the program's general purpose registers to the values which were stored in the OPEN SVRB.
10. The SVRB for the OPEN routine is deleted from the RB chain and various pointers are reset.
11. Finally, control is returned to the Task Dispatcher.

If the OPEN routines have completed successfully, the COBOL program can now issue other I/O requests, such as READ or WRITE, for the opened data set.

9.4.2 The Forward and Backward Merge

We have referred to the forward and backward merges several times in previous sections. The merging process combines DCB information from several places to construct a complete DCB which will be used when the program executes. It is important to note that incomplete or conflicting DCB information from the different sources may cause an I/O ABEND to occur.

Figure 9.10*a* illustrates what happens in the forward merge for an input file. Information from the data set label, either in the DSCB of the DASD VTOC or in the header label of a tape, is the starting point. This information is used to fill in any missing information in the JFCB which was built from information supplied in the JCL. The JFCB information is now used to fill in any missing information in the DCB which was created for the COBOL program by the compiler. The clauses in the COBOL program's FD and 01-levels for the data set were the original sources of this DCB information.

There are no overrides of any DCB information in the forward merge. The merging process simply fills in missing data. The program now runs with this completed DCB.

Figure 9.10*b* shows the processing that takes place in the backward merge for an output file. The starting point is the completed DCB. Information is rewritten into the JFCB with overrides from the DCB. Only the data set orga-

HEX OFFSET	LENGTH	DESCRIPTION
+04	4	PLHPT- Address of the PLH
+08	4	ECB- Address of the ECB or the actual ECB itself
+0D	3	FDBK- RPL feedback area with return and condition codes
+0F	1	ERRCD- Error code
+18	4	DACB- Address of the ACB
+20	4	AREA- Address of work area for current record or current record in buffer
+30	4	RLEN- Length of the record

Figure 9.9 Some fields in the VSAM Request Parameter List (RPL).

nization is not overridden. The new JFCB information is now used to create a new data set label. Again, values are rewritten with overrides from the JFCB.

There is potential for corrupting proper DCB parameters for a data set in both the forward and backward merge. For example, suppose the FD and 01-level for an input file are coded as follows in the COBOL program:

```
FD  IN-FILE
    RECORDING MODE IS F
    RECORD CONTAINS 80 CHARACTERS
    BLOCK CONTAINS 0 RECORDS
    LABEL RECORDS ARE STANDARD.
01  IN-REC               PIC X(80).
```

The JCL specifies the following DCB parameters:

```
DCB=(RECFM=FB,LRECL=50,BLKSIZE=450)
```

Figure 9.11 shows the completed DCB resulting from the forward merge. Because BLOCK CONTAINS 0 RECORDS is coded in the program, the block-

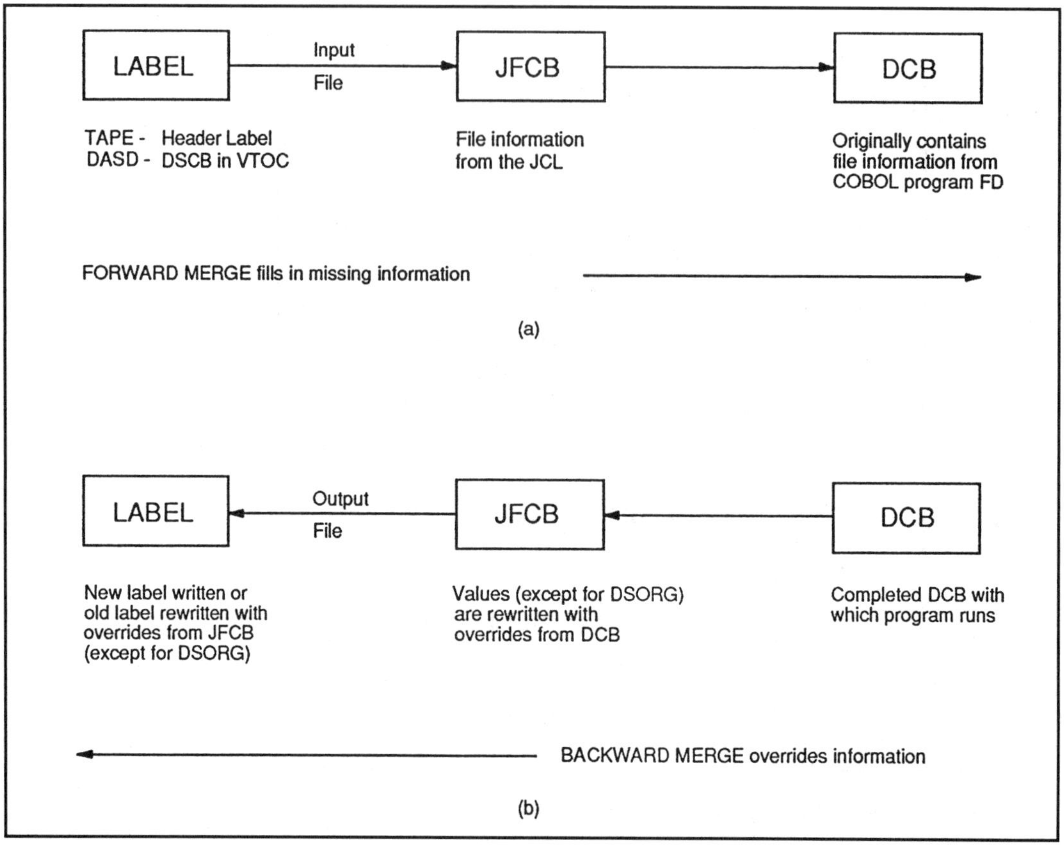

Figure 9.10 The merging process. (*a*) The forward merge which completes the DCB; (*b*) the backward merge which writes or updates data set labels.

size from the JCL is used to complete the DCB. The logical record length is not taken from the JCL because it is supplied by the program (it is 80 in the program). There is an error; a blocksize of 450 is not an even multiple of the logical record length of 80. An ABEND will occur on OPEN.

Conflicting information on the backward merge can also lead to error conditions when the program executes I/O operations. It is possible, for example, that an existing data set label may be overridden by incorrect DCB parameters. If a subsequent OPEN uses this invalid label on a forward merge, it may cause an ABEND.

9.4.3 OPEN Problems

The COBOL OPEN verb causes an SVC 19 (OPEN) interrupt. The hexadecimal equivalent of decimal 19 is 13. Problems due to OPEN often give system ×13 type ABENDs, with the last two digits of the completion code coming from the hexadecimal value of the SVC number.

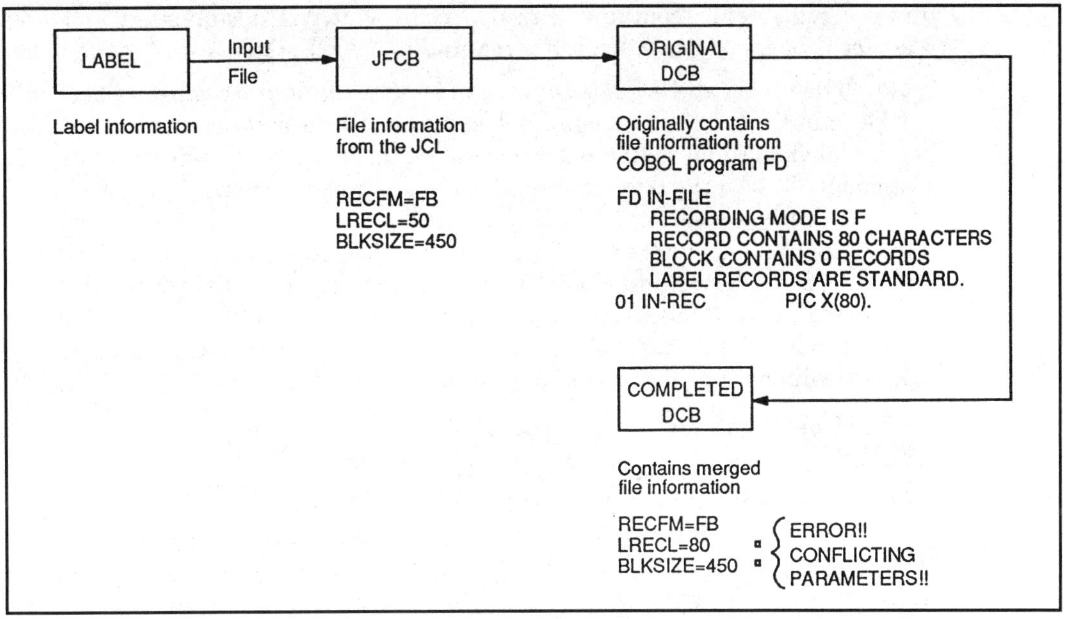

Figure 9.11 Errors in the DCB with which a program will run, resulting from conflicting information used in the forward merge.

Sometimes, after the TIOT lookup during OPEN processing, the message

```
IEC130I ddname - DD STATEMENT MISSING
```

may appear in the job log. This means that the DDname specified for the file in question was not found in the TIOT during OPEN processing. Although processing continues, an ABEND is likely for a subsequent READ or WRITE of the file.

Label verification problems may occur after the TIOT is checked. If the DSN on the JCL DD statement does not match that on the label, 213 or 813 ABENDs may occur.

213. There was an error in opening a DASD file because the data set could not be found. The data set may not exist or the DSCB in the VTOC may not match what was coded in the DSN parameter of the DD statement. To find the offending data set find the DDname in the DCB and TIOT as described in Secs. 9.2.1 and 9.2.2. If the DCB is not available in the formatted portion of the dump, it can be found from the compiler output or by going to the address in general-purpose register 2. At the address in general-purpose register 4 plus hexadecimal 64, the DSN specified in the JCL will be found. At the address in general-purpose register 4 plus hexadecimal DA, the volume serial number specified in the JCL will be found. You should carefully review the JCL and the program to look for errors and to see where conflicts exist. System message IEC143I with its reason code may supply additional help. In addition, general-purpose register 15 contains a return code which is documented in IBM's *Message Library: System Messages* manual.

813. There was an OPEN error on a tape data set because the data set could not be found. The data set may not exist or the data set name on the tape header label does not match what was coded in the DSN parameter on the DD statement. To find the offending data set look for the DDname in the DCB and TIOT as described earlier in Secs. 9.2.1 and 9.2.2. At the address in general-purpose register 4 plus hexadecimal 64, the DSN specified in the JCL will be found. At the address in general-purpose register 4 plus hexadecimal 4, the data set name from the header label will be found. You should carefully review the JCL to look for errors. An 813 completion code is accompanied by message IEC149I which may provide more information.

OPEN problems due to incorrect DCB information may result in an 013 ABEND.

013. This completion code indicates that the data set could not be successfully opened. The problem may be due to incorrect DCB information resulting from conflicts in the forward merge. Note that an incorrect label due to conflicts in the backward merge may cause an 013 ABEND if the file is later opened for input. To find information about the offending data set look for the DDname in the DCB and TIOT as described earlier in Secs. 9.2.1 and 9.2.2. You should look at system message IEC141I and its accompanying reason code, and carefully review the information supplied in the label, JCL, and program to see where conflicts exist. Also, general-purpose register 15 contains a return code which is documented in IBM's *Message Library: System Messages* manual.

9.4.4 CLOSE Processing

The events which occur when a file in a COBOL program is to be closed are summarized below. The actions which take place immediately before and after the actual CLOSE routine events are similar to those already described for OPEN interrupt processing (see Sec. 9.4.1). If you need to review any information about interrupt processing or Task Management control blocks turn back to Secs. 8.4 and Sec. 8.7.

1. The COBOL program issues a CLOSE statement. This causes a branch to a routine in the COBOL subroutine library which then initiates an SVC 20 (CLOSE) interrupt.
2. The PSW switch for an SVC occurs. An operating system instruction causes the system hardware to load a new PSW which puts the supervisor state into effect. Now a branch to other MVS operating system modules which execute privileged instructions can take place.
3. The SVRB for the CLOSE routine is built.
4. The RB pointer from the TCB is adjusted to point to the CLOSE SVRB instead of to the PRB.
5. The old SVC PSW from the PSA is stored in the OPSW field of the PRB.
6. The contents of the general-purpose registers are stored in the GPR fields of the SVRB for the CLOSE routine.

7. At this point, the SVC interrupt handler gives control to the CLOSE routine.
8. The CLOSE routine:
   a. Completes the processing of all the output buffers, writing out the remaining records
   b. Frees the storage used by the output buffers
   c. Takes the channel program and IOB off the queues
   d. If requested, writes a label for the output data set
   e. Restores the DCB to the condition it was in before OPEN so that the program can issue an OPEN statement in the same manner as the original OPEN
   f. Takes the DEB off the queue
9. The values of the program's general-purpose registers are then reset from the values which were placed in the SVRB for the CLOSE routine.
10. The CLOSE SVRB is deleted from the RB chain and various pointers are reset.
11. Finally, control returns to the Task Dispatcher.

9.4.5 CLOSE Problems

The COBOL CLOSE verb results in an SVC 20 (CLOSE) interrupt. Since the hexadecimal equivalent of decimal 20 is 14, problems due to CLOSE often give system ×14 type ABENDs. The last two digits of the completion code come from the hexadecimal value of the SVC number. One common CLOSE ABEND is the B14.

B14. This ABEND indicates a CLOSE problem with a partitioned data set (PDS). Possibilities are that the directory is full or the member name for a new member that is to be added already exists. Examine the DCB and TIOT as described earlier in Sec. 9.2.1 and 9.2.2 to find the DDname. Also, general-purpose register 6 has the address of the PDS member name. You should check the JCL to verify that the proper PDS and member names were used, or perhaps compress the data set, or delete unnecessary members and then compress the data set, or allocate more space and directory blocks and then copy the data set to the newly allocated data set. Message IEC217I and the return code in register 15, documented in IBM's *Message Library: System Messages* manual, may give additional information.

9.4.6 Miscellaneous I/O Problems

System completion codes of the ×37 type indicate problems with end-of-volume (EOV) processing. Because SVC 55 invokes the EOV routine, and the hexadecimal equivalent of decimal 55 is hexadecimal 37, the last two digits of EOV ABENDs are 37. Common EOV ABENDs are B37, D37, and E37.

B37. This type of ABEND usually occurs because there was insufficient space for an output data set on DASD or tape. It may be caused because not enough space was requested on DASD, the program was producing more output than was anticipated, a volume could not be mounted, or the DASD VTOC was full.

Examine the DCB and TIOT as described in Secs. 9.2.1 and 9.2.2 to find the DDname of the offending data set. Also inspect the associated DEB to examine the number of extents used. Actions which you can take if this ABEND occurs include examining the program for the possibility of an infinite WRITE loop, reestimating the space requirements and then increasing the space allocation, or deleting unnecessary data sets from the volume. Also note that this type of ABEND may be intercepted in a COBOL program writing to QSAM files by coding the INVALID KEY clause with the WRITE verb; if conditions for a B37 ABEND arise, the imperative statements associated with the INVALID KEY clause will be executed. System message IEC030I may provide additional information. The return code in register 15 may be helpful as well. Return codes are documented in IBM's *Message Library: System Messages* manual.

D37. A D37 completion code indicates that there was insufficient primary space for an output data set on DASD and no secondary space allocation was available. It may be caused if the directory for a PDS is full or its primary space allocation has been totally used, or if the program is producing more output than was anticipated (perhaps there was an infinite WRITE loop). You should follow the steps described for a B37 completion code. Message IEC031I and the return code in register 15 may provide additional information. Interpretation of the return codes is found in IBM's *Message Library: System Messages* manual.

E37. This completion code results from insufficient space or insufficient number of volumes for an output data set. It may be caused if the program is producing more output than was anticipated (perhaps there was an infinite WRITE loop), if a PDS has become fragmented resulting in excessive unusable space, or if all 16 extents of a PDS were used or fewer than 16 extents were used but no more space was available on the primary volume (a PDS must reside on one volume). You should follow the steps described for a B37 completion code. Message IEC032I may provide additional information. Also, the return code in register 15 may be helpful; see IBM's *Message Library: System Messages* manual for meanings.

I/O ABENDs accompanied by 001 and 002 completion codes may be related to DCB conflicts or physical I/O problems.

001. This completion code means that an I/O error has occurred, possibly because of conflicts in DCB parameters, incorrect usage of READ or WRITE statements, or actual physical I/O errors. It may be caused if an incorrect record length or blocksize was specified, if the COBOL program's FD clauses are incorrect, if there was an attempt to read a file after the AT END condition was encountered or after the file was closed, if there was an attempt to read a file opened for output, if there was a malfunctioning device or damaged storage medium, or if an out-of-space condition arose. Examine the DCB and TIOT for information on the data set as previously described in Secs. 9.2.1 and 9.2.2. Also, look at the following fields in the IOB for the current buffer (see Sec. 9.2.5) to determine if hardware errors occurred:

FLAG1; If this byte is hexadecimal 04, a permanent I/O error has occurred.

ECBCC; Unless this byte is hexadecimal 00 or 7F, a channel error has occurred.

Second word of the CSW, at hexadecimal offset +0C; This 1-byte field should be set to hexadecimal 04 or 08 if the I/O event completed successfully.

Register 15 contains a return code which may be useful; IBM's *Message Library: System Messages* manual gives interpretations of return codes. Examination of message IEC020I may provide additional information.

002. An 002 ABEND may occur when there is an I/O error, possibly due to conflicts in record or block size parameters, incorrect usage of READ or WRITE statements in the program, physical damage to the recording medium, or a device malfunction. In COBOL it may be caused if the FD information, DD statement, or actual data set characteristics conflict, an attempt was made to write a record larger than the track size or larger than the maximum record size allowed, or, for variable length records, there is an erroneous Record Descriptor Word (RDW). Examine the DCB and TIOT for data set information as previously described in Secs. 9.2.1 and 9.2.2. Register 15 contains a return code, documented in IBM's *Message Library: System Messages* manual, which may provide useful information. Also look at accompanying message IEC036I for additional information.

9.5 SUMMARY

It is important to understand MVS Data Management and the control blocks used by Data Management when dealing with I/O ABENDs because this part of the operating system is responsible for storing and retrieving all data.

Part of the function of the JES Interpreter is to create a control block to store information from the JCL. The initiator assigned by JES creates a table to identify DD statement information and file information for the job step.

As with Task Management control blocks, control blocks used by Data Management can be found in the hexadecimal portion of a system dump. Some can also be seen in the formatted section at the beginning of a dump, although some (such as the DCB) may not appear if the file is closed. The control blocks discussed in this chapter are the DCB, TIOT, DEB, IOB, UCB, and JFCB.

Some control blocks used exclusively by VSAM are also discussed, although it is uncommon to need to examine them because VSAM does not issue ABENDs; instead, it returns file status codes to the COBOL program or provides a number of system messages. The VSAM control blocks which are mentioned in this chapter are the ACB, AMB, PLH, and RPL.

The OPEN, CLOSE, and EOV macros use the O/C/EOV work area. This contains information copied from a number of the Data Management control blocks, and can be a convenient place to find information needed for debugging an I/O ABEND.

One of the important events which occur during OPEN processing is the completion of the DCB (recall that this control block is originally established by the

COBOL compiler). In the forward merge, information from the data set label fills in any missing information in the JFCB, and then this information is used to complete the DCB in the program. The program now runs with this completed DCB. In the backward merge, information is rewritten into the JFCB with overrides from the DCB. If requested, the new JFCB information is then used to create a new data set label with overrides from the JFCB. The only thing that doesn't get overridden is the data set organization. Any conflicting information from the different sources during the merging process gives the potential for error conditions when the program executes I/O instructions.

OPEN problems typically cause system ×13 type ABENDs. The 13 comes from the hexadecimal number of the OPEN SVC. The ×13 ABENDs discussed in this chapter include 013, 213, and 813.

One of the many events which occur during CLOSE processing is restoration of the DCB to the condition it was in before OPEN. A number of the control blocks which were available during OPEN are also taken off their respective queues, so that the information they contained is not readily available.

CLOSE problems often cause system ×14 type ABENDs. The 14 comes from the hexadecimal number of the CLOSE SVC. The ×14 ABEND covered in this chapter is B14.

Another category of I/O errors involves EOV processing. Because the EOV SVC number is 37 in hexadecimal, the last two digits of EOV ABENDs are 37. EOV ABENDs discussed in the current chapter are B37, D37, and E37.

Two final I/O ABENDs discussed are those resulting in 001 and 002 system completion codes. They may be related to conflicting file attributes or to hardware problems.

REVIEW QUESTIONS

1. What functions does JES provide?

2. How is the Data Control Block established? What type of information does it contain?

3. What is the VSAM equivalent of the Data Control Block?

4. Describe how to find the Data Control Block for a file which has been successfully opened.

5. Describe how to find the Data Control Block for an unopened COBOL file.

6. Give the purpose and acronym for each of the following system control blocks:
- **a.** Data Control Block
- **b.** Data Extent Block
- **c.** Task Input Output Table
- **d.** Input/Output Block
- **e.** Job File Control Block
- **f.** Unit Control Block

7. Name and give the acronyms for four VSAM control blocks described in this chapter.

8. Why is it usually unnecessary to examine VSAM control blocks to solve an I/O problem involving a VSAM file?

9. Define each of the following:
- **a.** channel
- **b.** O/C/EOV work area
- **c.** DSCB

10. Describe how the forward merge completes the DCB.

11. Indicate the contents of the data set label produced by the backward merge when the following information is used for a new data set:

From the JFCB

```
LRECL=80,RECFM=FB,BLKSIZE=800,DSORG=PS
```

From the DCB

```
LRECL=100,RECFM=FB,BLKSIZE=2000
```

12. For each of the following completion codes indicate whether the problem occurred during OPEN, CLOSE, or EOV processing.
- **a.** SD37
- **b.** S013
- **c.** S213
- **d.** SB14

13. Which of the following completion codes are most likely to be the result of hardware errors?
- **a.** S013
- **b.** S002
- **c.** S001
- **d.** SB37

Chapter

10

MVS System Dumps

The previous two chapters dealt with system control blocks and basic MVS operating system concepts. The purpose was to provide the background necessary for solving system dumps. If an ABEND occurs and it cannot be solved by any of the methods discussed in earlier portions of this book (e.g., use of COBOL language debugging tools, COBOL compiler options, COBOL formatted dumps, ABEND-AID, or interpretation of COBOL and system messages), or if these aids were not available, it may be necessary to look at system dumps. Understanding system dumps is not language-dependent; the same information is provided for COBOL, Assembler, PL1, or other languages. Since this book deals with COBOL debugging, we will use the information in the system dump and combine it with whatever debugging information is provided by COBOL in order to solve ABENDs.

First we will examine the types of MVS dumps you are most likely to encounter. Then we will solve two ABENDs to illustrate how to use what we have learned. Once you are familiar with the techniques we discuss, it should be easy to solve most system dumps.

10.1 SYMPTOM DUMPS

We mentioned in Sec. 1.4.2 that MVS prints a symptom dump when requested in the DUMP parameter of the ABEND macro. The symptom dump appears as part of message IEA995I in the job log, and contains information extracted from various system control blocks. You can often get relevant information about the ABEND from the summary information in the symptom dump, and avoid having to examine the formatted portion or the hexadecimal portion of the MVS system dump.

Figure 10.1 shows a symptom dump. At letter “A” is the completion code with its reason code. Letter “B” shows the time the ABEND occurred, the sequence number (SEQ), the number of the processor (CPU) (it is 0000 if the

```
                IEA995I SYMPTOM DUMP OUTPUT
                SYSTEM COMPLETION CODE=0C4  REASON CODE=00000004 <-- (A)
(B) ----------> TIME=10.21.24  SEQ=00083  CPU=0000  ASID=0053
                 PSW AT TIME OF ERROR  078D0000   0000A952  ILC 4  INTC 04 <-- (C)
(D) ----------> ACTIVE LOAD MODULE=GO          ADDRESS=0000A718  OFFSET=0000023A
                  DATA AT PSW  0000A94C - D1289240  30009240  3001D282 <-- (E)
                 (GPR  0-3   00000000  0000A815  0000FEF0  00000000
(F) ----------> { GPR  4-7   000180B0  008F75E0  0000A76C  0000FEF0
                 (GPR  8-11  00000000  0000AF70  0000A7A0  00015944
                 (GPR 12-15  0000A798  0000AB10  7000A94A  0000B148
                 END OF SYMPTOM DUMP
```

Figure 10.1 A symptom dump in the job log.

system did not determine the CPU number), and the address space id number (ASID). The two words of the PSW are shown at letter "C," followed by the instruction length code (ILC) of the instruction causing the ABEND, and the interrupt code (INTC). The name of the active load module at the time of the ABEND is pointed to by letter "D." If the system could not determine which load module was in control, the message NO ACTIVE MODULE FOUND is given instead. After the name of the active load module is its load-point address (LPA), and after that is the offset into the module of the next sequential instruction (NSI). The hexadecimal number after the words DATA AT PSW (at letter "E") is usually the address of the offending instruction, while the hexadecimal code following the address is the object code of that instruction as well as object code for the succeeding instructions. Letter "F" shows the contents of the general purpose registers at the time of the ABEND.

10.2 TYPES OF SYSTEM STORAGE DUMPS

IBM provides a number of dumping facilities for the MVS operating system. They are largely controlled by macro instructions, parameter libraries, and operator commands. An installation generally decides what type of dumps should be produced under certain conditions and may use different options for the macros, parameters, and operator commands to customize the dumps. In general, the installation may wish to control which parts of system storage are dumped and the format of the dumps. Two major types of system dumps encountered by applications programmers are those produced by the ABEND and SNAP macros.

The ABEND macro instruction initiates error-recovery routines for a task. When the DUMP parameter is requested, several types of storage dumps may be generated when the job step or a task within the job step is abnormally terminated. A SYSABEND, SYSMDUMP, or SYSUDUMP DD statement is placed in the JCL to define a data set to contain the ABEND dump. The type of dump going to each DD statement depends on IBM defaults for those DDnames, but is often adjusted at the installation by specifying different options in the ABEND macro, parameter library, or operator commands. Most shops designate SYSUDUMP as the preferred DD statement for applications programmers to use. The system storage dumps presented in this book were assigned to the SYSUDUMP DD statement and consist of a formatted portion at the beginning and limited regions of system storage given in hexadecimal format (with EBCDIC notation at the right). Some control over the dump generation was provided by information coming from the SNAP macro, which will be described shortly.

As previously mentioned, a symptom dump is also included with ABEND dumps; it does not require inclusion of any of the DD statements indicated in the last paragraph unless the installation changes certain parameters in the parameter library or in an operator command.

The SNAP macro instruction may be used to obtain a dump of system storage and then continue processing. As with the ABEND macro, parameters may be coded with the SNAP macro instruction to control the type of dump generated. A SNAP dump must be assigned to any DD statement except SYSABEND, SYSMDUMP, and SYSUDUMP. The DD statement which will receive the dump output is established by specifying a DCB address in one of the SNAP macro parameters; the DCB must be provided and an OPEN macro must be issued before the SNAP macro is issued.

Certain options may be coded in the SNAP macro when a dump is desired for a task that is to be abnormally terminated. A parameter list is created when the list form of the SNAP macro is executed. The DUMPOPT parameter in the ABEND macro points to this parameter list and uses the options in tailoring the dump. One useful piece of information from the SNAP macro is a dump index. You will notice this index in the system dumps analyzed later in this chapter. Also, it is interesting to see in the SVRB below the RB of the ABENDing task that the last 2 bytes of the field WLIC (at hexadecimal offset –2 from the beginning of the SVRB) contains 33. This is the hexadecimal value for the SNAP SVC.

Although Assembler programmers can request dumps by coding the SVCs for ABEND and SNAP macros within their programs, COBOL programmers cannot. MVS manages these dump services for COBOL. An exception is when a COBOL programmer indirectly invokes a system dump by calling ILBOABN0 (see Sec. 1.4.3).

10.3 SOLVING SYSTEM DUMPS

In this section we will solve two system dumps. We will follow the general debugging procedure outlined in Chap. 5 (see Sec. 5.3.2). Although we could shorten the debugging process by looking only at the symptom dump, I will point out relevant information in the system dump in order to give you practice in case you need to look at such a dump in your debugging activities.

I suggest that you approach dump analysis as you would a challenging puzzle. Choose the relevant pieces and fit them together to build a sensible picture of the problem, its causes, and finally the remedy.

10.3.1 A Word About Linkage-Editor Output

Although we will discuss linkage-editor output in greater depth in Chap. 11, we need to spend a moment now examining some useful information which is available from the linkage-editor diagnostic output. This will help in debugging the dumps to follow.

Near the bottom of the linkage-editor output listing is the length of the load module and the hexadecimal displacement of the entry point from the physical beginning of the load module. The module length, as well as the actual entry-point address, can also be found in the XTLST and CDE, respectively, in the system dump. When the address of the ABENDing instruction has been determined, its location within the load module must be found. Subtracting the load-point address (LPA) from the instruction address gives the instruction's offset from the beginning of the load module. This offset must be less than the total length of the module.

A load module normally contains a number of program units known as control sections (CSECTs). You should recognize the names of your COBOL programs in this CSECT listing. The linkage-editor module map gives the origin of each CSECT from the start of the module as well as each CSECT's length. By comparing the offset of the ABENDing instruction with the beginning and ending offsets of each CSECT you can find which CSECT the instruction is in.

10.3.2 Completion Codes Revisited

We discussed completion codes in Sec. 1.4.2. Recall that there are user completion codes and system completion codes. Documentation for completion codes should be reviewed before attempting to analyze the dump since the information provided may be specific enough to pinpoint the nature of the ABEND, or at least suggest a starting point for tackling the problem. Remember that user codes are documented (hopefully) by the creators of the program or application system. MVS system codes are documented in IBM's manual *MVS Message Library: System Codes.*

We can divide abnormal terminations into two general types: internal and external. Internal ABENDs generally occur within your program; a COBOL statement, or rather an Assembler instruction generated by the COBOL statement, resulted in an error condition which initiated abnormal termination processing. The problem may be due to invalid input data, uninitialized fields, faulty program logic, etc. System completion codes 0C1 through 0CF, the program checks, are of this type.

External ABENDs are external to your program, occurring within supervisor routines or utility programs invoked directly or indirectly by your program, or by the operating system in setting up the run-time environment. For example, a system ×13 type ABEND may be caused if your program invokes the OPEN macro with incorrect DCB attributes for a file. A system ×37 type ABEND may be the result of insufficient space allocation in the JCL.

10.3.3 The First System Dump

The first ABEND which we will debug occurred when a COBOL II program was executed under MVS/ESA. Figure 10.2 shows relevant portions of the JCL, job log, compiler output, linkage-editor listing, program output, and the system dump. Where necessary for clarity, the numbers of the steps we follow are printed and circled in the appropriate places of the figure to make it easier to follow.

1. Determine the type and location of the ABEND.

```
//S1         EXEC COB2UCLG,
//           PARM.COB2='XREF,MAP,LIST,OPTIMIZE',
//           PARM.GO='COBOL II DEBUGGING'                        (5b)
//***************************************************************
//*  SOURCE CODE IS COBOL.  PROC FOR COBOL II                   *
//***************************************************************
//COB2.SYSIN  DD DSN=MY.PROGLIB.COBOL(DMPCB21),DISP=SHR
//GO.NMFILE   DD *                                               (5a)
/*
//PRTFILE     DD SYSOUT=A
//SYSABOUT    DD DUMMY
//SYSDBOUT    DD DUMMY
//SYSOUT      DD SYSOUT=A
//SYSUDUMP    DD SYSOUT=A
                                    .
                                    .
                                    .
IEF142I DMPCB21 COB2 S1 - STEP WAS EXECUTED - COND CODE 0004
                                    .                        (1c)
                                    .
IEF142I DMPCB21 LKED S1 - STEP WAS EXECUTED - COND CODE 0000
                                    .                                   (1b)
                                    .
                                    .
IEA995I SYMPTOM DUMP OUTPUT                                  (6e)
SYSTEM COMPLETION CODE=0C7  REASON CODE=00000007
 TIME=13.38.58  SEQ=00357  CPU=0000  ASID=004D
 PSW AT TIME OF ERROR  078D0000   0000ADAA  ILC 6  INTC 07
   ACTIVE LOAD MODULE=GO          ADDRESS=0000AA48  OFFSET=00000362   (6a)
   DATA AT PSW  0000ADA4 - F811D1DE  D1DEF911  D1D6D1DE
   GPR  0-3  00000000  0000AB7B  00011B00  00000006
   GPR  4-7  0000B4C0  4000AD46  0000AA9C  00011B00
(1d) GPR  8-11 0001DE70  0000B698  0000AAD0  0000AD08
   GPR 12-15 0000AAC8  0000B120  4000AD96  0000BCF0
 END OF SYMPTOM DUMP
 IGZ038I AN ABEND WAS INTERCEPTED BY THE COBOL EXECUTION TIME ABEND
         HANDLER.
   THE COMPLETION CODE WAS = 'S0C7'  THE PSW AT ABEND WAS =
         '078D00000000ADAA'
   THE GP REGISTERS AT ENTRY TO ABEND WERE
      REGS 0-3   - '00000000  0000AB7B  00011B00  00000006'
      REGS 4-7   - '0000B4C0  4000AD46  0000AA9C  00011B00'
      REGS 8-11  - '0001DE70  0000B698  0000AAD0  0000AD08'
      REGS 12-15 - '0000AAC8  0000B120  4000AD96  0000BCF0'
                                    .
                                    .
                                    .
IEF472I DMPCB21 GO S1 - COMPLETION CODE - SYSTEM=0C7 USER=0000 REASON=00000007   (1a)
                                    .
                                    .
                                    .
PP 5668-958 REL. 2.0, 09/08/86, IBM VS COBOL II.                DATE 04/03/90  TIME 13.38.44   PAGE     1

       IGYOS4013-I   AN OPTIONS PARAMETER LIST WAS FOUND AS INPUT TO THE COMPILER AND WAS PROCESSED.

(1c(2)) IGYOS4020-W   OFFSET   OPTION DISCARDED DUE TO OPTION CONFLICT RESOLUTION. LIST     OPTION FROM COMPILER INPUT PARMLIST
                     TAKES PRECEDENCE.
                                    .
                                    .
                                    .
```

Figure 10.2 Portions of the JCL, job log, compiler output, linkage-editor listing, program output, and system dump for the first system dump example. (*Continued*)

```
PP 5668-958 REL. 2.0, 09/08/86, IBM VS COBOL II.                        DATE 04/03/90  TIME 13.38.44   PAGE     3
  000001  000100 IDENTIFICATION DIVISION.
  000002  000200  PROGRAM-ID.   DMPCB21.
  000003  000300  AUTHOR.         ALAN FRIEND.
  000004  000400  DATE-WRITTEN. 01/02/90.
  000005  000500 DATE-COMPILED. 04/03/90.
  000006  000600******************************************************************
  000007  000700* SYSTEM:                         STAND-ALONE                      *
  000008  000800* APPLICATION/SUBSYSTEM:          CERTIFICATE                      *
  000009  000900* PURPOSE/FUNCTIONS:              PRINTS A CERTIFICATE FOR EACH EMPLOYEE *
  000010  001000*                                 IN NAME FILE, LISTING AREA OF EXPERTISE. *
  000011  001100******************************************************************
  000012  001200* PARAMETERS RECEIVED :           AREA EXPERTISE, PASSED FROM JCL.  *
  000013  001300* ARGUMENTS  SENT:                NONE                             *
  000014  001400******************************************************************
  000015  001500*                                                                  *
  000016  001600*              DDNAME                    DESCRIPTION              *
  000017  001700*              ---------                 -----------              *
  000018  001800* INPUTS:      NMFILE                  EMPLOYEE NAME FILE; LAST NAME  *
  000019  001900*                                      FOLLOWED BY COMMA FOLLOWED BY  *
  000020  002000*                                      FIRST NAME.                    *
  000021  002100*                                                                  *
  000022  002200*                                                                  *
  000023  002300*                                                                  *
  000024  002400* OUTPUTS:     PRTFILE                 CERTIFICATE SENT TO PRINTER    *
  000025  002500******************************************************************
  000026  002600* ABNORMAL TERMINATION PROCESSING:     PROGRAM TERMINATES PROCESSING, *
  000027  002700*                                      ISSUES MESSAGE AND RETURNS TO  *
  000028  002800*                                      OPERATING SYSTEM IF LAST OR    *
  000029  002900*                                      FIRST NAME LONGER THAN MAXIMUM *
  000030  003000*                                      TABLE LENGTH FOR THE NAMES.    *
  000031  003100******************************************************************
  000032  003200*                      MODIFICATION HISTORY                        *
  000033  003300*                      --------------------                        *
  000034  003400* DATE         PROGRAMMER                DESCRIPTION              *
  000035  003500* ----         ----------                -----------              *
  000036  003600* N/A                                                              *
  000037  003700******************************************************************
PP 5668-958 REL. 2.0, 09/08/86, IBM VS COBOL II.              DMPCB21    DATE 04/03/90  TIME 13.38.44   PAGE     4

  000039  003900 ENVIRONMENT DIVISION.
  000040  004000  INPUT-OUTPUT SECTION.
  000041  004100   FILE-CONTROL.
  000042  004200     SELECT PRINT-FILE ASSIGN TO PRTFILE.
  000043  004300     SELECT NAME-FILE  ASSIGN TO NMFILE.

  000045  004500 DATA DIVISION.
  000046  004600  FILE SECTION.

  000048  004800  FD PRINT-FILE
  000049  004900     RECORDING MODE IS F
  000050  005000     RECORD CONTAINS 133 CHARACTERS
  000051  005100     BLOCK CONTAINS 0 RECORDS
  000052  005200     LABEL RECORDS ARE OMITTED
  000053  005300     DATA RECORD IS PRINT-FILE-REC.
  000054  005400  01 PRINT-FILE-REC                        PIC X(133).
  000055  005500  FD NAME-FILE
  000056  005600     RECORDING MODE IS F
  000057  005700     RECORD CONTAINS 80 CHARACTERS
  000058  005800     BLOCK CONTAINS 0 RECORDS
  000059  005900     LABEL RECORDS ARE OMITTED
  000060  006000     DATA RECORD IS NAME-FILE-REC.
  000061  006100  01 NAME-FILE-REC.
  000062  006200     05 NAME-FIELDS  OCCURS 80 TIMES       PIC X(01).
```

Figure 10.2 *(Continued)*

a. Scan the job log for a completion code. In this dump it is S0C7. This completion code indicates a program check, specifically a data exception. A decimal operation was attempted with invalid packed data.

b. Determine which step ABENDed. The GO step within procedure step S1. The JCL shows that S1 executed the COB2UCLG procedure.

c. Check the condition codes of the previous link and compile steps within the COB2UCLG procedure. It is 0 for the link, but 4 for the compile.

(1) Look at the compiler diagnostics. The warning does not involve the program source code.

(2) Look at the first page of compiler output. There was a compiler option conflict. LIST is overriding the default OFFSET.

```
PP 5668-958 REL. 2.0, 09/08/86, IBM VS COBOL II.                DMPCB21   DATE 04/03/90   TIME 13.38.44   PAGE     5

  000064  006400 WORKING-STORAGE SECTION.
  000065  006500  01 ACCUMULATORS    COMP SYNC.
  000066  006600      05 NAME-CNT                            PIC S9(02).
  000067  006700      05 LAST-NAME-CNT                       PIC S9(02).
  000068  006800      05 FIRST-NAME-CNT                      PIC S9(02).
  000069  006900      05 LAST-NAME-SUB                       PIC S9(02).
  000070  007000      05 FIRST-NAME-SUB                      PIC S9(02).
  000071  007100      05 FIRST-NAME-START                    PIC S9(02).
  000072  007200  01 SWITCHES.
  000073  007300      05 SW-EOF                              PIC X      VALUE 'N'.
  000074  007400         88 END-OF-FILE                                 VALUE 'Y'.
  000075  007500      05 SW-NM-LEN-ERR                       PIC X      VALUE 'N'.
  000076  007600         88 NAME-LENGTH-ERROR                           VALUE 'Y'.
  000077  007700  01 CONSTANTS.
(7g) ---> 000078  007800      05 LAST-NAME-MAX                       PIC S9(02).
  000079  007900      05 FIRST-NAME-MAX                      PIC S9(02).
  000080  008000  01 PRINT-LINES.
  000081  008100      05 PRINT-LINE1.
  000082  008200         10 FILLER                           PIC X(56)
  000083  008300                                                 VALUE SPACES.
  000084  008400         10 FILLER                           PIC X(23)
  000085  008500                              VALUE 'THIS IS TO CERTIFY THAT'.

  000087  008700

  000089  008900      05 PRINT-LINE3.
  000090  009000         10 FILLER                           PIC X(59)
  000091  009100                                                 VALUE SPACES.
  000092  009200         10 FILLER                           PIC X(15)
  000093  009300                                     VALUE 'IS AN EXPERT IN'.

  000095  009500      05 PRINT-LINE4.
  000096  009600         10 FILLER                           PIC X(57)
  000097  009700                                                 VALUE SPACES.
  000098  009800         10 EXPERTISE                        PIC X(30).
  000099  009900      05 PRINT-NAME-LINE.
  000100  010000         10 FILLER                           PIC X(59)
  000101  010100                                                 VALUE SPACES.
  000102  010200         10 PRT-NAME.
  000103  010300            15 PRT-FIRST-NAME OCCURS 1 TO 15 TIMES
  000104  010400                 DEPENDING ON FIRST-NAME-CNT
  000105  010500                 INDEXED BY PRT-FIRST-NAME-IND  PIC X.
  000106  010600            15 NAME-SEPARATOR                   PIC X.
  000107  010700            15 PRT-LAST-NAME OCCURS 1 TO 20 TIMES
  000108  010800                 DEPENDING ON LAST-NAME-CNT
  000109  010900                 INDEXED BY PRT-LAST-NAME-IND   PIC X.

  000111  011100 LINKAGE SECTION.
  000112  011200   01 INPARM.
  000113  011300       05 IN-PARM-LENGTH                     PIC S9(4) COMP SYNC.
  000114  011400       05 IN-PARM-EXPERTISE                  PIC X(30).
PP 5668-958 REL. 2.0, 09/08/86, IBM VS COBOL II.                DMPCB21   DATE 04/03/90   TIME 13.38.44   PAGE     6

  000115  011500 PROCEDURE DIVISION USING INPARM.
  000116  011600 0000-MAINLINE.

  000118  011800     OPEN INPUT  NAME-FILE
  000119  011900          OUTPUT PRINT-FILE
  000120  012000     MOVE IN-PARM-EXPERTISE TO EXPERTISE
  000121  012100     READ NAME-FILE
  000122  012200       AT END SET END-OF-FILE TO TRUE
  000123  012300     END-READ
  000124  012400     PERFORM 0050-PROCESS-NAMES THRU 0050-PROCESS-NAMES-EXIT
  000125  012500        UNTIL END-OF-FILE OR NAME-LENGTH-ERROR
  000126  012600     CLOSE PRINT-FILE
  000127  012700           NAME-FILE.
  000128  012800     GOBACK.
```

Figure 10.2 *(Continued)*

(3) There are no error messages from the linkage-editor. The length of the load module is F5B8.

d. Look for any system or COBOL messages in the job log. There is a symptom dump and a message from COBOL II, IGZ038I AN ABEND WAS INTERCEPTED BY THE COBOL EXECUTION TIME ABEND HANDLER.

2. Review your actions.

   a. No modifications were made in the program or the input data sets.

3. Check how far the program executed.

```
PP 5668-958 REL. 2.0, 09/08/86, IBM VS COBOL II.             DMPCB21   DATE 04/03/90  TIME 13.38.44   PAGE    7
  000130  013000*****************************************************************
  000131  013100* DETERMINE LENGTH OF ENTIRE NAME, INCLUDING COMMA  (NAME-CNT).  *
  000132  013200* DETERMINE LENGTH OF LAST NAME  (LAST-NAME-CNT).               *
  000133  013300* DETERMINE LENGTH OF FIRST NAME  (FIRST-NAME-CNT).             *
  000134  013400* DETERMINE STARTING POSITION OF FIRST NAME IN NAME-FILE-REC    *
  000135  013500*   (FIRST-NAME-START).                                         *
  000136  013600* TERMINATE PROCESSING IF LENGTH OF EITHER FIRST OR LAST NAMES  *
  000137  013700*   GREATER THAN MAXIMUM PERMITTED.  OTHERWISE PERFORM          *
  000138  013800*   PARAGRAPHS TO FORMAT PRT-NAME FIELDS AND THEN PRINT THE     *
  000139  013900*   CERTIFICATE.                                                *
  000140  014000*****************************************************************

  000142  014200 0050-PROCESS-NAMES.

  000144  014400     INITIALIZE   NAME-CNT
  000145  014500                  LAST-NAME-CNT
  000146  014600                  FIRST-NAME-CNT
  000147  014700     INSPECT NAME-FILE-REC
  000148  014800       TALLYING NAME-CNT
  000149  014900       FOR CHARACTERS BEFORE INITIAL SPACES
  000150  015000     INSPECT NAME-FILE-REC
  000151  015100       TALLYING LAST-NAME-CNT
  000152  015200       FOR CHARACTERS BEFORE INITIAL ','
(7b) -->  000153  015300     IF LAST-NAME-CNT GREATER THAN LAST-NAME-MAX
  000154  015400        DISPLAY 'LAST NAME TOO LONG'     <-- (3b)
  000155  015500        SET NAME-LENGTH-ERROR TO TRUE
  000156  015600     END-IF
  000157  015700     COMPUTE FIRST-NAME-CNT = (NAME-CNT - LAST-NAME-CNT) - +1
  000158  015800     IF FIRST-NAME-CNT GREATER THAN FIRST-NAME-MAX
  000159  015900        DISPLAY 'FIRST NAME TOO LONG'    <-- (3b)
  000160  016000        SET NAME-LENGTH-ERROR TO TRUE
  000161  016100     END-IF
  000162  016200     IF NAME-LENGTH-ERROR
  000163  016300        NEXT SENTENCE
  000164  016400     END-IF
  000165  016500     COMPUTE FIRST-NAME-START = (LAST-NAME-CNT + 2)
  000166  016600     SET PRT-FIRST-NAME-IND TO +1
  000167  016700     PERFORM 0100-MOVE-FIRST-NAME THRU 0100-MOVE-FIRST-NAME-EXIT
  000168  016800        VARYING FIRST-NAME-SUB FROM FIRST-NAME-START BY 1
  000169  016900           UNTIL FIRST-NAME-SUB GREATER THAN NAME-CNT
  000170  017000     PERFORM 0200-MOVE-LAST-NAME THRU 0200-MOVE-LAST-NAME-EXIT
  000171  017100        VARYING LAST-NAME-SUB FROM 1 BY 1
  000172  017200           UNTIL LAST-NAME-SUB GREATER THAN LAST-NAME-CNT
  000173  017300     MOVE SPACES TO NAME-SEPARATOR
  000174  017400     PERFORM 0300-PRINT THRU 0300-PRINT-EXIT
  000175  017500     READ NAME-FILE
  000176  017600       AT END SET END-OF-FILE TO TRUE
  000177  017700     END-READ.

  000179  017900 0050-PROCESS-NAMES-EXIT.
  000180  018000     EXIT.
PP 5668-958 REL. 2.0, 09/08/86, IBM VS COBOL II.             DMPCB21   DATE 04/03/90  TIME 13.38.44   PAGE    8
  000182  018200 0100-MOVE-FIRST-NAME.

  000184  018400     MOVE NAME-FIELDS (FIRST-NAME-SUB)
  000185  018500       TO  PRT-FIRST-NAME (PRT-FIRST-NAME-IND)
  000186  018600     SET PRT-FIRST-NAME-IND UP BY +1.

  000188  018800 0100-MOVE-FIRST-NAME-EXIT.
  000189  018900      EXIT.

  000191  019100 0200-MOVE-LAST-NAME.

  000193  019300     MOVE NAME-FIELDS (LAST-NAME-SUB)
  000194  019400       TO  PRT-LAST-NAME (LAST-NAME-SUB).

  000196  019600 0200-MOVE-LAST-NAME-EXIT.
  000197  019700      EXIT.

  000199  019900 0300-PRINT.

  000201  020100     WRITE PRINT-FILE-REC FROM PRINT-LINE1 AFTER ADVANCING PAGE  <-- (3b)
  000202  020200     WRITE PRINT-FILE-REC FROM PRINT-NAME-LINE AFTER ADVANCING 3
  000203  020300     WRITE PRINT-FILE-REC FROM PRINT-LINE3 AFTER ADVANCING 3
  000204  020400     WRITE PRINT-FILE-REC FROM PRINT-LINE4 AFTER ADVANCING 3.

  000206  020600 0300-PRINT-EXIT.
  000207  020700     EXIT.
```

Figure 10.2 *(Continued)*

```
PP 5668-958 REL. 2.0, 09/08/86, IBM VS COBOL II.            DMPCB21   DATE 04/03/90   TIME 13.38.44   PAGE     9

AN "M" PRECEDING A DATA-NAME REFERENCE INDICATES THAT THE DATA-NAME IS MODIFIED BY THIS REFERENCE.

 DEFINED   CROSS-REFERENCE OF DATA NAMES   REFERENCES
                                         .
                                         .
                                         .
     112   INPARM . . . . . . . . . . . .  115
      67   LAST-NAME-CNT. . . . . . . . .  108 M144 M150 153 157 165 170
7f -> 78   LAST-NAME-MAX. . . . . . . . .  153
      69   LAST-NAME-SUB. . . . . . . . .  M170 170 193 193
      66   NAME-CNT . . . . . . . . . . .  M144 M147 157 167
                                         .
                                         .
                                         .
PP 5668-958 REL. 2.0, 09/08/86, IBM VS COBOL II.            DMPCB21   DATE 04/03/90   TIME 13.38.44   PAGE    11

 DATA DIVISION MAP
 LINE     LEVEL NUMBER AND SOURCE NAME                      BASE      DISPL  STRCT DISP  DEFINITION    USAGE        R O D F
     48   FD PRINT-FILE. . . . . . . . . . . . . . . . . .            001                                QSAM              FB
     54   01 PRINT-FILE-REC. . . . . . . . . . . . . . . . BLF=0000   000                  DS 133C       DISPLAY
     55   FD NAME-FILE . . . . . . . . . . . . . . . . . .            001                                QSAM              FB
     61   01 NAME-FILE-REC . . . . . . . . . . . . . . . . BLF=0001   000                  DS 0CL80      GROUP
     62     02 NAME-FIELDS . . . . . . . . . . . . . . . . BLF=0001   000    0 000 000     DS 1C         DISPLAY        O
     65   01 ACCUMULATORS. . . . . . . . . . . . . . . . . BLW=0000   000                  DS 0CL12      GROUP            D
     66     02 NAME-CNT. . . . . . . . . . . . . . . . . . BLW=0000   000    0 000 000     DS 1H         COMP
     67     02 LAST-NAME-CNT . . . . . . . . . . . . . . . BLW=0000   002    0 000 002     DS 1H         COMP             D
     68     02 FIRST-NAME-CNT. . . . . . . . . . . . . . . BLW=0000   004    0 000 004     DS 1H         COMP             D
     69     02 LAST-NAME-SUB . . . . . . . . . . . . . . . BLW=0000   006    0 000 006     DS 1H         COMP
     70     02 FIRST-NAME-SUB. . . . . . . . . . . . . . . BLW=0000   008    0 000 008     DS 1H         COMP
7c   71     02 FIRST-NAME-START. . . . . . . . . . . . . . BLW=0000   00A    0 000 00A     DS 1H         COMP
     72   01 SWITCHES. . . . . . . . . . . . . . . . . . . BLW=0000   010                  DS 0CL2       GROUP
     73     02 SW-EOF. . . . . . . . . . . . . . . . . . . BLW=0000   010    0 000 000     DS 1C         DISPLAY
     74     88 END-OF-FILE . . . . . . . . . . . . . . . .
     75     02 SW-NM-LEN-ERR . . . . . . . . . . . . . . . BLW=0000   011    0 000 001     DS 1C         DISPLAY
     76     88 NAME-LENGTH-ERROR . . . . . . . . . . . . .
     77   01 CONSTANTS . . . . . . . . . . . . . . . . . . BLW=0000   018                  DS 0CL4       GROUP
     78     02 LAST-NAME-MAX . . . . . . . . . . . . . . . BLW=0000   018    0 000 000     DS 2C         DISP-NUM
     79     02 FIRST-NAME-MAX. . . . . . . . . . . . . . . BLW=0000   01A    0 000 002     DS 2C         DISP-NUM
                                         .
                                         .
                                         .
PP 5668-958 REL. 2.0, 09/08/86, IBM VS COBOL II.            DMPCB21   DATE 04/03/90   TIME 13.38.44   PAGE    16
                                                   .
                                                   .
                                                   .
   000352  4E30 D1D0             CVD   3,464(0,13)          TS2=0
000153  IF
   00034E  4830 9002             LH    3,2(0,9)             LAST-NAME-CNT
   000356  F211 D1DE 9018        PACK  478(2,13),24(2,9)    TS2=14                          LAST-NAME-MAX
7a ->000035C  F811 D1DE D1DE     ZAP   478(2,13),478(2,13)  TS2=14                          TS2=14   <- 7d
   000362  F911 D1D6 D1DE        CP    470(2,13),478(2,13)  TS2=6                           TS2=14
   000368  47D0 B0BA             BC    13,186(0,11)         GN=16(00037A)
000154  DISPLAY
   00036C  58F0 202C             L     15,44(0,2)           V(IGZCDSP )
                                                   .
                                                   .
                                                   .
PP 5668-958 REL. 2.0, 09/08/86, IBM VS COBOL II.            DMPCB21   DATE 04/03/90   TIME 13.38.44   PAGE    21

                *** TGT MEMORY MAP ***

        PGMLOC  TGTLOC
                                                   .
                                                   .
                                                   .
        000808  000130  BASE LOCATORS FOR SPECIAL REGISTERS
7e(1)-> 000810  000138  BASE LOCATORS FOR WORKING-STORAGE
        000814  00013C  BASE LOCATORS FOR LINKAGE-SECTION
        00081C  000144  BASE LOCATORS FOR FILES
                                                   .
                                                   .
                                                   .
```

Figure 10.2 *(Continued)*

```
PP 5668-958 REL. 2.0, 09/08/86, IBM VS COBOL II.              DMPCB21   DATE 04/03/90   TIME 13.38.44   PAGE    23

LINEID  MESSAGE CODE  MESSAGE TEXT ( IMBEDDED MESSAGES MAY BE IDENTIFIED BY THE <*> PRECEDING THE MESSAGE CODE )

        IGYDS0015-I   DIAGNOSTIC MESSAGES WERE ISSUED DURING PROCESSING OF COMPILER OPTIONS. THESE MESSAGES ARE LOCATED AT THE
                      BEGINNING OF THE LISTING.

TOTAL MESSAGES     INFORMATIONAL     WARNING     ERROR     SEVERE     TERMINATING

        3                2              [1]<-------------------------------------------------------- 1c(1)

* STATISTICS FOR COBOL PROGRAM DMPCB21 :
*     SOURCE RECORDS =  207
*     DATA DIVISION STATEMENTS =  31
*     PROCEDURE DIVISION STATEMENTS =  37

MVS/XA DFP VER 3 LINKAGE EDITOR                       13:38:52  TUE  APR 03, 1990
JOB DMPCB21     STEP S1           PROCEDURE LKED
INVOCATION PARAMETERS - LIST,XREF,LET,MAP
ACTUAL SIZE=(317440,86016)
OUTPUT DATA SET SYS90093.T133858.RA000.DMPCB21.GOSET IS ON VOLUME WKSH02

                                                      CROSS REFERENCE TABLE

 CONTROL SECTION                          ENTRY

   NAME    ORIGIN  LENGTH                   NAME   LOCATION      NAME   LOCATION      NAME   LOCATION      NAME   LOCATION

[DMPCB21        00     DF1]<-------------------------------------------- 6c
 IGZCDSP *     DF8     4AC
 IGZCINS *    12A8     98E
                                                      .
                                                      .
                                                      .

ENTRY ADDRESS        00

[TOTAL LENGTH      F5B8]<-------------------------------------------- 1c(3)
** GO          DID NOT PREVIOUSLY EXIST BUT WAS ADDED AND HAS AMODE 24
** LOAD MODULE HAS RMODE 24
** AUTHORIZATION CODE IS          0.
```

Figure 10.2 *(Continued)*

a. Check for program output. There is none.

b. Examine the program for WRITE and DISPLAY statements. The program did not get as far as the WRITE at line 201. The DISPLAY statements execute only if there is a field length error.

4. Review the output from any COBOL debugging aids which were in effect.

   a. As mentioned, no DISPLAYs were executed.

5. Check to see if the JCL is correct.

   a. Is the input data set the correct one? In-stream data were used.

   b. Look for anything else significant. A parameter is passed to the program.

6. Analyze the SYMPTOM DUMP or actual SYSTEM DUMP.

   a. Looking at the SYMPTOM DUMP shows that the name of the load module is GO, the ILC is 6, the LPA is AA48, and the offset of the NSI is 362.

   b. Check to see that the NSI is within the load module. It is, since the length of the module is F5B8.

   c. Looking back at the linkage-editor map we see that the CSECT containing the NSI is in DMPCB21, which is the name from the program's IDENTIFICATION DIVISION. DMPCB21 is located at the beginning of the load module.

   d. Subtract the ILC from the NSI offset. 362 – 6 = 35C. This is the offset of the ABENDing instruction within the program.

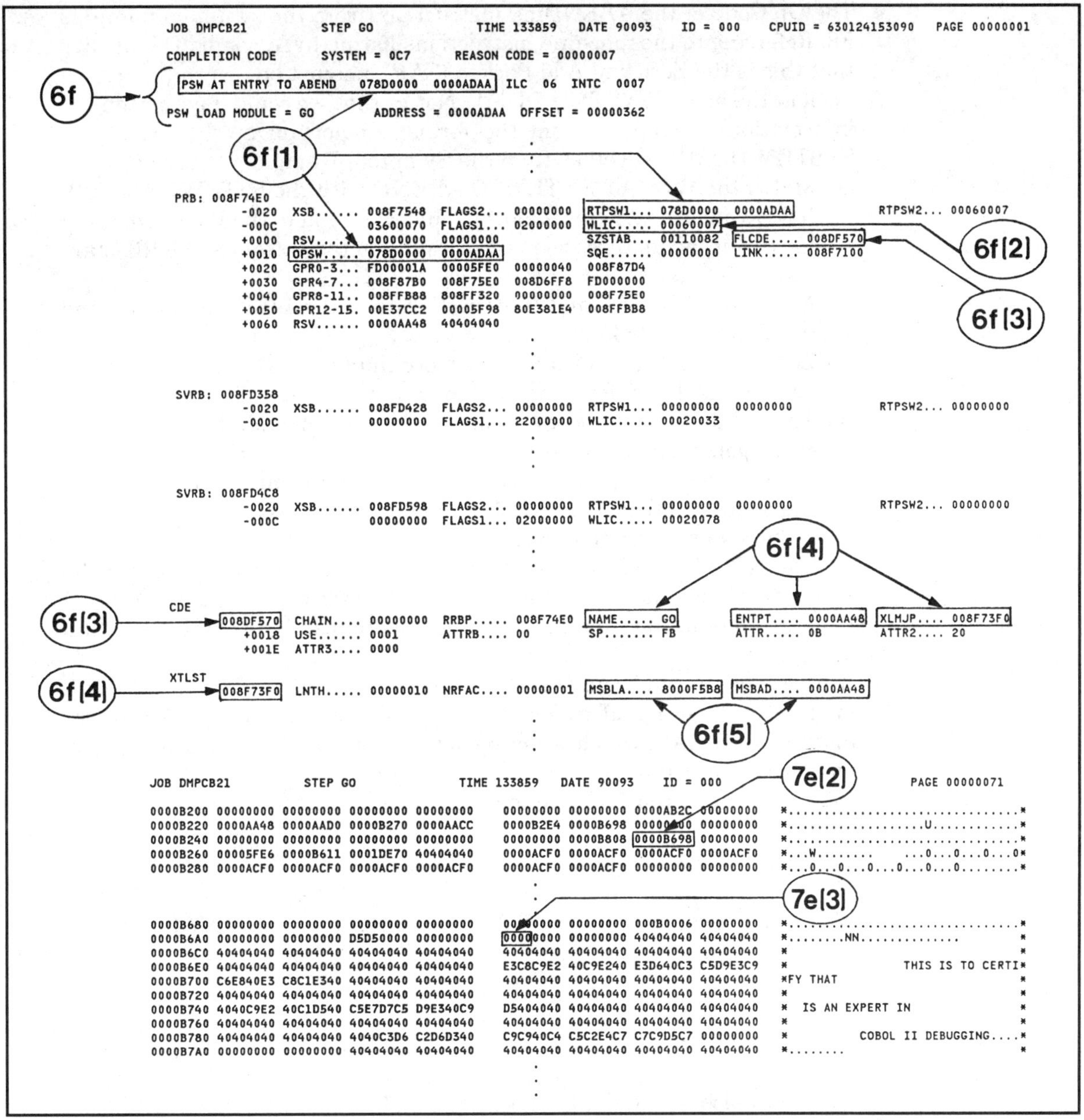


```
JOB DMPCB21          STEP GO              TIME 133859   DATE 90093    ID = 000    CPUID = 630124153090   PAGE 00000001

COMPLETION CODE      SYSTEM = 0C7     REASON CODE = 00000007

PSW AT ENTRY TO ABEND   078D0000  0000ADAA  ILC  06  INTC  0007

PSW LOAD MODULE = GO         ADDRESS = 0000ADAA  OFFSET = 00000362
                                            .
                                            .
                                            .
PRB: 008F74E0
        -0020  XSB...... 008F7548  FLAGS2... 00000000  RTPSW1... 078D0000  0000ADAA              RTPSW2... 00060007
        -000C            03600070  FLAGS1... 02000000  WLIC..... 00060007
        +0000  RSV...... 00000000  00000000            SZSTAB... 00110082  FLCDE.... 008DF570
        +0010  OPSW..... 078D0000  0000ADAA            SQE...... 00000000  LINK..... 008F7100
        +0020  GPR0-3... FD00001A  00005FE0  00000040  008F87D4
        +0030  GPR4-7... 008F87B0  008F75E0  008D6FF8  FD000000
        +0040  GPR8-11.. 008FFB88  808FF320  00000000  008F75E0
        +0050  GPR12-15. 00E37CC2  00005F98  80E381E4  008FFBB8
        +0060  RSV...... 0000AA48  40404040
                                            .
                                            .
                                            .

SVRB: 008FD358
        -0020  XSB...... 008FD428  FLAGS2... 00000000  RTPSW1... 00000000  00000000              RTPSW2... 00000000
        -000C            00000000  FLAGS1... 22000000  WLIC..... 00020033
                                            .
                                            .
                                            .

SVRB: 008FD4C8
        -0020  XSB...... 008FD598  FLAGS2... 00000000  RTPSW1... 00000000  00000000              RTPSW2... 00000000
        -000C            00000000  FLAGS1... 02000000  WLIC..... 00020078
                                            .
                                            .
                                            .
CDE
      008DF570  CHAIN.... 00000000  RRBP..... 008F74E0  NAME..... GO          ENTPT.... 0000AA48  XLMJP.... 008F73F0
         +0018  USE...... 0001      ATTRB.... 00        SP....... FB          ATTR..... 0B        ATTR2.... 20
         +001E  ATTR3.... 0000

XTLST
      008F73F0  LNTH..... 00000010  NRFAC.... 00000001  MSBLA.... 8000F5B8  MSBAD.... 0000AA48
                                            .
                                            .
                                            .

JOB DMPCB21            STEP GO              TIME 133859   DATE 90093    ID = 000                 PAGE 00000071

0000B200 00000000 00000000 00000000 00000000   00000000 00000000 0000AB2C 00000000  *................................*
0000B220 0000AA48 0000AAD0 0000B270 0000AACC   0000B2E4 0000B698 0000[illegible]00 00000000  *..................U.............*
0000B240 00000000 00000000 00000000 00000000   00000000 0000B808 0000B698 00000000  *................................*
0000B260 00005FE6 0000B611 0001DE70 40404040   0000ACF0 0000ACF0 0000ACF0 0000ACF0  *...W........     ...0...0...0...0*
0000B280 0000ACF0 0000ACF0 0000ACF0 0000ACF0   0000ACF0 0000ACF0 00000000 00000000  *...0...0...0...0...0...0........*
                                            .
                                            .
                                            .
0000B680 00000000 00000000 00000000 00000000   00[illegible]0000 00000000 000B0006 00000000  *................................*
0000B6A0 00000000 00000000 D5D50000 00000000   00000000 00000000 40404040 40404040  *........NN..............        *
0000B6C0 40404040 40404040 40404040 40404040   40404040 40404040 40404040 40404040  *                                *
0000B6E0 40404040 40404040 40404040 40404040   E3C8C9E2 40C9E240 E3D640C3 C5D9E3C9  *                THIS IS TO CERTI*
0000B700 C6E840E3 C8C1E340 40404040 40404040   40404040 40404040 40404040 40404040  *FY THAT                         *
0000B720 40404040 40404040 40404040 40404040   40404040 40404040 40404040 40404040  *                                *
0000B740 4040C9E2 40C1D540 C5E7D7C5 D9E340C9   D5404040 40404040 40404040 40404040  *  IS AN EXPERT IN               *
0000B760 40404040 40404040 40404040 40404040   40404040 40404040 40404040 40404040  *                                *
0000B780 40404040 40404040 4040C3D6 C2D6D340   C9C940C4 C5C2E4C7 C7C9D5C7 00000000  *          COBOL II DEBUGGING....*
0000B7A0 00000000 00000000 40404040 40404040   40404040 40404040 40404040 40404040  *........                        *
                                            .
                                            .
                                            .
```

Figure 10.2 *(Continued)*

e. The Op Code of the ABENDing instruction (from the symptom dump) is F8. Referring to the machine instructions listing in Appendix D indicates that this is the Zero and Add Packed (ZAP) instruction.

f. Look at the actual SYSTEM DUMP. Notice that we could have gotten the information in step 6*a* from the formatted portion at the top of the SYSTEM DUMP as well as from the Symptom Dump.

(1) Match the PSW AT ENTRY TO ABEND with the RTPSW1 or OPSW field in one of the request blocks. This leads you to the PRB. (We could have counted up three request blocks from the bottom of the RB chain instead.)

(2) Notice that the ILC and Interrupt Code in the WLIC field are 6 and 07, as we already know.

(3) Look for the CDE. (If there were more than one CDE entry, we would use the FLCDE field in the PRB to find the address of the correct one.)

(4) The CDE shows that the name of the load module is GO and the entry-point address (the point in the module where execution is to begin) is AA48. Find the corresponding XTLST entry. (We would use the pointer in the CDE's XLMJP field to find the correct XTLST entry if there were more than one.)

(5) The XTLST verifies a length of F5B8 and load-point address (the physical beginning of the module) of AA48 for load module GO.

7. Use the compiler output to examine the instruction and the operands within the program.

a. Look at the output from the LIST compiler option to find the COBOL instruction. Use the offset found in step 6*d* (35C). Notice the Assembler instruction is ZAP, which we previously determined. The COBOL statement number is 153.

b. Go to statement 153 in the source code. It is

```
IF LAST-NAME-CNT GREATER THAN LAST-NAME-MAX
```

c. We need to examine the two fields. Use output from the MAP compiler option.

```
LAST-NAME-CNT    BLW 0000    DISPL 2     2 bytes    COMP
LAST-NAME-MAX    BLW 0000    DISPL 18    2 bytes    DISP-NUM
```

(We could also verify the USAGE and PICTURE of each field by looking at lines 67 and 78 in the source code.)

d. Since the fields were not packed, COBOL generated instructions to convert them to packed format before comparing them. (See the Assembler instructions in the LIST output to verify this.) The operand in the ZAP instruction is in a temporary storage field which was used to PACK LAST-NAME-MAX in the previous instruction.

e. We need to check the contents of LAST-NAME-MAX in the storage dump.

(1) Go to the TGT MEMORY MAP to find the offset from the beginning of the program of BLW 0000. It is 810. Add this to the LPA (remember that program DMPCB21 is located at the beginning of the load module, at LPA AA48). AA48 + 810 = B258. This is the address of BLW 0000.

(2) Go to address B258 in the dump. This is the location of BLW 0000. The contents of this cell is B698. This is the base address for LAST-NAME-MAX.

(3) Add the displacement 18 to the base address B698. B698 + 18 = B6B0. Go to this address. The contents of LAST-NAME-MAX is 0000. The sign is invalid.

f. Return to the XREF output to determine why LAST-NAME-MAX has invalid data. It is defined at line 78 and is not modified in the Procedure Division.

g. Going to line 78 in the source code we see that LAST-NAME-MAX is coded without a VALUE clause. It is an uninitialized field.

10.3.4 The Second System Dump

The second ABEND we will examine occurred when another job involving a COBOL program was executed under MVS/ESA. Figure 10.3 shows relevant portions of the JCL, job log, compiler, linkage-editor and other job output, and the system dump. Again, the numbers of the steps we follow are printed and circled in the appropriate places of the figure to make it easier to follow.

1. Determine the type and location of the ABEND.
   a. Scan the job log for a completion code. In this dump it is S013. This signifies that an error occurred during execution of an OPEN macro instruction.
   b. Determine which step ABENDed. The GO step within procedure step S2. The JCL indicates that S2 executed the COBUCLG procedure.
   c. Check the condition codes of the previous job and procedure steps. They are all 0.
   d. Look for any system or COBOL messages in the job log. There is a symptom dump and a message

   ```
   IEC141I 013-20,IGG0191A,REPTIEB,GO,INFILE,506,PRIY07,MY.DATA.TEMP
   ```

   preceding the symptom dump. The reason code 20 means an OPEN macro was issued and either BLKSIZE is not an even multiple of LRECL, the LRECL=0 when RECFM=FB or FBS, or the BLKSIZE does not include four bytes for the RDW when RECFM=V. IGG0191A is the name of the module in which the error occurred, and the job name and step name are REPTIEB and GO, respectively. The DDname and data set name for the file are INFILE and MY.DATA.TEMP.
2. Review your actions.
   a. This is the first time this job was run.
3. Check how far the job executed.

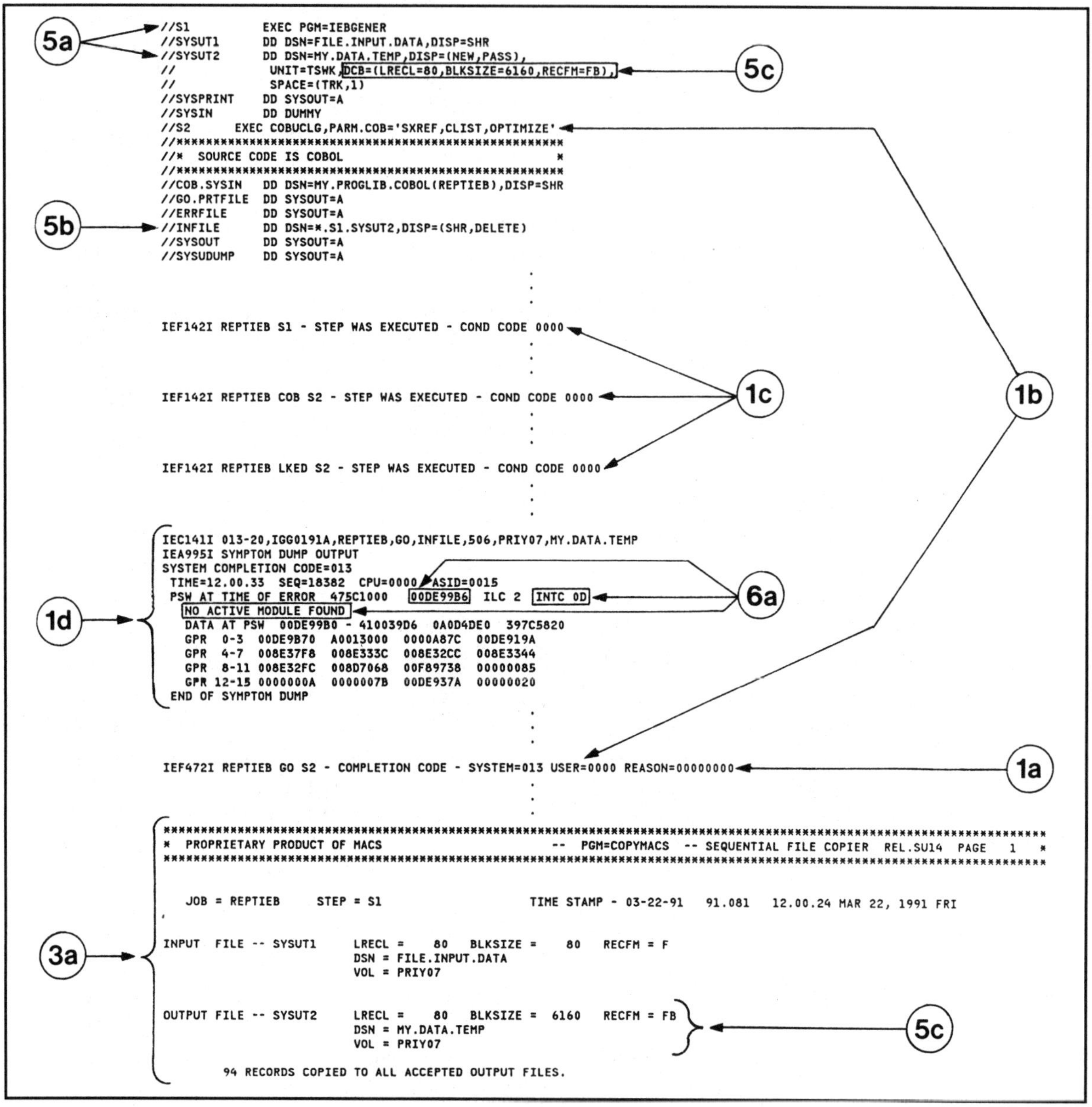

```
//S1         EXEC PGM=IEBGENER
//SYSUT1     DD DSN=FILE.INPUT.DATA,DISP=SHR
//SYSUT2     DD DSN=MY.DATA.TEMP,DISP=(NEW,PASS),
//              UNIT=TSWK,DCB=(LRECL=80,BLKSIZE=6160,RECFM=FB),
//              SPACE=(TRK,1)
//SYSPRINT   DD SYSOUT=A
//SYSIN      DD DUMMY
//S2      EXEC COBUCLG,PARM.COB='SXREF,CLIST,OPTIMIZE'
//**********************************************
//*  SOURCE CODE IS COBOL                       *
//**********************************************
//COB.SYSIN  DD DSN=MY.PROGLIB.COBOL(REPTIEB),DISP=SHR
//GO.PRTFILE DD SYSOUT=A
//ERRFILE    DD SYSOUT=A
//INFILE     DD DSN=*.S1.SYSUT2,DISP=(SHR,DELETE)
//SYSOUT     DD SYSOUT=A
//SYSUDUMP   DD SYSOUT=A
                        .
                        .
                        .
IEF142I REPTIEB S1 - STEP WAS EXECUTED - COND CODE 0000
                        .
                        .
IEF142I REPTIEB COB S2 - STEP WAS EXECUTED - COND CODE 0000
                        .
                        .
IEF142I REPTIEB LKED S2 - STEP WAS EXECUTED - COND CODE 0000
                        .
                        .
IEC141I 013-20,IGG0191A,REPTIEB,GO,INFILE,506,PRIY07,MY.DATA.TEMP
IEA995I SYMPTOM DUMP OUTPUT
SYSTEM COMPLETION CODE=013
 TIME=12.00.33  SEQ=18382  CPU=0000  ASID=0015
 PSW AT TIME OF ERROR  475C1000   00DE99B6  ILC 2  INTC 0D
  NO ACTIVE MODULE FOUND
   DATA AT PSW  00DE99B0 - 410039D6  0A0D4DE0  397C5820
   GPR  0-3  00DE9B70  A0013000  0000A87C  00DE919A
   GPR  4-7  008E37F8  008E333C  008E32CC  008E3344
   GPR  8-11 008E32FC  008D7068  00F89738  00000085
   GPR 12-15 0000000A  0000007B  00DE937A  00000020
 END OF SYMPTOM DUMP
                        .
                        .
IEF472I REPTIEB GO S2 - COMPLETION CODE - SYSTEM=013 USER=0000 REASON=00000000
                        .
                        .
*****************************************************************************************************
*  PROPRIETARY PRODUCT OF MACS                 --  PGM=COPYMACS  -- SEQUENTIAL FILE COPIER  REL.SU14  PAGE  1  *
*****************************************************************************************************

   JOB = REPTIEB     STEP = S1                  TIME STAMP - 03-22-91   91.081   12.00.24 MAR 22, 1991 FRI

INPUT  FILE -- SYSUT1      LRECL =    80   BLKSIZE =    80   RECFM = F
                           DSN = FILE.INPUT.DATA
                           VOL = PRIY07

OUTPUT FILE -- SYSUT2      LRECL =    80   BLKSIZE =  6160   RECFM = FB
                           DSN = MY.DATA.TEMP
                           VOL = PRIY07

        94 RECORDS COPIED TO ALL ACCEPTED OUTPUT FILES.
```


Figure 10.3 Portions of the JCL, job log, output from the compiler, linkage-editor and program, and parts of the system dump for the second system dump example.

a. There is output from a program called COPYMACS. This is not our COBOL program. We will need to check the JCL (see step 5).

b. So far evidence points to an OPEN problem for the file associated with DDname INFILE. The OPEN statement is at line 56 in the COBOL program.

```
PP 5740-CB1 RELEASE 2.4                          IBM OS/VS COBOL  JULY  1, 1982          12.00.26  DATE MAR 22,1991

  1                    12.00.26       MAR 22,1991

00001          IDENTIFICATION DIVISION.
00002           PROGRAM-ID.   REPTIEB.
00003           AUTHOR.        ALAN FRIEND.
00004           DATE-WRITTEN. 03/21/91
00005          ENVIRONMENT DIVISION.
00006           INPUT-OUTPUT SECTION.
00007           FILE-CONTROL.
00008              SELECT  CARD-FILE   ASSIGN  TO  INFILE.                     3c
00009              SELECT  PRINT-FILE  ASSIGN  TO  PRTFILE.
00010              SELECT  ERROR-FILE  ASSIGN  TO  ERRFILE.
00011          DATA DIVISION.
00012           FILE SECTION.
00013           FD  CARD-FILE
00014               BLOCK CONTAINS  0  RECORDS
00015               LABEL RECORDS ARE STANDARD                              5d
00016               RECORDING MODE IS F.
00017           01  CARD-FILE-REC                        PIC X(50).
00018           FD  PRINT-FILE
00019               BLOCK CONTAINS  0  RECORDS
00020               LABEL RECORDS ARE OMITTED
00021               RECORDING MODE IS F.
00022           01  PRINT-FILE-REC                       PIC X(133).
00023           FD  ERROR-FILE
00024               BLOCK CONTAINS  0  RECORDS
00025               LABEL RECORDS ARE OMITTED
00026               RECORDING MODE IS F.
00027           01  ERROR-FILE-REC                       PIC X(133).

  2        REPTIEB         12.00.26        MAR 22,1991

00029           WORKING-STORAGE SECTION.
00030           01 PRINT-OUT.
00031              05 CTRL-CHAR                  PIC X.
00032              05 CARD-TEXT                  PIC X(132).
00033           01 PRINT-STATS.
00034              05 FILLER                     PIC X(18)B
00035                                           VALUE 'TOTAL RECORDS READ'.
00036              05 REC-READ                   PIC ZZ9.
00037              05 FILLER                     PIC BX(21)B
00038                                           VALUE 'TOTAL RECORDS WRITTEN'.
00039              05 REC-WRITTEN                PIC ZZ9.
00040           01 CARD-IN.
00041              05 FILLER                     PIC X(80).
00042           01 SAVE-AREA.
00043              05 CARD-NO                    PIC S9(02) COMP-3.
00044              05 CTRL-CHAR                  PIC X.
00045              05 CARD-TEXT                  PIC X(132).
00046           01 COUNTERS  COMP-3.
00047              05 REC-READ                   PIC S9(03).
00048              05 REC-WRITTEN                PIC S9(03).
00049           01 SW-EOF                        PIC 9      VALUE 0.
```

Figure 10.3 *(Continued)*

c. The SELECT . . . ASSIGN clauses indicates that CARD-FILE was assigned to DDname INFILE.

d. Check for output from the COBOL program. Only PROGRAM REPTIEB BEGINNING appears.

e. Examine the COBOL program for WRITE and DISPLAY statements. The DISPLAY statement at line 55 was responsible for the data displayed in 3*d* above. There is no other output. Again, it seems that our COBOL program did not proceed beyond the OPEN at line 56.

4. Review the output from any COBOL debugging aids which were in effect.

   a. As mentioned, only the DISPLAY at line 55 executed.

5. Check for information in the JCL.

   a. Examination of the JCL shows that step S1 executes IEBGENER (an IBM copy utility program) and creates data set MY.DATA.TEMP with DISP=(NEW,PASS). It is assigned to the SYSUT2 DD statement.

```
   3       REPTIEB        12.00.26       MAR 22,1991
00051        PROCEDURE DIVISION.

00053        0000-MAINLINE.

00055            DISPLAY 'PROGRAM REPTIEB BEGINNING'
00056            OPEN OUTPUT PRINT-FILE
00057                        ERROR-FILE
00058                 INPUT  CARD-FILE
00059            PERFORM 0100-INITIALIZATION
00060            READ CARD-FILE INTO CARD-IN
00061              AT END MOVE 1 TO SW-EOF.
00062            PERFORM 0200-PROCESS UNTIL SW-EOF = 1
00063            MOVE REC-READ OF COUNTERS TO REC-READ OF PRINT-STATS
00064            MOVE REC-WRITTEN OF COUNTERS TO REC-WRITTEN OF PRINT-STATS
00065            WRITE PRINT-FILE-REC FROM PRINT-STATS
00066            CLOSE PRINT-FILE
00067                  CARD-FILE
00068                  ERROR-FILE
00069            GOBACK.

00071        0100-INITIALIZATION.

00073            MOVE ZERO TO COUNTERS
00074            MOVE SPACES TO PRINT-FILE-REC
00075            MOVE '-' TO CTRL-CHAR OF PRINT-OUT.

00077        0200-PROCESS.

00079            ADD +1 TO REC-READ OF COUNTERS
00080            IF CARD-IN ALPHABETIC
00081                MOVE SPACES TO CARD-TEXT OF PRINT-OUT
00082                MOVE CARD-IN TO CARD-TEXT OF PRINT-OUT
00083                WRITE PRINT-FILE-REC FROM PRINT-OUT
00084                ADD +1 TO REC-WRITTEN OF COUNTERS
00085             ELSE
00086                DISPLAY 'NON-NUMERIC RECORD'
00087                MOVE CARD-IN TO CARD-TEXT OF PRINT-OUT
00088                WRITE ERROR-FILE-REC FROM PRINT-OUT.
00089             READ CARD-FILE INTO CARD-IN
00090               AT END MOVE 1 TO SW-EOF
00091               DISPLAY 'NO MORE RECORDS'.
   4       REPTIEB        12.00.26       MAR 22,1991

    INTRNL NAME   LVL SOURCE NAME                  BASE   DISPL  INTRNL NAME   DEFINITION   USAGE     R O Q M
    DNM=1-097     FD  CARD-FILE                    DCB=01        DNM=1-097                  QSAM            F
    DNM=1-120     01  CARD-FILE-REC                BL=1   000    DNM=1-120     DS 50C       DISP

                                         .
                                         .
                                         .

             PGT                     007F8

         DEBUG LINKAGE AREA          007F8
         OVERFLOW CELLS              007F8
         VIRTUAL CELLS               007FC
         PROCEDURE NAME CELLS        0081C
         GENERATED NAME CELLS        0081C
         DCB ADDRESS CELLS           00824
                                         .
                                         .
                                         .

   8       REPTIEB        12.00.26       MAR 22,1991

                                    CONDENSED LISTING

 55    DISPLAY    000894          56    OPEN      0008AC          59    PERFORM    00093E
 60    READ       000956          61    MOVE      000990          62    PERFORM    000994
 63    MOVE       0009C0          64    MOVE      0009D2          65    WRITE      0009E4
                                         .
                                         .
                                         .

  10       REPTIEB        12.00.26       MAR 22,1991

                                CROSS-REFERENCE DICTIONARY

 DATA NAMES                    DEFN     REFERENCE


 CARD-FILE                     000008   000056  000060  000066  000089
 CARD-FILE-REC                 000017   000060  000089
 CARD-IN                       000040   000060  000080  000082  000087  000089
                                         .
                                         .
                                         .
```


Figure 10.3 *(Continued)*

```
MVS/DFP VERSION 3 RELEASE 2 LINKAGE EDITOR      12:00:32  FRI  MAR 22, 1991
JOB REPTIEB    STEP S2          PROCEDURE LKED
INVOCATION PARAMETERS - LIST,XREF,LET
ACTUAL SIZE=(317440,79872)
OUTPUT DATA SET SYS91081.T120033.RA000.REPTIEB.GOSET IS ON VOLUME WKSH10

                                        CROSS REFERENCE TABLE

 CONTROL SECTION                        ENTRY

   NAME     ORIGIN  LENGTH                NAME   LOCATION    NAME   LOCATION    NAME   LOCATION    NAME   LOCATION
(6b[7]) --> REPTIEB   00     E02
 ILBOATB *   E08     11A
                                         ILBOATB0    E0A
 ILBOCOM0*   F28     173
                                         ILBOCOM     F28
                                              .
                                              .
                                              .
(3d) --> PROGRAM REPTIEB BEGINNING

JOB REPTIEB          STEP GO             TIME 120035   DATE 91081    ID = 000    CPUID = 630724153090    PAGE 00000001

COMPLETION CODE      SYSTEM = 013

(6b) --> { PSW AT ENTRY TO ABEND   475C1000  00DE99B6   ILC  02   INTC  000D
         { PSW ADDRESS 00DE99B6 AT TIME OF ERROR DOES NOT POINT TO AN ACTIVE MODULE
                                              .
                                              .
                                              .
 PRB: 008FF5B0
          -0020  XSB...... 008FF618  FLAGS2... 00000000  RTPSW1... 00000000  00000000             RTPSW2... 00000000
          -000C            00000000  FLAGS1... 00000000  WLIC..... 00020013
          +0000  RSV...... 00000000  00000000            SZSTAB... 00110082  FLCDE.... 008FF008  <-- (6b[3])
          +0010  OPSW..... 478D0000  0000BD7E            SQE...... 00000000  LINK..... 008F3268
                                              .
(6b[1])                                       .
                                              .
 SVRB: 008FD4B8
          -0020  XSB...... 008FD588  FLAGS2... 00000080  RTPSW1... 00000000  00000000             RTPSW2... 00000000
          -000C            00000000  FLAGS1... 02000003  WLIC..... 0002000D
          +0000  RSV...... 00000000  00000000            SZSTAB... 001ED022  FLCDE.... 00C013E0
          +0010  OPSW..... 475C1000  00DE99B6            Q........ 00000000  LINK..... 008FF5B0
          +0020  GPR0-3... 00000000  0000ADE0  0000A87C  008F77D4
          +0030  GPR4-7... 0000A844  5000B3AC  0000A6A0  00000000
          +0040  GPR8-11.. 00000000  00000000  0000A600  0000AE94
          +0050  GPR12-15. 0000ADF8  0000AB98  5000AF02  0000BB22
                                              .
                                              .         (6b[6])
                                              .
 SVRB: 008FD628
          -0020  XSB...... 008FD6F8  FLAGS2... 00000000  RTPSW1... 00000000  00000000             RTPSW2... 00000000
          -000C            00000000  FLAGS1... 22000000  WLIC..... 00020033
          +0000  RSV...... 00000000  00000000            SZSTAB... 001ED022  FLCDE.... 00000000
          +0010  OPSW..... 470C1000  820A24C6            Q........ 00000000  LINK..... 008FD4B8
          +0020  GPR0-3... 00DE9B70  A0013000  0000A87C  00DE919A
          +0030  GPR4-7... 008E37F8  008E333C  008E3[illegible]CC  008E3344
          +0040  GPR8-11.. 008E3[illegible]FC  008D7068  00F89738  00000085
          +0050  GPR12-15. 0000000A  0000007B  00DE937A  00000020
                                   (6b[16])    .        (6b[10])
 SVRB: 008FD348
          -0020  XSB...... 008FD418  FLAGS2... 00000000  RTPSW1... 00000000  00000000             RTPSW2... 00000000
          -000C            00000000  FLAGS1... 02000000  WLIC..... 00020078
          +0000  RSV...... 00000000  00000000            SZSTAB... 001ED022  FLCDE.... 00000000
          +0010  OPSW..... 470C1000  80E6D91E            Q........ 00000000  LINK..... 008FD628
          +0020  GPR0-3... 008D3E68  7FFCB190  020A3348  008DFABC
          +0030  GPR4-7... 020A24DC  020A2349  820A134A  7FFCB090
          +0040  GPR8-11.. 008D3E68  00013000  008D3EC0  008D3EC0
          +0050  GPR12-15. 008DF760  7FFCB204  00F6BCFC  00000000
                                              .
                                              .
                                              .
```

Figure 10.3 *(Continued)*

```
         CDE
6b[3] -> 008FF008 CHAIN.... 00000000 RRBP..... 008FF5B0 NAME..... GO     ENTPT.... 0000A600 XLMJP.... 008FF528
             +0018 USE...... 0001     ATTRB.... 00       SP....... FB     ATTR.....0B        ATTR2...20
             +001E ATTR3.... 0000                                                               6b[4]
         XTLST
6b[4] -> 008FF528 LNTH..... 00000010 NRFAC.... 00000001 MSBLA.... 80002A00 MSBAD.... 0000A600
                                                                   6b[5]
          TIOT: 008D7000
                JOB...... REPTIEB   STEP..... GO                   S2

                      LN-STA    DDNAME    TTR-STC   STB-UCB
                +0018 14010100  PGM=*.DD  8EF1C000  80F77650
                +002C 14010100  STEPLIB   8E570000  80FBE930
                +0040 14010102  PRTFILE   8E558000  80000000
                +0054 14010102  ERRFILE   8E540000  80000000
6b[13] ->       +0068 14010100  INFILE    8E528000  80F89738
                +007C 14010102  SYSOUT    8E504000  80000000
                                              .
                                              .
                                              .

         -DEB-----------------------------------AT LOCATION  008E0CC8
         -----

         -8      EXTNSION 008E0040 LENGTH   11       AMTYPE   81       TBLOF    0004
         +0      TCBADR   008F3268 NEXTDEB  008E0838 IRBADR   088F8A40 PATB     0F000900
         +10     USRPG    00000000 RRQ      008D3E68 DCBADR   8F0057E8 APPADR   00E78000
                                              .
                                              .
                                              .

         *** FOR THIS DEB THERE IS NO DCB, THE CONTROL BLOCK POINTED TO BY THE DEB IS AN ACB ***


         -DEB-----------------------------------AT LOCATION  008E0838
         -----

         -8      EXTNSION 008E0940 LENGTH   11       AMTYPE   81       TBLOF    0003
         +0      TCBADR   008F3268 NEXTDEB  008E08C0 IRBADR   088F8BB0 PATB     0F000900
         +10     USRPG    00000000 RRQ      0000AAB4 DCBADR   8F005950 APPADR   00E78000
                                              .
                                              .
                                              .

         *** FOR THIS DEB THERE IS NO DCB, THE CONTROL BLOCK POINTED TO BY THE DEB IS AN ACB ***

                                              .
                                              .
                                              .

         JOB REPTIEB          STEP GO              TIME 120035   DATE 91081    ID = 000                 PAGE 00000079
6b[18] -> SP 230   KEY  00

         008E2FC0                                                      D5E4E2D9 288F3268   *                         NUSR....*
         008E2FE0 00000000 00000000 00000000 00009FE0    00000000 00000000 00000000 00000000   *................................*

         SP 230   KEY  05

         008E0040 004C0000 008D41B8 00002BE0 008E0CC8    00080000 00000000 00000000 00000000   *..............H.................*
         008E0060 0041F8A6 00000000 00000000 00000000    00000000 00000000 00000000 00000000   *..8.............................*
                                              .
                                              .
                                              .

         JOB REPTIEB          STEP GO              TIME 120035   DATE 91081    ID = 000                 PAGE 00000081

         008E3820 90201810 00500000 00828000 00000000    01E1C800 00010000 1B000500 1B000500   *..................H.............*
         008E3840 00000000 00000000 00000000 00000000    00000000 00000000 00000000 D4E84BC4   *............................MY.D*
         008E3860 C1E3C14B E3C5D4D7 40404040 40404040    40404040 40404040 40404040 40404040   *ATA.TEMP                        *
         008E3880 40404040 40404040 40404040 40404040    00000C1A 00000000 00000000 00000200   *                 ...............*
         008E38A0 00000000 20011EE0 82000000 5B005100    00000049 00420000 00000000 00004000   *................................*
         008E38C0 90201810 00500000 00000000 00000000    0001E3E2 D6C1F9F5 40404040 40404040   *..................TSOA95        *
6b[20] -> (0050)                              .
                                              .                                 6b[19] -> (MY.D)
                                              .
```

Figure 10.3 *(Continued)*

```
JOB REPTIEB          STEP GO               TIME 120035   DATE 91081    ID = 000                          PAGE 00000097

                                                     .
                                                     .
                                                     .
ACTIVE LOAD MODULES

LPA/JPA MODULE     GO
0000A600 90ECD00C 185D05F0 4580F010 D9C5D7E3    C9C5C240 E5E2D9F1 0700989F F02407FF    *.......0..0.REPTIEB VSR1....0...*
0000A620 96021034 07FE41F0 000107FE 0000B34E    0000A600 0000A600 0000ADF8 0000AB98    *.......0..................8....*
0000A640 0000AE94 0000B30E 00000000 00000000    00000000 00000000 00000000 00000000    *................................*
0000A660 00000000 00000000 00000000 00000000    00000000 00000000 00000000 00000000    *................................*
0000A680 00000000 00000000 F1F24BF0 F04BF2F6    D4C1D940 F2F26B40 F1F9F9F1 00000000    *........12.00.26MAR 22. 1991....*
0000A6A0 00000000 00000000 00000000 00000000    00000000 00000000 00000000 00000000    *................................*
      LINES 0000A6C0-0000A700  SAME AS ABOVE
0000A720 00000000 00000000 E3D6E3C1 D340D9C5    C3D6D9C4 E240D9C5 C1C44000 0000E3D6    *........TOTAL RECORDS READ ...TO*
0000A740 E3C1D340 D9C5C3D6 D9C4E240 E6D9C9E3    E3C5D540 40000000 00000000 00000000    *TAL RECORDS WRITTEN  ..........*
0000A760 00000000 00000000 00000000 00000000    00000000 00000000 00000000 00000000    *................................*
      LINES 0000A780-0000A800  SAME AS ABOVE
0000A820 00000000 00000000 00000000 00000000    00000000 00000000 F0000000 00000000    *.........................0.......*
0000A840 00000000 00000000 00000000 00000000    00000000 0500BABE 0000A626 00000001    *................................*
0000A860 00000001 00000000 00000000 00000000    00000000 00000000 80000000 00000000    *................................*
0000A880 00000000 00000000 00000000 00000000    00000001 00004000 00000001 40000001    *.....................  .........*
0000A8A0 9000A844 00684800 008E37F8 02004800    20000000 00000001 00001810 00000000    *..........8.....................*
0000A8C0 00000000 00000000 00000000 00000032    00000000 00000000 00000000 05EF0700    *................................*
0000A8E0 00000000 00000000 00000000 00000000    00000000 00900000 00000000 02000001    *................................*

6b[12]                 6b[14]        DUMP INDEX     6b[15]                         6b[11]
                                     ----------
 DATA AREAS                                PAGE NUMBER
 -----------                               -----------

 AREAS RELATED TO TCB AT: 008F3268 ....    00000001
 ENQ/DEQ CONTROL BLOCKS...............     00000011
 DATA MANAGEMENT CONTROL BLOCKS........    00000012
 IOS CONTROL BLOCKS...................     00000013
 RTM CONTROL BLOCKS...................     00000013
 PCLINK STACKS / SAVE AREAS...........     00000018
 INSTALLATION/SUBSYSTEM AREA..........     00000018
 LSQA.................................     00000018
6b[17] SWA AND SP229/230..................    00000076
 REGISTERS............................     00000097
 MODULES..............................     00000097
   GO     ............................     00000097
   IEAVTRF4...........................     00000103
   IEAVTRP2...........................     00000115
   IGG019DJ...........................     00000114
   IGG019DK...........................     00000105
   IGG0191A...........................     00000106
 TRACE TABLE..........................     00000119
 USER SUBPOOL STORAGE.................     00000124

END OF DUMP
```

Figure 10.3 *(Continued)*

b. Step S2 executes COBUCLG with DDname INFILE as a refer-back to MY.DATA.TEMP. In other words, the data set created in S1 is passed to the GO step in the OS/VS COBOL compile, link, and execute procedure. It is an input file for the COBOL program.

c. Since the completion code and reason code suggest conflicts in the DCB information for MY.DATA.TEMP, let us look at the DCB parameter for this data set in the JCL. It is

```
DCB=(LRECL=80,BLKSIZE=6160,RECFM=FB)
```

Notice that this is the same information as was supplied by the COPYMACS program (see 3*a* above). (Although the EXEC statement for Step S1 indicated that IEBGENER was to be executed, the installation replaced IEBGENER with COPYMACS, a program from another vendor which carries out functions similar to IBM's IEBGENER.)

d. Comparing this DCB information with the file attributes coded in the COBOL program's FD for this file shows that there is conflicting information; BLOCK CONTAINS 0 RECORDS means that the block size will come from the JCL in the forward merge, and the record length, taken from the 01-level, will be 50. A block size of 6160 is not an even multiple of 50. We have found the error.

6. Although it is not necessary to proceed any further, it should be instructive for us to analyze the SYMPTOM DUMP or actual SYSTEM DUMP.
   a. The SYMPTOM DUMP does not point to an active module. The NSI address in the PSW is DE99B6 and the interrupt code (INTC) is 0D, which is for the ABEND macro.
   b. Look at the actual SYSTEM DUMP. The information at the top of the formatted portion is the same as that reported in the Symptom Dump.
      (1) Use the PSW AT ENTRY TO ABEND to find the proper Request Block (the one for the ABENDing routine) by matching it with either the RTPSW1 or the OPSW field. In this case the RTPSW1 fields contain zeros because the PSW does not point to an active load module. The OPSW field helps us, however. We find that the request block in question is an SVRB. (We could have counted up three request blocks from the bottom of the RB chain instead.) Notice that the RB above is a PRB and the last 2 bytes in its WLIC field contains 13. This means that the program represented by this PRB called the OPEN macro (the hexadecimal value for the OPEN SVC is 13), and that the SVRB is for the OPEN macro.
      (2) The FLCDE field in the SVRB does not point us to any CDE in the dump.
      (3) Using the FLCDE field in the PRB directs us to the CDE entry at address 8FF008 (this is the only CDE entry shown).
      (4) This CDE entry shows the name of the load module is GO and the entry-point address is A600. We use the pointer in XLMJP to find the corresponding XTLST entry (this is the only one shown).
      (5) The XTLST specifies a length of 2A00 and load-point address of A600 for load module GO. Adding these values gives D000. The address of the NSI, DE99B6, is beyond the range of addresses for module GO. It is probably in a supervisor routine related to OPEN processing (remember message IEC141I in the job log pointed to a module named IGG019A).
      (6) If we wished to find the address of the instruction at which the program which invoked the OPEN macro was to resume execution, we could do so by either finding the return point address from general-purpose register 14 in the OPEN SVRB, from the address in the second word of the OPSW field of the PRB, or from the RET field in the appropriate Save Area of the SAVE AREA TRACE. One of these should give us the proper return point address. We will use the GPR 14 field in the SVRB. This field holds the contents of the program's register 14; it was stored by the OPEN routine in its SVRB so that

processing could continue in the program when OPEN services were completed. We will discuss how to locate the return point address further in Chap. 11. Suffice it to say that the address in register 14, AF02, is within the range for module GO (greater than A600 and less than D000), and if we subtract the GO module's LPA of A600 from AF02 we find that the offset into load module GO is 902.

(7) The linkage-editor map shows that this is indeed within our COBOL program REPTIEB. (We will examine linkage-editor output in Chap. 11.)

(8) The output from the OS/VS COBOL CLIST compiler option shows that the the instruction at offset 902 is generated by the COBOL statement at line 56 in the source module.

(9) Statement 56 is the first line for OPEN

```
00056        OPEN OUTPUT PRINT-FILE
00057                    ERROR-FILE
00058             INPUT  CARD-FILE
```

The instruction at which execution was to resume after the return from the OPEN routine follows the Assembler instruction generated by the COBOL OPEN which caused the branch to the OPEN routine.

(10) Although not necessary in the present case, we could examine the contents of the DCB in the dump. We can find the address of the DCB for INFILE either by looking at the OPEN macro's register 2 (it was saved by the next supervisor routine and is shown in the SVRB below the OPEN SVRB) or by looking for the DCB for CARD-FILE in the DMAP listing and then finding the offset to the pointer for that DCB in the PGT listing. We will do it the first way since it is easier. The address is A87C.

(11) There is no DCB in the formatted portion of the dump, so we go to address A87C in the hexadecimal storage dump. This is the beginning of the DCB.

(12) At hexadecimal offset 28 into the DCB we look for either a DDname or an offset into the TIOT for the file. A87C + 28 = A8A4. At that address is a value of 0068. The fact that this is an offset rather than a DDname indicates that OPEN was at work (see Sec. 9.2.1 for a discussion of the DCB and Sec. 9.2.2 for a discussion of the TIOT).

(13) Verify that this is the proper DCB by looking at offset 68 in the formatted TIOT in the dump. We see that it does say INFILE.

(14) Going back to the DCB, we can examine the flag at offset 30. A87C + 30 = A8AC. At address A8AC we see the value 02. This means that the file is closed (see Sec. 9.2.1). This verifies that the OPEN for INFILE failed.

(15) Since we are already looking at the DCB, let us examine the LRECL. It is at hexadecimal offset 52. A87C + 52 = A8CE. At address A8CE

is the hexadecimal value 0032. This is decimal 50. That is the record length that was coded in the COBOL program.

(16) We could also verify the LRECL that we saw in the JCL. It can be found in the JFCB which was copied into the O/C/EOV work area. This work area is pointed to by the OPEN macro's register 4. Look at register 4 in the SVRB below the one for OPEN. (Remember, that supervisor routine stored the contents of OPEN's registers in its own SVRB.) The contents of register 4 is 8E37F8.

(17) To find address 8E37F8 in the dump, recall that the O/C/EOV work area is in subpool 230 (Sec. 9.2.8); look at the dump index to find the approximate location of subpool 230. It is somewhere between pages 76 and 97.

(18) Scanning pages 76 to 97 we find that subpool 230 begins on page 79.

(19) At hexadecimal offset 64 into the O/E/EOV work area we will find the DSN from the JFCB. 8E37F8 + 64 = 8E385C. The EBCDIC portion of the dump at this address does give the name MY.DATA.TEMP.

(20) At hexadecimal offset CC into the O/E/EOV is the LRECL from the JFCB for the file. 8E37F8 + CC = 8E38C4. The LRECL is hexadecimal 0050, or decimal 80. This confirms what we saw in the JCL.

10.4 SUMMARY

The COBOL programmer who wishes to become competent at debugging should learn to solve system dumps. This is especially important when the COBOL debugging tools we have already dealt with in this book are not available. Because MVS system dumps are not language-specific, dump-solving techniques can be used for programs written in any language. Since this is a COBOL debugging book, however, the examples given here combine general system dump–solving techniques with COBOL aids.

There are several types of MVS system dumps. The symptom dump, generated by the ABEND macro, is printed in the job log. It is very concise and contains information extracted from various control blocks and system storage areas. Included is the completion code, name of the load module, LPA, PSW, offset into the module of the NSI, ILC of the ABENDing instruction, actual object code for the offending instruction, and contents of the general-purpose registers at the time of the ABEND.

System storage dumps commonly received by applications programmers are those generated by the ABEND and SNAP macros. The actual format and range of storage included is dependent on options specified in the macro instructions, parameter libraries, and operator commands.

Dumps produced by the ABEND macro instruction are placed on data sets associated with either the SYSABEND, SYSMDUMP, or SYSUDUMP DD statements. Most often, as in the examples in this book, SYSUDUMP is used. Some additional formatting control over the dump generated by the ABEND macro can be provided by information which comes from the SNAP macro.

```
//S1       EXEC COBUCLG,PARM.COB='NUM,DMAP,PMAP'
//COB.SYSIN    DD DSN=MY.PROGLIB.COBOL(TABOSVS1),DISP=SHR
//GO.OUTFILE   DD SYSOUT=A
//DEFILE       DD DSN=INPUT.DEFILE.DATA,DISP=SHR
//EMFILE       DD DSN=INPUT.EMFILE.DATA,DISP=SHR
//SYSUDUMP     DD SYSOUT=A
//SYSOUT       DD SYSOUT=A
                                          .
                                          .
                                          .

IEF142I COBOLTST COB S1 - STEP WAS EXECUTED - COND CODE 0000
                                          .
                                          .
                                          .

IEF142I COBOLTST LKED S1 - STEP WAS EXECUTED - COND CODE 0000
                                          .
                                          .
                                          .

IEA995I SYMPTOM DUMP OUTPUT
SYSTEM COMPLETION CODE=0CB  REASON CODE=0000000B
 TIME=13.33.01  SEQ=00235  CPU=0000  ASID=0069
 PSW AT TIME OF ERROR  478D0000   0000BEEA  ILC 6  INTC 0B
   ACTIVE LOAD MODULE=GO           ADDRESS=0000A9D0  OFFSET=0000151A
   DATA AT PSW  0000BEE4 - FD71D218  6004F875  D218D218
   GPR  0-3  0000BC52  0000BEDE  0000BD80  4000C0F0
   GPR  4-7  0000ABE0  0000BDE4  0000AA70  00016490
   GPR  8-11 0000B138  0002F040  0000A9D0  0000A9D0
   GPR 12-15 0000B588  0000B2C0  5000BDC2  0000B9D0
 END OF SYMPTOM DUMP
                                          .
                                          .
                                          .

IEF472I COBOLTST GO S1 - COMPLETION CODE - SYSTEM=0CB USER=0000 REASON=0000000B
                                          .
                                          .
                                          .

PP 5740-CB1 RELEASE 2.4                         IBM OS/VS COBOL  JULY  1, 1982          13.32.51  DATE APR  1,1991

  1                      13.32.51        APR  1,1991

      000100 IDENTIFICATION DIVISION.
      000200 PROGRAM-ID.       TABOSVS1.
      000300 AUTHOR.           ALAN FRIEND.
      000400 DATE-WRITTEN.     4/1/91.
                                          .
                                          .
                                          .

  2        TABOSVS1       13.32.51        APR  1,1991

      003800 WORKING-STORAGE SECTION.
      003900*************************************************************
      004000*          ACCUMULATORS AND SWITCHES                        *
      004100*************************************************************
      004200 01  MISC.
      004300     05  ACCUMULATORS       COMP-3.
      004400         10  LN-CTR            PIC 99          VALUE 60.
      004500         10  PG-CTR            PIC 9(3)        VALUE ZERO.
      004600         10  NO-DEPT-EMP       PIC S99         VALUE ZERO.
      004700         10  EMP-SALARY        PIC S9(6)V99    VALUE ZERO.
      004800         10  DEPT-SALARY       PIC S9(9)V99    VALUE ZERO.
      004900         10  AVE-DEPT-SALARY   PIC S9(6)V99    VALUE ZERO.
      005000         10  TOT-NO-EMP        PIC S9(6)V99    VALUE ZERO.
      005100         10  TOT-SALARY        PIC S9(9)V99    VALUE ZERO.
      005200         10  AVE-TOT-SALARY    PIC S9(6)V99    VALUE ZERO.
                                          .
                                          .
                                          .
```

Figure 10.4 Portions of the JCL, job log, compiler output, linkage-editor listing, program output, and system dump to be used in answering the review questions at the end of this chapter. (*Continued*)

```
4        TABOSVS1        13.32.51        APR  1,1991

       PROCEDURE DIVISION.
      *****************************************************************
      *     PROGRAM INITIALIZATION, LOAD DEPARTMENT TABLE, BEGIN TO   *
      *     PROCESS EMPLOYEE RECORDS IF TABLE SUCCESSFULLY LOADED.    *
      *****************************************************************
       1000-INIT.
           OPEN INPUT    EMPFILE
                         DEPTFILE
                OUTPUT   OUTFILE
           READ DEPTFILE INTO FIRST-REC
             AT END
                DISPLAY 'TABLE FILL ERROR - DEPARTMENT FILE EMPTY'
                DISPLAY '*** PROGRAM TERMINATED ***'
                MOVE 1 TO SW-EOF.
           IF NOT NO-MORE-DEPT-RECORDS
              PERFORM 1000-LOAD-TABLE THRU 1000-LOAD-TABLE-EXIT
                VARYING DEPT-IND FROM 1 BY 1
                UNTIL DEPT-IND GREATER THAN NO-OF-ENTRIES.
           IF NOT NO-MORE-DEPT-RECORDS
              READ EMPFILE INTO EMPREC-WS
                  AT END
                     MOVE 2 TO SW-EOF
                     DISPLAY 'EMPLOYEE FILE EMPTY'.
           MOVE EMP-DEPT-WS TO DEPT-HOLD
           MOVE 2 TO SEARCH-ERROR-SW
           PERFORM 3000-COMPARE-PROCESS THRU 3000-EXIT
              UNTIL NO-MORE-EMP-RECORDS
           PERFORM 6000-DEPT-SUMMARY THRU 6000-DEPT-SUMMARY-EXIT
           CLOSE    EMPFILE
                    OUTFILE
                    DEPTFILE
           GOBACK.
5        TABOSVS1        13.32.51        APR  1,1991

      *****************************************************************
      *     LOAD DEPARTMENT TABLE                                     *
      *****************************************************************
       1000-LOAD-TABLE.
                                                     .
                                                     .
                                                     .
      *****************************************************************
      *     HEADER ROUTINE                                            *
      *****************************************************************
       2500-HEADER.
                                                     .
                                                     .
                                                     .
       3000-COMPARE-PROCESS.
           IF EMP-DEPT-WS GREATER THAN DEPT-HOLD
              PERFORM 6000-DEPT-SUMMARY THRU 6000-DEPT-SUMMARY-EXIT
              MOVE 2 TO SEARCH-ERROR-SW
              MOVE ZERO TO NO-DEPT-EMP
                           DEPT-SALARY
                           AVE-DEPT-SALARY
              SET DEPT-IND TO 1
              SEARCH DEPT-REC
                AT END
                   DISPLAY 'ERROR FOR EMPLOYEE NO. ' EMPNO-WS
                   DISPLAY 'EMPLOYEE DEPARTMENT NO. ' EMP-DEPT-WS
                           ' NOT IN DEPARTMENT TABLE'
                   MOVE 1 TO SEARCH-ERROR-SW
                WHEN DEPT-CODE (DEPT-IND) IS EQUAL TO EMP-DEPT-WS
                   MOVE DEPT-CODE (DEPT-IND) TO DEPT-CODE-OUT
                   MOVE DEPT-NAME (DEPT-IND) TO DEPT-NAME-OUT
                   WRITE OUTREC FROM SUBHEADER-1
                      AFTER ADVANCING 3
                   ADD 3 TO LN-CTR.
           IF MATCH
              PERFORM 5000-DETAIL THRU 5000-EXIT.
           READ EMPFILE INTO EMPREC-WS
              AT END MOVE 2 TO SW-EOF.
       3000-EXIT.
           EXIT.
```

Figure 10.4 *(Continued)*

```
        6        TABOSVS1        13.32.51        APR  1,1991

      021100*****************************************************************
      021200*                  WRITE DETAIL LINE.                            *
      021300*****************************************************************
      021400 5000-DETAIL.
      021500     ADD +1 TO NO-DEPT-EMP
      021600               TOT-NO-EMP
      021700     MOVE EMP-SALARY-WS TO EMP-SALARY
      021800     ADD EMP-SALARY TO DEPT-SALARY
      021900                       TOT-SALARY
      022000     IF LN-CTR GREATER THAN 55
      022100        PERFORM 2500-HEADER THRU 2500-EXIT.
      022200     MOVE EMPNO-WS TO EMPNO-OUT
      022300     MOVE EMP-NAME-WS TO EMP-NAME-OUT
      022400     MOVE EMP-SALARY-WS TO EMP-SALARY-OUT
      022500     WRITE OUTREC FROM DETAIL-1
      022600        AFTER ADVANCING 2
      022700     ADD 2 TO LN-CTR
      022800     MOVE EMP-DEPT-WS TO DEPT-HOLD.
      022900 5000-EXIT.
      023000     EXIT.
      023100*****************************************************************
      023200*             WRITE DEPARTMENT SUMMARY DETAIL LINE.              *
      023300*   IF END OF EMPLOYEE FILE, WRITE COMPANY SUMMARY DETAIL LINE  *
      023400*****************************************************************
      023500 6000-DEPT-SUMMARY.
      023600     DIVIDE DEPT-SALARY BY NO-DEPT-EMP
      023700        GIVING AVE-DEPT-SALARY
      023800     IF LN-CTR GREATER THAN 55
      023900        PERFORM 2500-HEADER THRU 2500-EXIT
      024000        MOVE AVE-DEPT-SALARY TO AVE-DEPT-SALARY-OUT
      024100        WRITE OUTREC FROM DETAIL-2
      024200           AFTER ADVANCING 2
      024300        ADD 2 TO LN-CTR
      024400     ELSE
      024500        MOVE AVE-DEPT-SALARY TO AVE-DEPT-SALARY-OUT
      024600        WRITE OUTREC FROM DETAIL-2
      024700           AFTER ADVANCING 2
      024800        ADD 2 TO LN-CTR.
      024900     IF NO-MORE-EMP-RECORDS
      025000        DIVIDE TOT-SALARY BY TOT-NO-EMP
      025100           GIVING AVE-TOT-SALARY
      025200        PERFORM 2500-HEADER THRU 2500-EXIT
      025300        MOVE AVE-TOT-SALARY TO AVE-COMPANY-SALARY-OUT
      025400        WRITE OUTREC FROM DETAIL-3
      025500           AFTER ADVANCING 2.
      025600 6000-DEPT-SUMMARY-EXIT.
      025700     EXIT.
```

Figure 10.4 *(Continued)*

The SNAP macro instruction may be used to obtain a dump of system storage without terminating the job. The dump is taken and then processing continues. A SNAP dump must be assigned to any DD statement but SYSABEND, SYSMDUMP, and SYSUDUMP. A DCB for the dump data set must be provided, and the OPEN macro must be issued before the SNAP macro is issued. As already mentioned, the SNAP macro can be used in conjunction with the ABEND macro for a task that is to be abnormally terminated.

Although Assembler programmers can issue supervisor calls for the SNAP and ABEND macro instructions to control error and dump processing in their programs, COBOL programmers usually rely on MVS to provide dump services. When necessary, however, a COBOL programmer can indirectly invoke a system dump by calling ILBOABN0.

In order to solve a system dump, it helps to follow a step-by-step debugging process. A suggested procedure is

```
  7        TABOSVS1         13.32.51         APR  1,1991

     INTRNL NAME    LVL SOURCE NAME                          BASE    DISPL    INTRNL NAME     DEFINITION    USAGE        R  O  Q  M
                                                                       .
                                                                       .
                                                                       .
     DNM=1-374      01  MISC                                 BL=4     000     DNM=1-374       DS 0CL42      GROUP
     DNM=1-394      02  ACCUMULATORS                         BL=4     000     DNM=1-394       DS 0CL38      GROUP
     DNM=1-419      03  LN-CTR                               BL=4     000     DNM=1-419       DS 2P         COMP-3
     DNM=1-435      03  PG-CTR                               BL=4     002     DNM=1-435       DS 2P         COMP-3
     DNM=1-451      03  NO-DEPT-EMP                          BL=4     004     DNM=1-451       DS 2P         COMP-3
     DNM=1-472      03  EMP-SALARY                           BL=4     006     DNM=1-472       DS 5P         COMP-3
     DNM=2-000      03  DEPT-SALARY                          BL=4     00B     DNM=2-000       DS 6P         COMP-3
     DNM=2-021      03  AVE-DEPT-SALARY                      BL=4     011     DNM=2-021       DS 5P         COMP-3
     DNM=2-046      03  TOT-NO-EMP                           BL=4     016     DNM=2-046       DS 5P         COMP-3
     DNM=2-066      03  TOT-SALARY                           BL=4     01B     DNM=2-066       DS 6P         COMP-3
     DNM=2-086      03  AVE-TOT-SALARY                       BL=4     021     DNM=2-086       DS 5P         COMP-3
                                                 .
                                                 .
                                                 .

  9        TABOSVS1         13.32.51         APR  1,1991

                        MEMORY MAP

                   TGT                      008F0
                                              .
                                              .
                                              .
               OVERFLOW CELLS               00AF0
               BL CELLS                     00AF0
               DECBADR CELLS                00B00
                                              .
                                              .
                                              .

23500   *6000-DEPT-SUMMARY
                   00150E                    PN=07    EQU    *
23600   DIVIDE     00150E  F8 75 D 218 6 00B          ZAP    218(8,13),00B(6,6)     TS=09           DNM=2-0
                   001514  FD 71 D 218 6 004          DP     218(8,13),004(2,6)     TS=09           DNM=1-451
                   00151A  F8 75 D 218 D 218          ZAP    218(8,13),218(6,13)    TS=09           TS=09
                   001520  F8 44 6 011 D 21B          ZAP    011(5,6),21B(5,13)     DNM=2-21        TS=011+1
                                              .
                                              .
                                              .
                   001526  94 0F 6 011                NI     011(6),X'0F'           DNM=2-21
24800   ADD        001604                    GN=034   EQU    *
                   001604  FA 10 6 000 C 13C          AP     000(2,6),13C(1,12)     DNM=1-419       LIT+4
                                              .
                                              .
                                              .
25000   DIVIDE     001624  F8 75 D 218 6 01B          ZAP    218(8,13),01B(6,6)     TS=09           DNM=2-66
                   00162A  F0 60 D 219 0 002          SRP    219(7,13),002(0),0     TS=010
                   001630  F8 F6 D 220 D 219          ZAP    220(16,13),219(7,13)   TS=017          TS=010
                                              .
                                              .
                                              .
  MVS/DFP VERSION 3 RELEASE 2 LINKAGE EDITOR     13:32:59  MON  APR 01, 1991
  JOB COBOLTST    STEP S1         PROCEDURE LKED
  INVOCATION PARAMETERS - LIST,XREF,LET
  ACTUAL SIZE=(317440,79872)
  OUTPUT DATA SET SYS91091.T133251.RA000.COBOLTST.GOSET IS ON VOLUME WKSH13

                                                   CROSS REFERENCE TABLE

   CONTROL SECTION                          ENTRY

     NAME     ORIGIN  LENGTH                  NAME    LOCATION      NAME    LOCATION      NAME    LOCATION      NAME    LOCATION

   TABOSVS1       00     1810
   ILBOCOM0*    1810      173
                                            ILBOCOM      1810
   ILBODSP *    1988      A08
                                            ILBODSP0     198A     ILBODSS0     198A
                                              .
                                              .
                                              .
```

Figure 10.4 *(Continued)*

```
                    D E P A R T M E N T   L I S T I N G                                    PAGE  1

10100     ALBERT J. KOPACKA               $28900.00

10200     KENNETH P. DYKSTRA              $39000.00

                    AVERAGE DEPARTMENT SALARY =  $33950.00


DEPARTMENT 20       FINANCIAL SERVICES

20100     JERILYN M. HERBERT              $37600.00

20200     DOROTHEE BURCHARTZ              $40100.00

                    AVERAGE DEPARTMENT SALARY =  $38850.00


DEPARTMENT 30       HUMAN RESOURCES

30100     JANET BAZEWICZ                  $39250.00

30200     ALAN SWEIFACH                   $27000.00

                    AVERAGE DEPARTMENT SALARY =  $33125.00


DEPARTMENT 40       ACTUARIAL SERVICES

40100     JOHNSON R. PHIPPS               $28000.00

40200     PHYLLIS E. VICKERY              $30500.00

ERROR FOR EMPLOYEE NO. 41200
EMPLOYEE DEPARTMENT NO. 41 NOT IN DEPARTMENT TABLE

JOB COBOLTST          STEP GO              TIME 133302   DATE 91091    ID = 000    CPUID = 630724153090    PAGE 00000001


COMPLETION CODE       SYSTEM = 0CB       REASON CODE = 0000000B

  PSW AT ENTRY TO ABEND   478D0000  0000BEEA  ILC  06  INTC  000B


PSW LOAD MODULE = GO         ADDRESS = 0000BEEA  OFFSET = 0000151A
                                                 .
                                                 .
                                                 .

 PRB: 008FA2A8
          -0020  XSB...... 008FA310  FLAGS2... 00000000  RTPSW1... 478D0000  0000BEEA            RTPSW2... 0006000B
          -000C            03900070  FLAGS1... 00000000  WLIC..... 0006000B
          +0000  RSV...... 00000000  00000000            SZSTAB... 00110082  FLCDE.... 008FE000
          +0010  OPSW..... 478D0000  0000BEEA            SQE...... 00000000  LINK..... 008FA3A8
                                                 .
                                                 .
                                                 .

 SVRB: 008FD348
          -0020  XSB...... 008FD418  FLAGS2... 00000000  RTPSW1... 00000000  00000000            RTPSW2... 00000000
          -000C            00000000  FLAGS1... 22000000  WLIC..... 00020033
          +0000  RSV...... 00000000  00000000            SZSTAB... 001ED022  FLCDE.... 00000000
          +0010  OPSW..... 470C1000  820A24C6            Q........ 00000000  LINK..... 008FA2A8
                                                 .
                                                 .
                                                 .

 SVRB: 008FD4B8
          -0020  XSB...... 008FD588  FLAGS2... 00000000  RTPSW1... 00000000  00000000            RTPSW2... 00000000
          -000C            00000000  FLAGS1... 02000000  WLIC..... 00020078
          +0000  RSV...... 00000000  00000000            SZSTAB... 001ED022  FLCDE.... 00000000
          +0010  OPSW..... 470C1000  80E7291E            Q........ 00000000  LINK..... 008FD348
                                                 .
                                                 .
                                                 .
CDE
       008FE000  CHAIN.... 00000000  RRBP..... 008FA2A8  NAME..... GO        ENTPT.... 0000A9D0  XLMJP.... 008E1020
          +0018  USE...... 0001      ATTRB.... 00        SP....... FB        ATTR..... 0B        ATTR2.... 20
          +001E  ATTR3.... 0000

XTLST
       008E1020  LNTH..... 00000010  NRFAC.... 00000001  MSBLA.... 80004630  MSBAD.... 0000A9D0

                                                 .
                                                 .
                                                 .
```

Figure 10.4 *(Continued)*

```
JOB COBOLTST          STEP GO              TIME 133302   DATE 91091     ID = 000                          PAGE 00000082

ACTIVE LOAD MODULES

LPA/JPA MODULE    GO
0000A9C0                                        90ECD00C 185D05F0 4580F010 E3C1C2D6   *                .......0..0.TABO*
0000A9E0 E2E5E2F1 E5E2D9F1 0700989F F02407FF    96021034 07FE41F0 000107FE 0000C132   *SVS1VSR1....0..........0......A.*
0000AA00 0000A9D0 0000A9D0 0000B588 0000B2C0    0000B7DC 0000C0F2 00000000 00000000   *.......................2........*
0000AA20 00000000 00000000 00000000 00000000    00000000 00000000 00000000 00000000   *................................*
0000AA40 00000000 00000000 00000000 00000000    00000000 00000000 F1F34BF3 F24BF5F1   *........................13.32.51*
0000AA60 C1D7D940 40F16B40 F1F9F9F1 00000000    034F001F 000C0030 50000C00 00000000   *APR  1. 1991....................*
0000AA80 0C000000 000C0000 00800C00 02703500    0C000000 000CF4F0 F0F10000 00000000   *......................4001......*
0000AAA0 F1F04040 40404040 40404040 40404040    40404040 40404040 40404040 40404040   *10                              *
0000AAC0 F1F0C4C1 E3C140D7 D9D6C3C5 E2E2C9D5    C7404040 40404040 40404040 40404040   *10DATA PROCESSING               *
0000AAE0 F1F5C1E4 C4C9E3C9 D5C74040 40404040    40404040 40404040 40404040 40404040   *15AUDITING                      *
0000AB00 F2F0C6C9 D5C1D5C3 C9C1D340 E2C5D9E5    C9C3C5E2 40404040 40404040 40404040   *20FINANCIAL SERVICES            *
0000AB20 F2F5C8C5 C1D3E3C8 40E2C5D9 E5C9C3C5    E2404040 40404040 40404040 40404040   *25HEALTH SERVICES               *
0000AB40 F3F0C8E4 D4C1D540 D9C5E2D6 E4D9C3C5    E2404040 40404040 40404040 40404040   *30HUMAN RESOURCES               *
0000AB60 F3F5C2E4 C9D3C4C9 D5C740E2 C5D9E5C9    C3C5E240 40404040 40404040 40404040   *35BUILDING SERVICES             *
0000AB80 F4F0C1C3 E3E4C1D9 C9C1D340 E2C5D9E5    C9C3C5E2 40404040 40404040 40404040   *40ACTUARIAL SERVICES            *
0000ABA0 F5F0D9C5 E2C5C1D9 C3C840C1 D5C440C4    C5E5C5D3 D6D7D4C5 D5E34040 40404040   *50RESEARCH AND DEVELOPMENT      *
0000ABC0 F6F0D4C1 D9D2C5E3 C9D5C740 40404040    40404040 40404040 40404040 40404040   *60MARKETING                     *
0000ABE0 F7F0D7E4 C2D3C9C3 40D9C5D3 C1E3C9D6    D5E24040 40404040 40404040 40404040   *70PUBLIC RELATIONS              *
0000AC00 00000000 00000000 00000000 00000000    00000000 00000000 00000000 00000000   *................................*
                                                        .
                                                        .
                                                        .
0000B460 00000000 00000000 00000000 4000C776    0000A9D0 00000000 0000C1E0 E2E8E2D6   *............ .G...........A.SYSO*
0000B480 E4E34040 E380000C 0000AA58 00000000    00000000 00000000 00000000 00000000   *UT  T...........................*
0000B4A0 00000000 00000000 00000000 00000000    00000000 00000000 00000000 00000000   *................................*
0000B4C0 00016490 0000B138 0002F040 0000AA70    00000000 0000000F 00000000 0000000C   *..........0 ....................*
0000B4E0 00000000 00000000 00000000 00000000    00000000 0000010F F04BF0F0 00000000   *.......................0.00.....*
0000B500 00000000 00000000 01400000 00000140    0000ABE0 0000AB82 0000BBD8 0000BDEA   *......... ..... ...........Q....*
0000B520 00000000 0000C08E 0000BEDE 0000BC30    00000000 00000000 0000BBD8 00000000   *...........................Q....*
0000B540 0000B9B8 00000000 0000BC52 00000000    0000BC30 00000000 0000BEDE 00000000   *................................*
0000B560 0000AF34 0000B1DC 8F00B050 00000000    1400B137 00000002 8000B050 00000000   *................................*
0000B580 00000000 00000000 0000DDDA 0000CDCE    0000DDDA 0000CD66 0000D5C2 0000CDCA   *.........................NB....*
0000B5A0 0000C35A 0000DDDE 0000E2AA 0000BB52    0000BBD2 0000BBD8 0000BC30 0000BDE4   *..C.......S........K...Q.......U*
0000B5C0 0000BDEA 0000BEDE 0000C088 0000C08E    0000C0A4 0000C0EA 0000B8AA 0000B8D6   *...............................O*
0000B5E0 0000B940 0000B90A 0000B92A 0000B8FC    0000B938 0000B99A 0000B982 0000B9B8   *... ............................*
0000B600 0000B9D0 0000B9EE 0000BB92 0000BC24    0000BD80 0000BC52 0000BD60 0000BC7C   *................................*
0000B620 0000BCCC 0000BD52 0000BD3E 0000BDB0    0000BDA8 0000BDE0 0000BE60 0000BE58   *................................*
0000B640 0000BEC0 0000BF86 0000BF1C 0000BF72    0000BFE2 0000BFD4 0000C032 0000B89C   *..................S...M.........*
0000B660 0000B97C 0000BA18 0000BA4E 0000BAAC    0000BAE6 0000BB28 0000BB28 0000BB8C   *..................W.............*
0000B680 0000BDDA 0000C0E8 0000C0E4 0000AF34    0000B050 0000B1DC 0000BBD8 00000000   *.......Y...U...............Q....*
0000B6A0 0000BDEA 00000000 0000C08E 00000000    0000BC30 00000000 0000BEDE 00000000   *................................*
```

Figure 10.4 *(Continued)*

1. Determine the type and location of the ABEND.
2. Review your actions.
3. Check how far the program executed.
4. Review the output from any COBOL debugging aids which were in effect.
5. Check to see if the JCL is correct.
6. Analyze the SYMPTOM DUMP.
7. If necessary, examine the actual system dump.
8. Examine the COBOL instruction and operands within the program.

With a plan in hand and a bit of practice, you should become a capable system dump solver.

REVIEW QUESTIONS

A job involving a COBOL program ABENDed. The following questions are based on the job output shown in Fig. 10.4.

1. What is the completion code? What does this completion code signify?

2. Which step ABENDed? Are there indications that any previous job or procedure steps had problems?

3. What is the name of the active load module? What is its LPA?

4. What is the PSW? What is the address of the NSI?

5. What is the address of the ABENDing instruction? What is its Op Code? Which Assembler instruction is this?

6. What is the name of the load module where the ABENDing instruction is located? What is its offset into the module? What CSECT is it in?

7. Under which version of COBOL was this program compiled? Write the complete COBOL instruction which was executing at the time of the ABEND.

8. Name any COBOL fields which need to be examined. Find their hexadecimal storage addresses.

9. Examine the contents of the problem field in the dump. What is its value?

10. How did the problem field get the value you found in question 9? Identify any line numbers in the source module where the field was changed.

11. What would you do to prevent this ABEND in the future?

Chapter

11

Multimodule Dumps

The last chapter covered system dump solving. We assumed that only one COBOL program was being executed. Solving system dumps for jobs with multiple load modules or with load modules containing more than one COBOL program involves some additional considerations. The main program may call one or more subprograms; it is necessary to determine whether the call is static or dynamic, to find the load module with the ABENDing instruction, and to find the actual COBOL program containing the ABENDing instruction.

In this chapter we will discuss standard program linkage conventions, the purpose and contents of the Save Area, general-purpose register assignments, how to trace through called programs using the Save Area trace, and linkage-editor output. We will then give examples of solving multimodule dumps.

11.1 THE SAVE AREA

As previously discussed (Sec. 2.2.1.11), the Save Area for a COBOL program is at the beginning of the TGT. It is pointed to by general-purpose register 13. In order to follow standard linkage conventions, all programs, regardless of the language, must have a Save Area. Unlike an Assembler programmer, who must provide for the Save Area within the source code, a COBOL programmer does not need to be concerned with creating or maintaining it; COBOL handles Save Area requirements automatically. Many COBOL programmers, in fact, are unaware of its existence or its importance.

The Save Area must contain information which enables the operating system and each calling program to keep track of the flow of control as programs branch to and return from other programs. The Save Area is 18 fullwords (72 bytes) in size.

Upon entering your program, standard linkage conventions require that your program:

- Save the contents of the calling program's general-purpose registers in the calling program's Save Area. Recall our analysis of the first Assembler instruction in an OS/VS COBOL program and the second instruction in a COBOL II program in Secs. 8.2.1 and 8.2.2; it was

  ```
  STM 14,12,12(13)
  ```

  This instruction put the contents of registers 14, 15, and 0 through 12 into word 4 through word 18 of the calling program's Save Area, pointed to by the address in register 13. The calling program may be an operating system routine.
- Create a Save Area for subsequent subprograms.
- Store the address of the caller's Save Area in your program's Save Area.
- Place the address of your Save Area in register 13.

Upon exiting your program, your program must:

- Adjust the contents of register 13 to point back to the caller's Save Area.
- Restore the general-purpose registers (other than register 15) to the contents as they were in the calling program. This is done by retrieving the data from the calling program's Save Area.
- Establish a return code in register 15.
- Return to the caller through the address in register 14.

Figure 11.1 shows the format of a Save Area. In a COBOL II program, the first word of the Save Area will always contain hexadecimal 00108001. This makes it easy to verify that you are looking at the Save Area for a COBOL II program when debugging a module containing programs of several languages. The first word of an OS/VS COBOL Save Area contains 00300000.

Word 2 of a Save Area is known as the High Save Area (HSA) pointer. It contains the address of the Save Area of the program which called the current program.

Word 3 of a Save Area is referred to as the Low Save Area (LSA) pointer. It contains the address of the Save Area for a program called by the current program. As can be seen, the HSA and LSA establish a forward and backward Save Area chain which permits a Save Area trace to be generated. We will discuss this further in Sec. 11.3.

Word 4 contains the return point address into the current program (a called program will return control to this address) taken from register 14, and word 5 contains the entry point address into the next called subprogram taken from register 15 (see Sec. 11.2 for more about registers 14 and 15).

The remainder of the Save Area contains the contents of registers 0 through 12 for the current program at the time it called the subprogram.

Figure 11.2 illustrates what the Save Areas for a main program (SaveMain), the subprogram it calls (SaveSub1), and the next subprogram called by the

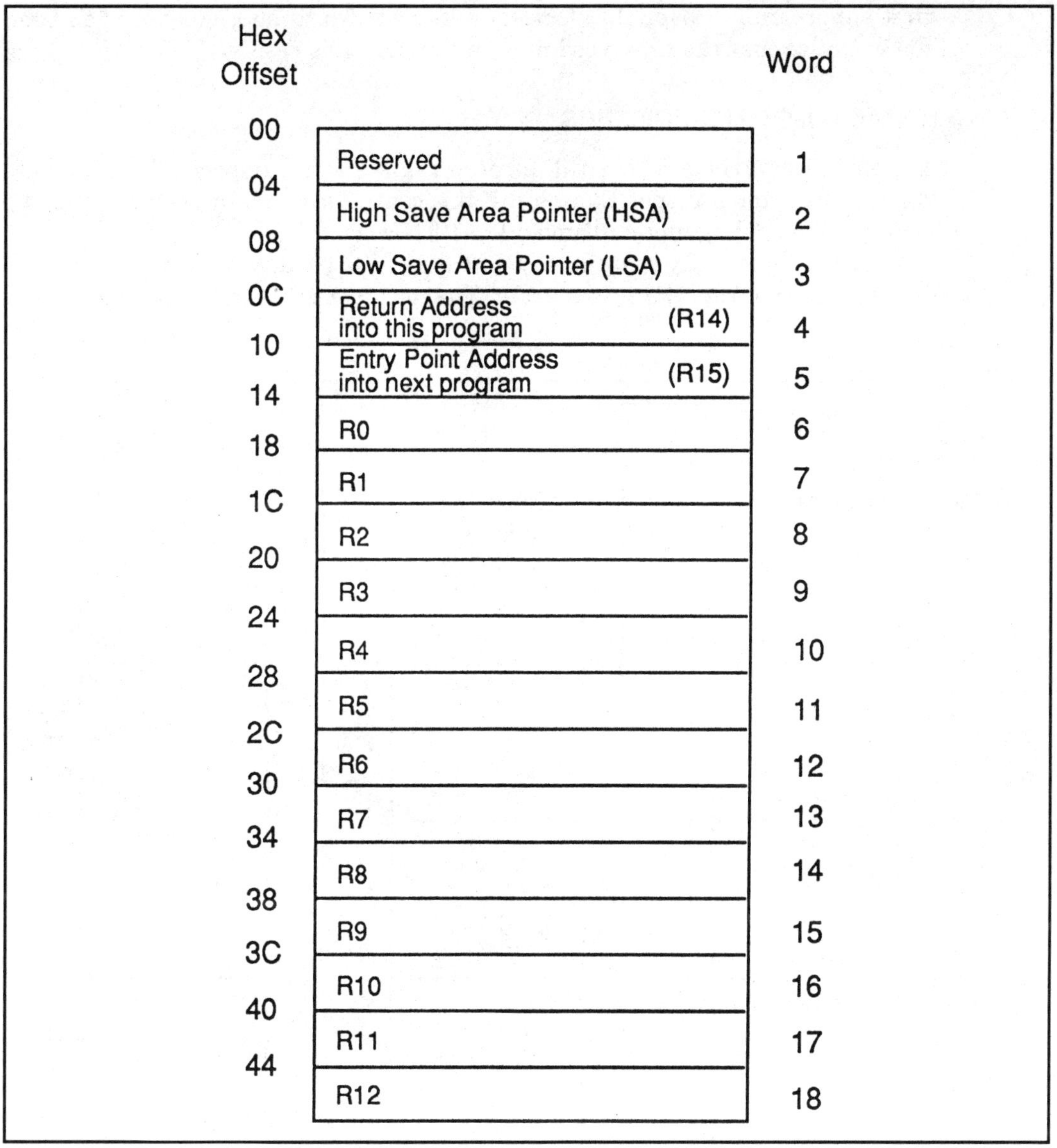

Figure 11.1 A program Save Area.

first subprogram (SaveSub2) look like after standard housekeeping has been done. Notice that the first word in each Save Area is reserved.

11.2 GENERAL-PURPOSE REGISTERS

By convention, certain general-purpose registers have specific assignments during program linkage. Examining the contents of these registers can be helpful when debugging multimodule ABENDs.

Register 1 generally contains the address of the parameter list used in passing data to and from the subprogram. The parameter list consists of the actual

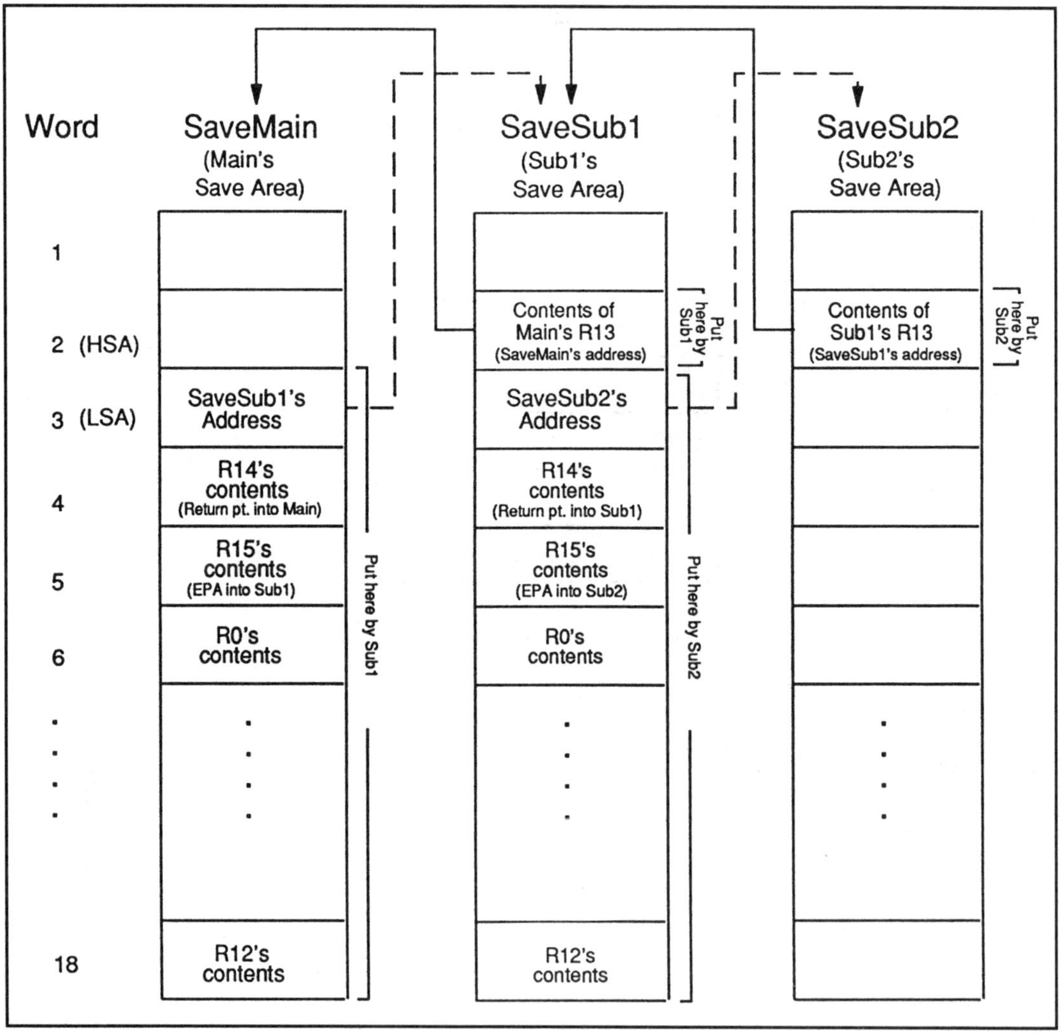

Figure 11.2 The Save Areas for a main program and two subprograms after standard housekeeping has been done.

addresses of the parameters. When a COBOL program issues a CALL. . . USING data names, the calling program is passing the addresses of the parameters (data names) in the calling program to the subprogram, not the actual values of parameters. This is referred to as a CALL "by reference." This is the only type of CALL available in OS/VS COBOL and is the default in COBOL II.

Because COBOL II also allows a CALL. . .USING BY CONTENT. . . , in which the addresses of copies of the parameters (COBOL places the copies in TEMPORARY STORAGE-2) are passed to the subprogram, the USING BY REFERENCE phrase can be coded to avoid any possible confusion.

Figure 11.3 illustrates a CALL for the statement

```
CALL 'SUB' USING FIELD-A
                 FIELD-B
                 FIELD-C
```

Register 1 points to the start of the parameter list, and the parameter list itself consists of fullword addresses for the beginning locations of FIELD-A, FIELD-B, and FIELD-C. Note that the high-order bit of the last address in the list will be 1, designating the end of the list; the high-order bits of the preceding addresses will be 0.

Recall (see Secs. 2.2.1.3 and 2.2.1.4) that base locator cells in the main and called programs can be used to find the base addresses of any program fields in a COBOL program. In the event that the cells for passed parameters are overlaid, register 1 may be examined to verify the integrity of the parameter addresses at the time of an ABEND.

If a parameter is passed to the main program through JCL, register 1 at the entry to the program will contain the address of the data given in the PARM clause in the JCL. The first halfword at that address will be the length of the parameter string in binary, calculated and placed there by the operating sys-

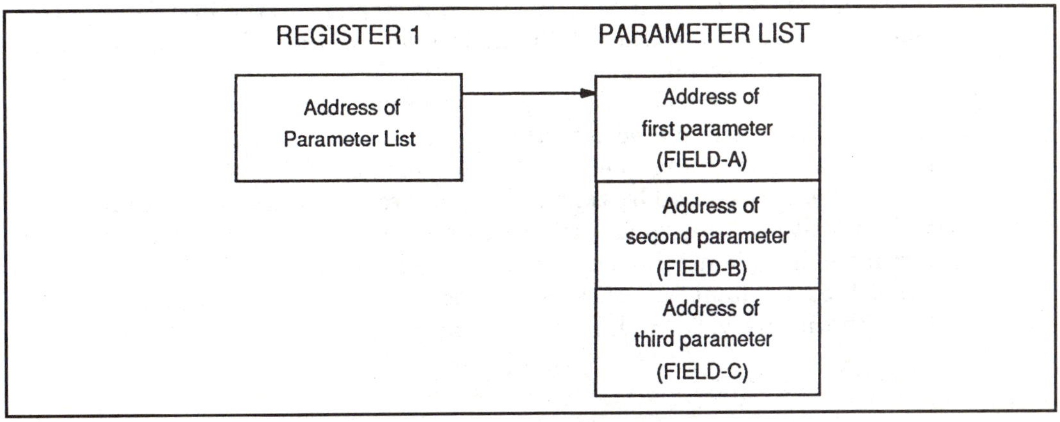

Figure 11.3 General-purpose register 1 pointing to a parameter list in a COBOL CALL statement.

tem. The following bytes will contain the actual parameter string up to the allowable maximum of 100 bytes.

Register 0 is generally used for passing additional parameters to certain supervisor routines.

Register 13, as already mentioned, contains the address of the Save Area. In COBOL it also points to the TGT since the Save Area is at the beginning of the TGT. Register 13 can be used to locate the Save Area, although we will see in Sec. 11.3 that there is another way to find the Save Area.

Upon entering a program, register 14 contains the return-point address into the program which called it. This is the address of the instruction following that which caused the branch to the current program. It was stored in register 14 by an Assembler instruction just before the transfer took place so that execution could resume at the next instruction in the calling program. The called program saves the contents of register 14 in word 4 of the calling program's Save Area. Knowing this address can be important when you need to find out in what program the transfer of control originated, as when a "wild" branch causes control to be given to a location in protected storage (a protection exception, or S0C4 ABEND).

When a program is entered, register 15 contains the entry point address of this called program. It was placed there by an Assembler instruction just before control was transferred to this program from the calling program. The called program saves the contents of register 15 in word 5 of the caller's Save Area.

The Assembler instruction

```
BALR 14,15
```

may be seen when you scan the calling program's PROCEDURE DIVISION map. BALR is the Branch And Link Registers instruction. Its format is

```
BALR first register, second register
```

It places the address of the instruction following it into the first register (register 14) and then branches to the instruction whose address was previously loaded into the second register (register 15). An instruction at the end of the called routine causes a branch back to the return point, that is, the instruction whose address was placed into the first register (register 14) by the BALR instruction. Examining the contents of registers 15 and 14 will give the intended entry-point address and return address for a transfer of control.

Upon exiting a program, a return code is placed into register 15. Although Assembler programmers code an instruction to load a value in register 15, COBOL as a default will set a return code of 0 to indicate successful completion. Alternatively, COBOL programmers can code

```
MOVE value TO RETURN-CODE
```

to set their own return code. RETURN-CODE, as described in Sec. 1.3, is a special COBOL register. When COBOL is ready to transfer control back to the operating system, the return code is moved to register 15.

11.3 THE SAVE AREA TRACE

The Save Area Trace appears near the end of the formatted portion of a system dump. It can be helpful when dealing with a multimodule ABEND because it shows the chain of Save Areas for calling and called modules including, in the case of COBOL, subroutines from the COBOL subroutine library. Information available for each Save Area in the chain includes the standard items expected in a Save Area, namely the contents of the HSA and LSA, the return-point address into the the present program, the entry-point address into the next called program, and the contents of the registers for the current program when it passed control to the next program in the chain.

Figure 11.4 illustrates a Save Area trace. The forward trace is shown between the headings SAVE AREA TRACE and INTERRUPT AT. The first Save Area, pointed to by letter "A" in the figure, is that of the supervisor (an operating system program). Its contents were put there by the next called program. Following Save Areas are for modules which are called or linked to. The last Save Area is the one most recently created. The item at letter "B," DMPCOB2B WAS ENTERED VIA LINK, specifies that the supervisor passed control to the next program, DMPCOB2B, by means of the LINK macro. The item AT EP DMPCOB2B, shown at letter "C," is the name of the entry point into the called program, and its entry-point address is shown by the field EPA in the present Save Area (letter "D").

The Save Area pointed to by letter "E" in Fig. 11.4 is that of the program called by the supervisor, DMPCOB2B. Words 3 through 18 were filled in by the next called program in the chain, IGZCPAC. (Prefix IGZ is used for routines in the COBOL II subroutine library.) The value in word 2 was put there by DMPCOB2B. Notice that word 1 in this Save Area contains the value 00108001; this signifies that the Save Area is for a COBOL II program. To verify that this is the Save Area for DMPCOB2B, you can go 5 bytes past the entry-point address (indicated by letter "D") in the dump. You will find the name DMPCOB2B, copied there from the IDENTIFICATION DIVISION by the COBOL II initialization routine generated by the compiler. For an OS/VS COBOL program, the name will be at hexadecimal displacement 12 from the entry-point address.

The format for the succeeding Save Areas normally follows the same conventions. Each HSA and LSA points to its preceding and succeeding Save Area. Note, however, that the Save Area trace is not always useful since there is no guarantee that a called subroutine has actually followed standard linkage conventions. The message at letter "F," "INVALID (or INCORRECT) BACK CHAIN" indicates the next Save Area printed may be invalid because its HSA does not point to the previous Save Area. It seems ironic that some IBM routines do not adhere to the "standard" linkage conventions. Some registers may be used for dual purposes.

```
                                                              (C)
    SAVE AREA TRACE                                                                                       (D)
(B)→DMPCOB2B WAS ENTERED VIA LINK       AT EP DMPCOB2B.C2.1.2.0.10.21.88.11.43.03

    SA    00005FA8  WD1 00000000   HSA 00000000   LSA 00006410   RET 80FCF548   EPA 80006138   R0  FD00000F
(A)→                R1  00005FF0   R2  00000040   R3  008F6774   R4  008F6750   R5  008FB8A8   R6  008DAFF8
                    R7  FD000000   R8  008D0140   R9  8089DE50   R10 00000000   R11 008FB8A8   R12 00E509AA
                                                                                                          (J)
    IGZCPAC  WAS ENTERED VIA CALL       AT EP .IGZCLNK...C22.012.15.87.09.13...N.....

    SA    00006410  WD1 00108001   HSA 00005FA8   LSA 00038FF0   RET 8000634A   EPA 8000A290   R0  80006DBE
(E)→                R1  00006254   R2  000052E4   R3  00006B34   R4  0000618C   R5  00038CC8   R6  008DAFF8
                    R7  FD000000   R8  00005FF6   R9  00006728   R10 000061C4   R11 00000000   R12 000061B8

    DMPCOB26 WAS ENTERED VIA CALL       AT EP subcob26.C2.1.2.0.10.21.88.11.43.43

    SA    00038FF0  WD1 00102401   HSA 00006410   LSA 000077A0   RET 8000A7B8   EPA 80007520   R0  000000F8
(I)→                R1  0000656C   R2  80007E14   R3  00006138   R4  00006254   R5  000390E8   R6  000390E8
                    R7  00000000   R8  8000A7BA   R9  00006410   R10 00038CC8   R11 00000000   R12 8000A2C2

    IGZCPAC  WAS ENTERED VIA CALL       AT EP .IGZCDSP...C22.011.25.87.14.25...N.....

    SA    000077A0  WD1 00108001   HSA 00038FF0   LSA 000380B0   RET 80007730   EPA 80009DE0   R0  00007C06
(H)→                R1  000076E3   R2  000052E4   R3  00006138   R4  00007574   R5  00038FF0   R6  000390E8
                    R7  00FCF4F8   R8  00005FF6   R9  000078F8   R10 000075A8   R11 000052E4   R12 000075A0

    IGZCPCO  WAS ENTERED VIA CALL       AT EP .IGZEOUT...C22.009.29.87.12.14...O.....

    SA    000380B0  WD1 00100001   HSA 000077A0   LSA 000381A0   RET 8000A174   EPA 00026158   R0  00007C06
                    R1  00038134   R2  00000013   R3  000075B0   R4  000075B0   R5  00000000   R6  0003AF94
                    R7  00000065   R8  80007E14   R9  000077A0   R10 00038CC8   R11 000052E4   R12 80009E12

    SA    000381A0  WD1 00101001   HSA 000380B0   LSA 8001D1C0   RET 4002643C   EPA 92CB50B8   R0  00007C06
                    R1  0003AF80   R2  00038F50   R3  000075B0   R4  000075B0   R5  00000000   R6  00038134
                    R7  00000065   R8  80007E14   R9  000077A0   R10 00000004   R11 000052E4   R12 5002618A

(F)→INVALID BACK CHAIN

    SA    0001D1C0  WD1 47F0F02C   HSA 2740C9C7   LSA E9C3E5D3   RET C4404200   EPA C3F2F24B   R0  F0F1F061
                    R1  F1F461F8   R2  F640F1F9   R3  4BF3F040   R4  4040D500   R5  00000000   R6  90ECD00C
                    R7  05B050D0   R8  80905820   R9  B29658D0   R10 818C1A2D   R11 59208188   R12 4740B024

(G)→INTERRUPT AT 80007778

    PROCEEDING BACK VIA REG 13

    IGZCPAC  WAS ENTERED VIA CALL       AT EP .IGZCDSP...C22.011.25.87.14.25...N.....

    SA    000077A0  WD1 00108001   HSA 00038FF0   LSA 000380B0   RET 80007730   EPA 80009DE0   R0  00007C06
                    R1  000076E3   R2  000052E4   R3  00006138   R4  00007574   R5  00038FF0   R6  000390E8
                    R7  00FCF4F8   R8  00005FF6   R9  000078F8   R10 000075A8   R11 000052E4   R12 000075A0

    DMPCOB26 WAS ENTERED VIA CALL       AT EP subcob26.C2.1.2.0.10.21.88.11.43.43

    SA    00038FF0  WD1 00102401   HSA 00006410   LSA 000077A0   RET 8000A7B8   EPA 80007520   R0  000000F8
                    R1  0000656C   R2  80007E14   R3  00006138   R4  00006254   R5  000390E8   R6  000390E8
                    R7  00000000   R8  8000A7BA   R9  00006410   R10 00038CC8   R11 00000000   R12 8000A2C2
```

Figure 11.4 The Save Area trace in a system dump.

The message shown at letter "G" in Fig. 11.4, INTERRUPT AT, marks the end of the forward trace. The instruction address is taken from the OPSW field in the last PRB in the RB queue, and is that of the next instruction to be executed in the last module that was entered. It is not necessarily the NSI address from the PSW AT ENTRY TO ABEND, and may not point to the address of the instruction which follows the ABENDing instruction in either the application program or a supervisor routine.

The backward trace follows the heading PROCEEDING BACK VIA REGISTER 13. Save Areas appear in the reverse order of that for the forward trace.

Here is an example of how we might use the Save Area trace (see Fig. 11.4). Assume that we suspect our COBOL subprogram ABENDed because it received a bad parameter from the calling COBOL program. We would like to locate the CALL statement in the main COBOL program. Subprogram DMPCOB26 contains the ABENDing instruction. Its Save Area is at letter "H" in the figure. We see that DMPCOB26 received control from IGZCPAC, whose save area is shown at letter "I." IGZCPAC in turn received control from DMPCOB2B, whose Save Area is pointed to by letter "E." We can tell that both DMPCOB26 and DMPCOB2B are COBOL II programs because word 1 of their Save Areas contain 00108001. The intermediate module, IGZCPAC, comes from the COBOL II subroutine library, as evidenced by its prefix; it contains numerous general library routines. The entry point IGZCLNK is the linkage manager routine; its purpose is to provide execution-time support for the CALL verb which effects the transfer of control to DMPCOB26.

Subtracting the beginning address of DMPCOB2B (this is the LPA, taken from the XTLST entry for DMPCOB2B) from the return address into DMPCOB2B, given in the RET field in DMPCOB2B's Save Area (at letter "J") gives the offset into DMPCOB2B for the instruction following the CALL to IGZCPAC. In the present example, program DMPCOB2B is the first CSECT in load module DMPCOB2B, and the LPA and EPA are the same. (The field labeled EPA in the Supervisor's Save Area, at letter "D," gives the EPA for DMPCOB2D.) 634A – 6138 = 212. The instruction is at offset 212 in program DMPCOB2B. Note that the EPA is not necessarily at the physical beginning of a load module; you can determine this by examining the LPA and EPA given in the XTLST and CDE, respectively.

11.4 LINKAGE-EDITOR OUTPUT

The purpose of the linkage-editor is to create an executable load module from the object module produced by the compiler. The object module is relocatable, but is composed of machine code which cannot be executed. Relocatable means that the addresses of the code can be adjusted to make up for a change in the code's origin. The load module is both relocatable and has machine code in an executable format.

A load module normally consists of many relocatable program units known as control sections (CSECTs). Each compiled COBOL (or other language) program comprises one or more CSECTs. Also, each routine from the COBOL subroutine library (or other language subroutine library) comprises a CSECT. Because CSECTs may have instructions which refer to other CSECTS, as when a CALL statement is issued, there must be a mechanism which allows CSECTs to find one another. The linkage-editor assigns consecutive relative displacements from the origin of the load module to all CSECTs and resolves all references between statically linked CSECTs. Thus a COBOL CALL statement referring to another CSECT in the load module has that CSECT's location available to it. When a load module is to be executed, it is fetched into virtual storage at a specific location. For all relocatable code in the load module, program fetch increments all relative displacements from the origin of the load module by the actual virtual storage address.

The linkage-editor also generates maps and diagnostic output. We saw parts of this output when we were solving the ABENDs in Chap. 10. We will look at it more closely now.

11.4.1 Linkage-Editor Maps and Diagnostic Output

Figure 11.5 shows part of the diagnostic output produced by the linkage-editor. It is comprised of a series of messages, maps, and cross-reference tables. Letter "A" shows linkage-editor options and attributes which were in effect. Options can be passed to the linkage-editor from the JCL. In this example, the options were LIST, XREF, LET, and MAP.

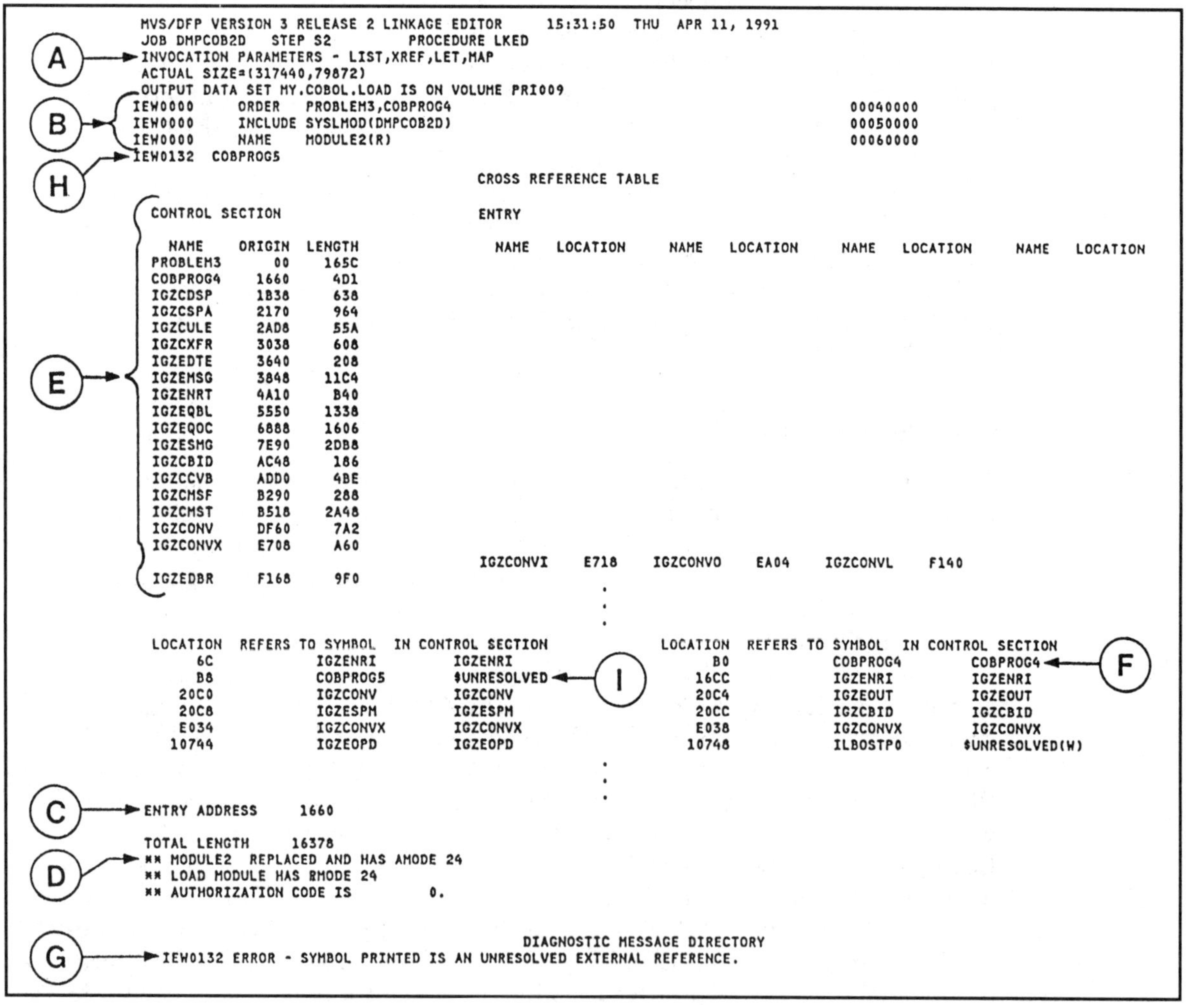


```
MVS/DFP VERSION 3 RELEASE 2 LINKAGE EDITOR      15:31:50  THU  APR 11, 1991
JOB DMPCOB2D    STEP S2         PROCEDURE LKED
INVOCATION PARAMETERS - LIST,XREF,LET,MAP
ACTUAL SIZE=(317440,79872)
OUTPUT DATA SET MY.COBOL.LOAD IS ON VOLUME PRI009
IEW0000      ORDER    PROBLEM3,COBPROG4                                   00040000
IEW0000      INCLUDE SYSLMOD(DMPCOB2D)                                    00050000
IEW0000      NAME     MODULE2(R)                                          00060000
IEW0132   COBPROG5
                                          CROSS REFERENCE TABLE

 CONTROL SECTION                          ENTRY

   NAME     ORIGIN   LENGTH                 NAME   LOCATION     NAME   LOCATION     NAME   LOCATION     NAME   LOCATION
 PROBLEM3       00     165C
 COBPROG4     1660      4D1
 IGZCDSP      1B38      638
 IGZCSPA      2170      964
 IGZCULE      2AD8      55A
 IGZCXFR      3038      608
 IGZEDTE      3640      208
 IGZEMSG      3848     11C4
 IGZENRT      4A10      B40
 IGZEQBL      5550     1338
 IGZEQOC      6888     1606
 IGZESMG      7E90     2DB8
 IGZCBID      AC48      186
 IGZCCVB      ADD0      4BE
 IGZCMSF      B290      288
 IGZCMST      B518     2A48
 IGZCONV      DF60      7A2
 IGZCONVX     E708      A60
                                          IGZCONVI      E718    IGZCONVO      EA04    IGZCONVL      F140
 IGZEDBR      F168      9F0
                                                   .
                                                   .
                                                   .

 LOCATION  REFERS TO SYMBOL  IN CONTROL SECTION          LOCATION  REFERS TO SYMBOL  IN CONTROL SECTION
       6C          IGZENRI         IGZENRI                       B0          COBPROG4         COBPROG4
       B8          COBPROG5        $UNRESOLVED                 16CC          IGZENRI          IGZENRI
     20C0          IGZCONV         IGZCONV                     20C4          IGZEOUT          IGZEOUT
     20C8          IGZESPM         IGZESPM                     20CC          IGZCBID          IGZCBID
     E034          IGZCONVX        IGZCONVX                    E038          IGZCONVX         IGZCONVX
    10744          IGZEOPD         IGZEOPD                    10748          ILBOSTP0         $UNRESOLVED(W)
                                                   .
                                                   .
                                                   .
 ENTRY ADDRESS      1660

 TOTAL LENGTH      16378
 ** MODULE2  REPLACED AND HAS AMODE 24
 ** LOAD MODULE HAS RMODE 24
 ** AUTHORIZATION CODE IS          0.

                                              DIAGNOSTIC MESSAGE DIRECTORY
   IEW0132 ERROR - SYMBOL PRINTED IS AN UNRESOLVED EXTERNAL REFERENCE.
```

Figure 11.5 Portions of the diagnostic output generated by the linkage-editor.

LIST produces a listing of the linkage-editor control statements which were used as input to the linkage-editor. The message code IEW0000 and the control statement appear near the top of the output, as shown by letter "B" in the figure. Typical control statements used are INCLUDE, ORDER, ENTRY, and NAME.

The INCLUDE statement specifies what physical sequential data sets and libraries are to be used as additional input to the linkage-editor. The INCLUDE statement in Fig. 11.5 refers to DD card SYSLMOD which is assigned to a load library containing the module DMPCOB2D. Either load modules or object modules can be included.

The ORDER statement is used to indicate in what sequence the CSECTs are to be positioned in the load module. It may be used to minimize paging by placing CSECTs which call one another near each other. When ORDER is not specified, the CSECTs will be placed in the order in which the linkage-editor receives and processes them.

Although the first statement in the first CSECT in a load module is normally where execution can be expected to start, this is not necessarily the case, particularly when a load module has been reprocessed. The ENTRY statement is used to indicate explicitly where execution is to begin. A message near the end of the linkage-editor output indicates the relative entry-point location for the load module (see letter "C" in Fig. 11.5). In the current case (see Fig. 11.5) no ENTRY statement was in effect. Notice that the module was replaced (reprocessed) (letter "D") and that the entry point is at offset 1660. This is the origin of the second CSECT, COBPROG4.

I remember a problem in which a program intermittently ABENDed with an S0C4 completion code (protection exception). The big mystery was that the program terminated normally the first time the load module was executed but ABENDed the second time. In my testing, I changed a compiler option, recompiled, and relinked. Again, the program terminated normally. After verifying that neither the program nor the input data set had been changed, I found that the ABEND was caused because execution of the load module was beginning with a called program instead of the main program; the ABEND occurred when the called program tried to access parameters which were to have come from the main program but which were not available because the main program had never executed. Although the main program was the first CSECT in the load module, execution had begun elsewhere. No ENTRY statement had been coded. The moral: Be safe; always code an ENTRY statement.

The NAME statement names the load module produced by the linkage-editor. This is the name referred to on the PGM= parameter of the JCL EXEC statement which invokes execution of the load module. The module's name, and whether or not it replaced an existing module with that name in the load library, is printed near the bottom of the diagnostic output (letter "D").

Getting back to linkage-editor options, the XREF option produces what is commonly called the link-edit map; it actually consists of both a cross-reference table and a module map. As is seen at letter "E" in Fig. 11.5, the first three columns of the module map list CSECT names, relative positions within the load module, and CSECT lengths. Any names followed by an asterisk (*) are resolved using the automatic library-call mechanism; this mechanism searches libraries defined on the SYSLIB DD statement or named in the LIBRARY control statement for external references. The columns to the right give names and locations of any entry points within CSECTs. In Fig. 11.5 the CSECTS PROBLEM3 and COBPROG4 are the names of COBOL programs as coded in the IDENTIFICATION DIVISION. CSECTS with the prefix IGZ are subroutines that were brought in from the COBOL II subroutine library (those in the OS/VS COBOL subroutine library have the prefix ILBO).

As an example of how to use the module map, refer again to Fig. 11.5. Suppose it is determined that the NSI address at the time of an ABEND is B190 and that the LPA of the load module is 9A90. Subtracting the LPA from the NSI address gives the displacement from the beginning of the module for the NSI; B190 – 9A90 = 1700. Comparing this offset with the origin of each CSECT, we see that it is greater than COBPROG4's origin (1660) and less than IGZCDSP's origin (1B38). Therefore the relative position of the NSI falls somewhere in CSECT COBPROG4. (Notice that CSECTs start on a doubleword boundary; the offsets end with either 0 or 8. If the location you have calculated falls in the slack bytes between the end of one CSECT and the beginning of the next, you have made a mistake.) Thus, when dealing with an ABEND involving multiple programs, examining the module map enables you to find which CSECT contains an instruction.

The cross-reference table appears below the module map. Each entry shows the offset into the load module where there is a reference to a symbol in a specified CSECT. For example, the entry at letter "F" in Fig. 11.5 indicates that there is reference to symbol COBPROG4 in CSECT COBPROG4 at hexadecimal offset B0 from the origin of the load module. If you add B0 to the LPA and examine the contents of storage at that address in the dump, you will find an address which points to the entry point COBPROG4. In this case, the entry point is the beginning of CSECT COBPROG4 since the entry-point name is the same as the CSECT name.

There is a diagnostic message at the bottom of the linkage-editor output in Fig. 11.5 (letter "G"). Message IEW0132 ERROR – SYMBOL PRINTED IS AN UNRESOLVED EXTERNAL REFERENCE means that the linkage-editor could not find a reference to an entry point named in one of the CSECTs included in the load module. This results in a linkage-editor return code of 08. If a COBOL CALL statement or any branch to such an unresolved external reference is issued, an ABEND will occur. The symbol referred to in the message is printed near the top of the output, shown by letter "H." In the present example, the unresolved reference is COBOL program COBPROG5. It does not appear in the module map and is labeled $UNRESOLVED in the cross-reference table at letter "I." The object module for COBPROG5 or a load module containing it was never made available for processing by the current invocation of the linkage-editor.

Sometimes an unresolved external reference is not a problem. It may be acceptable if the current load module is to be combined with another load module which contains that reference. If you wish to mark a load module as executable even though there is an unresolved external reference, specify the linkage-editor option LET.

There is a special type of external reference known as a weak external reference. A weak external reference is one that is left unresolved by the Automatic call library mechanism unless an ordinary external reference to the same symbol is found. It is labeled $UNRESOLVED(W) in the cross-reference table. A load module is marked as executable even if there are unresolved weak external references.

The linkage-editor option MAP generates a module map. If XREF is in effect, it is unnecessary to specify MAP since both the module map and the cross-reference table will be printed.

The linkage-editor output listing also gives the length of the load module. It appears below the entry address specification. Remember that the module length can also be found in the XTLST in the system dump.

11.5 STATIC AND DYNAMIC CALLS

In debugging a situation involving calling and called programs it is important to know whether the calls are static or dynamic. Briefly, static calls involve a single load module containing all the programs. The linkage-editor should have resolved all external references so that the locations of all entry points are known at execution time. The COBOL instruction causing an ABEND is therefore in that load module, and the module map can be used to find the correct CSECT.

With dynamic calls, the compiler does not generate external references. Although the main COBOL program may call other programs, the subprograms are in separate load modules and the linkage-editor has not resolved any of these references. A called program gains control dynamically at execution time. That is, a CALL statement causes the load module containing the subprogram to be loaded into main storage (unless it is already there from a prior CALL) followed by a branch to the subprogram. To find the COBOL instruction causing an ABEND, it is necessary to find the proper load module. Examining the CDE and XTLST in the dump becomes important in this case.

11.6 SOME TYPICAL MULTIMODULE PROBLEMS

Some common multimodule errors may result from simple coding errors. For example, if a CALL literal is intended, leaving out the quotes (or apostrophes) will convert it into a CALL identifier. If an identifier with that name exists in the program, COBOL will attempt a dynamic call to the value of that identifier. Another problem may occur if you specify the wrong type of call, e.g., a static call instead of a dynamic call or a dynamic call instead of a static call. Still another mistake may be in specifying the wrong load library in the JCL. In all these cases the system will not be able to locate the called program.

One error that can occur in a dynamic calling situation with COBOL II is if the run unit contains a mixture of RESIDENT and NONRESIDENT COBOL II programs. Dynamic calls require that all the programs be compiled with the RESIDENT option. COBOL II will issue the message

```
IGZ1005I RUN UNIT CONTAINS A MIX OF RES AND NORES PROGRAMS
```

and cause a U1005 completion code if there is a conflict in this COBOL II compiler option. It is recommended, but not required, that in a run unit containing only OS/VS COBOL programs that all the COBOL programs have RESIDENT in effect. In any case, RESIDENT is always required for the calling program. A run unit containing both COBOL II and OS/VS COBOL programs must have RESIDENT in effect for all the programs.

A typical system completion code often associated with multimodule ABENDs is S806. The 806 occurs if an error is encountered during execution of the LINK, XCTL, ATTACH, or LOAD macro instruction. Occasionally S0C1, S0C2, and S0C4, which are program exceptions, will occur in a multimodule system due to attempted access of, or transfer of control to, a storage area which is invalid for the program.

806. This completion code means that a requested load module could not be found. The module may be a called subprogram or a system routine. In COBOL, a dynamic CALL may have been made to a module which does not exist, perhaps because a previous link was unsuccessful. Also, the name may have been misspelled in the CALL statement, or a library containing the module was not available or not specified. Check the JCL to be sure that the COND parameter, which would prevent a step from executing if a previous link step was unsuccessful, is properly coded. Also be sure that JOBLIB or STEPLIB DD statements include the proper data sets in the correct concatenation. Examine the COBOL CALL statement to be sure that the module to be called was spelled correctly. The return code in register 15 may provide useful information. These codes are documented in IBM's *Message Library: System Messages* manual. Message IEA703I may also give more information.

0C1. This is a program check known as an operation exception. It results from an attempt to execute an invalid instruction. Check the Op Code to see if the instruction is valid for your operating system. The problem may be caused by an invalid branch to a data area rather than to an instruction, a call to a module that is not available (also refer to the previous paragraph on the 806 ABEND), an attempt to access an instruction which was overlaid by an incorrectly subscripted or indexed field, attempt to access an unopened data set, or failure to reinitialize fields in a dynamically called subprogram. In COBOL, check the program logic: there may be a CALL to a nonexistent subprogram, a DD statement may be missing (SYSIN for ACCEPT verb or SYSOUT for DISPLAY, EXHIBIT, or TRACE verbs), or an out-of-range subscripted or indexed field may have overlaid the instruction. Note that it is not always possible to pinpoint the exact ABENDing instruction by subtracting the ILC from the NSI address, since the ILC is not always meaningful for an 0C1 ABEND. When the NSI is within a COBOL program, you may be able to find a BALR instruction before the NSI (use the PROCEDURE DIVISION map); the address in the first register is the intended return point and the address in the second register may be the EPA to a procedure close to the NSI address. When the NSI is in another module or at a very low or high storage address, look at the contents of register 14 in REGISTERS AT ENTRY TO ABEND for the intended return point to the instruction following the one that caused the branch. If a problem with an unopened data set is suspected, examine the DCB as explained in Chap. 9.

0C2. This is a privileged-operation exception. It occurs when a program is in the problem state and attempts to execute a privileged instruction. Privileged instructions are valid only when the CPU is running in supervisor state. This type of ABEND may result from an uninitialized address causing a branch to an area which contains a privileged instruction, or from an attempt to access an unopened file. Additional causes as well as actions you can take to solve the problem are similar to those previously described in the paragraph on the 0C1 completion code.

0C4. An 0C4 represents a protection exception. It occurs when a program attempts to access storage which is beyond the range permitted for the program. The problem may be caused by an attempt to execute a module with unresolved external references or a module that is not available (also refer to the previous information on the 806 ABEND), an incorrect or unmatched parameter list in the USING clauses of calling and called programs, an incorrectly placed or missing LINKAGE SECTION header preventing parameters from being accessed, an incorrect subscript or index which has violated storage beyond the permissible range of the program, a STOP RUN or GOBACK in an INPUT or OUTPUT PROCEDURE when using the COBOL SORT verb, or an attempt to access an unopened data set. Check the COBOL program for valid CALL statements and parameter lists, and check table-handling logic. If a data set problem is suspected, examine the DCB as explained in Chap. 9. Also see the previous paragraph on 0C1 ABENDs.

11.7 SOLVING A MULTIMODULE DUMP

Some time ago I was given a dump to solve. A quick analysis showed that this was a multimodule situation. Although I solved that ABEND, there were many other problems with the programs. I have used that system for the examples in the following sections to illustrate how to deal with multimodule ABENDs. After going through the solutions presented here, I will leave it to you to look further at the program logic to see what else is wrong, for even after fixing the problems described here, errors will occur in subsequent execution.

The system consists of a main program and a subprogram. The main program passes a number of parameters, including a course code, to a subprogram. The subprogram checks the values in the parameters it has received. If the subprogram finds an error in a parameter, it passes an error code back to the calling program. If it finds no error, it loads a course table and finds all student numbers within the course matching the course code it has received; it passes those student numbers back to the main program. If the main program has not received an error indicator from the subprogram, it loads a table containing student records, searches it for student numbers matching those it has received from the subprogram, and writes out records for those students in the course.

11.7.1 The First ABEND

Figure 11.6 shows the output produced the first time the system was run under MVS/ESA. Shown are pertinent portions of the JCL, job log, compiler and linkage-editor listings, program output, and the system dump. Numbers of the debugging steps we follow are circled in the figure for clarity.

1. Determine the type and location of the ABEND.
   a. Scanning the job log shows that the completion code is S0C1. This indicates a program check, specifically an operation exception. The system found an invalid Op Code for an instruction.
   b. Determine which step ABENDed. Step S2 in this ABEND.
   c. The JCL shows that step S2 executed PGM STUDCRSA and that step S1 executed the COBUCL procedure. COBUCL does an OS/VS COBOL compile and link.
   d. Check the condition codes for the previous compile and link steps within COBUCL. It is 0 for the compile, but 8 for the link.
   e. Examining the linkage-editor output, we see:
      (1) message IEW0132 indicating that CRSPROC is an unresolved external reference.
      (2) The entry point into load module STUDCRSA is in CSECT STUDCRSA (from the IDENTIFICATION DIVISION of the OS/VS COBOL program). Does STUDCRSA CALL the unresolved external reference, CRSPROC?
      (3) The LET option was in effect. This is why the load module was able to begin execution.
   f. See if there is a CALL statement in STUDCRSA. There is. At line 60 is a CALL CRSPROC. . . statement.
   g. Look for any system or COBOL messages in the job log. There are no messages from COBOL, but the symptom dump indicates NO ACTIVE MODULE FOUND. Thus far it looks like the missing unresolved external reference CRSPROC is the culprit. Although we could stop here, we will continue in order to verify that we have isolated the reason for the ABEND and to demonstrate how to find additional related information.
2. Review your actions.
   a. This is the first time this job was run. The linkage-editor reports that STUDCRSA DID NOT PREVIOUSLY EXIST BUT WAS ADDED. . .

```
//S1       EXEC COBUCL,PARM.COB='XREF,CLIST,OPTIMIZE'
//COB.SYSIN    DD DSN=MY.PROGLIB.COBOL(STUDCRSA),DISP=SHR
//LKED.SYSLMOD DD DSN=MY.COBOL.LOAD,UNIT=TSWK,
//          DISP=SHR
//LKED.SYSIN  DD *
/*
//S2         EXEC PGM=STUDCRSA
//STEPLIB        DD DSN=MY.COBOL.LOAD,DISP=SHR
//TABFILE        DD SYSOUT=A
//OUTFILE        DD SYSOUT=A
//SYSUDUMP       DD SYSOUT=A
//SYSOUT         DD SYSOUT=A
                                               .
                                               .
                                               .
IEF142I STUDCRSA COB S1 - STEP WAS EXECUTED - COND CODE 0000
                                               .
                                               .
                                               .
IEF142I STUDCRSA LKED S1 - STEP WAS EXECUTED - COND CODE 0008
                                               .
                                               .
                                               .
IEA995I SYMPTOM DUMP OUTPUT
SYSTEM COMPLETION CODE=0C1  REASON CODE=00000001
 TIME=11.40.30  SEQ=01637  CPU=0000  ASID=006D
 PSW AT TIME OF ERROR  478D0000   00000004  ILC 2  INTC 01
   NO ACTIVE MODULE FOUND
   DATA AT PSW  00000000 - 040C0000  81168B70  00000000
   GPR  0-3  00001AA9  00010D80  00000040  900113F0
   GPR  4-7  00005FF8  80005FFE  0000AF88  00000000
   GPR  8-11 0000FF88  80005FFE  00000000  00010E54
   GPR 12-15 00010D98  00010B00  50010EBC  00000000
 END OF SYMPTOM DUMP
                                               .
                                               .
                                               .
IEF472I STUDCRSA S2 - COMPLETION CODE - SYSTEM=0C1 USER=0000 REASON=00000001
                                               .
                                               .
                                               .
PP 5740-CB1 RELEASE 2.4                    IBM OS/VS COBOL  JULY  1, 1982          11.40.19  DATE APR 15,1991

   1                       11.40.19       APR 15,1991

00001    000100 IDENTIFICATION DIVISION.
00002    000200 PROGRAM-ID. STUDCRSA.
00003    000300 ENVIRONMENT DIVISION.
00004    000500 INPUT-OUTPUT SECTION.
00005    000600 FILE-CONTROL.
00006    000700        SELECT  TAB-FILE  ASSIGN  TO  TABFILE.
00007    000710        SELECT  OUT-FILE  ASSIGN  TO  OUTFILE.
00008    000800 DATA DIVISION.
00009    000900 FILE SECTION.
00010    001000 FD  TAB-FILE
00011    001100        BLOCK CONTAINS  0  RECORDS
00012    001200        LABEL RECORDS ARE OMITTED
00013    001300        RECORDING MODE IS F.
00014    001400 01  TAB-RECORD                          PIC X(500).
00015    001410 FD  OUT-FILE
00016    001420        BLOCK CONTAINS  0  RECORDS
00017    001430        LABEL RECORDS ARE OMITTED
00018    001440        RECORDING MODE IS F.
00019    001450 01  OUT-RECORD                          PIC X(500).
```

Figure 11.6 Portions of the JCL, job log, compiler listings, linkage-editor output, program output, and system dump for the first multiprogram system dump example (see Sec. 11.7.1). (*Continued*)

```
  2         STUDCRSA        11.40.19        APR 15,1991

00021    001600 WORKING-STORAGE SECTION.
00022    001800 01  FILLER                                   PIC  X(32)
00023    001900                       VALUE 'STUDCRSA WORKING-STORAGE STARTS*'.
00024    002000 01  CONSTANTS                   COMP-3.
00025    002210     05  MAX-TAB-ENTRIES                      PIC S9(2) VALUE +15.
00026    002220 01  COUNTERS                    COMP-3.
00027    002230     05  REC-READ                             PIC S9(2).
00028    002231     05  REC-WRITTEN                          PIC S9(2).
00029    002240     05  TAB-ENTRIES                          PIC S9(2).
00030    002300 01  STUD-DATA.
00031    002400     05  STUD-ENTRIES OCCURS 50 TIMES
00032    002410                      DEPENDING ON MAX-TAB-ENTRIES
00033    002420                      INDEXED BY STUD-IND.
00034    002430         10  STUD-NUMBER                      PIC X(5).
00035    002500         10  FILLER                           PIC X(450).
00036    002800 01  SWITCHES.
00037    002900     05  SW-EOF                               PIC X     VALUE 'N'.
00038    002910         88  END-OF-FILE                                VALUE 'Y'.
00039    002920     05  SW-SEARCH                            PIC X     VALUE 'Y'.
00040    003000         88  CONTINUE-SEARCH                            VALUE 'Y'.
00041    003100         88  END-SEARCH                                 VALUE 'N'.
00042    003200 01  HOLD-AREA.
00043    003210     05  HOLD-STUD-NUMBER                     PIC X(5).
00044    003300 01  FILLER                                   PIC  X(32)
00045    003410                       VALUE 'STUDCRSA WORKING-STORAGES ENDS *'.
00046    003500 LINKAGE SECTION. <------------------------------------------ (5c)
00047    003600 01  IN-PARM.
00048    003700     05  PARM-LENGTH                          PIC S9(4) COMP.
00049    003800     05  PARM-DATE                            PIC X(06).
00050    003810     05  PARM-COURSE                          PIC X(05).

  3         STUDCRSA        11.40.19        APR 15,1991

00052    004000 PROCEDURE DIVISION USING IN-PARM.
00053    004100 0000-MAINLINE.
(3b) --> 00055    004200     DISPLAY 'STUDCRSA BEGINNING'
00056    004201     MOVE ZERO TO COUNTERS
00057    004210*****************************************************************
00058    004300*  CALL ROUTINE TO CHECK PARMS                                  *
00059    004310*****************************************************************
(1f)(7b) --> 00060    004400     CALL 'CRSPROC' USING  PARM-DATE
00061    004500                           PARM-COURSE
00062    004600                           MAX-TAB-ENTRIES
00063    004610                           HOLD-STUD-NUMBER
00064    004700     IF  RETURN-CODE  EQUAL  0
00065    004710         OPEN  OUTPUT  OUT-FILE}
00066    004720                       TAB-FILE} <---------------------------- (5b)
00067    004800         PERFORM 1000-LOAD-TABLE
00068    004801            UNTIL REC-READ EQUAL MAX-TAB-ENTRIES
00069    004802         PERFORM 1500-SEARCH-FOR-STUD
00070    004803            UNTIL END-SEARCH OR STUD-IND GREATER MAX-TAB-ENTRIES
00071    004804         PERFORM 2000-WRITE-RECORD
00072    004805            VARYING STUD-IND FROM 1 BY 1
00073    004806            UNTIL END-OF-FILE OR STUD-IND GREATER MAX-TAB-ENTRIES
00074    004810     ELSE
00075    004900          DISPLAY 'ERROR -- BAD PARM PASSED'.
00076    005500     CLOSE  OUT-FILE
00077    005510            TAB-FILE
00078    005600     DISPLAY  'STUDCRSA ENDING'
00079    005700     GOBACK.

00081    005800 1000-LOAD-TABLE.
00082    005900     WRITE  OUT-RECORD  FROM STUD-DATA <------------------------ (5b)
00083    006000     ADD  +1  TO  REC-READ.

00085    006110 1500-SEARCH-FOR-STUD.
00086    006130     SEARCH STUD-ENTRIES
00087    006140       AT END MOVE 'N' TO SW-SEARCH
00088    006150       DISPLAY 'ERROR -- STUDENT NOT IN TABLE'
00089    006160     WHEN HOLD-STUD-NUMBER = STUD-NUMBER (STUD-IND)
00090    006170       PERFORM 2000-WRITE-RECORD.

00092    006200 2000-WRITE-RECORD.
00093    006400     WRITE  TAB-RECORD  FROM STUD-ENTRIES (STUD-IND) <---------- (5b)
00094    006500     ADD  +1  TO  REC-WRITTEN.
                                     .
                                     .
                                     .
```

Figure 11.6 *(Continued)*

```
        8          STUDCRSA           11.40.19          APR 15,1991

                                                    CONDENSED LISTING

      52       ENTRY      005F6C                55       DISPLAY     005F84                56       MOVE       005F98
      60       CALL       005FA2                64       IF          005FEC                65       OPEN       005FFC
                                                    .
                                                    .
                                                    .

 MVS/DFP VERSION 3 RELEASE 2 LINKAGE EDITOR      11:40:25  MON  APR 15, 1991
 JOB STUDCRSA    STEP S1             PROCEDURE LKED
 INVOCATION PARAMETERS - LIST,XREF,LET
 ACTUAL SIZE=(317440,79872)
 OUTPUT DATA SET MY.COBOL.LOAD IS ON VOLUME PRI008
IEW0000       NAME STUDCRSA(R)                                                        00030001
IEW0132   CRSPROC

                                                    CROSS REFERENCE TABLE

  CONTROL SECTION                           ENTRY

    NAME      ORIGIN  LENGTH              NAME    LOCATION      NAME    LOCATION     NAME    LOCATION     NAME    LOCATION
  STUDCRSA      00     651C
  ILBOCOM0*   6520      173               ILBOCOM       6520

  ILBODSS *   6698      418               ILBODSS0      669A

  ILBOEXT *   6AB0       68               ILBOEXT0      6AB2      ILBOEXT1      6AB6

  ILBOITB *   6B18      11A               ILBOITB0      6B1A

  ILBOQIO *   6C38      7F4               ILBOQIO0      6C3A      ILBOQIO1      6C3E
                                          ILBOMSG0      801A
                                                    .
                                                    .
                                                    .

  LOCATION   REFERS TO SYMBOL   IN CONTROL SECTION               LOCATION   REFERS TO SYMBOL   IN CONTROL SECTION
     5EB4           ILBOSRV0          ILBOSRV                        5EB8          ILBOQIO1           ILBOQIO
     5EBC           ILBOSR5           ILBOSRV                        5EC0          ILBODSS0           ILBODSS
     5EC4           CRSPROC          $UNRESOLVED                     5EC8          ILBOEXT1           ILBOEXT
                                                    .
                                                    .
                                                    .

 ENTRY ADDRESS          00

 TOTAL LENGTH         8118
 ** STUDCRSA DID NOT PREVIOUSLY EXIST BUT WAS ADDED AND HAS AMODE 24
 ** LOAD MODULE HAS RMODE 24
 ** AUTHORIZATION CODE IS          0.

                                                 DIAGNOSTIC MESSAGE DIRECTORY

   IEW0132 ERROR - SYMBOL PRINTED IS AN UNRESOLVED EXTERNAL REFERENCE.

 STUDCRSA BEGINNING
```

Figure 11.6 *(Continued)*

3. Check how far the program executed.
   a. Only the message STUDCRSA BEGINNING appears.
   b. Examine the COBOL program for WRITE and DISPLAY statements. The DISPLAY at line 55 was responsible for the message in 3*a* above. There is no other output.
4. Review the output from any COBOL debugging aids which were in effect.
   a. As mentioned, only the DISPLAY at the beginning of the program executed.

```
JOB STUDCRSA        STEP S2           TIME 114031   DATE 91105    ID = 000    CPUID = 630724153090    PAGE 00000001

COMPLETION CODE     SYSTEM = 0C1      REASON CODE = 00000001

  PSW AT ENTRY TO ABEND   478D0000  00000004  ILC  02  INTC  0001

PSW ADDRESS 00000004 AT TIME OF ERROR DOES NOT POINT TO AN ACTIVE MODULE
                                        .
                                        .
                                        .
 PRB: 008FA038
          -0020  XSB...... 008FA0A0  FLAGS2... 00000000  RTPSW1... 478D0000  00000004            RTPSW2... 00020001
          -000C            00189CF0  FLAGS1... 00000000  WLIC..... 00020001
          +0000  RSV...... 00000000  00000000            SZSTAB... 00110082  FLCDE.... 008FE000  <-- 6d
          +0010  OPSW..... 478D0000  00000004            SQE...... 00000000  LINK..... 008F3400
                                        .
                                        .
                                        .
 SVRB: 008FD348
          -0020  XSB...... 008FD418  FLAGS2... 00000000  RTPSW1... 00000000  00000000            RTPSW2... 00000000
          -000C            00000000  FLAGS1... 22000000  WLIC..... 00020033
          +0000  RSV...... 00000000  00000000            SZSTAB... 001ED022  FLCDE.... 00000000
          +0010  OPSW..... 470C1000  820A24C6            Q........ 00000000  LINK..... 008FA038
          +0020  GPR0-3... 00001AA9  00010D80  00000040  900113F0
          +0030  GPR4-7... 00005FF8  80005FFE  0000AF88  00000000
          +0040  GPR8-11.. 0000FF88  80005FFE  00000000  00010E54
          +0050  GPR12-15. 00010D98  00010B00  50010EBC  00000000
          +0060  EXSAVE... 00001AA9  00010D80  00000000  008F3400  008FD348  00F28500  00FF8C80  01BE1B28  7FFCD090
                                        .               6g
                                        .
                                        .
 SVRB: 008FD4B8
          -0020  XSB...... 008FD588  FLAGS2... 00000000  RTPSW1... 00000000  00000000            RTPSW2... 00000000
          -000C            00000000  FLAGS1... 02000000  WLIC..... 00020078
          +0000  RSV...... 00000000  00000000            SZSTAB... 001ED022  FLCDE.... 00000000
          +0010  OPSW..... 470C1000  80C180FE            Q........ 00000000  LINK..... 008FD348
                                        .
                                        .                          6e
                                        .
CDE
      008FE000  CHAIN.... 00000000  RRBP..... 008FA038  NAME..... STUDCRSA  ENTPT.... 0000AEE8  XLMJP.... 008FF2F8
          +0018  USE...... 0001      ATTRB.... 00        SP....... FB        ATTR..... 0B        ATTR2.... 20
          +001E  ATTR3.... 0000
                                                  6d
XTLST
      008FF2F8  LNTH..... 00000010  NRFAC.... 00000001  MSBLA.... 80008118  MSBAD.... 0000AEE8  <-- 6f
                                        .
                                        .
                                        .
  REGISTERS AT ENTRY TO ABEND

  FLOATING POINT REGISTER VALUES
      0-6  00000000 00000000    00000000 00000000    00000000 00000000    00000000 00000000

  GPR VALUES
      0-3  00001AA9  00010D80  00000040  900113F0
      4-7  00005FF8  80005FFE  0000AF88  00000000
     8-11  0000FF88  80005FFE  00000000  00010E54
    12-15  00010D98  00010B00  50010EBC  00000000

  ACCESS REGISTER VALUES
      0-3  00000000  00000000  00000000  00000000
      4-7  00000000  00000000  00000000  00000000
     8-11  00000000  00000000  00000000  00000000
    12-15  00000000  00000000  00000000  00000000

ACTIVE LOAD MODULES

LPA/JPA MODULE    STUDCRSA
0000AEE0                    90ECD00C 185D05F0    4580F010 C4D4D7C3 C2F2C140 E5E2D9F1   *        .......0..0.STUDCRSA VSR1*
0000AF00 0700989F F02407FF 96021034 07FE41F0    000107FE 0001133C 0000AEE8 0000AEE8   *....0..........0...........Y...Y*
0000AF20 00010D98 00010B00 00010E54 000112FC    00000000 00000000 00000000 00000000   *................................*
0000AF40 00000000 00000000 00000000 00000000    00000000 00000000 00000000 00000000   *................................*
0000AF60 00000000 00000000 00000000 00010D38    F1F14BF4 F04BF1F9 C1D7D940 F1F56B40   *...............11.40.19APR 15. *
0000AF80 F1F9F9F1 00000000 E2E3E4C4 C3D9E2C1    40E6D6D9 D2C9D5C7 60E2E3D6 D9C1C7C5   *1991....STUDCRSA WORKING.STORAGE*
0000AFA0 40E2E3C1 D9E3E25C 015C0000 00000000    F0F0F0F0 F0F00000 00000000 00000000   * STARTS.........000000..........*
0000AFC0 00000000 00000000 00000000 00000000    00000000 00000000 00000000 00000000   *................................*
                                        .
                                        .
                                        .
```

Figure 11.6 *(Continued)*

5. Check for information in the JCL.
   a. We already know that the first step, S1 compiled program STUDCRSA and produced a load module with STUDCRSA as the entry point. The program called by STUDCRSA was not included in the load module.
   b. Both of the program files in step S2 (DDnames TABFILE and OUTFILE) are output files. A check of the program verifies that the files were opened for output and that WRITEs are issued to them.
   c. Although program STUDCRSA has a LINKAGE SECTION, no parameters were passed from the JCL. At this point it looks like there is no input to the program. Is STUDCRSA called by another program?
6. Let us analyze the SYMPTOM and actual SYSTEM dumps.
   a. As previously mentioned (step 1*g*), the SYMPTOM DUMP shows NO ACTIVE MODULE FOUND. There is no LPA printed.
   b. The NSI address from the PSW is 4. This is in low memory, protected storage.
   c. The DATA AT PSW indicates an address of 0 for the instruction which was executed at the time of the ABEND. How did the program get there?
   d. Going to the SYSTEM DUMP, we follow the PRB for the failing program to the CDE and the XTLST.
   e. The CDE shows an EPA of AEE8 for module STUDCRSA.
   f. The XTLST reports that the LPA is also AEE8.
   g. Subtracting the LPA from the NSI address of 4 gets us nowhere. Recall that however we got to this place in low memory, we should expect to return to the instruction following the branch. Register 14 should contain the return point address. We can find the contents of register 14 in several places; in the SYMPTOM DUMP, in the SVRB below the PRB, and in the REGISTERS AT ENTRY TO ABEND before the storage contents of STUDCRSA in the hexadecimal portion of the dump. Since we are looking at the formatted portion of the system dump, let's get the address from the SVRB below the PRB. It is 10EBC.
   h. Subtract the LPA from the return address. 10EBC – AEE8 = 5FD4. This should be the displacement of an instruction following a CALL statement.
   i. Going back to the linkage-editor module map, we see that offset 5FD4 is within CSECT STUDCRSA.
7. Use the compiler output to examine the instruction in the COBOL program.
   a. Use the CLIST output to find the COBOL instruction. The instruction at offset 5FD4 is generated by the CALL statement at line 60.
   b. Look at lines 60 through 63. They are

```
CALL 'CRSPROC' USING PARM-DATE
                     PARM-COURSE
                     MAX-TAB-ENTRIES
                     HOLD-STUD-NUMBER
```

   c. This verifies our previous conclusion. Control was to return to an Assembler instruction following the one generated by CALL which caused the branch.

It is interesting to look more closely at how this ABEND occurred. Because the external reference to CRSPROC was not resolved, the address to which control was to be transferred remained at 0. Note that the instruction at that address, taken from the DATA AT PSW in the symptom dump, has an Op Code of 04. We see from Appendix D that this is a valid Op Code; the instruction is Set Program Mask (SPM) with a length of 2 bytes. The IBM manual *Principles of Operation* indicates that SPM is not subject to program exceptions. After incrementing the NSI address in the PSW by 2 and executing this instruction, the system encounters 00 as the first byte of the next "instruction." This translates to a length of 2, causing the NSI address to be adjusted to 4. However, there is no instruction with an Op Code of 00, so a protection exception now occurs.

11.7.2 The Second ABEND

After the JCL was changed to make subprogram CRSPROC available, the job was run again. It ABENDed a second time. The relevant output is shown in Fig. 11.7. Numbers of the steps we follow in debugging the ABEND are circled in the figure for clarity.

1. Determine the type and location of the ABEND.
   a. Scanning the job log shows that the completion code is S0C7. This represents a program check, specifically a data exception. An instruction was attempting an operation with invalid packed data.
   b. Determine which step ABENDed. It was Step S3.
   c. The JCL shows that this was a three-step job. Step S3 executed PGM STUDCRSA, step S2 executed COB2UCL, the COBOL II compile and link procedure, and step S1 executed COBUCL, the OS/VS COBOL compile and link procedure.
   d. Check the condition codes for all previous job and procedure steps. They were all 0.
   e. Examining output from the linkage-editor we see that:
      (1) Step S1 produced the load module STUDCRSA with the CSECT STUDCRSA. This is the main program. There are no error messages.
      (2) Step S2 produced a separate load module named CRSPROC containing the CSECTs CRSPROC and IGZEBST. CRSPROC is the subprogram. There are no error messages.
   f. Look for any system or COBOL messages in the job log. There are no messages from COBOL, but there is a symptom dump.
2. Review your actions.
   a. This is the second time the job was run. The first time it ABENDed because the subprogram was an unresolved external reference. This time the subprogram was compiled and linked using COB2UCL. We will examine the JCL in step 5.
3. Check how far the program executed.
   a. Only the two literals STUDCRSA BEGINNING and PROGRAM CRSPROC BEGINNING appear.

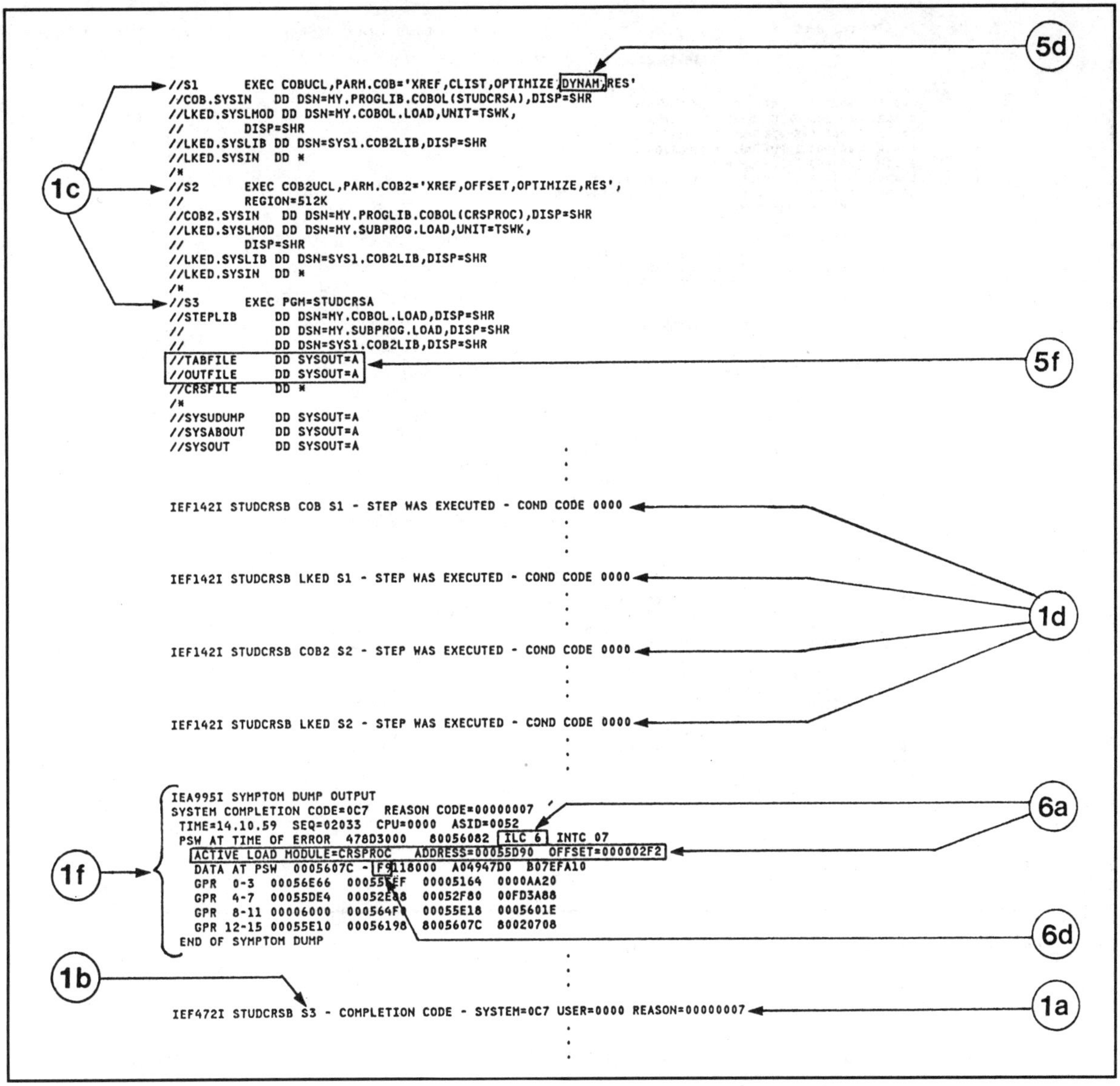


```
//S1       EXEC COBUCL,PARM.COB='XREF,CLIST,OPTIMIZE,DYNAM,RES'
//COB.SYSIN    DD DSN=MY.PROGLIB.COBOL(STUDCRSA),DISP=SHR
//LKED.SYSLMOD DD DSN=MY.COBOL.LOAD,UNIT=TSWK,
//           DISP=SHR
//LKED.SYSLIB DD DSN=SYS1.COB2LIB,DISP=SHR
//LKED.SYSIN   DD *
/*
//S2       EXEC COB2UCL,PARM.COB2='XREF,OFFSET,OPTIMIZE,RES',
//           REGION=512K
//COB2.SYSIN    DD DSN=MY.PROGLIB.COBOL(CRSPROC),DISP=SHR
//LKED.SYSLMOD DD DSN=MY.SUBPROG.LOAD,UNIT=TSWK,
//           DISP=SHR
//LKED.SYSLIB DD DSN=SYS1.COB2LIB,DISP=SHR
//LKED.SYSIN   DD *
/*
//S3       EXEC PGM=STUDCRSA
//STEPLIB       DD DSN=MY.COBOL.LOAD,DISP=SHR
//              DD DSN=MY.SUBPROG.LOAD,DISP=SHR
//              DD DSN=SYS1.COB2LIB,DISP=SHR
//TABFILE       DD SYSOUT=A
//OUTFILE       DD SYSOUT=A
//CRSFILE       DD *
/*
//SYSUDUMP      DD SYSOUT=A
//SYSABOUT      DD SYSOUT=A
//SYSOUT        DD SYSOUT=A
                                                    .
                                                    .
                                                    .
IEF142I STUDCRSB COB S1 - STEP WAS EXECUTED - COND CODE 0000
                                                    .
                                                    .
                                                    .
IEF142I STUDCRSB LKED S1 - STEP WAS EXECUTED - COND CODE 0000
                                                    .
                                                    .
                                                    .
IEF142I STUDCRSB COB2 S2 - STEP WAS EXECUTED - COND CODE 0000
                                                    .
                                                    .
                                                    .
IEF142I STUDCRSB LKED S2 - STEP WAS EXECUTED - COND CODE 0000
                                                    .
                                                    .
                                                    .
IEA995I SYMPTOM DUMP OUTPUT
SYSTEM COMPLETION CODE=0C7  REASON CODE=00000007
 TIME=14.10.59  SEQ=02033  CPU=0000  ASID=0052
 PSW AT TIME OF ERROR  478D3000   80056082  ILC 6  INTC 07
  ACTIVE LOAD MODULE=CRSPROC    ADDRESS=00055D90  OFFSET=000002F2
  DATA AT PSW  0005607C - F9118000  A04947D0  B07EFA10
  GPR  0-3  00056E66  00055EEF  00005164  0000AA20
  GPR  4-7  00055DE4  00052E88  00052F80  00FD3A88
  GPR  8-11 00006000  000564F0  00055E18  0005601E
  GPR 12-15 00055E10  00056198  8005607C  80020708
 END OF SYMPTOM DUMP
                                                    .
                                                    .
                                                    .
IEF472I STUDCRSB S3 - COMPLETION CODE - SYSTEM=0C7 USER=0000 REASON=00000007
                                                    .
                                                    .
                                                    .
```

Figure 11.7 Portions of the JCL, job log, compiler listings, linkage-editor output, program output, and system dump for the second multiprogram system dump example (see Sec. 11.7.2). This ABEND occurred on the same application system as in Fig. 11.6, but after the first ABEND was fixed. (*Continued*)

```
PP 5740-CB1 RELEASE 2.4                       IBM OS/VS COBOL  JULY  1, 1982       14.10.28  DATE APR 15,1991

   1                      14.10.28        APR 15,1991

00001   000100 IDENTIFICATION DIVISION.
00002   000200 PROGRAM-ID. STUDCRSA.
00003   000300 ENVIRONMENT DIVISION.
00004   000500 INPUT-OUTPUT SECTION.
00005   000600 FILE-CONTROL.
00006   000700      SELECT  TAB-FILE  ASSIGN  TO  TABFILE.
00007   000710      SELECT  OUT-FILE  ASSIGN  TO  OUTFILE.
00008   000800 DATA DIVISION.
00009   000900 FILE SECTION.
00010   001000 FD  TAB-FILE
00011   001100      BLOCK CONTAINS  0  RECORDS
00012   001200      LABEL RECORDS ARE OMITTED
00013   001300      RECORDING MODE IS F.
00014   001400 01  TAB-RECORD                             PIC X(500).
00015   001410 FD  OUT-FILE
00016   001420      BLOCK CONTAINS  0  RECORDS
00017   001430      LABEL RECORDS ARE OMITTED
00018   001440      RECORDING MODE IS F.
00019   001450 01  OUT-RECORD                             PIC X(500).

   2        STUDCRSA        14.10.28        APR 15,1991

00021   001600 WORKING-STORAGE SECTION.
00022   001800 01  FILLER                                 PIC  X(32)
00023   001900                        VALUE 'STUDCRSA WORKING-STORAGE STARTS*'.
00024   002000 01  CONSTANTS                      COMP-3.
00025   002210      05  MAX-TAB-ENTRIES                   PIC S9(2) VALUE +15.   <-- 7g(5)
00026   002220 01  COUNTERS                       COMP-3.
00027   002230      05  REC-READ                          PIC S9(2).
00028   002231      05  REC-WRITTEN                       PIC S9(2).
00029   002240      05  TAB-ENTRIES                       PIC S9(2).
00030   002300 01  STUD-DATA.
00031   002400      05  STUD-ENTRIES OCCURS 50 TIMES
00032   002410                     DEPENDING ON MAX-TAB-ENTRIES
00033   002420                     INDEXED BY STUD-IND.
00034   002430          10  STUD-NUMBER                   PIC X(5).
00035   002500          10  FILLER                        PIC X(450).
00036   002800 01  SWITCHES.
00037   002900      05  SW-EOF                            PIC X     VALUE 'N'.
00038   002910          88  END-OF-FILE                             VALUE 'Y'.
00039   002920      05  SW-SEARCH                         PIC X     VALUE 'Y'.
00040   003000          88  CONTINUE-SEARCH                         VALUE 'Y'.
00041   003100          88  END-SEARCH                              VALUE 'N'.
00042   003200 01  HOLD-AREA.
00043   003210      05  HOLD-STUD-NUMBER                  PIC X(5).
00044   003300 01  FILLER                                 PIC  X(32)
00045   003410                        VALUE 'STUDCRSA WORKING-STORAGES ENDS *'.
00046   003500 LINKAGE SECTION.   <-- 5g
00047   003600 01  IN-PARM.
00048   003700      05  PARM-LENGTH                       PIC S9(4) COMP.
00049   003800      05  PARM-DATE                         PIC X(06).   <-- 7h
00050   003810      05  PARM-COURSE                       PIC X(05).
```

Figure 11.7 *(Continued)*

b. Examine both COBOL programs for WRITE and DISPLAY statements.

(1) The DISPLAY at line 55 in the main program STUDCRSA was responsible for the first literal. No other DISPLAY or WRITE statements in STUDCRSA were executed.

(2) The DISPLAY at line 50 in the subprogram CRSPROC was responsible for the second literal. The DISPLAY at line 61 did not execute. There are no WRITEs in CRSPROC. It looks like the main program called the subprogram and the ABEND occurred before control returned to the main program.

4. Review the output from any COBOL debugging aids which were in effect.

a. As mentioned, only the DISPLAY at the beginning of each program executed.

```
       3          STUDCRSA           14.10.28          APR 15,1991

      00052    004000 PROCEDURE DIVISION USING IN-PARM.
      00053    004100 0000-MAINLINE.
3b(1)→00055    004200        DISPLAY 'STUDCRSA BEGINNING'
      00056    004201        MOVE ZERO TO COUNTERS
      00057    004210*****************************************************************
      00058    004300*  CALL ROUTINE TO CHECK PARMS                                     *
      00059    004310*****************************************************************
   7f→00060    004400        CALL 'CRSPROC' USING  PARM-DATE
      00061    004500                              PARM-COURSE
      00062    004600                              MAX-TAB-ENTRIES
      00063    004610                              HOLD-STUD-NUMBER
      00064    004700        IF  RETURN-CODE  EQUAL  0
      00065    004710            OPEN  OUTPUT  OUT-FILE  ←5f
      00066    004720                          TAB-FILE
      00067    004800            PERFORM 1000-LOAD-TABLE
      00068    004801               UNTIL REC-READ EQUAL MAX-TAB-ENTRIES
      00069    004802            PERFORM 1500-SEARCH-FOR-STUD
      00070    004803               UNTIL END-SEARCH OR STUD-IND GREATER MAX-TAB-ENTRIES
      00071    004804            PERFORM 2000-WRITE-RECORD
      00072    004805               VARYING STUD-IND FROM 1 BY 1
      00073    004806               UNTIL END-OF-FILE OR STUD-IND GREATER MAX-TAB-ENTRIES
      00074    004810        ELSE
      00075    004900              DISPLAY 'ERROR -- BAD PARM PASSED'.
      00076    005500        CLOSE  OUT-FILE
      00077    005510               TAB-FILE
      00078    005600        DISPLAY  'STUDCRSA ENDING'
      00079    005700        GOBACK.

      00081    005800 1000-LOAD-TABLE.
      00082    005900        WRITE  OUT-RECORD  FROM STUD-DATA  ←5f
      00083    006000        ADD  +1  TO  REC-READ.

      00085    006110 1500-SEARCH-FOR-STUD.
      00086    006130        SEARCH STUD-ENTRIES
      00087    006140          AT END MOVE 'N' TO SW-SEARCH
      00088    006150          DISPLAY 'ERROR -- STUDENT NOT IN TABLE'
      00089    006160        WHEN HOLD-STUD-NUMBER = STUD-NUMBER (STUD-IND)
      00090    006170          PERFORM 2000-WRITE-RECORD.

      00092    006200 2000-WRITE-RECORD.
      00093    006400        WRITE  TAB-RECORD  FROM STUD-ENTRIES (STUD-IND)  ←5f
      00094    006500        ADD  +1  TO  REC-WRITTEN.

       4          STUDCRSA           14.10.28          APR 15,1991

        INTRNL NAME   LVL SOURCE NAME              BASE   DISPL  INTRNL NAME  DEFINITION  USAGE     R O Q M
        DNM=1-125     FD  TAB-FILE                 DCB=01        DNM=1-125                QSAM            F
        DNM=1-147     01  TAB-RECORD               BL=1    000   DNM=1-147    DS 500C     DISP
        DNM=1-167     FD  OUT-FILE                 DCB=02        DNM=1-167                QSAM            F
        DNM=1-189     01  OUT-RECORD               BL=2    000   DNM=1-189    DS 500C     DISP
        DNM=1-209     01  FILLER                   BL=3    000   DNM=1-209    DS 32C      DISP
        DNM=1-220     01  CONSTANTS                BL=3    020   DNM=1-220    DS 0CL2     GROUP         Q
7g(1)→  DNM=1-242     02  MAX-TAB-ENTRIES          BL=3    020   DNM=1-242    DS 2P       COMP-3        Q
                                        .
                                        .
                                        .
        DNM=2-153     01  IN-PARM                  BLL=3   000   DNM=2-153    DS 0CL13    GROUP
        DNM=2-173     02  PARM-LENGTH              BLL=3   000   DNM=2-173    DS 2C       COMP
        DNM=2-194     02  PARM-DATE                BLL=3   002   DNM=2-194    DS 6C       DISP
        DNM=2-216     02  PARM-COURSE              BLL=3   008   DNM=2-216    DS 5C       DISP
```

Figure 11.7 *(Continued)*

5. Check for information in the JCL.
   a. We already know that the first step, S1 compiled the main program STUDCRSA and produced a load module with that name as the entry point. The program called by STUDCRSA was not included in the load module.
   b. The second step, S2, compiled the subprogram CRSPROC producing a load module with that name as the entry point.
   c. The third step, S3, executed load module STUDCRSA. This contains the main program which issues the call to CRSPROC.

```
      5          STUDCRSA        14.10.28        APR 15,1991

                           MEMORY MAP

                     TGT                         05C18
                                                    .
                                                    .
                                                    .
                BL CELLS                         05E18  <---------------- (7g(2))
                DECBADR CELLS                    05E38
                FIB CELLS                        05E38
                TEMP STORAGE                     05E40
                TEMP STORAGE-2                   05E40
                TEMP STORAGE-3                   05E48
                TEMP STORAGE-4                   05E48
                BLL CELLS                        05E48
                                                    .
                                                    .
                                                    .

      8          STUDCRSA        14.10.28        APR 15,1991
                                                       CONDENSED LISTING

 52       ENTRY       005FAC              55     DISPLAY     005FC4              56     MOVE      005FD8
 60       CALL        005FE2              64     IF          00603A              65     OPEN      00604A
                                                    .
                                                    .
                                                    .

      9          STUDCRSA        14.10.28        APR 15,1991
*STATISTICS*     SOURCE RECORDS =    94     DATA DIVISION STATEMENTS =    28     PROCEDURE DIVISION STATEMENTS =    21
*OPTIONS IN EFFECT*     SIZE =  196608  BUF =   28672  LINECNT = 57  SPACE1, FLAGW, NOSEQ,   SOURCE
*OPTIONS IN EFFECT*       DMAP, NOPMAP,   CLIST, NOSUPMAP,   XREF, NOSXREF,   LOAD, NODECK, APOST, NOTRUNC, NOFLOW
*OPTIONS IN EFFECT*     NOTERM, NONUM, NOBATCH, NONAME, COMPILE=01, NOSTATE,   RESIDENT,  [DYNAM,] NOLIB, NOSYNTAX
*OPTIONS IN EFFECT*       OPTIMIZE, NOSYMDMP, NOTEST,   VERB,   ZWB, SYST, NOENDJOB, NOMIGR, NOLVL
                                                    .                                        \
                                                    .                                         \
                                                    .                                          ---- (5e)

 MVS/DFP VERSION 3 RELEASE 2 LINKAGE EDITOR      14:10:36  MON  APR 15, 1991
 JOB STUDCRSB   STEP S1          PROCEDURE LKED
 INVOCATION PARAMETERS - LIST,XREF,LET
 ACTUAL SIZE=(317440,79872)
 OUTPUT DATA SET MY.COBOL.LOAD IS ON VOLUME PRI008
IEW0000      NAME STUDCRSA(R)                                                  00032001

                                                 CROSS REFERENCE TABLE

  CONTROL SECTION                        ENTRY

    NAME     ORIGIN  LENGTH                 NAME    LOCATION     NAME    LOCATION     NAME    LOCATION     NAME    LOCATION
  --->STUDCRSA   00     65E0

(1e(1))

  LOCATION   REFERS TO SYMBOL   IN CONTROL SECTION            LOCATION   REFERS TO SYMBOL   IN CONTROL SECTION

 ENTRY ADDRESS        00

 TOTAL LENGTH       65E0
--->** STUDCRSA REPLACED AND HAS AMODE 24
 ** LOAD MODULE HAS RMODE 24
 ** AUTHORIZATION CODE IS          0.
```

Figure 11.7 *(Continued)*

d. The JCL indicates that a dynamic CALL was requested.

e. The compiler options in effect listing states that DYNAM is active for the main program.

f. Recall from the first ABEND that all of the program files in STUDCRSA were output files (DDnames TABFILE and OUTFILE). A check of the program verifies that the same files were opened for output and that WRITEs are issued to them.

```
PP 5668-958 IBM VS COBOL II Release 3.0 09/13/88                              Date 04/15/91  Time 14:10:39   Page    1

Invocation parameters:
XREF,OFFSET,OPTIMIZE,RES

Options in effect:
      ADV
      APOST
    NOAWO
      BUFSIZE(4096)
    NOCMPR2
    NOCOMPILE(S)
      DATA(31)
    NODBCS
    NODECK
    NODUMP
    NODYNAM
    NOEXIT
    NOFASTSRT
    NOFDUMP
      FLAG(I)
    NOFLAGMIG
    NOFLAGSAA
    NOFLAGSTD
      LANGUAGE(EN)
    NOLIB
      LINECOUNT(60)
    NOLIST
      MAP
    NONAME
    NONUMBER
      NUMPROC(NOPFD)
      OBJECT
      OFFSET
      OPTIMIZE
      OUTDD(SYSOUT)
    NORENT
      RESIDENT
    NOSEQUENCE
      SIZE(MAX)
      SOURCE
      SPACE(1)
    NOSSRANGE
    NOTERM
    NOTEST
      TRUNC(OPT)
    NOVBREF
    NOWORD
      XREF
      ZWB

PP 5668-958 IBM VS COBOL II Release 3.0 09/13/88                   CRSPROC   Date 04/15/91  Time 14:10:39   Page    2
  LineID  PL SL  ----+-*A-1-B--+----2----+----3----+----4----+----5----+----6----+----7-|--+----8 Cross Reference

  000001         000100 IDENTIFICATION DIVISION.
  000002         000200 PROGRAM-ID. CRSPROC.
  000003         000300 DATE-COMPILED. 04/15/91.
  000004         000400*****************************************************************
  000005         000500*  THIS PROGRAM VALIDATES THE PASSED PARM PASSED-MAX-TAB-ENTRIES*
  000006         000600*  AND EITHER SETS A RETURN-CODE OF 5 IF IT IS IN ERROR OR      *
  000007         000601*  PROCESSES THE COURSE-FILE IF THERE IS NO ERROR.              *
  000008         000610*****************************************************************
  000009         000800 ENVIRONMENT DIVISION.
  000010         000900 INPUT-OUTPUT SECTION.
  000011         000910 FILE-CONTROL.
  000012         000920     SELECT COURSE-FILE ASSIGN TO CRSFILE.                              15
  000013         001000 DATA DIVISION.
  000014         001010 FILE SECTION.
  000015         001020 FD  COURSE-FILE
  000016         001030     BLOCK CONTAINS 0 RECORDS
  000017         001040     LABEL RECORDS ARE OMITTED
  000018         001050     RECORDING MODE IS F.
  000019         001060 01  COURSE-RECORD                          PIC X(100).
```

Figure 11.7 *(Continued)*

```
PP 5668-958 IBM VS COBOL II Release 3.0 09/13/88              CRSPROC   Date 04/15/91  Time 14:10:39   Page    3
  LineID  PL SL  ----+-*A-1-B--+----2----+----3----+----4----+----5----+----6----+----7-|--+----8  Cross Reference
  000021         001200 WORKING-STORAGE SECTION.
  000022         001400 01  FILLER                                PIC  X(32)
  000023         001500                        VALUE '*CRSPROC WORKING-STORAGE STARTS*'.
  000024         001510 01  COURSE-DATA.
  000025         001520     05  COURSE-ENTRIES OCCURS 16 TIMES
  000026         001530                         DEPENDING ON MAX-ENROLLMENT                     36
  000027         001540                         INDEXED BY COURSE-IND.
  000028         001550         10  STUD-NUMBER                   PIC X(05).
  000029         001560         10  FILLER                        PIC X(95).
  000030         001600 01  HOLD-AREA.
  000031         001700     05  HOLD-DATE                         PIC 9(06).
  000032         001800     05  HOLD-COURSE-CODE                  PIC X(15).
  000033         001900 01  ERROR-CNT                             PIC S9(3) COMP-3.
  000034         001910 01  SW-EOF                                PIC X   VALUE 'N'.
  000035         001920     88  END-OF-FILE                               VALUE 'Y'.
  000036         001930 01  MAX-ENROLLMENT                        PIC S9(3) COMP-3.
  000037         002000 01  FILLER                                PIC X(32)
  000038         002100                        VALUE '* CRSPROC WORKING-STORAGE ENDS *'.

PP 5668-958 IBM VS COBOL II Release 3.0 09/13/88              CRSPROC   Date 04/15/91  Time 14:10:39   Page    4
  LineID  PL SL  ----+-*A-1-B--+----2----+----3----+----4----+----5----+----6----+----7-|--+----8  Cross Reference
  000040         002300 LINKAGE SECTION.
  000041         002400 01  PASSED-COURSE-CODE                    PIC X(15).
  000042         002500 01  PASSED-MAX-TAB-ENTRIES                PIC S9(2) COMP-3.
  000043         002600 01  PASSED-DATE                           PIC 9(06).
  000044         002610 01  PASSED-HOLD-STUD-NUMBER               PIC 9(05).

PP 5668-958 IBM VS COBOL II Release 3.0 09/13/88              CRSPROC   Date 04/15/91  Time 14:10:39   Page    5
  LineID  PL SL  ----+-*A-1-B--+----2----+----3----+----4----+----5----+----6----+----7-|--+----8  Cross Reference
(7e)--> 000046   002800 PROCEDURE DIVISION USING PASSED-MAX-TAB-ENTRIES                        42
  000047         002900                          PASSED-COURSE-CODE                            41
  000048         003000                          PASSED-DATE                                   43
  000049         003010                          PASSED-HOLD-STUD-NUMBER.                      44
(3b(2))--> 000050 003100     DISPLAY 'PROGRAM CRSPROC BEGINNING'
(7b)--> 000051   003200     IF  PASSED-MAX-TAB-ENTRIES   GREATER THAN +15                      42
  000052      1  003300         PERFORM 1000-ERROR-TOO-GREAT                                   65
  000053         003400     ELSE
  000054      1  003401         OPEN INPUT COURSE-FILE                                         15
  000055      1  003402         PERFORM 2000-LOAD-TABLE                                        69
  000056      1  003403            UNTIL END-OF-FILE                                           35
  000057      1  003404         PERFORM 3000-PROCESS-COURSE                                    74
  000058      1  003405            VARYING COURSE-IND FROM 1 BY 1                              27
  000059      1  003406               UNTIL COURSE-IND GREATER PASSED-MAX-TAB-ENTRIES          27 42
  000060         003407     END-IF
  000061         003410     DISPLAY 'PROGRAM CRSPROC ENDING'
  000062         003420     CLOSE COURSE-FILE                                                  15
  000063         003500     GOBACK.

  000065         003600 1000-ERROR-TOO-GREAT.
  000066         003700     ADD  +1  TO ERROR-CNT                                              33
  000067         003900     MOVE 5  TO  RETURN-CODE.                                           IMP

  000069         003920 2000-LOAD-TABLE.
  000070         003930     READ COURSE-FILE INTO COURSE-ENTRIES (COURSE-IND)                  15 25 27
  000071      1  003940        AT END SET END-OF-FILE TO TRUE                                  35
  000072         003950     END-READ.

  000074         004000 3000-PROCESS-COURSE.
  000075         004200     MOVE PASSED-COURSE-CODE TO HOLD-COURSE-CODE                        41 32
  000076         004300     MOVE PASSED-DATE  TO HOLD-DATE                                     43 31
  000077         004400     MOVE STUD-NUMBER (COURSE-IND) TO PASSED-HOLD-STUD-NUMBER.          28 27 44
                                              .
                                              .
                                              .

PP 5668-958 IBM VS COBOL II Release 3.0 09/13/88              CRSPROC   Date 04/15/91  Time 14:10:39   Page    8

  Defined   Cross-reference of programs     References

       2    CRSPROC
```

Figure 11.7 *(Continued)*

```
PP 5668-958 IBM VS COBOL II Release 3.0 09/13/88            CRSPROC   Date 04/15/91  Time 14:10:39   Page     9

Data Division Map

Data Definition Attribute codes (rightmost column) have the following meanings:
    D = Object of OCCURS DEPENDING     G = GLOBAL                            S = Spanned file
    E = EXTERNAL                       O = Has OCCURS clause                 U = Undefined format file
    F = Fixed length file              OG= Group has own length definition   V = Variable length file
    FB= Fixed length blocked file      R = REDEFINES                         VB= Variable length blocked file

Source   Hierarchy and                                  Base       Hex-Displacement  Asmblr Data                  Data Def
LineID   Data Name                                      Locator    Blk   Structure   Definition    Data Type      Attributes
     2   PROGRAM-ID CRSPROC ------------------------------------------------------------------------------------------------*
                                                     .
                                                     .
                                                     .
    41   01 PASSED-COURSE-CODE. . . . . . . . . . . . . BLL=0001   000               DS 15C        Display
(7c) --> 42   01 PASSED-MAX-TAB-ENTRIES. . . . . . . . . BLL=0002   000               DS 2P         Packed-Dec
(7g[6]) --> 43   01 PASSED-DATE . . . . . . . . . . . . BLL=0003   000               DS 6C         Disp-Num
    44   01 PASSED-HOLD-STUD-NUMBER . . . . . . . . . . BLL=0004   000               DS 5C         Disp-Num
                                                     .
                                                     .
                                                     .
LINE #  HEXLOC  VERB                        LINE #  HEXLOC  VERB                        LINE #  HEXLOC  VERB
000050 0002DE DISPLAY                       000051 0002EC IF   <-- (7a)                 000052 0002F6 PERFORM
000066 0002F6 ADD                           000067 000302 MOVE                          000054 00030C OPEN
                                                     .
                                                     .
                                                     .
PP 5668-958 IBM VS COBOL II Release 3.0 09/13/88            CRSPROC   Date 04/15/91  Time 14:10:39   Page    12

                     *** TGT MEMORY MAP ***
           PGMLOC    TGTLOC

                     *** VARIABLE PORTION OF TGT ***

           000534    00012C   BASE LOCATORS FOR SPECIAL REGISTERS
           00053C    000134   BASE LOCATORS FOR WORKING-STORAGE
(7d[1]) -->000540    000138   BASE LOCATORS FOR LINKAGE-SECTION
           000554    00014C   BASE LOCATORS FOR FILES
                                                     .
                                                     .
                                                     .

 MVS/DFP VERSION 3 RELEASE 2 LINKAGE EDITOR     14:10:55  MON  APR 15, 1991
 JOB STUDCRSB    STEP S2          PROCEDURE LKED
 INVOCATION PARAMETERS - LIST,XREF,LET,MAP
 ACTUAL SIZE=(317440,79872)
 OUTPUT DATA SET MY.SUBPROG.LOAD IS ON VOLUME PRIY11
IEW0000     NAME CRSPROC(R)                                                     00036801

                                         CROSS REFERENCE TABLE

  CONTROL SECTION                             ENTRY

    NAME      ORIGIN  LENGTH                    NAME    LOCATION     NAME   LOCATION     NAME   LOCATION     NAME   LOCATION
  { CRSPROC     00      E41   <-- (6c)
  { IGZEBST *   E48     428                     IGZEBS2     10D6

(1e[2])
  LOCATION   REFERS TO SYMBOL   IN CONTROL SECTION             LOCATION   REFERS TO SYMBOL   IN CONTROL SECTION
      6C          IGZEBST          IGZEBST                        1244          IGZETUN          $UNRESOLVED(W)
    1248          IGZEOPT        $UNRESOLVED(W)
 ENTRY ADDRESS        00

 TOTAL LENGTH       1270
 ** CRSPROC  DID NOT PREVIOUSLY EXIST BUT WAS ADDED AND HAS AMODE ANY
 ** LOAD MODULE HAS RMODE 24
 ** AUTHORIZATION CODE IS          0.

(3a) -->{STUDCRSA BEGINNING
        {PROGRAM CRSPROC BEGINNING
```

Figure 11.7 *(Continued)*

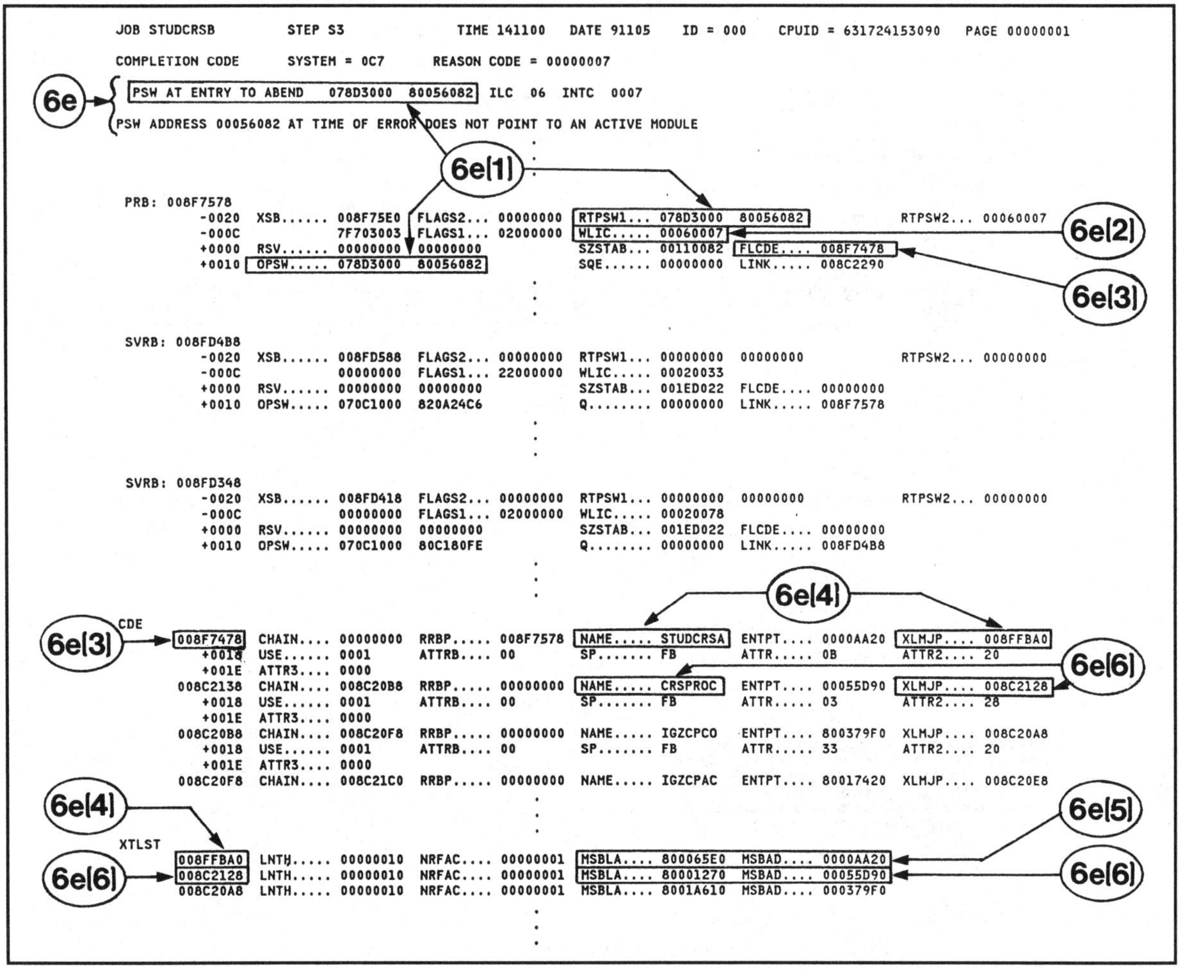

```
JOB STUDCRSB       STEP S3        TIME 141100   DATE 91105   ID = 000   CPUID = 631724153090   PAGE 00000001

COMPLETION CODE    SYSTEM = 0C7   REASON CODE = 00000007

PSW AT ENTRY TO ABEND   078D3000  80056082  ILC  06  INTC  0007
PSW ADDRESS 00056082 AT TIME OF ERROR DOES NOT POINT TO AN ACTIVE MODULE
                                   .
                                   .
 PRB: 008F7578
        -0020  XSB...... 008F75E0  FLAGS2... 00000000  RTPSW1... 078D3000  80056082        RTPSW2... 00060007
        -000C            7F703003  FLAGS1... 02000000  WLIC..... 00060007
        +0000  RSV...... 00000000  00000000            SZSTAB... 00110082  FLCDE.... 008F7478
        +0010  OPSW..... 078D3000  80056082            SQE...... 00000000  LINK..... 008C2290
                                   .
                                   .
                                   .
 SVRB: 008FD4B8
        -0020  XSB...... 008FD588  FLAGS2... 00000000  RTPSW1... 00000000  00000000        RTPSW2... 00000000
        -000C            00000000  FLAGS1... 22000000  WLIC..... 00020033
        +0000  RSV...... 00000000  00000000            SZSTAB... 001ED022  FLCDE.... 00000000
        +0010  OPSW..... 070C1000  820A24C6            Q........ 00000000  LINK..... 008F7578
                                   .
                                   .
                                   .
 SVRB: 008FD348
        -0020  XSB...... 008FD418  FLAGS2... 00000000  RTPSW1... 00000000  00000000        RTPSW2... 00000000
        -000C            00000000  FLAGS1... 02000000  WLIC..... 00020078
        +0000  RSV...... 00000000  00000000            SZSTAB... 001ED022  FLCDE.... 00000000
        +0010  OPSW..... 070C1000  80C180FE            Q........ 00000000  LINK..... 008FD4B8
                                   .
                                   .
                                   .
 CDE
      008F7478  CHAIN.... 00000000  RRBP..... 008F7578  NAME..... STUDCRSA  ENTPT.... 0000AA20  XLMJP.... 008FFBA0
         +0018  USE...... 0001      ATTRB.... 00        SP....... FB        ATTR..... 0B        ATTR2.... 20
         +001E  ATTR3.... 0000
      008C2138  CHAIN.... 008C20B8  RRBP..... 00000000  NAME..... CRSPROC   ENTPT.... 00055D90  XLMJP.... 008C2128
         +0018  USE...... 0001      ATTRB.... 00        SP....... FB        ATTR..... 03        ATTR2.... 28
         +001E  ATTR3.... 0000
      008C20B8  CHAIN.... 008C20F8  RRBP..... 00000000  NAME..... IGZCPCO   ENTPT.... 800379F0  XLMJP.... 008C20A8
         +0018  USE...... 0001      ATTRB.... 00        SP....... FB        ATTR..... 33        ATTR2.... 20
         +001E  ATTR3.... 0000
      008C20F8  CHAIN.... 008C21C0  RRBP..... 00000000  NAME..... IGZCPAC   ENTPT.... 80017420  XLMJP.... 008C20E8
                                   .
                                   .
                                   .
 XTLST
      008FFBA0  LNTH..... 00000010  NRFAC.... 00000001  MSBLA.... 800065E0  MSBAD.... 0000AA20
      008C2128  LNTH..... 00000010  NRFAC.... 00000001  MSBLA.... 80001270  MSBAD.... 00055D90
      008C20A8  LNTH..... 00000010  NRFAC.... 00000001  MSBLA.... 8001A610  MSBAD.... 000379F0
                                   .
                                   .
                                   .
```


Figure 11.7 *(Continued)*

g. Although program STUDCRSA has a LINKAGE SECTION, no parameters were passed from the JCL. At this point it looks like there is no input to the main program. Is STUDCRSA to be called by another program? Is there a potential problem here?

6. Let us analyze the SYMPTOM and actual SYSTEM dumps.

   a. The symptom dump shows us that the name of the active load module is CRSPROC, its LPA is 55D90, the offset of the NSI is 2F2, and the ILC is 6. We already know from the DISPLAY statement examined in step 3*b*(2) that the subprogram CRSPROC began execution.

   b. Subtract the ILC from the NSI offset. 2F2 − 6 = 2EC. This is the offset of the ABENDing instruction within module CRSPROC.

   c. We can look back at the linkage-editor map from step S2 to see that this instruction is in CSECT CRSPROC.

```
SAVE AREA TRACE

PROCEEDING FORWARD FROM TCBFSAB

STUDCRSA WAS ENTERED VIA LINK

SA   00005FB0 WD1 00000000  HSA 00000000  LSA 00010638  RET 80FD3AD8  EPA 0000AA20  R0  FD000008
              R1  00005FF8  R2  00000040  R3  008F6654  R4  008F6630  R5  008FF0B8  R6  008CEFF8
              R7  FD000000  R8  008F1030  R9  808FF3F0  R10 00000000  R11 008FF0B8  R12 00E1BCDA

IGZCPAC  WAS ENTERED VIA CALL        AT EP .IGZCLNK...C23.012.08.89.15.15...N.....

SA   00010638 WD1 00300000  HSA 00005FB0  LSA 00052E88  RET 50010A42  EPA 80035950  R0  00001AA9
              R1  00010798  R2  0000A8B0  R3  0000003C  R4  00000000  R5  80005FFE  R6  0000AAC0
              R7  00000000  R8  0000FAC0  R9  80005FFE  R10 00000000  R11 000109CC  R12 000108D0

CRSPROC  WAS ENTERED VIA CALL        AT EP CRSPROC..C2.1.3.0.05.01.91.15.21.30

SA   00052E88 WD1 00102401  HSA 00010638  LSA 00056198  RET 80035E78  EPA 80055D90  R0  00000000
(7h(1)) ----> R1  000108B8  R2  00052F1D  R3  0000AA20  R4  00010798  R5  00052F80  R6  00052F80
              R7  80055D90  R8  80035E7A  R9  00010638  R10 00052CC8  R11 000109CC  R12 80035982

IGZCPAC  WAS ENTERED VIA CALL        AT EP .IGZCDSP...C23.009.29.88.20.03...N.....

SA   00056198 WD1 00108001  HSA 00052E88  LSA 000520B0  RET 8005607C  EPA 80020708  R0  00056E66
              R1  00055EEF  R2  00005164  R3  0000AA20  R4  00055DE4  R5  00052E88  R6  00052F80
              R7  00FD3A88  R8  00006000  R9  000564F0  R10 00055E18  R11 0005601E  R12 00055E10

IGZCPCO  WAS ENTERED VIA CALL        AT EP .IGZEOUT...C23.009.29.88.22.13...O.....

SA   000520B0 WD1 00100001  HSA 00056198  LSA 000521B8  RET 80020B28  EPA 00048420  R0  00056E66
              R1  0005214C  R2  00000019  R3  00055E32  R4  00055E32  R5  00000000  R6  00054F9A
              R7  0000005F  R8  000113EC  R9  00056198  R10 00052CC8  R11 00005164  R12 8002073A

SA   000521B8 WD1 00101001  HSA 000520B0  LSA 00056318  RET 40048704  EPA 92DD0968  R0  00056E66
              R1  00054F80  R2  00005028  R3  00055E32  R4  00055E32  R5  00000000  R6  0005214C
              R7  0000005F  R8  000113EC  R9  00056198  R10 00000004  R11 00005164  R12 50048452

INVALID BACK CHAIN

SA   00056318 WD1 000563A0  HSA C0000000  LSA 00000000  RET 00000000  EPA 000564A0  R0  00000000
              R1  00000000  R2  00000000  R3  00000000  R4  00000000  R5  00000000  R6  00000000
              R7  00000000  R8  00000000  R9  00000000  R10 00000001  R11 00004000  R12 00000001

INTERRUPT AT 80056082
                                          .
                                          .
                                          .
```

Figure 11.7 *(Continued)*

d. The Op Code of the ABENDing instruction, taken from DATA AT PSW in the symptom dump, is F9. Referring to Appendix D shows us that this is the decimal Compare Packed (CP) instruction.

e. Although it is not necessary to do so, it will be instructive to look at the actual system dump. Notice that the PSW, ILC, and completion code printed at the top of the system dump are the same as was reported in the symptom dump, but that there is a message indicating that the PSW at the time of the error does not point to an active load module. This is typical when an ABEND occurs in a module which was called dynamically.

(1) Use the PSW AT ENTRY TO ABEND to find the proper Request Block by matching it with the RTPSW1 or OPSW field. This leads you to the PRB. (We could have counted up three request blocks from the bottom of the RB chain instead.)

(2) Notice that the ILC and interrupt code in the WLIC field are 6 and 07, as we already knew.

(3) Use the FLCDE field to find the proper CDE entry. Notice that there are many CDE entries.

(4) The entry in the CDE indicates that the load module associated with

```
LPA/JPA MODULE     STUDCRSA
0000AA20 90ECD00C 185D05F0 4580F010 E2E3E4C4   C3D9E2C1 E5E2D9F1 0700989F F02407FF   *.......0..0.STUDCRSAVSR1....0...*
0000AA40 96021034 07FE41F0 000107FE 00012E94   0000AA20 0000AA20 000108D0 00010638   *.......0........................*
0000AA60 000109CC 00010E82 00000000 00000000   00000000 00000000 00000000 00000000   *................................*
0000AA80 00000000 00000000 00000000 00000000   00000000 00000000 00000000 00000000   *................................*
0000AAA0 00000000 00010870 F1F54BF2 F14BF1F7   D4C1E840 40F16B40 F1F9F9F1 00000000   *........15.21.17MAY  1. 1991....*
0000AAC0 E2E3E4C4 C3D9E2C1 40E6D6D9 D2C9D5C7   60E2E3D6 D9C1C7C5 40E2E3C1 D9E3E25C   *STUDCRSA WORKING.STORAGE STARTS.*
0000AAE0 015C0000 00000000 F0F0F0F0 F0F00000   00000000 00000000 00000000 00000000   *........000000..................*
0000AB00 00000000 00000000 00000000 00000000   00000000 00000000 00000000 00000000   *................................*
(7g(4))                                            .
                                                   .
                                                   .
00010800 0000AAA8 00000000 00000000 00000000   00000000 00000000 000109C8 00000000   *..........................H....*
00010820 00000000 00000000 00000000 00000000   00000000 00000000 00000000 00000000   *................................*
00010840 0000AAC0 0000BAC0 0000CAC0 0000DAC0   0000EAC0 0000FAC0 00000000 00000000   *................................*
00010860 00000000 0000015C 00000000 00000000   80005FFE 00000000 1AA90000 00000000   *................................*
00010880 00000000 00000000 00000000 00000000   00000000 00010D28 00000000 00010DB2   *................................*
000108A0 00000000 00010E20 00000000 00000000   00000000 00000000 00006000 00006006   *................................*
                                                   .
(7g(3))                                            .          (7h(2))
                                                   .
LPA/JPA MODULE     CRSPROC
00055D80                                       47F0F070 23C3D9E2 D7D9D6C3 4040C3F2   *                .00..CRSPROC  C2*
00055DA0 40F14BF3 4BF040F0 F561F0F1 61F9F140   F1F54BF2 F14BF3F0 00055DE4 E02E2C0C   * 1.3.0 05.01.91 15.21.30...U....*
00055DC0 00810000 4208010B 81000000 08000000   00000000 0000000F 00000010 00000000   *................................*
00055DE0 40404040 00055D90 00055E10 00056198   00055D95 00055D90 00055FC0 00056BD8   *     ...........................Q*
00055E00 90ECD00C 5810F028 98EFF068 07FF0000   00055E18 0005601E 00055FC0 00055FC0   *......0...0.....................*
                                                   .
                                                   .      (7d(2))   (7g(8))
                                                   .
00056280 00000000 00000001 0005631C 00000000   00055E64 00000000 00055D90 00055E18   *................................*
000562A0 000562E8 00055E14 00056318 000564F0   00000000 40404040 40404040 40404040   *...Y..........0....             *
000562C0 40404040 40404040 00056BA0 000564F0   00000000 00006006 00006000 0000AAE0   *        .......0................*
000562E0 000103D8 00000000 00055FC0 00055FC0   00055FC0 00055FC0 00055FC0 00000000   *...Q............................*
00056300 00000000 00000000 00000000 00000000   00000000 80000001 000563A0 C0000000   *................................*
00056320 00000000 00000000 000564A0 00000000   00000000 00000000 00000000 00000000   *................................*
00056340 00000000 00000000 00000000 00000000   00000000 00000001 00004000 00000001   *...........................  .....*
                                                   .
                                                   .
                                                   .
USER SUBPOOL STORAGE

00005020 00005E28 00000090 00000000 00000000   00000000 00000000 00000000 01054F78   *................................*
00005040 00794000 00016FE8 46000001 94013DD4   00CC0048 008DD458 92DD0968 00000001   *.. ....Y.......M......M.........*
                                                   .
              (7d(3)),(7h(3))                      .
                                                   .
00006000 00000000 00000000 00000000 00000000   00000000 00000000 00000000 00000000   *................................*
       LINES 00006020-00009B00  SAME AS ABOVE
00009B20 00010000 00000000 00000000 00000000   03010000 00000000 00000000 00000000   *................................*
                                                   .
                                                   .
                                                   .
```

Figure 11.7 *(Continued)*

the PRB is STUDCRSA. This is the module containing the main program; however, we have already determined that the module containing the subprogram is where the ABEND occurred. Using the XLMJP we find the XTLST entry associated with the current CDE. Notice that there are many XTLST entries.

(5) The XTLST specifies a length of 65E0 and an LPA of AA20 for STUDCRSA. Adding these together gives the ending address for STUDCRSA. AA20 + 65E0 = 11000. The address of the ABENDing instruction is the ILC subtracted from the NSI in the PSW (this should be the same as the address in the DATA AT PSW field in the symptom dump). 56082 – 6 = 5607C. This is beyond the address range for STUDCRSA.

(6) Scan the list of CDE entries for module CRSPROC; remember the symptom dump specified that CRSPROC was in control. Find the corresponding XTLST entry. The module's LPA is 55D90 and its length

is 1270. Adding them together gives CRSPROC's ending address. 55D90 + 1270 = 57000. The address of the ABENDing instruction, 5607D, falls within this range. This confirms that the ABEND did indeed occur within CRSPROC.

7. Use the compiler output to examine the instruction and operands in the COBOL program.
   a. Use the OFFSET compiler output to find the COBOL instruction in CRSPROC. Recall that the offset is 2EC (from step 6*b*). The instruction at offset 2EC is generated by the IF statement at line 51.
   b. Statement 51 is

```
IF PASSED-MAX-TAB-ENTRIES GREATER THAN +15 . . .
```

   c. Let us examine field PASSED-MAX-TAB-ENTRIES. Use the output from the MAP compiler option.

```
PASSED-MAX-TAB-ENTRIES BLL 0002 DISP 000 2 bytes PACKED
```

   (We could also verify this definition by looking at line 42 in the source code.)
   d. In order to examine the contents of the field in the storage dump:
      (1) Go to the TGT MEMORY MAP to find the offset of BLL 0000. It is 540. Since we are interested in BLL cell 0002, we add 8 bytes to this (each cell is 4 bytes in length). 540 + 8 = 548. Adding 548 to the LPA of CRSPROC gives the address of BLL 0002. 548 + 55D90 = 562D8.
      (2) Go to address 562D8 in the dump. This is the location of BLL 0002. Its contents is 6000. This is the base address for PASSED-MAX-TAB-ENTRIES.
      (3) Since the displacement from BLL 0002 is 0, we can go directly to address 6000 in the dump. Recall that the main program was compiled under OS/VS COBOL. A CALL statement in OS/VS COBOL makes the address of the field in the main program available to the subprogram. Thus address 6000 should be the location of the field in STUDCRSA which was passed to subprogram CRSPROC as PASSED-MAX-TAB-ENTRIES. However, this address is not in STUDCRSA (remember that the LPA of STUDCRSA is AA20). Scanning the dump we find that 6000 is in user subpool storage, and that its contents is 0000. We have found out why the program ABENDed with a S0C7, the value 0000 is invalid packed data, but why does PASSED-MAX-TAB-ENTRIES appear in such an unexpected place in storage?
   e. Let us look carefully at the parameters received by the subprogram. Line 46 in CRSPROC is coded as

```
PROCEDURE DIVISION USING     PASSED-MAX-TAB-ENTRIES
                             PASSED-COURSE-CODE
                             PASSED-DATE
                             PASSED-HOLD-STUD-NUMBER.
```

PASSED-MAX-TAB-ENTRIES, a 2-byte packed field is the first field appearing in the USING clause of the subprogram.

f. The CALL statement starting at line 60 in STUDCRSA is coded as

```
CALL 'CRSPROC' USING PARM-DATE
                     PARM-COURSE
                     MAX-TAB-ENTRIES
                     HOLD-STUD-NUMBER
```

COBOL matches the parameters by position, not by name. Thus PASSED-MAX-TAB-ENTRIES is matched with PARM-DATE, the first field in the USING clause of the main program. Logically, the program was supposed to have passed MAX-TAB-ENTRIES to PASSED-MAX-TAB-ENTRIES.

g. Let us verify that MAX-TAB-ENTRIES, the third field in the main program's USING clause, was unintentionally matched with PASSED-DATE, the third field in the subprogram's USING clause. We will examine the field's contents in the storage dump.

(1) First let us examine MAX-TAB-ENTRIES. The DATA DIVISION map in STUDCRSA gives the following information for MAX-TAB-ENTRIES:

```
MAX-TAB-ENTRIES    BL 3    DISP 20    2 bytes COMP-3
```

(2) Go to the TGT MEMORY MAP to find the offset of BL cell 1. It is 5E18. Since we are interested in BL cell 3, we add 8 bytes to this. 5E18 + 8 = 5E20. Adding 5E20 to the LPA of STUDCRSA gives the address of BL 3. 5E20 + AA20 = 10840.

(3) Go to address 10840 in the dump. This is the location of BL cell 3. Its contents is AAC0. This is the base address for MAX-TAB-ENTRIES.

(4) Since the displacement from BL 3 is 20, we add it to the base address. AAC0 = 20 = AAE0. Go to this address. The contents of MAX-TAB-ENTRIES is 015C. This is equivalent to +15.

(5) We see that MAX-TAB-ENTRIES is defined at line 25 in STUDCRSA as a COMP-3 field with a VALUE clause of +15.

(6) Now let us look at PASSED-DATE. The Data DIVISION map in CRSPROC gives the following information for PASSED-DATE:

```
PASSED-DATE BLL 0003 DISP 000 6 bytes Disp-Num
```

(7) We already know from step 7*d*(1) that the offset of BLL 0000 is 540. Since we are interested in BLL cell 0003, we add 12 bytes (C in hexadecimal) to this. 540 + C = 54C. Adding 54C to the LPA of CRSPROC gives the address of BLL 0003. 54C + 55D90 = 562DC.

(8) Go to address 562DC in the dump. This is the location of BLL 0003. Its contents is AAE0. This is the base address for PASSED-DATE. Since the displacement is 000, AAE0 is the actual address of PASSED-DATE. This is the same address as MAX-TAB-ENTRIES in the main program.

h. Now, since the main program's field PARM-DATE was used in the subprogram's IF statement instead of the proper field, let's look more closely at PARM-DATE. PARM-DATE is at line 49 in the LINKAGE SECTION of the main program. Apparently it was to be passed to STUDCRSA from either another program or from the JCL. Since STUDCRSA is the main program in this system, we must assume that a parameter was supposed to be passed from the JCL. We mentioned in step 5*g* that no parameters were passed to STUDCRSA and that this could be a potential problem. We have discovered that this was indeed a problem; there were no valid data available in PARM-DATE. Let us check the parameter list.

(1) Look at the Save Area trace. Register 1 in the program that called CRSPROC will contain the address of the parameter list. The Save Area trace indicates that STUDCRSA called the COBOL II subroutine IGZCLNK and IGZCLNK then transferred control to CRSPROC. Remember, the purpose of IGZCLNK is to provide execution-time support for the CALL verb which effects the transfer of control to subprogram CRSPROC (see Sec. 11.3). The contents of IGZCLNK's register 1 is 108B8.

```
SAVE AREA TRACE


PROCEEDING FORWARD FROM TCBFSAB

INTER33  WAS ENTERED VIA LINK          AT EP INTER33.....C2.1.3.0.05.14.91.13.44.38

SA    00005FB0  WD1 00000000   HSA 00000000   LSA 0000AA08   RET 80FD3AD8   EPA 8000A7F0   R0  FD000008
                R1  00005FF8   R2  00000040   R3  008F6654   R4  008F6630   R5  008FF0B8   R6  008D3FF8
                R7  FD000000   R8  008FF288   R9  808F74A8   R10 00000000   R11 008FF0B8   R12 00E1BCDA

IGZCPAC  WAS ENTERED VIA CALL          AT EP .IGZCLNK...C23.012.08.89.15.15...N.....

SA    0000AA08  WD1 00108001   HSA 00005FB0   LSA 00048F28   RET 8000A9CC   EPA 8002B950   R0  8000AE06
                R1  0000A8FF   R2  000052EC   R3  0000A9AA   R4  0000A844   R5  00048CC8   R6  008D3FF8
                R7  FD000000   R8  8000A604   R9  0000AA08   R10 0000A878   R11 0000A938   R12 0000A870

SLIP03   WAS ENTERED VIA CALL          AT EP SLIP03...C2.1.3.0.05.14.91.13.44.44

SA    00048F28  WD1 00102401   HSA 0000AA08   LSA 0000CA50   RET 8002BE78   EPA 8000C878   R0  000000F8
                R1  00000000   R2  00048FBD   R3  0000A7F0   R4  0000A8FF   R5  00049020   R6  00049020
                R7  8000C878   R8  8002BE7A   R9  0000AA08   R10 00048CC8   R11 0000A938   R12 8002B982

IGZCPAC  WAS ENTERED VIA CALL          AT EP .IGZCDSP...C23.009.29.88.20.03...N.....

SA    0000CA50  WD1 00108001   HSA 00048F28   LSA 000480B0   RET 8000CA12   EPA 80016708   R0  0000CE66
                R1  0000C95E   R2  000052EC   R3  0000C9FA   R4  0000C8CC   R5  00048F28   R6  00049020
                R7  00FD3A88   R8  8000A604   R9  0000CA50   R10 0000C900   R11 0000C988   R12 0000C8F8

IGZCPCO  WAS ENTERED VIA CALL          AT EP .IGZEOUT...C23.009.29.88.22.13...O.....

SA    000480B0  WD1 00100001   HSA 0000CA50   LSA 000481B8   RET 80016B28   EPA 0003E420   R0  0000CE66
                R1  0004814C   R2  0000000F   R3  0000C910   R4  0000C910   R5  00000000   R6  0000BF90
                R7  00000069   R8  8000A604   R9  0000CA50   R10 00048CC8   R11 000052EC   R12 8001673A
                                                            .
                                                            .
                                                            .
```

Figure 11.8 A Save Area trace to be used in answering review question 5.

```
MVS/XA DFP VER 2 LINKAGE EDITOR                13:22:32  THU  OCT 27, 1988
JOB DMPCOB2D    STEP S1          PROCEDURE LKED
INVOCATION PARAMETERS - LIST,XREF,LET,MAP
ACTUAL SIZE=(317440,86016)
OUTPUT DATA SET MY.COBOL.LOAD IS ON VOLUME TYOYN2
IEW0000     NAME DMPCOB2D(R)                                            00030000
IEW0132  SALES09


                                              CROSS REFERENCE TABLE

 CONTROL SECTION                      ENTRY

   NAME    ORIGIN  LENGTH               NAME    LOCATION     NAME    LOCATION     NAME    LOCATION     NAME    LOCATION
 SALES033     00     1384
 IGZCDSP *   1388     4AC
 IGZCSPA *   1838     7AC
                                                          .
                                                          .
                                                          .

 LOCATION   REFERS TO SYMBOL   IN CONTROL SECTION             LOCATION   REFERS TO SYMBOL   IN CONTROL SECTION
     6C            IGZENRI          IGZENRI                         A4           SALES09         $UNRESOLVED
   17AC            IGZCONV          IGZCONV                       17B0           IGZEOUT          IGZEOUT
   17B4            IGZESPM          IGZESPM                       ACBC           IGZCONVX         IGZCONVX
   ACC0            IGZCONVX         IGZCONVX                      D2D0           IGZEOPD          IGZEOPD
   D2D4            ILBOSTP0       $UNRESOLVED(W)                  D2C8           ILBOCOM         $UNRESOLVED(W)
                                                          .
                                                          .
                                                          .
ENTRY ADDRESS       00

TOTAL LENGTH      12410
** SALES033 REPLACED AND HAS AMODE 24
** LOAD MODULE HAS RMODE 24
** AUTHORIZATION CODE IS          0.


                                           DIAGNOSTIC MESSAGE DIRECTORY
  IEW0132 ERROR - SYMBOL PRINTED IS AN UNRESOLVED EXTERNAL REFERENCE.
```

Figure 11.9 Linkage-editor diagnostic output to be used in answering review question 7.

(2) Go to address 108B8. The contents is 6000. This is the address of the first parameter passed to CRSPROC. Since the parameter PARM-DATE should have come from the JCL, the first halfword at that address will be the length of the parameter string and the next halfword will contain the actual parameter string (see Sec. 11.2).

(3) Go to address 6000. As we saw in step 7*d*(3), its contents is 0000. No parameter was passed from the JCL.

Thus the S0C7 ABEND resulted from a double problem; the parameters were passed incorrectly from the main program and the value in the field (supposed parameter) in the IF statement was improper.

11.8 A FINAL WORD ON SYSTEM DUMPS

This concludes the series of chapters on system dumps. We have looked at numerous control blocks and several dumps. Our tour of system dump solving has given many alternative methods for finding relevant debugging information. Armed with these techniques and information sources, you should be in a good position to handle most system dump situations.

```
//S1       EXEC COBUCL,
//         PARM.COB='DYNAM,RES'
//COB.SYSIN    DD DSN=MY.PROGLIB.COBOL'(CH11EX8),DISP=SHR
//LKED.SYSLMOD DD DSN=MY.COBOL.LOAD,DISP=SHR
//LKED.SYSLIB  DD
//              DD DSN=MY.SUBPROG.LOAD,DISP=SHR
//LKED.SYSIN  DD *
/*
//S2       EXEC PGM=CH11EX8,PARM='N'
//STEPLIB      DD DSN=MY.COBOL.LOAD,DISP=SHR
//             DD DSN=MY.SUBPROG.LOAD,DISP=SHR
//INFILE       DD *
/*
//OUTFILE      DD SYSOUT=A
//SYSOUT       DD SYSOUT=A
//SYSUDUMP     DD SYSOUT=A
                                                       .
                                                       .
                                                       .

IEF142I CH11EX8 COB S1 - STEP WAS EXECUTED - COND CODE 0000
                                                       .
                                                       .
                                                       .

IEF142I CH11EX8 LKED S1 - STEP WAS EXECUTED - COND CODE 0000
                                                       .
                                                       .
                                                       .

CSV003I REQUESTED MODULE DATERTN  NOT FOUND
CSV028I JOBNAME=CH11EX8   STEPNAME=S2        ABEND806-04
IEA995I SYMPTOM DUMP OUTPUT
SYSTEM COMPLETION CODE=806  REASON CODE=00000004
 TIME=15.31.27  SEQ=21067  CPU=0000  ASID=004A
 PSW AT TIME OF ERROR  070C1000   811434DC  ILC 2  INTC 0D
   NO ACTIVE MODULE FOUND
   DATA AT PSW  011434D6 - A6261810  0A0D186D  58E002FC
   GPR  0-3  84806000  84806000  0004DF1D  00000000
   GPR  4-7  00000010  008FD348  008D0450  0004DF1D
   GPR  8-11 00000000  008D0450  81142FAA  01143ED2
   GPR 12-15 01143ED6  008D0450  8114338A  00000004
 END OF SYMPTOM DUMP
                                                       .
                                                       .
                                                       .

IEF472I CH11EX8 S2 - COMPLETION CODE - SYSTEM=806 USER=0000 REASON=00000004
                                                       .
                                                       .
                                                       .
```

Figure 11.10 Portions of the JCL, job log, compiler listing, and linkage-editor output to be used in answering review question 8. (*Continued*)

11.9 SUMMARY

Solving system dumps involving multiple load modules or multiple programs within a load module requires an understanding of program linkage conventions. All programs must establish a Save Area to enable MVS to keep track of information as programs branch to and return from other programs. When your program receives control, it must save the contents of its caller's general-purpose registers in the caller's Save area, create a Save Area for the next called program, store the address of the callers's Save Area, and put the address of your Save Area in register 13.

```
PP 5740-CB1 RELEASE 2.4                     IBM OS/VS COBOL  JULY  1, 1982          15.31.22  DATE MAY 11,1991

   1                    15.31.22        MAY 11,1991

004900 IDENTIFICATION DIVISION.
005000  PROGRAM-ID.    CH11EX8.
005100  AUTHOR.        ALAN FRIEND.
005200  DATE-WRITTEN. SEPTEMBER 1990.
005300 DATE-COMPILED. MAY 11,1991.

005500 ENVIRONMENT DIVISION.
005600  INPUT-OUTPUT SECTION.
005700   FILE-CONTROL.
005800     SELECT INPUT-FILE        ASSIGN TO INFILE.
005810     SELECT PRINT-FILE        ASSIGN TO OUTFILE.

006000 DATA DIVISION.
006100  FILE SECTION.
006200  FD INPUT-FILE
006300     RECORDING MODE IS F
006400     RECORD CONTAINS 80 CHARACTERS
006500     BLOCK CONTAINS 0 RECORDS
006600     LABEL RECORDS ARE OMITTED
006700     DATA RECORD IS  INPUT-FILE-REC.
006800  01 INPUT-FILE-REC.
006801     05 RECORD-TYPE              PIC X.
006802     05 FILLER                   PIC X(79).
006810  FD PRINT-FILE
006820     RECORDING MODE IS F
006830     RECORD CONTAINS 133 CHARACTERS
006840     BLOCK CONTAINS 0 RECORDS
006850     LABEL RECORDS ARE OMITTED
006860     DATA RECORD IS  PRINT-FILE-REC.
006870  01 PRINT-FILE-REC              PIC X(133).
```

Figure 11.10 *(Continued)*

When your program relinquishes control, it must restore the contents of the caller's registers, adjust register 13 to point back to the caller's Save Area, and set a return code.

Because Save Areas point to one another, examining the Save Area trace in a dump can enable you to determine pertinent information which was stored in the calling and called programs' Save Areas. Important information from a debugging standpoint includes entry-point and return addresses. Unfortunately, the Save Area trace is not always reliable; although COBOL automatically adheres to standard linkage conventions, there is no guarantee that other programs have.

When standard linkage conventions are followed, certain general-purpose registers have specific assignments. Register 1 normally contains the address of the parameter list used in passing parameters in a CALL. Register 0 is often used to pass additional parameters to certain supervisor routines. Register 13 points to the Save Area which, in a COBOL program, is at the beginning of the TGT. Register 14 contains the return address. This is the point at which execution should resume after a return from a called program. At entry into a subprogram register 15 contains the entry-point address. Upon leaving a program register 15 usually contains a return code.

The contents of the general-purpose registers for a program which has ABENDed can be found in several places: the program's Save Area, the symp-

```
    2        CH11EX8          15.31.22        MAY 11,1991

007000 WORKING-STORAGE SECTION.

007200*****************************************************************
007300*    DATA AREAS FOR DATE INFO RECEIVED FROM SUBPROGRAM          *
007600*****************************************************************
007700 01 FIRST-DATE.
007800    05 FIRST-DATE-TYPE             PIC X(9).
007900    05 FIRST-DATE-RECEIVED         PIC X(6).
008000 01 SECOND-DATE.
008100    05 SECOND-DATE-TYPE            PIC X(9).
008200    05 SECOND-DATE-RECEIVED        PIC X(5).

008700*****************************************************************
008800*    OUTPUT DETAIL LINES                                        *
008900*****************************************************************

009110 01 WS-RECORD-TYPE-A.
009200    05 FILLER                      PIC X(20)
009300                                            VALUE 'GREGORIAN DATE: '.
009400    05 GREGORIAN-OUT               PIC X(6)  VALUE SPACES.
009401    05 GREGORIAN-RECORD            PIC X(6)  VALUE SPACES.

009600 01 WS-RECORD-TYPE-B.
009700    05 FILLER                      PIC X(20)   VALUE 'JULIAN DATE: '.
009800    05 JULIAN-OUT                  PIC X(5)  VALUE SPACES.
009900    05 JULIAN-RECORD               PIC X(5)  VALUE SPACES.

010300*****************************************************************
010400*    SWITCH AND HOLD-AREA                                       *
010500*****************************************************************

010700 01 SWITCH-AND-HOLD-AREA.
010710    05 SWEOF                       PIC X       VALUE '0'.
010800       88 END-OF-FILE                          VALUE '1'.
010810    05 GREGORIAN-HOLD              PIC X(6).
010820    05 JULIAN-HOLD                 PIC X(5).

011100 LINKAGE SECTION.

011300*****************************************************************
011400*    PARM PASSED THROUGH JCL                                    *
011500*****************************************************************

011700 01 JCL-PARM.
011800    05 PARM-LENGTH                 PIC S9(4)   COMP SYNC.
011900    05 PROCESS-TYPE                PIC X.
```

Figure 11.10 *(Continued)*

tom dump, in the SVRB below the RB for the program, and in REGISTERS AT ENTRY TO ABEND right before the storage contents of the ABENDing module in the hexadecimal storage dump.

The linkage-editor is responsible for creating an executable load module from one or more object modules, load modules, or both. Individual program units within the load module are called CSECTs; after an instruction is known to be within a module it is necessary to determine which CSECT it is in.

Besides generating a load module, the linkage-editor produces diagnostic output. When the LIST option is in effect, a listing of the control statements used is given. Some common control statements are INCLUDE, ORDER, ENTRY, and NAME. The ENTRY statement should always be coded since it explicitly establishes the entry point for execution to begin in the module. Failure to code it may sometimes cause execution to begin other than where it was intended.

```
            3        CH11EX8         15.31.22        MAY 11,1991

          00079    012800 PROCEDURE DIVISION USING JCL-PARM.
          00080    012900**************************************************************
          00081    013000*    MAINLINE CONTROL PARAGRAPH                               *
          00082    013100**************************************************************

          00084    013300 0000-MAINLINE.

          00086    013500        OPEN OUTPUT PRINT-FILE
          00087    013600             INPUT  INPUT-FILE
          00088    013700        CALL 'DATERTN' USING  FIRST-DATE
          00089    013900                              SECOND-DATE
          00090    014100        MOVE FIRST-DATE-RECEIVED TO GREGORIAN-HOLD
          00091    014200        MOVE SECOND-DATE-RECEIVED TO JULIAN-HOLD
          00092    014210        READ INPUT-FILE
          00093    014220           AT END MOVE '1' TO SWEOF.
          00094    014230        PERFORM 0100-PROCESS UNTIL END-OF-FILE
          00095    014240        MOVE ZERO TO RETURN-CODE
          00096    014250        CLOSE PRINT-FILE
          00097    014260              INPUT-FILE
          00098    014270        GOBACK.

          00100    014290 0100-PROCESS.

          00102    014292        IF PROCESS-TYPE = 'A' AND RECORD-TYPE = 'A'
          00103    014300           MOVE GREGORIAN-HOLD TO GREGORIAN-OUT
          00104    014301           MOVE INPUT-FILE-REC TO GREGORIAN-RECORD
          00105    014302           WRITE PRINT-FILE-REC FROM WS-RECORD-TYPE-A
          00106    014303                AFTER ADVANCING PAGE
          00107    014304        ELSE
          00108    014310           MOVE JULIAN-HOLD TO JULIAN-OUT
          00109    014320           MOVE INPUT-FILE-REC TO JULIAN-RECORD
          00110    014600           WRITE PRINT-FILE-REC FROM WS-RECORD-TYPE-B
          00111    014700                AFTER ADVANCING PAGE.
          00112    014800        READ INPUT-FILE
          00113    014900           AT END MOVE '1' TO SWEOF.
                                                        .
                                                        .
                                                        .

  7        CH11EX8         15.31.22        MAY 11,1991

                                         CONDENSED LISTING

 79     ENTRY      0006E0            86     OPEN       0006F0            88     CALL       00075E
 90     MOVE       00079E            91     MOVE       0007A4            92     READ       0007AA
 93     MOVE       0007D4            94     PERFORM    0007D8            95     MOVE       000800
 96     CLOSE      000806            98     GOBACK     0008CC            102    IF         0008F6
 103    MOVE       00090E            104    MOVE       000914            105    WRITE      00091A
 108    MOVE       00095A            109    MOVE       000960            110    WRITE      000966
 112    READ       0009A0            113    MOVE       0009CA
                                           .
                                           .
                                           .
```

Figure 11.10 *(Continued)*

The NAME statement is used to assign a name to the load module. INCLUDE designates additional input to the linkage-editor. ORDER explicitly designates the order in which CSECTs are to be placed in the module.

The linkage-editor module map and cross-reference table are generated if the XREF option is in effect. The module map shows you the CSECT names, origins, and lengths; it is used to locate the CSECT in which an instruction lies. The cross-reference indicates entry-point offsets and names for CSECTs in the load module.

```
 MVS/DFP VERSION 3 RELEASE 2 LINKAGE EDITOR     15:31:26  SAT  MAY 11, 1991
 JOB CH11EX8     STEP S1          PROCEDURE LKED
 INVOCATION PARAMETERS - LIST,XREF,LET
 ACTUAL SIZE=(317440,79872)
 OUTPUT DATA SET MY.COBOL.LOAD IS ON VOLUME PRIY08
IEW0000     NAME CH11EX8(R)                                                          00035001

                                                      CROSS REFERENCE TABLE


  CONTROL SECTION                      ENTRY

    NAME    ORIGIN  LENGTH               NAME   LOCATION     NAME   LOCATION     NAME   LOCATION     NAME   LOCATION
  CH11EX8       00     B3C


  LOCATION  REFERS TO SYMBOL  IN CONTROL SECTION              LOCATION  REFERS TO SYMBOL  IN CONTROL SECTION

 ENTRY ADDRESS       00

 TOTAL LENGTH       B40
 ** CH11EX8  REPLACED AND HAS AMODE 24
 ** LOAD MODULE HAS RMODE 24
 ** AUTHORIZATION CODE IS         0.
```

Figure 11.10 *(Continued)*

One diagnostic message which indicates a potential problem is SYMBOL PRINTED IS AN UNRESOLVED EXTERNAL REFERENCE. An attempt to access an unresolved reference will result in an ABEND. If you wish to mark a load module as executable even though there are unresolved external references, use the LET linkage-editor option.

When debugging a problem involving multiple programs it is necessary to determine whether CALLs are static or dynamic. Statically called programs reside in the same load module; programs called dynamically reside in separate load modules.

Simple coding errors may cause multimodule problems. Often these errors prevent the system from locating the called program.

For dynamic calls, the RESIDENT compiler option must always be in effect for a calling COBOL program; if the run unit contains only COBOL II programs, RESIDENT is required for all programs.

A typical system completion code which may occur in a multimodule situation is S806. Occasionally, an S0C1, S0C2, or S0C4 may occur.

In the last four chapters we have discussed a variety of system dump–solving techniques. You should now be in a position to handle most system dumps that come your way.

REVIEW QUESTIONS

1. When following standard linkage conventions, what functions are assigned to the following general-purpose registers?

- **a.** Register 0
- **b.** Register 1

c. Register 13
d. Register 14
e. Register 15

2. What is the purpose of a Save Area? Why must programs have a Save Area?

3. Describe differences between static and dynamic calls.

4. Answer these questions about the code for two COBOL programs shown below:
a. What type of call is being requested?
b. Should PROG1 be compiled with the RESIDENT or NORESIDENT option?
c. If PROG2 receives control from PROG1, what may happen when PROG2 accesses FLD-B?

Coded in PROG1:

```
CALL PROG2 USING FLD-1
```

Coded in PROG2:

```
PROCEDURE DIVISION USING    FLD-A
                            FLD-B.
```

5. Refer to the Save Area trace in Fig. 11.8.
a. What is the name of the main COBOL program? Under which version of COBOL was it compiled?
b. What is the name of the called COBOL program? Is it a COBOL II or OS/VS COBOL program?
c. What is the EPA of INTER33? SLIP03?
d. What is the return point address in the main COBOL program to which the called COBOL program will pass control when it reaches a GOBACK statement?

6. What is the purpose of the linkage-editor?

7. Refer to the output given in Fig. 11.9.
a. What is the name of the load module?
b. What linkage-editor options were in effect?
c. In which CSECT will execution begin in the load module?
d. What is the load module's length?
e. Are there any unresolved external references? If so, name them.
f. What linkage-editor option marks a load module as executable even if there are unresolved ordinary external references?

8. Examine Fig. 11.10.
a. What type of ABEND occurred?
b. What is the probable reason for this type of ABEND?
c. What is the name of the load module which was inaccessible?
d. Find the statement in CH11EX8 which caused the ABEND.
e. How would you fix the problem which caused the ABEND?

Part

3

Interactive Debugging

Chapter

12

Debugging OS/VS COBOL Programs with TESTCOB

This is the first of three chapters on interactive debugging. Interactive debuggers make the debugging process more efficient by allowing you to halt program execution, test the current program status (e.g., contents of fields and OPEN/CLOSE status of files), make changes, and then continue execution.

It amazes me how few COBOL programmers, especially those writing batch systems, use interactive debugging facilities. For many years, especially before COBOL II became available, there seemed to be a general lack of familiarity with the use and benefits of interactive debugging. When programmer productivity is important, it makes sense to utilize facilities which speed up the testing and debugging process. This chapter will deal with one of the first interactive debuggers specifically designed for use with OS/VS COBOL, TESTCOB.

12.1 SOME TESTCOB BACKGROUND

Initially, IBM provided OS COBOL Interactive Debug, consisting of the TESTCOB command and its subcommands, for programs compiled under the OS Full American National Standard COBOL Version 4 compiler. It was then extended for use under OS/VS COBOL. Commonly called TESTCOB by programmers, this tool enabled programmers to monitor and interact with programs by entering commands from the terminal while the program executed. Few programmers took advantage of TESTCOB. I suspect their reluctance arose out of unfamiliarity: many COBOL programmers either originally learned their COBOL in schools which did not offer instruction in this tool, or worked in shops which did not encourage TESTCOB's use because of limited resources. Today, when online interactive applications have become the norm rather than the exception, it behooves all programmers coding in OS/VS COBOL to become familiar with the online interactive capabilities of TESTCOB as a viable tool for testing and debugging their programs.

TESTCOB enables you to interrupt program execution at predetermined points and check the contents of program variables and the status of program files. Although the DISPLAY and EXHIBIT verbs can be used for these functions, TESTCOB permits you to specify at the terminal where in the program you wish to halt execution and what you wish to monitor. As with other interactive functions, it is not necessary for the program to run to completion in order to review the results of your inquiries. Also, and this is a big advantage in debugging interactively, TESTCOB allows you to change the contents of program variables and then resume execution to see what will happen with the new values. The TESTCOB trace function provides more information and flexibility than the READY TRACE and RESET TRACE statements. It is also possible to display program source code at the terminal during the debugging session.

One of the beauties of TESTCOB is that the tasks just mentioned are done without coding them in the program, and therefore there is no need to recompile the program when the "test" code needs to be changed or removed. There are trade-offs; in order to use TESTCOB the TEST compiler must be in effect. With TEST in effect FLOW, STATE, COUNT, or SYMDMP compiler options should not be specified since they will be nullified by TEST. Most likely the assumption is that those compiler options will not be needed since you intend to use the interactive debugger.

12.2 TESTCOB COMMANDS

TESTCOB is available for programmers using a terminal under the Time Sharing Option (TSO) of the MVS operating system or under Conversational Monitor System (CMS). We will assume that debugging is being done in a TSO environment. Prerequisite for running TESTCOB under TSO is an understanding of basic TSO concepts, including the use of the ALLOCATE command.

A brief description of all TESTCOB commands is given in Fig. 12.1. Additional information, including complete syntax and usage examples, can be found in *IBM OS COBOL Interactive Debug Terminal User's Guide and Reference.* There is also online information which you can access by entering HELP or HELP *subcommand name* at the terminal.

Figure 12.2 shows the commands that would be used to carry out the various TESTCOB debugging functions.

The following sections will illustrate how to prepare a program for testing under TESTCOB, how to invoke TESTCOB and how to run a TESTCOB session. The sample TESTCOB session will demonstrate most of the common TESTCOB tasks and commands.

12.3 PREPARING FOR THE TESTCOB SESSION

12.3.1 Compiling and Linking the Program

The OS/VS COBOL program to be tested or debugged under TESTCOB must be compiled using the TEST compiler option. It is also strongly recommended

SUBCOMMAND	PURPOSE
AT	Set break points
DROP	Delete symbols created with the EQUATE command
DUMP	Terminate the debugging session and give a snap dump
END	Terminate the TESTCOB debugging session without a dump
EQUATE	Establish symbols for program data-names, indexes or special registers
GO	Start or resume execution, recognizing breakpoints
HELP	Provide information about TESTCOB commands
IF	Cause immediate evaluation of an expression with conditional execution of the program
LIST	Display attributes and values of selected storage
LISTBRKS	List the current breakpoints
LISTFILE	Display the current status and attributes of a file
NEXT	Set temporary breakpoint at the next program verb to be executed
OFF	Remove AT breakpoints
OFFWN	Remove WHEN breakpoints
QUALIFY	Change qualification of names or line numbers used in TESTCOB sub-commands
RUN	Execute the program without interrupts caused by active breakpoints, in effect turning them off
SET	Initialize or change values of program variables
SOURCE	Display one or more program source statements
TRACE	Display a flow of program execution
WHEN	Set up continuous monitoring of an expression or value before each verb in the program executes, with establishment of a conditional breakpoint

Figure 12.1 Alphabetical list and brief description of all TESTCOB subcommands.

that the SOURCE compiler option be requested as well. This will enable you to view the program source code during the debugging session. Figure 12.3 shows sample JCL.

A SYSUT5 DD statement must be included in the compile JCL (see letter "A" in Fig. 12.3). This provides a work file needed by TESTCOB; it is where the compiler will place a debug data set. Unlike the SYSUT1 through SYSUT4 data sets, which are the default work files supplied in the IBM compile procedures and which are temporary work data sets used for compiler processing, the SYSUT5 data set must be available at TESTCOB execution time. SYSUT5 allows you to make symbolic references during the debugging session. The data set assigned to SYSUT5 has a default low-level qualifier name of SYM.

TESTCOB TASK	SUBCOMMANDS
Setting Breakpoints	AT NEXT WHEN
Removing Breakpoints	OFF OFFWN
Resuming Program Execution	GO RUN
Analyzing Program Flow	TRACE
Testing Program Conditions	IF WHEN
Referring to Other OS/VS COBOL Programs	QUALIFY
Setting Values of Program Variables	SET
Displaying Values of Program Data	LIST LISTFILE
Creating and Deleting Alias Names	EQUATE DROP
Determining Active TESTCOB Breakpoints	LISTBRKS
Terminating TESTCOB Session	DUMP END

Figure 12.2 TESTCOB subcommands used to carry out various TESTCOB debugging tasks.

A SYSPRINT DD statement, which is provided in the IBM compile procedures, is where the compiler places the program source listing. The low-level qualifier suggested in the TESTCOB documentation is LIST, but you can use any other valid low-level qualifier (see letter "B" in Fig. 12.3).

After compilation the object module must be link-edited. Do not use the TEST linkage-editor option. Since the TESTCOB routines are in the OS/VS COBOL subroutine library, be sure to include a SYSLIB DD statement pointing to that library (normally SYS1.COBLIB, unless your installation has changed the library name).

If you wish, instead of compiling using JCL, you may use the TSO ALLOCATE and CALL commands to identify the necessary files to the system and to

```
      //S1        EXEC COBUCL,PARM.COB='SXREF,SOURCE,NUM,TEST'
(B)-->//COB.SYSPRINT DD DSN=MY.TSTCB1.LIST,DISP=(,CATLG),
      //             UNIT=TSOW,SPACE=(TRK,(5,5),RLSE),
      //             DCB=(LRECL=121,RECFM=FB,BLKSIZE=1210)
(A)-->//COB.SYSUT5   DD DSN=MY.TSTCB1.SYM,DISP=(NEW,CATLG),
      //             UNIT=TSOW,SPACE=(CYL,(1,1),RLSE)
      //COB.SYSIN    DD DSN=MY.PROGLIB.COBOL(TSTCB1),DISP=SHR
      //LKED.SYSLMOD DD DSN=MY.COBOL.LOAD(TSTCB1),DISP=SHR
      //LKED.SYSLIB  DD DSN=SYS1.COB2LIB,DISP=SHR
      //
```

Figure 12.3 JCL to compile and link in preparation for a TESTCOB debugging session.

execute the COBOL compiler. Alternatively, if your installation is equipped with the TSO COBOL Prompter, you may compile using the COBOL Prompter. [See the *IBM OS(TSO) COBOL Prompter Terminal User's Guide* for information on how to execute the OS/VS COBOL compiler.] After compiling you can issue the TSO LINK command to create a load module.

12.3.2 Allocating Files

Before invoking TESTCOB a number of files must be allocated to the system. These include input and output data sets used by the COBOL program and files needed by TESTCOB. It is easiest to include all the necessary ALLOCATE commands in a CLIST (a program written in the CLIST language; it may contain TSO commands) as illustrated in Fig. 12.4.

The first 10 lines in the figure show the appropriate TSO ALLOCATE commands. The last line is the TESTCOB command. This command will be discussed in Sec. 12.3.3.

The top four lines specify files defined in the application program. The first two lines allocate input files. The next two lines allocate PRTFILE and SYSOUT, which will contain program output, to the terminal.

The next six lines allocate files required by TESTCOB. DEBUG is the DDname allocated to the SYM file which was assigned to SYSUT5; it contains the symbolic debug file. SOURCE is the DDname representing the LIST data set assigned to SYSPRINT; it contains the program source listing. The DDname LOAD points to the load library containing the load module. PRINT is the DDname allocated to the data set which will contain output of certain TESTCOB subcommands if the PRINT option is used on those subcommands. The LRECL and RECFM of the PRINT data set must be as given in the figure; BLKSIZE must be a multiple of 121. SYSUDUMP will receive a system dump of the region in which the COBOL program is executing if the TESTCOB DUMP command is issued. DEBUG, SOURCE, LOAD, and PRINT are programmer-selected DDnames; you can use any valid DDname. The name SYSUDUMP (or SYSABEND) is the required DDname for DUMP output.

```
ALLOC DD(CARDFLE) DA(INPUT.TAXTAB.DATA) SHR REU
ALLOC DD(DISKFLE) DA(INPUT.INCOME.DATA) SHR REU
ALLOC DD(PRTFILE) DA(*) REU
ALLOC DD(SYSOUT)  DA(*) REU
ALLOC DD(DEBUG)   DA(MY.TSTCB1.SYM) SHR REU
ALLOC DD(SOURCE)  DA(MY.TSTCB1.LIST) SHR REU
ALLOC DD(LOAD)    DA(MY.COBOL.LOAD) SHR REU
ALLOC DD(PRINT)   DA(MY.PRINT.DATA) NEW +
      LRECL(121) BLKSIZE(6171) RECFM(F B A) TRACKS SP(1 1)
ALLOC DD(SYSUDUMP) SYSOUT(F) REU
TESTCOB (TSTCB1:DEBUG) LOAD(TSTCB1:LOAD) PRINT(PRINT)
```

Figure 12.4 A CLIST which allocates the necessary files for a TESTCOB session and then invokes TESTCOB.

12.3.3 The TESTCOB Command

Once all files have been allocated, the TESTCOB command can be issued. As shown in Fig. 12.4, it can be the last command in a CLIST.

There are two different formats for the TESTCOB command under TSO. The format used in Fig. 12.4 is

```
TESTCOB  (program-name:DDname,...) LOAD (module-name:DDname)
         [PRINT(DDname)] [PARM('parameter')]
```

Operands in brackets are optional. Program-name is the name from the IDENTIFICATION DIVISION of the OS/VS COBOL program being debugged. It is followed by the DDname of the SYM file specified in the ALLOCATE command. More than one program name and DDname can be specified. Following the LOAD keyword is the name of the load module and the DDname of the load library coded in the ALLOCATE statement. If a data set is desired for holding the output of TESTCOB commands which have the PRINT option, the PRINT keyword and the DDname of the output data set specified in the ALLOCATE command can be coded. If a parameter is normally passed to the program from the JCL, the PARM keyword and parameter string can be coded. Neither PRINT nor PARM is required.

The second format is

```
TESTCOB  (load-module-name) (program-name:DDname,...)
         [PRINT(DDname)] [PARM('parameter')]
```

Load-module-name is the name of the load module which will receive control when the debugging session begins. It resides in a STEPLIB (or LINKLIB) library allocated to your terminal session. In this case it is unnecessary to allocate the load library as we did in Fig. 12.4. The other operands are the same as in the previous format.

12.4 SOME MISCELLANEOUS TESTCOB NOTES

Syntax errors are the source of many TESTCOB subcommand failures. There are a few simple syntax rules to be aware of. Subcommands within a subcommand list must be separated by semicolons (;). Operands must be separated by at least one space or a comma (,). Some operands must be enclosed in parentheses.

The following examples illustrate these rules.

```
AT 250 (LISTBRKS;GO) COUNT(5) NONOTIFY
LIST (FLD-A,FLD-B)
EQUATE EMP EMPLOYEE
DROP (TP SV NM)
```

The first command sets a breakpoint at line 250 and executes the commands in the parentheses; COUNT and NONOTIFY are AT command options. The second command lists the contents of FLD-A and FLD-B. The third command establishes the symbol EMP for the program variable EMPLOYEE. The fourth command drops three previously established EQUATE symbols. Syntax rules for all subcommands are given in *IBM OS COBOL Interactive Debug Terminal User's Guide and Reference* and in the online TESTCOB HELP facility.

Some COBOL verbs and compiler-directing statements are not recognized by TESTCOB. They are BASIS, COPY, DEBUG, DELETE, EJECT, ENTER, INSERT, NOTE, READY TRACE, RESET TRACE, SKIP1, SKIP2, and SKIP3.

12.5 A SAMPLE TESTCOB SESSION

Let us assume that we are testing a new program. Its purpose is to load a tax rate schedule table and calculate the tax owed by each employee. We will use an employee input file containing only a few records for our test session. If an employee's taxable income is within the limits of the tax table, the employee's owed tax is calculated; otherwise error processing is done. Employee records processed and error messages indicating employee records out of range are printed in an output report. The report also includes summary statistics. Figure 12.5 shows the program.

To review, the steps we need to take to initiate our debugging session are

1. Compile the program under OS/VS COBOL using the TEST and SOURCE compiler options. Be sure to code a SYSUT5 DD statement; the IBM default name of the low-level qualifier of the data set assigned to SYSUT5 is SYM. Assign a data set to the SYSPRINT DD statement; the default low-level qualifier name of this data set is LIST.
2. Run the object module through the linkage-editor to create an executable load module.
3. ALLOCATE input and output files used by the program, the SYM file, and, if you will use format 1 of the TESTCOB command, the load library.
4. Enter the TESTCOB command in TSO READY mode or as a TSO command from within ISPF.

Assume the program has been compiled and linked as shown in Fig. 12.3. The CLIST in Fig. 12.4 has been run to allocate all necessary files (with the output allocated to the terminal) and to invoke TESTCOB. When the TESTCOB prompt, which is simply the word "TESTCOB," appears on the terminal, we can enter any of the TESTCOB commands.

We enter

```
GO
```

TESTCOB responds by sending the following output to the terminal.

```
                EMPLOYEE      TAXABLE       TAX         NET
                NUMBER        INCOME        OWED        INCOME
```

```
IDENTIFICATION DIVISION.
 PROGRAM-ID. TSTCB1.
 DATE-WRITTEN. APRIL 1991.
 DATE-COMPILED.
    SKIP1.
ENVIRONMENT DIVISION.
 INPUT-OUTPUT SECTION.
  FILE-CONTROL.
    SELECT CARD-FILE  ASSIGN TO CARDFLE.
    SELECT DISK-FILE  ASSIGN TO DISKFLE.
    SELECT PRINT-FILE ASSIGN TO PRTFILE.
     SKIP1
DATA DIVISION.
 FILE SECTION.
 FD CARD-FILE
    RECORDING MODE IS F
    RECORD CONTAINS 80 CHARACTERS
    BLOCK CONTAINS 0 RECORDS
    LABEL RECORDS ARE OMITTED
    DATA RECORD IS CARD-FILE-REC.
 01 CARD-FILE-REC                      PIC X(80).
 FD DISK-FILE
    RECORDING MODE IS F
    RECORD CONTAINS 80 CHARACTERS
    BLOCK CONTAINS 0 RECORDS
    LABEL RECORDS ARE OMITTED
    DATA RECORD IS DISK-FILE-REC.
 01 DISK-FILE-REC                      PIC X(80).
 FD PRINT-FILE
    RECORDING MODE IS F
    RECORD CONTAINS 133 CHARACTERS
    BLOCK CONTAINS 0 RECORDS
    LABEL RECORDS ARE OMITTED
    DATA RECORD IS PRINT-FILE-REC.
 01 PRINT-FILE-REC                     PIC X(133).
     EJECT
WORKING-STORAGE SECTION.
***************************************************************************
*                  WORK  AREAS                                            *
***************************************************************************
 01 WORK-AREAS.
    05 SUB                             PIC S9(4) COMP SYNC VALUE +0.
    05 SW-EOF                          PIC 9 VALUE 0.
       88 NO-MORE-RECORDS                    VALUE 1.
    05 WK-TAX-CONSTANT                 PIC S9(3)  COMP-3 VALUE +10.
    05 WK-INC-TAX-AMT                  PIC S9(5)V99 COMP-3.
    05 WK-TAX-PERCENT                  PIC SV99     COMP-3.
    05 WK-MIN-TAX-AMT                  PIC S9(5)V99 COMP-3.
    05 WK-TAX                          PIC S9(5)V99 COMP-3.
    05 WK-NET-INCOME                   PIC S9(5)V99 COMP-3.
    05 WK-NOT-PROCESSED                PIC S9(5)    COMP-3 VALUE +0.
    05 WK-PROCESSED                    PIC S9(5)    COMP-3 VALUE +0.
     SKIP1
***************************************************************************
*             INPUT EMPLOYEE  RECORD LAYOUT                               *
***************************************************************************
 01 WS-DISK-REC.
    05 EMP-NO                           PIC X(5).
    05 FILLER                           PIC X(18).
    05 INC-TAX-AMT                      PIC 9(5)V99.
    05 FILLER                           PIC X(50).
     SKIP1
```

Figure 12.5 Source code for the OS/VS COBOL program used in the TESTCOB session described in Sec. 12.5.

```
******************************************************************
*                      PRINT FILE LAYOUT                         *
******************************************************************
  01 MESSAGE-LINE.
     05 FILLER                        PIC X(25) VALUE SPACES.
     05 PRT-EMP-NO                    PIC X(6).
     05 PRT-MESSAGE                   PIC X(102)
        VALUE 'TAXABLE   INCOME   OUT   OF   RANGE'.
  01 HEADER.
     05 FIELD1                        PIC X(25).
     05 FIELD2                        PIC X(108).
  01 DETAIL-LINE REDEFINES HEADER.
     05 FILLER                        PIC X(25).
     05 EMP-NO                        PIC X(13).
     05 INC-TAX-AMT                   PIC ZZ999.99BBB.
     05 TAX                           PIC ZZZZ99.99BBB.
     05 NET-INCOME                    PIC ZZZZ99.99B(63).
  01 SUMMARY-LINE REDEFINES HEADER.
     05 FILLER                        PIC X(25).
     05 PROCESSED                     PIC ZZZZ9B(15).
     05 NOT-PROCESSED                 PIC ZZZZ9B(83).
      SKIP1
******************************************************************
*   FIRST RECORD ON CARD DETERMINES NUMBER OF TABLE ENTRIES      *
******************************************************************
  01 CARDIN.
     05 NUM-RECORDS                   PIC 9(3).
     05 FILLER                        PIC X(77).
******************************************************************
*                         TAX TABLE                              *
******************************************************************
  01 TAX-TABLE.
     05 TAX-REC OCCURS 25 TIMES.
        10 TAX-CODE                   PIC X.
        10 MIN-TAX-AMT                PIC 9(6)V99.
        10 MAX-TAX-AMT                PIC 9(6)V99.
        10 IGNORE                     PIC 9(6)V99.
        10 TAX-PERCENT                PIC V99.
        10 FILLER                     PIC X(53).
     EJECT
 PROCEDURE DIVISION.
******************************************************************
*                    MAINLINE LOGIC SECTION                      *
******************************************************************
 0000-MAINLINE.
     OPEN INPUT  CARD-FILE
                 DISK-FILE
          OUTPUT PRINT-FILE.
     PERFORM 0050-HEADER-ROUTINE THRU 0050-EXIT.
     READ CARD-FILE INTO CARDIN.
     PERFORM 0100-FILL-TABLE THRU 0100-EXIT
       VARYING SUB FROM 1 BY 1 UNTIL SUB GREATER THAN NUM-RECORDS.
     DISPLAY 'TAX TABLE FILLED'.
     CLOSE CARD-FILE.
     PERFORM 0200-READ-DISK THRU 0200-EXIT.
     PERFORM 0300-PROCESS-DISK THRU 0300-EXIT
       UNTIL NO-MORE-RECORDS.
     PERFORM 0500-SUMMARY THRU 0500-EXIT.
     CLOSE DISK-FILE
           PRINT-FILE.
     STOP RUN.
     SKIP1
 0000-EXIT.
      EXIT.
     EJECT
```

Figure 12.5 *(Continued)*

```
****************************************************************
*          REPORT HEADER AND SUMMARY HEADER ROUTINES           *
****************************************************************
 0050-HEADER-ROUTINE.
         MOVE SPACES TO FIELD1.
         MOVE 'EMPLOYEE      TAXABLE      TAX         NET' TO
           FIELD2.
         WRITE PRINT-FILE-REC FROM HEADER AFTER ADVANCING
           PAGE.
         MOVE 'NUMBER        INCOME       OWED        INCOME' TO
           FIELD2.
         WRITE PRINT-FILE-REC FROM HEADER AFTER ADVANCING 1.
         MOVE SPACES TO HEADER.
         WRITE PRINT-FILE-REC FROM HEADER AFTER ADVANCING 5.
 0050-EXIT.
        EXIT.
       SKIP1
 0060-SUMMARY-HEADERS.
         MOVE SPACES TO FIELD1.
         MOVE 'EMPLOYEES              EMPLOYEES'     TO FIELD2.
         WRITE PRINT-FILE-REC FROM HEADER AFTER ADVANCING
           PAGE.
         MOVE 'PROCESSED              NOT PROCESSED' TO FIELD2.
         WRITE PRINT-FILE-REC FROM HEADER AFTER ADVANCING 1.
         MOVE SPACES TO HEADER.
         WRITE PRINT-FILE-REC FROM HEADER AFTER ADVANCING 5.
 0060-EXIT.
        EXIT.
       SKIP1
****************************************************************
*         THIS ROUTINE FILLS THE TAX TABLE                     *
****************************************************************
 0100-FILL-TABLE.
       READ CARD-FILE INTO TAX-REC(SUB).
 0100-EXIT.
        EXIT.
       SKIP1
****************************************************************
*  THIS ROUTINE READS THE DISK FILE CONTAINING EMPLOYEE INFO.  *
*  AT END OF FILE SET SW-EOF TO 1 (NO-MORE-RECORDS)            *
****************************************************************
 0200-READ-DISK.
       READ DISK-FILE INTO WS-DISK-REC
         AT END MOVE 1 TO SW-EOF.
 0200-EXIT.
        EXIT.
       SKIP1
****************************************************************
*          THIS ROUTINE CHECKS TO SEE IF THE EMPLOYEE'S        *
*          INCOME IS OUT OF RANGE OF THE TAX TABLE             *
****************************************************************
 0300-PROCESS-DISK.
       IF INC-TAX-AMT OF WS-DISK-REC  > MAX-TAX-AMT (NUM-RECORDS)
          MOVE EMP-NO OF WS-DISK-REC TO PRT-EMP-NO
          WRITE PRINT-FILE-REC FROM MESSAGE-LINE
            AFTER ADVANCING 2
          ADD +1 TO WK-NOT-PROCESSED
       ELSE
          PERFORM 0400-CALCULATE-TAX THRU 0400-EXIT
            VARYING SUB FROM 1 BY 1 UNTIL SUB > NUM-RECORDS.
          ADD +1 TO WK-PROCESSED
       PERFORM 0200-READ-DISK THRU 0200-EXIT.
 0300-EXIT.
        EXIT.
       SKIP1
```

Figure 12.5 *(Continued)*

```
019300**********************************************************************
019400*         THIS ROUTINE WILL SEARCH THE TAX TABLE FOR                 *
019500*         THE EMPLOYEE'S INCOME BRACKET AND CALCULATE                *
019600*         THE NET INCOME AND TAX OWED.                               *
019700**********************************************************************
019800 0400-CALCULATE-TAX.
019900     IF INC-TAX-AMT OF WS-DISK-REC < MAX-TAX-AMT (SUB) OR
020000     INC-TAX-AMT OF WS-DISK-REC = MAX-TAX-AMT (SUB) THEN
020100       MOVE INC-TAX-AMT OF WS-DISK-REC TO WK-INC-TAX-AMT
020200       MOVE TAX-PERCENT (SUB) TO WK-TAX-PERCENT
020300       MOVE MIN-TAX-AMT (SUB) TO WK-MIN-TAX-AMT
020400       COMPUTE WK-TAX ROUNDED =
020500         (WK-INC-TAX-AMT - WK-MIN-TAX-AMT) * WK-TAX-PERCENT
020600                                         + WK-TAX-CONSTANT
020700       COMPUTE WK-NET-INCOME = WK-INC-TAX-AMT - WK-TAX
020800       MOVE CORR WS-DISK-REC TO DETAIL-LINE
020900       MOVE WK-INC-TAX-AMT TO INC-TAX-AMT OF DETAIL-LINE
021000       MOVE WK-NET-INCOME TO NET-INCOME
021100       MOVE WK-TAX TO TAX
021200       WRITE PRINT-FILE-REC FROM DETAIL-LINE AFTER ADVANCING 2
021300       ADD NUM-RECORDS TO SUB.
021400 0400-EXIT.
021500      EXIT.
021600      SKIP1
021700 0500-SUMMARY.
021800     PERFORM 0050-HEADER-ROUTINE THRU 0050-EXIT.
021900     MOVE WK-PROCESSED     TO PROCESSED.
022000     MOVE WK-NOT-PROCESSED TO NOT-PROCESSED.
022100     WRITE PRINT-FILE-REC FROM SUMMARY-LINE AFTER ADVANCING 2.
022200 0500-EXIT.
022300      EXIT.
```

Figure 12.5 *(Continued)*

```
TAX TABLE FILLED

                 00123        100.00       21.00        79.00
                 00124      12345.67       61.70     12283.97
                 00125        124.53       23.70       100.83
                 00126      15888.88      152.06     15736.82
                 12345        124.53       23.70       100.83
                 12346 TAXABLE INCOME OUT OF RANGE
                 12578      12500.00       84.85     12415.15
                 12854 TAXABLE INCOME OUT OF RANGE
                 21345        147.52       26.23       121.29

PROGRAM UNDER TESTCOB ENDED ABNORMALLY, SYSTEM CODE 0C7
LAST PSW BEFORE ABEND FF850007E0051782
TSTCB1.020200.1
```

We see that the program produced some output from the WRITE statements in the program as well as from the DISPLAY statement indicating that the tax table was filled. It then ABENDed at line 020200.

At the TESTCOB prompt we enter

```
SOURCE 19800:20600 SOURCE
```

in order to display lines 19800 through 20600 of the source code. Line 020200 (see Fig. 12.5) is

```
MOVE TAX-PERCENT (SUB) TO WK-TAX-PERCENT
```

Since the program ABENDed with an S0C7 (data exception), we know that an operation was attempted with invalid packed data. We decide to examine both fields in the MOVE statement. First we enter

```
EQUATE TP TAX-PERCENT
```

to permit us to enter TP instead of TAX-PERCENT at the terminal (this will save a few key strokes, since we may need to enter this field name a few more times in our debugging session).

Then we enter

```
LIST (TP(SUB),WK-TAX-PERCENT)
```

in order to view information about the fields. (We could also have entered the full name TAX-PERCENT instead of TP.) TESTCOB indicates that TAX-PERCENT is defined as a numeric field with USAGE DISPLAY and displays the contents in hexadecimal as F140. This is invalid data since the hexadecimal 40 represents a space. The value of the subscript SUB is given as 20.

The receiving field is defined as packed. We realize that the cause of the ABEND was an attempt to execute an instruction generated by the MOVE statement which converts the numeric DISPLAY field into packed format (most likely the ZAP, or Zero and Add Packed, instruction; we could verify this by looking at a PMAP compiler listing). The twentieth occurrence of TAX-PERCENT in the tax table contained bad data.

In order to examine the employee record being processed we enter

```
LIST WS-DISK-REC
```

WS-DISK-REC is a group identifier containing the employee record layout. TESTCOB shows us that the field INC-TAX-AMT, which contains the income on which the tax is calculated, is 19024.00, and that the employee number in the field EMP-NO is 49000.

Entering

```
LIST TAX-REC(SUB)
```

shows us the twentieth entry in the tax table. We learn that the employee tax amount of 19024.00 falls within the range of incomes for the TAX-PERCENT being used in the tax calculation; MIN-TAX-AMT is reported as 019001.00 and MAX-TAX-AMT is reported as being 020000.99.

In order to test the program with a valid numeric value in the field TAX-PERCENT(SUB), we enter the TESTCOB command

```
SET TP(SUB) = .18
```

This puts .18 in TAX-PERCENT, replacing the space in the second byte with the number 8.

We now enter

```
GO
```

to resume execution at the COBOL statement which caused the ABEND. After an ABEND, entering GO or RUN causes TESTCOB to reexecute the last program statement.

TESTCOB continues displaying program output at the terminal (shown below), including the tax calculation for employee number 49000, and gives us the reassuring message that the program ended normally.

```
          45678          12024.53       13.53          12011.00
          49000          19024.00       14.14          19009.86
          EMPLOYEE       TAXABLE        TAX            NET
          NUMBER         INCOME         OWED           INCOME



            11                       2

PROGRAM UNDER TESTCOB ENDED NORMALLY
```

But wait! The headers above the numbers 11 and 2 are incorrect. They are supposed to be column headers for the end-of-job summary statistics. It appears as though paragraph 0050-HEADER-ROUTINE, at line 013100 in the source code, was executed instead of paragraph 0060-SUMMARY-HEADERS at line 014500. We will have to end the current TESTCOB session and then invoke TESTCOB again for additional testing.

Entering

```
END
```

terminates the current debugging session.

We will start a new TESTCOB session using the TRACE command to check the flow of control as the program executes. We invoke TESTCOB again, but before entering GO we must establish a breakpoint so that we can set the twentieth occurrence of TAX-PERCENT to a numeric value and begin the trace. We put the breakpoint at the first statement in the PROCEDURE DIVISION with the command

```
AT 10800
```

We then enter

```
GO
```

When program execution halts at line 010800, we enter the command

```
WHEN W1 (EMP-NO OF WS-DISK-REC EQ '49000')
```

WHEN tests the condition before each COBOL verb executes (quite inefficient). It will return control to the terminal when the employee record which was being processed when the S0C7 occurred in the previous TESTCOB session, number 49000, is read into the program.

We enter

```
GO
```

As before, TESTCOB sends output to the terminal, but this time it halts at line 017300 as a result of the WHEN command. This is the statement following the READ.

We now turn off the WHEN command and set the twentieth occurrence of TAX-PERCENT to a valid numeric value with the commands

```
OFFWN
SET TAX-PERCENT(20) = .18
```

Since the incorrect column headers were written as a result of executing the end-of-job summary routine, we now wish to begin tracing program flow at the PERFORM statement which begins execution of that routine. We enter

```
AT 12000 (TRACE NAME;NEXT)
```

The TRACE NAME command will give a trace showing the line number of each paragraph entry point as well as the name of the paragraph. The NEXT command can be used to set a temporary breakpoint at the next COBOL statement to be executed. Entering NEXT subcommands followed by GO subcommands permits us to step through the program one instruction at a time.

We now enter

```
GO
```

to resume execution.

When we reach the NEXT breakpoint we enter

```
NEXT
GO
```

to continue stepping through the program.

As in the previous debugging session, TESTCOB sends program output to the terminal. It also gives the following TRACE information:

```
021700 0500-SUMMARY
013100 0050-HEADER-ROUTINE
014200 0050-EXIT
022200 0500-EXIT
```

We see that 0050-HEADER-ROUTINE received control from 0500-SUMMARY; remember that 0060-SUMMARY-HEADERS was supposed to receive control. Examining the source code shows us that the first statement in paragraph 0500-SUMMARY, at line 021800, is

```
PERFORM 0050-HEADER-ROUTINE THRU 0050-EXIT.
```

Thus we have found that the PERFORM statement was coded incorrectly.

TESTCOB has enabled us to isolate two errors in a relatively quick and easy fashion. The next steps would be to correct the input data set from which the tax table was loaded and the program code at line 021800, then recompile, relink, and test again to verify that the problems have been fixed.

The preceding example demonstrates the power and flexibility of interactive debugging. This chapter dealt with IBM's TESTCOB facility for OS/VS COBOL. We will look at other tools in the following chapters.

12.6 SUMMARY

TESTCOB is IBM's interactive debug tool for OS/VS COBOL programs. Advantages of interactive debugging are the ability to interrupt program execution, test the current status of the program, make changes, and then continue execution. Although programmers often do not utilize such tools, the savings in time and the gain in programmer productivity makes them desirable additions to the programmer's toolkit.

Once TESTCOB is invoked, subcommands can be entered at the terminal to do such things as halt program execution at predetermined points, view the current contents of program variables and the status of program files, change the values of identifiers, set up condition tests, and trace the logical flow of control of the program.

To use TESTCOB, the program must be compiled with the TEST compiler option. This requires some adjustments to the usual compile JCL; an additional work file must be assigned to a SYSUT5 DD statement, and a file should be assigned to the SYSPRINT DD to contain the source code.

Alternatives to using JCL to compile are to use the TSO CALL command or the TSO COBOL Prompter.

After compiling and link-editing the program, and before invoking TESTCOB, a number of files must be allocated using the TSO ALLOCATE command. These include files used by the program, the file which was assigned to the SYSUT5 DD statement, the file which was assigned to the SYSPRINT DD statement, and the library containing the load module. Typically, program output files are allocated to the terminal so that program output can be viewed during program execution.

The TESTCOB debugging session can then be started.

REVIEW QUESTIONS

1. What OS/VS COBOL compiler option must be specified in order to use TESTCOB? Which compiler options will be overridden when that option is in effect?

2. When using TESTCOB:

- **a.** What is the DDname of the work file where the compiler will create symbolic references. What is the default low-level qualifier name of this work file?
- **b.** What is the DDname of file where the compiler will place the source code? What is the default low-level qualifier name of this file?
- **c.** What is the TESTCOB prompt?

3. Assume that you wish to test an OS/VS COBOL program named PROGTEST using the TESTCOB facility. It has been compiled with the proper compiler option to allow it to be run under TESTCOB, has been link-edited and placed in a load library called YOUR.PROGLIB.LOAD, and been given the module name LOADTEST. The symbolic debug file YOUR.PROGTEST.SYM is to be assigned to the DDname SYMB, and the source listing file YOUR.PROGTEST.LIST is to be assigned to the DDname SRC. You will use the PRINT option on some of the TESTCOB subcommands to place output from those subcommands in a data set named YOUR.OUTPUT.DATA, assigned to the DDname PRT. You wish to view output from the program, assigned to a file with the DDname PROGOUT, at the terminal.

- **a.** Write all the necessary TSO ALLOCATE commands.
- **b.** Write the TESTCOB command.

4. You intend to test the OS/VS COBOL program PROGTEST under TESTCOB. The program has been compiled and link-edited, and all necessary files have been allocated as specified in question 3. You have just entered TESTCOB. Perform the following tasks during your debugging session.

- **a.** Write the subcommand which displays source lines 100 through 200 at the terminal.
- **b.** Establish the symbol IFR for the field INPUT-FILE-REC and the symbol PS for the field PROCESS-SWITCH.
- **c.** If the file named INPUT-FILE is OPENed at line 5500, write the TESTCOB subcommand which will establish a breakpoint at the COBOL statement immediately following the OPEN.
- **d.** Identify the command that will begin executing the program under TESTCOB.
- **e.** Assuming that you were successful in halting execution at the statement following line 5500, write the subcommand that will display the status of INPUT-FILE.
- **f.** If the first READ for INPUT-FILE is at line 6600, write the subcommand to halt execution immediately after the READ and to display the contents of the field END-OF-FILE-SWITCH.
- **g.** Write the subcommand to continue program execution.

h. Assuming that you succeeded in halting execution following the READ, display the contents of INPUT-FILE-REC.
i. At this point, remove any breakpoints you have set.
j. Write the TESTCOB subcommand to verify that you were successful in removing all breakpoints.
k. Set the value of PROCESS-SWITCH to 'YES'.
l. Write the command which will return control to you at the terminal whenever the contents of PROCESS-SWITCH becomes 'NO'.
m. Write the subcommand to resume execution.
n. Write the subcommand to end the debugging session.

Chapter

13

Debugging COBOL II Programs with COBTEST

In this chapter we continue our discussion of interactive debuggers. As explained in Chap. 12, an interactive debugger typically allows you to halt program execution, test the current status of the program, make changes, and then continue execution. This often makes testing and debugging a program much quicker and easier than when using batch debugging aids. The current chapter will deal with IBM's COBOL II interactive debugging facility, COBTEST.

13.1 SOME BACKGROUND

When IBM introduced Release 1 of VS COBOL II, they provided the VS COBOL II Debug Tool. This debugging facility, often referred to as COBTEST by programmers, enabled the programmer to debug and test interactively by entering commands at the terminal, or to debug by executing the program under COBTEST in batch mode. The interactive line mode was quite similar to the OS/VS COBOL debugger TESTCOB, discussed in Chap. 12.

With Release 2 of VS COBOL II, the Debug Tool was officially called COBTEST in the IBM manuals. It was greatly enhanced to allow testing and debugging to be done interactively in full-screen mode as well as in interactive line and batch modes. Release 3 provided no significant changes. We will deal here with COBTEST as it was designed for full-screen, line, and batch mode debugging.

13.2 WHY USE COBTEST?

When testing or debugging a program, it is helpful to be able to trace the logical flow of the program, list the contents of selected identifiers at specific points in the execution, and make changes to the values of identifiers to see what the effect will be. OS/VS COBOL has a number of debugging statements for these tasks which can be placed directly in the program code: READY TRACE, RESET TRACE, DISPLAY, and EXHIBIT. Although the COBOL II compiler checks the syntax when READY TRACE and RESET TRACE are coded, it ignores them during program execution. EXHIBIT is not available in COBOL II. That limits COBOL II programmers to using the DISPLAY verb.

Because of the near absence of debugging statements in COBOL II, it is important that COBOL II programmers learn to use COBTEST facilities to debug and test. COBTEST allows you to suspend execution of the program at any COBOL verb, list the values and attributes of identifiers and the status of files, alter the values of identifiers at any time, and trace the logical flow of the program. The beauty of this is that these tasks are done without coding them in the program, and therefore without the need to recompile the program when the "test" code needs to be changed or removed. You merely specify the appropriate COBTEST commands in an input data set for batch mode, or at the terminal for the interactive modes, and run the program.

Some caveats need to be mentioned: the TEST compiler option must be in effect in order to use COBTEST; because this option reduces program efficiency, the program should be recompiled without TEST when debugging is completed. Also, although the output from COBTEST commands is essentially the same whether batch mode or one of the interactive modes is used, it is not possible to interrupt the program to interact with it at the terminal once execution of the program under COBTEST in batch mode has begun.

13.3 COBTEST COMMANDS

Figure 13.1 contains an alphabetical list of all COBTEST commands available in Release 2 and Release 3. It indicates in which mode each command can be used, and gives a capsule explanation of its use. Further information, including complete syntax and usage examples, can be found in the IBM manual *VS COBOL II Application Programming: Debugging* (use the manual for the release of COBOL II that you are using). Information about commands is also available in line mode by entering HELP or HELP *command name* at the terminal. Information is available in full-screen mode by entering HELP on the command line, or hitting the PF key defined for the help function; a Main Help Menu will then be presented from which a topic or command can be selected by number.

Figure 13.2 shows the commands that would be used to perform the various COBTEST tasks.

We will use most of the common COBTEST tasks and commands in the sample debugging session in Sec. 13.7.

13.4 USING COBTEST IN BATCH MODE

Programs running under COBTEST in batch mode are noninteractive; the debugging session is invoked by submitting COBTEST as a batch job through a JCL EXEC statement. A batch COBTEST session requires careful planning of debugging strategy before the job is submitted. When running under MVS,

COMMAND	MODE	PURPOSE
AT	All Modes	Set break points
AUTO	Full-Screen	List variables in the Auto-Monitoring area
COBTEST	Batch, Line	Invoke the COBOL II debug tool
COLOR	Full-Screen	Set color and intensity attributes
COMMENT	All Modes	Insert comments into COBTEST debugging input and output
DROP	All Modes	Delete symbols created with the EQUATE command
DUMP	All Modes	Terminate the debugging session and give a snap dump
EQUATE	All Modes	Establish symbols for program data-names, indexes, or special registers
FLOW	All Modes	Trace control flow of selected portions of the program
FREQ	All Modes	Tally verb use during program execution
GO	All Modes	Start or resume execution, recognizing breakpoints
HELP	Line, Full-Screen	Provide information about COBTEST commands
IF	All Modes	Cause conditional execution of COBTEST commands based on the immediate evaluation of an expression
LINK	All Modes	Simulate a non-existent calling program
LIST	All Modes	Display attributes and values of selected storage
LISTBRKS	All Modes	List the current breakpoints
LISTEQ	All Modes	List active symbols created by the EQUATE command
LISTFREQ	All Modes	List tally of verb usage if FREQ was turned on
LISTINGS	Full-Screen	Access panel to make associations between source listings and debuggable program units
MOVECURS	Full-Screen	Move cursor between the last position in the Source or Auto-monitoring area and the command line
NEXT	All Modes	Set temporary breakpoint at the next program verb to be executed
OFF	All Modes	Remove AT breakpoints
OFFWN	All Modes	Remove WHEN breakpoints
ONABEND	All Modes	Permit execution of a command list if the program ABENDs
PEEK	Full-Screen	Allow viewing of the line number obscured by AT breakpoint feedback
POSITION	Full-Screen	Cause specified line in Source, Auto-Monitoring or Log area to move to top of its area
PREVDISP	Full-Screen	Allow redisplay of a previous panel displayed by program if ISPF Services were used
PRINTDD	All Modes	Specify file where output from RECORD or commands with PRINT option will be directed
PROC	All Modes	Trap calls to a non-existent subprogram
PROFILE	Full-Screen	Access panel to allow setting of COBTEST session parameters
QUALIFY	All Modes	Change qualification of names or line numbers used in COBTEST commands
QUIT	All Modes	Terminate the COBTEST debugging session
RECORD	All Modes	Activate or deactivate logging of the COBTEST session

Figure 13.1 Alphabetical list and brief description of all COBTEST commands. (*Continued*)

RESTART	Line, Full-Screen	Load new copy of program and begin execution, recognizing previous COBTEST settings
RESTORE	Full-Screen	Restore the Source area to last point of execution
RUN	All Modes	Execute the program without interrupts caused by active breakpoints, in effect turning them off
SEARCH	Full-Screen	Search the Source, Log or Auto Monitoring area for a given character string
SELECT	Full-Screen	Allow viewing of frequency count on a line with multiple statements
SET	All Modes	Initialize or change values of program variables
SOURCE	Full-Screen	Open, close or change the size of the Source area
STEP	All Modes	Cause execution of a specific number of program statements
SUFFIX	Full-Screen	Open or close the suffix area within the Source area
TRACE	All Modes	Display a flow of program execution
VTRACE	Full-Screen	Allow dynamic viewing of program execution
WHEN	All Modes	Set up continuous monitoring of a condition before each verb in the program executes with conditional execution of an optional COBTEST command list or transfer of control to the terminal
WHERE	All Modes	Show where execution has been suspended

Figure 13.1 *(Continued)*

the debugging commands must be placed in a data set or instream in the JCL, with no chance for second thoughts once the job has begun execution. Output from the commands is sent to a data set which can be reviewed after the program has either terminated successfully or ABENDed.

You might question why you would use batch mode rather than the COBOL language debugging features explained in Chap. 5 (DISPLAY statements, DEBUGGING LINES, DECLARATIVES, etc.). First, under batch mode no commands are inserted into the program source code; hence the program does not need to be recompiled when changes in the debugging strategy become necessary. Second, the COBTEST commands provide a great deal of flexibility and give more debugging information than is available with the COBOL language debugging aids.

Batch mode uses fewer resources than either of the interactive modes. You may prefer it to an interactive session when you do not want to tie up your terminal for long periods of time or when you wish to use COBTEST facilities to gather information about program execution for later review.

13.4.1 Invoking COBTEST in Batch Mode

The following procedure explains how to prepare for and invoke batch mode.

1. Compile the source module. You must compile with the TEST compiler option.
2. Run the object module through the linkage-editor in order to create an executable load module.

COBTEST TASK	COMMANDS
Setting Breakpoints	AT NEXT ONABEND PROC WHEN
Removing Breakpoints	OFF OFFWN
Resuming Program Execution	GO RESTART RUN
Analyzing Program Behavior and Flow	FLOW FREQ STEP TRACE VTRACE
Testing Program Conditions	IF WHEN
Referring to Other COBOL II Programs	QUALIFY
Simulating Non-Existent Calling or Called Programs	LINK PROC
Setting Values of Program Variables	SET
Displaying Values of Program Variables	LIST
Creating and Deleting Alias Names	EQUATE DROP
Determining Status of COBTEST settings	LISTBRKS LISTEQ LISTFREQ WHERE
Directing COBTEST Output to Datasets	PRINTDD
Logging COBTEST Session	RECORD
Terminating COBTEST Session	DUMP QUIT

Figure 13.2 COBTEST commands used to carry out various COBTEST debugging tasks.

3. Enter the COBTEST commands you intend to use in a data set (or instream in the JCL) with a record length of 80. It should be assigned to the DDname SYSDBIN. Place the commands in the following order:
   a. COBTEST *load-module-name*
   b. If you wish, you may now specify RECORD.
   c. QUALIFY *program-id.* Use the program-id from the IDENTIFICATION DIVISION of the first program being tested. It is possible to debug more than one COBOL II program in a COBTEST session. This is particularly useful when you wish to test calling and called programs. QUALIFY identifies the COBOL II program in the load module to which the following debugging commands apply.
   d. Now supply the additional COBTEST commands for this first program being tested.
   e. If you wish to test other COBOL II programs, use additional QUALIFY commands for each one. Use the same format as above—QUALIFY *program-id.* Follow this with the COBTEST commands to be used for that program.
4. Activate the debug commands by submitting a job with the JCL statement:

```
//  EXEC  PGM=COBDBG
```

5. The debugging test will be done when the program completes execution or when an ABEND occurs. The data set assigned to the SYSDBOUT DDname will contain the data generated by COBTEST.

13.4.2 COBTEST Commands in Batch Mode

Since you are operating in batch, you will have less flexibility than with one of the interactive modes. Be aware that all COBTEST commands specified will be read and processed before the execution of any instruction in the program you are testing occurs. Some of these commands will take effect immediately while others will be delayed. As an example, consider the LIST and AT commands. LIST displays the contents and attributes of selected storage areas. AT sets a breakpoint (a place where program execution is to be interrupted). A LIST FLD-1 command will take effect and give the contents of FLD-1 as soon as it is read in, but AT 100 (LIST FLD-1) will not give the contents of FLD-1 until the AT command takes effect at line 100. In the latter case, this is because the LIST command is part of a command list; commands in a command list execute only when the specified breakpoint is reached.

The "immediate" commands, which become effective and complete their processing as soon as they are read, can be divided into two groups: those which have no further effect once they are first encountered and executed, and those which may have an effect on subsequent program execution. The immediate commands having no further effect are DUMP, IF, LIST, LISTBRKS, LISTEQ, LISTFREQ, and WHERE. Those which may have a subsequent effect are DROP, EQUATE, FLOW ON, FREQ, GO, LINK, OFF, OFFWN, PRINTDD, QUALIFY, QUIT, RECORD, RUN, SET, STEP, and TRACE.

The "delayed-action" commands do not perform their functions when first entered. They set up conditions which must be met before they will process. The delayed commands are AT, NEXT, ONABEND, PROC, and WHEN.

Although most COBTEST commands operate essentially the same in batch mode as in the interactive modes, there is an implied GO in batch mode whenever the interactive modes would have expected you to provide input at the terminal.

Based on the preceding discussion, you should note that a number of commands are not useful in batch mode outside of a command list. They are GO, IF, QUIT, RUN, SET, and WHERE. It is also important to remember that commands will be executed in the same sequence as they appear in SYSDBIN.

13.4.3 An Example of COBTEST in Batch Mode

Shown in Fig. 13.3 is sample JCL for a simple batch COBTEST session. The dataset containing the program source code is MY.PROGLIB.COBOL(COBTAB2) and the name of the load library is MY.LOADLIB.LOAD. The name of the COBOL II subroutine library, which may be different for your installation, is SYS1.COB2LIB.

The job compiles and links a COBOL II program in STEP1 and invokes the debug tool in STEP2. Note that the STEPLIB statement in STEP2 includes the load library where the load module resides as well as the COBOL II subroutine library containing COBDBG. Also, the separator for commands within a command list is the semicolon.

The COBTEST commands in the example do the following:

```
//**************************************************
//*     EXECUTE PROC FOR COBOL II COMPILE AND LINK   *
//**************************************************
//STEP1    EXEC COB2UCL,REGION=512K,
//              PARM.COB2='XREF,TEST'
//COB2.SYSIN    DD DSN=MY.PROGLIB.COBOL(COBTAB2),DISP=SHR
//LKED.SYSLMOD DD DSN=MY.LOADLIB.LOAD,DISP=SHR
//LKED.SYSIN    DD *
 NAME BATCHDBG(R)
/*
//***************************************************
//*        THIS INVOKES COBTEST IN BATCH MODE         *
//***************************************************
//STEP2    EXEC PGM=COBDBG
//STEPLIB       DD DSN=MY.LOADLIB.LOAD,DISP=SHR
//              DD DSN=SYS1.COB2LIB,DISP=SHR
//SYSDBIN       DD *
 COBTEST BATCHDBG
 QUALIFY COBTAB2
 FREQ
 TRACE NAME
 AT 174  (TRACE OFF;LIST NO-OF-ENTRIES)
 ONABEND (LIST (NO-OF-ENTRIES,DEPT-TABLE,INREC-WS))
 AT 178  (LISTBRKS;LIST (DEPT-IND,EMP-DEPT-WS))
 AT 181  (LISTFREQ)
/*
//EMPFILE      DD DSN=INPUT.EMPTABLE.DATA,DISP=SHR
//DPTFILE      DD DSN=INPUT.DPTTABLE.DATA,DISP=SHR
//LENFILE      DD DSN=INPUT.LEN.DATA,DISP=SHR
//OUTFILE      DD SYSOUT=A
//SYSOUT       DD SYSOUT=A
//SYSDBOUT     DD SYSOUT=A
//SYSUDUMP     DD SYSOUT=A
//
```

Figure 13.3 JCL to compile, link, and invoke a batch COBTEST debugging session.

- COBTEST BATCHDBG identifies the load module created in STEP1.
- QUALIFY COBTAB2 names the COBOL II program being debugged.
- FREQ tallies the verb use during program execution.
- TRACE NAME displays the flow of program execution, giving line numbers and paragraph names.
- AT 174 (TRACE OFF;LIST NO-OF-ENTRIES) turns the trace off and lists the contents of the variable NO-OF-ENTRIES when line 174 is reached.
- ONABEND (LIST (NO-OF-ENTRIES,DEPT-TABLE,INREC-WS)) will list the contents of the three variables specified if the program ABENDs.
- AT 178 (LISTBRKS;LIST (DEPT-IND,EMP-DEPT-WS)) lists the active breakpoints and lists the contents of the two variables specified when line 178 is reached.
- AT 181 (LISTFREQ) lists the verb frequency table, created as a result of the previous FREQ command, when line 181 is reached.

The output from the COBTEST commands, appearing on the data set named in the SYSDBOUT DDname, is shown in Fig. 13.4. Note that the first line states that COBTEST Release 2.0 was used. The third line from the top identifies the program being debugged as COBTAB2 and indicates that the first executable statement is at 000142.1, meaning the first verb on line 142 of the source code. The next line in the COBTEST output indicates that COBTEST is tracing the program flow. Note that each time a breakpoint is reached, you are notified (NOTIFY is the default option for the AT command), and that the output from any command in a command list is then displayed. Thus, the LIST command executed as a result of the breakpoint at line 174 indicates that pro-

```
IGZ100I PP - 5668-958 VS COBOL II DEBUG FACILITY -- REL 2.0
IGZ100I (C) COPYRIGHT IBM CORPORATION 1986
IGZ102I COBTAB2.000142.1
IGZ106I TRACING COBTAB2
IGZ109I 000152.1
IGZ109I 000154.1
IGZ109I 000157.1
IGZ109I 000157.1
IGZ109I 000157.1
IGZ109I 000157.1
IGZ109I 000157.1
IGZ109I 000167.1
IGZ109I 000168.1
IGZ109I 000173.1
IGZ109I 000187.1 2500-HEADER
IGZ109I 000193.1 2500-EXIT
IGZ105I AT COBTAB2.000174.1
000089 02 COBTAB2.NO-OF-ENTRIES                            99
       DISP     ===>10
IGZ105I AT COBTAB2.000178.1
FREQ IS SET ON FOR PROGRAMS:
 ALL
AT COBTAB2  000174.1
AT COBTAB2  000178.1
AT COBTAB2  000181.1
000094 00 COBTAB2.DEPT-IND                                 IX
          ===>8
000102 03 COBTAB2.EMP-DEPT-WS                              XX
       DISP     ===>50
IGZ105I AT COBTAB2.000181.1
FREQUENCY OF VERB EXECUTIONS IN COBTAB2
000142.1=1          000145.1=1          000146.1=1          000152.1=1
000154.1=1          000157.1=5          000167.1=1          000168.1=1
000173.1=1          000174.1=1          000178.1=1          000187.1=1
000188.1=1          000189.1=1          000191.1=1          000193.1=1
000200.1=11         000201.1=11         000203.1=6          000204.1=6
000206.1=1          000207.1=1          000209.1=1          000211.1=5
000212.1=5          000213.1=5          000215.1=5          000218.1=11
000219.1=10         000221.1=11         000222.1=1          000225.1=11
000230.1=10         000233.1=10         000234.1=10         000235.1=10
000236.1=10         000238.1=10         000239.1=10         000241.1=10
TOTAL VERBS=50         TOTAL VERBS EXECUTED=40          PERCENT EXECUTED=80
IGZ129I PROGRAM UNDER COBTEST ENDED NORMALLY
IGZ350I ******** END OF COBTEST ********
```

Figure 13.4 Output from the COBTEST commands executed in the batch COBTEST session invoked by the JCL in Fig. 13.3.

gram variable NO-OF-ENTRIES is defined at line 89 in the program as a PIC 99 field with USAGE DISPLAY at an 02 "normalized" level (instead of the 05 level which was actually coded in the program) and currently has a value of 10. The LIST command executed as a result of the breakpoint at line 178 shows that DEPT-IND is an index (IX) containing the value 8, and that EMP-DEPT-WS is defined as PIC XX USAGE DISPLAY and has a value of 50. LISTBRKS, which is also in the command list for the AT 178 command, displays the active breakpoints, and LISTFREQ, executed because of the AT 181 command, displays the frequency table created as a result of the FREQ command.

13.5 USING COBTEST IN INTERACTIVE LINE MODE

COBTEST in line mode is similar to TESTCOB in OS/VS COBOL (see Chap. 12). In an interactive line mode session, the debugging commands are entered sequentially at the terminal, one line at a time, with the responses from COBTEST also appearing sequentially at the terminal. You can set break points to halt execution at any time and perform COBTEST functions in a true interactive fashion. In order to use line mode under MVS, you must be operating in a TSO environment.

Use of COBTEST in line mode is intended primarily for programmers who only have access to a teletype terminal, or for installations which do not have ISPF. A disadvantage of line mode is that source code cannot be viewed at the terminal.

13.5.1 Invoking COBTEST in Line Mode

Here is an outline of how to prepare for and invoke line mode.

1. Compile using the TEST compiler option.
2. Use the linkage-editor to create an executable load module.
3. Use the TSO ALLOCATE command to identify to the system all input and output data sets used by the program as well as the library where the load module resides. If you wish to see program output on-line as the program executes, allocate program output to the terminal rather than to a data set.
4. Enter the line-mode version of the COBTEST command at the terminal in either TSO READY mode or from within ISPF. This activates the debug tool. (See Sec. 13.5.2 for the syntax of the COBTEST command.)
5. When the COBTEST prompt appears, enter any COBTEST commands that work in line mode. The prompt is simply the message "COBTEST."
6. After entering the debugging commands you need, issue a command to begin program execution (such as GO).
7. You can continue entering COBTEST commands, including RESTART, to resume testing from the beginning, until you have determined the nature of your program's problems.

8. The session will end when you enter QUIT or if you enter two attention interrupts in a row.
9. After you have terminated COBTEST, you will return to the point from which you invoked COBTEST, either TSO or ISPF.

Figure 13.5 shows a sample setup for using COBTEST in interactive line mode. This can be written and run as a CLIST. The same DDnames and dataset names as in the previous batch mode example (Sec. 13.4.3) are used. OUTFILE and SYSOUT, which will contain output, have been allocated to the terminal. Remember that you must allocate the load library and any input/output files used by your program before invoking COBTEST.

13.5.2 The COBTEST Command in Line Mode

Once all files have been allocated, the COBTEST command is issued. It can be placed, as shown in Fig. 13.5, as the last line in a CLIST. The COBTEST command has been coded using the format:

```
COBTEST LOAD(load-module-name:DDname) [PARM('parameter')]
```

The LOAD keyword is followed by the name of the load module which will receive control when the COBTEST command is executed, and the DDname of the load library coded in the ALLOCATE statement. If a parameter is normally passed to the program from the JCL, the PARM keyword and parameter string can be coded. PARM is optional.

A second format of the COBTEST command in line mode is

```
COBTEST load-module-name [PARM('parameter')]
```

Load-module-name is the name of the load module which will receive control when the debugging session begins. It resides in a STEPLIB library allocated to your terminal session. In this case it is unnecessary to allocate the load library as was done in Fig. 13.5. Again, PARM is optional.

13.5.3 The COBTEST Session in Line Mode

Once the COBTEST session has been activated, the COBTEST prompt will appear on the terminal. Any COBTEST commands which are valid for line

```
ALC     DD(LOADLIB)    DS(MY.LOADLIB.LOAD) SHR REU
ALC     DD(EMPFILE)    DS(INPUT.EMPTABLE.DATA) SHR REU
ALC     DD(DPTFILE)    DS(INPUT.DPTTABLE.DATA) SHR REU
ALC     DD(LENFILE)    DS(INPUT.LEN.DATA) SHR REU
ALC     DD(OUTFILE)    DS(*) REU
ALC     DD(SYSOUT)     DS(*) REU
COBTEST LOAD(INTERDBG:LOADLIB)
```

Figure 13.5 A CLIST which allocates the necessary files for a COBTEST session in line mode and then invokes COBTEST.

mode can now be entered (see Fig. 13.1 for a list of valid commands). Most of the commands which are available in full-screen mode and not in line mode are for special viewing and customization of a full-screen environment. Note that because the program source code cannot be viewed on the terminal, it is usually necessary to have a hard copy of the program with you during the debugging session.

A sample debugging session is given in Sec. 13.7. Rather than give an example explicitly for line mode, the sample session in Sec. 13.7 will serve for both line and full-screen modes. The commands entered in that example and the responses from COBTEST are the same for both modes.

13.6 USING COBTEST IN INTERACTIVE FULL-SCREEN MODE

Interactive full-screen mode is the most powerful of the three COBTEST modes. Additional commands, many of them relating to setting screen options or requesting special functions are available in full-screen mode. The screen can be divided into three windows of varying size and shape: the Source Area contains program source code, the Log Area lists COBTEST commands you have entered along with their output, and the Auto-Monitoring Area shows the contents of selected program variables.

Full-screen mode allows you to dynamically step through the program, watching the source code scroll by as it executes, with the executing line of code highlighted. While this is occurring you can view the Log area to see the output of COBTEST commands as they execute and monitor the values of program variables in the Auto-Monitoring Area as they change. If PDF is installed, you can also split the physical screen into two logical screens in order to do other tasks. Thus you can edit a data set or view source code in one logical screen while remaining in COBTEST in the other.

In order to use full-screen mode, ISPF Version 2 or higher under MVS-TSO, MVS/XA-TSO or MVS/ESA-TSO must be installed.

Figures 13.7 through 13.13, referred to in the following discussion of full-screen mode, show the relevant ISPF panels.

13.6.1 Invoking and Running COBTEST in Full-Screen Mode

As with the other COBTEST modes, you must first compile the program using the TEST compiler option. Since you will probably want to view the source code during the debugging session, you must be sure that the compiler output is in a data set which will be available during your debugging session (LIST is the default low-level qualifier specified in the IBM documentation, but you can use any valid low-level qualifier name). Next, link-edit your object module; be sure that the COBOL II subroutine library is included. Sample JCL to compile and link is given in Fig. 13.6.

To invoke COBTEST, select the foreground option in the ISPF Primary Option Menu. When the Foreground Selection Panel appears, select the COBTEST option.

```
//**************************************************
//*      EXECUTE PROC FOR COBOL II COMPILE AND LINK     *
//**************************************************
//STEP1    EXEC COB2UCL,REGION=512K,
//              PARM.COB2='XREF,TEST'
//COB.SYSPRINT DD DSN=MY.program.LIST,DISP=(,CATLG),
//             UNIT=TSWK,SPACE=(TRK,(5,5),RLSE),
//             DCB=(LRECL=121,RECFM=FB,BLKSIZE=1210)
//COB2.SYSIN    DD DSN=MY.PROGLIB.COBOL(program),DISP=SHR
//LKED.SYSLMOD DD DSN=MY.LOADLIB.LOAD,DISP=SHR
//LKED.SYSIN    DD *
 NAME module-name(R)
/*
```

Figure 13.6 JCL to compile and link a COBOL II program in preparation for a COBTEST session in full-screen mode.

You will now be in the VS COBOL II Debug Invocation Panel (see Fig. 13.7). Enter the name of your load library and load module. You can also enter program parameters, specify that you wish to log the debugging session, or restart the session using a previously created file containing COBTEST commands. Logging the session enables you to retain the debugging information for review at a later time. It also enables you to use the same COBTEST commands for a restart file; using a restart file permits you to duplicate the debugging session commands in another test, avoiding the need to reenter them.

Be aware that indicating you will "log" the session and naming a data set to receive the log information works independently from "recording" the session using the RECORD/NORECORD commands from within the COBTEST session; output goes to a different data set and you cannot turn off the logging feature. You can turn on the recording of your session, and turn it off again, by using the RECORD/NORECORD commands. If you intend to restart using a restart data set, each COBTEST command must be preceded with an asterisk. The logging feature inserts the asterisk automatically when it logs the session. The RECORD command places the symbol ⟩⟩⟩ before each command; to use the commands in a restart file, you will have to replace each ⟩⟩⟩ with an asterisk so that COBTEST will recognize the commands as valid input. Obviously you can also create your own restart data set independently from using the logging feature or the RECORD command.

After pressing the ENTER key, you will be presented with the Main Full-Screen Panel, similar to that shown in Fig. 13.8. The Source Area will highlight the current line to be executed (first statement in the PROCEDURE DIVISION). The Log Area will give COBTEST identification information as well as the program name and line number of the first executable statement. The QUALIFY and WHERE fields will also display the program name and line number, respectively.

If you have not already done so, you must now allocate the program's input and output files. Remember to allocate SYSOUT if the program contains DISPLAY statements. Output data sets can be allocated to the terminal to allow

```
----------------------- VS COBOL II DEBUG INVOCATION -------------------------
COMMAND ===>

ISPF LIBRARY:
   PROJECT ===> MY
   GROUP   ===> COBOL
   TYPE    ===> LOAD
   MEMBER  ===>                        (Blank for member selection list)

OTHER PARTITIONED DATA SET:
   DATASET NAME  ===> LOADLIB.LOAD(TESTA2)


PASSWORD ===>                          MIXED MODE ===> NO  (YES or NO)

VS COBOL II PROGRAM PARAMETERS:
  ===>
  ===>

LOG     ===> NO   (Yes or No)
LOG DSN ===>
RESTART ===> NO   (Yes or No)
RESTART DSN ===>
```

Figure 13.7 The COBTEST Invocation Panel for a full-screen debugging session.

viewing of program output as the program executes. ISPF and TSO commands can be entered on the command line at the top of the Main Full-Screen Panel.

COBTEST commands can now be entered on the command line. The COBTEST commands, with their output and any messages, will be recorded in the Log Area. If you wish to have a permanent record of any portion of the debugging session, and you did not specify LOG in the Invocation Panel, you can specify RECORD and NORECORD at any time during the session.

The Auto-Monitoring Area can be opened up to continuously monitor the values of variables during execution of your program by entering

AUTO LIST *variable-name*

on the command line. The Auto Area will appear at the top of the Main Full-Screen Panel (see Fig. 13.9). You can specify more than one variable by using the appropriate form of the LIST command.

COBTEST permits you to set up windows of various sizes and shapes to contain the source listing, log information, and auto-monitoring data. This can be done at any time during your debugging session. To customize the panel, use the cursor-sensitive SOURCE and AUTO commands. To change the size and shape of the Source area for example, enter SOURCE on the command line, move the cursor to the position where you want the lower left corner of the Source Area to be, and press the enter key (see Fig. 13.10).

After opening up the areas you need and entering any COBTEST commands necessary, you can enter a command such as GO to begin program execution.

```
COBTEST   QUALIFY: TESTA2     WHERE: TESTA2.004900.1
COMMAND ===>                                                    SCROLL ===> CSR

SOURCE ----+----1----+----2----+----3----+----4----+----5----+- LINE: 44 OF 111
  4500 004500                          VALUE 'WORKING-STORAGE ENDS HERE'.
  4700 004700 PROCEDURE DIVISION.
  4800 004800 0000-MAINLINE.
  4900 004900     DISPLAY 'PROGRAM TESTA2 STARTS'
  5000 005000     OPEN  OUTPUT  OUT-FILE
  5100 005100     PERFORM  0100-PROCESS-TABLE
  5200 005200              UNTIL  NO-MORE-ENTRIES
  5300 005300     PERFORM  0200-PRINT-OUTPUT
  5400 005400     CLOSE  OUT-FILE
  5500 005500     DISPLAY  'PROGRAM TESTA2 ENDS'
  5600 005600     GOBACK.
LOG   0----+----1----+----2----+----3----+----4----+----5----+---- LINE: 0 OF 3
******************************** TOP OF LOG ********************************
000001 IGZ100I PP - 5668-958 VS COBOL II DEBUG FACILITY -- REL 2.0
000002 IGZ100I (C) COPYRIGHT IBM CORPORATION 1986
000003 IGZ102I TESTA2.004900.1
****************************** BOTTOM OF LOG *******************************
```

Figure 13.8 The Main Full-Screen Panel for a full-screen COBTEST debugging session. Shown are the Source and Log areas.

Monitor the Source, Log, and Auto areas as well as the ISPF message area right below the command line.

The RESTART command can be entered at any time to restart debugging at the beginning of the program. This command deletes and reloads the program that was invoked under COBTEST. Any breakpoints and other COBTEST settings remain intact from run to run unless they are explicitly changed by new commands.

```
COBTEST   QUALIFY: TESTA2     WHERE: TESTA2.004900.1
COMMAND ===>                                                    SCROLL ===> CSR

AUTO  0----+----1----+----2----+----3----+----4----+----5----+---- LINE: 1 OF 3
000001 002500 03 TESTA2.WS-FIELD-A                         S9(5)
000002                                       INVALID SIGN - POSITIVE VALUE IS
000003        CMP3    ===>+00000
****************************** BOTTOM OF AUTO *******************************

SOURCE ----+----1----+----2----+----3----+----4----+----5----+- LINE: 44 OF 111
  4500 004500                          VALUE 'WORKING-STORAGE ENDS HERE'.
  4700 004700 PROCEDURE DIVISION.
  4800 004800 0000-MAINLINE.
  4900 004900     DISPLAY 'PROGRAM TESTA2 STARTS'
  5000 005000     OPEN  OUTPUT  OUT-FILE
  5100 005100     PERFORM  0100-PROCESS-TABLE
  5200 005200              UNTIL  NO-MORE-ENTRIES
  5300 005300     PERFORM  0200-PRINT-OUTPUT
  5400 005400     CLOSE  OUT-FILE
  5500 005500     DISPLAY  'PROGRAM TESTA2 ENDS'
  5600 005600     GOBACK.
LOG   0----+----1----+----2----+----3----+----4----+----5----+---- LINE: 0 OF 7
******************************** TOP OF LOG ********************************
000001 IGZ100I PP - 5668-958 VS COBOL II DEBUG FACILITY -- REL 2.0
000002 IGZ100I (C) COPYRIGHT IBM CORPORATION 1986
```

Figure 13.9 The Main Full-Screen Panel for a full-screen COBTEST session, showing the Auto Area, Source Area, and Log Area.

```
COBTEST   QUALIFY: TESTA2     WHERE: TESTA2.004900.1
COMMAND ===>                                                  SCROLL ===> CSR

AUTO  0----+----1----+----2----+----3----+----4----+----5----+---- LINE: 1 OF 3
000001 002500 03 TESTA2.WS-FIELD-A                          S9(5)
000002                                           INVALID SIGN - POSITIVE VALUE IS
000003          CMP3      ===>+00000
****************************** BOTTOM OF AUTO ********************************

LOG   0----+----1----+- LINE: 0 OF 8| SOURCE ----+----1----+--- LINE: 44 OF 111
************ TOP OF LOG ************|   4500 004500                         ....
000001 IGZ100I PP - 5668-958 VS COBO|   4700 004700 PROCEDURE DIVISION.     ....
000002 IGZ100I (C) COPYRIGHT IBM COR|   4800 004800 0000-MAINLINE.          ....
000003 IGZ102I TESTA2.004900.1      |   4900 004900     DISPLAY 'PROGRAM T 0000
000004 * eq fa ws-field-a           |   5000 005000     OPEN  OUTPUT  OUT- 0000
000005 * at 58                      |_______________________________________________
000006 IGZ130I STATEMENT 58 NOT FOUND IN TESTA2
000007 * at 5800
000008 * freq
******************************* BOTTOM OF LOG ******************************
```

Figure 13.10 The Main Full-Screen Panel for a full-screen COBTEST session with the Source Area placed in a window.

At the start of the COBTEST session, or at any time during the session, the profile settings that affect the way the session runs can be displayed or changed by using the PROFILE command to access the Profile Panel (see Fig. 13.11). The settings include the number of columns and rows you want in the Source and Auto-Monitoring areas, whether or not you want log line numbers and default source module listings, and how long a delay you want between COBOL statements when you are executing the program using the VTRACE command. The initial value for each setting is shown in Fig. 13.11. To change a value, enter a new one in the field you wish to modify and follow the directions at the bottom of the panel.

If you wish to change the default source listing made available for viewing in the Source Area, you can explicitly name the program units to be shown in the Source Area by using the LISTINGS command to access the Listing Panel (see Fig. 13.12). Specify the desired TSO data set, enter the corresponding PROGRAM-ID in the PGM UNIT field, and indicate "YES" in the DISPLAY field.

If you wish, you can use ISPF split-screen mode to do other tasks while you are still in the debugging session (see Fig. 13.13). You can edit a data set and even recompile and relink the program you are debugging. To bring a new version of the program into COBTEST, access the LISTING Panel in your debugging session, delete the entry in the PGM UNIT field, press the enter key, reenter the name of the recompiled program unit, and press the enter key again. This will access the new version of your edited source listing. After leaving the LISTING Panel, entering the RESTART command from the Main Full-Screen Panel will access the new copy of the load module.

The session will end when you enter QUIT or if you enter an attention interrupt. After ending the debugging session, you will be returned to the ISPF VS COBOL II Debug Invocation Panel.

```
                 VS COBOL II DEBUG PROFILE PANEL
COMMAND ===>


                               CURRENT SETTING
                               ---------------
 Source area columns              80            (8 to screen width)
 Source area rows                 12            (0 to screen depth)
 Auto area rows                   6             (0 to screen depth)
 Auto line numbers                YES           (yes or no)
 Log line numbers                 YES           (yes or no)
 Default listings                 YES           (yes or no)
 Refresh screen                   NO            (yes or no)
 VTRACE delay                     50            (0 to 99999, 1 unit= .01 second)


 Enter:
    SAVE       to save your profile settings.
    DEFAULT    to restore default profile settings.
    END        to return to the debug session with current profile settings
               in effect.
```

Figure 13.11 The Profile Panel for a full-screen COBTEST session.

13.6.2 Miscellaneous Notes about Full-Screen Mode

There is a LIST command in ISPF. If you enter the COBTEST LIST command when you are in full-screen mode, ISPF may intercept it, assuming it was meant to be the ISPF LIST command. The command will fail and ISPF will return an error message. This problem can be avoided by changing the ISPF command list so that the ISPF LIST command is different from the COBTEST command. A much simpler alternative is to use the abbreviated COBTEST syntax "L."

The semicolon (;) is used as a command separator in COBTEST command lists. Because it is also the ISPF default command separator when stacking ISPF commands, ISPF assumes that the command following a semicolon is meant to be an ISPF command, not a COBTEST command. The COBTEST command will fail and you will receive an error message. A simple remedy to this annoyance is to change the ISPF command separator to a symbol other than the semicolon.

13.7 A SAMPLE COBTEST SESSION

Assume that the COBOL II program we have just completed has ABENDed with an S0C7. The purpose of the program is to read a record, process it, and write a detail line. A subprogram which has not yet been written is to be called after all record processing has been completed. The type of processing will be determined by a parameter passed from the JCL. For testing purposes, our input data set contains only 50 records. Figure 13.14 shows the COBOL II program.

We have allocated all files needed by the program, with the output files allocated to the terminal, and have entered one of the interactive COBTEST modes in order to solve the ABEND. We proceed as follows.

```
                 VS COBOL II DEBUG LISTING PANEL                        ROW 1 OF 2
COMMAND ===>                                                         SCROLL ===> CSR


PGM UNIT        MVS LISTING DATASET                        DISPLAY

TESTA2__  'MY.TESTA2.LIST'___________________________      YES
****************************** BOTTOM OF DATA  ********************************
```

Figure 13.12 The Listing Panel for a full-screen COBTEST session.

First, assuming the subprogram is called SUBPROG, we enter

```
PROC SUBPROG
```

to trap calls to the nonexistent submodule.

Since the COBOL II program is to receive a parameter from the JCL, we must establish addressability to the 01 identifier INPARM in the LINKAGE SECTION which will receive the parameter. The command that achieves this is

```
LINK INPARM
```

During testing we should be certain to try passing various parameters, both valid and invalid, to the program. For now, assume we enter the command

```
SET INPARM = 'B'
```

to simulate the passing of the parameter value 'B' to INPARM.

Entering either

```
GO or RUN
```

begins execution of the COBOL II program.

The program ABENDs. The output from COBTEST indicates a system completion code of 0C7 and displays the line number of the statement which was executing, line 007600. Looking at the source code, we find that the COBOL statement is

```
IF DETAIL-LINE-CNT GREATER THAN +55
```

Since an 0C7 is a data exception, we suspect that there is invalid data in DETAIL-LINE-CNT. We may want to enter the command

```
EQUATE L-C DETAIL-LINE-CNT
```

to permit us to enter L-C instead of DETAIL-LINE-CNT at the terminal (this saves a few key strokes if we will refer to this field again).

```
COBTEST   QUALIFY: TESTA2      WHERE: TESTA2.008400.1

COMMAND ===>                                                  SCROLL ===> CSR
AUTO   0----+----1----+----2----+----3----+----4----+----5----+---- LINE: 1 OF 3
000001 002500 03 TESTA2.WS-FIELD-A                       S9(5)
000002                                        INVALID SIGN - POSITIVE VALUE IS
000003         CMP3      ===>+00000
****************************** BOTTOM OF AUTO **********************************

LOG    0----+----1----+ LINE: 0 OF 14| SOURCE ----+----1----+--- LINE: 81 OF 111
************ TOP OF LOG ************|  8300 008300      END-COMPUTE          ....
000001 IGZ100I PP - 5668-958 VS COBO|  8400 008400      IF  WS-FIELD-A GRE 0001
000002 IGZ100I (C) COPYRIGHT IBM COR|  8500 008500      THEN                 ....
000003 IGZ102I TESTA2.004900.1      |  8600 008600            SET NO-MORE- 0000
000004 * eq fa ws-field-a           |  8700 008700      END-IF               ....
000005 * at 58                      |
000006 IGZ130I STATEMENT 58 NOT FOUND IN TESTA2
000007 * at 5800
000008 * freq
.  .  .  .  .  .  .  .  .  .  .  .  .  .  .  .  .  .  .  .  .  .  .  .  .  .  .
----------------------- ISPF/PDF PRIMARY OPTION MENU -----------------------
OPTION ===>
                                                      USERID   - xxxxxx
   0  ISPF PARMS  - Specify terminal and user parameters  TIME     - 14:38
   1  BROWSE      - Display source data or output listings TERMINAL - 3278
```

Figure 13.13 Screen with COBTEST in the top part and ISPF in the bottom part.

To view information about DETAIL-LINE-CNT, we now enter

```
LIST L-C
```

(We could also have entered the full name DETAIL-LINE-CNT instead of L-C.) COBTEST indicates that this is a PIC S99 COMP-3 field and displays the contents in hexadecimal format as F0F0. COBTEST specifies that this is invalid data for this data type; the data are not packed.

To determine why DETAIL-LINE-CNT contained unpacked zeros, we must examine the source code. If we are using line mode we must look at the hard-copy program listing (the source code cannot be viewed at the terminal). In full-screen mode we can place the cursor in the source area and enter

```
SEARCH DETAIL-LINE-CNT
```

to locate the character string DETAIL-LINE-CNT. We find that DETAIL-LINE-CNT is defined as an elementary item within the COMP-3 group item COUNTERS. In line mode we scan our hard-copy listing for COUNTERS; in full-screen mode we enter the command

```
SEARCH COUNTERS
```

This reveals that

```
MOVE ZERO TO COUNTERS
```

was coded at line 006800 in the program.

```
IDENTIFICATION DIVISION.
 PROGRAM-ID.   CH13F14.
 AUTHOR.       ALAN FRIEND.
 DATE-WRITTEN. JULY, 1989.
 DATE-COMPILED.
    SKIP1
ENVIRONMENT DIVISION.
 INPUT-OUTPUT SECTION.
  FILE-CONTROL.
    SELECT INFILE    ASSIGN TO  INFILE.
    SELECT OUTFILE   ASSIGN TO  OUTFILE.
    SKIP1
DATA DIVISION.
 FILE SECTION.
 FD INFILE
    RECORDING MODE IS F
    RECORD CONTAINS 80 CHARACTERS
    BLOCK CONTAINS 0 RECORDS
    LABEL RECORDS ARE OMITTED
    DATA RECORD IS INFILE-REC.
 01 INFILE-REC.
    05 INFILE-REC-NO          PIC S9(5).
    05 FILLER                 PIC X(75).
 FD OUTFILE
    RECORDING MODE IS F
    RECORD CONTAINS 80 CHARACTERS
    BLOCK CONTAINS 0 RECORDS
    LABEL RECORDS ARE OMITTED
    DATA RECORD IS OUTFILE-REC.
 01 OUTFILE-REC.
    05 OUTFILE-PAGE-NO        PIC X(5).
    05 OUTFILE-REC-NO  REDEFINES
          OUTFILE-PAGE-NO     PIC X(5).
    05 EMP-CLASSIFICATION     PIC BBXBB.
    05 REST-OF-OUTFILE-REC    PIC X(70).
    EJECT
 WORKING-STORAGE SECTION.
    SKIP1
 01 SWITCH-STATUS-AREA.
    05 SW-EOF                 PIC X       VALUE 'N'.
       88 INFILE-EOF                      VALUE 'Y'.
 01 COUNTERS         COMP-3.
    05 DETAIL-LINE-CNT        PIC S99.
    05 PAGE-CNT               PIC S99.
    05 A-RECORDS-WRITTEN      PIC S9(5).
    05 B-RECORDS-WRITTEN      PIC S9(5).
    05 C-RECORDS-WRITTEN      PIC S9(5).
    SKIP1
 LINKAGE SECTION.
    SKIP1
 01 PASSED-PARM.
    05 FILLER                 PIC S9(4) COMP.
    05 INPARM                 PIC X.
    EJECT
```

Figure 13.14 Source code for the COBOL II program used in the COBTEST debugging session described in Sec. 13.7. *(Continued)*

```
005500 PROCEDURE DIVISION USING PASSED-PARM.
005600     SKIP1
005700*****************************************************************
005800*    MAINLINE CONTROL PARAGRAPH - HOUSE-KEEPING, READ EACH        *
005900*    RECORD AND PROCESS BASED ON VALUE IN INPARM RECEIVED FROM    *
006000*    CALLING PROGRAM.     AT END OF INPUT FILE, CALL 'SUBPROG'    *
006100*    TO DO SUMMARY REPORT PROCESSING.                             *
006200*****************************************************************
006300     SKIP1
006400 0000-MAINLINE.
006500     SKIP1
006600     OPEN INPUT  INFILE
006700          OUTPUT OUTFILE
006800     MOVE ZERO TO COUNTERS
006900     MOVE SPACES TO INFILE-REC
007000                    OUTFILE-REC
007100     PERFORM 0500-REPORT-TITLE-RTN
007200     PERFORM    UNTIL INFILE-EOF
007300        READ INFILE
007400             AT END SET INFILE-EOF TO TRUE
007500        END-READ
007600        IF DETAIL-LINE-CNT GREATER THAN +55
007700           MOVE ZERO TO DETAIL-LINE-CNT
007800           PERFORM 0400-HEADER-RTN
007900        END-IF
008000        EVALUATE INPARM
008100           WHEN    'A'
008200              PERFORM 0100-PARA-A
008300           WHEN    'B'
008400              PERFORM 0100-PARA-A
008500           WHEN    'C'
008600              PERFORM 0300-PARA-C
008700        END-EVALUATE
008800     END-PERFORM
009900     CALL 'SUBPROG'
009000     CLOSE INFILE
009100           OUTFILE
009200     GOBACK.
009300     EJECT
```

Figure 13.14 *(Continued)*

A group move is treated as an alphanumeric move, hence DETAIL-LINE-CNT was improperly initialized to unpacked zero.

To change the contents of DETAIL-LINE-CNT to packed zero, we enter

```
SET L-C = 0
```

Entering the LIST command again verifies that the contents of the field are properly packed.

We enter similar SET commands for the other elementary items in COUNTERS.

We now enter

```
GO or RUN
```

to resume execution at the same statement which caused the ABEND. After an ABEND, entering GO or RUN causes COBTEST to reexecute the last COBOL statement.

```
******************************************************************
*    0100-PARA-A, 0200-PARA-B, AND 0300-PARA-C PROCESS AND       *
*    WRITE THE OUTPUT RECORD.  PROCESSING DEPENDS ON THE         *
*    RESOLUTION OF EVALUATE STATEMENT IN 0000-MAINLINE           *
*    PARAGRAPH:  IF INPARM IS 'A', 0100-PARA-A IS PERFORMED      *
*                IF INPARM IS 'B', 0200-PARA-B IS PERFORMED      *
*                IF INPARM IS 'C', 0300-PARA-C IS PERFORMED      *
******************************************************************
     SKIP1
 0100-PARA-A.
     SKIP1
     MOVE INFILE-REC-NO TO OUTFILE-REC-NO
     MOVE 'EMPLOYEE CLASS A' TO REST-OF-OUTFILE-REC
     IF DETAIL-LINE-CNT GREATER THAN +55
        MOVE ZERO TO DETAIL-LINE-CNT
        PERFORM 0400-HEADER-RTN
     END-IF
     WRITE OUTFILE-REC
     ADD +1 TO DETAIL-LINE-CNT  A-RECORDS-WRITTEN.
     SKIP1
 0200-PARA-B.
     SKIP1
     MOVE INFILE-REC-NO TO OUTFILE-REC-NO
     MOVE 'EMPLOYEE CLASS B' TO REST-OF-OUTFILE-REC
     IF DETAIL-LINE-CNT GREATER THAN +55
        MOVE ZERO TO DETAIL-LINE-CNT
        PERFORM 0400-HEADER-RTN
     END-IF
     WRITE OUTFILE-REC
     ADD +1 TO DETAIL-LINE-CNT  B-RECORDS-WRITTEN.
     SKIP1
 0300-PARA-C.
     SKIP1
     MOVE INFILE-REC-NO TO OUTFILE-REC-NO
     MOVE 'EMPLOYEE CLASS C' TO REST-OF-OUTFILE-REC
     IF DETAIL-LINE-CNT GREATER THAN +55
        MOVE ZERO TO DETAIL-LINE-CNT
        PERFORM 0400-HEADER-RTN
     END-IF
     WRITE OUTFILE-REC
     ADD +1 TO DETAIL-LINE-CNT  C-RECORDS-WRITTEN.
     SKIP1
******************************************************************
* HEADER ROUTINE PERFORMED WHEN DETAIL-LINE-CNT GREATER THAN 55. *
******************************************************************
     SKIP1
 0400-HEADER-RTN.
     SKIP1
     ADD +1 TO PAGE-CNT
     MOVE PAGE-CNT TO OUTFILE-PAGE-NO
     MOVE INPARM  TO EMP-CLASSIFICATION
     MOVE 'EMPLOYEE CLASSIFICATION' TO REST-OF-OUTFILE-REC
     WRITE OUTFILE-REC
        AFTER ADVANCING PAGE
     ADD +1 TO DETAIL-LINE-CNT.
     SKIP1
******************************************************************
* REPORT TITLE ROUTINE PERFORMED ONCE ONLY: BEFORE FIRST OUTPUT  *
* RECORD IS WRITTEN.                                             *
******************************************************************
     SKIP1
 0500-REPORT-TITLE-RTN.
     SKIP1
     MOVE +1 TO PAGE-CNT  OUTFILE-PAGE-NO
     MOVE 'EMPLOYEE CLASSIFICATION REPORT' TO REST-OF-OUTFILE-REC
     WRITE OUTFILE-REC.
```

Figure 13.14 *(Continued)*

The call to SUBPROG is trapped by the PROC command. We can enter

```
GO
```

again to continue. Since DETAIL-LINE-CNT and the other fields within COUNTERS now contain valid data, the program ends normally.

We realize we must change our program's code at line 007600, perhaps to

```
INITIALIZE COUNTERS
```

then recompile and relink, and then run the program through COBTEST again to verify our correction.

But wait! The program output displayed at the terminal is incorrect. The detail lines contain data that should only be written when the passed parameter is 'A'. However, we specified a value of 'B' for INPARM. Also, the last record was written twice.

We decide to reexecute the program with the TRACE command to check the control flow of the program as it executes. Entering the command

```
TRACE NAME
```

will give a trace showing the beginning line number of each paragraph and the paragraph name, as well as the line number of the first statement beginning each logical group of statements within each paragraph.

Before entering the RESTART command we must set breakpoints so we can halt execution at the beginning of the program and set the values of INPARM, DETAIL-LINE-CNT, and the other elementary fields in COUNTERS to their desired values. This is because RESTART loads a new copy of our program, thereby reinitializing program variables. All breakpoints and other COBTEST settings will remain in effect.

Entering

```
AT 006600
```

will halt execution at the first executable instruction in the PROCEDURE DIVISION.

We now enter

```
RESTART
```

When the new copy of the program halts at line 006600, we enter the commands

```
SET INPARM = 'B'
FREQ
AT 007600 (NEXT)
```

The FREQ command turns on tallying of verbs; this may be useful to determine how many READS and WRITES have been executed.

Since we found that the COBOL statement at line 007600 moved alphanumeric zero to DETAIL-LINE-CNT, we enter the AT statement with the subcommand NEXT to halt execution at the following COBOL statement. This will allow us to reset DETAIL-LINE-CNT and the other items in COUNTERS to properly packed zeros.

We now enter

```
GO
```

When execution halts at the statement following line 007600, we enter

```
SET L-C = 0
```

as well as the other necessary SET commands.

We then enter

```
GO
```

to continue execution until the PROC SUBPROG command interrupts the program at the COBOL call statement, and

```
GO
```

again to proceed to end-of-job.

Since TRACE NAME has been in effect, we can view the log area to see the flow of execution of the program. We learn that the program never executed the paragraph that should have been performed if INPARM was 'B'. Instead, it executed the paragraph that should only have been performed when INPARM had a value of 'A'. We find that the EVALUATE statement in the program was coded incorrectly; the trace reveals that the proper WHEN clause at line 008300 was executed, but that it caused a branch to the wrong paragraph because the wrong paragraph was named on line 008400:

```
PERFORM 0100-PARA-A
```

instead of

```
PERFORM 0200-PARA-B
```

This explains the incorrect program output. Now we enter the COBTEST command

```
LISTFREQ
```

and find that, as we suspected, 51 READ and 51 WRITE statements were executed by the program. This means a program logic error since our input data set contains only 50 records. Examining the code reveals that the fifty-first READ hit end-of-file, but we continued processing and wrote the fiftieth record an extra time.

To verify this we restart the program as described above and use the command

```
AT 007200 COUNT (50,1)
```

to set a breakpoint at the beginning of the in-line perform which controls reading and writing of records. The breakpoint will be in effect the fiftieth time this procedure is reached and every time thereafter. Now we enter

```
GO
```

The READ will be executed 49 times, and execution will be interrupted before it is executed the fiftieth time.

When execution halts at line 007200 we enter

```
STEP
```

repeatedly to step through the procedure one statement at a time. Following the flow of execution in this paragraph, we find that

```
READ INFILE
  AT END SET INFILE-EOF TO TRUE
```

was coded at the beginning of the procedure instead of at the end. Further examination of our source code reveals that there was no initial READ statement, and that we coded the PERFORM at line 007200 UNTIL INFILE-EOF.

We have thus been able to isolate several problems in our COBOL program in one COBTEST session. Our next steps would be to make the necessary corrections to the source module, recompile and relink, and execute the module again to test the changes.

The preceding example demonstrates the power and flexibility of the COBTEST tool. Note that it represents only one possible method for debugging the sample program.

13.8 SUMMARY

COBTEST is IBM's interactive debugging facility for COBOL II programs. This chapter deals with COBTEST in its full-screen, line, and batch modes.

Some of the tasks available in COBTEST are suspension of program execution at any COBOL verb, listing of values and attributes of identifiers and the status of files, modifying the values of identifiers at any time, and tracing of the logical flow of the program. Whenever COBTEST is to be used, the COBOL II program must be compiled with the TEST option.

When using COBTEST in batch mode, it is not possible to interrupt the program or interact with it at the terminal. Debugging commands are read into the COBTEST job and are executed according to the rules described in this chapter. Debugging in batch mode differs from using COBOL language debugging statements (DISPLAY, DEBUGGING LINES, DECLARATIVES, etc.) in that no commands are inserted into the program source code. The COBTEST commands also offer quite a bit of flexibility and provide a great deal of debugging information.

Batch mode might be used when you do not want to tie up your terminal or when you wish to gather performance statistics about your program for later review. It is less resource-intensive than line or full-screen modes.

COBTEST in line mode is truly interactive. The COBTEST debugging commands are entered sequentially at the terminal, one line at a time, and the output from COBTEST also appears sequentially at the terminal. It is possible to set breakpoints to halt execution at any point and then perform the various COBTEST debugging tasks.

Use of COBTEST in line mode is similar to the use of the TESTCOB facility for OS/VS COBOL programs. It is intended primarily for programmers who only have access to a teletype terminal, or for installations which do not have ISPF. One disadvantage of line mode is that source code cannot be viewed at the terminal.

The full-screen mode of COBTEST is the most powerful and flexible of the three COBTEST modes. It is also the most resource-intensive. It operates under ISPF, allowing you to divide the screen into three areas: as the program executes under COBTEST control, you may view the contents of selected variables in one area, the source code in a second area, and the output from COBTEST commands in a third area. If PDF is available, you can also split the physical screen into two logical screens in order to do other tasks.

REVIEW QUESTIONS

1. What COBOL II compiler option must be specified in order to use COBTEST?

2. Which of the three COBTEST modes uses the most resources? Which uses the least resources?

3. How do the logging feature and the RECORD command differ in full-screen mode?

4. Assume you wish to test a COBOL II load module in a library named YOUR.COBOL.LOAD. Also assume that you will want to send output from COBTEST commands which have the PRINT option to a data set named COBTEST.OUTPUT.DATA with a DDname of OUTPUT. Write the TSO ALLOCATE commands necessary before you will be able to invoke COBTEST in interactive line mode with the following command.

```
COBTEST LOAD(INTER1:LOAD) PARM('PASSED INFORMATION')
```

5. You need to test a new COBOL II program. Assume that you have already compiled and link-edited the program and are presently in the COBTEST Main Full-Screen Panel. Perform the following tasks during your debugging session.

a. Write a command that will allow you to find DDnames of input and output files in the program.

b. The program contains DISPLAY statements. Write the ALLOCATE command that will send output from the DISPLAY statement to the terminal.
c. Write a command to search for any CALL statements in the program.
d. Write the command to trap calls to a program named CALLED1.
e. Write a command to determine whether the program you are testing will receive parameters.
f. Write the command necessary to establish addressability to an 01-level item named PASSED-INFO in the Linkage Section of the program you are testing.
g. Write a command to redisplay the first executable COBOL statement in the source area of the COBTEST panel.
h. Establish the symbol I-S for the field named INFILE-STATUS.
i. If the first READ statement is at line 7680, write the command that sets a breakpoint to halt execution immediately before the READ and displays the contents of the field INFILE-STATUS.
j. Now write the command to execute the program from the beginning.
k. Assuming that you were successful in halting execution at line 7680, write a command to suspend execution immediately following the READ so you will be able to display the contents of INFILE-STATUS again.
l. Write a command to resume execution.
m. Assuming that you were successful in halting execution immediately following the first READ, write the command that will display the contents of INFILE-STATUS.
n. At this point, write the command to remove any breakpoints you set.
o. Write the command which will verify that you were successful in removing all breakpoints.
p. Write the command to resume execution.
q. Assuming that the program has halted at the point where it called a subprogram, write a command to continue execution to the end of the program you are testing.
r. Write the command to execute a fresh copy of the program you are testing.

Chapter

14

Debugging with XPEDITER/TSO

There are a number of debugging products from vendors other than IBM. Included are VIA/SmartTest from Viasoft, SIMON from Symark International, Inc., and XPEDITER/TSO from Compuware Corporation. This chapter will discuss XPEDITER/TSO, one of the more widely used products, as an example of the functions that are usually available in current, non-IBM debugging products.

Like IBM's TESTCOB and COBTEST, XPEDITER/TSO is an interactive debugger which permits you to set breakpoints, check program status, change variables, and then continue execution. It can be used with OS/VS COBOL or COBOL II programs. XPEDITER/TSO is available in batch mode and interactive mode.

Although XPEDITER/TSO supports COBOL, Assembler, and several data bases, we will look only at the common features and the COBOL-specific features. The discussion and examples presented will be based on XPEDITER/TSO Release 5.1 running under MVS/ESA.

14.1 XPEDITER/TSO FEATURES

Although XPEDITER/TSO can be run in batch mode or interactive mode, you need to test a program in interactive mode in order to take advantage of the more powerful features of the product. These features include the ability to

- Intercept program ABENDs before the offending instruction actually executes. This permits you to fix the problem on-line and then continue execution.
- Set conditional or unconditional breakpoints to interrupt execution at any point in your program.
- Display or modify the contents of program variables and general-purpose registers.
- See file status information.

- Trace program execution flow.
- Review program execution in the reverse direction. This allows you to step through the program backward from the point at which it ABENDed, displaying the contents of program variables which may have contributed to the problem.
- Temporarily insert XPEDITER/TSO debugging statements to alter the COBOL program logic.

14.2 THE SIR PROCESSOR

To use XPEDITER/TSO, you must compile the program with Compuware's Shared Information Repository (SIR) compiler. This processor invokes the COBOL compiler to produce an object module and compiler listings, and then creates SIR records from the compiler output. These records are placed in a partitioned data set. The SIR records contain information required by XPEDITER, including program data relationships, execution paths, and program structures, and symbolic information such as source code, the DATA DIVISION map, and the PROCEDURE DIVISION map.

Certain COBOL compiler options must be used when the SIR processor is invoked. For OS/VS COBOL they are NOCOUNT, NOFLOW, NOPRINT, SOURCE, NOSTATE, NOSYMDMP, NOTEST, VERB, BUF=256K (256K is the minimum; it may be set higher) and SIZE=512K (512K is minimum; it may be set higher). If you did not specify DMAP, the SIR processor forces it on. If you did not specify either CLIST or PMAP, the SIR processor puts CLIST in effect. If you specified NUM, the SIR processor changes it to NONUM.

For COBOL II, the required compiler options are MAP, either LIST or OFFSET if NOOPTIMIZE is used and LIST if OPTIMIZE is used, SOURCE, NONUMBER, and NOTEST.

14.3 XPEDITER/TSO COMMANDS

Figure 14.1 contains an alphabetical list of all XPEDITER/TSO primary commands. It indicates in which mode each command can be used, whether there is an equivalent line command in interactive mode, and how the command is used. Further information, including complete syntax and usage examples, can be found in the *XPEDITER/TSO Release 5.1 COBOL Version Reference Manual* and, in interactive mode, by entering HELP on the command line or pressing the PF key defined for the help function.

Figure 14.2 shows the line commands available in interactive mode.

Figure 14.3 shows the commands that would be used to perform the various XPEDITER/TSO tasks.

We will illustrate the use of many of the common XPEDITER tasks and commands in the sample debugging session in Sec. 14.6.

COMMAND	MODE	PURPOSE
ACCEPT	Interactive	Assign a value from a preallocated file to a data item
AFTER*	Both Modes	Set a break point after execution of a statement, paragraph or module
ALLOCATE	Interactive	Access the File Allocation Utility from within the full-screen session
BEFORE*	Both Modes	Set a break point before execution of a statement, paragraph or module
BROWSE	Interactive	Browse a data set
COUNT*	Both Modes	Count the number of times a statement, paragraph, module or entry point is executed
DISPLAY*	Both Modes	View the contents of program variables
DISPLAYE*	Both Modes	View the contents of the elementary items in a group level variable
DISPLAYH*	Both Modes	View the contents of program variables in hexadecimal format
DISPLAYP*	Interactive	View a specified area of memory in dump format
DLI	Interactive	Issue calls to IMS using IBM's standard CBLTDLI interface
DOWN	Interactive	Scroll down, towards the bottom of the screen display
END	Interactive	Terminate the current function and return to the source display screen
EXCLUDE*	Interactive	Suppress the display of a line or range of lines from the source display screen
FIND	Interactive	Search for character strings, data names or COBOL structures in the source display screen
GEN*	Interactive	Display the translator-generated COBOL statements for an EXEC DLI or EXEC SQL statement
GO	Both Modes**	Start or resume execution, recognizing breakpoints
GPREGS	Interactive	Continuously display the contents of the general purpose registers in the source display screen
HELP	Interactive	Provide information about XPEDITER/TSO commands and messages
IF	Interactive	Establish a conditional expression within a block of lines INSERTed into the source code
INCLUDE	Both Modes	Include a predefined test script member containing XPEDITER/TSO commands
INSERT*	Both Modes**	Temporarily insert XPEDITER/TSO commands within the COBOL source code
INTERCEPT	Both Modes**	Load a module and set BEFORE and AFTER breakpoints
KEEP*	Both Modes	Continuously display the contents of program variables in a window at every breakpoint or pause
KEEPE*	Both Modes	Continuously display the contents of the elementary items in a group level variable in a window at every breakpoint or pause
KEEPH*	Both Modes	Continuously display the contents of program variables in hexadecimal format in a window at every breakpoint or pause
LEFT*	Interactive	Scroll the contents of DISPLAYed program variables to the left in the source display screen
LOAD	Interactive	Dynamically load a module
LOCATE	Interactive	Scroll the source display screen to a designated line number or to the current execution point
LOG	Interactive	Browse the XPEDITER session log
MONITOR	Interactive	Record the execution history in a buffer, enabling you to execute in review mode later

Figure 14.1 Alphabetical list and brief description of all XPEDITER/TSO primary commands. (*Continued*)

MOVE	Both Modes	Change the value of program variables
NOLINES	Interactive	Suppress the message line "xxx LINES NOT DISPLAYED" which appears in the source display screen following an EXCLUDE command or keyword
PAUSE	Both Modes**	Set a pause breakpoint within a block of INSERTed XPEDITER commands
QUIT	Both Modes	Terminate the current test session
RESET*	Both Modes**	Turn off the effect of other XPEDITER/TSO commands
RESUME	Interactive	Exit the review mode and return to your current execution position
RETEST	Interactive	Begin a new test session with the same module or with a new copy of the same module even if the current test was not completed
REVERSE	Interactive	Change the current execution direction in order to review the sequence of instructions leading to the current breakpoint. MONITOR must have been previously entered to establish review mode.
RIGHT*	Interactive	Scroll the contents of DISPLAYed program variables to the right in the source display screen
SET	Both Modes**	Temporarily override XPEDITER/TSO defaults for the current session
SHOW	Both Modes**	Display breakpoints, SET options or environmentally dependent information
SKIP*	Both Modes	Bypass statements, paragraphs or modules to prevent them from being executed
SOURCE	Both Modes	Display the source or change the qualification for the following XPEDITER/TSO commands
SQL	Interactive	Enter the SQLizer/TSO Primary menu from XPEDITER/TSO
SQL EXPLAIN*	Interactive	Capture and display DB2 access path information about SQL statements coded in the program
TEST	Batch Mode	Identify the program to be tested in batch mode, along with any necessary test parameters
TRACE	Both Modes	Monitor the execution flow of control in the program
TSO	Interactive	Execute a TSO command from within the XPEDITER/TSO test session
UP	Interactive	Scroll up, towards the top of the screen display
USE	Both Modes	Establish addressability to data base PCBs in the LINKAGE SECTION when testing an IMS program
WHEN	Both Modes**	Set up continuous monitoring of a condition or a program variable after each verb in the program executes
XPED	Batch Mode	Set up the test environment for batch mode

* A line command version of the command exists
** There are differences between the batch mode version and the line mode version

Figure 14.1 *(Continued)*

COMMAND	PURPOSE
)	Scroll a data line to the right one column
)n	Scroll a data line to the right n columns
))	Scroll a block of data lines to the right one column
))n	Scroll a block of data lines to the right n columns
(	Scroll a data line to the left one column
(n	Scroll a data line to the left n columns
((	Scroll a block of data lines to the left one column
((n	Scroll a block of data lines to the left n columns
:	Freeze a line at the current column position
:n	Scroll a line to column n
A	Establish an AFTER breakpoint on a line
AA	Establish AFTER breakpoints on a block of lines
B	Establish an BEFORE breakpoint on a line
BB	Establish BEFORE breakpoints on a block of lines
C	Establish a COUNT breakpoint on a line
CC	Establish COUNT breakpoints on a block of lines
D	DISPLAY the first variable on the line
Dn	DISPLAY variable n on the line
DD	DISPLAY the variables on each line in a block of lines
DE	DISPLAY the elementary items for the variable on the line
DEn	DISPLAY the elementary items for group level n on the line
DH	DISPLAY the variable on the line in hexadecimal format
DHn	DISPLAY variable n on the line in hexadecimal format
E	DISPLAY the elementary items for the variable on the line
En	DISPLAY the elementary items for group level n on the line
EX	Capture and display information about an EXEC SQL statement
F	Reshow the first line in a block of excluded lines
Fn	Reshow the first n lines in a block of excluded lines
G	Show translated code and comment out the original code for an EXEC DLI or EXEC SQL statement
GG	Show translated code and comment out the original code for EXEC DLI or EXEC SQL statements within a block
H	DISPLAY the variable on the line in hexadecimal format
Hn	DISPLAY variable n on the line in hexadecimal format
I	Insert a single line below the current line
In	Insert n lines below the current line
K	KEEP the first variable on the line

Figure 14.2 Alphabetical list and brief description of all XPEDITER/TSO line commands available in interactive mode. *(Continued)*

Kn	KEEP variable n on the line
KK	KEEP the variables on each line in a block of lines
KE	KEEP the elementary items for the variable on the line
KEn	KEEP the elementary items for group level n on the line
KH	KEEP the variable on the line in hexadecimal format
KHn	KEEP variable n on the line in hexadecimal format
L	Reshow the last line in a block of excluded lines
Ln	Reshow the last n lines in a block of excluded lines
P	Display memory starting from the address associated with the current line
R	On a PROCEDURE DIVISION line, reset all breakpoints
R	On a DISPLAYed line, remove the displayed value
R	On an INSERTed line, remove the line
R	On a KEEP line, remove the kept line
R	On a SKIPped line, remove the SKIP breakpoint
R	On an EXCLUDEd range of lines, reshow all the excluded lines
R:	On a frozen line, enable scrolling to the left and right
RA	RESET the AFTER breakpoint on the line
RAB	RESET the AFTER and BEFORE breakpoints on the line
RAC	RESET the AFTER and COUNT breakpoints on the line
RB	RESET the BEFORE breakpoint on the line
RBC	RESET the BEFORE and COUNT breakpoints on the line
RC	RESET the COUNT breakpoint on the line
RE	Change a DISPLAYE command to a DISPLAY command
RH	Change a DISPLAYH command to a DISPLAY command
RR	RESET a block of lines
RT	Remove the column template from above a DISPLAYed variable
S	Set a SKIP breakpoint on the current line
SS	Set SKIP breakpoints on a block of lines
T	Set a column template above a DISPLAYed value
TT	Set a column template above each of a block of DISPLAYed values
X	EXCLUDE a line
XX	EXCLUDE a block of lines

Figure 14.2 *(Continued)*

XPEDITER/TSO TASK	COMMANDS
Set Breakpoints	AFTER BEFORE COUNT GOn INSERT INTERCEPT SKIP TRACE WHEN
Control the Test Session	GO INTERCEPT QUIT MONITOR RESET RESUME RETEST REVERSE SOURCE SQL TEST USE XPED
Manipulate or Display Program Data	ACCEPT DISPLAY KEEP MOVE SQL EXPLAIN T
Perform Utility Functions	ALLOCATE BROWSE DISPLAYP DLI GEN GPREGS HELP INCLUDE LOAD LOG SHOW
Manipulate the Screen	DOWN END EXCLUDE F FIND L LEFT LOCATE NOLINES RIGHT UP

Figure 14.3 XPEDITER/TSO commands used to carry out various XPEDITER/TSO debugging tasks.

14.4 USING XPEDITER/TSO IN BATCH MODE

Programs running under XPEDITER/TSO in batch mode are noninteractive. Therefore, you must plan your debugging strategy carefully before the job is submitted. The XPEDITER commands must be placed in a test script file (a script contains prewritten XPEDITER/TSO commands) or in-stream in the JCL, with no opportunity to change them once the job starts executing. Output from the commands is written to a log file which can be reviewed after the program has either terminated successfully or ABENDed.

You might not think it desirable to use batch mode until you see its versatility. The commands provide more flexibility and useful debugging information than the COBOL language debugging elements (DISPLAY statements, DEBUGGING LINES, DECLARATIVES, etc.) described in Chap. 5. Also, it is not necessary to insert commands in the COBOL source code and then remove them when the test is done.

Because batch mode uses less resources than interactive mode, it is helpful to use it when you do not want to tie up your terminal or when you intend to gather program execution information returned from XPEDITER for later review.

14.4.1 Invoking XPEDITER/TSO in Batch Mode

The following procedure explains how to prepare for and invoke batch mode in a standard environment.

1. Set up JCL as shown in Fig. 14.4. This JCL prepares a COBOL II program, as evidenced by the COBOL II libraries SYS1.COB2COMP and SYS1.COB2LIB in the JCL. The libraries may have different names at your installation.
   a. Step S1 compiles the program with the XPEDITER SIR processor.
   b. Step S2 link-edits the object module created in step S1, placing the load module in a load library (MY.LOADLIB.LOAD in this example).
   c. Step S3 creates a dynamic work area (see letter "A" in the figure) which is required by XPEDITER/TSO at execution time. It is passed to the

```
//*****************************************************************
//* XPEDITER COMPILE STEP
//*****************************************************************
//S1  EXEC  PGM=ADSRA327,REGION=1024K,
//            PARM='OBJECT,LIST,MAP,NONUMBER,SOURCE,NOTEST,NORENT'
//STEPLIB   DD DSNAME=SYS1.COB2COMP,DISP=SHR
//          DD DISP=SHR,DSN=INSTALL.XPEDIT5.LOADLIB
//SYSIN     DD DSN=MY.PROGLIB.COBOL(COB2BAT),DISP=SHR
//SYSPRINT DD SYSOUT=A,
//           DCB=(BLKSIZE=3509),UNIT=(WORK,SEP=(SYSUT1,SYSPUNCH))
//SYSLIN    DD DISP=(,CATLG),UNIT=TSWK,SPACE=(TRK,(75,5,0)),
//            DCB=(RECFM=FB,LRECL=80,BLKSIZE=3120),
//            DSN=MY.COB2BAT.OBJ
//SYSUT1    DD UNIT=WORK,SPACE=(CYL,(1,1))
//SYSUT2    DD UNIT=WORK,SPACE=(CYL,(1,1))
//SYSUT3    DD UNIT=WORK,SPACE=(CYL,(1,1))
//SYSUT4    DD UNIT=WORK,SPACE=(CYL,(1,1))
//SYSUT5    DD UNIT=WORK,SPACE=(CYL,(1,1))
//SYSUT6    DD UNIT=WORK,SPACE=(CYL,(1,1))
//SYSUT7    DD UNIT=WORK,SPACE=(CYL,(1,1))
//*****************************************************************
//* FILES FOR XPEDITER COMPILE STEP
//*****************************************************************
//MSGPRINT DD SYSOUT=A
//XCOMPILE DD DISP=SHR,DSN=MY.XPEDSIR.DATA(XPEDBAT)
//XMSG      DD DISP=SHR,DSN=INSTALL.XPEDIT5.XMESSAGE
//XOPTIONS DD DISP=SHR,DSN=INSTALL.XPEDIT5.XOPTIONS
//XSOURCE   DD UNIT=WORK,SPACE=(TRK,(20,10))
//XUTILITY DD UNIT=WORK,SPACE=(TRK,(20,10)),
//            DISP=(NEW,PASS),
//            DCB=(RECFM=FBA,LRECL=133,BLKSIZE=16093)
//*****************************************************************
//* LINK-EDIT STEP
//*****************************************************************
//S2 EXEC PGM=IEWL,
//         PARM='LET,LIST,MAP,XREF,SIZE=(196608,65536)'
//SYSPRINT DD SYSOUT=A
//SYSUT1    DD UNIT=WORK,SPACE=(CYL,(1,1))
//SYSUT2    DD UNIT=WORK,SPACE=(CYL,(1,1))
//SYSUT3    DD UNIT=WORK,SPACE=(CYL,(1,1))
//SYSUT4    DD UNIT=WORK,SPACE=(CYL,(1,1))
//SYSUT5    DD UNIT=WORK,SPACE=(CYL,(1,1))
//SYSLMOD   DD DISP=SHR,DSN=MY.LOADLIB.LOAD
//SYSLIB    DD DISP=SHR,DSN=SYS1.COB2LIB
//OBJ1      DD DISP=SHR,DSN=MY.XPEDBAT.OBJ
//SYSLIN    DD *
 INCLUDE OBJ1
 NAME XPEDBAT(R)
/*
```

Figure 14.4 JCL to compile, link, and invoke a batch XPEDITER/TSO debugging session.

STEPLIB in step S4 (see letter "B"), assigned to the DDname XDYNAMIC (see letter "C"), and finally deleted at the end of the job.

d. Step S4 executes the program XPBATCH. This performs the XPEDITER/TSO batch debugging test. The STEPLIB must have the dynamic work area created in step S3 first in the concatenation of libraries. Also,

```
//******************************************************************
//* CREATE TEMPORARY WORK FILE
//******************************************************************
//S3          EXEC PGM=IEFBR14
//XDYNAMIC DD DSN=&&XDYNAM,
//               DISP=(NEW,PASS,DELETE),UNIT=SYSDA,
//               SPACE=(CYL,(5,1,10)),
//               DCB=(RECFM=U,BLKSIZE=19069,DSORG=PO)
//******************************************************************
//* INVOKE EPEDITER BATCH MODE
//******************************************************************
//S4         EXEC PGM=XPBATCH,REGION=1000K
//STEPLIB   DD DSN=&&XDYNAM,DISP=(OLD,PASS)
//          DD DSN=INSTALL.XPEDIT5.LOADLIB,DISP=SHR
//          DD DSN=MY.LOADLIB.LOAD,DISP=SHR
//EMFILE    DD DSN=MY.NEWTABEM.DATA,DISP=SHR
//DEFILE    DD DSN=MY.NEWTABDE.DATA,DISP=SHR
//OUTFILE   DD SYSOUT=A
//SYSOUT    DD SYSOUT=A
//XCOMPILE DD DISP=SHR,DSN=MY.XPEDSIR.DATA
//XDYNAMIC DD DSN=&&XDYNAM,DISP=(OLD,DELETE),
//             VOL=REF=*.S3.XDYNAMIC
//XINCLUDE DD DISP=SHR,DSN=MY.XSCRIPT.DATA
//XMSG      DD DISP=SHR,DSN=INSTALL.XPEDIT5.XMESSAGE
//XOPTIONS DD DISP=SHR,DSN=INSTALL.XPEDIT5.XOPTIONS
//XPOUT     DD SYSOUT=A
//XPIN      DD *
 XPED BATCH
 TEST COB2BAT
      LOADM  XPEDBAT
      POSTSCR SHOWCNT
 COUNT ALL PARAGRAPHS
 AFTER  174,178
 KEEPH NUM-ENTRIES
 KEEPH EMPLOYEE-DEPT-WS
 GO
 QUIT
/*
//
```

Figure 14.4 *(Continued)*

the XPEDITER/TSO load library containing XPBATCH (it may be named differently at your installation than that shown at letter "D") and the library containing your program's load module (at letter "E") must exist in the STEPLIB concatenation. Step S4 must have DDnames for your program's input and output data sets (pointed to by letter "F" in the figure) and the DDnames needed by XPEDITER/TSO. The XPEDITER DDnames and their associated data sets are

XCOMPILE — The SIR PDS.

XDYNAMIC — Temporary work data set for XPEDITER/TSO. This is the same data set that was created in step S3, and it is also concatenated to the beginning of the STEPLIB in step S4.

XINCLUDE	Optional test script library, used for the INCLUDE command and for scripts specified in the TEST command.
XMSG	The error message data set.
XOPTIONS	The options data set for enhanced FIND parameters.
XPOUT	The log data set which will receive the debugging output.
XPIN	Input command stream for entering XPEDITER/TSO commands.

2. Put the XPEDITER commands you intend to use either in a script file (a script contains prewritten XPEDITER/TSO commands) assigned to the DDname XPIN or in-stream assigned to the DDname XPIN. Place the commands in the following order:
   a. XPED BATCH (BATCH corresponds to the interactive STANDARD environment).
   b. TEST *program-name.* Program-name is the name of the module being tested. If your COBOL program is part of a statically linked load module, also code the keyword LOADM followed by the composite load-module name. Execution will start with the program-name specified. If the program-name is the same as the load-module name, the LOADM parameter is not necessary. It is also possible to specify INITSCR, the initial-script name; POSTSCR, post-script name; and ABENDSCR, ABEND-script name, to issue a set of XPEDITER command scripts before the debugging session, at the conclusion of the session, and when an ABEND occurs. A script can also be issued during the session by using the INCLUDE command. All script names must be members of the library assigned to the XINCLUDE DD statement in the JCL.
   c. Now supply the additional XPEDITER commands for the program being tested.
   d. If there are other programs you wish to test in the same batch session, use additional TEST commands for each one. Use the same format as above. Follow this with the XPEDITER/TSO commands to be used for that program.
3. Activate the XPEDITER/TSO test by submitting the JCL.
4. The debugging test will be done when the program completes execution or when an ABEND occurs. You can now look at the data generated by XPEDITER in the log data set assigned to the XPOUT DDname.

14.4.2 XPEDITER/TSO Commands in Batch Mode

A batch session does not offer as much flexibility as an interactive session. This is because all XPEDITER commands specified will be read and processed before the first instruction in the program you are testing executes. DISPLAY, for example, will display information to the log as soon as it is encountered. DISPLAY is most useful if you want to see the contents of a field at the very beginning of the program. The INSERT command allows XPEDITER/TSO commands to have a "delayed" effect. It allows you to temporarily embed XPE-

DITER commands within the COBOL program code. (See the *XPEDITER/TSO Release 5.1 COBOL Version Reference Manual* for restrictions on the permitted commands.) It is coded

```
INSERT program statement number
               .
               .
               .
        valid XPEDITER/TSO commands
               .
               .
               .
END-INS
```

The commands within an INSERT are executed after the specified program statement number is executed. Thus DISPLAY might be placed within inserted code, causing it to be delayed until after the specified statement number executes.

KEEP is usually more helpful than DISPLAY because KEEP can show the value of a program variable repeatedly. It displays a value only when a breakpoint is reached and when a value has changed. You can monitor the changing contents of variables by setting breakpoints (AFTER, BEFORE, or TRACE) at key program statements and specifying KEEP for the variables you wish to observe.

Although AFTER, BEFORE, and TRACE all update the KEEP window with similar information, there are minor differences. AFTER identifies the statement both before and after the breakpoint, making it ideal for tracking execution flow before and after conditional statements when you are uncertain of the execution path. BEFORE and TRACE give less output, making it easier to read the log.

The COUNT command can be used to monitor the number of times a statement, paragraph, or module executes. The results of the COUNT command are reported by issuing SHOW COUNTS at the end of the debugging session.

Not all XPEDITER/TSO commands are valid in batch mode. In addition, some commands operate differently in batch than in interactive mode. Figure 14.1 indicates which primary commands can be used in batch mode, and specifies which are significantly different in their actions. See the *XPEDITER/TSO Release 5.1 XPEDITER/IMS Release 5.1 COBOL Version User Guide* and the *XPEDITER/TSO Release 5.1 COBOL Version Reference Manual* for further details.

14.4.3 An Example of XPEDITER/TSO in Batch Mode

Figure 14.4 shows the JCL for conducting a test in batch mode. The XPIN DD statement in step S4 contains the XPEDITER/TSO commands.

- XPED BATCH specifies a standard batch environment for the test.

- TEST COB2BAT
  LOADM XPEDBAT
  POSTSCR SHOWCNT identifies the program being tested as COB2BAT, indicating it is part of load module XPEDBAT. A post script named SHOWCNT in the XINCLUDE library is to perform additional XPEDITER/TSO tasks at the conclusion of program execution. In our current example, we will see that the post-script contains the SHOW COUNTS command.
- COUNT ALL PARAGRAPHS monitors execution counts for all paragraphs in the program. The SHOW COUNTS command must be issued at the conclusion of program execution to see the results; that is the purpose of the post script.
- AFTER 174, 178 sets breakpoints which will update the KEEP window after source lines 174 and 178 have executed.
- KEEPH NUM-ENTRIES establishes a KEEP window for the COBOL variable NUM-ENTRIES. The "H" at the end of the command specifies that the variable's contents are to be given in both EBCDIC and hexadecimal notation.
- KEEPH EMPLOYEE-DEPT-WS establishes a KEEP window for the COBOL variable EMPLOYEE-DEPT-WS. The variable's contents will be given in EBCDIC and hexadecimal notation.
- GO begins execution.
- QUIT terminates the debugging session for the current program.

The output from the XPEDITER/TSO commands is shown in Fig. 14.5. It appears on the data set assigned to the XPOUT DD statement. The first several lines identify the XPEDITER release and your installation, and give a time-date stamp. Following this is a list of the commands which have been read in and which will execute when the test begins. Notice that XPEDITER/TSO has changed the program-name COB2BAT to the load module name XPEDBAT for the duration of the test. XPEDITER automatically sets a BEFORE breakpoint before the first COBOL statement executes. The KEEP window is displayed at that breakpoint. The window specifies the lines where the variables EMPLOYEE-DEPT-WS and NUM-ENTRIES are defined, their level numbers and their contents. Because the variables were not initialized with VALUE clauses, they contain binary zeros. The "INVALID DECIMAL" message for NUM-ENTRIES occurs because the field was defined as COMP-3 and does not contain valid packed data when program execution begins.

Updated KEEP windows are displayed as a result of the two AFTER breakpoints as well. The lines where the breakpoints were taken are indicated. Following the last KEEP window are messages indicating completion of the test and the application program. Because a post-script containing SHOW COUNTS was specified, we see the SHOW COUNTS command listed after the QUIT command. The output from SHOW COUNTS consists of the PROCE-

```
+------------------------------------------------------------------------------+
:                                                              JOB: XPEDBAT   :
: XPEDITER/TSO RELEASE  5.01.00        CUSTOMER # 333333       STEP: S4       :
: TAPE CREATE DATE 91022                                       DATE: 07/01/91 :
: MY COMPANY NAME                                              TIME: 16.24.39 :
:                                                                             :
+------------------------------------------------------------------------------+

   XPED BATCH
   TEST COB2BAT
        LOADM XPEDBAT
        POSTSCR SHOWCNT
*** XPEDBAT  FROM MY.LOADLIB.LOAD                                 LINK 07/01/91
 XPD0582 RA151       PROGRAM-ID COB2BAT IN MODULE XPEDBAT CHANGED TO THE MODULE
                      NAME
   BEFORE XPEDBAT.
   AFTER  XPEDBAT.
   COUNT ALL PARAGRAPHS
   AFTER 174,178
   KEEPH NUM-ENTRIES
   KEEPH EMPLOYEE-DEPT-WS
   GO
PAUSE BEFORE XPEDBAT
BEFORE BREAKPOINT ENCOUNTERED
-------------------------------------------------------- XPEDBAT  KEPT ITEMS ---

                                                --
   00102 10 EMPLOYEE-DEPT-WS               ===> ..
                                              > 00
                                              > 00
                                                --
   00089 05 NUM-ENTRIES                    ===> ..               INVALID DECIMAL
                                              > 00
                                              > 00
--------------------------------------------------------------------------------


   GO
PAUSE AFTER XPEDBAT.174 IN 1000-INIT
             NEXT LOGICAL INSTRUCTION IS XPEDBAT.199
-------------------------------------------------------- XPEDBAT  KEPT ITEMS ---

                                                --
   00102 10 EMPLOYEE-DEPT-WS               ===> 10
                                              > FF
                                              > 10
                                                --
   00089 05 NUM-ENTRIES                    ===> 10                       DECIMAL
                                              > FF
                                              > 10
--------------------------------------------------------------------------------


   GO
PAUSE AFTER XPEDBAT.178 IN 1000-INIT
             NEXT LOGICAL INSTRUCTION IS XPEDBAT.181
-------------------------------------------------------- XPEDBAT  KEPT ITEMS ---

                                                --
   00102 10 EMPLOYEE-DEPT-WS               ===> 50
                                              > FF
                                              > 50

   00089 05 NUM-ENTRIES                    ===> UNCHANGED
--------------------------------------------------------------------------------


   GO
PAUSE AFTER XPEDBAT IN 1000-INIT
              TEST COMPLETED
   GO
*** APPLICATION PROGRAM HAS COMPLETED ***
```

Figure 14.5 Output from the XPEDITER/TSO commands executed in the batch XPEDITER/TSO session invoked by the JCL in Fig. 14.4. (*Continued*)

```
QUIT
SHOW COUNTS
                    *** EXECUTION COUNTS FOR MODULE XPEDBAT  ***
* 00136 PROCEDURE DIVISION.
* 00137*****************************************************************
* 00138*     PROGRAM INITIALIZATION, LOAD DEPARTMENT TABLE, BEGIN TO    *
* 00139*     PROCESS EMPLOYEE RECORDS IF TABLE SUCCESSFULLY LOADED.     *
* 00140*****************************************************************
* 00141 1000-INIT.                                                       0000001
* 00142      OPEN INPUT    EMPFILE
* 00143                    DEPTFILE
* 00144           OUTPUT   OUTFILE
* 00145      INITIALIZE MISC
* 00146      READ DEPTFILE INTO FIRST-REC
* 00147        AT END
                                    .
                                    .
                                    .
* 00183*****************************************************************
* 00184*     HEADER ROUTINE                                             *
* 00185*****************************************************************
* 00186 2500-HEADER.                                                     0000001
* 00187      ADD 1 TO PG-CTR
* 00188      MOVE PG-CTR TO PG-OUT
* 00189      WRITE OUTREC FROM HEADER-1
* 00190        AFTER ADVANCING PAGE
* 00191      MOVE 1 TO LN-CTR.
* 00192 2500-EXIT.                                                       0000001
* 00193      EXIT.
* 00194*****************************************************************
* 00195*    COMPARE EMPLOYEE DEPARTMENT NUMBER WITH DEPARTMENT TABLE    *
* 00196*    ENTRIES; REFORMAT AND WRITE EMPLOYEE RECORD IF THERE IS A   *
* 00197*    MATCH AND DISPLAY ERROR MESSAGE IF NO MATCH                 *
* 00198*****************************************************************
* 00199 3000-COMPARE-PROCESS.                                            0000011
* 00200      SET MATCH TO TRUE
* 00201      EVALUATE TRUE
* 00202         WHEN EMPLOYEE-DEPT-WS GREATER THAN DEPT-HOLD
* 00203            SET DEPT-IND TO 1
* 00204            SEARCH DEPT-REC
* 00205              AT END
                                    .
                                    .
                                    .
                    *** END OF EXECUTION COUNTS ***
*** END OF XPEDITER/TSO RELEASE 5.1 SESSION ***
```

Figure 14.5 (*Continued*)

DURE DIVISION code (only portions of it are illustrated in the figure) with execution counts to the right of each paragraph header.

14.5 USING XPEDITER/TSO IN INTERACTIVE MODE

On the surface, XPEDITER/TSO in interactive mode is similar to COBTEST in full-screen mode. It interfaces with ISPF and allows you to debug interactively using full-screen capabilities. However, it offers more debugging options in more operating environments than COBTEST and consequently is a little more difficult to set up. It possesses some features not available with COBTEST, such as the ability to insert XPEDITER/TSO commands within COBOL code as if they were part of the program, and the ability to display the contents of any storage area within the program in hexadecimal and EBCDIC dump format, even items in the literal pool; the storage contents can also be changed. XPEDITER/TSO lacks a few COBTEST features which I find useful, such as the ability to EQUATE a program variable with a shorter symbol. Because it is easier to set up, I prefer to use COBTEST when I am testing relatively simple programs which are all compiled under COBOL II. I use XPEDITER/TSO for more complex situations where the extra capabilities (e.g., the ability to view or change any part of the program's storage area and the ability to debug both COBOL II and OS/VS COBOL programs) give me extra debugging flexibility.

Interactive mode is more powerful than batch mode and provides more XPEDITER/TSO commands; some of them are for setting screen options or for requesting functions only available in interactive mode. The screen contains program source code and can optionally be set up with a KEEP window to show the contents of selected program variables continuously.

Interactive mode allows you to step dynamically through the program, watching the source code scroll by as it executes, with the executing line of code highlighted. While this is occurring you can monitor the values of program variables in the KEEP window as they change.

In order to use interactive mode, ISPF Version 2 or 3 under MVS-TSO, MVS/XA-TSO or MVS/ESA-TSO must be installed.

Figures 14.6 through 14.14, referred to in the following discussion of interactive mode, show the relevant XPEDITER panels.

14.5.1 Setting up and Running XPEDITER/TSO in Interactive Mode

Before invoking XPEDITER/TSO, you may wish to allocate a partitioned data set with your own choice of name to contain the SIR records. If you do not create it at this time, one will be created for you with the low-level qualifier name SIR when you invoke the SIR processor; the rest of the name will be the same as that of the data set containing the COBOL source code.

To invoke XPEDITER/TSO, select the ISPF option required by your installation. This will take you into the XPEDITER/TSO Primary Menu (see Fig. 14.6). The menu will not have option 4, SQLIZER (a Compuware product used for development and performance analysis of DB2 applications) unless your installation has licensed that product from Compuware.

The first time you use XPEDITER you should choose option 0, Defaults, in order to specify default settings for your terminal, PF keys, profile, and screen colors. You can verify your ISPF PF key assignments and establish different PF key assignments for various XPEDITER functions which will be in effect only when you are in an XPEDITER/TSO test session.

```
COMPUWARE ---------------------- PRIMARY MENU -------------------- COMPUWARE
OPTION  ===> 0

         0    DEFAULTS    -  Specify Defaults
         1    ALLOCATE    -  Create and Maintain File Allocation Lists
         2    XPEDITER    -  Test an Application Using Full Screen Commands
         3    UTILITIES   -  Execute Utility Functions
         4    SQLizer     -  Perform DB2 Table Manipulation/Program Development


         8    COMPILE     -  Compile, Assemble, Create SIR, Link Edit Programs
         9    BIND        -  BIND Application Plan with SQLizer/TSO

         B    BULLETIN    -  Display General Product Info, New Features, Etc.
         T    TUTORIAL    -  Display Information on Compuware Products
         X    EXIT        -  Exit Compuware Menu         (PROFILE ID: 0)

                            Compuware Corporation
                               (800) 538-7822



           Press ENTER to Process  or  Enter END Command to Terminate
```

Figure 14.6 The XPEDITER/TSO PRIMARY MENU for an interactive debugging session.

Select option 8, Compile, from the Primary Menu in order to compile your COBOL program, create the SIR records and place them in a SIR PDS, and link-edit the program. Panels will prompt you for the compiler options, input data set name, SIR data set name, linkage-editor options, load library name, and compiler and linkage-editor SYSLIB data set names. You will be able to edit the generated JCL before submitting it for execution.

```
COMPUWARE ---------------------- ALLOCATE (1) ------------------ Empty Table
COMMAND ===> COPY                                              SCROLL ===> CSR

                UP, DOWN, LEFT, and RIGHT Scrolling Available
LINE COMMANDS: D (Delete)    PRIMARY COMMANDS: CAN   (Quit without saving)
               I (Insert)                      COPY  (Retrieve existing list)
               R (Repeat)                      ALLOC (Allocate and continue)
                                               END   (Save and End)

                ---------------------- DSNAME ----------------------
       DDNAME    DUMMY, TEMP, TERM, SYSOUT, OR A FULLY QUALIFIED DSNAME   DISP
------------------------------------------------------------------------------
'''''
'''''
'''''
'''''
'''''
'''''
'''''
'''''
'''''
'''''
'''''
'''''
```

Figure 14.7 ALLOCATE (1) screen for an interactive XPEDITER/TSO debugging session. The COPY command will access a screen in which the data set to be copied is specified.

You may now choose option 1 from the Primary Menu to allocate program files or option 2 in order to invoke XPEDITER/TSO and begin testing. If you do not allocate files now, you can allocate them when you are in the test environment by using the ALLOCATE command, or just before starting the debugging session by naming a preexisting file allocation list or JCL containing the file names. Whichever allocation technique you use puts you into the XPEDITER/TSO File Allocation Utility (FAU).

The FAU will place you into the Allocate (1) screen (see Fig. 14.7). You can either enter the necessary DSNAME information or use the COPY command (as illustrated) to copy allocations from an existing allocation file list, CLIST, or JCL. Entering COPY places you into a screen where you specify the name of the data set to be copied. After entering the name and pressing the enter key you are placed into the ALLOCATE/COPY screen (see Fig. 14.8). By selecting the DDnames on the ALLOCATE/COPY screen and entering END to return you to the ALLOCATE (1) screen, you can overtype data and use the line commands specified at the top of the screen to change existing information (see Fig. 14.9). Scrolling to the right you will see additional allocation screens; ALLOCATE (2) is used to enter space and catalog information, ALLOCATE (3) for DCB parameters, ALLOCATE (4) for model DCB information, and ALLOCATE (5) for subsystem information. When you have entered all necessary information, you can issue the ALLOC command to allocate the files (Fig. 14.9). Notice in the figure that OUTFILE and SYSOUT, which will contain program output, have been given DSNAMEs of TERM. This assigns them to the terminal so you can view the output during the debugging session. After the files have been allocated, entering END will access the ALLOCATE/SAVE panel which allows you to save the file allocation list for future use (see Fig. 14.10).

```
COMPUWARE -----------------  ALLOCATE/COPY (DDNAME)  ------------ Row 3 Of 17
COMMAND ===> END                                              SCROLL ===> CSR

LINE COMMAND: S (Select)   PRIMARY COMMANDS: END  (Process selected statements)
                                             CAN  (Quit without processing)
                                             Edit (Edit JCL using ISPF Editor)
                                             EXP  (Expand JCL procedures)

            SELECT THE DDNAMES TO BE COPIED TO THE ALLOCATE SCREEN

SEL   JCL DATA SET:  'MY.JCLLIB.DATA(ROYALTY)'
------------------------------------------------------------------------------
''''' //*********************************************************************
''''' //* PROCEDURE FOR COBOL II RELEASE 3.
''''' //*********************************************************************
''''' //S1      EXEC COB2UCLG,
''''' //              PARM.COB2='NUM',
''''' //         REGION.LKED=512K,
''''' //              PARM.GO='30004500'
''''' //SYSIN          DD DSN=MY.PROGLIB.COBOL(CH14ROY),DISP=SHR
SS''' //GO.INFILE      DD DSN=MY.INPUT.DATA,DISP=SHR
''''' //OUTFILE        DD SYSOUT=T
SS''' //SYSOUT         DD SYSOUT=T
```

Figure 14.8 The ALLOCATE/COPY screen for an interactive XPEDITER/TSO debugging session. Shown is the JCL from which DDnames will be selected for allocation.

```
COMPUWARE ---------------------- ALLOCATE (1) -------------------- Row 1 Of 3
COMMAND ===> ALLOC                                                 SCROLL ===> CSR

LINE COMMANDS: D (Delete)     PRIMARY COMMANDS: CAN    (Quit without saving)
               I (Insert)                       COPY   (Retrieve existing list)
               R (Repeat)                       ALLOC  (Allocate and continue)
                                                END    (Save and End)

                        ---------------------- DSNAME ----------------------
        DDNAME     DUMMY, TEMP, TERM, SYSOUT, OR A FULLY QUALIFIED DSNAME   DISP
-------------------------------------------------------------------------------
'''''   INFILE     'MY.INPUT.DATA'                                         SHR
'''''   OUTFILE    TERM
'''''   SYSOUT     TERM
'''''
'''''
'''''
'''''
'''''
'''''
'''''
'''''
'''''
'''''
```

Figure 14.9 The ALLOCATE (1) screen for an interactive XPEDITER/TSO session showing the edited DDnames selected from the ALLOCATE/COPY screen in Fig. 14.8. The ALLOC command performs the allocations.

Option 2 from the XPEDITER/TSO Primary Menu places you into a submenu from which you specify the environment under which your program is to be tested (see Fig. 14.11). We will assume that there are no special environmental requirements, and choose option 1, Standard. Batch programs that process QSAM or VSAM files, and batch programs that issue data base calls other than IMS/DB may be executed in the standard environment. Selecting

```
COMPUWARE -------------------- ALLOCATE/SAVE -------------------- COMPUWARE
COMMAND ===>


      Your files have been allocated... Save the file allocation list?


  Enter/Verify partitioned or sequential dataset to save the file allocations

      DSNAME ===> 'MY.ALLOC.DATA(CH14ROY)'
      VOLUME ===>                                    (If not cataloged)




          Press ENTER to Process or  END to  Terminate Without Saving
```

Figure 14.10 The ALLOCATE/SAVE screen which allows the file allocation list to be saved.

```
COMPUWARE ------------  FULL SCREEN ENVIRONMENTS MENU  ------------ COMPUWARE
OPTION  ===> 1

  Select Environment

    XPEDITER/TSO
        1   STANDARD   -  Test a Program With No Special Environment Services
        2   DIALOG     -  Test Programs That Make ISPF Dialog Manager Calls
        3   IMS        -  Test a Program That Makes IMS/DB Calls
        4   BTS        -  Test Programs Using BTS
        5   BATCHPEM   -  Test a Program in a HOGAN BATCHPEM Environment
        6   DLIPEM     -  Test a Program in a HOGAN DLIPEM/BMPPEM Environment
        7   IMSPEM     -  Test a Program in a HOGAN BTS IMSPEM Environment


    XPEDITER/IMS
        8   MPP        -  Test Programs in an IMS Message Region
        9   BMP/IFP    -  Test a Program in a BMP or Fast Path Region
        10  IMSPEM     -  Test HOGAN IMSPEM in an IMS Message Region
        11  BMPPEM     -  Test HOGAN BMPPEM in a BMP Region


           Press ENTER to Process   or   Enter END Command to Terminate
```

Figure 14.11 The FULL-SCREEN ENVIRONMENTS MENU for an interactive XPEDITER/TSO session. The Standard environment is chosen.

option 1 and pressing the enter key accesses the TEST (STANDARD) panel (see Fig. 14.12).

Before entering the test selection criteria on the TEST (STANDARD) panel, it is advisable to enter the SETUP command. This brings up screens which allow you to verify or modify the data set names and defaults that will be needed for processing during the test, or that will be needed to establish the dispositions of the log and script data sets at the test's conclusion. The log data set contains the XPEDITER/TSO commands entered and the responses which were automatically recorded by XPEDITER during a debugging session. This can serve as documentation or can be used for review after the session is over.

The script data set contains the XPEDITER/TSO commands you entered which were automatically recorded by XPEDITER during the session. At the conclusion of the current session, the script data set can be saved and used as input to another debugging session.

As with batch mode, a test script must be a member of an INCLUDE library allocated to the XINCLUDE DDname; the library is listed in the Test Script Libraries screen (see Fig. 14.13), accessed by choosing option 3 after the SETUP command is issued. In the TEST (STANDARD) screen the fields Initial Script and Post Script may be filled in with the member names containing initial and post scripts in the INCLUDE library.

The initial script is used to specify an initial set of XPEDITER/TSO commands to be executed before the source display screen appears at the start of the test session. If a RETEST NEWCOPY command is issued, the initial script will also be executed.

```
COMPUWARE -------------------- TEST (STANDARD) -------------------- COMPUWARE
COMMAND ===> SETUP

COMMANDS:  SEtup (Display Setup Menu)

TEST SELECTION CRITERIA:
                Program ===> CH14ROY
            Entry Point ===>
            Load Module ===>

         Initial Script ===>
            Post Script ===>

            PARM String ===> '30004500'

   File Allocation List ===> 'MY.ALLOC.DATA(CH14ROY)'

    Is This a DB2 Test? ===> NO     Plan ===>             System ===>


           Press ENTER to Process   or   Enter END Command to Terminate
```

Figure 14.12 The TEST (STANDARD) screen in an interactive XPEDITER/TSO session. This is where the program name and other options which will begin the debugging session are specified. The SETUP command has been entered to allow setting up of session defaults.

The post script lets you specify XPEDITER/TSO commands to be executed at the end of a test. The post script will be executed after the QUIT command has been entered but while you are still in the testing environment.

You can also issue the INCLUDE command to copy a script into your debugging session. This script must also reside in a member of the INCLUDE library.

To begin the XPEDITER test session, an entry in the program field of the TEST (STANDARD) panel is required. It may be either the load module name

```
COMPUWARE ----------------- TEST SCRIPT LIBRARIES ----------------- COMPUWARE
COMMAND ===>



User Libraries:
      (1) ===> 'MY.XSCRIPT.DATA'
      (2) ===>
      (3) ===>

Installation Libraries: (Changes made to this list override installed default
      (4) ===> 'INSTALL.XPED51C.INCLUDE'
      (5) ===>
      (6) ===>







           Press ENTER to Process   or   Enter END Command to Terminate
```

Figure 14.13 The TEST SCRIPT LIBRARIES screen for an interactive XPEDITER/TSO session in which script libraries for initial, post, and INCLUDE scripts are specified.

or, if the program to be tested is a member of a statically linked load module, the program ID from the IDENTIFICATION DIVISION; in the latter case enter the name of the load module in the load module field. Enter an alternate entry point in the entry-point field if execution is to start at a point other than the link-edited entry point in the load module. In addition, you may specify a file list to allocate the files used by your program (if you haven't already done so), predefined scripts to be executed before and after the test session, and parameters to be passed to the program.

When you press the ENTER key, you will see a message indicating that you are entering the XPEDITER/TSO test environment. You will then be placed in the source display screen (see Fig. 14.14). You will see a BEFORE breakpoint (marked with the letter "B") and an AFTER breakpoint (marked with the letter "A"), which were automatically set by XPEDITER, at the PROCEDURE DIVISION header and the program terminating statement, respectively. An arrow will point to the statement where execution is currently paused. Primary XPEDITER/TSO commands or TSO commands (prefixed by TSO) can now be entered on the primary command line, and XPEDITER/TSO line commands can be entered on the lines to the left of the source code. If necessary, program variables can be altered explicitly with the MOVE command, or implicitly by overtyping the current value after the variable has been accessed by DISPLAY or KEEP. You can alter program logic by INSERTing XPEDITER commands in the COBOL code. You can also use the MONITOR command to record the execution history in a buffer, and later replay the test session in reverse. In addition, you can view the session log at any time by entering the LOG command, restart the test of the current copy of the module by entering RETEST, or restart with a new copy by entering RETEST NEWCOPY.

```
Source: CH14ROY -------------- XPEDITER/TSO ------------------- Before CH14ROY
COMMAND ===>                                                   SCROLL ===> CSR

====> PROCEDURE DIVISION USING PASSED-PARMS.                                B
00126 ****************************************************************
00127 *    MAINLINE CONTROL PARAGRAPH                                  *
00128 ****************************************************************
00130 0000-MAINLINE.
00131     OPEN INPUT  INFILE
00132          OUTPUT OUTFILE
00133     IF PARM-LENGTH GREATER THAN ZERO
00134        MOVE PASSED-NET-RECEIPTS TO PRT-NET-RECEIPTS
00135                                    NET-RECEIPTS
00136        MOVE PASSED-LIST-PRICE   TO PRT-LIST-PRICE
00137                                    LIST-PRICE
00138     ELSE
00139        DISPLAY 'NO PARM PASSED'
00140        SET PARM-ERROR TO TRUE
00141     END-IF
00142     IF NOT PARM-ERROR
00143        READ INFILE INTO WS-INFILE-REC
00144           AT END
00145              SET END-OF-FILE TO TRUE
00146              DISPLAY 'END OF FILE ON FIRST READ'
```

Figure 14.14 The Source Display screen for an interactive XPEDITER/TSO debugging session.

If you wish, you can use ISPF split-screen mode. This will enable you to do other tasks in the second screen while you are in the debugging session on the first screen. Thus you can view the log from a previous XPEDITER test or even edit the original copy of the program you are debugging.

Your debugging session will end when you enter QUIT. After exiting the source display screen you can examine the log and script data sets. Panels will appear which give you the option of deleting, keeping, or printing these data sets.

14.5.2 Miscellaneous Notes about Interactive Mode

Many of the primary commands have counterparts in line commands. Also, it is usually more convenient to overtype field values which are in KEEP windows or which are DISPLAYed rather than to enter MOVE commands. XPEDITER/TSO also permits you to overtype data in any program storage area which is displayed with the DISPLAYP command; you can overtype either the hexadecimal or EBCDIC data.

The GPREGS command shows the contents of the general-purpose registers. Although you can overtype values in the registers, I do not recommend doing this unless you are sure what consequences the new values will have; incorrect data in general-purpose registers can produce unpredictable results when the program is executed. The ability to change register contents is more valuable for Assembler programmers who often use general-purpose registers in instructions.

The command delimiter is the same as that used in ISPF; normally the default is the semicolon (;). Recall that you may alter ISPF and XPEDITER session defaults and PF key assignments by accessing the Defaults screen from the XPEDITER/TSO primary menu.

14.6 A SAMPLE INTERACTIVE XPEDITER/TSO DEBUGGING SESSION

The COBOL II program used for the test session was written to estimate the income from new book sales. The projected net receipts and list price for each copy are passed as a parameter from the JCL. Each input record contains numbers representing percentages of the proceeds due to the author for specific numbers of books sold, and estimated numbers of copies sold. The program is illustrated in Fig. 14.15.

In order to test the program we prepare it for execution as described in Sec. 14.5.1. When we are in the source display screen we enter

```
GO
```

to begin execution. XPEDITER reports that an S0C7 ABEND was encountered at line 136 in the source code. Entering

```
LOG
```

```
000100 IDENTIFICATION DIVISION.
000200  PROGRAM-ID.   CH14ROY.
000300  AUTHOR.       ALAN FRIEND.
000400  DATE-WRITTEN. JULY, 1990.
000500  DATE-COMPILED.
000600     SKIP1
000700 ENVIRONMENT DIVISION.
000800  INPUT-OUTPUT SECTION.
000900   FILE-CONTROL.
001000     SELECT INFILE          ASSIGN TO   INFILE.
001100     SELECT OUTFILE         ASSIGN TO   OUTFILE.
001200     SKIP1
001300 DATA DIVISION.
001400  FILE SECTION.
001500  FD INFILE
001600     RECORDING MODE IS F
001700     RECORD CONTAINS 80 CHARACTERS
001800     BLOCK CONTAINS 0 RECORDS
001900     LABEL RECORDS ARE OMITTED
002000     DATA RECORD IS INFILE-REC.
002100  01 INFILE-REC                 PIC X(80).
002200  FD OUTFILE
002300     RECORDING MODE IS F
002400     RECORD CONTAINS 133 CHARACTERS
002500     BLOCK CONTAINS 0 RECORDS
002600     LABEL RECORDS ARE OMITTED
002700     DATA RECORD IS OUTFILE-REC.
002800  01 OUTFILE-REC                PIC X(133).
002900     EJECT
003000  WORKING-STORAGE SECTION.
003100  01 WS-INFILE-REC.
003200     05 DOMESTIC-INFO.
003300        10 DOMESTIC-PCENT-1       PIC SV9(03).
003400        10 FILLER                 PIC X.
003500        10 DOMESTIC-PCENT-2       PIC SV9(03).
003600        10 FILLER                 PIC X.
003700        10 DOMESTIC-PCENT-3       PIC SV9(03).
003800        10 FILLER                 PIC X.
003900        10 DOMESTIC-CP-1          PIC S9(04).
004000        10 FILLER                 PIC X.
004100        10 DOMESTIC-CP-2          PIC S9(04).
004200  01 HEADER-LINE-1.
004300     05 FILLER                    PIC X(20) VALUE 'DOMESTIC SALES -'.
004400     05 FILLER                    PIC X(12) VALUE 'LIST PRICE'.
004500     05 PRT-LIST-PRICE            PIC $Z9.99.
004600     05 FILLER                    PIC X(10) VALUE  SPACES.
004700     05 FILLER                    PIC X(14) VALUE 'NET RECEIPTS'.
004800     05 PRT-NET-RECEIPTS          PIC $Z9.99.
004900     05 FILLER                    PIC X(50) VALUE  SPACES.
005000     05 FILLER                    PIC X(05) VALUE 'PAGE '.
005100     05 PRT-PAGE-NO               PIC ZZ9.
```

Figure 14.15 The COBOL II source code for the interactive XPEDITER/TSO debugging session described in Sec. 14.6. *(Continued)*

accesses the data that XPEDITER has sent to the log data set. The log information verifies the location of the ABEND, reports the contents of the PSW and general-purpose registers, and indicates that the ABENDing Assembler instruction was Zero and Add Packed (ZAP).

The COBOL statement which ABENDed is

```
MOVE PASSED-LIST-PRICE TO PRT-LIST-PRICE
```

```
01 DETAIL-LINE-1.
   05 FILLER                  PIC X(10) VALUE SPACES.
   05 DTL-DOMESTIC-PERCENT-1  PIC 99.9.
   05 FILLER                  PIC X     VALUE SPACES.
   05 FILLER                  PIC X(03) VALUE '%'.
   05 FILLER                  PIC X(14) VALUE 'ON THE FIRST'.
   05 DTL-DOMESTIC-COPIES-1   PIC ZZ,Z99.
   05 FILLER                  PIC X(14) VALUE '  COPIES  ='.
   05 DTL-DOMESTIC-MONEY-1    PIC ZZ,Z99.99.
01 DETAIL-LINE-2.
   05 FILLER                  PIC X(10) VALUE SPACES.
   05 DTL-DOMESTIC-PERCENT-2  PIC 99.9.
   05 FILLER                  PIC X     VALUE SPACES.
   05 FILLER                  PIC X(03) VALUE '%'.
   05 FILLER                  PIC X(14) VALUE 'ON THE NEXT'.
   05 DTL-DOMESTIC-COPIES-2   PIC ZZ,Z99.
   05 FILLER                  PIC X(14) VALUE '  COPIES  ='.
   05 DTL-DOMESTIC-MONEY-2    PIC ZZ,Z99.99.
01 DETAIL-LINE-3.
   05 FILLER                  PIC X(10) VALUE SPACES.
   05 DTL-DOMESTIC-PERCENT-3  PIC 99.9.
   05 FILLER                  PIC X     VALUE SPACES.
   05 FILLER                  PIC X(03) VALUE '%'.
   05 FILLER                  PIC X(21)
                                 VALUE 'ON ALL COPIES AFTER'.
   05 DTL-DOMESTIC-COPIES-3   PIC ZZ,Z99.
   05 FILLER                  PIC X(07) VALUE '   =   '.
   05 DTL-DOMESTIC-MONEY-3    PIC ZZ,Z99.99.
   05 FILLER                  PIC X(02) VALUE SPACES.
   05 FILLER                  PIC X(10)
                                 VALUE '(MAXIMUM  '.
   05 DTL-MAX-COPIES          PIC ZZ,Z99BB.
   05 FILLER                  PIC X(34)
                VALUE 'COPIES ASSUMED FOR THESE EXAMPLES)'.
01 DETAIL-LINE-4.
   05 FILLER                  PIC X(51) VALUE SPACES.
   05 FILLER                  PIC X(10) VALUE ALL '-'.
01 DETAIL-LINE-5.
   05 FILLER                  PIC X(51) VALUE SPACES.
   05 DTL-DOMESTIC-MONEY-TOT  PIC $ZZZ,Z99.99.
01 DETAIL-LINE-6.
   05 FILLER                  PIC X(133) VALUE ALL '-'.
01 MAX-VALUES               COMP-3.
   05 MAX-COPIES              PIC S9(05) VALUE +10000.
   05 MAX-LINES               PIC S9(02) VALUE +56.
01 SWITCHES.
   05 SW-EOF                  PIC X     VALUE 'N'.
      88 END-OF-FILE                    VALUE 'Y'.
   05 SW-PARM                 PIC X     VALUE 'N'.
      88 PARM-ERROR                     VALUE 'Y'.
01 COUNTERS                 COMP-3.
   05 LINE-CNT                PIC S9(02) VALUE +60.
   05 PAGE-NO                 PIC S9(03).
01 WORK-AREAS               COMP-3.
   05 DOMESTIC-PERCENT-1    PIC SV9(03).
   05 DOMESTIC-PERCENT-2    PIC SV9(03).
   05 DOMESTIC-PERCENT-3    PIC SV9(03).
   05 DOMESTIC-COPIES-1     PIC S9(05).
   05 DOMESTIC-COPIES-2     PIC S9(05).
   05 DOMESTIC-COPIES-3     PIC S9(05).
   05 NET-RECEIPTS          PIC S9(03)V99.
   05 LIST-PRICE            PIC S9(03)V99.
   05 DOMESTIC-MONEY-INT    PIC S9(05)V99.
   05 DOMESTIC-MONEY-TOT    PIC S9(05)V99.
   EJECT
```

Figure 14.15 *(Continued)*

```
011700  LINKAGE SECTION.
011800
011900  01 PASSED-PARMS.
012000      05 PARM-LENGTH            PIC S9(04)          COMP.
012100      05 PASSED-NET-RECEIPTS    PIC S9(02)V99.
012200      05 PASSED-LIST-PRICE      PIC S9(02)V99.
012300      EJECT
012400 PROCEDURE DIVISION USING PASSED-PARMS.
012500      SKIP1
012600*****************************************************************
012700*     MAINLINE CONTROL PARAGRAPH                               *
012800*****************************************************************
012900      SKIP1
013000 0000-MAINLINE.
013100      OPEN INPUT  INFILE
013200           OUTPUT OUTFILE
013300      IF PARM-LENGTH GREATER THAN ZERO
013400         MOVE PASSED-NET-RECEIPTS TO PRT-NET-RECEIPTS
013500                                     NET-RECEIPTS
013600         MOVE PASSED-LIST-PRICE   TO PRT-LIST-PRICE
013700                                     LIST-PRICE
013800      ELSE
013900         DISPLAY 'NO PARM PASSED'
014000         SET PARM-ERROR TO TRUE
014100      END-IF
014200      IF NOT PARM-ERROR
014300         READ INFILE INTO WS-INFILE-REC
014400            AT END
014500               SET END-OF-FILE TO TRUE
014600               DISPLAY 'END OF FILE ON FIRST READ'
014700            NOT AT END
014800               PERFORM 0100-PROCESS-RECORD
014900                  THRU 0100-PROCESS-RECORD-EXIT
015000                     UNTIL END-OF-FILE
015100         END-READ
015200      END-IF
015300      CLOSE INFILE
015400            OUTFILE
015500      GOBACK.
015600      EJECT
```

Figure 14.15 *(Continued)*

Since an S0C7 is a data exception, we realize that we must examine the field PASSED-LIST-PRICE. Entering

```
FIND PASSED-LIST-PRICE DEFINE
```

causes XPEDITER to scroll the source display screen to line 122, where the field is defined. We see that it is an elementary field in the group item PASSED-PARMS. In order to examine the parameters passed to the program we enter the line command

```
DH
```

on the lines where the first and second parameters, PASSED-NET-RECEIPTS and PASSED-LIST-PRICE are defined. XPEDITER displays the contents in EBCDIC and hexadecimal notation. PASSED-NET-RECEIPTS contains 3045

```
******************************************************************
*    OTHER PARAGRAPHS NEEDED FOR PROCESSING.                     *
******************************************************************
         SKIP1
 0100-PROCESS-RECORD.
         SKIP1
         MOVE DOMESTIC-PCENT-1 TO DOMESTIC-PERCENT-1
         MOVE DOMESTIC-PCENT-2 TO DOMESTIC-PERCENT-2
         MOVE DOMESTIC-PCENT-3 TO DOMESTIC-PERCENT-3
         MOVE DOMESTIC-CP-1    TO DOMESTIC-COPIES-1
         MOVE DOMESTIC-CP-2    TO DOMESTIC-COPIES-2
         COMPUTE DTL-DOMESTIC-MONEY-1  DOMESTIC-MONEY-INT =
            DOMESTIC-PERCENT-1    * DOMESTIC-COPIES-1 * NET-RECEIPTS
         MOVE DOMESTIC-MONEY-INT TO DOMESTIC-MONEY-TOT
         COMPUTE DTL-DOMESTIC-MONEY-2  DOMESTIC-MONEY-INT =
            DOMESTIC-PERCENT-2    * DOMESTIC-COPIES-2 * NET-RECEIPTS
         ADD  DOMESTIC-MONEY-INT TO DOMESTIC-MONEY-TOT
         ADD DOMESTIC-COPIES-1 DOMESTIC-COPIES-2
                               GIVING   DOMESTIC-COPIES-3
         COMPUTE DTL-DOMESTIC-MONEY-3  DOMESTIC-MONEY-INT =
            DOMESTIC-PERCENT-3 *
            (MAX-COPIES - DOMESTIC-COPIES-3) * NET-RECEIPTS
         ADD  DOMESTIC-MONEY-INT DOMESTIC-MONEY-TOT
            GIVING DTL-DOMESTIC-MONEY-TOT
         PERFORM 0200-PRINT THRU 0200-PRINT-EXIT
         READ INFILE INTO WS-INFILE-REC
              AT END
                 SET END-OF-FILE TO TRUE
         END-READ.
 0100-PROCESS-RECORD-EXIT.
         EXIT.

 0200-PRINT.
         MOVE SPACES TO OUTFILE-REC
         MULTIPLY DOMESTIC-PCENT-1 BY +100
             GIVING DTL-DOMESTIC-PERCENT-1
         MULTIPLY DOMESTIC-PCENT-2 BY +100
             GIVING DTL-DOMESTIC-PERCENT-2
         MULTIPLY DOMESTIC-PCENT-3 BY +100
             GIVING DTL-DOMESTIC-PERCENT-3
         MOVE DOMESTIC-CP-1      TO DTL-DOMESTIC-COPIES-1
         MOVE DOMESTIC-CP-2      TO DTL-DOMESTIC-COPIES-2
         MOVE DOMESTIC-COPIES-3 TO DTL-DOMESTIC-COPIES-3
         MOVE MAX-COPIES         TO DTL-MAX-COPIES
         IF LINE-CNT  GREATER THAN MAX-LINES
            ADD +1 TO PAGE-NO
            MOVE PAGE-NO TO PRT-PAGE-NO
            WRITE OUTFILE-REC FROM HEADER-LINE-1
              AFTER ADVANCING PAGE
            MOVE +1 TO LINE-CNT
         END-IF
         WRITE OUTFILE-REC  FROM DETAIL-LINE-1
           AFTER ADVANCING 2 LINES
         WRITE OUTFILE-REC  FROM DETAIL-LINE-2
           AFTER ADVANCING 1 LINES
         WRITE OUTFILE-REC  FROM DETAIL-LINE-3
           AFTER ADVANCING 1 LINES
         WRITE OUTFILE-REC  FROM DETAIL-LINE-4
           AFTER ADVANCING 1 LINES
         WRITE OUTFILE-REC  FROM DETAIL-LINE-5
           AFTER ADVANCING 1 LINES
         WRITE OUTFILE-REC  FROM DETAIL-LINE-6
           AFTER ADVANCING 2 LINES
         ADD +8 TO LINE-CNT.
 0200-PRINT-EXIT.
```

Figure 14.15 *(Continued)*

and PASSED-LIST-PRICE contains spaces. The invalid data (spaces) in PASSED-LIST-PRICE caused the ABEND. The parameter passed to the program should have been 30004500 (representing $30.00 for net receipts and $45.00 for list price).

Overtyping the displayed values with 3000 and 4500, respectively, sets the two fields to their proper numeric values. We could have entered the primary commands

```
MOVE 3000 TO PASSED-NET-RECEIPTS
MOVE 4500 TO PASSED-LIST-PRICE
```

instead.

We enter

```
GO
```

to resume execution from line 136. XPEDITER intercepts another S0C7 ABEND at line 202. The COBOL statement at line 202 is

```
ADD +1 TO PAGE-NO
```

We enter the line command

```
DH
```

on line 202. XPEDITER reports the contents of PAGE-NO as hexadecimal 0000. This invalid packed data caused the second S0C7. Examining the source code for PAGE-NO shows that there was no VALUE clause for PAGE-NO.

Entering

```
FIND PAGE-NO ALL
```

allows us to verify that there were no statements which initialized PAGE-NO before the ADD was executed.

Overtyping the hexadecimal value in PAGE-NO with 000C or entering the primary command

```
MOVE 0 TO PAGE-NO
```

sets the field to packed zero.

Entering

```
GO
```

continues execution. XPEDITER/TSO shows the program output on the terminal and we notice that one set of output lines has 0 for all percentages, numbers of copies, and calculated amounts. This is incorrect. Did an input record contain zeros instead of proper numeric values? After the rest of the program output has been displayed, XPEDITER gives the message TEST COMPLETED.

We decide to reexecute the program from the beginning, this time checking for zeros in an input record. Entering

```
RETEST
```

refreshes the source display screen with execution paused at the beginning of the PROCEDURE DIVISION. We enter the line command

```
DH
```

on lines containing all variables we modified in the previous test. XPEDITER displays the correct values that we established for the passed parameters, but shows that PAGE-NO has been set back to its original value of hexadecimal 0000. As before, we modify PAGE-NO to contain packed zeros. Now the program should execute without any S0C7 ABEND.

We wish to halt execution if an input record containing zeros is read. Because the primary command we will enter is too long for the space provided, we enter

```
SET CMDSIZE 2
```

to open the primary command area to two lines. Now we enter

```
WHEN ((DOMESTIC-PCENT-1 = 0) AND (DOMESTIC-PCENT-2 = 0)
  AND (DOMESTIC-PCENT-3 = 0))
```

This will halt execution and return control to us at the terminal when a record with values of 0 in all the percentage fields is read.

Entering

```
MONITOR
```

turns on the recording feature so that program execution history will be stored in a buffer when execution resumes. This will permit us to execute in review mode later to do a backward trace of portions of the program execution.

We enter

```
GO
```

to begin execution. XPEDITER displays several sets of program output at the terminal and then pauses with a message indicating that the WHEN condition has been met after line 182 executed. Line 182 is the READ statement,

```
READ INFILE INTO WS-INFILE-REC
```

Entering either a primary KEEP command or a line KEEP command on line 182,

```
KEEPE WS-INFILE-REC
```

or

```
KE2
```

opens a KEEP window for WS-INFILE-REC (the “E” at the end of the command directs XPEDITER to show elementary fields in WS-INFILE-REC). As suspected, all elementary fields in WS-INFILE-REC contain zero.

We would like to see the previous input record values. Entering

```
REVERSE
```

changes the direction of execution. XPEDITER extracts the values that were recorded for WS-INFILE-REC from its review mode buffer and displays them in the KEEP window. We can now identify the previous valid input record.

We enter

```
RESUME
```

to exit review mode and resume our current execution position. The zeros reappear for the fields in the KEEP window. Overtyping the values with correct ones, or entering the appropriate MOVE commands, replaces the values with the proper numeric data. Entering

```
GO
```

causes the program to execute successfully to completion. The command

```
QUIT
```

terminates the XPEDITER/TSO debugging session.

The preceding example demonstrates some of the powerful capabilities of XPEDITER/TSO and concludes our discussion of interactive debuggers. There are other interactive debuggers besides those discussed in Chaps. 12 through 14; any such tool which your site has installed can be invaluable in your testing and debugging activities if you invest the time to learn it.

14.7 SUMMARY

XPEDITER/TSO is an interactive debugging facility from Compuware Corporation. This chapter deals with its general features and those which apply to COBOL debugging.

Tasks available in XPEDITER/TSO include the suspension of program execution before or after any COBOL verb, the listing of the contents of fields, program storage areas and general-purpose registers, the listing of the status of files, the modifying of the values of identifiers and storage areas at any time, the tracing of the logical flow of the program, the review of program execution in the reverse direction, and the temporary insertion of XPEDITER/TSO commands within the COBOL code. In order to use XPEDITER/TSO, the program to be tested must be compiled with the XPEDITER SIR processor.

XPEDITER/TSO can be run in batch mode or interactive mode. In batch mode, it is not possible to interrupt the program or interact with it at the terminal. Your debugging strategy must therefore be planned before you execute the job. The XPEDITER/TSO commands in batch mode offer quite a bit of flexibility and provide a great deal of debugging information.

Batch mode might be used when you do not want to tie up your terminal for a long time or when you wish to gather performance statistics about program execution for later review. It uses fewer resources than interactive mode.

Like COBTEST in full-screen mode, XPEDITER/TSO in interactive mode operates under ISPF. It shows the executing program code in the source display screen and allows you to see the contents of variables in KEEP windows or in the source display screen. It provides very powerful interactive testing facilities. Features include the ability to overtype the contents of variables and storage areas which have been accessed, the ability to temporarily insert XPEDITER/TSO commands in the program code, and the ability to review program execution in the reverse direction one statement at a time. It is also possible to split the physical screen into two logical screens in order to do other tasks within the ISPF environment while remaining in XPEDITER.

The benefits of interactive debugging, no matter which product you use, are well worth the time spent in learning it.

REVIEW QUESTIONS

1. What is the purpose of the XPEDITER/TSO SIR processor?

2. Indicate the purpose of each of the following DD statements in the JCL to run XPEDITER/TSO in batch mode:

- **a.** XCOMPILE
- **b.** XPIN
- **c.** XPOUT
- **d.** XINCLUDE

3. Describe the purpose of an XPEDITER/TSO:

- **a.** post script
- **b.** initial script
- **c.** log data set

4. How are line commands entered when debugging in interactive mode? How are primary commands entered?

5. Describe how program files may be allocated before you begin execution in an interactive XPEDITER/TSO session.

6. You have entered the source display screen in order to test a COBOL program in XPEDITER/TSO interactive mode. Perform the following tasks during your debugging session.

a. Write the command that will access the file allocation utility.

b. Write a command that will record the execution history of your session.

c. Establish a breakpoint that will interrupt program execution after the READ statement at line 200.

d. Write a primary command to open up a window that will continuously monitor the values in the elementary fields of group item EMPLOYEE-DATA.

e. Write a command that will tally the number of times each paragraph in the program executes.

f. Now write the command to execute the program from the beginning.

g. Assuming that you successfully halted execution after the READ statement, write a command to show the contents of EMPLOYEE-INPUT-RECORD in hexadecimal notation.

h. Write a command that will return control to the terminal when EOF-SWITCH equals 'Y.'

i. Write the command to remove the breakpoint at line 200.

j. Write the command to resume execution of your program.

k. Assuming that the condition in "h" was met and you received control, write the command that will permit you to replay program execution in reverse.

l. Write the command to execute the prior statement before your current paused position.

m. Write the command that will reestablish your paused execution position.

n. Write the command that moves the value 'N' to EOF-SWITCH.

o. Write the command that will execute the program in the forward direction from your current paused position.

p. Write the command that will display the tally of paragraph executions when the program has completed execution.

q. Write a command to begin a new test of the program.

Appendix

A

List of Abbreviations and Acronyms

There is a virtual "alphabet soup" of abbreviations and acronyms in the documentation and literature relating to IBM products. Knowing what an abbreviation or acronym stands for may be helpful in understanding its purpose or function. This list is provided in order to help you make some sense out of it all. More complete information about each item is provided in the text of the book.

ABEND	ABnormal ENDing
ACB	Access Method Control Block (a VSAM control block)
ALU	Arithmetic Logic Unit
AMB	Access Method Block (a VSAM control block)
ASCB	Address Space Control Block (an MVS control block)
BL	Base Locator (used in OS/VS COBOL and COBOL II)
BLF	Base Locator for File (used in COBOL II)
BLL	Base Locator for Linkage (used in OS/VS COBOL and COBOL II)
BLW	Base Locator for Working-Storage (used in COBOL II)
CCW	Channel Command Word
CDE	Contents Directory Entry (an MVS control block)
CGT	Constant Global Table (a COBOL II control block)
CLIST	Command List (a programming language)
COBOL	COmmon Business-Oriented Language
CPU	Central Processing Unit
CSECT	Control Section
CSW	Channel Status Word
DASD	Direct Access Storage Device
DAT	Dynamic Address Translation
DCB	Data Control Block (an MVS control block)
DD	Data Definition (a JCL statement)

DEB	Data Extent Block (an MVS control block)
DSCB	Data Set Control Block (DASD label)
EBCDIC	Extended Binary-Coded Decimal Interchange Code
ECB	Event Control Block (an MVS control block)
EOV	End-of-Volume
EPA	Entry-Point Address
EXCP	Execute Channel Program
FCB	File Control Block (a COBOL II control block)
FD	File Description (used in COBOL)
FIB	File Information Block (an OS/VS COBOL and COBOL II control block)
FLIH	First-Level Interrupt Handler
HIPO	Hierarchy plus Input-Process-Output
HSA	High Save Area
ILC	Instruction Length Code
I/O	Input/Output
IOB	Input/Output Block (an MVS control block)
ISPF	Interactive System Productivity Facility
JCL	Job Control Language
JES	Job Entry Subsystem
JFCB	Job File Control Block (an MVS control block)
LPA	Load-Point Address
LSA	Low Save Area
MVS	Multiple Virtual Storage (operating system)
MVS/ESA	MVS Enterprise Systems Architecture (operating system)
MVS/XA	MVS Extended Architecture (operating system)
O/C/EO	Open/Close/End-of-Volume
NSI	Next Sequential Instruction
PDS	Partitioned Data Set
PER	Program Event Recording
PGT	Program Global Table (a COBOL control block)
PLH	Place Holder (a VSAM control block)
PRB	Program Request Block (an MVS control block)
PSA	Prefixed Save Area (or Prefixed Storage Area)
PSW	Program Status Word
QSAM	Queued Sequential Access Method
RB	Request Block (an MVS control block)
RDW	Record Descriptor Word
RPL	Request Parameter List (a VSAM control block)
SAM	Sequential Access Method

SVC	Supervisor Call Instruction
SVRB	Supervisor Request Block (an MVS control block)
TCB	Task Control Block (an MVS control block)
TGT	Task Global Table (a COBOL control block)
TIOT	Task Input/Output Table (an MVS control block)
TSO	Time-Sharing Option
UCB	Unit Control Block (an MVS control block)
VSAM	Virtual Storage Access Method
VTOC	Volume Table of Contents
XTLST	Extent List (an MVS control block)

Appendix

B

Common MVS System Completion Codes

This list of system completion codes (system ABEND codes) includes the most common ones likely to be encountered by the COBOL programmer executing under MVS. For those discussed elsewhere in the text, only a brief description is given here and the section in the book giving more complete information is indicated. If you receive a code not listed here, or need further information about any completion code, see the IBM *Message Library: System Codes* manual appropriate for your version of MVS.

001 An I/O error has occurred, possibly due to conflicts in DCB parameters, incorrect usage of READ or WRITE statements in the program, or actual physical I/O errors. See Sec. 9.4.6.

002 There is an I/O error, possibly because of conflicts in record or block size parameters, incorrect usage of READ or WRITE statements in the program, physical damage to the recording medium, or a device malfunction. See Sec. 9.4.6.

013 A data set could not be successfully opened, usually due to conflicting or insufficient DCB parameters. See Sec. 9.4.3.

0C1 Operation exception: There was an attempt to execute an instruction with an operation code not valid for the hardware. See Sec. 11.6.

0C2 Privileged-operation exception: An attempt was made to execute a privileged instruction in the problem state. See Sec. 11.6.

0C4 Protection exception: An attempt was made to access a protected area in memory. See Sec. 11.6.

0C7 Data exception: An operation was attempted with invalid packed decimal data. Common causes are failure to initialize a field, invalid input data, initializing a group item rather than initializing the COMP-3 elementary fields, or moving a COMP-3 field to a group item containing fields defined as DISPLAY numeric. Check the program logic to see how the field was initialized, updated, or accessed, or check the definition of the field. This is one of the most common completion codes. See the following sections for further information and for examples of solving S0C7 ABENDs: 3.3.2.3, 6.1.2, 6.2.2, 7.1.2, 8.2, 10.3.3, 11.7.2, 12.5, 13.7, and 14.6.

0CB Decimal-divide exception: The quotient in a division using a decimal operand is greater than the size of the receiving field, or division by zero was attempted. The operation is suppressed. Possible causes include dividing by zero, dividing by a very small packed number, too small a specification of a COMP-3 receiving field, improper placement of the V in the receiving field definition, or failure to code the ON SIZE ERROR clause. Check the program logic to see if the divisor was correctly initialized or updated, whether a runaway program loop caused the dividend to become too large relative to the divisor, whether the receiving field was incorrectly defined, or whether a fractional value was loaded into an integer divisor with truncation of the fractional part resulting in a zero divisor. Note that an 0CB ABEND caused by attempting to divide by zero may be intercepted by COBOL library subroutines; the subroutines check for zero before dividing. Rather than ABENDing (leading you to think there is a problem in the library subroutine) they issue a user completion code. The code is U0203 in OS/VS COBOL or U1061 in COBOL II.

122 The operator cancelled the job for unspecified reasons and requested a dump. The job may have appeared to be in an infinite loop, as evidenced by an abnormal quantity of output, it may have been deadlocked or in a wait state, it may have attempted to access unauthorized or unavailable resources, or it may have violated installation procedures. It is also possible that the operator erred. It is quite possible that nothing is wrong with the program. Speak to the operator to find out why the job was cancelled, make any necessary corrections, and submit again.

213 There is an error in opening a DASD file because the file could not be found. See Sec. 9.4.3.

222 The operator cancelled the job for unspecified reasons and did not request a dump. Depending on which supervisor routine was active when the job was cancelled, a dump may have been produced. The job may have appeared to be in an infinite loop, as evidenced by an abnormal quantity of output, it may have been deadlocked or in a wait state, it may have attempted to access unauthorized or unavailable resources, or it may have violated installation procedures. It is also possible that the operator erred. It is quite possible that nothing is wrong with the program. Speak to the operator to find out why the job was cancelled, make any necessary corrections, and submit again.

322 The default or specified CPU time limit for a job, job step, or procedure was exceeded. Check to see if the time specified in the JCL was too low, if an endless loop was coded, if inefficient repetitive code was used, if the job was run on a slower CPU, or if the access times for the I/O devices were too slow. If the the program logic and coding techniques are good, try increasing the time requested in the JCL. If a very large amount of processing is being done (e.g., you are now processing one million records when previously you processed 100,000 records) and you have already checked the program logic, program efficiency, and CPU time requested in the JCL, you may wish to consider breaking up the job or job step into smaller units. Also, speak to the operators and try to find out if the job was run on a slower CPU, or if data sets were placed on devices with slower access time.

706 The error occurred during execution of a LINK, XCTL, ATTACH, or LOAD macro instruction because a requested load module was marked as not exe-

cutable by the linkage-editor. It may have been marked nonexecutable because of an unresolved external reference. Check the linkage-editor messages and correct any errors. Specify the LET linkage-editor option if you wish to mark the module as executable even if it does contain unresolved external references. Be sure that the correct module name was specified for execution.

806 The error occurred during execution of a LINK, XCTL, ATTACH, or LOAD macro instruction because a requested load module could not be found. See Sec. 11.6.

813 There is an open error on a tape data set because the data set could not be found. See Sec. 9.4.3.

B14 A close error occurred for a partitioned data set opened for output. See Sec. 9.4.5.

B37 The error was detected by the end-of-volume routine because there was insufficient space for an output data set on DASD or tape. See Sec. 9.4.6.

D37 The error was detected by the end-of-volume routine because there was insufficient primary space for an output data set on DASD and no secondary space allocation was available. See Sec. 9.4.6.

E37 The error was detected by the end-of-volume routine because the amount of space or the number of volumes allocated for an output data set on DASD or tape was inadequate. See Sec. 9.4.6.

Appendix

C

Selected MVS/XA Supervisor Calls

SVC Dec.	SVC Hex.	Associated macro
0	00	EXCP/XDAP
1	01	WAIT/WAITR/PRTOV
4	04	GETMAIN
5	05	FREEMAIN
6	06	LINK
7	07	XCTL
8	08	LOAD
9	09	DELETE
10	0A	GETMAIN/FREEMAIN (with R operand)
13	0D	ABEND
19	13	OPEN
20	14	CLOSE
42	2A	ATTACH
51	33	SNAP/SDUMP
55	37	EOV
62	3E	DETACH
68	44	SYNADAF/SYNADRLS
99	63	DYNALLOC

Appendix

D

Machine Instructions under MVS/ESA*

*Reprinted by permission from *ENTERPRISE SYSTEMS ARCHITECTURE/370 REFERENCE SUMMARY,* © 1989 by International Business Machines Corporation.

TABLE D.1 Machine Instruction Formats

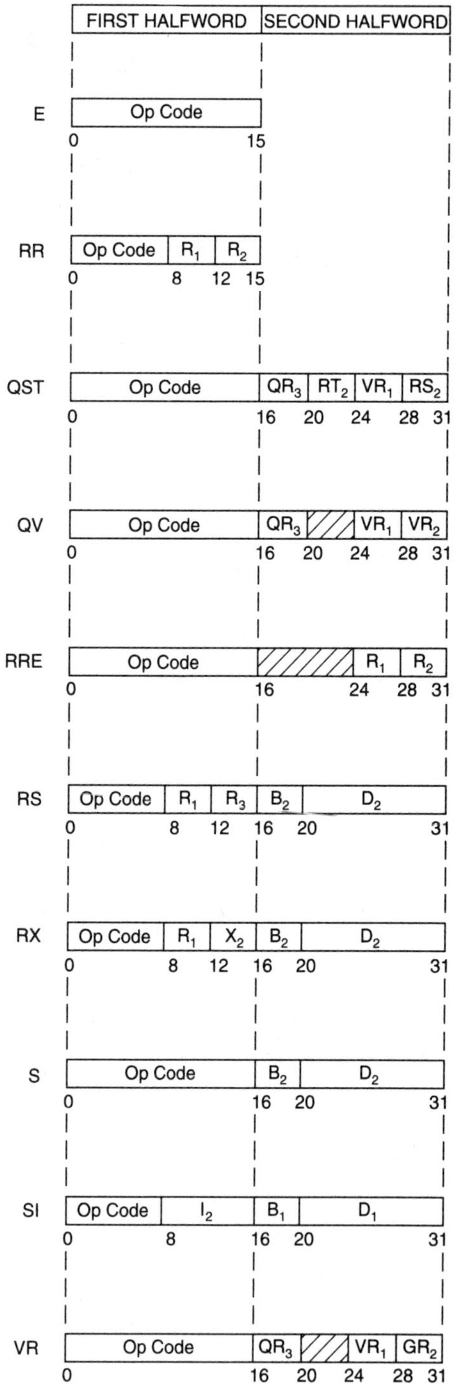

TABLE D.1 Machine Instruction Formats (*Continued*)

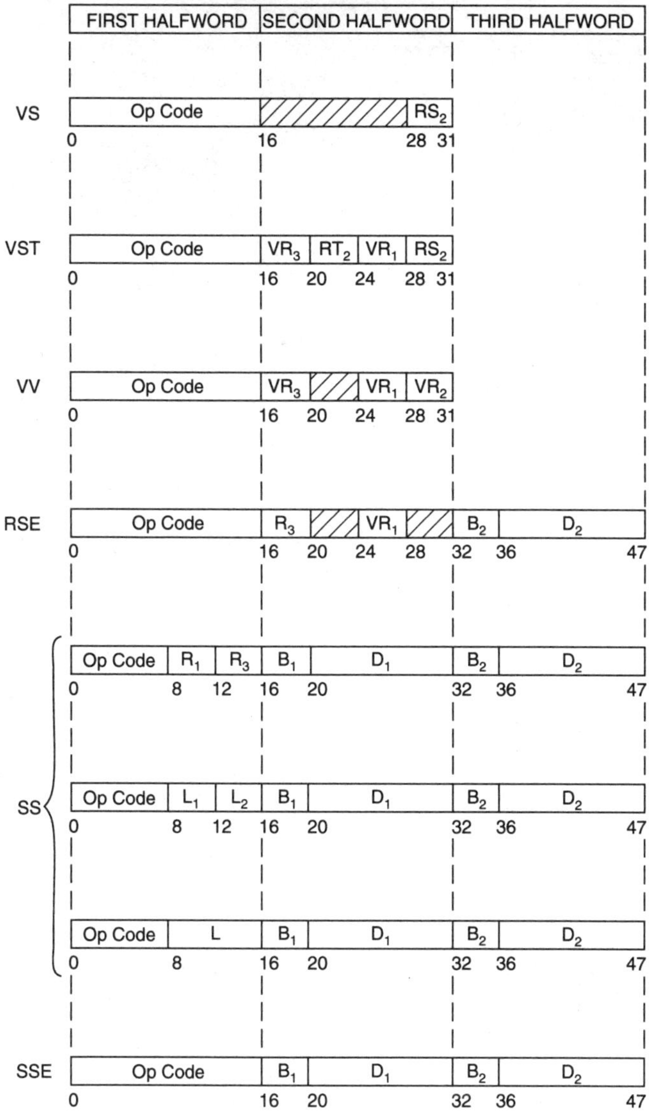

1, 2, 3: Denotes association with first, second, or third operand
B_1, B_2: Base register designation field
D_1, D_2: Displacement field
GR_2: Register designation field (general register)
I_2: Immediate operand field
L, L_1, L_2: Length field
QR_3: Register designation field (equivalent to GR_3 if general register, or FR_3 if floating-point register)
R_1, R_2, R_3: Register designation field
RS_2: Register designation field (starting address of vector)
RT_2: Register designation field (stride of vector)
VR_1, VR_2, VR_3: Register designation field (vector register)
X_2: Index register designation field

TABLE D.2 Machine Instructions by Mnemonic

Mnemonic	Operands	Name	Format	Op Code	Class & Notes
A	$R_1, D_2(X_2, B_2)$	Add	RX	5A	c
AD	$R_1, D_2(X_2, B_2)$	Add Normalized (L)	RX	6A	c
ADR	R_1, R_2	Add Normalized (L)	RR	2A	c
AE	$R_1, D_2(X_2, B_2)$	Add Normalized (S)	RX	7A	c
AER	R_1, R_2	Add Normalized (S)	RR	3A	c
AH	$R_1, D_2(X_2, B_2)$	Add Halfword	RX	4A	c
AL	$R_1, D_2(X_2, B_2)$	Add Logical	RX	5E	c
ALR	R_1, R_2	Add Logical	RR	1E	c
AP	$D_1(L_1, B_1), D_2(L_2, B_2)$	Add Decimal	SS	FA	c
AR	R_1, R_2	Add	RR	1A	c
AU	$R_1, D_2(X_2, B_2)$	Add Unnormalized (S)	RX	7E	c
AUR	R_1, R_2	Add Unnormalized (S)	RR	3E	c
AW	$R_1, D_2(X_2, B_2)$	Add Unnormalized (L)	RX	6E	c
AWR	R_1, R_2	Add Unnormalized (L)	RR	2E	c
AXR	R_1, R_2	Add Unnormalized (L)	RR	36	c
BAKR	R_1, R_2	Branch and Stack	RRE	B240	q
BAL	$R_1, D_2(X_2, B_2)$	Branch and Link	RX	45	
BALR	R_1, R_2	Branch and Link	RR	05	
BAS	$R_1, D_2(X_2, B_2)$	Branch and Save	RX	4D	
BASR	R_1, R_2	Branch and Save	RR	0D	
BASSM	R_1, R_2	Branch and Save and Set Mode	RR	0C	
BC	$M_1, D_2(X_2, B_2)$	Branch on Condition	RX	47	
BCR	M_1, R_2	Branch on Condition	RR	07	
BCT	$R_1, D_2(X_2, B_2)$	Branch on Count	RX	46	
BCTR	R_1, R_2	Branch on Count	RR	06	
BSM	R_1, R_2	Branch and Set Mode	RR	0B	
BXH	$R_1, R_3, D_2(B_2)$	Branch on Index High	RS	86	
BXLE	$R_1, R_3, D_2(B_2)$	Branch on Index Low or Equal	RS	87	
C	$R_1, D_2(X_2, B_2)$	Compare	RX	59	c
CD	$R_1, D_2(X_2, B_2)$	Compare (L)	RX	69	c
CDR	R_1, R_2	Compare (L)	RR	29	c
CDS	R_1, R3, $D_2(B_2)$	Compare Double and Swap	RS	BB	c
CE	$R_1, D_2(X_2, B_2)$	Compare (S)	RX	79	c
CER	R_1, R_2	Compare (S)	RR	39	c
CFC	$D_2(B_2)$	Compare and Form Codeword	S	B21A	i c
CH	$R_1, D_2(X_2, B_2)$	Compare Halfword	RX	49	c
CL	$R_1, D_2(X_2, B_2)$	Compare Logical	RX	55	c
CLC	$D_1(L, B_1), D_2(B_2)$	Compare Logical	SS	D5	c
CLCL	R_1, R_2	Compare Logical Long	RR	0F	i c
CLI	$D_1(B_1), I_2$	Compare Logical	SI	95	c
CLM	$R_1, M_3, D_2(B_2)$	Compare Logical Characters under Mask	RS	BD	c
CLR	R_1, R_2	Compare Logical	RR	15	c
CP	$D_1(L_1, B_1), D_2(L_2, B_2)$	Compare Decimal	SS	F9	c
CPYA	R_1, R_2	Copy Access	RRE	B24D	
CR	R_1, R_2	Compare	RR	19	c
CS	$R_1, R_3, D_2(B_2)$	Compare and Swap	RS	BA	c
CSCH		Clear Subchannel	S	B230	pc
CVB	$R_1, D_2(X_2, B_2)$	Convert to Binary	RX	4F	
CVD	$R_1, D_2(X_2, B_2)$	Convert to Decimal	RX	4E	
D	$R_1, D_2(X_2, B_2)$	Divide	RX	5D	
DD	$R_1, D_2(X_2, B_2)$	Divide (L)	RX	6D	
DDR	R_1, R_2	Divide (L)	RR	2D	
DE	$R_1, D_2(X_2, B_2)$	Divide (S)	RX	7D	
DER	R_1, R_2	Divide (S)	RR	3D	
DP	$D_1(L_1, B_1), D_2(L_2, B_2)$	Divide Decimal	SS	FD	
DR	R_1, R_2	Divide	RR	1D	
DXR	R_1, R_2	Divide (E)	RRE	B22D	
EAR	R_1, R_2	Extract Access	RRE	B24F	
ED	$D_1(L, B_1), D_2(B_2)$	Edit	SS	DE	c
EDMK	$D_1(L, B_1), D_2(B_2)$	Edit and Mark	SS	DF	c
EPAR	R_1	Extract Primary ASN	RRE	B226	q
EREG	R_1, R_2	Extract Stacked Registers	RRE	B249	q
ESAR	R_1	Extract Secondary ASN	RRE	B227	q
ESTA	R_1, R_2	Extract Stacked State	RRE	B24A	qc

TABLE D.2 Machine Instructions by Mnemonic (*Continued*)

Mnemonic	Operands	Name	Format	Op Code	Class & Notes
EX	$R_1, D_2(X_2, B_2)$	Execute	RX	44	
HDR	R_1, R_2	Halve(L)	RR	24	
HER	R_1, R_2	Halve (S)	RR	34	
HSCH		Halt Subchannel	S	B231	pc
IAC	R_1	Insert Address Space Control	RRE	B224	qc
IC	$R_1, D_2(X_2B_2)$	Insert Character	RX	43	
ICM	$R_1, M_3, D_2(B_2)$	Insert Characters under Mask	RS	BF	c
IPK		Insert PSW Key	S	B20B	q
IPM	R_1	Insert Program Mask	RRE	B222	
IPTE	R_1, R_2	Invalidate Page Table Entry	RRE	B221	p
ISKE	R_1, R_2	Insert Storage Key Extended	RRE	B229	p
IVSK	R_1, R_2	Insert Virtual Storage Key	RRE	B223	q
L	$R_1, D_2(X_2, B_2)$	Load	RX	58	
LA	$R_1, D_2(X_2, B_2)$	Load Address	RX	41	
LAE	$R_1, D_2(X_2, B_2)$	Load Address Extended	RX	51	
LAM	$R_1, R_3, D_2(B_2)$	Load Access Multiple	RS	9A	
LASP	$D_1(B_1), D_2(B_2)$	Load Address Space Parameters	SSE	E500	pc
LCDR	R_1, R_2	Load Complement (L)	RR	23	c
LCER	R_1, R_2	Load Complement (S)	RR	33	c
LCR	R_1, R_2	Load Complement	RR	13	c
LCTL	$R_1, R_3, D_2(B_2)$	Load Control	RS	B7	p
LD	$R_1, D_2(X_2, B_2)$	Load (L)	RX	68	
LDR	R_1, R_2	Load(L)	RR	28	
LE	$R_1, D_2(X_2, B_2)$	Load (S)	RX	78	
LER	R_1, R_2	Load (S)	RR	38	
LH	$R_1, D_2(X_2, B_2)$	Load Halfword	RX	48	
LM	$R_1, R_3, D_2(B_2)$	Load Multiple	RS	98	
LNDR	R_1, R_2	Load Negative (L)	RR	21	c
LNER	R_1, R_2	Load Negative (S)	RR	31	c
LNR	R_1, R_2	Load, Negative	RR	11	c
LPDR	R_1, R_2	Load Positive (L)	RR	20	c
LPER	R_1, R_2	Load Positive (S)	RR	30	c
LPR	R_1, R_2	Load Positive	RR	10	c
LPSW	$D_2(B_2)$	Load PSW	S	82	pn
LR	R_1, R_2	Load	RR	18	
LRA	$R_1, D_2(X_2, B_2)$	Load Real Address	RX	B1	pc
LRDR	RI, R_2	Load Rounded (E/L)	RR	25	
LRER	R_1, R_2	Load Rounded (L/S)	RR	35	
LTDR	R_1, R_2	Load and Test (L)	RR	22	c
LTER	R_1, R_2	Load and Test (S)	RR	32	c
LTR	R_1, R_2	Load and Test	RR	12	c
LURA	R_1, R_2	Load Using Real Address	RRE	B24B	p
M	$R_1, D_2(X_2, B_2)$	Multiply	RX	5C	

Floating-point operand lengths:
(E) Extended source and result.
(E/L) Extended source, long result.
(L/E) Long source, extended result.
(L) Long source and result.
(L/S) Long source, short result.
(S/L) Short source, long result.
(S) Short source and result.

Notes:
c. Condition code set.
i Interruptible instruction.
n. New condition code loaded.
p. Privileged instruction.
q. Semiprivileged instruction.
x. Execution in problem state and supervisor state differs.
y. Condition code may be set.
z. Condition code is unpredictable.

Class (for instructions subject to vector-control bit, CR 0 bit 14)
IC: Interruptible; (VCT — VIX) elements processed.
IG: Interruptible; either (bit count in a general register) elements or (section-size — VIX) elements processed, whichever is fewer.
IM: Interruptible; (VCT — VIX) elements processed, vector-mask mode.
IP: Interruptible; (partial-sum-number — VIX) elements processed.
IZ: Interruptible; (section-size) elements processed.
NC: Not interruptible; (VCT) elements processed.
NZ: Not interruptible; (section-size) elements processed.
N0: Not interruptible; no elements processed (VSR/VAC housekeeping).
N1: Not interruptible; one element processed.

TABLE D.2 Machine Instructions by Mnemonic (*Continued*)

Mnemonic	Operands	Name	Format	Op Code	Class & Notes
MC	$D_1(B_1)$, I_2	Monitor Call	SI	AF	
MD	R_1, $D_2(X_2, B_2)$	Multiply (L)	RX	6C	
MDR	R_1, R_2	Multiply (L)	RR	2C	
ME	R_1, $D_2(X_2, B_2)$	Multiply (S/L)	RX	7C	
MER	R_1, R_2	Multiply (S/L)	RR	3C	
MH	R_1, $D_2(X_2, B_2)$	Multiply Halfword	RX	4C	
MP	D_1, (L_1,B_1), $D_2(L_2, B_2)$	Multiply Decimal	SS	FC	
MR	R_1, R_2	Multiply	RR	1C	
MSCH	$D_2(B_2)$	Modify Subchannel	S	B232	pc
MSTA	R_1	Modify Stacked State	RRE	B247	q
MVC	$D_1(L, B_1)$, $D_2(B_2)$	Move	SS	D2	
MVCDK	$D_1(B_1)$, $D_2(B_2)$	Move with Destination Key	SSE	E50F	q
MVCIN	$D_1(L, B_1)$, $D_2(B_2)$	Move Inverse	SS	E8	
MVCK	$D_1(R_1, B_1)$, $D_2(B_2)$, R_3	Move with Key	SS	D9	qc
MVCL	R_1, R_2	Move Long	RR	0E	i c
MVCP	$D_1(R_1, B_1)$, $D_2(B_2)$, R_3	Move to Primary	SS	DA	qc
MVCS	$D_1(R_1, B_1)$, $D_2(B_2)$, R_3	Move to Secondary	SS	DB	qc
MVCSK	$D_1(B_1)$, $D_2(B_2)$	Move with Source Key	SSE	E50E	q
MVI	$D_1(B_1)$, I_2	Move	SI	92	
MVN	$D_1(L, B_1)$, $D_2(B_2)$	Move Numerics	SS	D1	
MVO	$D_1(L_1, B_1)$, $D_2(L_2, B_2)$	Move with Offset	SS	F1	
MVZ	$D_1(L, B_1)$, $D_2(B_2)$	Move Zones	SS	D3	
MXD	R_1, $D_2(X_2, B_2)$	Multiply (L/E)	RX	67	
MXDR	R_1, R_2	Multiply (L/E)	RR	27	
MXR	R_1, R_2	Multiply (E)	RR	26	
N	R_1, $D_2(X_2, B_2)$	AND	RX	54	c
NC	$D_1(L, B_1)$, $D_2(B_2)$	AND	SS	D4	c
NI	$D_1(B_1)$, I_2	AND	SI	94	c
NR	R_1, R_2	AND	RR	14	c
O	R_1, $D_2(X_2, B_2)$	OR	RX	56	c
OC	$D_1(L, B_1)$, $D_2(B_2)$	OR	SS	D6	c
OI	$D_1(B_1)$, I_2	OR	SI	96	c
OR	R_1, R_2	OR	RR	16	c
PACK	$D_1(L_1, B_1)$, $D_2(L_2, B_2)$	Pack	SS	F2	
PALB		Purge ALB	RRE	B248	p
PC	$D_2(B_2)$	Program Call	S	B218	q
PR		Program Return	E	0101	qz
PT	R_1, R_2	Program Transfer	RRE	B22B	q
PTLB		Purge TLB	S	B2OD	p
RCHP		Reset Channel Path	S	B23B	pc
RRBE	R_1, R_2	Reset Reference Bit Extended	RRE	B22A	pc
RSCH		Resume Subchannel	S	B238	pc
S	R_1, $D_2(X_2, B_2)$	Subtract	RX	5B	c
SAC	$D_2(B_2)$	Set Address Space Control	S	B219	q
SAL		Set Address Limit	S	B237	p
SAR	R_1, R_2	Set Access	RRE	B24E	
SCHM		Set Channel Monitor	S	B23C	p
SCK	$D_2(B_2)$	Set Clock	S	B204	pc
SCKC	$D_2(B_2)$	Set Clock Comparator	S	B206	p
SD	R_1, $D_2(X_2, B_2)$	Subtract Normalized (L)	RX	6B	c
SDR	R_1, R_2	Subtract Normalized (L)	RR	2B	c
SE	R_1, $D_2(X_2, B_2)$	Subtract Normalized (S)	RX	7B	c
SER	R_1, R_2	Subtract Normalized (S)	RR	3B	c
SH	R_1, $D_2(X_2, B_2)$	Subtract Halfword	RX	4B	c
SIE	$D_2(B_2)$	Start Interpretive Execution	S	B214	i p
SIGP	R_1, R_3, $D_2(B_2)$	Signal Processor	RS	AE	pc
SL	R_1, $D_2(X_2, B_2)$	Subtract Logical	RX	5F	c
SLA	R_1, $D_2(B_2)$	Shift Left Single	RS	8B	c
SLDA	R_1, $D_2(B_2)$	Shift Left Double	RS	8F	c
SLDL	R_1, $D_2(B_2)$	Shift Left Double Logical	RS	8D	
SLL	R_1, $D_2(B_2)$	Shift Left Single Logical	RS	89	
SLR	R_1, R_2	Subtract Logical	RR	1F	c
SP	$D_1(L_1, B_1)$, $D_2(L_2, B_2)$	Subtract Decimal	SS	FB	c

TABLE D.2 Machine Instructions by Mnemonic (*Continued*)

Mnemonic	Operands	Name	Format	Op Code	Class & Notes
SPKA	$D_2(B_2)$	Set PSW Key from Address	S	B20A	q
SPM	R_1	Set Program Mask	RR	04	n
SPT	$D_2(B_2)$	Set CPU Timer	S	B208	p
SPX	$D_2(B_2)$	Set Prefix	S	B210	p
SR	R_1, R_2	Subtract	RR	1B	c
SRA	$R_1, D_2(B_2)$	Shift Right Single	RS	8A	c
SRDA	$R_1, D_2(B_2)$	Shift Right Double	RS	8E	c
SRDL	$R_1, D_2(B_2)$	Shift Right Double Logical	RS	8C	
SRL	$R_1, D_2(B_2)$	Shift Right Single Logical	RS	88	
SRP	$D_1(L_1, B_1), D_2(B_2), I_3$	Shift and Round Decimal	SS	F0	c
SSAR	R_1	Set Secondary ASN	RRE	B225	q
SSCH	$D_2(B_2)$	Start Subchannel	S	B233	pc
SSKE	R_1, R_2	Set Storage Key Extended	RRE	B22B	p
SSM	$D_2(B_2)$	Set System Mask	S	80	p
ST	$R_1, D_2(X_2, B_2)$	Store	RX	50	
STAM	$R_1, R_3, D_2(B_2)$	Store Access Multiple	RS	9B	
STAP	$D_2(B_2)$	Store CPU Address	S	B212	p
STC	$R_1, D_2(X_2, B_2)$	Store Character	RX	42	
STCK	$D_2(B_2)$	Store Clock	S	B205	c
STCKC	$D_2(B_2)$	Store Clock Comparator	S	B207	p
STCM	$R_1, M_3, D_2(B_2)$	Store Characters under Mask	RS	BE	
STCPS	$D_2(B_2)$	Store Channel Path Status	S	B23A	p
STCRW	$D_2(B_2)$	Store Channel Report Word	S	B239	pc
STCTL	$R_1, R_3, D_2(B_2)$	Store Control	RS	B6	p
STD	$R_1, D_2(X_2, B_2)$	Store (L)	RX	60	
STE	$R_1, D_2(X_2, B_2)$	Store (S)	RX	70	
STH	$R_1, D_2(X_2, B_2)$	Store Halfword	RX	40	
STIDP	$D_2(B_2)$	Store CPU ID	S	B202	p
STM	$R_1, R_3, D_2(B_2)$	Store Multiple	RS	90	
STNSM	$D_1(B_1), I_2$	Store Then AND System Mask	SI	AC	p
STOSM	$D_1(B_1), I_2$	Store Then OR System Mask	SI	AD	p
STPT	$D_2(B_2)$	Store CPU Timer	S	B209	p
STPX	$D_2(B_2)$	Store Prefix	S	B211	p
STSCH	$D_2(B_2)$	Store Subchannel	S	B234	pc
STURA	R_1, R_2	Store Using Real Address	RRE	B246	p
SU	$R_1, D_2(X_2B_2)$	Subtract Unnormalized (S)	RX	7F	c
SUR	R_1, R_2	Subtract Unnormalized (S)	RR	3F	c
SVC	I	Supervisor Call	RR	0A	
SW	$R_1, D_2(X_2, B_2)$	Subtract Unnormalized (L)	RX	6F	c
SWR	R_1, R_2	Subtract Unnormalized (L)	RR	2F	c
SXR	R_1, R_2	Subtract Normalized (E)	RR	37	c
TAR	R_1, R_2	Test Access	RRE	B24C	qc

Floating-point operand lengths:
(E) Extended source and result.
(E/L) Extended source, long result.
(L/E) Long source, extended result.
(L) Long source and result.
(L/S) Long source, short result.
(S/L) Short source, long result.
(S) Short source and result.

Notes:
c. Condition code set.
i. Interruptible instruction.
n. New condition code loaded.
p. Privileged instruction.
q. Semiprivileged instruction.
x. Execution in problem state and supervisor state differs.
y. Condition code may be set.
z. Condition code is unpredictable.

Class (for instructions subject to vector-control bit, CR 0 bit 14)
IC: Interruptible; (VCT — VIX) elements processed.
IG: Interruptible; either (bit count in a general register) elements or (section-size — VIX) elements processed, whichever is fewer.
IM: Interruptible; (VCT — VIX) elements processed, vector-mask mode.
IP: Interruptible; (partial-sum-number —VIX) elements processed.
IZ: Interruptible; (section-size) elements processed.
NC: Not interruptible; (VCT) elements processed.
NZ: Not interruptible; (section-size) elements processed.
NO: Not interruptible; no elements processed (VSR/VAC housekeeping).
N1: Not interruptible; one element processed.

TABLE D.2 Machine Instructions by Mnemonic (*Continued*)

Mne-monic	Operands	Name	For-mat	Op Code	Class & Notes
TB	R_1, R_2	Test Block	RRE	B22C	ipc
TM	$D_1(B_1), I_2$	Test under Mask	SI	91	c
TPI	$D_2(B_2)$	Test Pending Interruption	S	B236	pc
TPROT	$D_1(B_1), D_2(B_2)$	Test Protection	SSE	E501	pc
TR	$D_1(L, B_1), D_2(B_2)$	Translate	SS	DC	
TRACE	R_1, R3, $(D_2(B_2)$	Trace	RS	99	p
TRT	$D_1(L, B_1), D_2(B_2)$	Translate and Test	SS	DD	c
TS	$D_2(B_2)$	Test and Set	S	93	c
TSCH	$D_2(B_2)$	Test Subchannel	S	B235	pc
UNPK	$D_1(L_1, B_1), D_2(L_2, B_2)$	Unpack	SS	F3	
UPT		Update Tree	E	0102	i c
VA	$VR_1, VR_3, RS_2(RT_2)$	Add	VST	A420	IM
VACD	$VR_1, RS_2(RT_2)$	Accumulate (L)	VST	A417	IM
VACDR	VR_1, VR_2	Accumulate (L)	VV	A517	IM
VACE	$VR_1, RS_2(RT_2)$	Accumulate (S/L)	VST	A407	IM
VACER	VR_1, VR_2	Accumulate (S/L)	VV	A507	IM
VACRS	$D_2(B_2)$	Restore VAC	S	A6CB	N0 p
VACSV	$D_2(B_2)$	Save VAC	S	A6CA	N0 p
VAD	$VR_1, VR_3, RS_2(RT_2)$	Add (L)	VST	A410	IM
VADQ	VR_1, FR_3, VR_2	Add (L)	QV	A590	IM
VADR	VR_1, VR_3, VR_2	Add (L)	VV	A510	IM
VADS	$VR_1, FR_3, RS_2(RT_2)$	Add (L)	QST	A490	IM
VAE	$VR_1, VR_3, RS_2(RT_2)$	Add (S)	VST	A400	IM
VAEQ	VR_1, FR_3, VR_2	Add (S)	QV	A580	IM
VAER	VR_1, VR_3, VR_2	Add (S)	VV	A500	IM
VAES	$VR_1, FR_3, RS_2(RT_2)$	Add (S)	QST	A480	IM
VAQ	VR_1, GR_3, VR_2	Add	QV	A5A0	IM
VAR	VR_1, VR_3, VR_2	Add	VV	A520	IM
VAS	$VR_1, GR_3, RS_2(RT_2)$	Add	QST	A4AO	IM
VC	$M_1, VR_3, RS_2(RT_2)$	Compare	VST	A428	IC
VCD	$M_1, VR_3, RS_2(RT_2)$	Compare (L)	VST	A418	IC
VCDQ	M_1, FR_3, VR_2	Compare (L)	QV	A598	IC
VCDR	M_1, VR_3, VR_2	Compare (L)	VV	A518	IC
VCDS	$M_1, FR_3, RS_2(RT_2)$	Compare (L)	QST	A498	IC
VCE	$M_1, VR_3, RS_2(RT_2)$	Compare (S)	VST	A408	IC
VCEQ	M_1, FR_3, VR_2	Compare (S)	QV	A588	IC
VCER	M_1, VR_3, VR_2	Compare (S)	VV	A508	IC
VCES	$M_1, FR_3, RS_2, (RT_2)$	Compare (S)	QST	A488	IC
VCOVM	GR_1	Count Ones in VMR	RRE	A643	NC c
VCQ	M_1, GR_3, VR_2	Compare	QV	A5A8	IC
VCR	M_1, VR_3, VR_2	Compare	VV	A528	IC
VCS	$M_1, GR_3, RS_2(RT_2)$	Compare	QST	A4A8	IC
VCVM		Complement VMR	RRE	A641	NC
VCZVM	GR_1	Count Left Zeros in VMR	RRE	A642	NC c
VDD	$VR_1, VR_3, RS_2(RT_2)$	Divide (L)	VST	A413	IM
VDDQ	VR_1, FR_3, VR_2	Divide (L)	QV	A593	IM
VDDR	VR_1, VR_3, VR_2	Divide (L)	VV	A513	IM
VDDS	$VR_1, FR_3, RS_2(RT_2)$	Divide (L)	QST	A493	IM
VDE	$VR_1, VR_3, RS_2(RT_2)$	Divide (S)	VST	A403	IM
VDEQ	VR_1, FR_3, VR_2	Divide (S)	QV	A583	IM
VDER	VR_1, VR_3, VR_2	Divide (S)	VV	A503	IM
VDES	$VR_1, FR_3, RS_2(RT_2)$	Divide (S)	QST	A483	IM
VL	$VR_1, RS_2(RT_2)$	Load	VST	A409	IC
VLBIX	$VR_1, GR_3, D_2(B_2)$	Load Bit Index	RSE	E428	IG c
VLCDR	VR_1, VR_2	Load Complement (L)	VV	A552	IM
VLCER	VR_1, VR_2	Load Complement (S)	VV	A542	IM
VLCR	VR_1, VR_2	Load Complement	VV	A562	IM
VLCVM	RS_2	Load VMR Complement	VS	A681	NC
VLD	$VR_1, RS_2(RT_2)$	Load (L)	VST	A419	IC
VLDQ	VR_1, FR_2	Load (L)	QV	A599	IC
VLDR	VR_1, VR_2	Load (L)	VV	A519	IC
VLE	$VR_1, RS_2(RT_2)$	Load (S)	VST	A409	IC
VLEL	VR_1, GR_3, GR_2	Load Element	VR	A628	N1
VLELD	VR_1, FR_3, GR_2	Load Element (L)	VR	A618	N1
VLELE	VR_1, FR_3, GR_2	Load Element (S)	VR	A608	N1
VLEQ	VR_1, FR_2	Load (S)	QV	A589	IC
VLER	VR_1, VR_2	Load (S)	VV	A509	IC

TABLE D.2 Machine Instructions by Mnemonic (*Continued*)

Mnemonic	Operands	Name	Format	Op Code	Class & Notes
VLH	VR_1, $RS_2(RT_2)$	Load Halfword	VST	A429	IC
VLI	VR_1, VR_3, $D_2(B_2)$	Load Indirect	RSE	E400	IC
VLID	VR_1, VR_3, $D_2(B_2)$	Load Indirect (L)	RSE	E410	IC
VLIE	VR_1, VR_3, $D_2(B_2)$	Load Indirect (S)	RSE	E400	IC
VLINT	VR_1, $RS_2(RT_2)$	Load Integer Vector	VST	A42A	IC
VLM	VR_1, $RS_2(RT_2)$	Load Matched	VST	A40A	IC
VLMD	VR_1, $RS_2(RT_2)$	Load Matched (L)	VST	A41A	IC
VLMDQ	VR_1, FR_2	Load Matched (L)	QV	A59A	IC
VLMDR	VR_1, VR_2	Load Matched (L)	VV	A51A	IC
VLME	VR_1, $RS_2(RT_2)$	Load Matched (S)	VST	A40A	IC
VLMEQ	VR_1, FR_2	Load Matched (S)	QV	A58A	IC
VLMER	VR_1, VR_2	Load Matched (S)	VV	A50A	IC
VLMQ	VR_1, GR_2	Load Matched	QV	A5AA	IC
VLMR	VR_1, VR_2	Load Matched	VV	A50A	IC
VLNDR	VR_1, VR_2	Load Negative (L)	VV	A551	IM
VLNER	VR_1, VR_2	Load Negative (S)	VV	A541	IM
VLNR	VR_1, VR_2	Load Negative	VV	A561	IM
VLPDR	VR_1, VR_2	Load Positive (L)	VV	A550	IM
VLPER	VR_1, VR_2	Load Positive (S)	VV	A540	IM
VLPR	VR_1, VR_2	Load Positive	VV	A560	IM
VLQ	VR_1, GR_2	Load	QV	A5A9	IC
VLR	VR_1, VR_2	Load	VV	A509	IC
VLVCA	$D_2(B_2)$	Load VCT from Address	S	A6C4	NO c
VLVCU	GR_1	Load VCT and Update	RRE	A645	NO c
VLVM	RS_2	Load VMR	VS	A680	NC
VLY	VR_1, $RS_2(RT_2)$	Load Expanded	VST	A40B	IC
VLYD	VR_1, $RS_2(RT_2)$	Load Expanded (L)	VST	A41B	IC
VLYE	VR_1, $RS_2(RT_2)$	Load Expanded (S)	VST	A40B	IC
VLZDR	VR_1	Load Zero (L)	VV	A51B	IC
VLZER	VR_1	Load Zero (S)	VV	A50B	IC
VLZR	VR_1	Load Zero	VV	A50B	IC
VM	VR_1, VR_3, $RS_2(RT_2)$	Multiply	VST	A422	IM
VMAD	VR_1, VR_3, $RS_2(RT_2)$	Multiply and Add (L)	VST	A414	IM
VMADQ	VR_1, FR_3, VR_2	Multiply and Add (L)	QV	A594	IM
VMADS	VR_1, FR_3, $RS_2(RT_2)$	Multiply and Add (L)	QST	A494	IM
VMAE	VR_1, VR_3, $RS_2(RT_2)$	Multiply and Add (S/L)	VST	A404	IM
VMAEQ	VR_1, FR_3, VR_2	Multiply and Add (S/L)	QV	A584	IM
VMAES	VR_1, FR_3, $RS_2(RT_2)$	Multiply and Add (S/L)	QST	A484	IM
VMCD	VR_1, VR_3, $RS_2(RT_2)$	Multiply and Accumulate (L)	VST	A416	IM
VMCDR	VR_1, VR_3, VR_2	Multiply and Accumulate (L)	VV	A516	IM
VMCE	VR_1, VR_3, $RS_2(RT_2)$	Multiply and Accumulate (S/L)	VST	A406	IM
VMCER	VR_1, VR_3, VR_2	Multiply and Accumulate (S/L)	VV	A506	IM

Floating-point operand lengths:
(E) Extended source and result.
(E/L) Extended source, long result.
(L/E) Long source, extended result.
(L) Long source and result.
(L/S) Long source, short result.
(S/L) Short source, long result.
(S) Short source and result.

Notes:
c. Condition code set.
i. Interruptible instruction.
n. New condition code loaded.
p. Privileged instruction.
q. Semiprivileged instruction.
x. Execution in problem state and supervisor state differs.
y. Condition code may be set.
z. Condition code is unpredictable.

Class (for instructions subject to vector-control bit, CR 0 bit 14)
IC: Interruptible; (VCT — VIX) elements processed.
IG: Interruptible; either (bit count in a general register) elements or (section-size — VIX) elements processed, whichever is fewer.
IM: Interruptible; (VCT — VIX) elements processed, vector-mask mode.
IP: Interruptible; (partial-sum-number — VIX) elements processed.
IZ: Interruptible; (section-size) elements processed.
NC: Not interruptible; (VCT) elements processed.
NZ: Not interruptible; (section-size) elements processed.
NO: Not interruptible; no elements processed (VSR/VAC housekeeping)
N1: Not interruptible; one element processed.

TABLE D.2 Machine Instructions by Mnemonic (*Continued*)

Mnemonic	Operands	Name	Format	Op Code	Class & Notes
VMD	$VR_1, VR_3, RS_2(RT_2)$	Multiply (L)	VST	A412	IM
VMDQ	VR_1, FR_3, VR_2	Multiply (L)	QV	A592	IM
VMDR	VR_1, FR_3, VR_2	Multiply (L)	VV	A512	IM
VMDS	$VR_1, FR_3, RS_2(RT_2)$	Multiply (L)	QST	A492	IM
VME	$VR_1, VR_3, RS_2(RT_2)$	Multiply (S/L)	VST	A402	IM
VMEQ	VR_1, FR_3, VR_2	Multiply (S/L)	QV	A582	IM
VMER	VR_1, VR_3, VR_2	Multiply (S/L)	VV	A502	IM
VMES	$VR_1, FR_3, RS_2(RT_2)$	Multiply (S/L)	QST	A482	IM
VMNSD	VR_1, FR_3, GR_2	Minimum Signed (L)	VR	A611	IM
VMNSE	VR_1, FR_3, GR_2	Minimum Signed (S)	VR	A601	IM
VMQ	VR_1, GR_3, VR_2	Multiply	QV	A5A2	IM
VMR	VR_1, VR_3, VR_2	Multiply	VV	A522	IM
VMRRS	$D_2(B_2)$	Restore VMR	S	A6C3	NZ
VMRSV	$D_2(B_2)$	Save VMR	S	A6C1	NZ
VMS	$VR_1, GR_3, RS_2(RT_2)$	Multiply	QST	A4A2	IM
VMSD	$VR_1, VR_3, RS_2(RT_2)$	Multiply and Subtract (L)	VST	A415	IM
VMSDQ	VR_1, FR_3, VR_2	Multiply and Subtract (L)	QV	A595	IM
VMSDS	$VR_1, FR_3, RS_2(RT_2)$	Multiply and Subtract (L)	QST	A495	IM
VMSE	$VR_1, VR_3, RS_2(RT_2)$	Multiply and Subtract (S/L)	VST	A405	IM
VMSEQ	VR_1, FR_3, VR_2	Multiply and Subtract (S/L)	QV	A585	IM
VMSES	$VR_1, FR_3, RS_2(RT_2)$	Multiply and Subtract (S/L)	QST	A485	IM
VMXAD	VR_1, FR_3, GR_2	Maximum Absolute (L)	VR	A612	IM
VMXAE	VR_1, FR_3, GR_2	Maximum Absolute (S)	VR	A602	IM
VMXSD	VR_1, FR_3, GR_2	Maximum Signed (L)	VR	A610	IM
VMXSE	VR_1, FR_3, GR_2	Maximum Signed (S)	VR	A600	IM
VN	$VR_1, VR_3, RS_2(RT_2)$	AND	VST	A424	IM
VNQ	VR_1, GR_3, VR_2	AND	QV	A5A4	IM
VNR	VR_1, VR_3, VR_2	AND	VV	A524	IM
VNS	$VR_1, GR_3, RS_2(RT_2)$	AND	QST	A4A4	IM
VNVM	RS_2	AND to VMR	VS	A684	NC
VO	$VR_1, VR_3, RS_2(RT_2)$	OR	VST	A425	IM
VOQ	VR_1, GR_2, VR_2	OR	QV	A5A5	IM
VOR	VR_1, VR_3, VR_2	OR	VV	A525	IM
VOS	$VR_1, GR_3, RS_2(RT_2)$	OR	QST	A4A5	IM
VOVM	RS_2	OR to VMR	VS	A685	NC
VRCL	$D_2(B_2)$	Clear VR	S	A6C5	IZ
VRRS	GR_1	Restore VR	RRE	A648	IZ xc
VRSV	GR_1	Save VR	RRE	A64A	IZ c
VRSVC	GR_1	Save Changed VR	RRE	A649	IZ pc
VS	$VR_1, VR_3, RS_2(RT_2)$	Subtract	VST	A421	IM
VSD	$VR_1, VR_3, RS_2(RT_2)$	Subtract (L)	VST	A411	IM
VSDQ	VR_1, FR_3, VR_2	Subtract (L)	QV	A591	IM
VSDR	VR_1, VR_3, VR_2	Subtract (L)	VV	A511	IM
VSDS	$VR_1, FR_3, RS_2(RT_2)$	Subtract (L)	QST	A491	IM
VSE	$VR_1, VR_3, RS_2(RT_2)$	Subtract (S)	VST	A401	IM
VSEQ	VR_1, FR_3, VR_2	Subtract (S)	QV	A581	IM
VSER	VR_1, VR_3, VR_2	Subtract (S)	VV	A501	IM
VSES	$VR_1, FR_3, RS_2(RT_2)$	Subtract (S)	QST	A481	IM
VSLL	$VR_1, VR_3, D_2(B_2)$	Shift Left Single Logical	RSE	E425	IM
VSPSD	VR_1, FR_2	Sum Partial Sums (L)	VR	A61A	IP
VSQ	VR_1, GR_3, VR_2	Subtract	QV	A5A1	IM
VSR	VR_1, VR_3, VR_2	Subtract	VV	A521	IM
VSRL	$VR_1, VR_3, D_2(B_2)$	Shift Right Single Logical	RSE	E424	IM
VSRRS	$D_2(B_2)$	Restore VSR	S	A6C2	IZ x
VSRSV	$D_2(B_2)$	Save VSR	S	A6C0	NO x
VSS	$VR_1, GR_3, RS_2(RT_2)$	Subtract	QST	A4A1	IM
VST	$VR_1, RS_2(RT_2)$	Store	VST	A40D	IC
VSTD	$VR_1, RS_2(RT_2)$	Store (L)	VST	A41D	IC
VSTE	$VR_1, RS_2(RT_2)$	Store (S)	VST	A40D	IC
VSTH	$VR_1, RS_2(RT_2)$	Store Halfword	VST	A42D	IC
VSTI	$VR_1, VR_3, D_2(B_2)$	Store Indirect	RSE	E401	IC
VSTID	$VR_1, VR_3, D_2(B_2)$	Store Indirect (L)	RSE	E411	IC
VSTIE	$VR_1, VR_3, D_2(B_2)$	Store Indirect (S)	RSE	E401	IC
VSTK	$VR_1, RS_2(RT_2)$	Store Compressed	VST	A40F	IC
VSTKD	$VR_1, RS_2(RT_2)$	Store Compressed (L)	VST	A41F	IC
VSTKE	$VR_1, RS_2(RT_2)$	Store Compressed (S)	VST	A40F	IC

TABLE D.2 Machine Instructions by Mnemonic (*Continued*)

Mnemonic	Operands	Name	Format	Op Code	Class & Notes
VSTM	VR_1, $RS_2(RT_2)$	Store Matched	VST	A40E	IC
VSTMD	VR_1, $RS_2(RT_2)$	Store Matched (L)	VST	A41E	IC
VSTME	VR_1, $RS_2(RT_2)$	Store Matched (S)	VST	A40E	IC
VSTVM	RS_2	Store VMR	VS	A682	NC
VSTVP	$D_2(B_2)$	Store Vector Parameters	S	A6C8	N0
VSVMM	$D_2(B_2)$	Set Vector Mask Mode	S	A6C6	N0
VTVM		Test VMR	RRE	A640	NC c
VX	VR_1, VR_3, $RS_2(RT_2)$	Exclusive OR	VST	A426	IM
VXEL	VR_1, GR_3, GR_2	Extract Element	VR	A629	N1
VXELD	VR_1, FR_3, GR_2	Extract Element (L)	VR	A619	N1
VXELE	VR_1, FR_3, GR_2	Extract Element (S)	VR	A609	N1
VXQ	VR_1, GR_3, VR_2	Exclusive OR	QV	A5A6	IM
VXR	VR_1, VR_3, VR_2	Exclusive OR	VV	A526	IM
VXS	VR_1, GR_3, $RS_2(RT_2)$	Exclusive OR	QST	A4A6	IM
VXVC	GR_1	Extract VCT	RRE	A644	N0
VXVM	RS_2	Exclusive OR to VMR	VS	A686	NC
VXVMM	GR_1	Extract Vector Mask Mode	RRE	A646	N0
VZPSD	VR_1	Zero Partial Sums (L)	VR	A61B	IP
X	R_1, $D_2(X_2, B_2)$	Exclusive OR	RX	57	c
XC	$D_1(L, B_1)$, $D_2(B_2)$	Exclusive OR	SS	D7	c
XI	$D_1(B_1)$, I_2	Exclusive OR	SI	97	c
XR	R_1, R_2	Exclusive OR	RR	17	c
ZAP	$D_1(L_1, B_1)$, $D_2(LC, B_2)$	Zero and Add	SS	F8	c
--	Model-dependent	Diagnose	--	83	py

Floating-point operand lengths:

(E) Extended source and result.
(E/L) Extended source, long result.
(L/E) Long source, extended result.
(L) Long source and result.
(L/S) Long source, short result.
(S/L) Short source, long result.
(S) Short source and result.

Notes:

c. Condition code set.
i. Interruptible instruction.
n. New condition code loaded.
p. Privileged instruction.
q. Semiprivileged instruction.
x. Execution in problem state and supervisor state differs.
y. Condition code may be set.
z. Condition code is unpredictable.

Class (for instructions subject to vector-control bit, CR 0 bit 14)

IC: Interruptible; (VCT — VIX) elements processed.
IG: Interruptible; either (bit count in a general register) elements or (section-size — VIX) elements processed, whichever is fewer.
IM: Interruptible; (VCT — VIX) elements processed, vector-mask mode.
IP: Interruptible; (partial-sum-number — VIX) elements processed.
IZ: Interruptible; (section-size) elements processed.
NC: Not interruptible; (VCT) elements processed.
NZ: Not interruptible; (section-size) elements processed.
N0: Not interruptible; no elements processed (VSR/VAC housekeeping).
N1: Not interruptible; one element processed.

TABLE D.3 Machine Instructions by Operation Code

Op Code	Mnemonic
0101	PR
0102	UPT
04	SPM
05	BALR
06	BCTR
07	BCR
0A	SVC
0B	BSM
0C	BASSM
0D	BASR
0E	MVCL
0F	CLCL
10	LPR
11	LNR
12	LTR
13	LCR
14	NR
15	CLR
16	OR
17	XR
18	LR
19	CR
1A	AR
1B	SR
1C	MR
1D	DR
1E	ALR
1F	SLR
20	LPDR
21	LNDR
22	LTDR
23	LCDR
24	HDR
25	LRDR
26	MXR
27	MXDR
28	LDR
29	CDR
2A	ADR
2B	SDR
2C	MDR
2D	DDR
2E	AWR
2F	SWR
30	LPER
31	LNER
32	LTER
33	LCER
34	HER
35	LRER
36	AXR
37	SXR
38	LER
39	CER
3A	AER
3B	SER
3C	MER
3D	DER
3E	AUR
3F	SUR
40	STH
41	LA
42	STC
43	IC
44	EX
45	BAL
46	BCT
47	BC
48	LH
49	CH
4A	AH
4B	SH
4C	MH
4D	BAS
4E	CVD
4F	CVB
50	ST
51	LAE
54	N
55	CL
56	O
57	X
58	L
59	C
5A	A
5B	S
5C	M
5D	D
5E	AL
5F	SL
60	STD
67	MXD
68	LD
69	CD
6A	AD
6B	SD
6C	MD
6D	DD
6E	AW
6F	SW
70	STE
78	LE
79	CE
7A	AE
7B	SE
7C	ME
7D	DE
7E	AU
7F	SU
80	SSM
82	LPSW
83	Diagnose
86	BXH
87	BXLE
88	SRL
89	SLL
8A	SRA
8B	SLA
8C	SRDL
8D	SLDL
8E	SRDA
8F	SLDA
90	STM
91	TM
92	MVI
93	TS
94	NI
95	CLI
96	OI
97	XI
98	LM
99	TRACE
9A	LAM
9B	STAM
A400	VAE
A401	VSE
A402	VME
A403	VDE
A404	VMAE
A405	VMSE
A406	VMCE
A407	VACE
A408	VCE
A409	VL
A409	VLE
A40A	VLM
A40A	VLME
A40B	VLY
A40B	VLYE
A40D	VST
A40D	VSTE
A40E	VSTM
A40E	VSTME
A40F	VSTK
A40F	VSTKE
A410	VAD
A411	VSD
A412	VMD
A412	VDD
A414	VMAD
A415	VMSD
A416	VMCD
A417	VACD
A418	VCD
A419	VLD
A41A	VLMD
A41B	VLYD
A41D	VSTD
A41E	VSTMD
A41F	VSTKD
A420	VA
A421	VS
A422	VM
A424	VN
A425	VO
A426	VX
A428	VC
A429	VLH
A42A	VLINT
A42D	VSTH
A480	VAES
A481	VSES
A482	VMES
A483	VDES
A484	VMAES
A485	VMSES
A488	VCES
A490	VADS
A491	VSDS
A492	VMDS
A493	VDDS
A494	VMADS
A495	VMSDS
A498	VCDS
A4A0	VAS
A4A1	VSS
A4A2	VMS
A4A4	VNS
A4A5	VOS
A4A6	VXS
A4A8	VCS
A500	VAER
A501	VSER
A502	VMER
A503	VDER
A506	VMCER
A507	VACER

TABLE D.3 Machine Instructions by Operation Code (*Continued*)

Op Code	Mnemonic
A508	VCER
A509	VLER
A509	VLR
A50A	VLMER
A50A	VLMR
A50B	VLZER
A50B	VLZR
A510	BADR
A511	VSDR
A512	VMDR
A513	VDDR
A516	VMCDR
A517	VACDR
A518	VCDR
A519	VLDR
A51A	VLMDR
A51B	VLZDR
A520	VAR
A521	VSR
A522	VMR
A524	VNR
A525	VOR
A526	VXR
A528	VCR
A540	VLPER
A541	VLNER
A542	VLCER
A550	VLPDR
A551	VLNDR
A552	VLCDR
A560	VLPR
A561	VLNR
A562	VLCR
A580	VAFQ
A581	VSEQ
A582	VMEQ
A583	VDEQ
A584	VMAEQ
A585	VMSEQ
A588	VCEQ
A589	VLEQ
A58A	VLMEQ
A590	VADQ
A591	VSDQ
A592	VMDQ
A593	VDDQ
A594	VMADQ
A595	VMSDQ
A598	VCDQ
A599	VLDQ
A59A	VLMDQ
A5A0	VAQ
A5A1	VSQ
A5A2	VMQ
A5A4	VNQ
A5A5	VOQ
A5A6	VXQ
A5A8	VCQ
A5A9	VLQ
A5AA	VLMQ
A600	VMXSE
A601	VMNSE
A602	VMXAE
A608	VLELE
A609	VXELE
A610	VMXSD
A611	VMNSD
A612	VMXAD
A618	VLELD

Op Code	Mnemonic
A619	VXELD
A61A	VSPSD
A61B	VZPSD
A628	VLEL
A629	VXEL
A640	VTVM
A641	VCVM
A642	VCZVM
A643	VCOVM
A644	VXVC
A645	VLVCU
A646	VXVMM
A648	VRRS
A649	VRSVC
A64A	VRSV
A680	VLVM
A681	VLCVM
A682	VSTVM
A684	VNVM
A685	VOVM
A686	VXVM
A6C0	VSRSV
A6C1	VMRSV
A6C2	VSRRS
A6C3	VMRRS
A6C4	VLVCA
A6C5	VRCL
A6C6	VSVMM
A6C8	VSTVP
A6CA	VACSV
A6CB	VACRS
AC	STNSM
AD	STOSM
AE	SIGP
AF	MC
B1	LRA
B202	STIDP
B204	SCK
B205	STCK
B206	SCKC
B207	STCKC
B208	SPT
B209	STPT
B20A	SPKA
B20B	IPK
B20D	PTLB
B210	SPX
B211	STPX
B212	STAP
B214	SIE
B218	PC
B219	SAC
B21A	CFC
B221	IPTE
B222	IPM
B223	IVSK
B224	IAC
B225	SSAR
B226	EPAR
B227	ESAR
B228	PT
B229	ISKE
B22A	RRBE
B22B	SSKE
B22C	TB
B22D	DXR
B230	CSCH
B231	HSCH
B232	MSCH

Op Code	Mnemonic
B233	SSCH
B234	STSCH
B235	TSCH
B236	TPI
B237	SAL
B238	RSCH
B239	STCRW
B23A	STCPS
B23B	RCHP
B23C	SCHM
B240	BAKR
B246	STURA
B247	MSTA
B248	PALB
B249	EREG
B24A	ESTA
B24B	LURA
B24C	TAR
B24D	CPYA
B24E	SAR
B24F	EAR
B6	STCTL
B7	LCTL
BA	CS
BB	CDS
BD	CLM
BE	STCM
BF	ICM
D1	MVN
D2	MVC
D3	MVZ
D4	NC
D5	CLC
D6	OC
D7	XC
D9	MVCK
DA	MVCP
DB	MVCS
DC	TR
DD	TRT
DE	ED
DF	EDMK
E400	VLI
E400	VLIE
E401	VSTI
E401	VSTIE
E410	VLID
E411	VSTID
E424	VSRL
E425	VSLL
E428	VLBIX
E500	LASP
E501	TPROT
E50E	MVCSK
E50F	MVCDK
E8	MVCIN
F0	SRP
F1	MVO
F2	PACK
F3	UNPK
F8	ZAP
F9	CP
FA	AP
FB	SP
FC	MP
FD	DP

Index

ABOUT THE AUTHOR

Alan Friend is a Senior Data Processing Consultant with New York Life Insurance Company, where he has worked extensively in the areas of COBOL design, development, and instruction. He has also published articles on COBOL debugging in the *Enterprise Systems Journal,* and has served as a reviewer for McGraw-Hill's J. Ranade IBM Series.

ABOUT THE SERIES

The J. Ranade Series, with more than 75 published titles, are McGraw-Hill's primary vehicles for providing mini- and mainframe computing professionals with practical and timely concepts, solutions, and applications. The series cover DEC and IBM environments, communications, and networking.

Jay Ranade, Series Editor in Chief and best-selling computer author, is a Senior Systems Architect and Assistant V.P. at Merrill Lynch.